STEPTOE

THE VICTORS AND THE VANQUISHED ON THE TRAIL TO OREGON

(Revised Edition)

A Novel By

BOYD HARTMAN

Copyright © 2019 by Boyd Hartman.

ISBN Softcover   978-1-950580-84-2

All rights reserved. No part of this book may be reproduced or transmitted in any form or by any means, electronic or mechanical, including photocopying, recording, or by any information storage and retrieval system without express written permission from the author, except in the case of brief quotations embodied in critical reviews and certain other non-commercial uses permitted by copyright law.

Printed in the United States of America.

To order additional copies of this book, contact:
Bookwhip
1-855-339-3589
https://www.bookwhip.com

PREFACE

It has been the passion of man to seek new frontiers, to explore the unknown, to settle new lands and to conquer those who resist that drives the bold, the opportunists and the explorer ever beyond the limits of the known world. It was inevitable that the Americans, once freed from the constraints of their War of Revolution would look beyond the mountains that constrained them against the sea, and begin the great trek across the uncharted lands of the west. Lewis and Clark and Fremont charted the course. The trappers and adventures brought back stories of a great and bountiful land of limitless possibilities. The savages that possessed the lands were feared, but few respected their heritage to the land that would be claimed by the thousands of emigrants who would soon create a flood tide of humanity swarming across the trackless western plains.

The hardships endured by many are legend; the sacrifices they were called upon to endure were in many instances beyond our present comprehension. Many wandered into wastelands and were never heard from again. Thousands died of diseases spawned from the fetid water polluted by the hoards of cattle, horses and other livestock that accompanied the trains westward. Many died from contact with hostile tribes or were the victims of flood waters or trail accidents. These people we call pioneers, lived for days and weeks under the harsh rays of an unmerciful sun, choked down the dust clouds thrown up by the wagon trains. They slept on the ground, cooked over rude fires and most walked endless miles beside the wagons that bore their few possessions. They forded rivers; drug their wagons over rutted mountain trails and down treacherous slopes. They were men and women of great ingenuity who would confront problems and conditions that would discourage the humble and turn back the weak.

Each had a dream that surpassed their normal inclinations to hold onto the security of the present; the comforts of a home long established.

Some came from across the oceans from lands burdened with the prior claims of great Barons. The hope of land ownership drove them across the seas and into the growing tide of emigrants. They brought their families, their heritage, their courage and their independence and helped build a great nation. This is a story, molded according to the history that records their deeds. It is not intended to be factually accurate in a chronological scenes, it is intended rather to follow the broad outlines of history and to reveal once again a significant chapter in our nation's founding, a moment in time that erodes with each passing day. Where liberty is taken with actual facts and events I apologize to the historians who may take offence and remind them that this is a novel and not a history.

BOOK I

THE LAST CHRISTMAS

Jenny retired to the loft before the last guests had departed. She wanted to be in bed while the heat of the hearth still filled the house. Soon the December chill would invade the cabin and drive all within to the warmth of their beds. Come morning the water in her basin would be covered with a crust of ice. Tonight she felt melancholy and needed the comforting warmth of the quilts her grandmother had made with such loving care. Would she be able to take them with her? She forgot to ask father and would do so in the morning. So many of the things she loved would be left behind. Her pet horse, Lady had already been sold.

"No need feeding the critter over the winter, she ain't stout enough to be going with us," father had remarked when she pleaded with him.

She had received the same response to virtually every request she made. It seemed like all she would be allowed to take were her clothes and necessaries. Surely she would be allowed to take grandmother's quilt. To Jenny the entire subject brought heartache. She shared her mother's grief. What reasoning drove father to decide to sell everything and head west across the unknown plains and mountains to Oregon was beyond her mother's comprehension. Grandfather had homesteaded their farm and father had spent the last twenty years improving it when it became his inheritance. It was a prosperous farm and Uncle Ed was quick to offer father's asking price.

For the last several years father had read everything he could find about the west and the trail to Oregon. He even sent away for a copy of Fremont's maps of the west and became absorbed in the reports of his journeys with Kit Carson to map the trail for the westward migration. Father would ride miles from home to converse with any stranger reported to have been west of the Mississippi. Last summer when the crop was sold, father sat them all down one Sunday and told them of his decision.

"Were selling out and going to Oregon. There's land and opportunity. I can't do more with this place. There's big trouble brewing over slavery in this territory. People about here are not going to tolerate each other much longer and I don't plan on being a part of what's about to happen."

Mother cried for days every time the subject of leaving was broached. Her heart seemed near broken when she was told that all she could take with her of her many treasures was her cooking ware and her tableware.

"Can't afford but one wagon and team. The boy here can't drive a wagon and I can't afford to pay a driver and buy another wagon and set of oxen. Don't intend to take much more then my own tools and implements myself. Hear most folks end up dumping most of the furniture and stoves and such they try to haul along anyways."

Papa had contracted for a Studebaker wagon that would be ready early in the spring. He scoured the country for the best oxen he could find. He'd spent the last two months packing his tools and sorting out the things that would be sold and what would be taken. Seeing him go about this appointed task left the rest of the family despondent, yet every objection others offered only hardened his resolve.

At dinner this evening, none of the relatives and friends offered further objections. They had all used their best arguments with father before and had not altered his commitment. The talk was of politics, the weather and the prospects for the spring planting. Jamie, her brother was allowed on this occasion to stay up late and listen to the discussions. Unlike Jenny, who like the rest of the women were assumed to have no interest in men's affairs, Jamie was allowed to join the men, but his silence was the price.

Jenny, if anyone cared to ask, would have also enjoyed the man's talk, but women's presence was not invited when men talked of serious matters. Her mother and the other women were expected to sit elsewhere and concern themselves with the more mundane things that consumed their days. To Jenny, such talk was boring. Raising kids, making soap, canning foods, spring cleaning and the other tasks that consumed her mother's days and those of her friends, lacked the romanticism that occupied her thoughts and her passions.

Jenny knew she would never be seeing these friends and relatives again. Although that knowledge saddened her, she knew that she could not change that fact. Staying up to be with them for the last moments would be an agony she could not endure. Her mother may need her companionship when that eventful moment of departure came, but Jenny knew she could do nothing to alleviate the pain of parting. Let father suffer the consequences of what he was doing to them. Let him console mother.

The tears that had stained her pillow so many nights before did not come tonight. Jenny had exhausted her emotions over the past months and felt depleted of further suffering. She heard the guest departing now. Fortunately they were saying their goodbye on the porch or out at the gate because she could no longer hear the murmur of voices. Jamie was climbing the ladder to the loft. She could hear the familiar creaking of the treads and the rustling of his straw mattress as he scrambled beneath the covers and struggled to remove his britches.

Jamie was small and sickly growing up and was only now gaining stature and strength. Mother called him delicate and sensitive. He had long suffered from breathing trouble and hard labor would soon leave him gasping for breath. She and mother would, on such occasions, hold his head in their laps, wiping away the sweat and spittle until he calmed down. Father treated him with indifference and had long since despaired of his attempts to make him a farmer. Jamie was relegated to those task that were helpful to mother. To mother that was just fine. She adored Jamie and was his buffer against the harshness of the demands about the farm. If father needed help with the plowing, harvesting, butchering or other tasks, mother thought it quite proper that he should hire help. She had even suggested one day that he could buy himself a slave if he needed a farm hand, but that suggestion had been met with a fierce, firm rejection.

The discussion of slavery was avoided around father. His opinions were definite, his arguments heated. The Reverend Jackson had forbidden further discussions of the subject at church and father and those of like mind necessitated the edict. Other Missouri farmers were not so intolerant and had purchased slaves. Of those who did, father would no longer associate.

Wayne had served in the militia that drove the Mormons from Daviess County and then out of Missouri. He had received a flesh wound at the

Battle of Crooked River. His experience with the Mormon uprising and its brutal suppression gave him a perspective of what the intrusion of slavery into Missouri would eventually bring. Fear and hate, once fed by the flames of passion, would blind men of their humanity and allow them to glory in the excesses of violence. Wayne had no desire to participate further in such events and did not want his family around when the inevitable conflict between the freeholders and slave owners erupted. The same men who so willingly slaughtered Mormons were still about in the state and were even now agitating against the slave owners.

Jenny had fallen into a light slumber, but was awakened by the rattling of the roof shakes. A cold wind was blowing and gusts of frigid air were permeating the loft, driving away the last of the warmth from the failing fire in the hearth below. Jamie was getting restless. When they were but toddlers, she and Jamie would share their blankets and warmth against the deepening chill of the night. Since Jamie was two years old they had slept together on these cold winter nights. Puberty had brought a halt to these intimacies. Father had built a partition between their sleeping mats to afford Jenny her privacy as her modesty increased with the blooming of her body. She no longer had the body of a small girl. Her breasts were now formed, and her body and emotions were no longer those of an adolescent.

She often, on these cold nights, wanted another's warmth and tonight she longed for the embrace and compassion of another but knew not the source of her emotions. Her thoughts and emotions were confused. Jamie was equally saddened by the prospect of leaving the farm, the animals he loved, the extended family and friends that were a comfort to him. Although he and Jenny now had a partition between them, they would often spend much of the night and would again on this night, discussing their disappointments and apprehensions at leaving Missouri.

Jenny and Jamie did talk long into the night until there was nothing more to be said and each then sought the escape of slumber. Jenny, deep in sleep, became gradually aware of the clanking of pans, the shuttling of the stove grates and the various smells that emanated from the kitchen below as her mother began the preparations for the morning meal. Her first reaction was to pull her head deeper under the covers. Jamie was still asleep buried under his covers. Frost would be clinging to the shingles above her head and would soon be melting and dripping on her bed. It was the resonant sound of her father's voice that brought to her an awareness of the hour and the need to be up tending to the many chores that awaited her and Jamie. She pounded on the partition to awaken Jamie. It seemed a mean thing to do to a warm sleeping Jamie, but Jenny had given up on coaxing him to get up and get dressed with gentleness. Jamie would merely crawl deeper under the covers and cling to sleep no matter what attempts were made to coax him into getting up to do his chores.

"Papa is up," Jenny admonished him, "Don't be late again or he'll send you off without your breakfast."

At this reminder, Jamie stumbled to his feet and pulled on his trousers. Jenny slipped back under her quilts and pulled on her clothes. The warm quilts provided to her what little privacy there was in the loft.

"Mix up some soda biscuits, Hon," her mother directed as Jenny walked into the kitchen. Jenny nodded to her mother and set to work. Jamie went to retrieve wood for the stove and fireplace. Father had already left for the barn to milk the two cows that remained of their once generous herd. Jenny glanced over at her mother. She noticed the growing strain that had been bearing heavily upon her mother of late. Her clear, silken complexion that was Jenny's inheritance, now bore a grayish pallor, worry lines were forming about her mouth and furrowing her brow. Carla was thirty-eight years old, and had remained frail after her last birth bore a stillborn child. It was one of those unstated sorrows that weighed heavily upon the household that Clara would bear no more children. Jenny knew that the trip across the continent that father had in mind would not be easy on her mother and she vowed to herself that she would do all she could to relieve her mother's burdens during the journey west. He mother's homespun dress appeared to fit her slender frame more loosely. The veins in her hands and arms seemed more prominent. She was still a pretty woman, but would not hold her beauty without more flesh on her waning frame.

Her mother had to use both hands to place the iron skillet on the stove. The smell of fresh brewed coffee was filling the air as her mother placed strips of thick cut bacon in the skillet. When the bacon was done, she would pour out some of the grease and then fry the eggs in the remainder. Jenny placed her biscuits on a sheet and placed them in the oven and proceeded to set the table. The butter was taken from the window box where it was kept overnight. The milk was in the pantry, covered with a cloth, she would have to mix in the cream after she spooned off some of the rich thick cream for her father's coffee. Honey her father had gathered from a hive found in the woods would be applied to the warm biscuits.

A burst of cold air entered the room as Jamie hurried across the floor with a scuttle filled with wood. Mother gave him a warm smile and tousled his hair as he passed her.

"Don't forget, your father wanted you to bring in the apple wood for the fireplace," she reminded him.

"Yes, Mama, I remembered, but I can hardly split it. He knows I can't."

"Do try, maybe Jenny can help you, I don't really need her help with the churning this morning with just two cows to tend too."

"But Mama, I can do the churning after I help Jamie. You leave it to me; you don't look like you feel well."

Jamie did not respond to the suggestion. He was aware of his mother's sheltering embrace and over time had come to accept it. But of late he was coming to the realization that he accepted that embrace not because he was still the sickly youth that had fostered his mother's concern, but because he did in fact find little interest in farming or in helping his father.

"I'll do just fine, please help Jamie, you know how it will go with Papa if he doesn't get the wood in."

Although Jenny bundled up in her father's old coat that hung on the peg by the kitchen door, the December morning had a cold, penetrating chill that made her catch her breath as she walked hurriedly to the wood shed. The sky was silver blue, the sun shown dimly through a murky haze. The wood shed was just a lean-to attached to the back of the barn. Ten cords of wood of various specie was stacked neatly in rows against the side of the barn. Jamie was awkwardly straddling the chopping block struggling mightily to dislodge the ax from where father had driven it.

"Never leave the blade exposed," Father had advised, "keeps it from rusting and don't cause no accidents."

Jenny added her weight to his efforts and freed the blade. Although his body had put on a growing streak of late and his pants and shirt were a size too small, his strength had lagged behind his growth. "You go ahead and gather the eggs, Jamie, and I'll split the wood, when you're finished you can carry it in and papa will never be the wiser. He's out in the field checking the fences in the far pasture. Hurry now."

Jamie gladly left the woodshed and headed to the chicken coop at the far side of the yard. Grandfather had built the coop, placing twelve by twelve cubicles along the wall where the hens could build their nests. Father liked to keep about thirty laying hens at a time. The excess eggs would be sold in town after they were sorted. Jamie loved to gather the eggs, he had a name for each of the hens and when they were not in their nest he would be quick to find their hidden nest, buried in the hayloft, in a manger, or in some other secret spot. On cold mornings, reaching under the warm hens was pleasing on his cold hands. He would talk to them as he took their eggs; call them by their name. He liked to think that he was talking them out of their eggs rather than taking them. It was the one task his father conceded he did well, for the egg production had greatly increased when Jamie took over the task of egg gathering. Before he left the coop with the mornings egg collection, he was careful to inspect the coop to see that no fox or coyote had been digging about to get access to the chickens. Papa said he could select the hens they would take west with them and he had been careful to observe which had been the best layers for the past few months. Jamie didn't want to know what would happen to the rest. Papa would be taking but six of the many hens each one of which Jamie had come to love.

Jamie added new straw to the nests, fed the chickens, broke the ice off the surface of their water container and left the door open so the hens could go about and scratch through the yard for gravel and what little feed they could find in the frozen ground. He checked each hen to make sure it had no sores. A chicken with an open sore would soon be pecked to death by the rest of the flock and an injured hen had to be put in a special cage until it had healed. Either that or Papa would butcher it for dinner. Jamie had watched his father kill a chicken only once and could not stand the thought of seeing him do it again.

As the spring weather warmed the land and gave its promise of renewal, the time was swiftly arriving when the trip westward would begin. And thus it was on the first week of April all the planning and preparation came to an end and the trip began. They were headed for Independence where they would join a wagon train yet to be organized. Independence was a struggling village nestled along the shores of the mighty Mississippi. It was a trading center where the produce from the farms were brought and would be carried downstream to New Orleans. The goods that were ordered from the East would be brought down the Ohio, onto the Mississippi and on to Independence. The mighty river was their lifeline to the greater world beyond. Independence, St Louis, St Joseph, and Westport had become the jumping off points of the westward migration. Each town vied for the trade that would be plentiful when the spring thaws brought emigrants to the jumping off point to Oregon.

The road was still frozen and skiffs of snow lay beside the road. It was a jarring lurching ride in the back of the wagon where Jenny and Jamie huddled under a buffalo robe that was a hand-me-down from their grandfather's days when buffalo wandered across the open planes of Missouri. Father said there would be herds in the thousands on the way to Oregon. The prospect of seeing these great herds was one of the few delights both Jamie and Jenny looked forward to.

There was an air of expectancy about the town. Wagons were being unloaded in the storage sheds and merchandise was filling the stores in anticipation of the arriving emigrants. To Jamie the town was a dismal place, its muddy streets, clapboard store fronts, and the smells of the many defecating animals was offensive to him. He liked the clean smell about the farm, and the pleasant view of the rolling hills. Jenny on the other hand was eager to see the people, especially the women as they strolled about the town tending to their affairs. The colorful dresses, the shawls, the bonnets, the shoes the women wore were in stark contrast to the plain homespun she wore. One day she dreamed, she would have a fancy dress, a colorful bonnet and shoes that came up to her calf, just like these city ladies. Mother, on the other hand, Jenny noticed, looked at these women with a critical, disdainful eye.

Father drove the wagon on through the town to a large gathering place where hundreds of other wagons had preceded them. Everything was in a state of confusion. Children and animals were everywhere to be seen. Groups of men and women stood about in animated conversation. The contents of the wagons were set about in rough campsites and the pungent smell of burning green wood filled the air and burned Jenny's eyes. Father drove the team out near the edge of the gathering and prepared a campsite.

The air was cool and the sky held the threat of a coming storm. Jenny could not remember a time when she felt more despair and foreboding. Jamie was huddling close to her transfixed by the scene from the back of the wagon. The long tiring journey from home was for a short while at least at an end, but there was no joy in their hearts and no willingness to leave the relative security of the wagon and join the confusion without. Mother seemed to share their complacency and sat in silence on the wagon seat as father unhitched the team.

"Come, Jenny, let's set about making camp," mother called as she climbed down from the wagon. "At least father has found some solid ground. It will be supper time soon and we need to be getting about and find some fire wood."

It was an awkward process to climb over the crates and barrels stored in the wagon, climb over the front seat and to then lower herself down the side of the wagon using the wheel spokes as a ladder. As usual her skirts and petticoat got hung up in the process and she found herself standing on the ground with her bloomers exposed. As she struggled to free herself from her embarrassment, she noticed that her father was conversing with two men, one obviously the father to the other younger man, both of whom had turned to witness Jennie's struggle with her skirts. The younger man was tall, thin, and swarthy and had a fine sharply featured face. He stood next to her father and was half a head taller. She was momentarily stunned to find she was the center of attention and ceased her struggles. The younger man's amused smile suddenly angered her. She pulled herself free and stomped behind the wagon where she sat down on a crate and buried her face in her hands, tears coming without restraint to add to her perplexity and confusion.

Jenny's experience with the opposite sex was extremely limited. Growing up on their farm was limiting enough, but most of her cousins who came visiting were either female or boys years younger than her. Her instincts told her that she had exposed an important part of her anatomy that was not to be seen by the opposite sex, but beyond that her embarrassment was even confusing to her. Why should she feel mortified by having the young man see her bloomers, or was he merely amused because of her predicament? Her mother's call for help setting up camp forced her away from the relative security behind the wagon. Jenny was relieved when she peered around the wagon gate to see that the young man and her father were engrossed in conversation and had her out of mind.

"William here will help you with your animals and show you where to picket them," the elder man was saying. "There's a meeting after supper with some of the emigrants where them that wants to be Captains and Scouts will give their spiel. You got to join up with some group and select your leaders so's you can get moving out of here before the whole damn lot of emigrants show up. By then all the good Scouts will be gone. You were smart to get here early."

As Jenny was helping her mother spread a protective tarp from the wagon to protect their meager campsite from the impending rain, she couldn't resist stealing surreptitious glances at the tall stranger who had returned to his wagon and was walking his horse back to where the older men were still engaged in conversation. He walked with a light confident step; his shoulders were broad and tapered down to a slim waist. Although his shirt was homespun, his pants were of leather, the type she had seen the Plainsmen in town wearing. His boots were of black leather and came up his calf. He wore a large knife strapped to his waist and a wide brimmed hat. Jenny was fascinated by this young man who seemed to be so confident in his bearing.

Before she could return to her work and feign to ignore the stranger, her father startled her. "Jenny, you and mother come over here, I want you to meet the Andersons, they're from Illinois. Where's Jamie, he still hiding in the wagon?"

"He's gone to find some fire wood or find out where we can get some," mother responded as she walked over to where the men were standing.

"Your gonn'a have to walk up river a ways to find some now. These Pilgrims are cleaning out the stuff close in. Mostly Cottonwood left that just smokes and don't burn until you've done with it," the man introduced as Paul Anderson volunteered. Paul Anderson was clean shaven unlike so many of the men about camp. He was dressed in what Jenny knew must be store bought clothes that gave him the appearance of a man of substance. He also wore high black boots, but his pants and coat were light brown and his shirt was the whitest Jennie had ever seen. Everything her mother made or washed always came out a light gray even though to them it passed for white. Paul Anderson had intense blue eyes that drew your attention as he spoke.

"Heading west to start a newspaper in Oregon. Had one back home, but when the wife died, the boys and I decided it was time to move on. My other boy, Clay, is out scavenging for wood like your boy. I'll introduce him later. Tonight's his night to cook. Ain't too good at it yet, but he's learning. Too bad his mother passed on so soon. Had no time to teach the boys what they need to know."

When Jenny was introduced to William Anderson, she forced herself to look straight into his eyes; she wanted to know if he was looking at her as a girl or a woman. She saw only warmth that was indiscernible from interest or continued amusement at her prior predicament. He surprised her when he held out his hand upon being introduced. Jenny hesitated at first. This was something that she had only witnessed when men were introduced to each other. There was an intimacy in this touching that she was unprepared for. His hand was warm and firm.

"Miss Jenny I am most pleased to meet you. You will be a welcome fellow traveler; that is if your father joins our train." He held her hand for what seemed like an eternity as he spoke to her. She felt her face flush and was aware that her mother was watching her with something akin to amusement and interest. She could no longer look him in the face and dropped her eyes only to notice a golden locket about his neck, tied with a rawhide string. Her immediate thought was that he had a sweetheart back in Illinois and would have little interest in a shy, unworldly farm girl from Missouri. She felt a disappointment that puzzled her. He released her hand then and turned to her mother to whom he was next introduced.

"Do talk your husband into joining our train, Mrs. Rawlins. We need folks like you along. You got a sturdy team and a good wagon. That puts you ahead of most folks."

"Papa does know his animals," Jenny blurted out to her own surprise, feeling a need to be a part of adult conversation. Both of the Anderson's gave her an appraising look that again caused Jenny to flush.

"He does that, child," the elder Anderson said. "Now William, you best be getting along with Mr. Rawlins and tend to his stock." At that remark, Mr. Anderson tipped his hat to Jenny and her mother and walked back to his wagon.

Jenny became aware that her mother was staring at her. She had been standing as if immobilized as William road away with her father. "Come

Jenny; let's get back to our work. He is a handsome young man, I'll admit." Her mother had been reading her mind and she tried to shrug off her discomfort. "He's all right for an older man," Jenny responded trying to sound dismissive. Her mother gave her a knowing smile and set to work.

Jenny's mind was on William's urging that they should join the Anderson's going west. All of a sudden she found herself interested in the organization of the train and the decisions that had to be made. Jenny, despite her assumption that William Anderson had committed himself to another woman, felt nonetheless an interest in him that she could not dismiss. She wanted her father to join the Anderson train, but, of course, that was a matter she dared not broach with her father. Father would make that decision without her or her mother's advice.

Jenny could tell that her mother was concerned about Jamie; he had not returned from his wood gathering. Mother didn't intent to send Jamie out alone to gather wood, but she knew that father would insist that Jamie should shoulder his share of the work. About then Clay Anderson came riding up on a pinto mare leading a pack horse loaded with firewood strapped to the pack saddle. A buck saw and ax were tied to the side of the wood bundle. Clay was clearly doing some serious wood gathering. Mother's worried features relaxed when she saw Jamie riding on the back of Clay's saddle. Clay rode over to their camp and helped Jamie down.

"Found this young man out gathering wood. He couldn't carry back enough by his self to boil a pot of beans. We got plenty for both of us here. Found some dry stuff up river. Didn't know you folks were camped right next to us, I'm Clay Anderson. You met my paw?"

Clay swung his leg over the saddle and dropped to the ground. He removed his hat and extended his hand to Clara. Clay wasn't as tall as his brother, nor did he have the lean physic of his older brother. He was heavier set, with a round soft featured face that gave promise of a warm, friendly personality. His dress was much like his brother's but rather than a knife, he wore a side arm. Jenny stood back next to the wagon with her hand on Jamie's shoulder as mother thanked Clay for his help.

"Jenny come and meet Clay Anderson, you met the rest of the family. Clay was kind enough to help Jamie gather fire wood."

Jenny pushed Jamie aside and whispered to him that he should start the fire before father returned, and then stepped forward to where her mother was standing still in conversation with Clay. She felt none of the awkwardness that had overwhelmed her when she confronted Clay's brother William. Clay once again swept his hat from his head and extended his hand. Unlike his brother, Clay's expression was not enigmatic. His face exuded an open friendliness that put Jenny at ease.

"It was good of you to help Jamie," Jenny responded to his firm hand shake. "He isn't strong enough yet to handle all the chores he's given. I don't think he will ever be a wood cutter."

"Don't you worry none about him, Miss Jenny, Jamie and I worked just fine together. He has a good heart and there's more to that boy then you'd expect."

The pleasure evident on her mother's face in response to Clay's remark was matched by the warmth Jenny now felt for this stranger that had so readily assessed the spirit of her brother. Jamie was not strong in physical strength, but there was a sweetness of spirit and openness about Jamie that her father, obsessed with the need for physical strength in his son, could never appreciate.

Clay, noticing that Jamie was struggling to start the fire, stepped over to where he was and crouched down beside him. "Excuse us ladies, but us boys have work to do here."

Jenny and her mother watched with barely concealed pride as Jamie, following Clay's instruction, soon had the cook fire ready for the start of the evening meal. Their pride was exceeded only by Jamie's.

"I think he likes me mama," Jamie said after Clay and excused himself and returned to his own campsite. "He told me he would be my friend."

"You couldn't do no better," mother responded, her eyes moistening. "I like him too."

GETTING STARTED

The sky continued to darken and a misty rain was falling, dampening the spirits of those who were eagerly awaiting the start of their great adventure. In a large clearing among the wagons the crowd slowly gathered, the women in their shawls, capes and bonnets, the men in slickers or heavy coats. Most of the people had gathered in groups and were discussing the merits of the various scouts and wagon captains who would be vying for their loyalty and commitment on the trail west. Each group had prepared a list of articles and conditions that each member of their train must abide. Some of the team captains insisted on inspecting each wagon and requiring that each wagon carry a certain amount of food consisting of flour, beans, bacon, sugar, salt, hard tack and some even insisted that their members carried dried fish and beef. Most of the emigrants had brought along some livestock that would furnish some sustenance for the owners. Most had extra oxen, mules and horses and this was also taken into consideration. Extra wheels, single trees, double trees, yokes, axles and wagon tongues were also important items that most wagon owners had to have before starting their journey west. Water barrels, wagon loads, wagon condition and the condition of your teams would be inspected most carefully .Wheelwrights and blacksmiths were aggressively courted by each wagon master.

The murmuring and milling about abruptly ended when several men climbed aboard a buckboard that had been placed in the center of the clearing. One of them was beating on a pan with a large spoon to get their attention.

"Let's be get'n on with this meeting. You got things to decide and we didn't all come here to sit about and talk. I'm Lester Mapes. I've organized the Mapes train and this here gent beside me is the scout I've hired. His name is Cranston He's been across the plains with Freemont on his first trip and he spent time trapping along the Yellowstone. He led a train west last year and I find him an able scout. I'd tell you some about myself, but I been up here before and you know who I am. Our train is leaving in two days. We got forty wagons and expect to have fifty by then. Don't care to have more wagons as I intend on being the first train across the plains to Oregon. My wagon's the one just across the circle here. It has the "Oregon or Bust" banner on it there. Come see me when you make up your mind. It'll be $250 dollars to join the train." Having made this short, terse statement, he stepped down.

Several other wagon masters got up and gave their pitch. Father made little comment until a wagon master named Peterson gave a longwinded passionate appeal.

"I wouldn't follow that fellow across the street. He and that scout of his are just out here to do business. I want to follow a man who has a reason other than our money to get across the plains. That Mapes, I don't want to be a part of a train that wants to travel fast. You got to know the limitations of your teams. Neither Mapes nor that Peterson fellow impresses me as knowing diddle about animals and their limitations."

Father's comments surprised Jenny. Father had obviously been spending some time about camp checking out the train captains. No doubt his trip out to the picket line with William and his milling about camp waiting for supper had been put to good use."

"How did you learn all that much about Peterson," mother asked.

"I looked over that Peterson wagon and team and asked around about him and his scout. That scout don't know the Indians out there any better than I do. We'll be meet'n up with some tribes out there and I want to have a scout along who knows them and can talk Indian talk. Peterson's animals don't look cared for. That ain't no man I want selecting wagon teams on any train I'll be part of."

Father's comments gave Jenny a better understanding of the decisions that now had to be made and gave her a renewed confidence in her father and his knowledge so newly gained about wagon training west.

Jamie seemed distracted by the events. He was studying the people about him with an intense interest. "Is that man a preacher," he blurted out, pointing to a tall, stern looking man all dressed in black standing but a few feet away. The man, even though Jamie's remark could be overheard, ignored the comment, but a pleasant auburn haired, rather large but well proportioned women at his side turned about and smiled at Jamie.

"You are a good observer young man. This is the Reverend Markus Whitman. We are traveling west to his mission at Walla Walla on the Columbia River. I expect you'll be stopping there when you get to the Oregon Territory. My name is Narcissa, what is your name young man?"

Jamie, embarrassed now at being overheard, spoke in a bare whisper. "I'm James, but they call me Jamie."

The exchange led to introductions all around. The Reverend Whitman's response to the introductions was perfunctory until he was introduced to Jenny's father. "I overheard your comments about the wagon masters. I will be interested in who you find fit for the command of the train. I've been over the trail before, but I have a wife to travel with me this trip and I want to be sure I'm with the right train." (¹)

The knowledge that the Reverend Whitman had crossed the plains before caused father to engage him in an intense conversation that was interrupted when they heard the announcement, "My name is Paul Anderson. . ."

Jenny watched her father intently as Mr. Anderson gave his presentation. Would father select Mr. Anderson's train? When Mr. Anderson introduced his scout, a murmur spread through the crowd that drew Jenny's attention back to the wagon upon which Mr. Anderson was standing. Beside Mr. Anderson, dressed in buckskins with raven black hair and a swarthy complexion stood a man as erect as a soldier on parade. Someone behind her muttered, "That's a breed. I wouldn't have no Niger Indian leadin' no train I'm part of."

The remark was not unfamiliar to Jenny who had heard insults uttered against blacks. She didn't see the connection between blacks and Indians and studied the Scour harder. He had an almost hawkish nose, high cheek bones and a firm, thin lipped mouth. If he was a breed Jenny expected that he was more Indian then white. "Is he an Indian?" Jenny asked her father.

"Hear his father was French and his mother was a Sioux. William tells me he knows this country west to the Oregon Territory better than any man here. I don't give a damn whether he's white or brown; he talks several native languages and knows the tribes. Can't see why he can't do the job."

"They call him Johnny Two Shoes among the tribes," Reverend Whitman volunteered. "Met him at Fort Hall on my first trip. He scouted for Freemont. Understand he has issues with that scout on the Mapes train, but won't talk none about it."

"Our train will be leaving in four days," Paul Anderson was saying. "Once we break camp and get under way I intend to stop a few days and organize the train into sections and to perform a few exercises to acquaint you all on how to form a protective corral and how to break camp, how to keep pace and how to maintain your animals and wagons. Can't do those

---

[1] Marcus Whitman took several trips across the Oregon Trail, none by wagon train. Narcissa, along with the wife of Reverend Henry Spalding were the first white women to cross on the Oregon Trail to Oregon. End of the Oregon Trail Interpretive Center, http:// www. endoftheoregontrail. org

things here in camp. I got over fifty wagons committed and will take about ten or so more.

When the meeting broke up, Jenny noticed the Whitmans hurrying over to the Anderson wagon to sign up. She was disappointed when her father turned away and headed back to camp. "Papa, aren't we going to join a train?" Jenny demanded.

"I already joined the Anderson train. Just came here to listen to the rest of them to be sure I done right. He's the only one of them that want to be leaders who's had any experience leading men. He was with the Illinois Militia during the Mormon wars up there when they forced the Mormons out of Missouri. It was his doing that kept the militia from firing on the innocent like we did in Missouri. I respect a man that can keep hot heads from running loose."

It was while they were returning to their wagon; Jenny and her family had to walk past the wagon train where several people were in conversation with Harold Mapes. Mapes' scout, a tall rangy man in buckskins was leaning on a rifle watching the crowd as it passed. Jenny noticed his eyes were fixed on her. When she glanced at him he gave her a smile that to her seemed inappropriate. It was inviting and intimate. Jenny turned quickly away and moved closer to her father. No one had ever looked at her like that and it was unsettling. What did he see in her that made him look at her like that? His look would haunt her thoughts that night. When she asked her mother about it to try to understand her emotions, her mother reminded her that she was a young lady of marriage age and she should expect men to notice her. To Jennie, however, the looks she got from the scout went beyond mere interest or curiosity. Jenny was relieved when the Mapes train pulled out of camp and headed west. She did not want to see the Mapes scout again.

The Rawlins wagon that had been situated at the outer circle of the camp was now lost in a sea of wagons as more and more wagons and families arrived and crowded about the camps being abandoned by those now heading west and filling the space others felt belong to them. The friction in the camp was increased proportionally with the arrival of new immigrants and the desire of those now in camp to start their journey west. The Anderson train, to which Jenny's father had committed, was being delayed as Mr. Anderson insisted on various members buying more supplies or equipment in preparation for the trek west.

Jenny's father spent his time touring the camp with Mr. Anderson and assisting him in inspecting the wagons that would join the train. When not traveling about the camp, father was inspecting and repairing harnesses, sorting through the wagon for things that could be left behind to lighten the load or to make way for more needed supplies. It was four days after the meeting in the meadow that father came home and advised the family to get an early supper, they had to pack the wagon. Tomorrow at sunrise, they were heading west.

"We've got time for one more trip to town. The owner of the General Store sends a buggy out and hauls people to town who wants to shop at his store. We'll take the next wagon. I need to get some more powder and shot."

Jenny and her mother scurried to prepare for the trip to town. It was the only relief they would have from the boredom of camp life and the strain of the long trip from the family farm to the plot of muddy ground they now claimed as their earthly domain.

Jenny and Jamie were left to wander about the store and mother and father set about the more serious business of last minute shopping. They had never been in a store as large as the General Store and were dumb struck by the variety of goods on display.

Jenny had never seen store bought dresses on display, and there were a dozen or more hanging on a rack. She wanted to inspect each one and was fascinated by the variety of colors and styles. She touched the dresses to feel the material, satins, silks, cottons that had a texture in sharp contrast to the homespun she wore. The rows of material in various patterns, hues and textures invited her curiosity. How did it feel to wear a dress made out of these materials? Would she ever know? On the shelves near the dresses were undergarments that she would simply swoon to try on. The shoes with laces up the calf were in sharp contrast to the utilitarian boots she wore. Her imagination was carrying her into worlds beyond all her hopes. It was then she noticed several women enter the store who wore clothes similar to those she was admiring. Their faces were made up in a manor Jenny had never seen. Their lips were accented with something red, their cheeks had a reddish caste and their hair was captured under a strikingly elaborate hat that had a veil covering part of their face. Their dresses with ample bustles were of the quality Jenny admired on the dress rack. Long colorful gloves covered their arms to the elbows. Jenny backed to the rear of the store as the ladies approached the clothes rack. The store proprietor was at their elbow.

"These dresses just came in from New Orleans. They're the latest fashion," he was advising the ladies.

Before the ladies could see her in her simple garb, Jenny retreated further to the back of the store where Jamie was inspecting the rabbits and chicks. It was here that her mother took her by the elbow and told her it was time to leave. By the look mother gave the two ladies, Jenny was certain that they were the reason mother was hurrying her from the store.

"But who are those ladies," Jenny asked her mother, "And why are they dressed that way."

Mother hesitated before answering but finally blurted out. "Those are dance hall girls." Her mother would answer no more questions on the subject and hurried her down the board walk to where father stood watching a salesman extolling the virtues of a bottle of potions that would cure all ills from indigestion to snake bite.

"You girls finally done with all your gawking? Let's be getting back to camp. There's plenty to get done."

ON THE TRAIL

Forming up a wagon train turned out to be a problem of monumental proportions. First, the wagon owners had to sort out their animals from the large herd that had gathered outside of the camp, harness up teams and bring them into the camp area, hitch up and then maneuver through the hundreds of closely quartered wagons to the gathering point. Father had to get several nearby wagons pushed out of his way before he could proceed. Even then the halting effort to clear the camp with other wagon teams trying to form up or pull out of camp evoked a good deal of cursing and shouting that made the animals nervous and their drivers ill tempered. It was not until noon that the long line of wagons making up the Anderson train had formed in a long line along the muddy trench that made up the start of the road west. To aggravate matters, the rain that had been falling sporadically while they were in camp, came down now in torrents driven by a gusting wind that drove the dampness into wagons, dampening all within and drenching those who had to move about forming the wagons, moving the herds or were committed to riding or walking their way west.

The country they were moving through was impassable except along the crude roads that led first north along the river and then west forcing the train to proceed in file along the fast deteriorating road. The teams were laboring to pull the wagons and some were becoming mired and needed help to keep moving. The train had proceeded only a few miles when everything came to a halt. Clay Anderson, after an hour's delay came riding down the line and informed them that they had met up with a junction that lead down from St Louis and that another train was passing through. They should make camp where they were so the other train could pass and get well out of their way.

"They'll mess up the trail some; there must be a hundred wagons in that train. If the rain stops before morning the going will be easier."

There was no opportunity to build a camp fire, nor solid ground to form a camp site. The immigrants unhitched their teams and spent a wet, miserable night. Their dinner consisted of hard-tack and dried meat. The next morning, most of the wagoneers wanted to wait out the weather as their teams were suffering from the effort of pulling the wagons through the mire that made up the trail.

"Like to oblige you folks, but the Peterson train is coming on and will pass us if we don't get moving. That ain't going to make the trail no better," was Paul Anderson's response.

The rain had stopped, but the trail did not improve. The St Louis wagon train, with its hundreds of defecating animals made the trail little better than an endless barn yard. On the third morning, the clouds were gone, but the heat of the sun was drawing moisture from the ground shrouding the trail in a vaporous, odiferous fog bank. By the fourth day, the trail widened, the brush and shrubbery that had confined the wagons to a single track gave way to prairie lands that would ease their passage. The wagons could now form columns and leave the path of the trains that preceded them. On the fifth day, Mr. Anderson called a halt to rest the teams and organize the wagons into companies and organize the traveling order of the wagons. The graze was abundant and the animals would soon recover their strength.

"Where is that wood cutting partner of mine?" Clay Anderson inquired as he rode into their camp and spoke to Jenny. "I found some woods over yonder where we can get some dry firewood for you folks."

Jamie, who had been in the wagon fussing with his wet bedroll, hoping to get it into the sun light, jumped from the wagon in delight and was up behind Clay's saddle in a flurry.

The luxury of a warm camp fire drove the sadness from her mother's otherwise tired, ashen face. Soon there were ropes and poles strung around every campsite as the immigrants took the opportunity to dry out their possessions. Father had gone from camp to tend to the livestock. Lucy, the milk cow they brought along was still giving milk and needed milking to keep her from drying up. He would inspect and care for the oxen and the two horses that make up his share of the herd. William Anderson, who father now referred as Bill, was in charge of the herd and father, when not required to drive the wagon, would help William. Father was pleased to see a fire going in camp and relished the prospect of a warm meal.

"The boy get you this wood?" father asked as he settled next to the fire using a crate from the wagon as his chair.

"He went out with Clay Anderson and they both gathered the wood." Mother responded. "Clay asked if Jamie could ride with him tomorrow when he goes hunting for some fresh meat."

Father seemed somewhat incredulous when he looked at Jamie who was still glowing from Clay's attention, "You mean you want to go, boy? You ain't been too partial to butchering at the farm. You gott'a dress out them animals that get kilt and I don't think it'll sit well if you get sick when they's skinnin' the kill."

"Can't say's I'd object to seeing you learn some helpful things. Maybe you could be the family hunter. I ain't got time to be hunting and any extra meat will be appreciated. I'll saddle up Chester for you in the morning. You gonn'a want a rifle?"

Jenny and her mother could hardly believe how readily father was granting Jamie's request. Father would normally have dismissed such a request and surely would not be encouraging it as he was now. Of course father's attitude was no more difficult to comprehend than was Jamie's request. Jamie declined the rifle, surprised that it was offered. He had never been allowed to use one when he cried the one time father had tried to teach him to shoot. Besides, he doubted his father would let him have his Henry and his other rifle was so heavy only father could handle it.

"Can I take your hunting knife," Jamie asked.

At that request, they all looked again at Jamie with incredulity. Clay Anderson was definitely having a marked influence on Jamie.

The sun was burning off the early morning mist as Jamie and Clay crossed the prairie searching for some sign of game. The abundance of an early spring was everywhere in evidence. Fields of yellow, blue and purple flowers gave a vivid cast to green grass lands they were crossing. They were heading south of the wagon tracks where distant stands of cottonwood gave promise of good cover and good hunting.

"Franco our scout says he seen deer sign aplenty over yonder. There's a stream where the critters water. Should be far enough off the track so's not to have been bothered by hunters from them other trains," Clay advised Jamie. "Don't matter none that you're not wantin' to shoot no animals. We can't pack much back anyway. Sides, I don't mind doin' all the shootin"

Jamie was having some doubts about this hunting business, but his desire to be with Clay overrode his anxieties. He was glad that he was not going to have to do the shooting, but knew he would have to help dress the animals. He had helped his father some with the spring butchering, but his distaste for the work left him with little knowledge of the process. However, Jamie was coming to his own realization that he was no longer living an ordered life where everything the family needed was available on the farm. Living in a wagon and on the road, eating what was available, warm or cold, enduring the discomforts of wet and cold that had been their life in the wagon for the past month made Jamie want to do more to help. Above all he wanted to get away from the camp, the constants and intrusions of the close quarters they had to share. The prospect of hunting was a more appealing alternative then his existence within the train. On the farm, his mother and Jenny had been his comforters and would shelter him from many of the things he found distasteful. As the trip from home and the dreariness of the camp and now the traveling wore upon the energies of the women, Jamie found they had less and less time for him and were often too tired to console him.

And then he met Clay. When ordered to gather firewood that first day in camp, Jamie moved close along the river bank to find fallen wood. He hadn't brought an ax, that was just more weight and would mean that he couldn't carry the wood they needed. Jamie knew he would have to make several trips, but the distance he was moving away from camp made several trips before darkness doubtful. He had bundled together a quantity of loose sticks and limbs when he came upon the sound of a man sawing wood. Jamie walked carefully toward the sound and saw a man with a buck saw sawing away at a fallen tree. With his back still towards Jamie the man stopped sawing and without turning about called to him, "Come on over here boy and introduce yourself. Don't worry none about me stealing them sticks of yours."

Jamie was too startled to say anything and stood looking about. How did this man know he was behind him? By then the man had laid his saw aside and sat down on the log he was working on and faced Jamie.

"You're with them emigrants that just pulled into camp, aren't you son? Saw your wagon pulling in as I was leaving camp. Expect you folks will be wantin' a warm fire tonight. Think you got enough wood there to do the job?"

Jamie still stared at the man and gave no answer. Jamie was always shy with strangers and would usually have his mother or Jenny about to divert the attention of strangers from him. Finally Jamie managed to say,

"My name is Jamie. How'd you know I was here?"

At that the stranger smiled, "Now that's more like it. Can't carry on no conversation with a fella who don't talk. I'm Clay Anderson. Heard you comin' a spell ago and been watching you for a bit. You don't want to be out here in the woods not knowin' who's about with you. Set down that bundle you got there and come sit a moment."

Jamie set down his load and rather than sit next to the stranger found a stump a few feet away and sat looking at the stranger wondering what was expected of him.

Clay Anderson was still smiling at him. "You're a bit shy I see. No need to be. I was kind 'a hoping you was willing to help me get this here wood I cut back to camp. You're welcome to your share, of course."

Jamie suspected the man needed no help, but the prospect of bringing back enough wood to make a good fire was more then he could resist.

Anyway the man's outward friendliness was disarming and Jamie was warming up to this stranger.

Noting Jamie's shyness and wanting to help this shy boy who was sent out to do a task he wasn't up too, Clay reached across and offered his hand.

"O.K., lad lets shake on it and get to work. We are going to be good friends I expect. We got a long way to travel together."

When Paul Anderson saw Clay returning to camp with the young Rawlins boy, a knowing smile crossed his face. Clay had been close to his younger brother Arthur who had died of the same sickness that had swept through their Indiana town two springs ago. Clay, Mr. Anderson suspected, had adopted another brother. Unlike William, who was older and who had been studying for the law, Clay felt compassion for his younger brother and had taken to teaching him all about the things Clay loved, and that had to do with all things to do with the outdoors, hunting, fishing, exploring and spending days at a time away from home trapping for furs. The loss of both their mother and younger brother within days of each other had torn the family apart, but the loss to Clay seemed far worse than it had been to William. Clay took to brooding for days on end. It was because none of them cared to live with the memories of their lost loved ones that the father and the sons decided to head west to a new life.

"They're some deer over there in that thicket," Jamie said, halting his horse and pointing ahead.

Clay reigned in his pinto and looked to the spot where Jamie was pointing. "Don't see nothin', James, you sure?"

"Right there, by that big tree that got a broken top," Jamie assured him.

Clay studied the spot for a few moments. "By Jove, you're right lad, I see 'em now. You got you some good eyes. I'd walked right on and scared them off. Huntin' out here ain't like huntin' in the woods back home. You need good eyes to see them critters out here. I'll be needin' you along when I go hunting. Let's tether these horses and see if'n we can't get a little closer. This gun don't have the range to shoot from here. Sides, all them branches might deflect the ball."

Jamie stayed well behind Clay as they crept forward through the tall grass. "Careful where you step lad, them critters can hear you a mile off. We're down wind and ought to get in close if we don't spook 'em."

Jamie was almost crawling through the grass as they drew closer. In order to see better he spotted some high ground to his left and started to crawl towards it to get a better look. As he got closer, he noticed that the mound was not unoccupied. Dozens of furry little creatures were scurrying about the mound, darting in and out of holes that they had dug in the mound. They would occasional stop and stand on the hind legs, their front paws held against their chest and smell for sent. Jamie was engrossed in this scurry of activity until it was interrupted by the thundering report of Clay's rifle. In a second the mound was deserted; not a prairie dog in sight.

Jamie stood then and saw the large buck stagger a few steps and then crash to earth. Jamie's first inclination was to sink to the ground and hide his head in his hands. He pictured in his mind his last view of the beautiful buck that was grazing in the wood lot below unaware of the danger that faced it. Uncontrolled sobs were bursting from his chest and his body trembled with the hurt that possessed him. He forced himself to look up to where Clay was now standing reloading his rifle and slowly walking down toward his kill. Jamie didn't want Clay to see him in his distress and thought immediately of the horses and ran to where they were and led them down to where Clay was now inspecting his kill. Sobs were still contorting his body, but he was driving himself to face the reality that the killing must be accepted and he had to steel himself to the fact that his family needed the flesh that now laid quivering and dying before him. Clay stooped and deftly slit the animal's throat and pulled its hindquarters about so that the blood would drain from the carcass. Jamie felt the bile rise into his mouth and struggled to contain it.

Clay wiped the blood from the blade of his knife against the hide of the deer, sheathed it and then step over to Jamie and placed his hands on his shoulders forcing him to look him in the face.

"I knew this wasn't going to be easy on you son and I admire your courage in facing your demons. Ain't no pretty sight to kill one of these critters? I'll tell you a secret and it's just between you and me, understand?"

Jamie tried to avert his eyes, but Clays grip was firm and he waited until Jamie wiped the tears from his eyes. Clay then placed his arms about Jamie and gave him a reassuring hug.

"Now then you got to know I ain't bothered about how you been grieving' over this kill. Truth is when I shot my first critter, it be a big buck like this one, I blubbered about it just like you be doin'. It ain't man's nature to be a killin' things and if'n he git's so's he likes it or takes joy in it he got troubles. Anyways, I was sittin' there blubberin' of this here kill of mine when out of nowhere step this Winnidota brave, walks over to my kill and cuts its throat ignoring me like I was a stump. Then he kneels down and goes through some sign, raising his hands toward the sky and chanting some Indian song. Then he starts to dress the critter out and I came to my senses and asked him what the devil he was doing to my deer. 'Not your deer,' he said and continued to gut the critter. About then I got steamed and put my rifle on him, forgettin' I didn't reload the dam thing. The brave gave me a mean look and kept working on the carcass. He rolled the deer over and proceeded to pull and arrow out of its side. It was then I took a good look at that critter and there weren't no bullet holes in that carcass. I leant one lesson from that encounter and that's one you gotta' learn to. That critter was gonn'a get kilt and be someone's supper. Now that Injin' he thanked the spirit father for givin' him that kill. That made him accept the killin' he done. Now if it makes it easy for you, you can do as that brave done and thank the Lord for providin' us with this meat. Truth is he knows you need to eat and he accepts what we done. We don't eat this critter the coyotes and buzzards will, so what you say we get it back to camp. Our folks needs this meat too."

    Jamie rode back to camp in silence. Clay, knowing Jamie was fighting his demons left him to his thoughts. Last night when he announced his intentions to go on the hunt with Clay, Jamie wanted very much to be a part of what he now realized was a different world then he had known. He had watched the other boys about camp, frolicking about, playing games and showing an independence from the rigid constraints that had been his life on the farm. The older boys, not much older than himself were doing men's work and did not stay about camp to be with the women as Jamie had been doing. When Clay asked him to go hunting with him, he felt that perhaps he could emulate the other boys and become more of a man. He despaired that his inner nature failed him and when the deer was killed he felt the same sickness and revulsion that always plagued him when he saw animals killed or suffering. He knew his father would inspect his hunting knife when he returned it to him for signs of blood. Father always cleaned and sharpened his knife after butchering. Jamie wondered if he would ever be like those older boys and become a man like his father. But it was not his father he wanted to be like; he wanted to be like his new friend Clay. Jamie was certain he had disappointed Clay and that he would not be invited to accompany him on future trips away from camp hunting and exploring.

The joy in Jamie's heart almost brought him to tears, tears he knew he could no longer allow if he was going to be a man, when Clay announced, when the returned to camp,

"If you folks don't mind, I'll be askin' James to come along with me next time I go hunting. He has eyes like an eagle. I wouldn't even seen this deer but for James here spotting if for me."

Jamie was so overjoyed with the invitation that it was not until he sat down to dinner that he remembered that Clay had called him James, and not Jamie. Clay was still his friend and unlike his previous revulsions at eating the kill, Jamie ate his meal without hesitation.

GETTING STARTED

The weather continued to improve as the wagon train started out on the trail again. Other wagon trains could still be seen in the distance, some of them ahead of them and some behind. The scout, the Indians called Johnnie Two Shoes, but who Mr. Anderson called Franco, was guiding them along a trail that would afford them grass for their animals and fresh water. The further they could get away from the other trains, the better it would be. The moisture from the winter snow and spring rain allowed the wagon trains to move along the trail without the choking dust that would soon plague their travels. The scout, Franco, assured them that the Indians in this part of the country were friendly and that in any event; few would be seen on the prairies at this time of year. Their hunting grounds were to the north and only later in the summer would they come south to hunt for buffalo.

A monotonous routine was settling into the train. The train moved out at sunrise and encamped at sunset. Fire wood was getting scarce and the emigrants were soon acquainted with the many benefits of the buffalo as they collected buffalo chips as they traveled the plains and suffered the smoky, pungent campfires that offered barely sufficient heat to prepare their meals. Each morning, the wagon that trailed the train on the day before would move to the head of the column, but any team that couldn't keep the pace was ordered off the trail to follow the column. Each night the lagging wagons would join the camp and suffer the disadvantage of a short night's rest and early start.

"They'll learn to keep the pace," was Paul Anderson's response to the complaint that leaving wagons behind might attract Indian attacks when they got into hostile country. "My concern is to get this train to Oregon before winter sets in. If we get caught wintering along the trail there's gonna be a hell of a lot more lives lost then a few stragglers. No one asks these folks to go to Oregon. Gettin' them there is now my responsibility and they know my rules."

Jenny had early on found that the discomfort of riding in the wagon was not to be endured. She, along with most of the women, walked the trail beside the wagon, often wandering away from the train to collect buffalo chips and occasionally the fire wood that could be scavenged from the discarded furniture of the trains that passed before them. The further they proceeded along the trail, the more discards they came upon. When Jenny came across some of these discards she would appreciate the wisdom of her father when he refused to allow mother to take along the family heirlooms she felt she could not part with or start a new home without. Jenny could sympathize with the heartache that must have been felt by the many women who had to finally submit to the reality that they must at last part with those many possessions that had given substance to their young, more ordered lives. The wagon's owner that found it difficult to keep pace with the rest of the train were the ones that would be discarding the burdens that caused their teams to falter as the effort of keeping pace broke their teams down.

At night the wagons would be formed into a large circle and the teams, when water was available would be herded to the water course and then allowed to graze and rest. Franco insisted they circle the wagons even when there was no sign of Indians. "Can't be leaving the horses away from camp. You may not see any Indian sign, but you leave them horses loose and you'll soon enough find out they been here." And so it was that each night the horses and mules would be herded into the corral made by the circled wagons.

"They ain't gonna' try and steal them cows and sheep, they don't move along fast enough. They might butcher a few, but we'd run them down before they got far if'n they trys to steal 'em. If'n they get a horse or a mule though, you ain't likely to see it again," Franco advised them. "Some of them tribes can steal your horse while you be sittin' in the saddle."

Jamie was given permission by his father to ride along with Clay while Clay rode along the train to help keep the wagons up to pace. He was becoming more comfortable in the saddle and could now control Chester, who now seemed to accept Janie's commands without his usual contentiousness. Chester had been his mother's horse and though lacking in the spirit of Empress, his father's pride, Chester made up for it in orneriness. If he saw a tempting clump of grass, Chester would usually mosey over and graze, leaving Jamie helpless to pull him free. If Chester came to a suitable rock outcrop or wagon, Chester would rub along it trying to unseat Jamie. It was Clay who finally took a hand in the matter. "It ain't much matter what that critter does about camp, but you can't be lettin' him get by with that meanness when you get out on the prairie. It ain't no place to be left afoot. Teach him his manners or keep him in camp."

Jamie was chagrined to be admonished so by Clay, but he also knew he had been given some good advice. "I don't know what to do, Clay. He's so strong and bull headed."

"Horses is always stronger than us, you got to get them to know you're boss. Go talk to Franco. He knows more about horse ways then any man I know. I kin make Nancy here mind 'couse she knows I'm strong enough to bring her misery. You got to be like them Indian boys who know's horse's ways and can make 'em want to mind."

Carla Rawlins was becoming more and more concerned about her condition. She well knew she had never fully regained her strength and determination after her last miscarriage, but she was able to pace herself and with the help of Jenny, she could get by. Here on the trail to Oregon, she had no time to rest. When night came, it was the cold and the wind, or the rain would keep her from getting her rest. She was now always tired. Then there was her relationship with her husband Wayne. His father had named him after "Mad" Anthony Wayne with whom he had served at the Battle of Fallen Timbers. Perhaps it was the association with his name sake that made Wayne such a fiercely independent and determined man. Her husband, when told he could no longer have relations with his wife without fear of causing her death, withdrew from her and now treated her more like a sister or a friend.

It was hurtful to her that he no longer came to her for the companionship her love could offer. When they had conversations, it was as if between acquaintances and the exchanges gave her no comfort. Somehow she felt that this need to go to Oregon was caused by her inability to give him the sons he wanted to help tend and one day inherit the farm that had once been Wayne's great pride. The son she did give him turned out to be frail and unsuited for the awful burdens of farming. Going to Oregon, in Carla's mind would solve none of his problems; it would only amount to running away from one difficult situation to find them in a similar one. She did appreciate his concern for the mounting division over the issue of slavery, yet, on the trains heading west, many were bringing their slaves along with them. Would not Oregon become dependent on slavery like the south?

Her one comfort was seeing the change in Jamie, who had just the other day told his mother and Jenny that they should no longer call him Jamie. His name was James and that is what they should call him. Shortly thereafter, James had removed his bed roll from the wagon where he slept with her and Jenny and started sleeping under the wagon with his father. He even insisted on having Wayne's old rifle by his side, so like his father he could help defend the train if need arrived. James was spending more and more time with Franco and Clay Anderson and seemed to be always out with the animals or riding beside them. She had expected Wayne to object to his son frequent absence. Instead Wayne passed it off. "The boy needs men's company. I been a poor companion to the boy 'cause I always had to do his work too. Let him grow up. They's good men he's with."

Wayne's attitude confused her. If he wanted his son to have a man's company, shouldn't he be the one to give it. Was he really that alienated from his own son that he would let others raise him into manhood? Or was he really unconsciously upset with her for making James what Wayne called a mama's boy and expressing his feelings by turning away from his son. Although these concerns weighed heavily upon her mind, Carla was pleased to notice how fast James was now growing and filling out. Her greatest pleasure was seeing James ride home one afternoon wearing a pair of leather pants made out of the skins of some of the deer that he and Clay had killed. They were of the same style worn by Clay and Franco. James's pleasure was transformed into an even more mannish attitude toward her and Jenny. He no longer allowed them to hug him or to ruffle his hair, a habit they were much inclined toward. It almost felt to Carla, and she often thought of it, that her waning strength was somehow being transferred to her son. She wanted to believe that she was leaving to him the added strength he would need to survive the ordeal of the trail west. Carla was becoming more and more certain that at trails end, she would be with her family only as a memory. A memory that would give them a warmth and strength very different from what their father would be able to give them.

They were traveling six to ten miles a day. On some days they made no progress at all as time was spent fording a swift moving stream, swollen by the spring thaw. On one occasion the wagons had to be taken across one at a time, secured by ropes to keep them from floating away. Then there would be the frantic crossing of the herd. Some would not make it and be carried away by the current. Even on the trail itself, death had come unexpectedly one day when the young Clayton boy who was allowed to ride on the wagon seat, fell asleep and was crushed under the wagon wheel of the Clayton wagon. Another child died from stomach troubles. His cries, heard through the night, became less frequent and more muted as sunrise gave renewal to the land and finality to the child's passing.

But day upon day the train moved on until the movement itself was a numbness, a numbness that saved them from despair. Everything became a routine, interrupted only by another tragedy or hardship. It was a relief to them all when Franco announced that Fort Kearny lay just ahead and they would be reaching it in a couple of days.

Fort Kearny was a disappointment to those who were seeking a trace of civilization. It was made up of a number of sod walled structures along the banks of the Missouri River ([2]) Several hundred soldiers were stationed there to protect the immigrants from nearby Indians who were more

---

[2] Fort Kearny was located on the Missouri River in 1846 and was moved to the Platte River to protect the emigrants on the Oregon Trail in 1846. For a description of the fort see: Oregon-California Trails Association, http://www.octa-trails.org/JumpingOffToday/virtualTour/FortKearny.asp

interested in trading or stealing goods from the settlers then they were of attacking them. The relief if any Carla got from the Fort was the respite afforded by the brief stop and a chance to rest. Many of the emigrants were re-outfitting and buying supplies for the continued journey. As had been the case on the trail, the dust caused by the constant movement of wagons and horses was unrelenting; it was in their hair, their clothes, their bedding and even in their food.

Wayne was able to buy grain for the animals who were much in need of nourishment beyond what they received from the grass and brush along the trail. It was while at the fort that Carla had her first confrontation with her daughter's rapid maturity. The soldiers about the fort were, as Clay Anderson had warned, not the noblest of men. The army of the west was made up of the drunks and outcast that they culled from the eastern establishment. Not many were fit to fight then alone grace a uniform, uniforms which were usually dirty and worn with little respect.

"Keep your girls away from them," Clay warned.

Jenny had asked to go into the Fort compound to accompany several of her young acquaintances, all of whom would be escorted by Mrs. Estelle, as a more or less chaperone. They wanted to see the trade goods and see the River boats up close. Carla gave her permission, she wanted to lie down and rest awhile and for once be alone in the wagon. Her rest was shattered when she heard the excited, hysterical voices of the young ladies as the rushed back to the wagon. Carla, with great effort, made her way to the front of the wagon in time to see Jenny and the two Estelle girls rush into camp with Mrs. Estelle hurrying along behind them.

Jenny was sobbing and was incoherent, but Carla could see that a part of her dress along the waist was torn.

"Those damn soldiers," Mrs. Estelle was sputtering, "Those damn soldiers, we should have listened to Mr. Anderson."

Carla climbed down from the wagon and took the distraught Jenny into her arms.

"Dear, child, what on earth happened? Your dress is torn, who did this to you?"

Jenny didn't respond, she only sobbed harder. By now a crowd was gathering about them and Jenny was shying away. It was Mrs. Estelle who finally gave Carla the details. When they finished looking over the trade goods, they had gone down to the wharf to look at the riverboats.

"Some of them soldiers that come off the boat, no doubt replacements, was drinking before they got off. When they saw the girls they got downright nasty and started saying things to the girls that was insulting. I ain't about to repeat what they said. One of them grabbed Jenny and tried to pull her behind some boxes. That's when her dress got torn. That William Anderson was about, thank goodness. He picked up a shovel off'n one of them piles of goods and smacked that soldier square over the head and laid him out like a dressed duck. That plum took the fun out of things for the rest of them soldiers and when William pulled out that big knife he totes about, they ran off."

The men who were gathered about were about to storm over to the Fort and take matters into hand, when the strong, calming voice of Dr. Whitman intervened.

"It is a sad display them soldiers made of themselves, but don't go rushing over to the Fort with blood in your eye. I'll have a talk with the Commandant and we can get this settled. The girl was not hurt, just frightened. She ain't gonna' be no better off if a bunch of noses get broken."

When Dr. Whitman got to the Commandant's office he was surprised to see a crowed had already gathered. The unconscious soldier lay on the entry porch of the office. William was in a heated discussion with what appeared to be the Commandant's orderly, who was a Lieutenant. There was some argument as to why the soldier hadn't been taken to the infirmary rather than to the Commandant's quarters.

"I packed that carcass as far as I intend to. He's army property; you carry him the rest of the way. I brought him here so that the Major would have some cause to tell the rest of his soldiers why they should lay off of our women."

The major, who had been reading the latest reports delivered to him from the riverboat, hearing the commotion step out of his office,

"Is this man dead," he asked the Lieutenant looking at the inert body of the soldier. "And what the hell is he doing here?"

"He ain't dead, sir. This here pilgrim struck him over the head claiming he was mistreating some lady of his."

William was caught off guard by the suggestion that Jenny was his lady. Was that why he was quick to respond so violently to this soldier's actions? He realized that the soldier's conduct did have a savage reaction in him. He would give that matter some consideration, but now the Major was asking him a question.

"Is your young lady all right? Do you want to prefer any charges?"

Looking at the prostrate body of the soldier, who was now moaning and showing signs of recovery, William's anger left him. This man had had his punishment. He would have one hell of a head ache for some days. Besides, William had other things on his mind now.

"I guess this boy will know better next time, Major. I don't want any more of him." With that said, William turned and headed back to camp his mind unsettled by the suggestion that Jenny was his women. Several other members of the train company had heard the assertion made by the army officers. Should he have denied the suggestion or did he in fact fancy the thought. Jenny, in the short time he had known her, was transforming from the young shy girl he first saw in her embarrassment the time she exited the wagon, into an attractive young lady who was definitely coming of age. Life on the trail was forcing many of the young people into maturity, but that alone did not account for the change in Jenny. The vestiges of a robust, youthful body had given away to a tall slim stature with a well pronounced waist and bust. Her face was leaner, losing its fleshiness and now featured high cheek bones, sensuous lips, dark blue eyes with lashes, the longest William had seen. Her dark raven hair was allowed to cascade over her shoulders silhouetting her lightly tanned intense features. William would not be in a hurry to deny his interest in Jenny. He was going to see if this spark of interest was mutual and promising.

Jenny at this moment had other concerns about the intentions of men. Her mother had her climb into the wagon away from all the gawking people who had been drawn to the wagon by the commotion. When Carla dismissed the crowd, assuring them that things were under control and climbed into the wagon to comfort her daughter, Jenny was still shaking and sobbing.

"What did he mean mama, what did he want to do to me?" Jenny finally blurted out.

"Tell me what happened child, I only heard what Mrs. Estelle had to say."

Controlling her sobs after several deep breaths, Jenny told her mother that they had walked down to the peer to see the steamer unload its cargo when four soldiers came staggering out of one of the side rooms and shouting and cursing headed down the gang plank with one of the ships officers right behind them pushing them along. When they got half way down, they saw Jenny and her companions.

"Look boys," the largest of them shouted, "we got some young ladies from the Fort that come down to greet us. Now ain't that just like the Army."

Jenny told her mother that Mrs. Estelle immediately turned them about and headed back toward the Fort. That was when the soldier scrambled down the gang plank and grabbed Jenny by waist and tried to pull her back behind some shipping crates.

"He said he got a big hard on for me and wanted me to see it. He said my honey pot was wasting away and needed some man's attentions. What did he mean, mama and why was he trying to hurt me?"

Carla knew she had to talk to Jenny about the ways of men, but this was not the situation she had envisioned that would give rise to the occasion. When Jenny started having her periods, Carla told her how her body was preparing for child baring, but she had been purposely vague about how that matter was accomplished, knowing that the subject would be addressed again when Jenny needed to know more of the particulars. Carla had wanted to make the lovemaking between a man and a women sound special and natural. The vulgarness of the relationship that was common among drunks and scoundrels was something she had hoped to shelter her daughter from. That hope was now lost. Jenny had seen the lowest and bases of a man's desires and now Carla had to try to salvage her daughter's prospects for a happy future and marriage.

Perhaps it was her weariness, or maybe it was the growing knowledge that she may not be there when Jenny would need her that caused Carla to be blunt and more direct then was her nature.

"When he told you he wanted to show you his man thing, he was talking about his penis. When a man gets aroused it gets big. You seen it on the farm when the animals breed. When he said he wanted to put it in your honey pot he was talking about doing to you what men do to women when they make babies. He wanted to put his thing in you and place his seed in you. I don't know how else to put it to you child, but I want you to know that what happened to you today had nothing to do with what happens between a man and a women who fall in love. It ain't a cheap and vulgar thing that strangers do. When you love a man and he loves you these things ain't ugly and they ain't hurtful. What you went through today you can't let ruin the time when you find the man you want to marry. Men is different than women, at least most of them, they have a lust that don't need loving. A women needs to be thinking of the seed that's planted in her. She needs more permanent things like a home and family and she needs a man who can give her these things and not let his rootin' get control of him. Liquor makes some men like them soldiers more like hogs then men. You got to stay away from men who don't respect women and only want to pleasure them."

Jenny wanted to know more, but because of the long silence and the lines of fatigue that lined her mother's face, knew her mother would not or could not say more. She did, however, venture on more question. "How does it happen, I mean how will I know I have the right man and that he respects me?"

"You'll know in your bones, child, it's like a needin' you have that only God who made us wantin' to create more of our own can explain. The man that was meant for you will come along and you'll know. That's all I can tell you. Now get some rest and let me be.

BACK ON THE TRAIL

Wayne Rawlins was glad to be leaving Fort Kearny. If this was what civilization was like on the frontier, he wanted to be away from it as soon as possible. The Factor at the fort virtually stole from them with the prices he charged. Even though it wasn't proper to sell liquor to the Indians, there was no end to the drunkenness among the assorted tribes the hung around the Fort. The soldiers weren't much better than the savages and would sleep with the squaws in payment for the booze they got from the Factor. Fights over squaws and booze raged on through the night. The ferry boat that was moored at the wharf carried the first Army payroll since the Missouri froze over in the fall and there was no containing the solders. The confrontation Jenny had with the soldier was proof enough that they had to be away from the Fort as soon as possible. The thought of what happened to Jenny set his blood to boiling and he would have shot the soldier if William hadn't ended the matter.

Getting away from the Fort had also the advantage of getting on with the move to Oregon. Wayne, unlike Carla and his brother, knew that Missouri would soon be changing and farming as he and his father knew it wouldn't ever be the same as more and more slaves were being brought into the state. Besides, he couldn't get any more out of the farm and was getting tired of the effort to produce more for an uncertain posterity. James would never be a farmer and like as not Jenny would marry some man who had his own means and would take her away to some place where even her companionship and help would be lost to him. Jenny was a good girl and tried to be the son whose strong hands he was denied. But women weren't made for farming and they made their own homes, raised their own families and lived the lives their husbands made for them. Wayne saw the inconsistency in his thinking about Oregon. He had no certain future there either and farming in Oregon didn't provide any better prospects then farming in Missouri. But like so many men in the wagon trains heading west along the Oregon Trail, he thought not of the things that would be the same, but was obsessed instead on the hope of renewal.

The greatest concern he now had about leaving Missouri was the failing vigor of Carla. He had hoped that traveling west and leaving the dank summer humidity of Missouri that sapped the strength of even the strongest, would improve Carla's health. He was certain that she would prosper in Oregon, but would she survive the journey? This sobering thought weighed heavily upon his mind each day. Although it was customary for the emigrants to walk beside their wagons and save the teams from the extra burden of passengers, Wayne now insisted that Carla ride as much as possible, though he doubted that the discomfort of riding in the constantly bouncing, swaying wagon provided much comfort. James was another matter.

Each day Wayne could see the change in his son. James's companionship with Clay and Franco was an obvious inspiration to his son. There was no evidence that James was maturing into "a chip off the old block" as had been suggested of him when he was James's age. James would never be a farmer that was becoming more obvious every day. James's love and understanding of animals would lead him along another path, but that path was not clear to Wayne. For now he was satisfied to see his son progressing toward manhood.

While traveling four days out of Fort Kearney Franco came riding hard into camp and told them they had best circle their wagons and secure them against what he assured them was going to be a "hell of a storm." Wayne had noticed the sky darkening to the west, now when he looked ahead, he saw flashes of lightning and could hear the rumble of distant thunder. The animals were becoming nervous and hard to manage. "Don't put them in the wagon circle or they will be upsettin' your wagons," Franco advised them, "get them over to the shelter of that bluff. We'll have to round them up after the storm passes."

The wind was coming on fast and growing in intensity. Wayne had the animals unhitched and let them be herded away. He was busy securing the wagon cover that was taking a beating. Carla and Jenny were inside huddled between the cargo when the rain hit them in blinding sheets. The wind tore the canvas from his hand, ripped it off the wagon and into the driving wind. James, who had been helping with the herd was absent from the camp and was caught out in the open when a driving hail hit the train burying everything in a sheet of ice. Mixed in the din of the driving storm were the shouts of frantic men and the screams of the women and children, most of who were now exposed to the driving storm as more and more wagon covers were sent swirling into the wind. Wayne was helpless in the face of the raging storm and could think only of Carla and Jenny. He struggled into the wagon and remembering the buffalo robe under the wagon seat, took it back to where the women were huddled and wrapped them in the buffalo robe, finding enough room to cover himself as he huddled with the women. The storm raged on for what seemed an eternity and as it gradually subsided the members of the wagon train found escape in a fatigued slumber.

Wayne slowly gained consciousness form the depth of the sleep that came to him only after he surrendered to the merciless torment of the storm. Whether it was the gentle jostling of the wagon or his awareness of the snorting and movement of animals that awoke him, he felt comforted in the thought that the livestock that had taken flight in the storm was being returned. Pushing the robe away he forced his reluctant joints to bring him to a standing position in the wagon. For a moment, he could not comprehend the scene before him. The wagon train was an island in a sea of migrating buffalo, no doubt driven before the thunderstorm. Immediately he lunged to the front of the wagon where his Henry rifle was stored under the wagon seat. As he pulled it from its sheath, a familiar voice interrupted him.

"Don't go blastin' off that firearm. The last thing we need is to stir these critters into a stampede while we're sittin' here amongst them." It was Paul Anderson whose calming advice brought a sense of awareness to Wayne. He suddenly thought of James and the livestock.

"Where's the animals? My boy James ain't come back."

"Your boy is out there with Clay and Franco and them others that were looking after the livestock. We can't do nothing about them now till these buffalos get away from here unless you want to try walkin' through this mess," Paul admonished him.

"Best set tight for now. I asked them that can to start their fires so's these animals will shy away from the train. They don't cotton to the smell of smoke and we don't need them crowding the train."

It was not until noon when the last of the buffalo herd moved beyond the wagons. Shots would be heard as the emigrants were shooting the strays. Carla and Jenny made busy to repair the damage caused by the storm. People were wandering through the country side to retrieve wagon tarps. Wayne wandered to the top of a nearby hill where several of the wagon owners had gathered in a vain effort to locate their teams.

"It's like they was 'et up by that storm," one of the emigrants remarked. "You ain't gonna' find a trace of them after that storm and all them buffal'er tracks."

"It may take a day or two to get them all back, but they're out there hidin' in some ravine or down by the river in some thicket," remarked another.

Wayne returned slowly to the wagon, knowing that Carla would be near hysterics at the thought of James wandering about in this wilderness. Who knew what fate may have befallen him in a storm as severe as the one that hit them last night. Wayne, who was afoot now without his horse or livestock was helpless and could only sit with the women and hope for the best.

Near dinner time a commotion arose from the lead wagons. In the distance they could see the drovers driving in some of the livestock, though it was obvious only about half the animals were recovered. When the herd was settled inside the circled wagons and the owners sorted out their stock, Wayne found out that only two of his oxen were recovered. His horse Empress was missing as was his son. Franco and Clay were surrounded by anxious emigrants all wanting to know what had happened and where the rest of the animals were.

"When we saw the storm coming, we tried to drive the herd over behind that bluff over yonder," Franco was relating. "We didn't make it and the rain, thunder and lightning drove the animals crazy and they were scattering all over the place and then came that hail. We couldn't see nothin' and had to save ourselves. When the storm let up we couldn't even find hardly a foot print and just followed the storm path and found these critters."

It was then that Wayne noticed one of the horses that had been returned had a body draped over it. Since the body was mostly covered by a tarp, Wayne couldn't tell whose body it was and his heart froze.

"This here's Chester Bean, he got trampled by the herd when it stampeded, his horse must have throwed him."

As the weight lifted from Wayne's heart, a shriek and then a moaning wail was heard from the far side of the group as Chester's wife responded to the news that her husband had not survived the night.

"Where's the rest of the drovers," someone demanded, "Where's my Bill?" Wayne recognized the voice of Paul Anderson.

"We divided up, some went toward the river and some went west. All was accounted for except Bobby Mills and the Rawlins boy, we ain't seen neither of 'em, but that don't mean much now, they could be roundin' up strays and headin' back now."

As Franco had predicted, the next day more and more of the drovers drifted in and each group was welcomed with cheers. The men were virtually falling from their horses as they rode in, having suffered the storm in the open and then riding the rest of the night and the next day to round up the strays. As the sun cast is last rays of light across the western horizon, a small group stood outside the wagon loop and waited in vain for the sight of one more herd being driven back to camp. In all some thirty animals were still missing as were seven of the herders who had saddled up and left that morning, among the missing from the night before were William Anderson and James Rawlins. By noon the next morning all but six of the horses had been returned and all of the herders including William Anderson had returned.

"I saw your boy in a flash of lightning just before the hail stuck us. He was heading north toward the river after some horses that broke from the herd. I believe that horse of yours was among the bunch he was chasing," Bill Anderson was telling Wayne as he held a distraught Carla in his arms, trying to reassure her that he son would be returning.

"He's such a frail boy, he can't have done well in that storm," Carla murmured as her head was pressed against Wayne's chest. You have to find him."

"I ain't got no horse," Wayne responded, "or I'd been out there yesterday."

"Mine's near dead from running, or I'd let you have mine, "Bill Anderson volunteered, "I believe Dad's horse might be up to it though, you might ask him."

Paul Anderson readily agreed to loan his horse. "You best head out at first light. I can't be holding the train up, though; you'll have to catch up with the rest of us at Ash Hollow if you don't find your boy sooner. Franco will go with you long enough to show you where to start looking, but I can't spare him for much more than that. I wish you the best of luck and don't worry about that horse, your boys more important, but don't be leaving your Carla a widow, when hope's gone get back to the train. This is big country and many have been lost in it and there ain't no helping them."

Wayne, as he road north with Franco that next morning knew in his heart that his efforts would no doubt be futile. Bill Anderson and the other herders had searched the area at a time when a search would be more fruitful. Now two days later, who could guess which way James had gone or what fate may have dealt him. James had grown much during the weeks they had been on the trail, but he was just a boy, a boy in a land of endless hazards; hazards that would humble even the strong.

"Along this ridge is the last we saw of the herd and your boy," Franco was saying, interrupting Wayne's trance like state. "We looked pretty good along this side of the Platte. My guess is the boy followed them horses across the river while it was still low and couldn't get back 'couse that storm set it a floodin'. It still ain't fit to cross, but you might try crossin' downstream a bit as it gets wider and shallower down a ways. You keep that Henry of yours loaded and primed, over beyond that river is Sioux country and that bunch ain't all that friendly."

"You think they may have got my boy?" Wayne reluctantly asked not certain he wanted to know.

"I heard what your woman was saying about your boy. That boy ain't no tadpole. He's growed up a pacel out here on the trail. If he ain't met with no accident I s'pect you'll find 'im. I got these here spy glasses back at Fort Kearny off of that Lieutenant who don't Know an Ace from a Duce. You take them along and keep a good eye out," Franco urged as he handed the binoculars to Wayne. 'Look off toward that big sand hill. Beyond that's where you'll find that crossin' I was mentionin'."

Wayne held the glasses on the sand hill and fiddled with the adjustment trying to bring them into focus. Something was on that hill he couldn't see with his naked eye. "What is that on that hill? He asked Franco, handing him back the binoculars.

Franco studied the far off hill for some time and slowly lowered the glasses. "Its some horses, but I can't tell what's driving them. They're coming fast. It could be some of them Sioux I was tell' you about. We'd best take cover and keep an eye on 'em."

Both Wayne and Franco dismounted their horses and moved behind a rock outcropping nearby. They unlimbered their rifles and checked their load while keeping an eye on the movement to the east. For a long interval, the oncoming horses were hidden from view as they moved through a depression. When they became visible again, Wayne, grabbing the field glasses from Franco's grasp and concentrated on the scene before him. Slamming the glasses back into Franco's stomach, Wayne jumped on his horse and rode for the oncoming horses at a dead run. Franco trained the glasses on the horses now in clear view and as he did his face broke into a reassuring smile and he to mounted up and rode forward.

Although Wayne could not immediately recognize the rider on the black horse driving the herd, he recognized his horse Empress and as he raced closer he was certain that it was his son James driving the horses toward camp. As the small herd drew near they slowed to a walk as their path was blocked by the lone rider who stood dismounted before them.

James was slow to recognize this father. His eyes were clouded from the dust, the relentless sun and by the fatigue that enveloped him.

"Papa, they tried to steal your Empress. I brought her back for you," James muttered as he slipped off the horses back into his father's outstretched arms.

Wayne led James over to a nearby rock and set him down, but soon realized his son was too exhausted to even sit by himself. He was sitting on the ground holding his son as Franco rode up and dismounted. Franco pulled his bandana free from his neck and poured water from his canteen over it and began wiping James's face and neck.

"Try drinking some of this son," Franco told him as he held his canteen to James's parched lips. "Then maybe you can tell us what you been up to and why them braves back yonder are on your trail."

Wayne had paid no attention to the trail behind his son, being concerned only with James's return. Looking back along that trail, he could see three riders cresting the rise and now moving cautiously toward them. There could be no doubt now that they were Indians and that they were perusing James. Wayne laid his son down and pulled his rifle from the saddle scabbard.

"They don't have rifles and I don't think they will try to push their luck." Franco advised Wayne. "Keep your gun handy, but don't go to shootin'." The Indians had stopped some hundred yards from them and were engaged in heated discussion as Wayne and Franco stood waiting for them to make some move. Finally one of the braves moved forward and stopped some fifty yards from them.

"He wants to talk. You stay here and keep an eye on 'em." Franco said as he set his rifle aside and mounting his horse and rode forward.

Wayne stood beside his son warily watching the Indians for any sign of hostility. James was able to sit by himself now and was smiling to his father's surprise. "They're the one's who stole Empress," James told his father. "I suspect they thought they could get her back. It's a good thing you and Franco came along; I don't think I could have got back to the train."

"You just rest a bit more. Franco don't think them Indians are up to no fight. I didn't think I'd ever see you again and as soon as we deal with these hostels, I'll be wantin' to hear all about what you been up to."

Franco was returning now as the three braves turned their horses and rode off. "They don't want no trouble. They thought they could ride the boy down and get them horses back, but they weren't planning on no fight."

While they left James to regain his strength and eat some hardtack, Franco and Wayne gathered up the horses and inspected them. "These critters have had a hard few days. We best get then over to the river and water and rest 'em." Franco advised. "Then I'd best be gettin' back to the train. You can bring the horses and the boy along when their fit to travel."

They moved the herd slowly down to the river and hobbled several of them knowing the rest would stay close. They made a small camp, but decided against building a fire. James was walking about now and Wayne and Franco were now ready to hear him describe his ordeal.

"When the storm hit I seen Empress and these other horses separate from the herd and head toward the river," James started his story. "Before I could ketch up with them that storm hit and I couldn't seen nothin'. I found some trees and hunkered down to wait out the storm. When it was over and I took out after the strays I came to where they was, but them Indians had rounded them up and were taking them across the Platte. I rode back on my trail to find some help, but I couldn't find nobody. I went back and picked up the trail where the herd had crossed and followed it. The Indians took them north for about a day and then camped in a box canyon with the horses up ahead of them so's they wouldn't get past them. Franco taught me how Indians can move right up to a horse and steal it right from under a fella's nose. I knew Empress would know me, so when them Indians bedded down, I stole up the canyon behind them and mounted Empress and drove the herd right down through their camp. The Indian's ponies were in the group, but I couldn't handle all them horses so I cut out the Indian ponies. I wasn't wantin' to steal them horses anyways. I guess I should've driven them further away. I wasn't planin' on bein' followed."

Wayne could hardly believe the bravery and determination his son was relating to them. It was then Franco intervened. "Them Indians, they was Sioux by the way, was mighty impressed, especially when I told them they was foxed by a mere lad. They wanted me to give you this," Franco offered as he pulled from his pocket a rawhide necklace with some large bear claws dangling from it. "This here was worn by that fella I palavered with. He thinks it brings good luck and is proof of a brave heart. The story of your doin's will be told at his campfires for many moons and you will be called 'the boy with the heart of a grizzly'."

Hearing this evidence confirming his son's exploits brought moisture to Wayne's eyes. He stepped forward and tied the necklace about his son's neck and then drew the boy into his arms and exclaimed, "Son, don't ever do that again for the sake of a few horses, but your doin' it makes me mighty proud of you. I'm goin' to stay here with these horses until they're up to travel. You head on back to the train with Franco. I don't want your mother to spend any more time agonizin' over you then needs be. If Franco here don't mind he might send back a hand or two to help move these horses along. I ain't a gifted drover like you are son."

The heat waves driven from the vast land about them distorted their view, giving the impression that the wagon train was traveling along the crest of an ocean and not the drying prairie that was giving back to the heavens the last vestiges of moisture that had once turned all the land about them into verdant green. They had called a halt for the night close to a now trickling tributary of the Platte River. The evidence of the great storm that had brought such havoc to the train was evident now only by the deep gullies that now had to be crossed with great effort and delay. One of the men standing atop his wagon first noticed the riders moving across the flat land beyond the camp. It was hard to make out the horses because of the heat waves, but the shout was given of riders coming in. Jenny and her mother climbed onto their wagon to get a better view of the riders. Was it Franco and Wayne returning without word or trace of James? To Carla it was an eternity waiting for the first clear glimpse of the riders. The fact that there were only two was discomforting. In time it became evident that one of the riders was Franco and the other might have been Wayne. Then from the other end of the train, someone with a better view shouted, "Its Franco and that Rawlins boy."

Carla was at first filled with joy and then foreboding, "Where is your father?" she whispered to Jenny who held her hands clasped to her breast, suffering the same confusion of emotions as her mother.

Both Jenny and her mother hurried as best they could to the rear of the train to meet the riders. By now, both Jenny and her mother could make out James' features. He did not appear to be distressed, but did look dirty and tired. As he came nearer it was clear that James was indeed smiling and searching the many gathering faces for his mother. James dismounted short of the train and embraced his mother and Jenny as they ran forward to greet him. The story of his disappearance and reappearance could wait, Carla's first words were, "Your father, your father, he's out there looking for you, did you see him."

"He's fine mom," James responded in a confident strong voice that was new to Carla, "He stayed with the horses and will bring them along when there're fit to travel. Franco said they'll send some men out tomorrow to help him bring them in."

Franco said James was too tired and thirsty to tell the story of what had happened to him during and after the great storm. "When I get some vittles and rest, I'll tell you all what you're wantin' to know about James here. But now let us both alone for a while, we're plumb out of wind. I'll tell all I know when supper's over."

James had hardly gotten back to camp when he grabbed his bed roll for a pillow and fell fast asleep under the wagon. It was obvious that if they were going to find out what had happened to James that Jenny and Carla would have to join the other emigrants and hear Franco tell the story.

When the story was told, all who knew James as the young Rawlins boy would hence forward call him "Grizzly Rawlins", in deference to his Indian identity and his heroics when saving the horses.

Carla slept the sleep of the angels that evening confident that she had survived long enough to see her son grow into manhood even though he be yet in the body of a boy, a circumstance that was now changing daily before her eyes.

CROSSING THE PLATTE

The Anderson train, having traveled on as the search for James was in progress, came to the crest of Ash Hollow where the train would cross Platte River and continue its journey westward on the north side of the river. ([3]) Once again, they would have to descend a hazardous slope, but

---

[3] For a description of Ash Hollow on the Oregon Trail see: Oregon-California Trails Association: supra.

this time the descent was compounded by large rock outcrops that would smash any run away wagon into kindling. The teams were unhitched and the descent was made a wagon at a time with the rear wheels of the wagon locked for braking. The men let the wagons descend slowly by tying ropes to the axles and letting the wagon weight drag them down the slope while they struggled to impede the wagon from running free. It took most of the day to accomplish the descent, but once in the embrace of the hollow, they found the grass plentiful and the water sweet. Mr. Anderson called a halt at this point and ordered the emigrants to do their washing; repairing and let their animals feed before they proceeding to cross the river. It was at this point that Wayne Rawlins rejoined the train bringing with him the last of the animals lost during the recent storm.

Rejoining his family, Wayne once again retold the story of his son's ordeal adding to the events the circumstances that gave the story the flavor of a proud father. Herding seven horses across unfamiliar country with hostile Indians in pursuit was a feat, according to Wayne that few men could accomplish, let alone a boy who had seldom ventured beyond the safety of his family's embrace. To face up to hostiles and outsmart them and even run away with their own ponies was, to Wayne's interpretation a display of judgment and daring that would give James the respect that might cause the hostiles to let their train pass without challenge. It was Franco who added substance to these assertions when he confirmed the proposition that the Indians would indeed give respect to James feat and honor his presence where ever they met. Although James enjoyed the initial praise his action brought to him, he found it more and more discomforting to be a part of men's conversations and was soon absenting himself from camp to hunt and scout with Franco and Clay Anderson. He was ever eager to learn more about the land that held so many mysteries and adventures.

James and Franco, along with Clay had crossed the Platte and were scouting the trail ahead when they came upon a clearing where a lone wagon sat without any sign of life about. As James rode ahead to inspect the wagon, Franco called him back. "Don't go rushing into things without looking about to see why something that don't look right might not be a danger." At that, the scouts circled a distance beyond the lone wagon looking for signs.

"That wagon be part of a train passing on the north of the river, Franco pointed out as he inspected the tracks. It was cut out and abandoned. I suspect there may be dead folks in that wagon, the buzzards been about. My guess is that some folks met up with a fatal sickness elst the rest of the settlers wouldn't have driven off with their stock. I don't see no graves about, so I expect they was just left to die. You two stay put and I'll have a look."

As Franco rode nearer the wagon, he soon picked up the smell of rotting flesh. His horse became skittish and he knew he had guessed correctly. Holding his kerchief over his face he rode to the rear of the wagon and looking inside saw the bodies of what appeared to be a family of a man, women and two small infants. Their bodies were bloated, invested with vermin and carried the inescapable signs of cholera.

"We best burn that wagon," Franco told James and Clay as he rode back to join them. "They got the trail fever that is gonna' be a problem from here on."

James resisted the urge to peer into the wagon and he gathered clumps of grass and sticks and placed them about the wagon.

"Ain't nothin' you want to be remembering, son," Franco admonished him. "Just get on with the burnin'."

The Anderson train crossed the Platte without incident, except for the amusement provided when Grandma Murphy ungracefully fell off her wagon into the river. The train proceeded abreast of the Platte for several miles and then headed inland. It was about midday when it passed the spot where Franco had ordered the burning of the infested immigrant wagon. It was while they were passing the scene of the burning that the Whitman wagon pulled away from the train and stopped near the charred remains of a family that ended its trek to the land of promise in the valley of the Platte, yet hundreds of miles from its destination. Without the command to do so, the wagon train came to a halt and the emigrants left their wagons to surround the solemn, austere monument to a family that each knew could well have been and yet maybe theirs.

Dr. Whitman bent over the charred remnants and lifted to the sky a handful of the ashes that remained and letting them drift away in the wind began his oration.

Dear God in Heaven our blessed savior we beseech ye to take into your loving bosom the souls of these poor immigrants whose hope of renewal and promise have ended in this desolate place so far from their home and so far from their dream.

We know not what purpose you have in claiming these lost souls. We know not even who they be or why they have separated themselves from all that was familiar to them to lie at rest in obscurity.

We pray through you dear God that you will spare each of us the fate of this family and bless our journey to its conclusion. From ashes to ashes, from dust to dust, may God have mercy of these poor lost souls.

The train moved on, each member alone with the thought that they too could fall victim to some accident or malady that would end their journey in some remote soon forgotten grave. In spite of the compelling hopes and certainties that motivated their journey, none could purge from their minds the hazards of the trip west. Each day took them further away from the civilization that had added substance to their being and further into the uncertainty of trials yet unknown.

"I respect your concern for the souls of these poor creatures," Paul Anderson had announced to break up the prayer vigil, "but this is the last time we stop the train to lament some strangers death. We have our own to think of and that means we keep movin' and avoid these delays. Now back to your wagons and let's make some miles before sunset."

Whichever train it was that left behind the cholera victims; it became evident that it had not purged itself of the malady. After several days of travel the Anderson train passed the graves and abandoned possessions of other unfortunate members of the stricken train. There was no thought of halting of the train to pay respect to the stricken emigrants whose graves and abandoned possessions now marked the trail west. Franco insisted when possible that the grave markers be removed and that the trains pass over the grave sites to obliterate the last vestiges of evidence that one of God's own lay forever at rest beneath the earth that now claimed their remains.

"Them Indian's will dig 'em up for their valuables and get the pox from them corpses. They take the sickness back to their lodges and no tellin' how many of them will die. They'll soon be blaming these emigrants for the killing and be out for scalps. Ain't nobody but them that moved on knows who's buried in them graves and they ain't comin' back. Serves no purpose to mark them graves anyhow. This here's Indian territory now and we got to be taking our caution."

The Reverend Whitman and his admirers were much upset with what they called "desecration", but Paul Anderson followed Franco's advice. For that matter no member of the train was comfortable with the removal of the markers and the destruction of the last evidence of the grave sites. Each member of the train was well aware of the fact that the same fate would await them or their loved ones if they met with misfortune on the trail west. It was one thing to deal with the remembrances of strangers, it was quite another to contemplate leaving a loved one behind without a trace of their short tenure. On some date in the future there would be some small comfort in remembering a grave site as having a place and time to which at least memories could return.

But the train moved ever onward and each day brought forth its own difficulties and the memories of those left behind soon became as remote as the land that claimed them.

"See that spire off there in the distance," Franco said to James, "That be Chimney Rock. (⁴) In a day or so we'll be abreast of it. It's a marker to the way west that the mountin' men followed.' When we get there it'll plumb amaze you. Stands some five hundert feet tall and ain't no trace as to why it was put there."

The prospect of reaching one of the milestones often talked about on the way west brought a new excitement to the train. The eyes of each wagon member was glued to the horizon as they watched the spire inch ever higher into the heavens as they moved mile by mile closer to its base. It was indeed a marvel to behold as the train pulled into camp formation at its base on the second day of its first sighting. It looked like a great smoke stack sitting atop a large cone, a lone sentinel dominating the featureless prairie that surrounded it. It was composed of sandstone that belied its having been formed by volcanic action. What quirk of nature placed this monument at this point was the featured speculation of all who passed Chimney Rock on their way west. Jenny was among the many emigrants who walked along the base of the rock to view the mementoes left by those who passed before them. Some had carved their names into the

---

4   Chimney Rock is a slowly deteriorating monument that was one of the guide stones along the trail that is mentioned by most travelers and explorers that traveled along the Trail. Oregon-California Trails Association, supra.

sandstone rocks about the large cone; others had left wooden markers to evidence their moment of passage. To Carla and many other members of the train, it was but further confirmation of their faith. That night under the towering monument, the members of the train gathered about as the Reverend Whitman gave a rather long winded sermon extending their gratitude to the Lord for their safe passage and beseeching his blessing upon their further travels.

The passing of Chimney Rock soon brought the Anderson train into the virtual Eden surrounding of Scotts Bluff, but another of the wonders to be confronted on the trail to Oregon. The train camped for several days at the base of the bluff on the Platte River and let their animals fatten themselves on the lush grass. The women busied themselves with washing clothes and the men tended to the wagons, animals and some even had the leisure of hunting, shooting water fowl and other game to replenish their diminishing supplies. Across the river from the train was an encampment of Indians and brisk trading business was soon engaged in between the Indians and settlers. It was at this point that the Anderson Train first encountered the members of the Mapes Train that had left Independence before them with the commitment of being the first to reach Oregon. As Wayne had predicted, the pace that Mapes intended would bring disaster to many who tried to follow his lead. Their equipment was worn and in need of repair and their animals were suffering from sore feet and lack of rest and feed.

"He ain't stoppin' for no one," one of the members of the Mapes train informed them, "He'll be in Oregon first, but he'll be getting' there alone. God help the rest of his train."

Several members of the Mapes Train asked to join with the Anderson Train. It was not the first time the Anderson train encountered members of another train who were dissatisfied with the pace or demands of the train they had pledged to. Once the emigrants passed beyond the reach of civilized society, many gave vent to their independent spirit found the regimentation of the trail boss incompatible with their notions of justice and their feeling of independence. Invariably, Paul Anderson refused their entreaties.

"Most of them is just trouble makers and malcontents who will give us grief. It ain't an easy thing to follow my demands, I know that. But if everybody gets his say about how things get done we will end up a debating society and get nowhere," was Paul's justification for his rejection.

After leaving the valley below Scotts Bluff, the train once more crossed the Platte River. The river was low and the crossing was accomplished without incident. The members of the Anderson train felt their luck was holding, but a week before the crossing had spelled disaster for the train from St. Louis that they had confronted at the start of their trek. Seven wagons were lost and five members of the train were swept away by the raging water that followed a hail storm that the Anderson train saw only in the distance as they left Chimney Rock camp site. Their luck ran out on the second day out before they reached Fort Laramie when a thunderstorm caught the train before it could form a protective corral for the animals.

Wayne and James were sent out to help with the livestock and Jenny was left to fend off the affects of the storm as best she could. She insisted that her mother stay in the wagon secured in the old Buffalo robe while she brought the wagon into the protective circle and unhitched the oxen. The storm rage on for several hours and Jenny did her best to keep the wagon cover from blowing away. When all seemed hopeless as the wind was pulling the wagon cover out of her grasp, she felt a strong presence next to her. The rain driving hard into her face made it difficult to recognize the able hands that pulled the cover down and secured it. At first she thought it was her father, but then as he shouted at her to get in the wagon; she realized it was William Anderson who had come to her aid. Above the raging storm his voice did not carry and she only looked at him in puzzlement trying to understand his command. Realizing that she could not hear him, William took her swiftly into his arms and set her over the tail gate of the wagon and motioned for her to get under cover.

Jenny was more than glad to seek protection under the Buffalo robe and give what warmth and comfort she could to her mother who had also been drenched by the fast moving storm. The storm drove its unrelenting fury against the wagon for more than an hour and was gone as fast as it came. Jenny and Carla were alone in their small world under the robe and even when the storm subsided remained huddled together sharing a rare moment of intimacy that the rigors of travel had denied them. Jenny's thoughts were of her mother and how frail she had become. She could see her mother's vitality diminishing as each day's demands on her failing energy left her mother more listless and remote. Having this moment with her now gave Jenny great comfort.

But as she dozed between her thoughts and remembrances as her body warmth drove away her chill, she felt about her once again those strong arms that had rescued her from the lashing storm and placed her so effortlessly into the security of the wagon. This was the second time William had been there when she needed him. Although she often thought of William and how he had defended her when accosted by the drunken soldier at Fort Kearny, she looked upon him as a friend and guardian now and hesitated the think more of the matter. After all, there was still the matter of that gold necklace, no doubt a commitment gift from some women he loved. More than once Jenny had noticed William giving her appraising looks, looks that brought blood rushing to her cheeks and a flutter to her heart. She must look upon him more as a brother she had decided and not let her heart lead her astray. Yet, her thoughts continued to linger on his strength that protected her and his evident concern for her safety that suggested she possessed a place in his world, a thought that gave her comfort.

Jenny left her mother under the protection of the robe and did her best to scrounge a dinner for her father and James who had now returned to the train having settled the livestock for the night. A fire was out of the question, so it was back to hard tack and bacon rinds. The word was passing through the train that they were nearing Fort Laramie and would soon have a respite from their travails.

"What I hear tell," Franco remarked to Wayne and James as they rode back to the wagons, "it's becoming a real settlement with stores and all. We can provision up there and mend some of these wagons. They have a blacksmith there and they even sell wagons, teams and other necessaries."

The thought of reaching civilization again lifted Carla's sprits and she even began to show some of her lost vitality as the train headed once again on its journey west.

"You be lookin' a bit pert this mornin'," Wayne had remarked as Carla took her place on the wagon seat the day after the storm.

"I do feel some better, but you're not to go worrying' about me now, you have enough to tend to."

Wayne handed the reins over to Jenny, giving his wife an appraising look. He felt again the need for her warm body against him and for the reassurance of her presence in his bed. How long had it been since they last shared a bed? How long had it been since he had been able to possess her? He suddenly felt the great loss that misfortune had placed upon them. He must repay her a hundred fold for all the sufferings she endured. When they get to Oregon, all will be better he vowed. He will repay her the debt he owed her for the loss of her comfortable home and the denial of the comfort she deserved. Yes, Oregon was the answer and Oregon would be their redemption.

The joy of reaching Fort Laramie was quickly quashed when the wagon train passed an Indian encampment as they approached the fort. Small Pox had stricken the tribe and many of the Indians were dead or dying. A mother lay lifeless before her lodging with her baby crying at her side, a baby whose body was covered with the pustules of the rampant disease. The sight gave greater meaning to the advice Franco had given them regarding burial sites.

It was the Reverend Whitman who added a footnote to the scene. "They know not the evils that the white man brings to their villages. If it is not the measles and chicken pox, it is syphilis and drunkenness that we gift them. It will be a better day when they learn the ways of the Lord and have his help in averting the evils that decimate their tribes."

"I am a Christian man and try to follow the path ways to salvation," Paul Anderson muttered to Wayne, "but some ways that fellow festers on me. The Lord ain't killin' these poor soles and listening to that blow hard won't save them either."

Wayne was surprised to hear these sentiments expressed against Reverend Whitman. He was no less surprised to find that he agreed with Paul Anderson. The Reverend seemed to have intolerance for the Indians and their life style that was becoming more and more evident as they come into more frequent contact with the natives. Wayne's real problem with the Reverend was that he seemed to assume unto himself a personal knowledge of the ways of Christ that was not befitting of the humility one expected from a man of God. Tall and austere, always dressed in black, the Reverend set himself above the members of the train not only by his assertion of a divine presence, but also by his inability to suffer the misjudgments and unworthiness of others.

There was little doubt, however, but that the Reverend took his ordination seriously. He held religious services regularly and tended upon the sick and distressed members of the train. His sermons, to Wayne's notion, were too preachy, to long and to frequent. To Wayne's distress, Carla enthusiastically became one of his traveling congregation and insisted that the family attend each of the Reverend's often discomforting sermons. Wayne and Jenny attended the Reverend's revivals at Carla's request, but James was always conveniently absent attending to some more important undertaking. The good Reverend had once admonished James for his association with Franco and what the Reverend assumed to be James' taking up with older men who would lead him astray. He had also scolded James for his taking up the ways of the natives in his dress and habits.

"That trinket you wear around your neck was given to you by a heathen and has heathen meanings attached to it. You best throw it away or it may infect your eternal soul."

Although James could tolerate the Reverend's advice regarding his associations, which could be ignored, the Reverend's views regarding James' Bear Claw necklace was an intrusion in James' affairs that he could not forgive or tolerate.

James, who was invited to the Whitman wagon by Narcissa to enjoy a berry pudding she had made, abruptly stood up and threw his plate on the ground when confronted with the Reverend's opinion, and stalked out of his presence.

"That boy needs more than the hand of the Lord," he heard the Reverend remark as he mounted his horse and spurred it out of camp.

To the members of the train the Fort was an encouraging site. Its adobe walls gave the Fort an aura of permanence and strength that was comforting to travelers crossing the unmarked wilderness of the American West. Inside the Fort there was indeed the store, the grainary, the blacksmith shop and other businesses that they were told to expect. Unlike Fort Kearney, the Fort seemed to be well managed by its Commander Major Anderson. The streets were clean, the Fort well maintained and the contingent of some 250 soldiers was well disciplined. ([5]) Other wagon trains had passed through

---

[5]   For a description of the Fort, see Oregon-California Trails Association, supra.

before the Anderson train and a number or Oregon bound emigrants were re-outfitting and would join up with other trains passing through. This created a problem for those who wanted to use the services of the blacksmith as he had a huge back log and could not take on additional work.

A good number of wagons had been abandoned at the Fort and those in need of repairs scavenged these wagons or purchased new ones for the trip west. There was news of Indian troubles among the Blackfoot, Ute and Sioux tribes. This caused a brisk business at the settler's stores where rifles, powder and shot was readily available. Wayne, deciding that James should no longer ride about with a hand me down musket, bought a new, light weight rifle for James and was not surprised when James demonstrated immediate proficiency with the weapon. James' aversion to hunting had given way to the realization that even he was pray to the animals that prowled the night. Although his new rifle did not pack the punch of his father's Henry, it was more accurate and was effective up to 500 yards.

It was while the train was camped about the Fort that Jenny developed a special relationship with Narcissus Whitman. Narcissus canvassed the train to find women who had been previously affected by small pox and thus carried immunity. She wanted to go among the Indian village and offer what assistance and comfort she could to the stricken village they had passed on approaching the Fort. Jenny was one of the few who volunteered to assist Narcissa and in spite of the reservations of her father she, along with Narcissa, after consulting the Fort's surgeon, did their best to comfort those Indians who showed some signs of recovery. There was of course the sad duty of burying the dying and burning the belongings of those who were stricken. Fortunately, Major Anderson provided some volunteers for that purpose.

"They'll be in fever," the Fort Surgeon advised them, "and they'll want to throw their blankets off. That ain't good for fevered people. Keep then covered and see they get plenty of water. You can give them cold compresses about their face to fight the fever, other than that I can't offer no more advice. Don't let them scratch the sores if you can help it."

Narcissa took ready command of the effort and told Jenny that they would first enter each tent and determine if there were any survivors. If the inhabitants of the tepee were either dead or beyond help, they would mark the tent with a big "X" with a stick of charcoal and leave it up to the soldiers to handle the disposal detail. All the sick who could be helped would be moved to the large lodge in the center of the camp where they could be cared for. The children and babies were to be given the first consideration. Jenny was not surprised when James, Clay and Franco joined their effort and assisted in moving the infected to the major lodge.

Even though Jenny tried to prepare herself for what she expected to be a heart rendering experience, she was not prepared for the stench that permeated the tepees of the stricken Indians. In the first tepee, the corpse of a male lay naked with pustules erupted all over his body and flies thick as locus on his decomposing body. A young mother lay on her robe muttering incoherently as she became aware of Jenny's presence. Jenny could not understand the language, but the gesture was clear, she was trying to hand her baby to Jenny, no doubt hoping that Jenny could save the baby from the fate that awaited the young mother, whose condition was obviously hopeless. Jenny quickly grabbed the child and ran from the lodge. It was not until she was outside that she realized the baby was dead. She returned the child to the mother with tears streaming down her face, then marked the lodge with a large "X" and proceeded on the next tepee.

Jenny was relieved to find that among the stricken tribes there were some who had either survived the malady or had some immunity from the disease. These survivors were mostly older tribesmen although Jenny did find a few younger Indians able to afford assistance. For the most part these survivors were of little assistance to the stricken villagers. They had relied on medicine men whose chants and cures offered no relief. Many of them were engaged in singing death songs over the bodies of their loved ones and the village reverberated with their chants.

When Paul Anderson became aware of the nursing detail, he made it clear that he disapproved of the program.

"We can't be taking the time to nurse every Indian along the way. Were headed for Oregon and we can't be taking time to run no hospital. Them Indians that are going to get well will need weeks to recover and we ain't going to sit around and wait. In two days we got to be moving on."

Narcissa stood her ground to the consternation of Paul Anderson.

"We came west to serve the Lord and to do his work. This seems to me to be what we were called to do. If you have no patience for the Lord's work, you may go on without me."

Jenny knew she couldn't stay behind and tend to the Indians. Her father wouldn't have it and her mother's health concerned her more than her duties to the stricken Indians.

The solution to the dilemma came the next day. A number of the Indians not affected by the disease and those that had recovered, Narcissa decided, would be trained in the details of nursing the stricken. The Post Surgeon advised them that he would oversee the care of the Indians once the wagon train left.

"There ain't that much that can be done for them poor souls. Either they will recover or they will die. There ain't no cure but to survive," the Surgeon advised them.

LEAVING FORT LARAMIE

They were now at the halfway point of their westward journey. A few members of the train had turned back in discouragement. Indeed some of the emigrants who they met at Fort Laramie were selling their stock and turning back. To those who went on, there would be no turning back. But none who headed beyond the Fort had any inclination to do so. Even the warnings about Indian troubles would not discourage them. The lands that had offered them lush green pastures along the river courses were now behind them. The relentless, searing rays of the summer sun had now turned the vegetation into withering stocks of prairie grass and brittle outcroppings of sage and thorn bushes.

The dust that had bedeviled them became ever more pervasive as it swept across the plains driving sand and grit into every crevice and pore. It was impossible to wash one's self or one's clothes. Water had to be preserved as they left behind them the Platte River that they had followed westward to Fort Laramie. The enthusiasm that had pervaded the train as it began the trek westward had lasted only a short while and was replaced by dogged determination. Now as the train progressed slowly across the barren high desert country numbness set in that made their movements mechanical and their minds devoid of humor or wasted thought. If any motivation drove them forward it was the pervasive hope that the journeys end would find them immersed in the abundance of a new, verdant land where their lives would be leisurely and secure.

Such were the thoughts that dominated William Anderson as his large, graceful gelding Dominator, carried him with ease over the barren waste land that now lay ahead of the train. He had spent four years reading the law and following the circuit court that crisscrossed across the state of Illinois. His thoughts of setting up his own practice had come to an end with his mother's untimely death and the determination of the family to move west and start anew. His hopes, unlike most of the members of the train, did not evolve around the abundant land that would be theirs for the taking at the end of the journey. Opportunity for lawyers and other professional people was asserted to be promising in the new territories. He envisioned an active practice and an eventual life as a prominent politician, maybe even a Governor or a United States Senator when statehood came to Oregon. His father, who carried with him the printing press that would no doubt bring him some prominence, would be a help to William when it came time to move into a public life. William was not affected by the doubts that some men held regarding the future. He carried with him letters of recommendation and acknowledgement form many prominent lawyers in Illinois, including one aspiring lawyer like himself named Abraham Lincoln.

His usual certainty and confidence was shaken that day back at Fort Kearney, when the Commandant suggested that Jenny was "his woman." She had been on his mind on many occasions when he had moments for ruminations. The night during the recent storm when he came to her aid had rekindled his thoughts of Jenny. When he lifted her over the tail gate of her wagon he became suddenly aware of the femaleness of her. She submitted to his authority so readily and in fact had wrapped her arms around him as he first lifted her in his arms and she held him in a moment's close embrace that had more than a casual significance. But there remained the fact that Jenny was not the kind of woman he had envisioned as being the future Mrs. Anderson. Her father had no great prospects other than good husbandry of some yet to be claimed farmland.

Jenny, although attractive and agreeably shy, was unwise in the life he intended and would be of little assistance to him in claiming his future. None-the-less, her intrusion into his life was unsettling. Taken away from the burdens of a farmer's wife and given the finery which he intended to give to his wife, would she bloom into the vision he had for his wife? It was unsettling to William also to notice how the other young men in the train, and indeed even those who were neither young nor eligible, often looked upon Jenny with lustful, yearning, desire. Jenny would not long be able to resist the urges and pressures to select a husband. There was no certainty that he would ever find the woman he envisioned as the one to share his future in Oregon. After all, there would be no abundance of eligible women in Oregon. In fact there was a shortage of eligible ladies according to most reports.

A number of the younger men in the train were heading west to start a new life and would then call upon their intendeds back in the East to join them. William had no such prospects. He had been so intently engaged in learning his profession that he paid no attention to the young ladies that might have been eligible. At times he almost resented Jenny for having forced upon him this moment of decision when he had assumed that such matters could be shelved for future consideration at a time more suitable to his purposes.

William's thoughts were interrupted when he noticed several horsemen moving with haste over the scrubland toward him. He reigned up and watched them approach; noticing as they drew near that it was his brother Clay and James Rawlins. As they drew up to where he was awaiting them Clay told him, somewhat excitedly that there was a band of Indians headed their way. They were all braves and could be a war party, Clay remarked as they all turned and headed back to the train to give the alarm.

"How many were there?" Franco wanted to know when he met them.

"Can't rightly say," Clay responded, they came upon us all of sudden when we was followin' a steam bed looking for water. I'd guess there was a dozen or more."

"Was they painted up? Was their horses painted up?" Franco wanted to know.

It was James who answered obviously more certain of his observations than the excited Clay. "They looked pretty ordinary, more like the Indians at the Fort. I think they were as surprised to see us as we were to see them. They didn't chase us when we left, but they seemed to be headed this way."

"Well it don't sound like no raiding party or they'd been on you like flies. I spect I aught to ride on out there and see what they want. They may just be curious. I'd like to keep them away from the train, no knowing what some excited pilgrim may do when he sees all them hostiles," Franco remarked as he stepped up into his saddle.

James and the Anderson brothers joined him as he headed back across the plains from the direction Clay indicated.

As they approached the Indians, who seemed to be in no particular hurry to get to the train, Clay reached for his saddle gun.

"Best keep your hand away from that thing. These Indians don't seem to be lookin' for a fight. I count fifteen of them and they look to be a hunting party, not a war party," Franco admonished.

As the Indians had stopped at their approach and seemed to mill about uncertainly, Franco told the brothers and James to stay put while he checked them out. "I'll tell you when to come up if all goes well."

They could see Franco as he gave his peace greetings which were returned. Franco and several of the Indians then engaged in a long discussion, giving gestures and signs, until Franco turned to them and motioned them forward.

"These boys are a hunting party alright and they ain't had much luck. Seems the buffalo has been driven south by all these wagon trains. They want to trade. They say their babies are hungry and their lodges are without food. This here mean looking follow on the paint is their war chief and he ain't so friendly. He claims they have many warriors and will attack the train if we don't give them some food," Franco told them.

"That don't sound like trading to me," William responded.

"Well, it ain't like they got much to trade with," Franco responded, "so blusters got to do."

While they were talking, the War Chief slowly approached them and seemed to single out James as his point of interest. He pointed to the necklace about James' neck and spoke to Franco. Franco's response seemed to impress the Indian and more of the Indians came forward and studied the bear claw necklace about James throat. They grave a number of grunts and signs to which Franco responded.

"What's that all about?" Clay demanded.

"Seems like they're impressed with the lad here and have heard of his tussle with them Sioux back there. They'll be a bit easier to deal with I spect."

"Tell them we ain't giving them nothing and to stay clear of the train," William advised Franco.

"I can do that, but I don't think it's smart. If they be truly hungry, and I spect they be by the looks of 'em, they might just turn surly and there ain't no need to test them. Go back and get your paw and we'll see what's to be decided," Franco advised.

When William returned to the train and advised his father of the situation, Paul was relieved, but cautious.

"Did he want us to circle the wagons? Is there to be trouble?"

"No, I suspect they're not up to any trouble. They just want food. We could easily drive them off, but Franco thinks you should go out there and talk to them instead."

As Paul Anderson approached the group of Indians, now dismounted and sitting cross-legged on the ground, he was prepared to deal with them curtly and be on with his business. What he saw as he approached was not a threatening band of warriors, but a trail worn hunting party covered with dust and shabbily clothed in loin cloths and the remnants of leather leggings. A few had tattered shirts and several had silly hats that they no doubt got in trade with some passing train or trapper. Their horses were trail worn and tired with jutting ribs and shaggy mains and matted tails. This was no group to be feared and was in fact to be pitied. When Paul heard their tale of hardships he no longer could engender any hostility toward them. They were a peaceful band from the high plains to the north. They were continually raided by the Blackfoot tribes and occasionally by the Sioux. Their village was far to the northwest and consisted of near 200 nearly starved inhabitants.

"Cut out four steers and give them a keg or two of salt and sugar," Paul directed. "I doubt they will get it all back to their village, but that's their concern."

Having dealt with his problem, he road back to the train with William by his side.

"Why did you do that?" William demanded. "If word gets about that we pass out provisions, we will have hell to pay before we get out of this country."

"We're here to do the Lords work, I been told. Besides, I doubt that that group socializes much with the rest of the tribes to pass along the word of our generosity."

"I don't doubt that they will be back trying to steal more of our herd. Seems to me you got to show them the point of a gun and be rid of them. They don't look like they have much respect for our laws or property. The sooner the army gets out here and clears out these savages the better off we will all be."

"I don't get the feeling that the army is all that interested in fighting these savages. Back at the fort they seemed more inclined to advise the settlers to leave them alone and stay out of their hunting grounds and sacred places."

"All that's got to change," William declared dismissively. "If this land's to be settled we need to be rid of these savages."

"Those are harsh words, son. You best give some leeway for those who were here before us and who have done nothing to deserve such scorn."

William did not answer, and his father puzzled over what had caused his eldest son to have such a surly attitude toward the natives. There was a lot of land out here and there was little need to be driving people about to satisfy the ambitions of others. William's attitude was not exclusive among the emigrants. Paul had heard these thoughts expressed often when the men had the leisure to discuss such things. It appeared that few would tolerate interference with any claims they intended to file on the lands of Oregon. That, however, would not be Paul's concern once this train arrived in the Promised Land, yet a thousand miles away. His thoughts lay not in land claims, but in establishing his newspaper and once again gaining the respectability of an established publisher. The plight of the native Indians would be the concern of others, or so he thought.

As the train passed beyond Fort Laramie, the emigrants faced the vastness of the Great American Desert where the availability of the scare and random water sources would decide their fate. Franco's knowledge and instincts would be their salvation as they pressed on to Fort Hall. James and Clay Anderson were Franco's companions as they searched far beyond the train to find the water and suitable graze for the animals. Clay Anderson would spend much of his time hunting. Although James had lost his aversion to the hunt, he preferred to avoid the killing when his assistance was not needed. Clay, because of James' acute distance vision, would often urge James to accompany him. As for James, he was fascinated with Franco's knowledge of the land and ability to read sign and know instinctively where the most favored terrain lay. James after several days travel noticed that Franco was constantly riding through the washes and ravines only occasionally riding to the crest of a ridge where even then he hesitated to expose his entire silhouette. He admonished them to remain concealed.

"You expecting some trouble?" Clay asked when he was told not to ride out ahead and hunt Antelope.

"We ain't alone out here. I don't know yet if it means trouble, but we best be watchful. That dust way off to the left ain't no wagon train and it's been moving too fast to be an Indian village moving to new ground."

Peering over the ridge, James could see the dust as a mere discoloration on the horizon. Clay was the last to make out the dust cloud.

"It ain't that so much as the movement you see now and then between us and that cloud. It looks like a war party with its scouts riding lookout. The good thing is that they are moving away from the train. We best keep an eye on them to make sure they keep moving away. Were in the range of the Utes and Cheyenne and they say back at the Fort that they been getting' restless."

After a few hours ride, the small group of observers reached a prominent hillock and Franco was able to view the cause of the dust cloud through his field glasses.

"It's a war party alright, and they ain't up to much good. Let's hope they are raiding on another tribe and not on the track of the Mapes train that headed out of Fort Laramie ahead of us."

THE WRONG TURN

Cranston had been warned at the Fort about the possibility of hostile Indians, but when he confronted Harold Mapes about the necessity to stay close to the other trains, which would mean that they would have had to lie over at the Fort and allow the other trains to catch up, Mapes summarily rejected the suggestion. In response to the Indian threat, Mapes and the members of the train fell into the practice of shooting at any Indian that came in site of the train. Some of the immigrants claimed to have seen some of them hit and possibly killed.

"You shouldn't ought to be doin' that," Cranston advised, "Them ain't critters to be hunted like Antelope and they be more of them around here then they is of us."

"We been busting our butts to be the first into Oregon, and I ain't gonna' allow a bunch of savages to alter my plans. They need to know we won't be tolerating them around our wagons," was Mapes' response.

As it was the train was depleted when a number of the emigrants dropped out of the train at Fort Laramie complaining about the pace Mapes was demanding of them. Since they had entered the dry lands of the Great American Desert, their animals had suffered severely from a lack of feed and good water. Many had dropped from exhaustion and died on the trail. Others had sore feet and could not exert themselves to pull the wagons over the many rises and gullies that marked the trail. The dry air was drawing the moisture out of their wagon wheels and the wheels were constantly loosening and falling apart, a problem aggravated by the pace of the train. Of the forty wagons that made up the train when it left Independence, only thirty now remained. Unfortunately, those who went onward were obsessed, as was their leader of haste over caution.

Cranston, resting his mount on the summit of a ridge that had yet to be crossed by the train, first noticed the dust clouds following the train when he swung his leg over the saddle and had the advantage of a bit more elevation to view the back trail. At first he thought it might be a herd of buffalo, but soon rejected that thought as the cloud was not large enough and moving faster than a grazing herd of buffalo would be expected to move. With a sense of alarm, he rode back to the train to inform Mapes of his observation. The train had just started on the Sublette Cut Off, bypassing Fort Bridger. [6]

"I ain't running scared every time I see a dust cloud," was Mapes' response when Cranston suggested that they abandon the cut off and head by way of Fort Bridger. "There are Indians and whatever out there on the plains and I don't want you to be stirring up the folks every time

---

6   The Sublette Cut off saved the emigrants several days travel, but was a hazardous route that would take them to the Green River crossing that was also hazardous. The route that took them to Fort Bridger was considered safer. Fort Bridger was the jump off point for the trails to California. Oregon-California Trails Association, supra.

you see dust clouds. We got lots of rifles and ammunition and no Indian with any sense is going to get in our way. Now you get on ahead and find us a good camp spot like you're hired to do and quite getting' aggravated over your suspicions."

Cranston, as directed settled on a campsite he felt would be defensible if indeed his suspicions were justified. He knew Mapes would be upset because the site was not close to a water source and the grass was sparse. Cranston was out early the next morning to look for any sign of the source of yesterdays dust cloud. He felt little relief when he could find no trace of movement or other sign of danger. Although this lack of sign might prove reassuring to Mapes, Cranston knew that whatever had been following them did not vanish during the night and should be investigated. When he suggested that he take some men and scout their back trail, Mapes summarily dismissed the thought.

"Now how much sense does that take. You worry about hostiles on our trail and you want to go traipsing off with some of our guns and weaken our defense. I spect what you saw was a herd of wild horses or such and they settle down at some water hole, speaking of which you best find one for our camp site tonight. We can't keep up the pace with a puny campsite like you found us last night."

Cranston found it hard to bear the criticisms of Mapes. He had spent many years in the mountains north of the trail and was a private man inclined to following his own instincts. The obsession of Mapes to keep the train moving without regard for the animals or emigrants did not sit well with him. He had long ago come to the conclusion that haste often caused one to be incautious and that would always bring you grief out here in the wilderness.

"Why don't you send that Sherman fellow on ahead to find a camp site and I'll skedaddle back over our trail alone to see what's been making that dust cloud?"

"I didn't hire Sherman to do our scouting. He's got a team to tend and he's a good fellow to have about when we get into trouble getting' the wagons through these blamed washes. Now just do as you're told and quit fussin' about that sign you saw yesterday."

The sun was a bundle of golden rays on the eastern horizon as Cranston mounted his horse and rode off to the west to begin his scout. His mood was sour as he was still smarting from his rebuke by Mapes. What the hell was a scout for if you didn't want his advice? Mapes was a man driven by a purpose, but he was a green horn none-the-less. He stopped at a rise some distance from the wagon train and took a last look back. The camp was stirring and smoke wisps were rising in the still, cool air where it hung like a protective shroud. He could hear the call of the animals as they greeted yet another day of toil in the rising heat that would soon sap them of their vitality and add to their burden. "What the hell are these people doing out here?" Cranston mused to himself. Sitting out here in the middle of nowhere driven by hopes that few will ever realize, they were changing the wilderness he had come to love. Soon they would be carving the country into little plots and driving away the inhabitants that had wandered for centuries across these lands.

"It ain't no wonder the tribes is restless, it's just too bad that damn Mapes don't appreciate the dangers he asking these people to endure," he said to his horse as he spurred his mount onward. "You got more smarts than that Mapes."

The sun was at its midpoint, turning the land into a virtual furnace when Cranston headed off the trail to a far off clump of trees that he though held the promise of fresh water for a camp site. Riding along a ridge, he saw something that disturbed him in the arroyo below. The sage brush and clumps of grass had been trampled down. Something had recently passed through the arroyo. Pushing his horse over the crumpling side of the arroyo he dismounted as he inspected the tracks. They were horse tracks and there were a lot of them. They were not the tracks of wild horses. These horses carried a burden. It was hard to get a clear reading on the sign as so many animals had passed through the arroyo. From the volume of horse terds and the bent grass and trampled sage brush he knew that the tracks were but hours old and that there were some sixty to a hundred riders. He suspected that it was a band of raiding Utes and that in all probability they were moving ahead of the Mapes train to set up an ambush.

As Cranston recollected, there was a great site for an ambush but a short distance ahead where the train would pass through a valley of boulders and would have little chance of circling into a defensive circle. Cranston knew he must now ride like the wind to warn the train of the impending danger. As he set his foot into the stirrup to pull himself into the saddle there was a hiss and a Swack! Something had struck him in the back driving him to his knees. His horse bolted away startled by the sudden violence. Cranston staggered to his feet, dazed by the hit he had taken. An arrow was driven through his shoulder and he could see its head protruding from his body. He was not armed as his Navy revolver and Henry rifle were tied to his saddle. He turned to see the source of his agony when he was hit twice more with arrows from a source he could not see. He knew it was over for him. He could not rise from this last assault and remained on his hands and knees watching a Ute warrior run at him with his war club at the ready. It was over in a second and Cranston's scalp would now ride at the head of the war party tied to a war lance. It was good medicine and stirred the blood lust of the Ute war party.

Herald Mapes was extremely agitated as the sun turned to a golden orbit and raced to meet the horizon. "Where the hell was Cranston?" he kept muttering to himself. They had made a dry camp last night and Cranston was supposed to find them a good camp site tonight. From what he was told about the Sublette Cut Off, the trail would follow a narrow trail through a series of rock outcroppings. The wagons would be unable to form their normal defensive circle in a narrow canyon and yet here they were entering into what look to him like the entry into the canyon of rocks. Finally, he stopped the train and told the emigrants to form a circle as best they could for the night. Perhaps Cranston would show up soon and tell them where they could water the animals in the morning. One thing was for sure, Cranston would be in for a server rebuke for not performing his duty to find them a secure camp site with water and graze like he had been instructed. It was obvious to Harold Mapes that the camp site for the night was not the best. The rock outcroppings and bolder strewn terrain did not allow the wagons to draw together, they were instead, clustered in groups and the animals were, though contained by the surrounding slopes, going to be left to wander among the wagons and forage as best they could. His immediate thought, after the wagons were unhitched, was to send out a search party to find Cranston, but he had no idea which way to send them. In any event, he was certain the Cranston would show up, he was no doubt still peeved at the dressing down he had given him the night before and was trying to teach him a lesson. These Mountain Men were a stubborn bunch and had little sense of responsibility. That's why he was leading the train and not the likes of Cranston.

Rafe Matters had other things on his mind than the welfare of the train. For several weeks now, he had been obsessed with Melody Jenkins, a comely seventeen year old daughter of Christopher Jenkins, a surly old rock farmer who had the misfortune of settling on and trying to farm the unproductive, rock strewn lands in Eastern Main. Years of hard futile toil had gained him little but a broken hearts and broken dreams. His wife and three younger children remained behind him in shallow graves on the land that broke his heart and turned his soul into acidic turmoil and gave him a bitter disposition. Melody was the remaining light of his life, the only hope for his posterity, the only remembrance of his wife and the family that were once his only comfort. Christopher Jenkins was well aware of the comely countenance of his only daughter and knew that there were a number of young bucks on this train who had eyes for her. Christopher wasn't impressed with any of them, but the one he disliked the most and the one he admonished his daughter to avoid was Rafe Matters. Rafe was the son of a once well-to-do Tide Lands plantation owner from Carolina who had inherited a sizable estate and near a hundred slaves. The once rich soil that gave the plantation its wealth, however, was over farmed and the elder Matters inheritance soon wasted away. The debts had been paid by selling the slaves and the Matters family headed to Oregon. Rafe's father had three wagons in the train and had hired teamsters to drive them.

"That boy ain't done a day's honest work in his life. Look at the way he struts around in the tight pants and English riding boots sticking his nose into every camp with a young lady about. You stay away from that one, he'll only bring you grief," Jenkins advised his daughter.

Of course the very things that turned her father against Rafe were the very things that attracted Melody. She had seen too many men grow old before their time trying to create a livelihood tilling the unyielding fields of Maine. Melody was not interested in the sturdy farm stock that made up most of the eligible young men on the train. She had no desire to be a brood mare for some farmer and produce children whose life would be wasted tending to the land, a task that would be their only ambition.

It was difficult for two young people on a wagon train to share moments of solitude that would allow romance to bloom. The few respites along the trail where the fiddles were unlimbered and festive moments enjoyed were attended by all. The elder ladies would sit about and chatter and eagerly speculate on budding romances. To steal away from one of these gatherings and enjoy moments of passion was not a prospect a respectable young lady would undertake. Chattering old ladies would ruin the reputation of young ladies like Melody. None-the-less she and Rafe had stolen a moment or two behind a wagon or some sheltering tree or brush. A kiss or two was all that they had opportunity for, but those random kisses had stirred in Melody feelings of excitement and yearning she could not suppress. His strong arms about her pressing her to his hard muscular body left her breathless and yielding.

Rafe was not a young man without experience in these matters. He had lived the good life in a society where young enticing ladies, dressed in the finery of the day, openly flaunted their attractions at the numerous balls and cotillions that made up the social life on the Tide Lands. More than one of these young ladies had surrendered to his charms. To Rafe, Melody was one of the few attractive young ladies on the train. Whether she was single or married was no concern to him, his interest was in pursuit and the satiating of his loins, which had been too long without fulfillment of their lust. Most of the women on the train were as he would put it "shop worn", old before their time with skin of leather and the calloused hands of a man. They were a stern hard working lot whose passion for romantic endeavors had long since been blunted by long hours of toil and care.

In this group Melody stood out like a beam of hope and promise, drawing the attentions of would be suitors. To Rafe it was a question of availability, not love, a need for sex, not marriage that attracted him to Melody. While the camp was busy with preparations for the night's camp, Rafe slipped Melody a note telling her that when her father was asleep and the camp quite, to slip a pillow in her bed roll to make it look like she was occupying it and then to meet him near the large rock directly out from her camp. Rafe had discovered a semi cave carved out from under a small bluff that was hidden behind some heavy shrubbery. He had prepared a soft bed of bows and leaves and covered it with a blanket. It would be an ideal place to seduce Melody. Of course, he did not know if she would respond to his request.

Rafe sat long into the night waiting for Melody and was now concerned that she had waited too long. It would be daylight in a few hours and the camp would be stirring. He had about decided that Melody had declined his invitation, when he noticed a movement near her wagon, sure enough it was Melody and she was headed his way.

"Father was sleeping fitfully, his back is bothering him," Melody informed Rafe. "I couldn't get away any sooner."

Rafe pulled her to him and gave her a welcoming kiss to which she responded by gripping him tightly. Rafe then lead her to his secret place and settled her in. She had on a night dress, with pantaloons and a chemise underneath. She also had a heavy coat and demurred when he ask her to take it off. "It's to cold. Besides I don't have much else on," she responded.

"Let's see what we can do to warm you up then."

Melody had not been alone with a man before like this, and she did not know what was expected of her or how she should respond to this man. Soon, he was smothering her with kisses, first her lips, then he softly kissed her eyes and moved to her throat where he moved his tongue down to the top of her night dress. As she protested, he gave an amused chuckle.

"You are new at this aren't you?"

Melody now felt a bit defensive. Was there something she was supposed to do that she was not doing?

"I don't want you to go too far," she whispered.

"I won't hurt you, I just want you to like me and let me love you," he whispered back.

Her body was responding to his kisses and soon he was rubbing her breast through the thickness of her coat. She wanted to tell him to stop, but he stifled her protest with another kiss, this time parting her lips and putting his tongue in her mouth. At first she was shocked, but then yielded to this strange intimacy that set her heart racing and spread warmth through her body. Soon he was unbuttoning her coat. She grabbed at his hand, but instead of reaching for her breast, he let his hand rest on her stomach where he deftly massaged her flat, firm abdomen. The sensation caused by his caresses, his kisses was more pleasant than she imagined and she allowed his hand to slip up and grasp her breast. Soon he was rolling her extended nipple between his fingers and she begin to moan softly responding to his every move. He untied the bow strings of her nightgown and chemise and exposed her breast to the soft warmth of his eager lips. Now she was arching her back and pressing against him inviting more invasions, more pleasures. Rafe knew now that she would be his as he moved his hand down to that most vital spot to begin the final invasion. Suddenly his hand was no longer exploring but clamped firmly over her mouth stifling her moans, She knew instantly by the way he half sat upright that he was hearing someone approaching their secret place. My God, she shuddered; father had discovered her absence and was looking for her. She was ruined. Now Rafe was whispering softly into her ear, "Don't move, and don't utter a sound."

She was listening intently now and heard the sound of someone moving close to their hiding place. Something was wrong. It wasn't one person out there, there were many people moving down the slope past their hiding place. Close by she heard the sound of an owl hooting and it was soon answered from across the valley. It was no owl, Melody realized and terror gripped her turning her body just a moment ago fevered with passion stony cold. To Rafe it was all clear in an instant, having overheard the conversation between Cranston and Mapes about the possibility of being followed by a war party, he knew the wagon train would soon be under attack. How could he warn them? Any effort he made to reach the train would expose his hiding place and put him in the midst of who knew how many savages. Then there was Melody to consider. Would he dare expose their hiding place and allow these savages to have at her? He had left the camp without his rifle. He needed no weapon for the mission he was on that night. He could only hope that the sentinels were alert and would sound the alarm.

Rafe and Melody stayed huddled together as the first traces of morning light drove the darkness before it. Rafe could see but a few yards away the outline of a number of mounted warriors silently waiting for the moment of violence that would soon fall upon the wagon train. Then he heard the barked command of a sentinel, "Who goes there?" Then there was a warning shot and immediately the ground about them was alive with running horses, warriors charging and the war cries that curdled his blood. Below could be heard the shouts of men, the screaming of terrified women and children the braying of the startled mules and animals. Soon there were the sounds of small arms fire rising above the sounds of battle. Within what seemed like moments the report of firearms became distillatory and spasmodic and soon was replaced by the cries of anguish of those who would soon absorb the wrath of the hundred or so savages that were no doubt methodically butchering the emigrants.

Melody clung tightly to Rafe, tears streaming down her face. Her mind rejected any attempt to imagine the carnage that was taking place below their sanctuary. She murmured continually her words of protest: No! No! No!

After several hours, that seemed like years, the only noise that was heard from below was the occasional war hoops of the savages. Soon the warriors were riding past them and out of the valley, their horses and persons adorned with the spoils of their massacre, hats, bonnets, shirts, some even wearing women's apparel as well as pots, pans, weapons and the last vestiges of what had been the accumulation of dozens of families now dispossessed of even life itself. Rafe, obsessed with a boiling rage, but helpless to respond to his growing hate for these savages, was oblivious of Melody's need for comfort. There was no comfort he could offer. The man who had just hours before lived the life of comfort and pleasure, whose leisure moments had been spent in idleness and personal self indulgence died that day if not in life, surely in spirit.

When the eerie silence of death reined over the valley, Rafe emerged from the shelter where Melody was ordered to remain and ventured into the valley. The carnage was more then he could have imagined. All about lay the mutilated bodies of the emigrants. Women and children had not been spared, their naked abused bodies lying about in bloody heaps, some with arrows protruding from their bodies, others obviously bludgeoned to death or disemboweled. He found his father with a lance driven through his chest. He had been scalped and his testicles had been severed and shoved in his mouth. The depredations visited upon the women were even grosser. The savages had abused them and mutilated them, cutting off their breasts and driving arrows into their vaginas. The contents of the wagons were strewn about and some of the wagons had been set ablaze. Rafe came upon the body of Mapes who had been tied to a wagon wheel and disemboweled, no doubt while still alive. Rafe wondered through the scene of horror in a state of semi-shock unable accept that he been spared the fate of his father and the others whose death he deserved to have shared and would have shared except for his vanity and lust.

Rafe in anguish wondered about the remnants of the train for what seemed like an eternity as anger overcame his sense of loss. Searching among the discarded possessions, he selected clothing he thought suitable for Melody. They were boy's cloths and would allow her to move more freely over the terrain they would have to travel. Word of what happened here would have to reach Fort Bridger. There must be retribution for what had happened this day. Rafe found some hard tack among the wagons, a bit of bacon and fortunately a few canteens filled with water. Not a weapon was to be found except for the lances and arrows that the Indians had left in their victims.

When he was about to return to the hiding place he and Melody had shared, he heard the keening wail of a distressed woman and realized Melody had disregarded his command to stay away from the train and had ventured forth to find the body of her father and brother. He found her bent over the shattered remains of her father. His head was bare of the once abundant locks and was but a bloody mass. His clothes had been stripped away and he had been stabbed repeatedly in the chest. Melody's younger brother was laying nearby, his body undisturbed except for the large gash in the back of his head that allowed his life's essence to spill away. Rafe wanted to give her comfort, but was too submerged in his own grief to offer solace.

Rafe knew what he must do, but having led a life of idleness where he was seldom called upon for his opinion, he was ill prepared to venture into the wilderness to seek help and indeed to survive. It was Melody who, having recovered from her shock, realizing that Rafe was in a hopeless state of uncertainty, made the first suggestions that lead to a resolution and a decision as to what course they should take.

"Fort Bridger is to the south of us, but who knows what lies between us and the Fort if we head south. We could follow the trail on ahead, but we don't know how far it is to the next post which I think would be Fort Hall. I think we should back track in hopes of finding another train heading this way. If we don't find one we would at least be on the trail where we cut off and could get to Fort Bridger or meet another train going that way."

It was perhaps the first time in Rafe's life when a woman had taken command of a situation where he should have control and indeed spoke in the good sense terms that should have come from him.

"We best be doing it then," was his only response. "Take these clothes and boots and put them on. You can't be traveling in your night dress and slippers."

For a man accustomed to riding a horse whenever he needed locomotion, Rafe was finding it tedious to be walking back along the dusty sun baked trail to the junction of the cut off. He estimated that they must be at least thirty miles from the junction. For Melody, who had spent most of her travel time walking beside the wagon or in front of the train where she could avoid the choking dust, the walking was effortless and she soon found that their progress was being slowed by Rafe's continuing need to rest.

"Rafe," she admonished him, "we only been on the trail three hours and we've spent most of the time resting. You best keep up the pace or we will be out of water the way you been drinking it before we get half way back to the cut off."

The more time she was spending with him the more she realized that her father had been correct in his assessment of this man. How could she have so readily succumbed to his charms? She did not have it in her heart, however, to condemn him completely. Like her, his life had changed in a moment and he was having difficulties confronting the new reality that would be his life without family or position. She recognized in him a basic humanity that would eventually emerge from his current distress. He had after all, thought first of her safety when they were in crisis. He had confronted his terrible loss without going off the deep end which would have been understandable.

"Melody," he responded, "I will be better tomorrow. I need time to catch up to my feelings. Up yonder is some shade. I'm going to stop there for the night and come to terms with my emotions. I ain't going to tell you what to do, but I expect you could stand some thoughtful moments yourself. I'm sorry about the water, I ain't been too clear headed, but don't damn me yet. I know what we got to do and I'll be up to it."

When he did stop and removed his boots, Melody realized where part of the problem lay. His feet were bloody and blistered. He was indeed a tenderfoot. "We ain't got no way to tend to them feet," Melody remarked, "but I heard tell that you best soak them feet in your pee. It don't sound too comely, but it hardens 'em up I hear."

Their efforts at wrapping his feet in rags torn from Melody's chemise soaked with their urine gave them the only moments of humor, distracting them from thoughts of the hellish trek they must endure. Although the salty urine stung his wounds, Rafe endured the pain and found to his surprise the next morning that his feet were indeed healing and felt better. The second day of their trek took them through rugged rocky terrain with sparse vegetation and no hope of water or shade. By the end of the day, their water was gone, the temperature had dropped some forty degrees and a chill wind drove them into each others arms for what comfort and warmth could be had. Rafe realized that his estimate of the distance back to the tail junction was way off. There would be another day of walking at least and then who knew whether they would find any sign of a passing wagon train. Walking from the junction to Fort Bridger without water was a bleak prospect. Already their skin felt like parchment, their lips were splitting as the boiling sun sucked moisture from their bodies and burned their exposed skin.

"I see some movement off yonder," James remarked to Franco. It looks like buzzards."

Franco stopped his horse and through his field glasses studied the horizon in the direction James was pointing."

"Don't see nothin'," Clay remarked.

"It's Buzzards alright." Franco responded. "Best we head over and see what's got them interested. It ain't likely country to find no dead animal"

When the crested the ridge and looked down at the object of the birds interest, Franco drew his pistol and fired into the mass of buzzards to drive them off. It took some moments upon inspecting the corpse for Franco to pronounce that it was Cranston's body. Little was left of his features, but Franco recognized parts of the clothing as belonging to Cranston.

They buried him in a shallow grave they scraped out with their rifle butts and stacked rocks over the grave.

After studying the sign Franco told Clay. "You head back to the train and tell Anderson that there's a war party about and that they have probably set upon the Mapes train that was ahead of us. Tell him to get some men mounted and ride like hell to their aid. James, you head on to Fort Bridger and tell them there's a war party loose out here and they's probably after the Mapes people. I'll ride on ahead on their trail and see what I can find out. I don't want Anderson riding into no ambush."

At first Rafe thought it was an apparition, or maybe just some tall, forlorn bush that had somehow gained sustenance to prosper in this bleak wilderness so he ignored it and plodded determinedly on. He found it best to purge his mind of all thought and concentrate only on putting one foot ahead of the other. If thoughts came to him, they were not encouraging. He and Melody were out in the middle of nowhere, country claimed only by a band of marauding Indians who may yet appear. Even if the hostiles did not descend upon them, their chances of survival were diminishing as the unrelenting sun, absorbed their waning strength. Melody, who had tried to carry on an occasional conversation, had been silent for some time, no doubt finding it was taking all her concentration to just keep moving.

When Rafe raised his head to survey the trail before him, he drew up short and studied the apparition before him. It was no random bush out there it was a man on horseback and he was headed their way.

"Melody, we got company coming."

"Is it and Indian?" was Melody's fearful response. "Can't imagine no white man out here all alone."

"Can't tell from here, but since there ain't no place to hide I guess we will find out soon enough who it is. Damn, I wish I was armed, were helpless as babies."

Franco had noticed the travelers on the trail ahead of him and knew that they must be survivors from the Mapes train. Who else would be walking down this track heading back the way they had come. When he approached them, he noticed how the man moved the women behind him as if to protect her. It was one of the few times of late he had to acknowledge that he was part Indian and that these survivors would be wary of his approach. He was dressed more like and Indian then a white man. It was a good thing, he mused, that they were not armed.

"You folks from the Mapes train?" Franco asked as he dismounted and walked toward them.

"And who the hell are you?" was Rafe's wary response.

"I'm riding scout for the Anderson train, we bivouacked with your group back in Independence. We been trailing behind you since then."

I remember him," Melody volunteered. "We been walking for days. Our train was attacked by Indians. Rafe and me is the only ones left. They killed everyone, even the babies."

"The Anderson train's only about ten miles from here. There'll be some help for you folks in a couple hours. You best settle down and save your strength. Take some of this water, but be sparse as there ain't much to be had out here. I'm riding on ahead to make sure the trail is clear for them that's coming. Them Utes is a tricky bunch and may be settin' up an ambush for the rescue bunch."

"There ain't no rescuing to be done," was Rafe's response. "All that's needin' now is a burial detail. Them Indians didn't even leave a dog alive."

Rafe's remark peaked Franco's curiosity. "How's it that you folks got spared?"

"That ain't no matter to you," was Rafe's defensive response. "But if you must know we was away from the train and couldn't be of no help, so we hid out."

Rafe was irritated when Franco gave Melody and appraising look and an amused, knowing nod. "I best be going," Franco said and rode off.

Franco reigned in his horse on the ridge overlooking the campsite where the Mapes train made its last stand. From where he was at, the stench from the carnage below was palpable. He took out his field glasses and surveyed the scene below. It was obvious that the train was poorly led and that the massacre was greatly aided by the fact that the wagons could not be drawn into a defensive parameter. The killing of Cranston before he could warn the train of the danger was no doubt a factor. But, unbeknownst to Franco, Cranston had warned Mapes of the pending danger. When his glasses rested on the impaled body of Mapes, several Coyotes were fighting over his entrails. Franco felt no sympathy for the man. Mapes' foolish efforts to be the first train to Oregon put his people out here alone without the hope of assistance. He remembered Fremont's remark when he first found himself in the middle of a wilderness similar to this: "This here isn't no place for a fool. A man needs his wits about him to survive out here."

Franco scouted about the canyon reading sign and trying to find the path taken by the war party. As he suspected not far from the scene of the slaughter, the Indian band started breaking up into smaller and smaller groups. It would be a difficult and a long scout to run down and punish the murders of the Mapes train. In the distance he could now see the dust of the Anderson volunteers as they drove their horses toward the scene of the disaster. William Anderson was leading the group and as they drew up beside him at the head of the valley Franco observed that most of the riders had their rifles at the ready.

"You can put them guns away. There ain't nothing to shoot up ahead but buzzards and wolves. The pilgrims is all dead," Franco advised them.

William had not stopped to talk to Rafe and Melody when he came upon them. He instructed two men to stay with them and get them back to the train and rode on. He was stunned by what Franco now advised him. He and the other men came ready and eager for a fight. Upon them now fell the task of trying to identify the victims and to bury them, not a pleasant prospect. William's first instinct was to leave the scene and pursue the Utes who had caused this carnage. There must be retribution and it should be swift.

"Put them thoughts out of your head," Franco advised him. "Them Utes have scattered to the winds and you'll spend a month out there trying to track them all down. These men you have here ain't up to the task. Besides, they got family to get back too. Let the soldiers take care of this, it's their affair now."

"They need to be tracked down and wiped out for what they've done here. I don't expect you being a Breed would understand that."

Franco felt the sting of the remark. Under different circumstances he would have taught this cub a lesson. Now was not the time.

"We got one fool out there to bury. If you want to join him, take off. You ain't got enough provisions to last but a day or two or enough men to do the job if you run into them hostiles. You'll end up buzzard bate like these pilgrims, but if you think you're smarter than this Breed, go galloping after them Utes and I'll have the satisfaction of dancing on your grave." With that said Franco rode off to help with the burying.

William, with reluctance and a growing resentment toward Franco, accepted the wisdom of Franco's advice and joined in the burial detail.

William, like most of those engaged in the process became obsessed with a growing hatred toward those who had committed the atrocity they had to bare. Some would eventually accept what had happened here, but others would carry the memories to their grave and their hatred throughout their lives.

ON TO FORT BRIDGER

It was a trail weary, dust covered rider and horse that was first noticed to be seen approaching Fort Bridger from the northeast. Although there were no formal lookouts at the Fort, the traders at the Fort were on the alert for news of some Indian depredation. The Indian camps about the fort were teeming with excitement and it had been reported that many braves were riding though the camps with trophies, scalps, clothing and livestock taken in some recent raid.

"Best get the boss out here; I fear this rider is bringing some bad news." The trapper who had observed the rider approaching suggested to his mate.

When James first came into view of the Fort, he noticed the Indian encampments. There were a hundred teepees if not more about the Fort. The Fort itself was large and imposing, but James could see no sign of a military presence which he was expecting. Instead, as he rode into the Fort, he was confronted with a rag tag bunch of trappers and traders who had gathered in the center of a large compound in front of what appeared to be a headquarters building. When James reported that a large force of Indians had been gathering and might be preparing an ambush of the Mapes train, a silence fell over the gathering. The head factor turned aside and spit a large hock of tobacco juice at a passing beetle.

"I suspect, son, that what you feared has already happened. Them braves about camp is sportin' scalps and booty from some evil doin's. They mostly came ridin' in from the north," the head factor responded. "Where'd you come from?"

James explained that he had been part of a wagon train trailing the Mapes train, but he was sent to get help and didn't witness any Indian attack.

"There ain't much help we can be here," the factor responded, "As you can rightly see, were in the trading business. This ain't no army post.

Them Indians about here out number us fifty to one, so we ain't about to go among them and challenge all them hot headed braves that's been blooded. You can ride back to Fort Laramie where there's some soldiers."

"But you got to do something; those are white folks they killed, women and children. They need to be punished," James retorted indignantly.

"Son, you be new to these here parts. Ain't no one likin' what's happenin' out here since all these emigrant trains is passing through. They mostly just pass on, but some of these settlers are unkindly to the Indians, not to say the sickness they bring on to the tribes. Hundreds of them have died in awful misery. My business is tradin' and I can't be messin' with these hostilities less it involves me and my Fort here. What's to be done with them savages that done what's been done is Army business." Having said that, the factor walked away and the crowd, some shaking their heads and muttering epitaphs against the savages who would do such a thing and others indifferent to the tragedy, headed on about their business.

James then noticed a tall, bearded mountain man, clad in the usual buckskins, leaning against the hitching rail where he had been observing the confrontation between James and the Factor. At first James ignored him, now concerned about attending to his horse that needed water, feed and rest.

"Where'd you get that necklace you be wearin?" the mountain man asked as James stepped to the hitching post to retrieve his horse.

James was not receptive to these people who had shown indifference to the tragedy when he had ridden so hard in an effort to seek help. He did not respond to the question and started to walk past the man on the way to the livery stable.

The man stepped forward and seized him by the arm in a vice like grip. "I done asked a civil question and would like an answer."

James was not intimidated by the stranger and merely stood his ground and stared the man in the eyes for a long moment to show he did not fear him even though this mountain man was a full head taller.

"I've been told not to talk to strangers. Now let go of my arm or I'll cut your damn hand off."

To James' relief, the man took no offence at his remark, but released his grip. "I ain't meanin' no harm you feisty little cub, but I got reasons to ask about that necklace. I knowed a man who once wore what looks to be that same necklace. He was ambushed up on the Snake River by some Blackfoots and one of them took his scalp and his necklace. I am curious as to how it got around your neck if it be the same one which I suspect it be."

"Well, I didn't get no proper introduction from the savage that gave it to me, so I ain't certain as to how he got it. Let's say I bested him in a horse race and he thought it fittin' to give me this necklace as my prize.

The mountain man shrugged off the answer, "Look here young fella, I ain't wantin' to get you all ruffled. I suspect you be all out of sorts with what you been through. You jist give your horse to that Indian lad there who works for the livery and come along with me and I'll see if a little food and rest will cure your cantankerousness My name's Parker. What name do you go by?"

"James Rawlins," James responded curtly. "And I don't intend to leave my horse to no Indian's care. I'll take her to the livery myself and see she's properly treated."

"Suit yourself, but that boy knows horses and knows yours needs carin' for. Don't go thinkin' every red man you meet is like the last one you saw. This boy has been with the Factor for some time and is a good lad. He'll do right by your horse, now quit bein' testy and give him the horse."

Reluctantly James handed the reins to the Indian lad who James guessed was probably about his own age. "She needs grain and a good rub down, don't let her get too much water till she cools down," James admonished the Indian who merely nodded and walked away with the mare.

When James turned to follow Parker, accepting his invitation for some food, he was a bit surprised when Parker led him through the gate to the outside of the Fort rather than to one of the living quarters within the Fort. He followed him to a teepee where an Indian woman was fussing with a fire. She was a tall squaw dressed in a loose buckskin dress that revealed little of her features. The dress was adorned with blue and red beads. The dress had been bleached white, was clean, but showed signs of wear. Her raven black hair was tied behind her head with a leather thong, and her face, though not unpleasant displayed indifference at his presence. She gave him a cursory inspection, but after that would not look in his direction and busied herself with the contents of a large pot hanging over an open fire.

"Little Flower don't take much to strangers, especially white fella's like yourself, so don't mind her. She makes a good stew though and you need some the way you look."

Parker spoke to her in her language and she responded by filling a bowl from the contents of the pot and handed it to James without even looking at him. James sat holding the bowl confused as to what he was to do with it.

"Ain't no butler comin' around to give you your spoon and fork, you got to eat that stew from the bowl. Just slurp up the juice and pick out the big chunks with your fingers."

James hesitated until Parker was handed a bowl and followed his example in devouring the stew which he found to be quite tasty. After he had his second bowl and was feeling the fatigue of the long ride overwhelming him, Parker asked him again, "I'm still wantin to know how you come by that ornament around you neck. I know that them bear claws is strong medicine among the tribes and I don't cotton to that tale about a horse race. Now just how did you come by it?"

James related to him the events that lead up to the Indian giving him the necklace. "I didn't talk to the Indian or know much of his reasons for giving me the necklace. Franco, he was our guide with the train, did all the talking and didn't tell me anything other than the Indian gave it to me for what he thought was my bravery."

With the mention of Franco's name, Parker nearly choked on the broth he was sucking from the bowl of stew. When he recovered he spoke excitedly, "You mean that pole cat Franco is with the train that's coming after you?"

He addressed Little Flower in her language but the only thing James understood was the mention of the word "Franco" that brought the first signs of emotion in Little Flower's face. It was a smile of joy.

"Franco and me spent a winter or two up on the Yellowstone trapin' Beeves and wolves. He brung Little Flower to our camp. She is a Cree from Canada and was kidnapped by the Blackfoot. Franco found her wandering around near starved. He didn't want her so I took her as my wife. She's been a good woman to me and I got Franco to thank for that."

James felt immediately more comfortable with his new friends finding they had a common acquaintance, one they both respected. Having finished his stew, he felt the heavy weight of sleep overcoming him. Parker gave his wife instructions and she went into the lodge and prepared a bed for James which he gratefully accepted.

"You get you some rest and I'll go check on that critter of yours and make sure she's properly tended since you're not trusting that boy." Parker then left and James fell immediately into a deep sleep.

James didn't know how long he had slept but now lay half in and half out of sleep. His mind was struggling to familiarize itself with his surroundings. There was the smell of smoke and aroma of a meal he could not identify. The warmth and comfort of his bed held him in a cocoon like state that he was reluctant to leave. There was a commotion outside the lodge that had been the cause of his awakening. Suddenly he was wide awake as he recognized one of the voices as that Franco. He rushed outside the lodge to see Franco cavorting about with Little Flower in some facsimile of a dance while Parker sat on a robe with a whiskey jug in one hand while he was slapping it with his other hand to give the dancers their beat. James had never seen Franco in other than a serious demeanor and was delighted to see his friend in this rare moment of frivolity. It was then he noticed that the sun was setting and was in a state of confusion as to what time or what day it was. When Franco and Little Flower noticed him standing outside the lodge, Franco stopped his cavorting and walked over to him.

"I heard this Pole Cat had kidnapped you and was holding you in that there lodge of his, so I thought I best get over here and set you free. His lady here was trying to fend me off."

"She seemed to be getting the best of it," James responded. "Where's the train? It can't be here already."

At that remark, Parker laughed. "Boy, you done slept from sun set to sun set. I bet you could eat a skunk right now." At that he spoke to Little Flower who set about getting James another helping of the ever cooking stew.

"The train's on the other side of the Fort," Franco advised him. "Anderson was reluctant to bring the train in to close with the tribes camped about. I guess he didn't need to worry too much, most of the lodges were put down and the Indians pulled out last night. Seem the doin's up there with the Mapes train has them worried about the surliness of the settlers."

James looked about him and sure enough the area about the Fort where there had been groupings of lodges was mostly empty. The few lodges that remained were no doubt the lodges of the old, the young, the women and the infirm who were no longer up to moving about with the tribes.

After finishing his meal, James thanked Parker and Little Flower for their hospitality and headed off to rejoin his family, leaving the mountain men to their revelry.

He had yet to get the details regarding the fate that had befallen the Mapes train, but didn't want to wait around to hear the details from Franco, who seemed more in the mood for levity. He knew the news could not be heartening what with the report from the Factor that there were braves riding through the Indian encampments loaded with booty and scalps. When he returned to the train, his mother and Jenny were engaged in conversation with William Anderson whom James now recalled, had been spending more and more time lately by their campfire. It finally dawned on him that William was showing a special interest in Jenny. He didn't know if he liked this developing relationship. William was unlike his brother Clay and tended to treat him as a boy rather than the man he thought he had become. Jenny and his mother gave him a heartfelt welcome; they had been concerned about his lone ride to the Fort with the report of hostile Indians about. The fate of Cranston weighed heavily on their minds as they thought of James riding alone through a land where the smell of violence permeated the air.

"Poppa has gone to the Fort to arrange for supplies and get what news he can. That fellow Rafe who survived the raid on the Mapes train, headed back east with some group returning to St. Louis," Jenny advised him. "Mr. Anderson says we're to stay here for a bit until they's sure that the Indians have settled down. Franco and Clay head out tomorrow to scout the trail. I suppose you'll he going with him. Have you had anything to eat?"

"I did eat with a fella named Parker who's been friendly toward me. I been hearing all kinds of bad news about the Mapes train, but no one has told me what actually happened. I was hoping Dad would be here to fill me in on the details."

"William rode with the group that was to rescue them," Carla volunteered, "Let him tell you."

"I can't give you all the details," William responded, "not in front of the ladies. Franco guessed there was some three hundred or so Indians fell on the train at dawn and wiped it out to the man, except for that Rafe fella and his girl Melody. She's with the Whitmans now and is pretty broken up. She won't leave camp. She panics when an Indian looks at her. They even killed the animals they didn't herd off including the dogs. It was hell up there, if you'd seen it you wouldn't sleep well nor be kindly disposed to any savage you met. If it weren't for all them Indians taking off before we got here, things would be pretty bad around here right now. Every man that rode with me wanted to get an Indian in his sights and was mighty disappointed when they were gone."

James was not a witness to the site of the massacre and did not feel it his place to defend the Indians against a man who was a witness. He was none the less discomforted by the tone of William's voice as he spoke of the desire of men in the rescue party to kill Indians without regard to their guilt. Rather than get into an argument over the issue, James announced that his horse needed its shoes checked by the blacksmith and left the camp.

The next day when James and Franco were gone, the emigrants took advantage of the stopover at the fort to soak their wagon wheels in a nearby stream to tighten them up for the road ahead. The dry heat of the past month had loosened the wheel spokes and some had already fallen apart. This effort all went well enough until some of the men put their axes and mauls in the stream to let the wooden handles swell and secure the blades. It was then that the trouble started. Several Indian boys took to stealing the axes that were much prized by the Indians. When the theft was discovered, ten of the men gathered their guns and headed for the lone Indian encampment threatening to tear the camp apart unless their tools were returned.

"Them thieving' Indians got to be taught a lesson," was the leader's lament as they headed out of the camp.

There were only about forty scattered lodges left of the hundreds that had been there before the train arrived. The remaining Indians were mostly old or infirm or the women whose men had not returned from hunting. There were among the later, a number of children several of whom were guilty of the theft that was about to bring upon them all the retribution of the angered white man.

The disturbance that ensued when the men invaded the Indian camp soon came to the attention of the Factor who rushed out with about twenty other men from the Fort, some of whom were also armed. Among them were Parker and several other mountain men. When they arrived at the Indian lodges, several small Indian boys there had been rounded up and were being threatened by the emigrants. The boys, who could not speak the language of the white men, were in a state of great fear as they could not respond to the demands being made upon them. Their mothers were in a state of excitement also and there was much wailing and shouting among them. The crowd of Indians bout the scene was growing as the Factor arrived.

"What the hell you men doing with these Indian boys, and what are you doing in their camp?"

"These thieving little whelps has stole our axes and we aim to have them back." one of the whites responded.

"Why didn't you come to me about this? Those boys you got corralled is scared shitless. They don't understand a word you sayin' and they's mothers don't neither. Now you just back off and let me handle this."

"We don't need no Indian lover interfering in our affairs." One of the men holding an Indian boy shouted back. "These little savages need to be taught to stay away from our things and away from our camp."

Parker, who had come out to the camp out of curiosity, became agitated at the man's remarks and stepped forward and grabbed the man's arm and demanded that he release the child.

"Leave this boy be pilgrim. He ain't among them that sole your tools."

"Git your stinkin' hands off me you dirty squaw man," was the retort from the man named Fellows who was holding the boy.

It was an unfortunate utterance to make to a mountain man who had faced death a dozen times and instinctively responded to threats with immediate violence. Before Fellows knew what had happened he was on his back with Parker's knee at this throat looking at the blade of a huge knife.

Parker froze and rose slowly from the prostrate body of Fellows as he felt the cold steal of a rifle barrel pressing against his neck. One of Fellows' comrades had come to his aid. In a blaze of speed, Parker spun about and had the man disarmed and was threatening him with his own weapon. The Factor quickly stepped between them and called for quiet.

The rest of Fellow's supporters moved forward to aid him and his companion who was now looking down the barrel of his own rifle only to be confronted by the other mountain men and those who had accompanied them from the Fort. The men from the wagon train had ridden with William Anderson to assist the Mapes train and still had the bitter memories of the mutilated, bloated corpses that they had to bury. They wanted to let blood and if these men from the Fort were to interfere with their purpose, then they were ready to fight them too.

Paul Anderson, hearing the ruckus had hurried to the Indian village as had the Reverend Whitman. They joined with the Factor in separating the groups and brought some semblance of order to avoid the ugly scene that was about to occur.

"We have no fight with these men form the Fort and for that matter it isn't very prideful to be taking out your hate on these children and squaws. Those tools that were stolen were stolen by mere boys and they just didn't know what they were getting into. Now let's just ease back those hammers and start talking sense. I don't want any widows in my train whose husbands were killed fighting over some stupid ax that cost two dollars over at the Fort.

"I don't know why these here fellas get so testy over a bunch of damn Indians. They don't deserve no better than what them people on the Mapes train got." Fellows muttered after he got up from the ground and dusted himself off. He was still shaking from the encounter but unwilling to relent.

"I been trading with these Indians since before you got off your mothers teet. I aim to keep doing so and if you people don't care to get along with my rules, pack up and get on your way."

It was the Reverend Whitman who stepped forward then. "You need to be teaching these heathens some of God's commandments if they are to survive out here, what with all the people that will be coming this way. You may have been doing good business, but your future is with the white men and you should be teaching these Indians proper behavior if they are to survive."

"Reverend," the Factor retorted, "Shut your yap. It's you and your lot that's brought them nothing but disease, petulance and hunger. I ain't blaming them for getting' resentful of your comin'. Them braves that rode off before you got here was saying that them people on the Mapes train was shooting at them all along the way as if they were part of the game to be killed. I don't tolerate what happened to that Train, but the ignorance of them folks is like the ignorance you are displaying here. There's reasons the Indians got riled up and when riled up they settle their score the way you expect a heathen to do. You ain't in your own back yard out here so you best learn to treat them that were here before you more kindly. I ain't going to say no more. You men get back to your wagons or get down the trail. I'll see to them tools."

With that said, the Factor and his contingent walked back to the Fort leaving the settlers to return to their wagons humbled but resentful. The Reverend Whitman was seething with rage at having been lectured like a child over matters he believed to be in his special domain.

After Franco and James returned to report that there were no recent sign of Indians along the trail ahead, the Anderson train set forth on the last leg of its journey to Oregon. Most of the emigrants felt relieved to be leaving Fort Bridger which they deemed to be too tolerant of the Indians and too unfriendly toward them. Melody had a difficult time deciding what to do with her now altered future. She was tempted to head back East, but her only family was in the state of Maine and she had no desire to return there and take up life with what were rather distant relatives who may not have a place for her. The only friends she had that she felt close to were all killed in the Indian raid on their train. The decision to head on Westward with the Anderson train was made when Narcissa Whitman approached her and urged her to accompany the Reverend and her to their Mission and the Columbia River where there would be plenty to do while she decided what she could of her future. Although Melody was intimidated by the august presence of Dr. Whitman, she felt secure in the company of Narcissa and accepted the offer.

It was indeed tedious being back on the trail again. But ahead lay the promise of the fruitful lands they envisioned. Passing into what was designated the Oregon Territory gave encouragement that they would soon be reaching their destination. The hardships that they constantly endured seemed less severe as they drove on to Fort Hall a destination that would place them well beyond the halfway point of their journey. The terrain was dry and dusty, with little to commend it except for the steady pace they could maintain over land that was largely featureless except for the looming presence of the snow capped Rocky Mountains that grew ever closer and more dominant on the far horizon. It was on the third day on their passage from Fort Hall that Carla Rawlins called her small family about her and told them that she had made her peace with God and would likely not be with them beyond the morrow.

"My heart labors to keep me with you, but is not strong and is ever weaker. I fight to keep breath in my lungs and am tiring of the effort. My soul wants only peace and rest and I fear I must leave you, the will is no longer with me to live on."

Carla's confession of her condition drew immediate admonishment from her family. She must live on, her condition was sure to improve they urged her.

Taking Jenny's hand in hers, she pulled her close unable to raise her voice much above a whisper.

"Jenny, you have been a dear daughter and a faithful companion and I am saddened that I will leave you to face so much of your young life without my presence. You are a strong Christian girl and will find a good man like your father one day and my passing will not then be so great. Remember, honey that as a wife and one day a mother, you will be the rock that anchors your family. Give of yourself to your man and make him strong. We women give a man his humanity and his sense of purpose. Be your man's guiding light, now kiss me and be strong."

She then reached for James hand and pulled him down beside her. With insight into his thoughts that surprised him she whispered, pausing now and then to gain her strength and breath," I know you are punishing yourself for being away so much from camp while I have been declining. Don't be hard on yourself, James my dear child. My one great happiness these past days has been to see you pass from a shy child into manhood before my eyes. While you rode away from the train in this vast wild country, my heart was filled with joy knowing you were mine and I could be ever so proud. I must now ride with you in your heart and I will be part of you always, so there is no need to be missing me. Be strong and always ride ahead of the rest. Now James, please kiss me. You will one day be a man among men."

The effort of saying goodbye to her family was clearly taxing Carla's remaining strength. He voice was failing and when she called her husband to her side she had to wait to speak until she could gain her breath.

"Wayne, I know your heart is heavy with the thought that your decision to bring the family west and take me away from our home is what has brought me to this end. You are wrong, dear to blame yourself. My body was broken when we lost our last child and my time left in this life was by the Lord's blessing and he has allowed me the time to see my family on its way to a new land where they may prosper. Don't morn me long, dear, and find yourself a new help mate with the strength to serve you. You still have much living to do and I would be hurt deeply to think that you would be alone. I have only one last request I hope you will be able to grant me. I do not want to be buried alone out here in a land with out a trace of my passing. I heard tell there is a place close by called Soda Springs. It would be pleasing to me to think I should be laid to rest in a place where people go for renewal of their health; a place that has a marking on the map and where life is ever present. Can you do that for me Wayne?"

"I would carry you there all the way in my arms if need be," he assured her as he reached down to pull his failing wife to his chest. He could say no more for his throat was too constricted. His tears were wetting her cheeks and his heaving chest shook her body. James and Jenny fell upon their father and mother in a last embrace as the gathering dusk shrouded them in the privacy of its darkness.

The next morning James enquired of Franco the location of the springs that Carla had mentioned and was informed that they were only a day away from them, but that the springs were off the trail a short distance and he didn't think Paul Anderson intended to take that detour. However, when Paul heard of Carl's dying request he informed James that they would take that route and take a day's lay over so they could pay proper respects to their mother.

When they came to the site of the springs, the members of the Anderson train were not pleased to find that there were a number of Indians camped about the area. After the troubles with the with the Mapes train, the emigrants were not trustful of the tribes. Franco informed them, however, that they were mostly Canadian Indians and not likely to have been involved in the Mapes massacre.

To Wayne Rawlins and his family, they were the cause of other concerns. They had come to find a burial site for Carla and had heard stories about how the graves of many of the settlers along the trail had been desecrated. When Franco was advised of these concerns he led James over to a site where there were makings of a past grave.([7])

"These here emigrants were set upon by some renegade Indians who wanted their stock. There was a whole family of them as I hear that was buried in their wagon box. Ain't been no one bothering their grave, but if you have any concern there be a spring up the valley there where she could be buried without them viewing the doin's. There ain't no secure place unless you want to carry her on to Fort Hall and that be some days away."

Wayne tore the planking from an abandon wagon near the site and made a presentable coffin for his wife. Jenny dressed her mother in her best dress, but on the advice of Franco none of her treasures were buried with her as Wayne had wanted.

At Wayne's request only a few close friends attended the burial. He was afraid that a large crowd would draw the attention of the Indians camped nearby. A grave stone with her name and the date of her birth and death chiseled thereon was deliberately placed several yards away from the grave. It was a peaceful place that had a view of the valley below with a bubbling hot spring passing by the grave onto the valley below. After the other mourners had left, the members of the Rawlins family remained to emblazon into their hearts and memories the site where Carla would rest and pass onto her anticipated paradise. Although each of them had comfort in the fact that this spot could one day be located, unlike the many graves that marked the trail behind them, they knew the likelihood that they would ever pass this way again was indeed remote.

At their father's request, Jenny and James left their father alone beside their mother's grave and walked together in silence back to their camp. The other emigrants had made the best of the respite and many had soaked in the mineral springs, thereafter claiming that the curative properties of the

---

[7] For a description of Soda Springs campsite on the Oregon Trail and the Wagon Box Grave memorial see: Oregon-California Trails Association, supra.

hot springs had cured afflictions long suffered. Some, however, drank of the waters and soon found that benefits to be obtained were gained only from external contact.

Neither James nor Jenny could find words of consolation for the other and sat in lone silence at their wagon site awaiting the return of their father. Jenny knew that it was now her place to prepare the meals and manage the domestic affairs of their lonely camp. But tonight, there would be no warm meal, there would be no campfire, there would be only the over burdening sadness that dominated their every though. Jenny hardly noticed the presence of another beside her and became aware of Melody's presence only when Melody slipped a blanket about her.

"It is getting cold and you must have the comfort of some warmth," Melody spoke to her in a soft, consoling voice. "I wish I had words that would lift the weight of your mother's passing from your heart. I know there are no such words and only time can heal your aching heart. As you know I have recently lost my father and the hurt still possesses me. Please let us share our sorrow. I have had no one to help me. I think we need each other."

Jenny was slow to respond to Melody's entreaty. Her heart was heavy and her mind was searching the memories of a life that now seemed to be in a different universe; her life spent in the certainty and security of their home in Missouri. She stared for a moment at Melody, not immediately recognizing her. When she responded it was only a gesture, she raised the blanket and invited Melody to share it with her. Soon they were embracing each other and allowing their pent up emotions to take control of them and they wept together for the loss they could share. James who had been sitting in silence nearby picked up his rifle and saddle and headed off into the darkness. He would have to find his own way to bring healing for his loss.

It was but two days travel from Soda Springs to Fort Hall and the emigrants of the Anderson train were in no mood for further delays. Like Fort Bridger, Fort Hall was basically a trading post that had long served as a fur trading center first for the American Fur trading Company and then the Hudson Bay Company that was in control of the post when the Anderson train entered its environs. ([8]) Again the area about the Fort was habituated by Indian tribes, main Shoshone and Bannocks. The lingering

---

[8] The description of Fort Hall is from Oregon-California Trails Association, supra.

hostility toward the tribes as a result of their recent experience was an additional stimulant for the emigrants to move on as soon as possible. Wayne Rawlins was among the few who wanted to wait over a few days. James, who had headed out alone the night before they left Soda Springs, had not returned. Even Franco was ignorant as to James' whereabouts and was not inclined to go looking for him.

"The boy needs his time alone. He wouldn't welcome my coming after him. He knows by now how to take care of himself and will be along when he's feeling fit to be with us," was Franco's response when asked to go looking for James.

At that moment, far from their camp, James, having faced the loss of his mother had finally found comfort in her assurance that she was now imbedded in his heart where she would always be with him, had turned back toward the train. Unlike his travels of the previous several days, he was now more cautious and was riding along the ravines and staying off the high ground where he could be observed. He was quick to notice that his horse was beginning to get nervous and was snorting and shaking her head. Pulling his rifle from its scabbard, he dismounted and moved forward slowly along the sandy bottom of the ravine where his movement would be muffled. He instinctively knew that there as another presence about and his heart began to race and his breathing became labored. He was now regretting his decision to ride out alone. It was a dumb move and he would now have to pay the consequences. Something was moving toward him, but he could not make out what it was. What ever it was it was coming slowly and without caution and at a labored gate. It was then his horse whinnied, letting his presence be known. The movement ahead stopped, but then he heard a snorting as another horse responded to his horses call.

James moved to what cover was available behind a low bush and waited for the other horse and rider to come forward. Soon the movement ahead resumed and from around the bend of the ravine, a lone horse appeared, limping badly on what appeared to be an injured fore leg. It was a small pinto Indian pony, without saddle, its rope bridle dragging along beside it. James approached the horse slowly, letting it smell his scenes and get comfortable with his presence. James put some water in his hat and let the thirsty pony have a drink. After a time, the pony let James examine his leg and James was relieved to find that there were no broken bones, but only a sprain that would in time heal. If left alone, lame as it was, the pony would soon fall prey to the wolves that would discover its presence and its impediment. He made up a poultice using the juices of a small cactus that Franco had told him had healing properties.

James was in somewhat of a quandary. He wanted to get back to the train, but was reluctant to leave the pony alone. The pony needed to rest its leg for a few days, but James did not have the provisions to stay longer in the wilderness. He tied the two horses to a nearby bush. He was curious as to where the pony had come from and started tracing its path back up the ravine. The pony could not have been left out here alone with its bridle still on and no sign of a picket rope. After moving about half a mile up the ravine he came to a place where there was a high steep bank where he would read sign that this is where the pony had fallen over the side.

There was also sign that other animals had come over the side, it was buffalo sign. No doubt the rider had been hunting buffalo and had been forced over the side of the ravine by the stampeding herd. On the far side of the ravine, in the shade of a bush, he noticed a moccasined foot. He immediately dropped on one knee and aimed his rifle at the bush waiting for some reaction to his presence. None came. Slowly he moved forward with his finger tight on the trigger of his rifle. When he moved up beside the prostrate body of the brave, he could see that the Indian was unconscious and badly injured. The only weapon about was a large knife held in a scabbard at the Indian's waist. James recognized it as a Bowie knife and assumed it had been taken by the Indian on some raid. The scabbard was a piece of art with colorful beaded and designs and flowing thongs.

After removing the knife from the scabbard, he knelt down beside the brave and placed his hand on his chest. There was a heartbeat and labored breathing. Feeling his brow, James detected that the brave was in a fever and in no shape to cause him trouble. It was then he noticed that the brave had a broken leg. The thigh bone on his right side was protruding from the soiled leggings that had been soaked with blood. James had seen Dr. Whitman set broken bones and knew what he must do. As long as the Indian was unconscious, this would be the time to set the leg.

Returning to where he had picketed the horses, James cut several branches off of the stunted trees that grew in the ravine. It was while he was searching for material to make a splint that he noticed a place on the side of the Ravine where there was an outcropping of green grass. Upon investigating it, he let his horse loose and she began pawing the ground. James knew there was water under this soil but would wait to explore the source. The Indian brave was still unconscious when he returned to the place of where the brave had taken refuse from the blistering sun. James tore away the leggings from the right leg and then pulled firmly on the leg until with his hand he could feel that the broken bone had lined up and was set. Other than some groaning, the brave did not respond to what James knew must have been excruciating pain. He then strapped the leg with splints and the raw hide thongs he cut from his saddle. He then began to minister to other brave's other needs. He wiped him down with water from his canteen and put a compress on his forehead.

Having done what he could, James returned to where he though he found water and upon digging down and into the embankment, water began to ooze out of the ground. He watered his horse and then brought the Indian pony to the spot and let it drink its fill. Returning to the Indian brave, he poured a canteen full of water over him and then set off to see if he could shoot some game. He was successful in killing two rabbits and when he returned to the brave, he was moaning softly and was showing some signs of motion. His fever had gone down and James was certain he would recover. While preparing a fire to roast the rabbits, James had more leisure to inspect the brave. He was large for an Indian, over six feet in height, with a broad muscular frame. By Indian standards he was not very dark of skin suggesting some mixed blood. His hair was long and braided in back with eagle feathers tied to the end of the braid. He had a sharp nose that was somewhat large for his face, suggesting French blood lines.

It was while James was inspecting the brave from a distance that the brave's eyes suddenly snapped open. Noticing James, he tried to sit up and reached for the sheath where his knife should have been. James held up his hands, palms outward which was a gesture Franco had told him was a sign of peace. The brave looked at his wounded leg and then back at James, James then offered him his canteen, which after a moment of intense scrutiny of James face; he accepted and drank his fill. Seeing the rabbit on the spit, he made a sign of hunger. James tore a leg from the rabbit and the brave ate at it greedily. After his meal, the Indian lay back and fell into a deep sleep.

For three days James ministered to the brave. They were now able to communicate by sign language and what little of each other's language they knew. James had to get the brave back to his people and catch up to the train that would now be many miles away. The Indian brave confirmed James guess that he had been forced over the cliff like side of the ravine as he was riding in pursuit of a buffalo heard. The lodge where he was a guest was to the northeast near a river; James thought would be the Green River. It was in the opposite direction of the wagon trail and would take him more days away from the train. The next morning he helped the brave astride his pony and they headed off to his camp.

They had traveled most of the day with frequent stops to allow the Brave who indicated he was a Shoshone and was called Running Deer, to rest. James had dismounted in a grove of cottonwood trees and was helping Running Dear off of his pony when he heard the rustle of many feet in the bushes about him. Suddenly they were surrounded by a band of ten hostile looking braves. James knew better then to go for his gun and held his horse still while the Indians advanced with bows and arrows at the ready. A guttural protest arose from the throat of Running Dear and the braves drew back ignoring James and whooped and hollered dancing around Running Dear. James suspected they were members of Running Dear's lodge who had been searching for him, yet they were dressed differently in loin cloths and vests while Running Deer was dressed in buckskins more like his. It was during this exuberant greeting that James realized Running Dear was not just an ordinary brave and was probably a chief.

.The braves soon constructed a travois to transport their leader back to their village ignoring the presence of James who stood by watching. James was glad to be done with his responsibility but was uncertain as to what these Indians would do with him now that his usefulness had ended. After a long conversation among the braves, one of them went to where their horses were tethered and selected a beautiful white and gray stallion with a spotted rump. James would later find out that this was an Appaloosa horse of Nez Perce fame. The brave, a short bow legged warrior with a deep scar across his exposed chest, lead the horse over to James and handed him the tether rope.

The horse was a gift to him in gratitude for saving their Chief. It was then the brave noticed the necklace about James' neck. All of the braves came forward to inspect it. Again the Chief spoke to them and they nodded their heads and each placed a hand on James' chest and spoke in their language in a reverent, chanting tone with their faces turned heaven ward. The wounded brave then took his Bowie knife from about his waist and had one of the braves present it to James. At first James was reluctant to accept the knife suspecting it had been taken from some murdered settler, but the scabbard suggested that it had been the property of this brave for some time and may well have come to him in trade. It was a puzzlement as to how such a knife made its way to the Northwest, but James accepted it and tried to find a gift in return. When he drew some bullets from his saddle bag thinking they would accept them as a return gift they declined, mounted their ponies and without further ceremony, rode northward dragging their chief behind them.

As the Indians rode off to their lodges, James was troubled by the thought that he had walked right into what might have been and ambush. He inspected the grove of trees and discovered that he had virtually walked right into the camp site the braves had been using for the past several days. He was upset with himself for being so careless. The fact that he was distracted by the needs of the injured brave was no justification for his stupidity. He could hear the admonishments of Franco ring through his brain. He next inspected the Appaloosa that had been gifted to him. It was a handsome animal, a full hand taller then Molly and a good deal more spirited. James took the horse by its halter rope and sat on a fallen tree and spent an hour or so talking to the horse in soft comforting tones. The tension that James had sensed in the horse soon abated and James spent more time stroking the horse and still talking gently to it. He then mounted the horse and found that it would accept him and his commands. None-the-less he walked the horse about for a while stopping now and then to talk to it and stroke it. When he tethered it for the night, he was certain that indeed the horse had accepted him and was truly his. He decided he would name the Appaloosa Caesar after the Roman Emperor. To James there was a royalty about the horse that justified the name.

Having two horses to ride alternately would speed his trip back to the wagon train and early the next morning James set off riding westward to find the trail. He suspected that the train would be close to Fort Boise by the time he caught up with it.

Jenny was beside herself in grief over the loss of her mother and now by the absence of her brother who had been away far too long to assume that he had not fallen on some disaster. Her father was of little comfort. As had always been his condition, he was unable to open up his grieving to those about him and carried the loss of Carla like a great cold stone in his chest. Yet he too was vexed over the absence of his son and pleaded with Paul Anderson to send out a party to search for him.

"I can't go myself, I have Jenny to be concerned with," he told Paul.

"Your boy did a foolish thing. I know he was grieving and was not thinking good when he took off. But he told no one of his leaving and what with all the goings on about the Fort, picking up his trail was out of the question. Franco has got his responsibilities about the train and I need him here. I'd send one of my boys, but would it be smart to put them in the same pickle James is in and have us both grieving? I'm afraid we will just have to hope for the best and move on. We are already running late and I have the entire wagon train to think about."

What Paul said made sense, but was of little solace. Wayne could only take solace in the fact that James had survived by himself after that storm back on the Platte and hopefully he could survive this latest adventure. When he tried to share these thoughts with Jenny, she only stared at him in a disbelieving way and walked away from camp. She didn't have any purpose to her actions; she only knew she had to be alone. There was no comfort in her father's words and to her they seemed to be an abandonment of her brother. For the first time in her life she wished she were born a man and could to do the things men do. If she were, she would ride back along the trail to find her bother. As it was she was wandering aimlessly back along the trail with no conscious thought of what she intended. How long she had walked along the trail path, kicking up motes of dust with her bare feet, in the soft alluvial soil that had been turned into a powder by the passing of thousands of wagons and animals, she did not know. She was not even aware that she was over a mile from camp and that dusk was quickly falling upon the land.

"Are you walking back to Missouri or just out to donate your pretty scalp as a decoration on some buck's tepee?"

Jenny jumped with a start at the interruption and came quickly to her senses. She turned to see William Anderson mounted on his big gray mare close behind her. How had he gotten so close without her even hearing his horse approaching? She was for a moment disoriented and looking about her she realized she had wandered away from the train heading back East hoping somehow that she would find James riding toward her.

"I'm sorry, she murmured. I didn't realize where I was. I was being foolish wasn't I?"

"I understand you have been under a strain. It's a good thing Melody noticed your absence or you may have been wandering out here in the dark," William responded. "Now you best get up here behind me and let's get back to the train before we stir up the whole camp with our absence."

William removed his foot from the stirrup and reached his hand down to assist her onto the horse behind him. Jenny was again aware of his strength as he pulled her easily from the ground and swung her up behind him. She naturally threw her leg astraddle of the horse and realized her skirt was up about her waist and her pantalooned legs were exposed. Her face flushed. This was the second time she had exposed her legs to William and it was even more embarrassing now as she was helpless to pull her skirts down. William, however, didn't seem to notice or if he noticed he did he did not seem concerned about her predicament.

"You're going to fall off back there if you don't put your arms around my waist. I'm going to canter the horse so we can get back to camp before it turns dark," William instructed her.

Jenny was reluctant to comply with William's suggestion, but when his horse leapt ahead she had to grab hold of William's waist or fall unceremoniously to the ground. It took her several minutes before she felt confident enough to seize his waist tightly, pulling her body close to his. Soon she felt the rhythm of the horse's gate and responding to its motion, felt secure. She had never been this close to another man and the sensation was comforting. She laid her cheek against William's back and held on more firmly as the gated horse lulled her into a semi-slumber that allowed all of her pent up emotions of the last week to abate and the concerns for James and the hurt caused by the loss of her mother slip from her consciousnesses. The tingling feeling of her breasts rubbing up and down William's back, the manly smell of him, the firmness of his body all combined to make Jenny hope that this encounter would last and that she would not have to return to the train and the memories that would once more haunt her thoughts.

William, who had always avoided any intimate contact with members of the opposite sex, now remembered the advice of one of his mentors: "You have to dedicate your soul to the law and don't be letting any female distract you with her feminine ways or you will end up being just another middling lawyer."

This remembrance came to him because he suddenly felt himself becoming aroused by the presence of Jenny, the warmth and softness of her body as she clung tightly to his back. He willed himself to feel her breast as they gently rub against him. He now felt uncomfortable in the saddle as he needed to adjust his trousers for the swelling of his member but dared not make the move with Jenny hanging so tightly to him.

Jenny, with the chill of the evening air enveloping the land, clung even tighter to get more of the comforting warmth of Williams body and was not even aware of the fact that William had rained the horse in and was now walking it back to camp. William had a purpose in slowing the horse. He did not want this pleasant experience to end too soon. It was then he remembered a conversation he had with a Judge he was riding the circuit with when he mentioned the advice he had received from his mentor. The judge, it seemed wondered why he had never seen William with the other members of the traveling bar out in the evening socializing with the ladies that often attended the functions that were thrown when the Judge was in town.

"It's good advice you received and ought to followed when needed, but remember also that the lone plumb left on the tree turns into a prune. It isn't natural for a man to always ignore his emotions. A warn hearth and a warm bed are the comforts of a good woman. If you find one don't let your good sense deny you a meaningful life with a companionable woman."

Suddenly the comforting motion of the horse stopped and Jenny was slow in releasing her hold on William, not wanting to return to camp so soon. She was surprised when she opened her eyes and discovered she was not back at camp, but was some distance away. She could see the glimmer of the camp fires and smell the smoke as it moved on a soft breeze down the trail toward them.

"Why did we stop?" she asked William, thinking she might have done something wrong.

William replied in a husky voice, "Why don't we walk on in? I have a thing or two I'd like to discuss with you if you are in a mind to talk."

Jenny dismounted from the horse with William's assistance and quickly arranged her skirts. She noticed her bare feet and wished she had put on her shoes. She had not intended to meet anyone, particularly someone like William who seemed to be concerned about such matters evidenced by his dress and manners.

As they started to walk slowly back to the train William, having made up his mind about his intentions toward Jenny, suddenly found he could not find the words that usually came so readily when he wanted to address a subject. Jenny, for her part was curious as to what he had to say, but was quite content just to be walking along in his company.

"Jenny," he finally started. "You have been on my mind every since that day back in Independence when we first met."

Jenny remembering that moment when she exposed her undergarments upon debarking from the wagon, waited to hear what his remembrances of her from that date would be.

"You're a comely young lady and I know you have been receiving the attention of others. Have any of them expressed their intentions?"

The question confused Jenny. A number of the boys about camp had shown some interest in her, she knew that. But she considered them to be boys and wondered what these intentions were supposed to be.

"What do you mean by intentions?" Jenny enquired. "I have been asked to go for walks by a number of the boys. That young Hanson boy has been a bit of a nuisance but there is nothing I would describe as other than friendliness."

William smiled at her now. "I'm sure they had more than friendliness on their mind. Those boys probably were hoping you would show them some more serious attention. But it is about those more serious intentions I want to talk to you about.

"What do you mean, William? Are you saying you are interested in me for something more formal than friendship?"

William was taken aback by the direct question. He had not intended to broach the subject so directly, but than as one Judge told him when he was addressing the court with a many page argument he had carefully prepared: "Son, just put them papers aside and tell me what you are here for."

It was time to get to the point. "Yes, Jenny my intentions are more serious. I wish to ask your father if I may court you. Jenny, I am asking you to be my wife and to marry me after I get to Oregon and get set up. You have been through a lot lately and I could understand if you wanted to think my proposal over."

William had stopped walking now and turned to face her holding her gently by her arms as he spoke these last words directly at her wanting to study her face as the question was posed.

Instead of the hoped for expressions of joy he wanted to see in her face, he saw only concern and confusion. His heart skipped a beat. Had he exposed his sole only to be rejected? He was not prepared for this reaction.

Jenny turned away and started walking again. When he caught up with her she turned to him. "William, you said you found an interest in me when we were back in Independence. I would be lying if I did not admit that I felt the same toward you. But what of your girl back in Illinois?"

Now the look of confusion came across William's face. "What are you talking about? What girl back in Illinois?" William stammered.

Jenny looked at him carefully studying his face now. "You are wearing her locket about your neck. Some girl back in Illinois is waiting for you. What about her.?"

William reached for the pendent and suddenly smiled at her and started to chuckle. This reaction upset Jenny who thought such matters should be treated with more candor.

William removed the locket from his neck and opened it. "I know you can't see the picture in here with the light as it is, but if you could you would see an elderly, kindly, very sweet older lady. That would be my mother. She gave me this locket on her death bed and admonished me to give it one day to the lady I intended to marry so that she might be a part of our life. I am intending to give you this locket, Jenny, if you would take it."

Jenny was too taken aback by this sudden revelation to have an immediate response. After a long moment she squealed as she sprang into his arms. "Oh William, William, I am the happiest girl in the world. Please, Oh please let me be your wife."

Neither Jenny or William had any experience in the art of love making and their first attempts at a kiss was the pressing of two puckered firm lips that soon became a soft, deep and passionate search for the others inner self. They stood embraced in this manner for what seemed to Jenny like an eternity when William finally broke away, somewhat flustered and suggested that they best get back to camp. William was a bit unnerved at the emotions he was feeling. He wanted more, but was uncertain of his emotions and uncertain as to where this sudden passion would lead them.

Wayne Rawlins had been searching the train for his missing daughter after he'd returned from tending to his live stock. His search was becoming frantic as no one seemed to know where Jenny was. It was Melody, hearing of his enquiries that finally ran him down and told him that Jenny had walked back along the trail alone and that she had asked William to go searching for her. Although he was relieved to hear that William was out looking for her, he nonetheless felt compelled to go looking for her himself and as he was retrieving his rifle and saddle from the wagon, he turned to see Jenny and William walking arm and arm toward him. His first reaction was to admonish her for her foolishness, but upon seeing the young couple almost embracing as they walked back to camp, he lost his anger, realizing that something of importance was happening and he best hold his piece. He could see the euphoria written cross Jenny's face and it occurred to him that he had not seen his daughter's simile since they had started on this trip to Oregon.

When the joyous couple drew to a stop in front of Wayne, William removed his arm from about Jenny's waist and took her hand. "Mr. Rawlins I have asked Jenny to be my wife and I have come to ask your permission."

Wayne could think of nothing to say. He was still trying to accept the words he had just heard and to search his inner being to find a meaningful response. He studied Jenny's imploring happy face and knew what the answer must be. He stepped forward and clasped Williams extended hand and pulled him into an embrace that seemed a natural reaction but was also quickly broken as Wayne stepped quickly to his daughter and gave her a more heartfelt embrace.

Wayne murmured into her ear, "Jenny you can't believe how happy this makes me and how happy it would have made your mother. You both have my blessing. Have you informed Mr. Anderson?"

The small party moved on to the Anderson camp site where the news of the betrothal was announced again. Paul Anderson's elation was hard to contain. He embraced Jenny, sweeping her off her feet. "Damn, it's good to have a woman back in the family," he declared, "Especially such a pretty young thing as you."

The news of Jenny's commitment spread quickly through the train and it was not long before some fiddles and banjos were produced and some serious partying took hold of the emigrants who had had little to celebrate in recent months. Clay stepped forward when the announcement had been made and gave his congratulations to his brother and to Jenny. However, when the festivities commenced he remained silently in the background with a small group of casual observers. Paul and William Anderson were too consumed with the ecstasy of the occasion to notice his lack of participation. Jenny had never had such a good time. It seemed that every man in camp wanted to take his turn whirling her about on the dusty patch of ground that was their dance floor. She could hardly catch her breath before she was whisked away in another's arms. The ladies produced from nowhere, candy treats and sweets that had the children screaming with delight as they engaged in games of chase trying to steal the treats that each wanted to hoard. From the secret spots where such things were hidden in the wagons, jugs of spirits appeared and were being freely passed about. Paul Anderson, knowing that it would be useless to attempt to get the train moving at its usual dawn start, announced that the train would not set out until midmorning on the morrow.

But as such events of great exuberance usually do, the party ran out of steam as fast as it started and the emigrants began to filter back to their wagons around midnight and one o'clock. It was then William took Jenny in his embrace and led her away from the group and returned her to her wagon knowing that she was near exhaustion and was ready to drop.

"We have much to discuss, but it will wait now. We have a life time ahead of us," William told her as he helped her up into her wagon.

Jenny, knowing that she was covered with dust from head to toe, drew a pan of water and gave herself a sponge bath before she lie down on the robes and fell into a deep, blissful sleep.

The growing warmth of the sun upon the wagon canvas was slowly drawing Jenny from the depth of her slumber. She struggled to remain in her slumber with her dreams. She was feeling again that moment of surrender when she gave herself to William in that long passionate embrace after he had asked her to marry him. She didn't want to wake up and find that it was all just a dream. The murmur of familiar voices outside the wagon added to her feeling of well being. She was in a moment of life that she wanted to make a never ending experience. The familiarity of those murmuring voices was drawing her against her will to the reality of the life she must face. With a start, she jumped from her robes. Those familiar murmuring voices she now recognized as being those of her father and of James her brother. Jenny did not even hesitate to get dressed but jumped from the tail gate in her night dress and ran to her brother who had only half risen from his seat atop a keg when she spilled onto him tumbling them both onto the ground.

Jenny buried her head on James' chest and sobbed hysterically as she pounded him with her fist. "James, James, God I missed you. Why did you go away? Where have you been? Please, please don't ever do that again.'

James was rocking with laughter at his sister's reaction to his return and finally grabbed her face in his hands and kissed her tear streaked cheeks. "I'm back Jenny. I'm safe. Now tell me what you have been up to. I have been hearing reports about you and William. Is it true what I have heard?

"Oh, Yes James. It's true I'm going to be married and now you will be with me. That means so much. Don't ever leave us like that again."

As their conversation slipped into serious subjects, and they sat side by side on the ground, Jenny suddenly noticed that Franco and Clay were also present and that that she was still in her night shirt. She flushed with embarrassment as she saw the amusement on their faces. To her relief, her father had retrieved a blanket and draped it about her. "You best get dressed, Jenny. We're about to get under way."

As Jenny was trying to make a graceful retreat to the wagon, her attention was drawn to a large knife Franco was holding that was encased in a beautiful beaded sheath.

"This here's strong medicine," he was saying. "The Indian that gave you this meant that you are to be protected. This sign on the knife handle is a symbol of their spirit god of life. The scabbard has sign on it that I ain't really familiar with, but I know it to be the sign from some southern tribe, maybe Apache, but it does have a sun symbol also which I expect means the same thing. You wear this with pride."

"How did you get that knife?" Jenny asked her brother.

"I got a lot to tell you, Jenny. We best save it for later and get the wagon hitched up."

ON TO FORT BOISE

The train rolled on to its next destination which was Fort Boise, another trading post, but first they had to traverse the inhospitable lands along the Snake River gorge. At first the land was gentle rolling land, though sparse on feed and water for the animals. At a place called Glenns Ferry where they came to the dreaded Three Island Crossing. The Snake River at this point drove in swift and swirling fury about a series of islands. The only way to cross was to hitch each wagon to six or eight pairs of oxen, hoping they had the strength to pull the wagon across and that their numbers would allow some of the oxen to have purchase on the river bottom while a team of men on the opposite shore pulled them along with ropes. Unfortunately, even with their considerable effort, one of the wagons was swept away. The team and the driver were lost. ([9])

From then on to Fort Boise, they were in constant sight of the river, but forbidding canyon walls kept them from the life giving waters of the river. The smell of the water was driving the cattle to frenzy and there were continual problems of keeping the herd away from the canyon edge. The party looked forward to their arrival at Fort Boise as it drew them nearer and nearer to the end of the journey and would soon bring them to the Columbia River and the Whitman mission at Walla Walla where they could raft on down the river to their promised land. There was a new urgency to the train's movement and when the Fort finally came into site they were surprised to see the number of abandoned wagons and herds of

---

[9] Historic Sites on the Oregon-Trail, http://.isu.edu/%7Etrinmich/Sites.html

oxen that roamed about the place. When they arrived into the confines of the Fort they were virtually ignored amid the bustle of activity.

Paul, fearing that the frenzied activity meant Indian trouble, confronted the first man he could collar. "What the hell is going on here? Is there trouble ahead on the trail?"

The stranger gave him a hurried glance. "Ain't you heard? They's discovered gold in California. These trains is brake'n up and most of the folks is headed south to claim their fortune. They say the gold is thick as fleas on a dog on every stream down there." Having said that, the stranger hurried off leaving Paul Anderson in a state of bewilderment. He knew immediately that the news meant that the train he had shepparded so diligently through its many challenges may well end here. Paul led the wagon into camp and then called a meeting to inform them of the news. The news was at first taken matter of factly, but it was not long before the men were rushing into the fort for more news of the gold find. The rumors and speculation knew no bounds. They were told all kinds of outrageous stories about the gold fields that were of such abundance that claims would be available to all. Nuggets as big as your fist were lying about to be picked up by hand. Fortunes were being made overnight. Soon the land would be filled with millionaires and those who got there first would be the first to claim their fortune. The camp was a frenzy of activity that night as groups of men gathered to discuss their next move. It was useless for Paul to even contemplate organizing the group to move on to Oregon until this fever had abated.

Paul had made his own inquires at the Fort and was not surprised to find no one who had any firsthand knowledge of the situation in California. The rumors of gold were festering off of news that had reached Fort Bridger after they left and was carried by a messenger to Fort Boise. Paul, being a man of conservative instincts was quick to discount most of the alleged news, but found few who were willing to listen to his words of caution. A train was leaving the next day, back tracking the trail to join the wagons heading south to California. A number of the emigrants from his train were already preparing to join that train. Paul decided he would have to just sit back until this mess sorted itself out and then reorganize the group that would head on to Oregon. He had no desire himself to go to California on this get rich quick dream. He was a newspaper man that

that was his only interest. He was distressed to find that a number of men had actually abandoned their families at the Fort leaving them to head on alone as they went south to claim their fortune.

It was a sober and disheartened Paul Anderson who returned to his campsite that night to await the outcome of events. He found Wayne and James Rawlins in animated discussion with his sons and Franco. To his distress, the gold fever had gripped Wayne Rawlins and he was urging his boys to join him and James in an expedition to California.

"What of your Jenny," Paul asked Wayne when he was able to interject himself into the animated conversation.

"I've talked to the Reverend Whitman and he will take Jenny and Melody with him to his mission. They can help him there until William gets himself settled and calls for her. By then I should be back from California, hopefully with a pot of gold. She knows her letters and can help in the school Dr. Whitman has set up for the tribes."

Paul glanced at his son William unaware that all of these arrangements had been made without his knowledge. "Is that what you want?" He asked.

"I am not at all enthused that she will be mixing with savages, he responded, but if Wayne is going to leave her here, I don't know what else we can do now."

Paul started to offer his advice suggesting that he just marry Jenny now and she could go on with them as his wife, but then he thought to ask; "Don't tell me you are going on to California too?"

"I'm not that crazy. My calling is for the law and I intend to go on to Oregon with you. Clay here is of a different mind and I have been trying to talk sense into him."

Paul then looked at his younger son and waited until he addressed him. "I ain't trained for being no farmer and I don't have any schooling for other things. Whether there be gold in California or not, I would like to go there just to see the place."

Paul then looked to Wayne. "What on earth do you want to go off chasing rumors for? You know those fools running around spouting about all that gold are festering with dreams that will never come true. If there was all that gold lying around those Mexicans who have been living there for a century would have found it. There may be some findings, but I doubt that there is gold to be had for all."

Wayne took some moments to think over his answer before he spoke. "I lost my Clara, and by daughter is spoken for. I have nothing left to head on to Oregon for. I have no home to build for my wife and to be quite frank I no longer have the gumption to be a farmer. I suspect that was the reason I left Missouri where I already had a good farm. Like you, I don't doubt that a lot of what is being said is nonsense; but half a hope is better than none. As Clay here puts it, I can as well find land if I want it in California as in Oregon and on the way who knows what fortune may befall me if I get to California."

Paul knew it was pointless to argue the subject, but his reporter instincts caused him to look to James and Franco to see what their intentions were. They both gave the same response as had Wayne. They were adventures like Clay and wanted the excitement and experience that was now the lure of California.

BOOK II

Although short of stature and short on eloquence, his ambitions were larger than the nation. He had been elected to office with a slim majority, but assumed a mandate that would change forever the nation that had elected him. James Knox Polk was the youngest man to be elected to the presidency at age forty-nine, but came to office with a wealth of experience and political skill. Election of a Democratic House and Senate assured him that he could carry forth this plans of expansion that would give to America dominance of the continent from sea to sea. [10] Behind his large mahogany, uncluttered desk, he was giving his apt attention to his Secretary of War William Marcy. The latest dispatches from Veracruz had just arrived.

There had been much consternation over the invasion force led by Winfield Scott as it drove inland to Mexico City and a final resolution of the Mexican question. It was the largest military effort of the new and emerging nation and to President Polk it meant the realization of his ambition to secure New Mexico and California as part of the Union. It had all started innocently enough when it became apparent that the struggling Lone Star state of Texas could not survive without being incorporated into the Union. The meddling of Great Briton and Mexico in the Texas annexation question was a further concern of Congressional Democrats. The proposal to annex Texas to the Union drove the Mexican government to the limit and hostilities between America and Mexico gave Polk the pretext he had been waiting for to drive the Mexicans from the Southwest.

The savvy Secretary of War, a veteran of numerous political skirmishes in the patronage wars infesting New York politics, was astute enough to

---

[10] The American Presidents, Eighth Edition, David C. Whitney and Robin Vaughn Whitney, Readers Digest Association, Inc. e(1989, 1993) Doubleday.

address the subject he knew would soon be facing them in Congress as more southern territories were to be added to the Union.

"This won't sit all that well with the Wigs and the Yankees up north. All these territories we will be annexing to the Union will likely be slave states and upset the balance that has held the Union together." Secretary Marcy advised him. "The press is already turning against the Mexican war saying it was your scheme to turn the Congress over to the pro-slavery wing."

"I know what they are saying," the President responded. "But there is not one among those critics who did not know what my intentions were when I ran for this office. America has a destiny that must be fulfilled. Free or slave is not the issue, it is the power of a nation and its future that is at stake here. We need land. There are twenty-three million citizens all clamoring for land and more arrive at our shores each day. I would like to know how we are to stop these people who are now heading by the droves into these lands. Are we to leave them to the mercy of those capricious Mexicans?"

"It seems to me, Mr. President," Marcy continued, "that the answer to these critics lies in the Oregon territory. If we claim that land that is now under a joint treaty with Great Briton and add it to the Union we could allay the fears of the free state contingent that our purpose is to control Congress and dominate the slavery issue."

I've given thought to that, William, but we are in no position to extend our power to the Northwest at this time. The British have the power to destroy our attempts to take over that territory if we get too aggressive. We are over extended in Mexico and they know it."

"That don't mean we can't extend our presence there. After all, we have hundreds of emigrants flooding into that territory who need this nation's protection from the savages. We could establish Forts in the area and assert it was for the protection of the emigrants. Once the Forts are established, we own the territory."

"You have a good head on you William, but let's secure California first and get to Oregon next. As you suggest, we are invading the territory already with settlers and that alone should give us our claim. We will enforce it later. It might be a good idea to start moving our Forts westward. You see to it."

This comment by the President usually meant the meeting was over, but the Secretary of War remained seated which caused the President to look upon him with raised eyebrows and a somewhat incredulous look. He was late for a dinner party that was already in progress down stairs and was irritated at his Secretary's reluctance to leave.

"Is there something more?" the President asked with intended irritation in his voice.

"Yes, Mr. President there is more. As I was leaving to bring you the latest dispatches from Mexico, I was handed this dispatch forwarded from St Louis. The Secretary reached into his pocket and handed the President the dispatch he had referred to. "It seems that somewhere near Fort Bridger an emigrant train was attacked by an overwhelming number of savages. The report is that over three hundred emigrants were slaughtered. When the public gets wind of this, they will be demanding that we establish Forts along the Oregon Trail and into the Oregon Territory."

The President read the dispatch then slammed it down on his desk. "Those savages cannot be allowed to get by with this! That's open land and if we don't establish possession of it the British or Russians will!"

The President rose quickly from his desk almost tipping his chair over by his swift motion. He walked purposefully about the room with his hands clasped behind his back. He was in his thinking mode. The Senators, Ambassadors and other dignitaries who were awaiting his appearance below were of no moment to him now.

"I don't want to stir things up with the British right now. They have war ships on the coast and at Vancouver. But this attack on the Mapes train demands that we assert ourselves into the area. Secretary Buchanan was mentioning the other day that the Hudson Bay Company might we willing to sell their forts in the Oregon Territory. It seems they can no longer justify them what with the fur trade declining. Get with him and see if we can't buy those forts and insert ourselves into the territory by a less hostile means. The British would have little complaint if we bought out one of their own charter companies."

The President was standing before a large map now, a map that depicted his vision of the America he intended to create by war, annexation or purchase. As one newspaper had put it, it was America's "Manifest Destiny."

At that he strode to the door and held it open signaling the Secretary of War that his time was up. "Report to me in a week regarding your progress. And see what news there is from Colonel Kearny. He should be in California by now."

It seemed to the Mormons that they could find no sanctuary. They had been driven from Missouri and with the cooperation of the government in Illinois had found a new home and had built a community that afforded them a sanctuary compatible to their practices. But as the state burgeoned with settlements surrounding their Nauvoo community, tension rose and the intolerance that the Mormons suffered in Missouri soon drove the state authorities and local communities to demand more and more concessions from the Mormons and more conformance to the standards that were inimitable to the religious practices of the Mormons. When the rising prejudices brought forth the spilling of blood, and the murder of their spiritual leader Joseph Smith, the Mormons had little choice but to once again abandon their settlements and to move on. Brigham Young, their new leader sought permission from the federal government to move his flock through the Indian territories of Nebraska on to a new settlement far from the intolerance that had decimated their communities in Missouri and Illinois. Colonel Kearny, charged with the conquest of California saw in the appeal an opportunity. He needed an army to cross the southwestern desert from Santa Fe to California.

President Polk had received the request from Colonel Kearny that the government make it a condition for any permission granted to the Mormons to pass through the Indian Nations that they provide to the Army volunteers to fight in the Mexican War, more particularly to march with him to California and subdue and over through the Mexican government. Brigham Young, more concerned with the monetary advantage of the conscription, volunteered what came to be known as the Mormon Battalion that marched with soon to be General Kearny to California establishing what would become an extension of the Santa Fe trail onto California; a trail that would form a route for emigrants soon to come.([11])

"I've not heard from Kearny since he left Santa Fe," The Secretary responded as he passed through the door and hurried down the hall.

---

[11] Wagons West, Rank McLynn, Randon House (London) 2002, p 385-6.

Back at Fort Boise where the emigrants were in the throes of a great quandary regarding their continued journey to Oregon and the prospect of abandoning the dreams of free land for the promised riches of California, the events that were taking place in that distant and remote place called Washington D.C. would soon sweep them up in the history of the new Republic that President Polk had crafted from the failing revolution riddled Mexican nation and the declining Northwest fortunes of Great Briton's Hudson Bay Empire. Wayne Rawlins, Franco, James, Clay and a number of other unattached males were making plans to head directly to California from Fort Boise rather than join the trains heading through the Humboldt and over the Sierra Nevada's into California.

"It be a bad time to head through that country. Winter comes early in them mountains. Them folks is pressing their luck. Freemont near died when winter caught him out there on this third expedition that fortunately I wasn't on. Heading direct from here takes us into lands that I know nothing about and I ain't talked to no one who's been there. It would save us hundreds of miles and get us there ahead of the others if we could just head on from here."

"What about the Indians in that country. What do you know about them?" Clay asked.

"Well, there's Shoshone, Klamath, Modoc and Diggers that I know of, none too friendly far as I know except them Diggers who ain't much to speak of. I suspect there will be about thirty or so in our group and we'll go well armed. We would be a party about the size of Freemont's that went through some of that country. Ain't no way to California but what you ain't gonna' find unfriendlies."

"Well, so far you been pretty good at getting' us through to here findin' water and all. I spect we can rely upon you to get us to California," one of the adventurers declared.

"I'm not going as your guide so don't go along if you think I'm promisin' to get you to California. I ain't no Freemont and I'm done being a scout. I'm goin' to California for the same reason the rest of you are. If you want a guide, go find one."

This sober announcement should have had more effect upon the adventurers, but their enthusiasm for the venture and for gold overrode all caution. Within two days, the group heading south had grown to thirty-five well armed and well supplied men and was on its way southwest into uncharted territory.

Jenny stood in silence along with many of the remnants of the Anderson and other trains watching the small band of men leave the Fort and slowly vanish across the deserted plain. She was feeling abandonment and sadness at her father's abrupt decision to leave her to her own means in the care of a man she had no affection for. Narcissa was her friend, but Dr. Whitman's stern and demanding demeanor was not to her liking. Her only consolation was that she had William and Paul Anderson to rely upon and would be spending much of her time with them. She would miss James most of all. She remembered those days back in Missouri when they were close and she and her mother were his comfort against the harshness of a demanding world. Now he had grown up in a few short months and rode away a virtual stranger to her. She knew not when or if she would ever see her father and her brother again.

The train Paul Anderson organized from the remnants of his own train and that of others that had been left leaderless as the California gold rush depleted them, headed again westward to cross the Snake River for a final time and complete the trip to the Willamette Valley. Although her father had told her to sell the wagon and team and keep the funds, she was pleased when Paul Anderson decided to place the Rawlins wagon in his charge and take it on westward. It was still one of the stoutest wagons in the train and would be needed when the river crossings were confronted. Its tight construction allowed it to float like a raft. Jenny's pleasure was enhanced knowing that the remnants of her mother's possessions would ride on to Oregon and be there when she arrived to wed William.

SOUTH INTO OREGON AND ONTO THE GOLD OF CALIFORNIA

As the group of would be prospectors rode across the rolling hills west of the Fort Boise, it was Franco who advised the group that they were being followed and had best see who was on their trail. They were but two days out and Franco suspected that it was another emigrant trying to join them rather than anyone meaning them harm. The dust trail was but a wisp on the horizon behind them. Franco and James decided to ride their back trail and confront the strangers. The land over which they now traveled had not seen the benefit of rain for many months and the grass was withered and brown. The soil seemed ill suited to sustain even that small fading trace of life. The sage brush was short and scrubby and the stiff dry branches that graced it would scratch the horses flesh and would soon draw blood if care were not taken. They were a mere two miles on their back trail when Franco, riding to the crest of one of the seemingly endless rolling hills, got his first good look at the strangers trailing them. A smile came across his grizzled face.

"I'll be damned," he muttered turning to James, "That be that Pole Cat Parker with Little Flower. "Spect he got word of all that gold and be wantin' his share."

Looking closely now James could see the tall lanky from of Parker riding ahead of his wife Little Flower, who was astride a mule and leading a pack horse. Parker, when he spotted them on the hill, raised is rifle above his head, waving it back and forth to signal his acknowledgement of their presence and of his peaceful intentions. It was Little Flower who first recognized Franco and let out a whoop.

"That Parker got eyes like a badger," Franco muttered. "Good thing he don't travel alone. He'd ride off a cliff."

James had paid little attention to Little Flower during their last meeting, but then she would not look into his face and generally ignored him. As she drew near, dressed in a tight fitting white leather dress, he looked with more interest at her and realized she had a wild beauty about her. Her teeth, unlike many of the squaws he had seen were all present and white. Her face was more aquiline and her features more chiseled and distinct than had been the case of most of the plains Indians he had seen. It was perhaps the first time he had ever seriously studied the features of any woman and he found that his imagination was working overtime as he wondered what it would be like to have a woman. He no longer looked upon Parker, if he ever had, as a squaw man, for this was no mere squaw who's presence was but a passing convenience to those who would accept her company. As had been the case at their last meeting she generally ignored James but was exuberant in her greeting of Franco who again swung her about in a wild embrace as Parker laughed and shouted his encouragement.

"When I heard about all that gold in California, Little Flower and me meant to catch you at Fort Boise and talk you into going there with us. When we heard you'd already headed out we set off to find you. Ain't no more need for them furs that was our keep, so this here gold thing looks like a good bet," Parker remarked as the remounted and headed on to the main group that was now preparing camp for the night.

"I rather suspect that most of that talk be about as reliable as them tales we heard at rendezvous about all them beeves that fell into your traps up on the Yellow Stone, tales we was told when we were young and stupid," Franco remarked, "but than what else we got to do but go snooping around them rivers in California?"

When they returned to camp, most of the venturers were discomforted to have a squaw man among their group and avoided contact with Little Flower. The presence of another experienced mountain man in their group was an offsetting benefit so little friction was created. Several of the group remembered their confrontation with Parker back at Fort Bridger and were wary of confronting him over his choice of a wife.

As they headed further west, the land became even more uninhabitable. The lands they crossed were encrusted with alkali; what water they found aas brackish and undrinkable. They came upon a large lake where the soil all about was clay like and the water smelled of sulfur and alkali. The thirsty animals drank of it and suffered. It was Parker who told them to boil the water and collect the condensed steam for drinking purposes. This proved too tedious for many who drank of the water and with the animals suffered unsettled stomachs and slack bowels. Not only was fresh water scarce, but there was a decided lack of game for their camp fires. They could snare rabbits, but not enough to satisfy the appetites of the men. Little Flower was adept at finding roots and tubers that provided some sustenance, but men used to meat for their meals found little nourishment in her brew. It was because of this lack of food that caused Clay to volunteer to ride to the forested mountains to the north of them to hunt for game. As the group moved westward the next morning, Clay, leading a pack horse headed northward expecting to be back in camp within two or three days.

"Don't let your pants down out there, Parker advised him. There be game there, but there also be some pretty ugly tempered natives that wonder about them hills. Don't be startin' no fires unless you need to and keep one eye open when you sleep."

Clay had seen little sign of Indians about and was somewhat skeptical of the warning Parker had given him, but he knew enough by now to be cautious. James wanted to go with Clay, but Clay declined his urging saying that he felt he could move about better alone. Clay was soon but a speck on the endless landscape as the gold seekers moved on westward and southward. As they headed for what appeared to be the promise of fresh water and a distant gathering of cottonwoods, their progress was now under observation. A small group of warriors who had been encamped at the Cottonwoods, to which the adventures were headed, were quick to clean up their camp and ride off to report their observations to their village but a day's ride to the west.

The discovery of a fast flowing large stream abundant with gleaming trout gave the group of travelers fresh hope for the success of their endeavor. They were quick to decide that they had best spend a few days at this place to allow their animals to fatten on the abundant grass while they replenished their food supplies by catching and drying the trout. There was the promise of other game about. Unlike the rest of the group, Parker and Franco were more cautious and moved about the cottonwoods to look for sign. They were quick to discover the hastily evacuated camp where the band of Indians had recently left. They followed the trail of the Indians for a distance noting that they were heading in haste no doubt to give warning of their arrival.

When they reported their findings to the rest of the group, most gave little regard to the danger that the Indians presented.

"We no doubt scared them off," one replied.

"How do we know they ain't friendly," another interjected.

"Well, we're here now to stay awhile, so I guess we will know sooner or later what their intentions are," Wayne suggested. "If they intended to attack, I'd rather fight on this ground then out on that flat land."

Wayne suggested they set up some breastworks, but his suggestion was dismissed as needless caution.

Running Deer, still favoring his injured leg, came from his lodge as he heard the commotion caused by the return of the braves who had been hunting to the east of the village. He stood a head taller than most of the braves and it was evident by his commanding presence that he was the war chief of this tribe of Shoshone Indians. His appearance brought a hush to the gathering throng that was responding to the news the braves had brought to the village. Running Deer listened intently as the exhausted warriors gave him the news that a group of white men had invaded their hunting lands. Running Deer took the news stoically. He had recently returned from his visit to their cousins, the Bannocks to see for himself the veracity of the reports he had received that the white man was moving westward into their sacred lands.

Their odd looking wagons were growing in number each year bringing thousands of white settlers who were taking possession of the lands that had for so long been their sole province. For many years, the Shoshone had lived with the trappers from the British companies who wanted not their lands, but only the animal skins of which there was an abundance. The Hudson Bay trappers had respected their lands and rather than enter them would trade with them for the skins the Indians themselves had trapped. The trade goods the tribes received were for their skins were greatly valued by the tribes. These new white men were different. They came in uncontrolled numbers and respected no claim the tribes had to the lands they wished to possess. These things Running Deer had had confirmed when he traveled to the East. What concerned him even more was that these white men not only claimed their sacred lands as their own, they brought with them the diseases that decimated the tribes, leaving them helpless to resist the onslaught of the never ending stream of wagons.

To Running Deer, who had studied these matters and who had sought guidance from his spiritual leaders, knew that his duty to his heritage demanded that he expel these invaders from the lands of his fathers. He called a war council and soon the runners were moving across the land to advise their neighbors of the incursion. The council was well attended as the war chiefs from a dozen bands gathered. Running Deer told them of his observations and his fears and urged them to join his warriors in expelling the invaders. The war fever was upon them when he finished his comments and chief after chief joined in the call for action. That night the fires burned long into the night as the dancing braves gave demonstration of their courage and lust for white scalps. Running Deer took no part in these activities. He called the braves who had observed the intruders and questioned them at length as to their observations. He was planning his strategy well and he wanted to act without delay. But he would wait for the right moment. Scouts were sent out to observe the white men and report to Running Deer the any attempt to leave the Cottonwood grove.

Franco and Parker were the only ones about the camp who seemed concerned about their predicament. The rest of the group were in a festive mood as they fished and swam in the refreshing waters and hunted small game to enhance their larder. To the mountain men, there was that instinctive feeling that they were being observed and that their presence was not wanted in these lands. They scoured the land about and even though they found some sign that there were Indian scouts about, they could find none.

The problem that bothered Franco most was that this group of men had been too hastily thrown together and there was no one person in command of the group. Wayne Rawlins was the obvious leader, but he was reluctant to take charge. He had driven his family from its home and was still suffering from the consequences of his actions. He wanted no more of the burdens inherent in deciding the fate of others. It was only after Parker impressed upon them the need to move on and make their gold claims before the hoards of other gold seekers beat them into the best claims that the camp started packing to move out. The Indian scouts headed westward as soon as they noted the activity in the white men's camp to report their observation.

Franco was not familiar with the lands they would travel, but Parker had some familiarity with it and advised the group to head straight south and move around the lands of the Klamath Indians whom he knew to be hostile. His suggestions were ignored and the party moved out the next morning onto the still barren flat lands of the Central Oregon Territory. But then it was not the Klamath Indians they need to fear, for over three hundred warriors of the Shoshone Tribe were moving into position to meet them where the land broke into rolling hills and valleys where the Indians could move about without observation. Running Deer, who knew all these lands like the inside of his lodge, knew just where these white men would go and where they would probably make their camp sites and he arranged his ambush with methodical care.

As the white men moved toward what would be their last campsite, Running Deer moved with caution to a nearby ridge to watch what appeared to be a disorganized band of horseman having no regard for their danger. He was startled to observe among the many animals that would soon be their plunder, the large, spirited Appaloosa horse that had once been his, but had been given as a gift to the young white man who had saved his life. He moved closer now and confirmed this belief that the young man who had rescued him was still in possession of the horse and would be among those who he intended to kill. When the chiefs gathered that night to discuss their dawn attack, he admonished them all that the white boy who saved his life must be spared.

"He wears the large medicine knife I give to him. You will know it when you see it. He has about his neck the claws of the great bear of the north. Let no man harm him. The horse he rides was my gift to him and let no one claim it."

Franco was first to notice the restlessness of the animals and rose in the fading darkness of the coming day to see what was amiss. As he moved to the herd, he could just make out the Indian braves moving their horses away from the camp. He pointed his rifle in the air and fired a warning shot that brought the camp to its feet. The warning came too late to allow the camp to organize a defense, for there now rose in the air the cry of hundreds of warriors who stood in unison, leveled their bows or rifles and fired into the camp as they charged into the disorganized throng of terrified white men. Most of the men got off a shot or two at the advancing braves, but were unable to reload their rifles or pistols before the braves swarmed into the camp and overwhelmed them.

They fought to the last using their weapons as clubs or casting them aside in favor of knives or hatchets. James, having been one of the first to spring from his bedroll and grab his rifle was also one of the first struck by a random arrow that drove into his shoulder. Another arrow was soon imbedded in his thigh and he dropped to his knees trying to raise his rifle while at the same time locate his father among the tangle of bodies before him. Before he could even fire in defense, he was struck by a war club and fell unconscious as he was seized by the strong arms of several braves who now protected him from further harm. What resistance there was by the others was over in moments as the Indians, outnumbering their victims so greatly, were left to the plunder. Most were suffering from the frustration of having not blooded their weapons. They did not, as was the custom of many tribes, mutilate the bodies of the white men, but did set about stripping them of the clothing that was their prize.

James who briefly regained consciousness gave up struggling against the grasp of the braves who held him. He waited for the blow that would end his struggle, but none came. He would be saved for a latter more dreadful death, of that he was now certain. He had lost track of time and was trying to regain consciousness. He was losing blood from his wounds and the pain was now penetrating his brain. He then heard a familiar, comforting voice, but did not recognize who it was other than it was Indian. At the apparent command, the braves who held him pulled him to his feet and brought him face to face with Running Deer. Running Deer, raged in anger, pointing to the wounds James had received and the braves who had inflicted the wounds shuffled away to avoid the wrath of their chief.

Running Deer gave another command and two Braves advanced forward holding between them the shaking, sobbing, terrified Little Flower. She too had been spared no doubt because she was one of them and was better suited for slavery than death. The Chief addressed her and then shoved her toward James. He then advanced to James and placed his hand on his chest and said in broken English:

"We are brothers, go in peace."

Little Flower, realizing she was to be set free, pulled herself together and spoke to the Chief. He nodded agreement and gave further orders to the Braves nearby. They waited about as Little Flower extracted the arrows from the now inert form of James and ministered to his wounds. The Indians then strapped James to his horse and at the instructions of Running Deer moved him several miles away and made a shelter for him and Little Flower near a fresh flowing stream. Little Flower had told the Chief that James would be slow to recover from his wounds and that he should not be left to heal in the camp that was the graveyard of all his friends. The Chief had agreed.

Before he rode away, Running Deer provided to James and Little Flower provisions from the plundered camp and returned to them their animals and to James his weapons. The Indian Chief then rode away leaving the shattered Little Flower and the unconscious James alone to survive or die in the limitless wilderness of the Central Oregon territory.

James was in and out of consciousness for several days affected alternately with a fever or with chills. Little Flower treated his wounds with poultices she concocted from roots and herbs she found in abundance along the bank of the stream and in the prairie beyond. The cold, as the progressing fall consumed the night, was hovering near freezing and the lonely pair had few blankets or other covers to fend off the cold. On the third night of his ordeal, James awoke to see above his bed the crystal moon dominating a sky filled with the sparkling glittering stars of universes unknown. His mind filled with memories of those pleasant nights when as a young boy, a world away from his present circumstance, he and Jenny would share their bodily warmth to fend off the invasion of the cold that permeated the solitary nights on their farm back in Missouri. The warm comforting body that gave him warmth on this night he first thought to be Jenny, but the smell of her was different. There was the smoky smell of a dozen campfires in her hair and the musky sensual smells of the sage that dominated the land about him. The head that rested on his chest could not be Jenny's, for she would never allow such intimacy. This warm body that covered most of his was clad not in homespun, but in leather. James was reluctant to move, the sensations were far too pleasant.

He tried to remember where he was and get a perspective back into his life. It was then he remembered the clash at the Cottonwood campground, the cries of death and agony, the invasion of his flesh by the arrows of the charging Indians, the presence of Chief Running Deer and then the nothingness that preceded his present circumstance. The thought of the carnage caused him to make a feeble attempt to rise as if to fend off another attack, but his body would not respond. The weight of the body so intimate to his made movement even more difficult. The attempt at movement caused a stirring from the body that pressed against him. He heard a soft moan that was not familiar to him and wanted to know more, but his body commanded rest and he fell back into slumber.

The sun was out and at its apex when next James opened his eyes. His eyes were slow to focus and his senses were slow to react to his surroundings. He lay still for several moments and then reopened his eyes. His strength was returning and he raised himself on one elbow and studied his surroundings as his vision cleared. He first noticed the figure bent over a campfire tending to some familiar smelling concoction, perhaps a stew he had once eaten. He tried to say something to draw the attention of the figure bent over the fire, but his words came out a mere groan and he collapsed back onto his bed, but remained conscious. He was suddenly face to face with Little Flower who was holding up his head and placing tidbits of her stew into his mouth.

"You eat! Must travel soon!" she commanded.

James complied with her request finding his appetite was ravenous.

"Eat Slow!" she now demanded. "Get sick."

James stopped eating now aware of his surroundings, questions flooding through his mind.

"Where are we? Where is everybody?"

"Get well, talk later, eat more!" was her response.

James complied with her request, now savoring every morsel that she placed into his mouth. Now it occurred to him, Little Flower was speaking to him in his language. She had, on the few occasions he had met her before, remained mostly silent and when speaking to Parker or Franco had spoken in her own tongue. A flush came over him as he realized that that warm comforting presence in his bed had been Little Flower. Where, he asked himself, where are Parker and the rest of the men? He slept again with his questions unanswered. When he awoke again it was dark and he saw the slim silhouette of Little Flower huddled over the fire. He realized she had given him what covers were available and was actually shivering as she braved the cold night alone.

"Little Flower," he spoke softly, testing his voice and strength. He realized that now that he was conscious she was reverting to her modest ways and would not share his covers with him. "You must come to me and keep me warm."

He held the covers up and she scuttled beneath them, pressing her body close to his. He felt the chill that had consumed her and pulled her close to him. When she stopped shivering and felt warn to his touch, he asked her in a commanding voice.

"Now you must tell me what happened back at the Cottonwood Camp."

"They all die," she responded stoically. "Chief, he big man, say you live and that I be your woman and fix you."

"All? They are all dead?" he asked in disbelief.

"Parker, Franco, your Father all die. Too many braves."

James let the words settle in. He had not allowed his mind to pass this point before, but now he knew what he wanted to disbelieve had come to pass. Memories of his father now swept through his mind and tears formed in his eyes and slowly rolled down his cheeks. His father had been a stern and distant man during those years on the farm, but since those early days on the trail when he had returned to him his horse Empress, his father and he had grown close. It made his loss even more telling to James who was, despite all that had occurred, still no more than a youth just reaching his manhood.

It was long moments as he tried to relate to all the faces he would not again see, that he remembered that Clay had left the camp before the attack.

"What happened to Clay?" he asked Little Flower.

"No see. He not come back."

CLAY

Clay rode north for a day before he reached the timbered hills that he had seen from the Cottonwood camp. Ahead of him he could see the rising majesty of the forested mountains that cast their snow covered peaks to the heavens. He found little protection on the desert floor and was glad to finally reach the mountains and have the tree covered hills to hide his presence. By nightfall he found a large meadow with a brook meandering through it that he thought would be suitable place to set up camp and bag some game. Studying the ground about the brook it was evident that this place was a favorite spot for deer and elk to feed and water. He had gathered some dry wood for a campfire, intending to await the coming morning to make his kill, when he noticed that the horses were getting skittish.

First Clay suspected that some wandering bear or mountain lion might be about and the horses had picked up the scent. He looked in the direction that seemed to draw their attention and his heart missed a beat. Crossing the far side of the meadow was a large band of Indians. He quickly moved the horses further into the woods behind him and after tethering them, moved forward to observe the passing Indians. Franco had pressed upon him the field glasses that he had obtained from the unlucky officer back at For Kearny. Clay had seen no need for them when offered, but was glad to have them now.

Clay's worst fears were confirmed. The Indians that were moving across the far end of the meadow were dressed in war regalia. They had on their war bonnets, their faces were painted and their ponies were decorated in all forms of symbols that were intended to bring the warrior good luck. He counted at least forty of them and thought immediately of his comrades back at the Cottonwood camp ground. There would be no fire tonight and the chance of a good hunt in the morning was now lost. Until he was certain that this war party was well out of the territory, he dared not fire his rifle. The next morning, he rode out of the valley to high ground hoping he could observe the progress of the warriors he had seen the night before and hopefully gain some idea of their intentions.

The warriors had been moving westward and would be no threat to his comrades if they kept moving in that direction. To his surprise, he saw not the group that had crossed the valley, but yet another band of warriors on a trail leading from another valley moving also in a westerly direction. Something was definitely stirring up the tribes and he knew he must give warning to his comrades and head them south away from the gathering tribes. When he returned to the meadow to retrieve his pack horse and supplies, he did so taking a different route as was his custom when being cautious. He saw yet more sign of hostiles and decided he had best stay under cover for a day at least to be sure that he could not cross trails with one of the moving bands.

Clay trapped a few beaver and made a small smokeless fire that night to prepare his meal of the much maligned beaver. The tail, he was told was the best eating, but he had little appetite even for that. He was worried about his companions and wanted to be on his way. The next morning, however, he discovered more sign about the valley and decided that he would have to wait and move out that night. It was a perilous trek, moving down out the mountains in the darkness, but as he moved out onto the desert beyond, the moon at its half, provided more light and allowed him to move more rapidly. It was not until midmorning of the next day that he came into view of the campsite where he left his friends. He approached the camp site with caution as he noticed no movement and was not certain who he might confront if he rode in in haste. The camp was deserted, his companions had move on. He picked up their trail. They were moving westward. He felt no immediate fear for their safety. The Indians he had seen were all moving away from this camp, but he must nonetheless warn them that to proceed too far westward would not be wise.

After resting his horses, Clay headed along the path that his comrades had taken, knowing he would overtake them by nightfall or by the next day. They were not traveling in haste. By late afternoon, he became more concerned. He picked up the sign of Indian ponies moving ahead of him on the trail of his companions. The further he traveled the more sign became evident. His horses had been ridden hard for several days and he could not press them further to catch up to his friends without fear of ending up on foot.

That evening, he came upon what was the last campsite of the traveling caravan. He had not personally observed the carnage at the Mapes Train massacre and was unprepared for what faced him. The dead bodies of his friends were strewn about their campsite as if thrown about by a great storm. They lay in contorted shapes, most of them stripped of their clothing, though few had been mutilated as had been the case with the Mapes victims. Clay sat on a nearby boulder and felt the nausea overcome him. He pounded his fist on his thighs in frustration. He knew now that he should have thrown caution to the wind and rode to warn his comrades of the impending danger. The war parties he had observed were heading to intercept his friends. As he sat there, the carrion that had been scattered by the interruption of his arrival were returning to feast on the victims of the Indian's vengeance.

Caution was of no concern to him now, he grabbed his rifle and started shooting at the wolves and coyotes that hovered about, but he soon found this effort to be a waste of ammunition and effort. Instead he built a large fire in the midst of the tangled bodies to keep them away. He knew he must do something about a burial for all these men, but at the moment the task was too much for him. He was not capable of the gut retching effort that was required to embrace corpses of all these men and move them about. He bedded down close by and spent most of the night in fitful agony.

By morning he still despaired of the tasks of burying so many men. It was really quite pointless. The Indians had scavenged the camp site of all the tools and what was left was useless. He could not possibly give all these men a decent burial. Instead he searched about the remains for those who meant the most to him, Franco, Parker and Wayne Rawlins. He found their bodies and carried them to a ravine nearby and laid them to rest side by side. He spent most of that day hauling rocks to place over the graves to keep away the scavengers and provide to them some semblance of a monument. He had searched for the body of James, and could not find it, nor could he find the body of Little Flower and assumed that they had been carried off for some terrible purpose he did not want to contemplate.

Clay spent the rest of the day on a small knoll overlooking the campsite where his companions had made their last stand and wondered what it would have been like to have been among them. He realized, upon contemplation that even if he had been able to carry a warning to them that the number of braves that were gathering would have eventually wrought the disaster that lay before him. He was fortunate to be alive. At least now, with a good deal of luck he might be able to reach the Willamette Valley in Oregon and carry the news to loved ones that their husbands or sons would not be returning with a bounty of gold, but would indeed not be returning at all.

Soon this spot where the carrion were again devouring the flesh of his people would bear no evidence of what had happened here. The remaining bones of the victims would be scattered about the land and time, weather and the sun would obliterate what once had been the spirit and essence of men once vital in life. If he could not survive the trip back to their loved ones, they like so many others who ventured into this wilderness would merely vanish from the face of the earth and none would have knowledge of their fate. The next morning he turned his horse northward and began his long, hazardous trip back to civilization through a strange and now hostile land.

JAMES

In the early morning light, James observed the face of Little Flower as her head lay on his uninjured shoulder. He had had little opportunity to observe her this close before and was impressed by her fine featured face and the solemnity of her presence. She did not resemble the plains Indians he had seen around the Forts they had passed through. She looked a lot like his sister Jenny would have had she the deep tan that was Little Flower's heritage. Her brown, almost black eyes flicked open as though she was aware of his observations. She stared back at him for a moment with a quizzical look as if she was reading his thoughts.

"Make food," she whispered and moved quickly away from him.

He was disappointed when she left. Her presence was reassuring and comforting to James who was feeling alone and helpless in his present circumstance. He awaited her return and ate heartily of the meal she provided. He felt the need to move about and get away from the confining bed that had been his only world for many days. Little Flower came to him as he tried to rise from the bed and assisted him to his feet. He stood unsteadily for a long time before he ventured his first step. He felt the pain of his wounded leg race to his brain and let out a gasp. He had not even seen his wound but was now well aware that it had been severe. Little Flower supported him as he ventured about the small camp and returned him to his bed after he had taken only a few tentative steps.

"Good you walk. Must not stay." Little Flower admonished as she moved aside his split trousers and examined his leg.

"No bleed; that good," she said after her examination.

She added more of her poultice and rewrapped the wound.

"Shoulder heal good. No problem," she said after examining that wound also.

James tried to walk again several times that day and for two more days he kept testing his strength. On the third day, Little Flower gave him a stick to use as a cane and would no longer serve as his crutch.

"You better, walk alone," she scolded him when he reached for her. "Must not stay here longer."

The next morning after finishing the remainder of the rabbit stew, Little Flower left the camp and returned with James' horse and her mule. She saddled them and tied their meager possessions onto the pack horse that Running Deer had provided.

"We go now," she advised him as she mounted her mule, waiting for him to mount his horse.

James, to his surprise was able to mount Caesar with little difficulty, but once mounted he looked at Little Flower in confusion. Suddenly he had to decide where he was going and had no clue. The lust for gold was never in him and going on to California, now that his father was dead did not appeal to him. Heading back to Fort Boise or to Oregon also had little appeal.

"I must go back and bury my father," he advised Little Flower as he turned his horse in that direction. James was now feeling the uncertainty that circumstances had made of his life. He was now without family and the guidance of those who cared for him. He was fast growing into manhood, but was not prepared to take that last step away from the security of other's concerns.

"No go back," Little Flower insisted. "They all dead. Snow come soon. Must go."

James had given little thought to the weather, but now that Little Flower mentioned the subject, there was indeed the feeling of the changing season in the air. The nights were colder, the days now cool, the sun was setting earlier and the nights were longer.

"I don't know where to go," he told her.

"Shoshone Chief say we go south. Bad Indians to west. Klamath and Modoc. Soon snow in mountains that way." She said pointing to the northwest. "Must go way Chief say."

James thought for a long moment about the advice the Chief had given to Little Flower. Although he was certain Running Deer had saved his life and that of Little Flower, it was also Running Deer who had murdered his father and his friends. Why would he want to trust the Chief or heed his advice? Little Flower waited patiently for him to turn his horse and follow her admonition.

"Why should we go south?" He finally asked her.

"It warmer and snow not come so soon," she advised.

Finding he had no reason to protest and no particular interest in which direction he headed, James turned his horse southward and they started their long journey to a future that was less than certain. As they moved ever southward, James was wishing he had paid more attention to the maps that his father had gathered. He knew they would soon be in the high desert and would have to cross the Sierra Nevada Mountains to reach California, but what route they would take over the mountains would be their greatest challenge what with the promise of snow by the time they reached the mountain passes. They were ill prepared for a winter crossing of the high mountains and each day the temperature moved ever colder, they suffered the more.

On the third week of the journey, the skies were turning more threatening. Angry dark clouds swirled about the sky and the temperature at night was below freezing. They traveled slowly as James' healing wounds inhibited their progress. James had been successful in killing a few deer along the way, but now the hides were more important to them than the meat. They had little to provide shelter and what robes they had were used for warmth at night. The snow hit them hard the next morning and soon a howling wind was driving the snow into every crevice of their scant cover. James hobbled the horses and he and Little Flower huddled together in the shelter of a large rock that stood as a lone sentential in a land devoid of other shelter. It was an early winter storm and to their good fortune it abated that night. But the land they surveyed the next morning was a desert of white. The snow was as least a foot deep and drifted in spots higher than their horses could manage.

For the first time in the long journey he had taken from his home in Missouri, James' confidence in his survival was ebbing. He had faced a number of dangers, but being out in this open country with nature his enemy, he was losing faith in the good luck that had kept him alive so far. But as was common in the country they were traveling through, the weather suddenly turned warmer, the snow began to melt and their travels became less arduous. It was Little Flower's unbending will that help keep James from falling into complete despair.

"Be warmer soon." She kept telling him as they huddled together against the chill of the long nights.

To James, the intimate companionship he had with Little Flower during the cold nights was equated to those winter nights spent with Jenny in the loft of their Missouri home. He knew Little Flower was still in mourning over the loss of her Parker and would not be receptive to his advances, yet the more time they spent together, the more the stirrings of his loins demanded more. It was at those moments he forced himself to look upon Little Flower more as his sister like Jenny to whom a sibling relationship created its own boundaries. He was also concerned about what would be the result of a stronger more intimate relationship. He was not unmindful of the reception Parker had gotten from the members of his wagon train.

The intended slander hurled at Parker of being a "squaw man" was a chilling prospect to James who knew that these weeks or maybe months he was spending with her would place him in that category regardless of what their more intimate relationships might be. If they survived this ordeal, they would one day come into the company of white settlers. What would be the fate of Little Flower when this ordeal was over weighed heavily on James' mind? He was reluctant to compound the decisions that had to be made at that time by becoming more involved with Little Flower beyond the sisterly relationship that he now felt toward her. These were the things that dominated his thinking, but his body was sending other messages.

Another storm was gathering in the west moving inextricably toward them. It looked even more ominous than the storm they had recently survived. James and Little Flower knew that they must find suitable shelter and wait out the storm, but the land was devoid of suitable sites as it consisted of rolling hills and small washes. They dare not hover in a wash as the promised of a blizzard would mean they would be buried in drifts. The first flaks of snow were swirling about them as the temperature continued to drop. It was then they come to the crest of the range that they had been slowly climbing. Far below to the south was the great expanse of a green verdant valley. They drove their animals in haste downward along an ill defined game trail. The lower they descended into the valley the warmer the temperature became. The clouds that had threatened them were moving further to the north and the far end of the great valley was awash in sun light. It was their moment of deliverance and their spirits soared; even their animals picked up their pace. By night fall, they had entered the heart of the valley and made a hasty camp beside a cold mountain spring that cascaded down from the snow packed peaks that rimed the valley. The brook tumbled in noisy protest over the rocky bottom of the stream and provided to James and Little Flower a comforting contrast to the silence of the barren, bleak landscape that they had now left behind them.

The next morning, as Little Flower did what she could to prepare a shelter for the coming night, James rode about the valley to determine their prospects. The great lake that dominated the center of the valley, he found to be settled on alkali soil that made its waters brackish. The lake bed and the land about it was a silty gray soil that when exposed to moisture was hazardous. He could see the skeletons of many animals that had become hopelessly mired in the clay like essence of the silty soil. The heavy snow in the mountains above them had forced the game down into the valley. There would be plenty of meat to sustain them as long as they remained in the valley. He surveyed again the towering mountain ranges that dominated the horizon about the valley. The prospects of moving out of the valley into California were formidable. As James rode back into camp, he had already decided that this is the place where they would wait out the winter. When he made his decision clear to Little Flower, she nodded her head in agreement and proceeded with the task of preparing what would now be a more permanent camp,

As James' hunting brought in more and more hides, Little Flower soon had enough hides to construct an Indian type lodge. She gathered the grasses that had browned and withered in the fall and packed them about the base of the lodge and now with a small fire, they had the warmth and comfort that had been denied to them during their long travels. There was an abundance of mosses and pine boughs about and Little Flower lined the floor of their lodge with them and soon made them separate beds that James accepted with a growing disappointment. He accepted the fact that she was still in her mind Parker's woman and wanted no more of him.

James could not have been more misguided in his assessment of Little Flower's conduct. Little Flower did miss her Parker with a heart rendering agony, but he was dead. She had seen him fall and brutally bludgeoned by half a dozen savages. That memory haunted her nights. She needed the comfort of another human being to help heal the wounds branded into her sole. At first, she shared James' bed because he needed her warmth, but soon found she needed more than mere warmth. She needed the assurance and acceptance that James could afford her.

That night she was invited into his bed, she expected more, but then he was still healing and she suspected he could do no more. James' continued unwillingness to possess her in that lustful, lively way that Parker would have was a disappointment to her and she accepted James' hesitance as rejection. When she prepared their separate beds, she assumed that was what James would want. Little Flower had not been unaware of the insults that her Parker had to endure because of his relationship with her. She stoically accepted what she felt was James' unwillingness to suffer the enmity that her Parker had confronted with complete indifference.

Spring came with a perfusion of blossoms that carpeted the valley. The yellow, white and blue of the budding plants that adorned the sage and wild flowers, brought the buzz of a million honey gathering bees industriously gathering the nectar that was in abundance. James, relying upon the wisdom of Little Flower restrained his eagerness to resume their travels.

"Snow not done," she advised him, "Must wait."

James fought to restrain his impatience and rode in greater distances about the valley. On one of these trips, he stood on the crest of a small ridge and looking into the distance saw what he thought was the movement of a wandering animal that might be added to the larder. He was familiar now with the trails these animals followed and moved down the ridge to intercept the unsuspecting deer or elk. He tethered his horse in a nearby grove and waited to ambush what he assumed to be the approaching deer. Something, however, was going array with his expectations. As his pray drew closer, he could make out an uncommon noise which he soon recognized as a discordant attempt at singing. To his amazement there came meandered into his view the grizzled countenance of a wondering prospector leading a burrow heavily loaded with the prospector's belongings.

The prospector stopped abruptly and fell into silence when James stepped onto the trail in front of him. They were less than twenty yards apart by than and both men stood in silence studying the other. James guessed the prospector to be about five foot five and probably sixty or more years of age. He was slightly stooped and now stood looking at him with the obvious squint of a man troubled by poor eyesight.

The Prospector was the first to speak, "Well, you ain't no grizzly, be you a bandito?"

James realized then that he was holding his rifle in a threatening position, and dropped it butt first on the ground and raised his hand in the Indian sign of friendship.

"Don't mean you no harm, stranger. Just wasn't expecting guests. Thought you was my diner wondering along this game trail."

"I'd make poor victuals, stranger. Stringy as a horse tail." He responded moving closer, still squinting. "What brings you to his hell hole?"

James was surprised to hear this lush valley described as a hell hole. "This don't seem such a bad place to me. I came down from the Oregon Territory and got hung up here when winter set in."

"Well, you want to be moving on. When summer comes, this valley turns into an oven. Been prospecting about here long enough to know you want to be moving on before your bones get bleached."

James detected resentment in the man's voice as if he were trespassing on land the prospector claimed as his own.

"I have no reason to stay and intend to be leaving soon. I have made camp up ahead and welcome you to a meal if you ain't too cantankerous to be sociable." James responded.

The prospector chuckled then and stepped forward with his hand extended. "They call me Cactus Jack Slade," he announced. "Be glad to join you if you got some to spare."

James, perhaps because the prospector used a nickname responded with, "They call me Grizzly Rawlins. My name is James."

It was then the prospector noticed James' necklace and his large scabbarded knife. "You look like you could put harm on a grizzly," he remarked. James had paid little attention to the change that had overcome him, but standing in front of this crusty old prospector he realized his gain in height and stature. His expanding chest was stressing the seams of his buckskin shirt and his thighs tightly filled his deer skin pants. He was becoming a formidable presence.

He led Cactus Jack back to his camp. A feeling of relief was evident on Jack's face when James introduced him to Little Flower. It appears he had been expecting James to lead him into the hands of a bunch of brigands. James was anxious to get some news of events in California and the rest of the world outside what had been his limited domain these past months. Cactus Jack was not a good news source as he seemed little inclined to mingle with others.

"Last I was in California; Fremont was trying to drive the Mexes from power, but got his butt kicked trying to take San Francisco. That Kearny fellow, he brung a troop all the way from Santa Fe. Seems he whupped the Mexicans down south at San Pasqual and them Americans is claiming California as part of the United States. The place is flooding with them that's gold mad. Cain't tolerate them kind. They's soon shoot you for a pan of gold if you be lucky enough to find one."

"Is that what brought you out here to this remote spot?" James asked.

Cactus Jack looked at him with a hint of suspicion. He was not a man inclined to discuss his whereabouts and what he was up to.

"Just snoopin' around," was his only comment.

As night fall came, James invited Cactus Jack to bed down by their fire. He accepted the invitation and laid out his bed roll and tethered his burro.

Before he called it a night he produced from his pack a mouth harp and played a few tunes. Both James and Little Flower were impressed with his performance, Little Flower particularly. She moved over to Cactus Jack and touched the mouth harp as he played it as if trying to find where the music came from. Cactus Jack took the instrument from his mouth and wiped it on his sleeve and put it in Little Flower's hands and motioned for her to put it in her mouth and blow into it.

Little Flower was slow to respond, fearing some evil spirit might be inside the thing that made the noise. Eventually she was encouraged to comply and was enthralled with the result. She kept blowing into it. Despite the discord, she wouldn't stop blowing into it until James encouraged her to give it back to the one person who knew how to use it. The laughter and good fun that accompanied Little Flower's efforts brought to the small camp a bonding that broke down the resistance Cactus Jack had toward these strangers. The next morning he was in no hurry to leave and suggested that if they didn't mind him hanging around for a day or two, he would like to do a little panning in the stream that raced past their camp.

James was curious to see what prospecting was all about. After all it was the lust for gold that drove his group of adventurers into the vastness of a wilderness that consumed them. He intended to assist his father in whatever venture he undertook to find his fortune in the valleys of northern California. He knew nothing, however, about prospecting for gold and watched Cactus Jack with interest.

Cactus Jack had found a small pool where dark sand had settled and drove his pan into it filling it with the bottom grit. It was not long after he swirled the pan around and around that he began to look into the tailings with more interest. James could tell he had found something that interested Cactus Jack as Jack's activity became more vigorous. Jack placed the remains of his efforts on a flat rock nearby and studied it intently and then went back to work. Before the morning was over, he had accumulated a neat pile of gold dust which he scrapped into a small leather sack he retrieved from his bundle.

When James asked him about his findings and if they had any significance, Cactus Jack was noncommittal. "Don't mean nothin'" was his only comment. James, however, was certain that Cactus Jack was merely deflecting his interest and had indeed made a find of some interest. The excitement may not have been evident in how he spoke, but his face betrayed the excitement that was overtaking him.

For the rest of the afternoon, Jack did no more panning, but returned to the stream several times, moving up and down from the place he had done his panning using a stick to stir round the bottom of the various pools. When asked if he had found anything, Jack would deflect the question with some mumbled response.

One the second day, Cactus Jack said he would be heading up to the headwaters of the stream and maybe be gone for a day. He asked if they would watch over his possessions and tend to his burro. James assured him that they would do so, even though James was getting ready to break camp and move on.

"Don't be too long up there, Little Flower and I must be on our way. We don't intend to settle here."

The remark caused Cactus Jack to study James' face intently. "You don't see no reason to stay?" He asked with a trace of incredulity.

"We didn't land here by choice and don't chose to stay." James responded.

Jack gave James another long study and then turned and moved upstream.

Cactus Jack had been gone for two days and James was becoming concerned. The weather was good and he wanted to get on his way. Little Flower expressed her concern also.

"He not well, maybe have trouble." She volunteered when James expressed his eagerness to get on their way.

James knew Little Flower was more observant about such matters than he and having the subject brought forward he did recall that Cactus Jack did not show much energy and moved with deliberate steps and often stopped to rest. But then James had no idea how old the man was and how a man of Jack's age should be acting.

"He gets along pretty good. After all he walked all the way out to this Godforsaken place."

"Still not well," was her only response and no more was said.

That evening Jack wandered back into camp and sat down heavily on his bed roll obviously exhausted.

After Little Flower served their supper, Cactus Jack sat in silence a troubled look on his face. James decided to wait him out. If Jack had found anything, he probably did not want to talk about it and if he did want to talk about it he obviously wasn't ready to discuss the results of his trip.

That night Little Flower was solicitous to Jack's needs, helping him with his boots and seeing that he was comfortable before they turned in for the evening.

"I see pain on his face," Little Flower said as they returned to their lodge, "Give him medicine, maybe better tomorrow."

James recalled that Little Flower had been busy that day gathering some roots and herbs and fussing with some concoction over the fire. James was aware of Little Flower's perspicuity, but her knowledge of natural medicines was a mystery to him.

"If he gets better, we can get going," was James' only response.

The next morning Cactus Jack was up and seemed in renewed spirits. He had stirred up the fire and was brewing some coffee, a luxury James had not enjoyed for several months now. He also had a pan full of bacon frying in a big iron skillet. When the bacon was done, Jack threw some flour mixings into the grease and soon had some camp biscuits ready for their meal. James and Little Flower enjoyed this rare treat to Jack's approval. When the meal was over, James announced that he would be gone for the day; he saw sign of some prairie chicken and wanted a change in his diet of deer and elk.

"I'd bother you to stay for a piece if you might," Cactus Jack said, "I need to get some things said."

James put the saddle down he'd picked up as he was preparing to leave on his hunt and sat again next to Little Flower by the dwindling fire and waited for Jack to speak.

It took Jack long moments before the spoke. "I been wandering about these hills since '36 when I came out here from Philadelphia. My wife died of the blistering pox and my only boy wandered off to God knows where. I took to prospecting as it seemed suitable to a man who wanted to be left be."

Jack fell silent then and James could see he was having some difficulty finding the words he wanted.

"I made some finds, but not enough to excite anyone. Kept me in provisions was all," He continued. "I didn't really want much since I had no hankering for city life and didn't need much."

James's eyes and mind were returning to the mountains beyond. It was time to get moving and he wasn't much interested in sitting here listening to the remembrances of an old prospector."

"I ain't sayin' I wasn't looking for that big strike, it's just that I didn't have much hope for it and cause I seen what happened to them that made it. Saw men killed over a poke no bigger than that I got over there pannin' this stream.

Having referred to his poke, Jack walked over and retrieved it and threw it into James' hands. "I spect that there be five hundred dollars in that little sack you got there," he announced.

James hefted the leather pouch and felt its unusual weight. He was amazed that there could be so much wealth in that small sack.

He handed it back to Jack without comment.

"It don't impress you do it son?" Jack asked.

"It ain't mine, you found it," James replied.

James' response brought another long silence on Jack's part.

"You puzzle me lad. I left that sack there where a meddlesome man would have been at it. I see it ain't been bothered. As I say men been kilt for less than's in that sack."

"Well it's yours and you keep it," James replied as he rose again to be on his way.

"Not so fast son," Jack admonished, "I got a proposition for you."

James sat again impatient to be done with these proceedings. The suggestion of a proposition was of some interest and he was willing to listen.

There was again a long irritating silence that tested James' patience.

"Them findings I made the other day was the best I ever seen. There be lots of them tailings in that stream. I know enough to know that them tailings had to come from a deposit upstream, so I took a look. There's a mother load up at them headwaters and it's ours to be had."

James was slow to gather in the significance of what Jack now told him. It was unlike a prospector to reveal a strike or claim, yet here he was telling James of the find of a lifetime. But then there was the statement by Jack that the claim was "theirs."

It was James' turn to remain speechless as he contemplated the significance of Jack's statement.

"What's your proposition," he finally asked.

"I ain't been doin' too good. Doc said my ticker is getting' tired." Cactus Jack didn't speak again until he had cleared his throat several times and wiped his crusty hand over his eyes. "To be truthful, I didn't come out here to find me no pot of gold. I kind'a gave up on that. Why the Lord lead me to this spot when he knew I had no need of these riches puzzles me and I been thinkin' mighty heavy about that." Jack voice was wavering now and he was speaking with difficulty, his emotions were playing tricks on him.

"I says I'd be truthful and I'll be that. I came out here to die like a wounded animal goes away alone when it knows its time is up. But here I sit having found the riches that would buy a kingdom and can't make no use of it."

"You can't be all that bad off, Jack, you been getting about pretty good," James offered in encouragement.

"It be that brew your lady made for me that got me up and goin', that ain't the point now. To work this claim I need a partner with a strong back and an honest disposition. I'm thinking that be you and that and be why the Lord brought us together a sittin' here on a mother load."

Although James was aware of the fact that Cactus Jack had found gold, he had no conception of the extent of the find and was not prepared to make an immediate response to the offer now presented to him. He found it hard to believe that a wealth to the extent that Jack was talking about could come so easily and unexpectedly into his life. He and Jack spent the next two days talking about the extent of the find and the details of the partnership that was offered. Jack took him upstream to show him the core of gold he had found and assured him it was a large and deep vein.

"No need to go mining that core right off," Jack advised him, there be enough tailings in this stream to make us a good nest egg and get us enough capital to mine that core," he advised James. We'll pan this stream and get us a good poke and then you'll have to go to Sacramento and file a claim and make some business arrangements. I ain't sure if Sacramento be the place to file the claim, but that's where all the prospecting is goin' on and they must be a place there. If not, you may have to go to Buena Vista. We need a smart Lawyer and a good banker. I ain't up to the trip so it's you who will have to handle that end of it."

James' enthusiasm for the venture grew as he had time to digest the implications of the find Jack had made. They worked the stream for a week and Jack finally put a halt to the effort telling him that he dared not haul more of the gold dust they had panned than what they had accumulated. James prepared for his departure only after he and Jack had gone over the details of how they would file their claim and not reveal that the gold he carried came from that claim. If word got out, the valley would be inundated with prospectors and their claim would be in jeopardy.

Before leaving, James, as instructed by Jack returned to the vein that Jack had found and with a chisel removed several samples of the core that would be used to assay the claim. The black quartz laden rock was suffused with gold veins. As James was returning back to camp his trail led him past the large pool that formed below the falls where the stream gathered its might and created the hollow bed that formed the pool below. As he walked by with his thoughts on the trip he must now make, he came to a boulder upon which something lay that caught his attention. He stopped and looked at it; it was Little Flower's leather shift. He stopped and picked it up wondering what it was doing at this spot. He heard a splashing sound in the pool and looked to see Little Flower frolicking in the water below him. She had not noticed his presence and was uninhibited in the exposure of her lithe, firm body. James' first inclination was to drop the clothing and hurry away, but he could not remove his eyes from the beauty that presented itself so innocently in the pool below.

Little Flower instinctively felt the presence of another and looked about to see James holding her shift and gazing intently at her. She swam to the edge of the pool and stood with her breast exposed allowing him a better view of her nakedness. To his surprise, she seemed not to mind his voyeurism and instead of embarrassment, she motioned for him to join her.

"You need wash," she told him, "come, I help."

As if mesmerized, James walked slowly toward her and into the pool. Little Flower giggled. "No, No, must take off clothes."

James pulled his shirt over his head and threw it toward the bank, holding his gaze on the tantalizing presence of Little Flowers firm breasts, which because of the cold water thrust forth her dark bronze nipples. His trousers were wet and he was having some difficulty removing them when Little Flower joined in the effort soon exposing his manhood that had responded with an aching hardness to her ministrations. She grasped his maleness in both hands now and moved to him.

"You very big. Need woman," she said in a husky voice he hardly recognized.

She pushed him onto the sandy bank of the stream and onto his back and then guided his erection into her soft, receptive womb. James' passion rose in a great wave and Little Flower's deft movements drove him into a frenzy he had never known a man could experience. She drew from his loins every last measure of his essence and felt his body relax as he had no more to give, yet she drove on drawing him ever deeper into her until after shuddering gasps, she too had no more to give and fell in exhaustion upon his chest where his strong arms engulfed her drawing her tightly to his moist chest. The warmth of the noon day sun relaxed them even more and they dozed together on the sandy bank of the stream in loves embrace.

That night she came to James' bed and they made love long into the night. As the morning sun filled their lodge with warmth, James woke to find he was alone. Little Flower, however, was not far away, for he heard her humming one of those tunes that Cactus Jack had taught her. He missed her already and wanted her in his bed, but then he remembered this was the morning he was to depart on his trip to Sacramento. As he emerged from the lodge he found that Little Flower had his breakfast prepared and had even brought the horses into camp in preparation for his journey.

Jack, taking part of a flour sack, made a list of all the tools and supplies James would have to bring with him on his return trip."

"You best buy you another pack horse to haul all that," Jack advised, "And be sure no snoopy bastard follows your trail back here. All them supplies will make some varmints curious."

James found it difficult to say his goodbyes to Little Flower. They had shared a long, harrowing ordeal and had grown accustomed to their dependence on each other. Now that James and Little Flower had shared their bed, the bond was even stronger.

"I must bring you something," he told Little Flower, "What would you like?"

"Cook things, sew things," she responded, making sign so he would understand.

"You must want more than pots and pans and needles, but I'll find something just for you," he said as he mounted up and rode out of camp leaving Little Flower and Cactus Jack for what he knew would be several weeks.

ON TO SACREMENTO

James had no knowledge of the land across which he was to travel. Cactus Jack had given him some vague descriptions of Northern California, but even he had not traveled the route that James must take. "Once you get over the Sierras, you'll come upon a broad plane, just follow it south and you'll come to Sacramento," was the extent of Jack's directions. Getting over the mountains was, however, no easy matter. Snow still blocked most of the passes and James spent a week trying to find a pass that would allow him to broach the mountains. James' realized as he searched for a pass that his decision to pass the winter on the far side of these mountains had saved him and Little Flower from a miserable fate.

As James came out of the mountains and followed the streams to the valley below he began to encounter prospectors busy working the streams and at several places found mining operations of a more extensive nature where streams were diverted by sluices that separated the gold from the sands that made up the steam beds. He was assured by these men that there was a place to file claims and an assay office in Sacramento, but if he wanted bankers and lawyers he'd have to move on to Buena Vista or Los Angeles.

Some of the claims he came across had already been deserted, the evidence of a flurry of industry scattered about the claim doing violence to what had once been a pristine visage untouched by the ambitions of man. Hastily built shelters of little substance were rapidly crumbling and possessed only by rodents and vermin. Tins, emptied of their contents littered the ground in careless clusters. The lumber that had value had been scavenged and nothing was left but valueless remnants of man's presence. Already evident were the forces of nature rising to reclaim her domain as rust and rot were beginning the process of erasing the remaining evidence of man's invasion. James, who had spent several months removed from the intrusion of man's industry, was amazed that so much of man's presence had been driven into the remote reaches of the mountain by the frenzied quest for gold.

When he reached Sacramento he was disappointed to find not a city as he and envisioned it, but a collection of random structures, some complete, some half complete, some mere tents stretched about a lumber frame. When he rode down the muddy main street, he was caught up in a stream of commerce as wagons riders, buggies and pedestrians fought to gain their way along the busy street. He found the assayers office and decided to make that his first stop as he assumed it would take some time to get the core samples assayed. As he expected the office was busy and he had to wait. Being back in civilization with all sorts of humanity crowded about him, James became concerned for the gold that was being carried on his pack animal. He waited outside the assay office hoping the crowd inside would dissipate.

The discovery Cactus Jack had made, if revealed in this mass of humanity might well cause him harm if not the loss of his precious cargo. It was almost noon and as he entered the door, a clerk locked the door behind him and hung out a closed for lunch sign. James deliberately loitered until all those present had completed their business and had been let out the door. The harried clerk then looked at him and directed him to the counter where James set his satchel containing his ore samples. The samples made a big clunk as he set it on the counter to the clerk's obvious irritation.

"We don't need but a few rocks to make an assessment of your claim. What have you got in that bag, your whole claim?"

"I brung what I thought was needed," James replied with irritation. "If you don't care to look at it I'll be on my way."

From behind the counter at a desk where he had been occupied scrawling on a note pad, a tall lean, austere looking man, with an equally harried look that adorned the clerk's face looked up and asked in annoyance? "What's the trouble, just take the man's samples and be gone with him, I have to get to Alioto's and meet with someone."

In irritation, the clerk dumped the sample on the counter with a great clatter, but when he looked at the contents spread across the counter, he let out a long whistle.

"Where the hell did you find this ore?" he exclaimed in a voice that conveyed his amazement.

The reaction brought the man at the desk to the counter in a quick stride. He picked up the larger of the samples and examined it, then took it back to the far end of the office where he placed it on a bench and proceeded to strike it several times with a small pick. After fussing with the sample a few more minutes, he placed it in a box and brought it to the counter. "Clarence," he directed the Clerk, "get the particulars and give the man a receipt."

After the clerk left the counter, the other man looked at James with obvious interest. "Where did you find ore like this?"

James was not certain he need to tell the man what he wanted to know and hesitated. He remembered seeing some sailors on the street and the idea came to him. "I just come in from South America and brung these with me."

The man studies his face for a moment and then smiled. "That's a good story and you best stick with it. If word gets out about your find, this town will go nuts. You needn't worry about telling anybody where you got this ore; we don't need to know to make an assay. We keep such matters confidential, you best do so too. I'll be honest with you, from just an eyeball look at this sample, it's some of the richest I've seen since I been here, and I've seen a lot of this stuff. You come back this afternoon, say around four and I'll have some results for you."

When James turned to leave, he stopped for a moment and asked where the claims office could be found.

The tall man, who introduced himself as Robert Peters, gave him a conspiratorial smile and replied, "They don't accept filings on South American mines, but you'll find the office a block north of here. It'll be closed for lunch now, but if you have to wait around, why don't you join me and a friend of mine for lunch."

James' studied the man's face for several moments before he replied. "I've horses to attend to but if I can get them off the street, I could use some food." Mr. Peters directed him to the back of the building where he stabled his own animal and allowed James to leave his horses after providing them with feed and grain.

"I'm a bit late for lunch, so let's hoof it," Robert Peters urged him when they had tended to the horses. "You'll like meeting my friend."

The place where Mr. Peters led James turned out to be one of those hastily constructed structures, half tent and half frame construction. James had never been in a tavern in his life, but knew one when he saw it. The place was crowded with men sitting at make shift tables and benches where boisterous, hard looking men sat about, smoking, eating and shouting to each other over the din of dozens of conversations. Mr. Peters looked about for a moment and then directed James to the rear corner of the room where a man was waiving to Mr. Peters to get his attention.

The man at the table stood to greet Mr. Peters, barely concealing his irritation at his tardiness. "That beef steak will be all gone if we wait much longer to order," the stranger declared as he waved a waiter over.

The stranger was well dressed in a coat and tie, well polished boots, a well trimmed beard and mustache and intense blue eyes that now turned to James waiting to be introduced.

I want you to meet Charles Fremont," he said as he turned to James, "This is James, I'm sorry, what was the last name?"

James could tell by Mr. Fremont's expression that he was waiting for an explanation from Mr. Peters as to why he had brought this young man to lunch when he knew they had business matters to discuss.

It was then, when Fremont examined James more closely, that he noticed the bear claw necklace and the large knife and scabbard James carried at his waist. Fremont knew instinctively that the man before him was fresh from the frontier and being an explorer himself now waited with interest for an explanation of the man's presence.

Mr. Peters, true to his word said nothing of the ore sample. "This young man just got into town and needed a good meal. I have a feeling he'll have a great future here in California."

Freemont was astute enough to know that Peters was being evasive and knew more of this young man named James Rawlings than he could reveal.

"Where you hail from," he asked James.

"I started from Missouri and crossed the plains with my family to get to Oregon City. I got as far as Fort Boise, when we got word of the gold strike here in California and some of us headed this way. Not all of us made it; in fact, all but me was kilt in an Indian raid up in the Oregon Territory."

Fremont's interest in James' story was now acute and he started pelting him with questions. When he asked James if he could tell him who his companions were who were killed in the raid, he was clearly shocked and annoyed when James told him that Franco and Parker had been among those killed.

"Those boys were with me when I explored up through that country. I'm indeed depressed to hear they fell in an ambush. How was it you escaped?"

James told him the story of his experience with Running Deer, and Fremont again started with an intense series of questions.

"I heard of that chief, but never known him to be hostile. He's to be dealt with. Him and the rest. This country's to be made safe for the passage of the settlers. I need to know more about your travels. I'll be heading back to Washington soon and the President will want to know all the details."

"I don't suppose you knew it," Peters volunteered now, "but Mr. Freemont has been the acting governor here in California and has got some say over matters out west here. He's also a colonel in the army."

When James was first introduced to Fremont, he knew he was in the presence of one of the most prominent men in the West. It was Fremont who had published the maps and diaries that so inspired his father. James was raised to be respectful, but was at a loss to know how he should respond to this famous explorer, a man who was now the acting governor and who talked of meetings with the President of the United States. To James, who had seldom met a public official, and whose knowledge of Washington D.C. and Presidents came only from hearing adult conversation, this meeting with Freemont gave him his first vision of a world he would one day enter. James was impressed that Fremont would be interested in him at all, or that he would want to know all about his travels. When Fremont extended his sympathies upon hearing that James had lost his father in the Indian raid, James was impressed by the man's compassion and concern. Fremont was a man of his liking.

By the time the meeting broke up, the steaks had come and been consumed. James had had his first taste of hard liquor and found it not to his liking. "I tasted better water at Soda Springs," he remarked. "Does this stuff give you the runs too?"

"No," responded Fremont with a chuckle, "But those who don't tolerate it can have a heap of misery if they don't know when to quit."

James returned to the stable, leaving the other two men to deal with the business that had been the call for their meeting. He didn't want to leave his possession alone for long and was already worried about the safety of his gold. All was in order when he returned, so he ventured down the street to the claims office and filed the claim according to the description that Cactus Jack had provided.

"Ain't seen no claim filed up in that country," the official remarked. "Any good findings?"

"None yet," James lied, "Maybe some promise, but I don't know a damn thing about such matters, I'm filing for a friend."

"Well, most of these claims don't amount to nothing," the official volunteered, "but good luck to you anyway."

James had taken the opportunity to ask Fremont about a good banker and a lawyer in 'Yurba Buena and was told to look up a man named George Ramsdale.

"He's just come around the horn from New York and intends to open a bank. Probably already has. Seems a good sort with a good head for business. He'll no doubt know of some lawyer who can assist you. By the way, Yurba Buena is now called San Francisco. You'll find it a little more settled than this place, but it's growing like a rabbit colony also."

When Robert Peters returned to his office and completed his work on the ore sample, he was prepared to give his report to James that afternoon.

"As I suspected, this is indeed rich ore and will yield a fortune in gold. I estimate that the vein this sample came from is extensive. Do you have the capital to develop it?"

"I'll take that up with my backers when I get back to Bolivia," James said with a smile, but right now I couldn't pay for that meal you just bought me."

"I suspected as much," Peters said. "I'll tell you what I'll do. I'll give you five hundred dollars for this sample here. That will give you some idea of what your South American find is worth. That will give you a stake and get you back where you intend to go. If you come this way again, be sure to stop by. I expect you won't be needing any advance from me when you do. I'd like to hear the rest of the story about this foreign adventure of yours," he said, going along with the by now obvious ruse.

James followed the Sacramento River and reached San Francisco a few days later. He found San Francisco a larger version of Sacramento, a town as Fremont had put it, "growing like a colony of rabbits." Building activity was everywhere in evidence and the bustle of commerce was infectious as everyone seemed to be scurrying about at a hectic pace. Market Street was where the growth of the new territory of California was centered as its magnificent harbor was a clear invitation to worldwide enterprise. Yet, as James surveyed the harbor, he could see that it was crowded with ships, many in a state of obvious neglect, abandoned by the sailors that upon reaching the harbor, bolted for the gold fields, never to man these ships again. The masts of the ships bore the flags, now tattered and faded, of many nations, none of them known to James.

He had no trouble finding the Ramsdale Bank of Commerce and Industry as its prominent red and white sign dominated one corner of Market Street. James tied his animals to the hitching post in front of the bank along side of some fancy looking carriages, several of them guarded by liveried servants. James went into the bank to have a look around. Although there was evidence that the bank was still in the final stages of construction, it was a substantial looking and gave James confidence that it was a business that had solid prospects. James knew little of the ways of banks and watched with interest as the customers came and went, the five clerks at the caged counter efficiently dispatching their requests. While standing about alternately watching the proceedings and checking to see that his animals were being left alone, his suspicious activity attracted the attention of one of the guards who now approached him.

"What can we do for you stranger?" the large heavily built man, dressed in a business suit, but who carried a large pistol at his belt, asked.

James was surprised by the question and, unaware that he was drawing any interest, he was naturally defensive. All the warning he had received from Robert Peters and Fremont were having their effect. He didn't care for the man's intrusion and moved away toward one of the cages without responding. The large man then grabbed him by the arm and spun him about. James who had for the past months trained himself on the use of his Bowie Knife spun with blinding speed and had his knife at the man's throat before the stranger knew what had happened.

"I don't tolerate being handled, friend," he said menacingly to the guard. "I come to do business here if I'm taken to the place and you ain't making me comfortable."

Several other guards had hustled over upon noticing the disturbance and were preparing to come to the aid of the imperiled guard. Before things could progress any further, a man dressed in a blue striped business suit, came rushing from behind the counter.

"Let's hold on here stranger. There isn't any need for that knife. This man was only doing his duty; we don't want people loitering about here with no apparent business to do. What does bring you here?"

James, whose action had been instinctive, was now embarrassed by his actions and returned his knife to its scabbard. He now noticed that everyone in the bank had their eyes on him and he was ready to retreat from the bank, when the man in the business suit again spoke, this time in a more conciliatory voice.

"You had some purpose in mind when you came into the bank, surely you can state your business and we will be helpful if we can."

"Well, I did come to do some banking;" James responded hesitantly, "Colonel Fremont said your bank might be the place where I could do business."

At the mention of Fremont's name, the man extended his hand in friendship and waived away the guards. "Simon Oliver is my name. I am assistant manager here and welcome you to our bank. How is it you come to know the Governor?"

"I made his acquaintance in Sacramento where I went to file my claim." James responded noticing the man's growing interest.

"Why don't you come into my office? I'm sure Mr. Ramsdale would like to meet you. He's anxious to have new customers and likes to meet them all personally."

"I would be glad to oblige you, but I got animals out front and I don't want to leave them unattended what with all them people out there."

"That's no problem," the assistant manager advised him as he motioned the guard over who had first confronted James.

"The gentleman here owns those two horses tied to the rail outside, step outside and keep a watch on them while I introduce this gentleman to Mr. Ramsdale."

The guard, whose attitude had been hostile toward James but a few moments ago, now looked at him with a show of interest and nodding his head to the manager he walked outside as instructed.

James was led into a large walnut paneled office. For the first time in James' life he walked across a lush green carpet that felt like meadow grass to his moccasined feet. A large highly polished table dominated the room about which were a number of green leather covered chairs. A silver service sat in the middle of the table. James sat awkwardly on one of the chairs as instructed while the manager left the room to find Mr. Ramsdale.

James sat in discomfort in the ostentatious surroundings of the conference room and pondered the decision he would soon have to make. Is this the place where he would deposit his gold and the bank that would of necessity forge its place in what would be a long relationship? It would depend on this man Ramsdale who he was about to meet and what impression he made. The manager did not immediately return and James became restive and moved toward the door at about the time it swung open placing him face to face with the intensely earnest face of a stranger, who stopped abruptly and appraised him as the manager hurriedly introduced him as the bank's owner, George Ramsdale.

"I see you are a man of action and don't like to sit about," Mr. Ramsdale remarked as he shook his hand with a firm, strong grip. "But do come and sit for a moment so we can see what we can do for you. I see you are a man of the mountains. Have you just arrived in our fair city?"

James liked the man's friendly but businesslike manner and his mind was set on using this man's bank before the discussion about business even commenced.

"I have come a long way," James answered, "I don't know about me being a mountain man, but I have come over the mountains and intend on heading back when I can get some business done. I need a banker and a lawyer and you seem to fit one of the needs I got. There's some gold dust out there on one of my animals and I ain't wantin' to pack it about any longer."

George Ramsdale had dealt with many miners, some with a paltry bit of gold, others with a small fortune and he wondered which category this man would fall into.

"Why don't you go out and get that gold and we will see what we can do for you," Ramsdale suggested.

James hesitated. "It ain't that easy and I don't want to be packing that stuff about where everyone can get an eye on it."

This comment peaked the interest of the banker. Standing now to his full six foot, comfortably stout stature he strode to the door and called for another of the guards. When the man arrived he instructed him to go with James and show him the way around the building to the back entrance and assured James that he would meet him there and he would have help unloading his burden.

When James followed the bank guards around the building, leading his animals he was quick to notice that the large guard was now looking upon him with a more respectful look. He took a great interest in Caesar and asked him where he found a horse with such strange markings. Apparently an Appaloosa had not been seen this far south.

"It be and Indian breed. I hear the Nez Perce raise them. It was given to me by and Indian Chief who took to me after I saved him from becoming wolf bait." James replied to his inquiry.

"That so?" the man replied respectfully. "I suppose he gave you that fancy knife too. Ain't seen nothing like that around here either."

"Well, it came from the same people as a good luck symbol," James replied. "I'm sorry I pulled it on you back there. I ain't too civilized yet and was taking to my native ways."

"Ain't no mind. I should have knowed better than to grab at you like that. I ain't all that civilized either. Only been here for a short time and needed some work. I was captain of one of those ships out there, but it's just rottin' away without no hands and I had to come ashore or rot with it."

"Why didn't you join the rush to the gold fields with the rest of your men?"

"Owed some to the company that hired me and wanted to tend to the ship. They quit paying me when I couldn't haul cargo so I had to get on with my life. Sides, I ain't no prospector. I could stumble over a gold brick and toss it away. I suspect most of them sailors that ran off to the gold fields are gonna' lose their poke soon enough and go beggin' in the streets. My needs don't turn that way. Gettin' rich don't mean a thing unless you got something you want to spend it on. I just want to get back to sea."

When they arrived at the back door, Mr. Ramsdale and two clerks were waiting for him. After James tied up the horses he untied the pack on the pack horse and reached inside retrieving a leather sack and as instructed handed it to one of the clerks. Mr. Ramsdale was about to turn away and follow the clerk inside to get on with the accounting when James went back to the pack horse and retrieved another sack and handed that to the other clerk. When James returned again to the horse, Mr. Ramsdale himself step forward and retrieved the sack and handed it to one of the guards to take inside.

"Are there more?" he asked incredulously as James again returned to the horse.

"Yup." Was the short answer he received from James.

James retrieved three more sacks and then told the banker he was through.

The sacks had been carried into the large conference room where they awaited the weighing and counting that got under way when some scales were brought into the room. James and banker Ramsdale sat without comment as the two clerks went about the business of weighting and counting. Ramsdale watched James with a studied interest trying to see some reaction to the cataloging of what he knew to be a substantial fortune that lay spread across the table. When the clerks were done with the counting, they summed up their conclusions on a pad that they handed to the banker. The gold, now removed from the sacks was lined up neatly in a number of glass jars aligned on the table before him. Ramsdale dismissed the clerks and the manager after he studied the results of the counting. When the door was closed, he handed the pad to James for his reaction. To his amazement, there was no change in James' demeanor. He merely studied the figures for a moment and then placed the pad on the table and looked at the banker awaiting his reaction.

Ramsdale was for the first time in many years unable to find the words to convey his amazement and puzzlement.

"You are probably the richest man in San Francisco today. This gold will certainly make you our largest depositor. You are a very young man to fall into such a fortune. You may have been a humble mountain man when you walked in here, but you will leave with the power to buy a kingdom. What do you intend to do with yourself and with all this wealth?"

"Well" James replied without emotion, "I got a partner and need to draw up some papers. There's more gold than this where this was found. I expect I'll head back and bring you some more if you're likely to take it."

"Jesus!" the banker exclaimed rising to his feet. "It isn't that I don't intend to take it, I just can't believe there's more. You are taking so calmly what would drive most men into a frenzy of delight." The banker thought for a moment then wondered if James was illiterate and did not understand the material that had been presented to him on the note pad. "You can read and understand those conclusions on that pad, can't you?" he asked.

"I can read alright and understand them figures. I don't mean to be a disappointment to you, but all that gold there is just different colored sand and has value only to them that got the lust for having the things it can buy. I will just take my time finding out about what I can and want to do with it. Right now I just want it off my hands and in a safe place. As I say I got a partner and want to take care of his interest too."

On the banker's advice, James opened up an account in his name and that of Cactus Jack Slade and deposited one hundred fifty thousand dollars into it and put four of the jars of gold into a safe deposit box allowing James the opportunity to decide later what he would do with the remaining gold.

"Don't be letting that gold sit in there too long now," banker Ramsdale advised, " If you don't put it to good use, you might just as well have left it on the bottom of that pond where you found it."

As he was being escorted from the bank, Ramsdale thought to enquire as to his lodging. "I don't have any place to bunk up for the night, but I expect there be some lodging about," James replied.

"I don't want to have to tell you, but this town is short a thousand beds a night. Men like you wondering into town end up sharing a bed with two or three other men. I suggest you talk to Captain Roscoe Gray. He's the guard you nearly skewered. He's staying aboard that schooner he sailed and might have accommodations more suitable than you'll find in town"

As they walked out of the conference room, the bank was empty of customers and the guards were busy securing the bank for the evening, checking doors, closing the shutters and making sure no one was left inside as the bank was secured. Banker Ramsdale motioned for Captain Gray and soon had made arrangements for James to spend the night on the Captain's schooner. As they left together, the Captain suggested where James could stable his horses and then led the way to the docks. Even thought it was growing dark, James could not help but notice that many of the ships were in such bad condition that he doubted they would ever set sail again. Some had already been scavenged for the valuable planking that was much needed in town.

The Captain's schooner, as they boarded, appeared to be in fairly good condition and had escaped the enterprise of the scavengers. James was led into the main cabin and was impressed with the clean and orderly condition he observed. As the Captain entered he picked up a bell from a credenza and rang it, giving James a sudden start. A Chinese servant quickly appeared from a side door and bowed to the Captain.

"There'll be company for dinner Won, now bring us some of that heathen brew and let us be."

Noticing the quizzical look on James' face, the Captain chuckled and volunteered, "Won and a few other Chinese have worked on this Schooner for several passages now. Unlike the ruddy sailors that brought this ship in, they are indentured to service and will honor their agreement. Most of my pay goes to keeping them aboard. If not for them this vessel would be listing and settling like the rest of the vessels in the harbor."

Jack once again tried to partake of the grog that the Captain offered, but found it foul and declined to drink more. When the meal was served, James just stared at the plate of noodles, vegetables and meats that steamed temptingly on his plate and was at a loss as to what to do with it. Several long sticks were placed beside his plate, but no other utensils were in evidence. The Captain, noticing his distress called Won back into the room and in obvious good humor told him to bring the guest some heathen tools to eat with.

James spent the next three days wandering about the town speaking to various business men and merchants, having been given a letter of introduction from Banker Ramsdale. He also spent long hours talking to Captain Gray about his adventures at sea and about the ships abandoned in the harbor. He was surprised to be informed that many of the vessels still had on board the cargo that they brought into port, but because of the flight of the crews remained unloaded, much of it being destroyed by the elements. Jack was much impressed with the Captain. His solitary efforts to preserve his vessel when even the owners seemed to have abandoned the Captain and the vessel indicated to James that the man had a solid character. The fact that he used his own meager earnings to honor the commitment made to the indentured Chinese impressed him even more.

Having had lengthy conferences with the lawyer banker Ramsdale recommended, James had set his mind on how to put his fortune to good use as the banker had recommended.

When they finished their third meal aboard the vessel, James confronted the Captain with his plan.

"I need a man like yourself, Captain Gray, to go into business with me. I have some funds available and want to put them to use. I suspect that you are not suited to be a bank guard and would like to be back at sea or at least going about the business that sea merchants are most able to do."

The Captain, who had been morosely contemplating his cup of grog, pushed it aside and looked intently at James.

"What have you got in mind son, I'd walk the plank if it meant going to sea again."

James then advised him of the deposit of money and gold reserves he had available and how he intended to put a part of it to use. "You say there are ships with cargo yet to be unloaded. My lawyer tells me we can claim the cargo and the ships for unpaid moorage. I purchased the dockage about here today, and all of these vessel owners are owing to me for their moorage. Most won't pay. I want you to go aboard these vessels that are abandoned and claim and salvage the cargo. The vessels that won't sail again are to be stripped down and the lumber sold in town. They are frantic to have lumber and no ships are coming in. I know this is probably distasteful business for a man who made his living sailing these vessels, but they have got to be cleared out of the harbor. Now here comes the part I think you will like. I want you to pick out the five best schooners that are suitable for hauling lumber. Those vessels you are to command and move up the Pacific coast to the Oregon Territory and purchase all the lumber you can find and bring it back here to San Francisco and down to Los Angeles. Are you up to this task, Captain?"

James' answer came when the Captain sprang from the table upsetting his drink and pulled James from his chair and gave him a grizzly bear hug that took his breath away.

After several days conferring with lawyer Madison, who traced his linage to the late President, and a long conference with banker Ramsdale, the business venture was set in motion and James was on his way back to the Little Flower Claim, which was the name he gave the partnership between himself and Cactus Jack. At Sacramento he loaded up with the supplies Jack had requested and bought the sewing and cooking items that Little Flower had requested. He also bought for Little Flower some dresses, bonnets, shoes and bolts of cloth, not knowing what she would like but unconcerned if she chose to cast them all away. As an afterthought, he picked up several fashion magazines that were displayed on the counter of the merchandise company and added them to his purchases. By the time he was done with his purchasing, James needed two more pack animals to haul his purchases back to the claim. He spent that evening dining with Robert Peters, the assayer and in part satisfied his curiosity about the mining business. James had no idea how he could mine the ore and what equipment would be required to undertake that venture when it came time to expand the Little Flower Mine beyond the panning stage.

It took James two weeks to traverse the mountains and return to the claim and to Little Flower. After seeing the seamy side of the sex business practiced in the open along the water front in San Francisco, he was anxious to return to the arms of Little Flower where such matters could be conducted more discreetly and with the passion that he and Little Flower had found in each other's arms. As he rode into camp, he found that Little Flower and Cactus Jack had seen him crossing the desert headed toward them many miles away, and his arrival was met with whoops and hollers, back slapping from Jack and what was a first a tentative embrace from Little Flower. James had been gone for several months now and Little Flower was uncertain of her place in his life. When she felt his arms tighten about her lifting her off the ground in a grand embrace, she melted into his arms and buried her face in the hollow of his neck murmuring soft phrases that he couldn't understand but knew their meaning.

The rest of that day was spent unpacking the animals and examining the purchases James had made. To James' surprise, Little Flower was no longer talking in halting, fractured English, but was able to discourse in sentences although she had to stop occasionally until someone would supply her with the word she was intending. When asked about the change, Jack told him that they spent the evenings singing his long repertoire of songs and had learned more of the language singing along with him.

Little Flower was pleased with the pots and pans and sewing supplies James had purchased for her, but seemed mystified by the dresses and other items.

"It's what the ladies in San Francisco wear. It ain't no account, I thought you might like to get out of those buckskins one day, but use them for rags if you wish," James advised her. "Ain't no need to get gussied up out here."

Little Flower studied them carefully and then put them back in the bundles they were wrapped in and carried them into the tent where she remained for some time. When she returned to the camp fire and sat on the log beside James, she had the same questioning look about her that she had evidence when she first saw the garments he had bought for her. For the next several days when Jack and James got busy working the claim, Little Flower spent most of her time engrossed in the magazines that James had purchased.

James also noticed that Cactus Jack no longer had that tired, defeated look he wore when he first rode into camp. He looked younger, and possessed a good deal more energy. He had been busy panning gold during most of his absence and had accumulated four more bags of the precious metal tailings.

Jack and James spent several days falling trees and cutting them up into lumber slabs to build a sluice. James, having seen the other mines being worked, knew that the sluice would probably double their recovery efforts, but still harbored his general indifference to the riches that were being daily accumulated. When he asked Jack what he intended to do with all his riches, Jack had no coherent answer. It appeared to James that it was just Jack's nature to prospect and the riches had little value to him. Jack had told him a number of times that he had no desire to return to city life and at his age had no desire to return to the East where he could live in indolent luxury.

"Every since that lady of yours been feeding me that brew she makes, I been feeling like a sprout again. Someday I'll use some of that money to buy me a place in an old folk's home, or I may just pass my life here and let you have the fuss of spending all that money you say we got."

"We seem to be doing a lot of work to get richer than neither of us care to be." James offered, "When I take these latest tailings to San Francisco that banker's gonna' ask me again what I want to do with it. There must be something you would spend it on."

"Give it to them poor folks that's always beggin' in them streets," Jack responded dismissively, obviously disinterested in the topic of the conversation.

James knew that he must make another trip over the mountains to take their latest tailings to San Francisco, but was delaying the trip as long as possible. He was enjoying the companionship of Little Flower and the unaffected friendliness of Cactus Jack. San Francisco had been a trial to him yet he had a foreboding conviction that all this money would eventually draw him there and away from this idyllic life he was leading. And there still remained the question of Little Flower. She would not be accepted in San Francisco, yet he had not the heart to send her back to her people as was the custom of the mountain men when they tired of the company of their Indian wife. He could not ignore the fact that she had nursed him back to health and he owed to her his very life.

Both he and Little Flower, without the other's awareness, had been channeling their thoughts along the same path. Little Flower knew that she could not live much longer the life that had become so satisfying to her. She loved James in a way she could never have loved Parker. Parker was older than she and was a man without much cause for existence once the fur trade had declined. He had taken to living about the Forts, often drinking to excess and otherwise idling away his life. He was fun to be with, but she knew there was no future with Parker. She had urged him to go find his friend Franco in hopes that Franco could encourage him to take up some good purpose. When they arrived at Fort Boise and found that Franco had headed to California to the gold fields, she had been pleased when Parker set out after him.

The Indian attack that took Parker from her should have ended her life also. At the worst, she could have been taken by the Shoshone as a slave and returned to the deprivations that she had fled from when Franco had found her up on the Yellowstone. Her time with James had been quite different than she had expected. He treated her differently than the other men. At first, he would not even sleep with her and when he did he was not rough and demanding as the others had been. He was gentle and carrying around her at all times. At first she assumed that he was not interested in her, but she now knew he was a different kind of man and she never wanted to leave him. When James brought the finery that white women wore back from San Francisco, and the book with all the pictures of the fine ladies, Little Flower thought he was intending to convey to her a message. She assumed he wanted her to be like these ladies and that it would please him if she were.

And so it was that when the time for James' leaving drew near Little Flower decided that she would be his lady like the ladies in the books. She worked several days with great care to alter the red dress he had brought. She thought the bustle in back was silly and removed it. She took the fluff out of the sleeves and shortened the hem so it would not drag about on the ground. The shoes did not fit so she discarded them and put on the high topped beaded moccasins she had made while he was gone. Her long silken black hair she made into a braid and swirled it about her head in the fashion of one of the ladies in the book. Satisfied she had done her best, and knowing his time for leaving was near, she waited for him one afternoon in the lodge, knowing when she was not tending to the cooking; he could come looking for her.

When James returned to camp he did notice Little Flower's absence. Looking at the remnants of the dying cooking fire and the congealing stew that hung above it, he feared that some harm had befallen Little Flower. He dropped his tools and half sprinted to the lodge. Upon entering he stood totally immobilized by the sight before him. Little Flower was standing in the middle of the tent where the last rays of the western sun bathed her in a soft brilliance.

The red dress caught the sheen of her oaken skin; her dark luminous eyes that had the sparkle of the mischievous. James could not speak nor move; he had seen nothing so breathlessly beautiful in his life. Little Flower did not know what reaction she might get when she prepared her surprise, but was unprepared for the stunned look she received from James and had a momentary fear that she might have offended him. When he finally got his wits about him and spoke she was overjoyed.

"My God, Little Flower, you are beautiful!" He wanted to rush up to her and devour her, but looking at his grimy hands and sweat soiled clothes he held back.

"I'm going up to the pool and take a bath and shuck these dirty clothes. You wait right here until I get back and don't change a thing," he commanded as he grabbed clean pants and shirt and sprinted from the lodge.

Little Flower was so overjoyed that she wanted to rush to the pool with him, but thought better of the idea. She wanted him by her side in the privacy of their lodge when they were together again. Most of all she wanted him to be the one to remove the dress she had so carefully fashioned for this moment. In her heart she now had that warm certainty that she had now pulled James into her orbit and that he was now and would forever be, her man!

The return to the coast was a dutiful affair for James and he was anxious to get his business over with and return to the Claim and Little Flower. As he traveled over the mountains, he noticed more and more abandoned claims. Those that remained operational had turned to commercial mining and were disgorging the valleys of their substance and despoiling the waters that had once ran clear and sparkling to the valleys beyond. He thought of the valley that had been his home for more than a year now and tried to envision what it would look like if it were submitted to the extraction methods that raged through the northern valleys of California. It was not a prospect that gave him comfort.

When he reached Sacramento he met again with Robert Peters and got the latest mining news. The flurry of activity that had confronted him when he first came to Sacramento had abated and was replaced by more deliberate and sustainable endeavors. The main street had been paved with cobble stones which replaced the noise of cursing and shouting of the teamsters who slogged through the mud with the clattering rhythms of steel wheeled carriages and dozens of shod animals. The buildings were more substantial and there were no more tented structures in evidence.

"Lot of the mines has played out," Peters told him, "and those that lost out have come back to town and returned to their profession as carpenters and artisans. We even had a packet that goes daily between there and San Francisco carrying passengers and goods. You might want to take that and leave your animals here. It's a nuisance having them about in San Francisco now, besides they have carriage service that will take you where ever you want to go now."

Peters advised him that Fremont had gone back east and would probably not return. "They are already clamoring to make California a state of the Union and Fremont's meant to play a hand in that. Right now things are all tied up in the sticky business over slavery. Some want California to come in as a slave state and others not. Upsets the balance of power back there. A messy business that. California's a place for free men and I'd rather we stay a Territory than be committed to the travesty of allowing human bondage."

"My father was strong on that issue," James mused. "Caused him a peck of trouble and his fearing a rebellion over the matter was partly why we came west."

"We have a good number of those colored people fleeing out here to escape that abominable institution. Lot of them have been freed, thank God. Wouldn't want them bounty hunters running around here gathering them up and taking them back East. Be a bad business! Our laws don't allow it now."

After his conversation, and as he made arrangements for the care of his animals, James took notice that the population was becoming more mixed. There were several Chinese businesses and a number of black men were driving the carriages and working as labors about town. There was a distinctive Hispanic presence about the town. California was going to be a different kind of place.

San Francisco was, like Sacramento, catching up with its growth pains. Thousands of people a day had streamed through the town at the height of the gold rush. Many of them were now filtering back into town and taking up employment and occupations that benefited the formation of what was fast becoming a great trading center. Banker Ramsdale's bank had now been completed and a new floor was being added to the structure. James found a warm welcome there and after again going through the detailed process of depositing the new gold, he and the banker sat down for a long meeting.

"That move you made to purchase the water front was a master stroke. Captain Gray has made you a fortune. His deposit books are right here for your inspection. Selling those distressed ships for their lumber made you a profit right off. The cargo he recovered he made a lot of money on. He's a shrewd businessman and was able to avoid delays and hassle by accounting for his sales of the cargo and sharing the profits with the owner. Could still have the lawyers fighting over the spoils otherwise. Most important, he got the port cleared up. Now that the sailors are looking for work again the ships are carrying goods instead of being used as floating hotels and rats nests.

"Captain Gray is up north, but should be back in a week. He's got a real lumber operation going and there's people scrambling to get a piece of his next shipment. I loaned him money on your account to buy more ships so he could get down to Los Angeles where the demand for lumber is even greater than it is here. He's been a busy man."

James studied the bank's books covering the Captain's activities and was dizzied by the volume. He was impressed with the detail the Captain provided to the bank to support his dealings. He had made a good choice in the Captain, but now he had even greater plans for him.

The next day was spent with lawyer Madison, whose office had also expanded. There were now five lawyers busily engaged in servicing a variety of clients, most of them new businessmen eager for his services. Once again James found the records to be in good order. The Captain had been religious in complying with James' request that the lawyer be kept advised of his activities and finalizes any business relationships. Lawyer Madison was also very impressed with the Captain.

"I never met a more honest and capable man. You did well to employ him," The lawyer assured him.

James was able to find suitable hotel accommodations on this trip and without the Captain being in town, had time to spare as he waited for his return. There was little need for his intervention in the Captain's dealings, he only wanted to discuss them with him and talk to him about further expansion. The city was growing up around him. His appearance, in his buckskins, moccasins, and sheath knife, once common was now looked upon by passersby as threatening or inappropriate. When a dining room declined to seat him he was non-plused. He had the recourses to buy the whole building that housed the restaurant, but couldn't buy a meal. The next day he went to a tailor to order a suit of clothes. When he entered the shop, he was met with indifference and received the usual suspicious glances from the other patrons. James now had the message these people emoted. He was looked upon by them as part of the riff raff that the city no longer wanted in its better environment. After waiting several moments for service, James walked over to the counter, pulled from his belt pouch a handful of gold coins and slapped them with a clattering slam on the counter.

"I'll have some service," he demanded, "either that or I'll buy this damn place and throw you all out onto the street!"

There was a shocked silence as all eyes turned to him. No one moved until a nervous tailor who had been measuring a prosperous looking business man for a suit of clothes, dropped his tape and pin cushions and hurried over to where James was standing with every intention of demanding he leave the premises before he had him removed by the police. When the man approached James and realized that the clattering noise was made by dozens of gold coins that now lay scattered about the counter and the floor, he stopped abruptly and looked James over. His attitude immediately changed. This was not a man he wanted to tangle with. That bear claw necklace and huge knife was threatening evidence that this well built stranger should be treated with caution. It was all that gold that finally got the man's attention. With what dignity the man could manage by bent over and retrieved the coins, joined by another employee they soon had them all gathered up and placed on the counter in neat stacks. The proprietor, who had been the first to approach James, knew without counting that there was more than a year of his earning sitting on the counter.

James was learning fast that money had a power of its own, and those who had it could call the tune. He was not a second class citizen and he would no longer tolerate being treated like one.

"I'm sorry, sir," The tailor stammered, "I was measuring Mr. Pondexter for a new suit and meant to be right with you."

"Mr. Pondexter can wait, he already has a suit as you can plainly see," James retorted.

The tailor was clearly distressed now as he glanced first at the coins on the counter and then at the waiting Mr. Pondexter.

"Sir," the tailor said with a distressed sigh, "I apologize again for any discourteousy I've been responsible for and will be with you as soon as I can. May I ask you to look over our material samples while I finish with Mr. Pondexter? Would you like some tea while you wait?"

James was impressed with the pluck of the man who stood his ground and was not stampeded by his presence and money.

"You go ahead and take care of the gentleman. When you are through, perhaps you can come to my hotel room and we can take care of the measuring. I'll trust you to pick out the materials for a suitable set of clothes, but I'll need them promptly and will be glad to pay your price."

The proprietor was pleased at the way things were going; he had saved the prospects for a profitable business and in turn he didn't need to offend Mr. Pondexter, one of his better customers.

The tailor, who introduced himself as Frank Zimmerman, wrote down the address of James' hotel and promised to be there within the hour. He was curious as to whom this James Rawlins was and as he continued his measurements of Mr. Pondexter, asked Pondexter if he knew anything about the man.

"I can't say I know the man, but I saw him at the Ramsdale Bank the other day. I have the feeling he's a man we will be hearing from a lot more. When you go up to his hotel room, I'd appreciate it if you would give him my card." He handed the tailor his business card which was embossed with gold letters and read: "John Pondexter, Real Estate and Investment Co.," and gave an address nearby.

"Just tell him I'd like to meet him. Tell him I'd like to see his new suit."

The tailor smiled at the reference to the new suit. "I'm sure you will be impressed."

Tailor Zimmerman reached James hotel room within the hour as promised and did deliver Mr. Pondexter's card and message. James laid the card on the table and gave it no further thought and he and the tailor got about the business of measuring and discussing preferences.

"I knew you might be interested in having a suit you could wear right away while I complete your wardrobe, so I brought along a suit I made for another fellow about your size who had a misfortune and will not be able to pick up his suit. I can have it altered and deliver it this afternoon."

"I would appreciate it. I hope you will assist me in picking out the rest of my clothes. I've been living in the mountains for the past several years and don't have any of the clothes that these city people wear. I don't want any of them stiff collars or neck pieces they wear though; don't see how they breath with their necks all tied up like a strung up turkey."

When the tailor returned that afternoon he had underclothes, several white silk shirts, socks, tall leather boots and a low crowned, broad brimmed black hat.

By the time James had finished dressing as the tailor fussed about, he looked at himself in the mirror and was satisfied. When he reached for his bear claw necklace, the tailor told him that it wouldn't do.

"Every since I wore this piece, my luck has been more then tolerable. I don't aim to ever be without it," James responded. He then picked up the knife and belt and put that on also. It was partially hidden by the tail of the long tailed black coat that the tailor had fashioned for him. The tailor shook his head realizing his advice was not wanted when it came to necklace or the knife. He was dealing with a man of the frontier who would not be tamed overnight.

In spite of the tailor's concern, James made a striking presence in his black suit with his pants stuffed into the high, black, highly polished English riding boots. The necklace and belt knife added to the mystery and menace that he intended. The next day, James hired a buggy and instructed the driver to give him a tour of the city. He was taken to the Presidio where he expected to see a large military presence. The place was virtually deserted. The soldiers like the sailors had abandoned their positions in droves, but unlike the sailors, they would not be returning as they all faced charges of desertion. Many of the buildings had been abandoned only partially completed and were just now showing signs of renewed activity. It was while he was being driven through the better parts of the town, traveling the hills overlooking the city that he noticed a large home that was partially completed, but deserted. It had what appeared to be legal notices tacked to the door. James stopped the carriage and walked over the grounds and inspected what he could of the property. The view was outstanding and the house showed promise if completed. The notice on the door indicated that the property was in the state of foreclosure. James remembered then the card he had received from the tailor regarding some Real Estate company. When he returned to his room he retrieved the card and headed down the street to the offices of John Pondexter.

When he inquired of the receptionist regarding the property, she asked him to be seated and she would get someone to help him. The person who came from the outer office was the owner John Pondexter.

"I'll see to the gentleman, Miss Oliver, "he announced as he came forward to introduce himself. "I see you were able to get fitted." Pondexter remarked to give emphasis to the fact that he was the man in the tailor shop who was advised he already had a suit. "Mr. Zimmerman is the best tailor you'll find. Now how may I assist you?"

When told of his interest on the property atop Signal Hill, Mr. Pondexter acknowledged that he was aware of the property, but did not represent the seller whom he believed to be a mortgage company owned by a friend of his.

"May I look into the matter and get back to you?"

James agreed to come back the next day and find out what Pondexter discovered regarding the property.

"Yes, that property was just put on the market." Pondexter advised him the next morning. "A sad one that. A Mr. Bisbee was building that for his bride. She's in North Carolina. Poor fellow went down at sea when the boat he was traveling on floundered trying to make the passage around the horn of South America. He was returning to fetch his bride. Actually the bank owns it now having put up the money. You could make a good buy on that piece."

James arranged to have another look at the property, but asked Pondexter to find the builder and meet with them at the property.

"I may be interested in buying the property, but I have to know what's to be needed to complete it and how soon it could be done," James advised Pondexter. "It seems I will have to spend some time here and I don't cater to hotels."

They spent several hours going over the property and James listened to the architect and builders discuss the costs and details of the continued construction. James found all the talk about balustrades, candelabras, cornices, tera cotta, Walnut or Oak, Philippine Mahogany or Teak, all rather beyond him. He asked them to meet with him at Lawyer Madison's office the next day with their final estimates and be ready to close the deal. Pondexter, before setting up the arrangement to view the house, had taken the effort to find out who this brash stranger really was. His inquiry led him to the Ramsdale Bank where he was advised merely that James Rawlins was their largest depositor and not to worry about his ability to purchase any property he wanted. When Pondexter advised the architect, the builder and the mortgage company of James' worth, they were falling over each other to respond to his every request. They all had money owing to them and saw now not just the prospect of breaking even, but the hopes of laying the ground work for future profit.

When James entered the office, he wore a gray top coat that had black trim about the lapels, a black silk shirt with a ruffled front, gray trousers that he wore outside of his English boots. He was a picture of fashion. Even the necklace and Bowie knife added to the boldness of his attire.

"Gentlemen," he announced when the group met in Madison's plush conference room, "I have decided to buy the property and will pay you according to your estimates. I don't want to get messed up in all the details about what kind of wood I want here or what kind of marble I want there.

I don't know a damn thing about such matters, that's your business. You make the choices and if you need to change your estimates that will be no problem. I just advise you, I can be a good friend or an intolerable enemy. Just treat me fair and be honest with me and we will get along just fine. Mr. Ramsdale at the bank has been authorized to pay the vouchers you present as your progress justifies it. Just sign the papers Mr. Madison has prepared and we can get things going. I don't care for all that French stuff some here are crazy about. I am more impressed with the haciendas about here than I am with all that fancy, frilly stuff. I don't know if what I request will fit with the present structure. If it doesn't tear it down. I expect to be back in the spring and expect that you will have the place ready for me by then.

Having given these instructions, James said his goodbyes and left the conference leaving the details to be handled by lawyer Madison. James was getting restless and wanted to get back to Little Flower and away from the constant noise and endless activity of the city, yet in his heart, he knew the many commitments he was making would eventually bring an end to his carefree life in the mountains. To that end, he set about conferring with various businessmen who had some knowledge of the lumber business and timber industry. It was while meeting with his banker that he randomly brought up the subject of his partner and his lack of concern for his wealth, a part of which was in the accounts that James had set up.

"He tells me to give it to the beggars in the street and not bother him about it," James said intending humor.

To James' surprise, the banker was giving some thought to the suggestion. "There is a need for charity in this town. My wife, Linda, has a group of friends you may want to talk to about your friend. I don't pay much attention to what they're up to. They want to be a part of things and don't think we business people have enough care for the less fortunate in this community.

"Why don't you come to dinner at our house tonight and I will have you meet Linda. You might just get some ideas to present to your friend, this Cactus Jack fellow."

James accepted the invitation. He found the banker's home to be but a few blocks from the home he had just purchased. It was a large two story structure with a dozen gables graced with elaborate millwork. The house was as he anticipated; the banker and his wife liked that French furniture that he found frivolous. The heavy valet draperies and silk furniture coverings made him uncomfortable. On the other hand, he found Linda to be a small, intense, and warm hearted creature that he immediately felt comfortable with. She was an attractive woman but not one you would call beautiful, she had a high forehead, a nose a bit too large and thin lips that belied her natural humor. She had what one could call an austere appearance one would expect of a banker's wife. On the other hand, she would smile with ease and was inclined to be intimate enough with those she liked to touch them when engaged in serious discussions.

And so it was that at the dinner table, James found that she had placed her hand atop his as they discussed the needs of the underprivileged in the city. At first James' inclination was to withdraw his hand, but found he liked the warm intimacy of the gesture.

"They are not bad people," she was telling him, "Many of them came here with false hopes and have run out of money. Many can't find work even when there is such a need in this town because they have no tools and have no clothes to dress decent enough to work in a reputable establishment. Some are just passing through and have been robbed or lost their belongings and need food and lodging. We have all kinds, not all of them pleasant. But there just aren't enough business people who care about them and there certainly isn't enough money being donated to carry on with the mission we have established."

"What is the problem with the mission? James asked.

"We are about to lose our lease. When the ships weren't coming in, there was no need for the storage sheds by the dock and we were given one to use. Now the traffic is picking up and we have been told we will have to pay for the premises and the price is beyond our meager recourses."

The next day James and Linda went to the storage shed used by the charity and James found it not to his liking. It was unheated and rodent infested and indeed more suited for a warehouse than a place of charity.

"It is not a question of the money," James assured her, "My partner has enough to spare for you purposes. Let's have a visit with John Pondexter and see if he can find some more suitable facilities."

The next day James found himself back in Lawyer Madison's offices setting up yet another enterprise, this time a charitable trust in the name of Cactus Jack Slade. James made sure it was well funded and later that day approved of a site that Linda Ramsdale had selected, which was a small hotel that needed restoration. By the time this last business had been put to rest, James was anxious to be gone from the city, but still there was no Captain Gray.

James' activities, his dress and his inquiries about town combined to make his presence known. He was unaware of the attention he was getting until one morning a reporter from the *Chronicle* knocked on his hotel room door and asked to interview him for an article in the paper. James hadn't anticipated that his activities would be of any interest, and was taken aback by the request, but assented to an interview. He told the reporter about his travels along the Oregon Trail which he thought were of no consequence, but when the reporter started asking him about the necklace and the Knife and how he came into possession of them, he noticed that the reporter was showing a great deal more interest. He told him of the massacre at the Sublette Cutoff and the one in Oregon and his travels through the wilderness. When it came to questions regarding how he gained his fortune, however, James ended the interview.

A few days later, the clerk at the desk at his hotel stopped him as he was heading out of the lobby and asked him if he had read the article about himself in the paper. He gave James a copy of the local paper which James carried with him to breakfast where he intended to read it at leisure. James was stunned at the report. He was made out to be a western hero in the same league as Kit Carson and Charles Fremont. He was an Indian fighter and explorer, a fierce duelist and a philanthropist. His extensive business in the shipping business and ownership of the dockyards were revealed as was the fact that he had contracted for the construction of a "mansion." There was even a sketch of him in the paper that overplayed the necklace and the Bowie knife making him look almost like a desperado. The article made him overnight one of San Francisco's most sought after guests.

James suddenly found he could hardly walk the streets without people staring at him or pointing him out. It was a relief to him therefore when he walked from the hotel one morning and saw a large black sailing ship; its decks brimmed with lumber, coming into the harbor. Captain Gray was back in town. As he reached the dock, the vessel was already being moored. Passing beneath the bow of the ship, he looked up to see the gold letters of the ship's name. It was the *Grizzly Rawlins*. Captain Gray had remembered the story of James' first Indian encounter. James remembered that he'd mentioned, but only in passing and with intended incredulity, that the members of the wagon train had given him that name. James didn't know whether to be grateful or angry over this naming he had no part of. His recent experience brought on by the newspaper article did not please James and one more bit of notoriety was not welcome.

When the gang plank was lowered, James hurried aboard. The boson having no idea who he was and assuming him to be a prospective buyer for the cargo, halted him at the gangway and advised him that no one was allowed aboard until the customs officials had inspected the ships manifest and cleared the cargo.

"I'll see Captain Gray, if you don't mind. Advise him that Grizzly Rawlins is aboard."

The boson gave James a startled look and then did a quick about face, "Follow me sir, the Captain is on the forecastle reaming the helmsman for putting the ship too hard against the dock."

At the mention of the helmsman's distress, James could now hear the Captain berating the unfortunate helmsman in language James had not heard before. In the midst of the tirade, the Captain, looking over the shoulder of the helmsman, saw James being led toward him.

"I've had my say now lad," he told the helmsman. "Take mind of what I said and now be gone with you."

As the helmsman made a hasty retreat, Captain Gray's demeanor changed immediately as he strode quickly forward to greet James.

"By Jove, I wondered when I'd set eyes on you again. I've been spending your money like a sailor on liberty. I been needin' to get your opinion and approval on what I've been up to. Thought I'd have to go wandering over them mountains and find you. Come to my cabin, I got lots to go over. You may want to throw me to the sharks, but let's have a pint of grog a' for you do.

The Captain had indeed been spending his money, but, like banker Ramsdale had informed him, the Captain's efforts were now returning ample profit.

"When you left and gave me the purse strings, I went about them ships strung all over the place and found out which was the good ones and which one had cargo that was worth saving. I found a good number of them Chinese who was stranded when the crews ran off. I hired a passel of them and used them as the work crews to set about clearing out the cargos and dismantling them ships that wasn't worth salvaging. The owners was more'n glad to get some money for their cargo and ships. I ended up buying eight of them, more'n I needed right off, but you'd never be able to get them for that price again. Right now we may be need'n more. There's mills opening up north in California, along the Oregon coast and up to the Puget Sound. They can't keep up with what's needed here and down south in Los Angeles."

James was pleased at what he heard and after only a cursory review of the Captain's books which seemed in good order, James got down to the subject that had been highest on his mind every since he had made his enquiries about town and had a good idea of the growth potential once California became a state a prospect that was appearing more and more likely.

"We need to be sure we have a steady cargo for these vessels. If you need more ships, let's be for getting them. I want you to look at some of those mills that are opening up on the coast and see if you can buy them. Those mills will need a timber supply. See if timber lands can be bought. You may need to hire one of them operators that knows the timber business and get him to working on those acquisitions. I want you to concentrate on the shipping end of things and running this port. I've talked to Ramsdale about these ideas and he will make the money available. We'll be forming a corporation. We'll call it Little Flower Enterprises. I know it doesn't sound like much of a name, but I like it."

The Captain sat back and whistled when James had finished laying out his plans. "You are an ambitious rascal, and I love it. I don't know how long you think you can operate the kind of enterprise you are starting up and keep relying on other people to do your bidding. I'll be more than pleased to carry on with your plans. After all you saved me from becoming one of those wandering misfits you see about the docks. But it ain't comfortable spending the kind of money you are throwing my way without you being about to discuss matters. I'm a sea captain and you're relying on my smarts that ain't too abundant.'

James admired the Captain's candor and told him as much. James had come to the same conclusion himself, but was not ready to face up to the reality that he was no longer a man of the frontier and was being drawn forever away from the life he most desired. But the west was changing. The mountain men and explorers had had their day. The thousands upon thousands of emigrants flooding west along the Oregon Tail and the Santa Fe Trail would soon claim the lands that had once been the endless domain of the savage and the few brave white men who had opened the frontier. He remembered then the dying words of his mother foretelling a promising future for him that seemed now to be his.

The valley where he and Little Flower found their private paradise would soon be invaded by other prospectors and settlers who would challenge their possession and the wealth they and Cactus Jack had claimed. The decisions that had been made about the businesses he had launched seemed a natural consequence of trying to utilize the wealth that had come so effortlessly his way. But committing himself to the enterprises he had started affected not only his future, but that of Little Flower who had little appreciation for the dramatic alteration it would make to her life. Could he live a life half cosmopolitan and half native without destroying the possessor of either?"

BOOK III

CLAY GOES EAST

The dew of the morning rested heavily on the Clay's blankets as he rose for the last time in view of the camp site where his comrades had perished. He knew he must get moving as the horizon gave grim evidence that winter would soon envelop the land about him. The mountains off in the distance were no longer the verdant green that had dominated them just days ago. The snow had claimed the high mountains and filled the valleys. He also knew that the savages that had attacked the encampment below were to the northwest and would not tolerate his presence. His best chance was to backtrack or perhaps to head for the Mormon settlements around the Great Salt Sea. He decided the later route would serve him best as it would take him away from the descending storms driving winter onto the plains.

As he rode easterly that morning he made one last stop at the rock mounded grave site where he had interned his friends. He had been in the habit of riding alone for long periods while hunting, but such travels always ended when he returned to camp and to the company of friends. Other than his brother and father who had headed on to Oregon, he was now not only alone, he had been cast adrift and had only his own resourses to guide him. Tears formed in his eyes and his throat constricted as he tried to form the words that would at last commit the bodies of Franco, Parker and Wayne to their eternal rest. He wondered again what fate may have befallen James. One thing he was sure of, James would have suffered greatly at the hands of those who had overwhelmed the camp of the California bound gold seekers.

There seemed little need for caution as he traveled eastward. There was no sign that the barren lands he traveled had ever been inhabited or for that matter had ever been traversed by any but four legged creatures and as to them there was only slight evidence. Clay had the grim foreboding that he could travel this land forever and never see any sign of life. His recollection of the maps he had studied would have put the wagon trails to California well to the south and the trails to Oregon well to the north. At this time of year, he doubted that anyone would be traveling those routes, but finding a trail would at least give him guidance. As it was, he feared that he might travel in circles as there were few distinguishing land marks that he could use to guide him. With this thought in mind, he tried to steer a course more southerly to pick up a wagon trail into northern California and follow it toward the Mormon settlements.

On his third day of travel he came upon a large fresh water lake where he camped for several days and was able to shoot some water fowl and a small doe. He wandered the shores of the lake to find any sign of human presence, either friend of hostile. He found only faint sign of several old campsites, no doubt Indian. Having provided for his food needs, but before he could move on, he awoke the next morning to a threatening sky and a chill wind driving a large weather front toward the lake.

Clay took refuse in a nearby grove of trees and huddled within the embrace of some dead fall. As he anticipated, the storm brought a raging snow storm that soon covered the land and drove the temperature below freezing. The storm lasted for two days, but before he could move on, another storm was upon him. When the storm finally abated, the snow was too deep for his horses to manage. Clay struggled about the snow bound land attempting to build a better shelter and collect enough wood to keep a fire going. His biggest concern now was feed for his animals. They could not find graze under the heavy blanket of snow. As he burrowed into his scant shelter that night, he knew that on the morrow he would somehow have to move on or perish. He awoke the next morning to a drip, drip, drip on his blankets. Struggling out of his shelter, he stood awash in the sun's warming brightness. The storm had passed and a warm front was moving onto the plains. As Clay struggled through the melting, receding snow, he well knew that another cold front would soon be coming and would no doubt put him in the grip of a relentless winter from which he would not escape.

The skies had been overcast for the past several days and Clay was uncertain of his direction without the sun's guidance to give him his bearings. Thus it was that he wandered down into a high mountain meadow and followed the course of a meandering stream, thinking it would lead him to a larger water course and eventually to civilization. At the far end of the valley he came across Indian sign, and though not recent he estimated the sign to be several months old. As he progressed, the sign became more evident as the path he was on was no doubt traveled by the Indians. As he followed the trail, he came upon what appeared to be discarded cook ware and an occasional piece of cloth caught on the sage brush, fluttering in the gentle breeze. He realized then that he was following in the opposite direction the path made by a war party that had been returning from a raid. As he crested a small rise he came within sight of the object of the raiding party's objective.

It was a scene now familiar to him. The shattered remains of a wagon train lay scattered about the valley floor. He rode to the scene and dismounted then walked slowly among skeletal remains of what had once been a large wagon train. There was sign all about to give evidence of an Indian attack, but Clay found the evidence before him confusing. It appeared that many of the remains that appeared to be of the men were lying in a tight bunch. There were no arrow wounds evident. Most had died of bullet holes to the head. The women and children appeared to have died by wounds inflicted by Indian arrows, tomahawks, or from bludgeoning which one would expect from an Indian attack.

Although the sign was old, Clay could make out the sign of both unshod and shod hoof prints. Clay became convinced that some of the killing, especially of the men had been done by white men. The fact that their bodies were separate from the women and children convinced him that they had been unarmed and killed in execution style. ([12])

Clay was not unmindful of the persecution and killing that had driven the Mormons to the area around the Great Salt Sea. The Mormon Nauvoo Legion had been formed back in Nauvoo, Illinois to defend that community from the prejudices and hostility that drove the Mormons from Missouri. The Legion was known for its hostility toward the encroachment of the

---

[12] Review-Blood of the Prophets: Brigham Young and the Massacre at Mountain Meadows   http://atheism.about.com/library/books/full/aafprBloodProphets.htm?terms=go

emigrants onto their sanctuary lands. The brutality of their expulsion from Missouri festered in their memories. Clay suspected that these emigrants, whose remains and possessions lay scattered about, had somehow brought down upon themselves the vengeance of the Mormons. If his suspicions were correct, which be believed them to be, he may not be welcome around their settlements, especially if they suspected he had knowledge of the slaughter that had occurred about these meadows. This conviction caused him to turn north and attempt to reach Fort Boise and to winter within its confines.

Fort Boise, the scene of frenzied activity when he had last visited it in September, was now deserted by the Indians who had gone into winter camp. The wagon trains had all passed through and the Fort seemed almost deserted as Clay rode unnoticed through the gates. He rode to the factors office and upon knocking at the door was told to come in. To his surprise, it was not the factor he had met before who awaited him. A dragoon in the uniform of the United States army sat at a small desk and glanced at him suspiciously as he stood in the doorway gathering his composure.

"Shut the damn door you bumpkin!" the man at the desk who wore the stripes of a Sergeant demanded. "It's hard enough to keep this pest hole warm without that door being open."

Clay shut the door as requested and stood to size up the Sergeant who had insulted him. The Sergeant, who now stood up as Clay approached his desk in a swift stride, proved to be a half a head taller than Clay and equally menacing in his appearance.

Clay had his hand on the handle of the knife he wore at his belt as he addressed the Sergeant. "You've no call to be cantankerous. I've been away from this fort for the past several months and wasn't expecting to see that the United States Army had taken over the place. But army or no, I don't take to your attitude. Who commands this place you call a pest hole?"

The Sergeant, no doubt realizing he had no cause to confront this stranger and realizing also that his hostility at being stationed in this forsaken place for the winter was the burr under his blanket that caused his surliness, sat back down and waived Clay to the chair near the desk.

"Best have a sit. The Captain is over at the barracks checking on a soldier who damn near chopped his foot off trying to split fire wood. He'll be along any moment. Where you comin' from and what puts you out in this shitty weather?"

Clay, still smarting from the Sergeant's initial greeting, was not disposed to be conversant. He had a good deal to report, but didn't care to have the Sergeant included among those he would share his report.

"I came here believing the place was still owned by the Hudson Bay outfit and wanted to make arrangements to winter here. I wasn't expecting to see you sitting behind that desk and was a little surprised."

"Well, that's why we put that flag out there over the stockade," the Sergeant retorted reverting to his surliness. "Spect you'd have noticed."

"It did make me curious," Clay came back to match the insult," But when I came through the gate without a sign of the sentry or a uniform, I assumed no respectable army was in charge."

At that remark, the Sergeant jumped to his feet and slammed his fist on the desk causing Clay to grab for his knife and prepare to defend himself. To his relief, however, the Sergeants anger was not directed toward him.

"That goddamned Irishman! I'll find that bottle of his and bust him over the head with it!" He then stormed out of the office slamming the door behind him.

As Clay settled back down in the chair, he could hear the Sergeant bellowing, "Flannigan! Where the hell are you? I'll hang you by the ankles you bloody sot!"

The heat of the stove gave Clay the first real warmth he had had for months. What with that warmth, the fatigue of his long ride, and the sudden realization that he was no longer in imminent danger Clay began to doze while still sitting in the chair. When the door swung open and the Captain entered, Clay's reaction was instinctive. He jumped to his feet fully awake and ready to defend himself. The Captain, expecting to find only his Sergeant in attendance was equally startled, but quickly recovered.

"What did you do to the Sergeant? He asked. "And what may I ask is your business here?"

"Sorry," Clay said relaxing and taking his hand away from his knife. "I've been a time wandering about the wilderness. I fear I have forgotten my manners. I am Clay Anderson. I wasn't expecting to find an army post out here. I was looking for a place to ride out the winter. I guess I got some things to say that would be army business and am glad I don't have to go hunting you down."

"If you know anything about this country, you will be welcome to stay the winter. All the troopers I have in my command have never been in the west and get lost going to the latrine. They were what was left over when Taylor and Scott selected the best to fight the Mexicans. Come on into my office and let's hear what you have to say."

The Captain, who introduced himself as Captain Richardson, was a man of Clay's stature, with clear blue eyes, a prominent handle bar mustache and walked with a slight limp. As he sat down, he extended his leg and winched with evident pain. Seeing that Clay noticed his discomfort he remarked off handedly: "Took a musket ball at Vera Cruz. The army was intending to cahier me out, but instead gave me this unfortunate command. But forgive me for my grousing. What is it you think would interest the army?"

Clay related this experience with the ambush in Oregon Territory and the one at the Mountain Meadows. The Captain listened intently and when Clay was finished he remarked that he would have to make a report of the conversation.

"I'll have the Sergeant show you to some quarters. If you would be so kind as to be back here in the morning, I would like you to go over my report and make sure I have the details right. Meanwhile, you can mess with the men if you like. The Sergeant will see to your animals."

Clay declined the offer to bed down in the barracks after being shown about. "I think I'd rather sleep with my horse than be sleeping elbow to elbow with your men. I've been too long sleeping under the nearest bush to tolerate all that company."

"Well, can't say as I blame you," the Sergeant responded, "what with all the beans these troopers are fed, it ain't pleasant bunking with them. Sounds like a firing range and smells like an outhouse in July. You might talk to the suttler; he may let you sleep in his stock room. The grain sacks make a better mattress than them flee infested straw mattresses the men sleep on."

The next morning Clay was startled awake as the sound of revelry pierced the morning silence. He was surprised to find that for the first time in many months he had slept the night trough. The security of having bedded down in the suttler's storage room had given him the comfort to sleep the night away. Clay wandered over to the mess hall and shared the barely palatable breakfast of what was meant to be oatmeal or some semblance thereof. The coffee was bitter, but fortunately there was thick cream to dilute it. After he had finished his meal Sergeant Flannigan confronted him and conveyed to him the Captain's request that he join him at his convenience, which Clay understood to be army lingo for immediately.

The Captain greeted him warmly, asked about his satisfaction with the accommodations that had been offered and then handed him what he was told was to be the official report of the incidents that Clay had relayed to him the day of his arrival.

"I trust you are literate and will not have to have this document read aloud?"

Clay took the report without answering and having read it handed it back to the Captain. "You have put it down about as I remember it. I don't have any suggestions that would matter."

The Captain thanked him for his assistance and then settled back in his chair and gave Clay a long serious perusal.

"Is there something else?" Clay finally asked.

"Yes there is. This report must get back to Washington as soon as possible. As I mentioned before, I don't have any men in my command that are experienced enough to be trusted with the delivery of this dispatch."

It took Clay several minutes to pick up on the suggestion contained in the Captain's comment.

"You aren't asking me to do it are you?"

"You are perceptive. That's just exactly what I had in mind. I'm afraid that you are the only one in the Fort who could do it. Obviously you have had more than a little experience surviving in the wilderness. Winter has not set in in earnest yet and you could make it to the Platte and go by water to St. Louis and then by stage to Washington. What good men I have at the Fort will have to head down to that meadow where you found evidence of an atrocity. I will need a full report of what evidence you found. There's some burying to be done there and we will need to get the names of the murdered emigrants. I will give you government script to take care of your expenses and a voucher to present to the Secretary of War upon your arrival. I will give you a letter to the commanders of the Forts along the way and request that they assist you. I will recommend that you receive fifteen hundred dollars for your efforts. I can't promise what they will pay you. I wouldn't be honest with you if I did not advise you that now that the Mexican mess is over with, the army budget is being ravaged. Before you give me your answer, let me tell you why I think you should accept this assignment."

"When I left Washington to take this command, there was a big push to get the British out of the Oregon Territory and claim it for the United States. There was talk that the matter was settled. The Army of the West was being organized to protect the settlers and emigrants. That's why this Fort is now a United States Army post. Several other forts have been established and more are intended. The problem was that Congress has been unwilling to appropriate the money necessary to give substance to the Army deployment to the West. This report will demonstrate to them the necessity of a more serious commitment to the protection of the emigrants and settlers. I should think your experience and the murder of your friends would give you reason to take on this assignment. These Indians must be brought to heel."

Clay was unprepared for this challenge. He had expected to ride out the winter at the fort and then head on to Oregon to be with his father and brother. He had to admit he had no particular plans in mind once he got there. He had no intention of going into the newspaper business with his father. By now his brother William would be embroiled in his efforts to start his law practice and no doubt busy building a home for him and Jenny and would have no place for him.

"I have no idea what it would be like in Washington and how I would get along. I have never been a city boy and don't even know how to dress for a meeting with the people you suggest I contact."

"You needn't worry about that. While I was there last, Kit Carson was in town. They loved him. He dressed in his buckskins and drove the ladies to distraction. He was the toast of the town. I expect you would get the same treatment."

"I would need you to request that the Commandant at Fort Kearny take care of my horses until I return. I have no idea how long this trip of yours will take me, but if I'm to go by boat once I reach the Platte, I'll need caring for my horses."

Clay's request brought a smile to the Captains weathered face. "Then you will take the assignment?"

"The prospect of all those ladies falling at my feet is more then I can resist," Clay responded, extending his hand to seal the bargain.

The thought of traveling east with winter ever closer weighed heavily upon Clay's mind as he set about preparing for his departure the following morning. At the sutler's store he found a heavy sheepskin coat and boots, several heavy wool blankets, ammunition and food stuffs that he would need for the trip and had the bill taken to the Captain's office for approval. He saw to it that his horses were well grained and shod. The next morning when he was called to the Captain's office to be given the packet containing dispatches to the Secretary of War, the Captain was in a pensive mood.

"I am asking a lot of you, young man and if it weren't for the importance of these matters and the need to get better protection for the emigrant trains that will be heading this way in the spring, I wouldn't be sending you on such a difficult journey.

"In good conscience, I must offer you a chance to reconsider your commitment. I would do the same for one of my own men and I offer you this chance now."

"I thank you for your concerns, but you shouldn't worry about me. I have lived out doors since I was a tad and seen some severe weather. I'm more concerned about how I will get along in Washington D.C. Where do I stay when I get there? How do you go about a town so full of people who have no truck for a half savage stranger? If I can get by in a town so full of important people, getting there will be the easier part."

"You have a point there. In that packet there are some instructions for you when you get into town about how to contact the right people and there are some suggestions about places to stay and several letters of introduction. You will get along fine. Just follow your instincts and don't fall in with the scheming and infighting that is their life in that town. You are bringing an urgent call for more troops and a bigger budget for the Army of the West. There are those who don't want to spend a dime on the military and do not favor the westward expansion of the country. The extension of slavery into the new territories is always a troubling debate.

Don't let any of those politicians use you for their ill purposes. They are clever and they will use you if they can. You best not hang around that town any longer than necessary. But if you get the chance there are a few Senators and Representatives whose names are in you packet that you may want to talk to. But even as to them, let it be known that you are just a messenger and don't intend to be put upon."

Clay gave these words some consideration. "Like I said, getting there will be the easy part."

"You are going to be bringing to Washington news that is most likely to rile up sentiments against the Indians. I don't know what your feelings are toward those that killed your friends. You've been witness to three different Indian attacks now and I expect you're a bit bitter toward the red men," the Captain continued, "there are those back east who have no idea what the conditions are out here, but they all have a certainty that they know how to deal with what they are inclined to call the savages. Some want to exterminate them. One of them eastern papers was raging on about the only good Indian is a dead Indian. They assume that the land out here is theirs for the taking and America must dominate the land from sea to sea. I hope you can shed some light on the real conditions out here and give them some appreciation for the fact that the Army of the West, as they like to call this measly force they have sent out here, is outnumbered a thousand to one or more. We don't need more killing; we need to find some better way to deal with the situation out here. I tell you these things because I suspect that you will be, like Carson before you, treated like hero to some and a demigod to others depending on which view point you take on these Indian matters. You'll want to be giving some thought to these things as you travel east. What may I ask are your feelings toward the natives?"

Clay had been struggling with this same question for some time. He had spent much of his time in Illinois trapping and exploring. He'd been in contact with a number of tribes in the northern part of the state and around the Great Lakes region. He had eaten at their camps and slept in their lodges. These Indians were peaceful and had come to terms with the white man. Many of the Indians he had encountered moving west were peaceful also, but he had to admit that the hostility of some of the tribes was a thing he was not prepared for. The loss of his friends in Oregon was senseless. They were there to claim no land and were attacked without warning and given no mercy. The Mapes train had met with the same fate as had the emigrants at the mountain meadow in Utah Territory. Yet, he had seen also the devastation brought upon the western tribes by the white man and his diseases. The white man gave no regard to the land rights of the natives and killed without reason the game that the Indians needed to survive. His mind was still unsettled as to who had the right or the wrong of the matter and he said so to the Captain.

"You are wise beyond your years, young man and I have confidence in you. I hope upon your return you will come this way and favor me with a report on your encounter with the scallywags and damsels, one, I might suggest, is as dangerous as the other."

On the trip away from the Fort, Clay was in a melancholy mood. He was worried about his father's progress to Oregon City. There were several hazardous river crossings to be made as he headed west and he had lost some of his best men to the gold rush. He was headed in the opposite direction from that he had intended and would soon be in the jaws of winter as it swept across the endless expanses of the land that had been challenging enough in the summer. Like so many men before him, he may be riding onto his eternity by challenging the forces of an uncertain nature.

The weather, though cold and wind driven, was favorable until he reached Fort Hall, where he found the Fort, like Fort Boise to be nearly deserted. The Indians who had been camped about the Fort in the summer were now in the mountains secured against the oncoming winter. There were no emigrants passing through and the store and blacksmith shop were virtually closed down. There were no soldiers about, but the sutler accepted his script for supplies and wished him well as he rode on the next morning.

"You best move on as fast as you can, the weather out here on the plains ain't hospitable. You can have days on end when you can't see your hand in front of your face when them blizzards hit. It you get in one you best sit it out or you will wonder in circles and spend your critters in the process."

He had reached the vicinity of Scotts Bluff when his luck ran out. The storm clouds had been gathering all day and were swirling in the frenzy of the gathering storm when he sought shelter on the leeward side of a large bluff. To his surprise, he found an abandoned shelter that some trapper had probably used to ride out the winter several years before. Clay found shelter for his horses against the bluff and spent some time as the snow started to fall to shore up the shelter and gather wood. By mid afternoon the storm hit in all its furry and the land was soon blanketed with a wind driven snow that filtered through every crack of his scant shelter. The storm lasted for three days and when he awoke on the third day, the sky was clear and the temperature rose. Clay headed again eastward, but this time his progress was considerably slower as the snow in places was drifted and impassable. As long as he could stay on ridge lines the snow, driven by the wind was passable, but still the horses labored. The sutler at Fort Hall had persuaded him to buy snow shoes which he now found to be the better way to travel as the horses did not need added weight. That night Clay camped in the open, burrowing into a snow drift as protection from the still relentless wind.

The temperature dropped well below freezing and the snow which had partially melted from the sun during the day had a frozen crust in the morning which made travel even more difficult for the animals. As it was, the animals were suffering from the lack of graze which lay buried under the snow. Whenever he found a light covering of snow, he allowed that horses to paw through the curst and obtain what nourishment they could. He had some grain that he fed to the horses, but that alone would not last long nor be a sufficient diet if he could not reach Fort Laramie within a few more days. Clay had lost track of how long he had been traveling and when the sun failed to penetrate a gathering cloud layer the next day, he had the additional concern that he would lose his sense of direction. For two more days he labored on. The curst on the snow was becoming harder as the freezing weather was dehydrating the top layer.

As Clay stopped to rest on top of a ridge he looked back at his tracks. The horses were leaving a trail of blood as the hard crust they broke through was cutting their ankles. He had no choice but to cut up one of his blankets and wrap the legs of the horses. As he traveled onward he had to stop again and again to secure the wrapping. He was not making good progress and both he and the animals were reaching their limit. That night he got little rest as he had to get up occasionally to keep from freezing and to move the horses about to so they would not lay down and submit to the cold.

The next day he labored on even more slowly. Although the sky was still overcast, there had been no more snow which he thought to be a blessing until he looked at his back trail and saw that the blood left by the horses as their fetlocks continued to bleed had attracted a pack of wolves that was now moving ever closer as their hunger mounted.

Clay had no way of knowing how far he was traveling each day, but thought he could be covering no more the five or ten miles at which rate the wolves would have them before he could reach Fort Laramie. That night he was able to build a fire as he found a clump of aspen and cottonwood near a small frozen stream. The wolves stayed just beyond the glow of the fire, but kept the horses nervous and Clay ever alert. As dawn struggled against the gloom of the still present cloud cover, Clay moved beyond the camp to try to get a shot at the wolves, but they were too wary and not yet ready to confront him.

Clay traveled that day constantly checking his back trail, hoping to get a shot at the wolves. He was reminded of a comment made by Franco that when a pack of wolves was on to you, you had to select their leader, usually the larger of the pack and kill him first. Later that morning, Clay let the horses wander on ward and waited behind a clump of bushes and got in several shots that brought down the leader and one other of the wolves. That night, they did not bother him, but the next morning they were back on his trail, but where the pack was only eight in number before, there were over a dozen now and their numbers would make them more aggressive. Several times that day, he stopped to take a shot or two at the wolf pack, but could see that his efforts were not overly productive. Fatigue and the relentless wind and chill were affecting his aim. As darkness overcame him that night, he found no suitable shelter and camped in a small ravine without a fire to ward off the wolves.

He had no other defense except to remain awake and fire a shot at any suspected movement. Unfortunately this meant that he had to stay awake throughout the night. His mind slowly responded to a great commotion, the squealing of his pack horse and the growling, yapping of the wolves who where now within his small camp. He had fallen asleep. He rose up with a start with his rifle at the ready to discover that the wolf pack had his pack animal on the ground and tearing it to pieces as it cried out in protest. His saddle horse had fended off several wolves that were after it. Clay, slow to respond finally raised his rifle to kill the intruders, but his rifle's breach was frozen and would not respond. Panic quickly over came him. Instinctively he ran to his saddle horse, beating away the wolves with his rifle butt, swung astride the terrified animal, unsheathed his knife, cut the tether rope and rode frantically away from his camp. He rode hard for several minutes until the horse's fright was overcome by its poor condition.

The wolves had not followed him as the blood and flesh of his pack horse drew the remaining wolves onto the kill. He dismounted and walked his horse on into the night and toward the slowly graying eastern horizon that would soon give him the advantage of daylight to assess his situation and hopefully rest. He had fallen asleep and the wolf pack made its move. He was coming to grips with his limitations. He had always felt he could handle himself in any situation. He had done it many times before when he had had to confront danger. But this situation was entirely different. His enemy now was nature itself and the feeling of helplessness was overwhelming him. He knew the wolf pack, once satiated would pick up his scent and press relentlessly on until he was once more in the grip of their overwhelming need of his very flesh.

He collapsed on top of a ridge to let the increasing light from the now visible sun light his route ahead. It was time to make an assessment. He had lost all of his provisions including his extra ammunition. He had only three bullets left and none in his rifle. He had not reloaded before falling asleep. He searched his pockets, but found only empty casings. There was neither food for himself nor grain for his horse. Clearly he could not travel much further before his fate would be sealed. Looking up, he saw his horses ears pricked up as it looked off to the east. Something was out there drawing his horse's attention. Pulling his hood down, he now heard a strange sound; it was familiar, but he could not place it for it was quite faint. Shortly it stopped and all was silent. Was it the wind he had heard or his imagination? That couldn't be for his horse had heard it also. Clay was far too exhausted to think straight and muddled long moments over the possible source of the sound he had heard. Then it came to him. It was the sound of a bugle calling reveille. It had to be coming from Fort Laramie. He pulled his horse half running toward the sound, his fatigue no longer and obstacle with salvation within his grasp.

But no matter how hard he tried or how strong was his desire to make it to the Fort; his body did not have the reserve strength to make it. He was in sight of the Fort when he collapsed and could move no further. He could make out the flag that rode the freshening breeze. He had never given much thought to the presence of the flag and the strength of the nation that it represented. Seeing it flutter above the Fort made him appreciate the security and order that it presented as the Army of the West moved into its post on the expanding frontier.

He worked the breach of his rifle until he could chamber a cartridge then fired three times into the air.

As he expected, the gates of the fort soon opened and a troop of mounted soldiers appeared heading his way. He sat in the snow awaiting their arrival, his eyes misting with tears of gratitude. When the troop arrived, he found he did not have the strength to rise to greet them.

"Pilgrim, what the hell are you doing out here at this time of year?" The young Lieutenant asked as he dismounted and approached him. Clay was too dizzy and weak to even respond. The soldiers placed him on a horse in front of a strong trooper who held him in the saddle as they headed back to the Fort. Another trooper was dispatched to lead his horse slowly to the Fort.

Major Anderson stood on the porch of his headquarters building and watched the procession of troopers pass by him on to the infirmary. He walked slowly behind the procession and stood aside as Clay was helped from his horse and carried inside. It was obvious to the Major that the man they had brought into the Fort was only half alive and badly in need of medical attention, yet he had to know who he was and what his business was in the eventuality that stranger did not survive. The "saw bones" as the soldiers referred to the surgeon, immediately instructed the orderlies who had gathered to take the man's outer garments off and to wrap him in warm blankets.

"Give him a shot of spirits and start rubbing his arms and legs. Pedro, you stoke up that fire and keep it cooking hot," The surgeon commanded. "Take off them boots you fool," he shouted at another orderly. "You can't get circulation going in his limbs rubbing those damn boots."

The Major stepped forward and by his presence took command of the situation. "We must get his name and reason for approaching the Fort in this damnable weather."

After a couple of swigs of whiskey were administered and Clay reacted by choking and sputtering, the Major bent over him and asked:" Who are you and what brings you to the Fort Laramie?"

Clay looked at him for a moment as if to gather his strength and then murmured. "Dispatches from Fort Hall. They're in my saddle bags."

At that the Major left the patient to the surgeon's care and headed out the door and waited impatiently for the trooper to arrive with Clay's exhausted, feeble horse. "Bring the saddle bags to my office." He instructed the trooper that led the horse into the compound.

After the Major reviewed the dispatches, he returned to the infirmary with a renewed interest in the welfare of Clay Anderson. The man was on government business and was to be given special consideration. He left instructions for the surgeon to advise him immediately when the patient was able to converse with him.

By the next morning, Clay was up and about making plans for the renewal of his journey. While he was at the stable checking on the condition of his horse, he was approached by a corporal who informed him that Major Anderson sends his compliments and requests his presence at headquarters. Clay responded intending to present his need for assistance to complete his journey. The Major had respected the privacy of the material in the dispatches directed to the Secretary of War and was aware only of the request from the Commandant at Fort Hall for his assistance in facilitating Clay's journey to Washington. After Clay recited the facts of his encounters in the Oregon Territory and at the mountain meadows, the Major informed him that unfortunately Clay was too late to travel on to St Louis by river as the Platte was frozen over.

"I do have a contingent of troopers whose enlistments are about to terminate who want to move out as soon as the weather is more promising. I suggest you travel east with them. I'm sure you can make it to the Mandan villages without much trouble. From then on you should have little trouble getting to St Louis. From the looks of your horse, it will be a few more days before you are ready to travel, so if it's satisfactory with you I will make arrangements to get that troop prepared to move in two days time and you can accompany them. I will prepare a letter of instructions for you to deliver to the Commander at Fort Leavenworth for the care of your horse while you travel east."

Clay gladly accepted the offer. He had no further desire to travel alone across the frozen plains of Nebraska. The advantage of traveling with the troopers, Clay soon found was that he no longer needed to do his own cooking and could sleep at night knowing others were posted on watch to protect them and their animals from interference by savages or wild animals. Clay found he had little in common with these troopers who had no experience in the west beyond garrison duty and who hailed from points unfamiliar to him on the eastern seaboard. The frenzied scrambling to get to the gold fields of California that infected most of the people on the Anderson and other trains heading west seemed to be of little interest to these men.

Some had served in Mexico and had their fill of regimented army life; others had families back east they had not seen in many months. All of them were interested only in returning home not in further adventurers in the west. He did observe that there was a subtle division between the troopers who had southern ancestry and those who hailed from the north. Few could perceive that this difference would soon enflame the nation in one of man's greatest conflicts and thrust these very men who were now comrades in arms onto the killing fields of Virginia and Pennsylvania and across the south where they would vent their anger and distrust in bloody conflict. Once they reached St Louis and arrangements were made to care for his horse with the army detachment located at nearby Fort Leavenworth, Clay left the company of these soldiers and set about arranging for this travels beyond with the assistance of the quartermaster at the fort who had some knowledge of transportation facilities that would carry him eastward.

Clay found St Louis to be confining and the noise; smell and bustling crowds unsettled him. He found the offices of the Chicago & St. Louis Rail Road Company and arranged for transportation eastward. The train schedule assured him that he would be in Chicago in a mere twelve hours. From Chicago, he would make a connection with a stagecoach that would take him into Pennsylvania where he would connect with another railroad that would take him to Baltimore and then on to Washington D.C. Clay had been to St Louis once before with his father, but found that he recognized nothing of the frontier town he had visited in his youth. There were now dance halls, gambling halls, haberdashers, merchandise stores, and an assortment of offices that tended to your every need. Many of the structures that were once false front frame buildings before were now constructed of stone or brick.

Boarding houses and hotels were plentiful and he found himself a room for the night. The clerk at the desk was dressed in formal attire that was unfamiliar to him with high colored shirts, a bow tie and a suit coat that buttoned up the front. The clerk looked somewhat askance at Clay and his frontier attire and when Clay laid his rifle on the counter to sign the register, the Clerk curtly asked him to remove it.

"Don't be going about with that thing. You will frighten the guests," he was instructed. "You are fortunate to be arriving at this time of the year; we can give you a private room. Come spring, you would have to share your bed." He gave Clay a further inspection and then condescendingly suggested, "I assume the gentleman will want a bath. That would be fifty cent extra."

Clay gave him a cold calculating look what caused the clerk to step back a pace. "I've come a long hard way and have had to put up with many discomforts and don't look favorable to your attitude, but I will have that bath if the water is hot and the soap mild. You may send a steward to the room and I will give him my order for dinner. I will expect my laundry to be done by first light. When my bath is done, send a barber to my room and after that don't disturb me!"

Clay then slammed a five dollar gold piece on the counter. "That should take care of it, now show me to my room," he commanded.

Clay was up at first light, had a quick breakfast and then headed to the train station. He had never ridden on a train and had seen a locomotive only once before when his father covered for his newspaper the initial run of the Lake Erie and Mad River Railway. He was traveling on his government vouchers and was shown to a seat in the third class car where he was crowded in with a number of families, itinerate salesman, and a an assortment of farmers, merchants and what appeared to be railway employees. Clay found a seat on the far end of the car away from the one stove that provided what little heat was available. Although the train had been advertised as having new facilities including rail cars, the car Clay rode in seemed the worse for wear. The floors were not swept, the windows were coated with the film of the ever billowing smoke from the engine and the seats were unpadded and about as comfortable as riding a saw boned horse without a saddle.(13)

The train started with a jerk that sent some of the children screeching and an adult or two onto the aisle. By the time it built up speed it swayed back and forth on the road bed like a small boat on rough seas. Clay had little room to store his gear and had to hold his rifle upright between his knees, a circumstance that caused a number of wary glances. If there was a way to abandon the coach, Clay would have taken it gladly and walked to Chicago, especially when the swaying train kept casting him against a stuffy looking matron who obviously was offended by his proximity and contact. Clay soon tired of excusing himself and rode glumly onto Chicago. The train stopped frequently to take on fuel and water and to disembark and pick up passengers. By the time he reached Chicago in the late of night, he was rattled and tired. Unlike the other passengers, he had not brought his own food along and was also suffering from hunger pangs. After seeking accommodations at what was recommended to be one of the better hotels by the station master, Clay got a sandwich at one of the all night bars, had his first cold beer and then retired for the night. He awoke to the clatter of steel wheeled carriages wagons and the clop, clop of shod horses on the cobble stones of the street below.

He realized that he could no longer walk about carrying his rifle. Although a few men wore side arms, the rifle was seen as threatening and indeed it was awkward to carry about and in the city it was completely without use. He traded it for a side arm at a gunsmith, gathered his belongings and boarded and eastbound stage. It was winter and the roads were frozen and firm except where travel was frequent and the road bed had broken down. Although the stage had a motion of its own, Clay found little comfort in the smaller conveyance except for the fact that he had better companionship. A tall lean intense looking railroad lawyer named Lincoln had introduced himself and when the lawyer heard Clay had

---

13 For a description of the early railroads see: History of Railroads and Maps, http://memory.loc.gov/ammem/gmdhtml/rrhtml/rrintro.hotml; Baltimore and Ohio Railroad-Wikipedia, http://en.wikipedia.org/wiki/Altimore_and_Ohio_Railroad; Advertisement: The Alton Railroad, 1860, hppt://www.uic.edu/ors/LockZero/3image/CAASTKKRKRR_ad.html

recently been in the Oregon Territory, he quizzed Clay intently about his travels and opinions.

"We will surely have a railroad covering that land one day, they are sprouting up all over the east now and will soon be replacing this dubious conveyance and linking up all the cities about," he assured Clay.

Lincoln was familiar with Paul Anderson and his newspaper and said he was sorry he closed it and headed to Oregon. "We need more newspapermen like your pa. Most of these fella's are prone to be a little inventive. But of course, we lawyers can't complain too loudly about a bit of fabrication," he said with a chuckle. "A stirring tale has won a good deal of bounty in the field of law." Lincoln, upon hearing that Clay had business with the War Department acknowledged that he had served in the Congress for two years but that "the prudence of men wiser than he declined to return him to that office."

"This nation is torn between the conflicting interests of the rural south and the expanding industrialized north. The middle ground is shrinking and the stance of the partisans is growing ever more rigid. The great promise of this nation is hostage to the question of slavery an issue that must be resolved sooner than later if this nation is to survive." Lincoln observed in a tone that evidenced his distress over an issue that seemed to defy even his capacity to resolve.

It was from Lincoln that he received the advice that he should abandon stage travel at Pittsburg, Pennsylvania and ride on to Washington on the Baltimore and Ohio Rail Road. As if to emphasize the wisdom of Lincoln's advice, the coach, coming upon a hilly section of the road which had thawed during the day to form a veritable quagmire, stopped and the driver asked the passengers to proceed by foot up the grade to lighten the load for the struggling mule team. By the time they reached Detroit, the stops to change teams, feed and exchange passengers and coaches rendered the travel by coach far too tedious for Clay to bear. When they arrived at Inns where he was expected to sleep like cord wood in the same bed with the other male patrons, Clay bought a horse and rode on alone. Better, he decided, to sleep in the woods than in the flea infested roadhouses that provided accommodations along the stage route.

When he finally reached Pittsburg, he was again confronted with the smells of the assembling multitudes that make up a city. But in Pittsburg there were the added smells of coal and coke from the mills that lined the river and gave evidence of a burgeoning industrial center. As he entered the outskirts of the city the small farms still mantled with the snows of winter, gave way to the paved roads and cobble stone streets, brick and stone building, trams and the usual horse drawn conveyances that carried the merchandise of the community and the citizens of the city. He found a stable where he arranged for the sale of his recently acquired horse and asked direction to the B & O depot. He arrived just prior to its departure and was wise enough to ask for better accommodations and was informed that his government voucher would not be honored except for third class.

Clay, whose father had given him a small sack of gold coin when they parted at Fort Boise, gladly tendered the fare for a first class seat. The cars of the B & O were larger and in first class even had padded seats, adequate heat from two stoves, one on each end of the car, and a private privy where a passenger could even relieve themselves through the questionable practice of littering the trackage. Of course, the facilities were closed while the train rested at the station.

By the time the train commenced its journey, Clay had settled himself into a well upholstered comfortable seat next to a window where he could watch the passing countryside he had not seen before. The rail car was larger than that of the St. Louis, Alton and Chicago Rail Road that he had ridden before and the train was making better speed. Although the windows would open, the cool weather and flying cinders from the locomotive riding just ahead of the coach discouraged riding with open windows even when the air became foul with the smoke of a dozen or so cigars.

Clay observed that the closer they got to their destination the more likely it was that the passengers joining them along the route would be attired in more formal ware, with top hats, fir trimmed over coats, suit coats, vests, gold watch fobs and chains and other evidences of their prosperity and importance. The homespun trappings and deerskins of the frontier were seldom seen. His attire, with his high boots, store bought trousers and deerskin shirt generated disdainful glances from his fellow travelers. The knife and revolver at his belt did cause some of the passengers to give him a wide, respectful birth.

After switching trains twice he arrived in Washington D.C. in less than a day's travel. Clay could now understand the enthusiasm the lawyer Lincoln had for the future of the railroad. He had traveled from St. Louis to Washington D.C. in a third of the time it took him to travel from Fort Laramie to St. Louis. When the rails eventually connected through to Chicago the time would be even shorter.

When Clay left the station he hired a carriage to take him to the Willard Hotel that had been recommended to him by Captain Richardson at Fort Boise.

The desk clerk who had seen Clay enter the lobby deliberately ignored him when he came to the counter, busying himself with some paper work with his back to him. Clay waited for a few moments and then shouted at him in a voice that startled not only the clerk whose reaction scattered his papers about, but also startled several of the patrons seated in the lobby.

"Are you asleep, or just being a jackass?"

The clerk, once he had gathered his composure, responded, "Perhaps, sir, you have the wrong hotel. As you can see, we cater to the gentlemen's trade." He then gave Clay a disdainful look and started to suggest that he head on down the street to another hotel when Clay responded.

"You may find my attire ungentlemanly, and my manner abrasive, but be assured, I'm here on the business of the United States government and this is the place I was told would honor the gold of the realm and favor its government."

The clerk appeared puzzled at Clay's use of the language and by his message. "What business would you have with the government?" he asked testily.

"I'm not of the impression that whatever business I have with the government is to be discussed with hotel clerks. Now are you giving me a room or must I speak with someone with better manners?"

The insult drew the clerk's ire but before he could respond, Clay set his official pouch on the counter and instructed the clerk, "And when you have shown me to my room, send a messenger to deliver this dispatch to the office of the Secretary of War at first light. You may also recommend a haberdasher I may call upon in the morning. Before I retire, I expect to have a hot bath and shave. Can this place accommodate a gentleman's request?" He said with intentional sarcasm.

Without further discourse the clerk placed the register before Clay and inquired with his own invective, "Can the *gentleman* sign his name, if not and "X" will do."

At that remark, Clay chuckled and signed his name with a flourish. "My name is Anderson, not "X". And I am able to read so please send a newspaper to my room. Oh, yes, and you might be so good as to send up some of those cigars these *gentlemen* about here smoke."

Clay was not surprised when he didn't receive the best room in the hotel, and he didn't particularly care. The room had a view of the building across an alley way, but was a large room with a large, double bed, a sitting area and large armoire. The drapes were of a red velvet material that matched the bed spread and what Clay guessed to be a Persian carpet. The woodwork was a reddish wood he guessed to be cherry. A tub was brought into his room and filled with hot water that sudsed up when the maid sprinkled some powders into it. The newspaper and cigars arrived in time to be enjoyed as he luxuriated in the tub.

Clay had not even seen a newspaper than alone read one in over a year. After reading the several papers that had been delivered it became evident to Clay that the events concerning slavery that gripped the nation when he left for the west had not changed a great deal, but it was obvious that the emotions of the participants had escalated and the positions of the advocates had become more entrenched. The actions of the Polk Administration in what was asserted by some to be the "unjust war with Mexico" had not only expanded the territories of the United States, it had expanded the festering issue of slavery.

Congress had been equally balanced between Free states and Slave states and the annexation of Texas, New Mexico and now the petitioning of California to be entered into the Union as full fledged states threatened that balance. The settlement of the border dispute with Great Britain in the Northwest would soon bring Oregon into play. In the past, the new states were created into territories that allowed the luxury of time and bargaining to form the character of the state before its union with the rest of the country. The new states, however, demanded immediate entry without going through the territorial period of adjustments. The issues that all had tried to avoid, but was ever pressing upon the nation had reached the point of critical confrontation. The issue had become not one of the merits of the union, but of the balance of national power between the northern states and the southern states.

The debates between the eloquent advocates of the positions of the several parties were now raging in Congress with Senators Clay, Calhoun, and Webster mesmerizing the nation with their passionate, intense oratory. The Mason-Dixon Line that had long established the division of the states between Free and Slave and north and south was no longer meaningful as the nation expanded ever westward. As Clay read the text of their speeches and the reports of the other proceedings in Congress he had difficulty deciding the right of the issue. The Southern states had a persuasive cause in claiming that the States had certain rights that should not be subject to interference by other states or the Federal government. Unfortunately their argument skirted around the compelling question of slavery and their right to preserve and continue that "damnable institution" as it was referred to by Webster and others from the north.

The Southern delegates to Congress were even suggesting that their right to sovereignty exceeded their obligation to the union and gave them the right to secede from that union to avoid intrusion by the growing militancy of the northern states that wanted slavery abolished. The failure of the northern states to respect the property rights the southern states claimed was inherent in slave ownership was a vexing question, particularly so when groups in the north were organizing what was referred to as the Underground Railroad to channel runaway slaves through the northern states and into Canada. President Taylor, upon hearing of the talk of succession, advised the Congress that he would use the army to quell any such rebellion and "he would hang . . . with less reluctance than he had hanged deserters and spies in Mexico" those who rebelled against the union. ([14])

Clay recalled the conversations his father had had with Wayne Rawlins and the grim prediction that Wayne had made that the slavery question would not be resolved without the spilling of blood. It appeared to Clay upon reviewing the news, that the country was indeed destined to validate the prediction Wayne had made. It was a good thing his family was in

---

[14] Biography of Zachary Taylor, http://www.whitehouse.gov/history/presidents/zt12.html.

Oregon and that was where he intended to be before the bloodletting began.

Clay had read long into the night and was jarred from a deep sleep by a firm knocking on his door. When he awoke he was disoriented and confused. Where was he and why was he here. The knocking came again and he regained his senses, pulled on his trousers and answered the door. A short young man or maybe it was a mere boy, dressed in what appeared to be a uniform confronted him.

"I was advised, sir, that you had a parcel to deliver to a government office. I am with the messenger service and am here to assist you."

Clay gave the boy his dispatches and the address to which they should be delivered and then dressed and went down to the dining room for breakfast. As he passed the desk, another clerk was on duty, but upon seeing him motioned him to the desk.

"Mr. Simpson, the night clerk asked me to watch for you. You ask for the name of a haberdashers and I have it here."

He handed Clay a slip of paper with the name of a nearby store and returned to his work of sorting some messages and placing them in a series of cubbyholes where the guests would find them. Clay finished his breakfast and headed out to do his shopping. He bought what he was assured would be a suitable wardrobe and returned to his room and dressed. He expected it would be some time before he would be called to the office of the Secretary of War if called at all and decided to hire a carriage and do some sightseeing. The sky was overcast and a chill was in the air. Outside of the Capital district, where there were rows of stately, mostly antebellum mansions, Clay got his first glimpse of how the wealthy and influential citizens of Washington lived. Carriages were coming and going from these stately mansions all driven by liveried colored men in splendid uniforms.

Clay got glimpses of finely dressed ladies in the passing carriages, coiffured and splendidly dressed with elaborate hats and veils that only partially hide their faces from the glances of passersby. The carriage driver was able to recite the names of the personages who resided in the various houses and give Clay a brief account of their eminence.

"That be Millard Fillmore's home there. He's the Vice-President. Over there is the house of Senator Thomas Hart Benton. He's a man of great influence in this town. And over here . . ."

The recitation went on and Clay soon lost interest. "I saw an advertisement in the newspaper that says there's a slave market in this town. Is that a fact?" he asked the driver.

"Oh, yes it's true. President Tyler is all for closing it down, but it's over in Maryland and the law that governs the District don't allow him any say in the matter." The driver responded.

"Take me to it," he instructed the driver.

"It ain't no good place to be seeing, especially for a gentleman. You'd best let me take you some other place." The driver responded. "It's a dirty business they carry on there."

"It's the business that seems to be driving the nation toward division, and I best know what it's all about. I came from the west and am ignorant of these matters. Now don't worry about my sensitivities and let's be on our way."

The driver headed down toward the water front on the Potomac River. Gone now were the homes of the influential and spread in mass were the homes of the workers that performed all the labor that made for the commerce of public affairs. The houses were closer, the streets were unpaved and the smell of animals, privies, and coal smoke was enough to cause Clay to pull his handkerchief over his nose and mouth. The snow that had been clean and white, was now gray and covered with the grit of a thousand coal and wood fires. Children played about in the street engaged in games of tag, kick ball and snow ball fights. Some of the boys even threw snow balls at his carriage as it passed. The children's clothes were grimy and tattered, but gave them what protection they would have against the chill of winter.

The driver brought them into the warehouse district. The elegant carriages gave way to the stout drayage wagons that that moved the goods of commerce to and from the docks. The air was filled with the sounds of cursing men urging animals to and fro, the sounds of protesting animals and the shouts and commands of stevedores. At the far end of one of the piers, there was an assemblage of well dressed citizens and the carriages that conveyed them. The horses were attended by liveried black servants who stood well back of the crowed that had gathered.

"This is the place you was lookin' for, sir. Do you want me to wait for you?" The driver asked.

"Yes, I don't think I shall be long." Clay replied as he dismounted from the carriage and moved off through the crowd.

Clay noticed that most of the participants in the auctioning of the slaves were well dressed in the striking dress of the southern gentlemen, with maroon or green felt hats, matching breaches, and coats in tans and gray. They carried walking sticks or canes and some were using snuff boxes or taking a sip now and then from a flask. The ladies that were present and he was surprised to see that there were a few of these were decked out in brightly colored calicos, silks and laces. It was evident that these people looked upon this event, as solemn as it was to the slaves, as a social occasion.

Clay watched as several male slaves were auctioned off for three and five hundred dollars. The auctioneer then called forward a large black, almost blue black male that stood well over six feet tall, had a strong well proportioned physical features and a look of insolence that evidenced his disdain and hatred for those who now held him in subjugation. The auctioneer spouted forth with recitations of the slave's attributes which included his incredible strength and breeding prospects and concluded by stating he had been a prince or king among his people.

There was a lot of murmuring among the participants. One among the crowd called out, "Let's see those attributes he has as a breeder."

At the potential bidder's request, the auctioneer nodded at one of the handlers who stepped forward and stripped the slave of his loin cloth to expose his privates to the prospective bidders. If that was not enough to encourage the bidding, the handler stepped forward and with the butt end of a ridding quirt, lifted the slave's flaccid penis to expose its size. Clay was stunned by this exhibition, but noticed little revulsion from the crowed; even the ladies looked upon the demonstration without a blush. Upon given back his loin cloth, the slave, without a change of expression tied it back on and continued his disdainful stare at the audience.

"That one will be nothing but trouble," he heard one among the crowd mutter.

"A good whipping or two will bring him to heal." Another responded. "Ain't no Niger you can't bring to heal with a good application of the cat."

The bidding for the powerful slave started at five hundred and soon reached fifteen hundred dollars and he was finally sold for eighteen hundred dollars. Clay had had enough and was turning to leave when he saw a young female slave ushered forward clutching two small boys. The auctioneer extolled once again the virtues of the woman and her two small boys that he asked not be separated from her mother, but as he conceded, separate bidding would be allowed.

At the request on one of the bidders he was allowed to come upon the stage and inspect the prospects more closely.

The bidder, a middle aged man dressed in breaches, coat and top hat of gray with thigh lengthen black ridding boots strode importantly across the stage and inspected the teeth of the mother and her boys and then felt their bodies for firmness. He then asked that the female be disrobed for further inspection. The young boys seem horrified at their mother's predicament as she tried to resist the efforts to disrobe her. She was quickly subdued and stripped naked before the crowd. The young boys began to wail and try to grasp on to their mother's legs, but were pulled away by attendants so the crowd could get a good look at the naked slave.

"Why do they have to do that?" Clay asked a man standing beside him.

"I suppose that fellow wants a house Niger and don't want one that's been marked by the whip. Shows their disrespectful and of a strong will if they's been whupped. Besides, she may be branded and that makes her worth less. One's got to inspect what he's gonn'a own, she's a comely little thing ain't she?"

When the bidding started, it was obvious the little family was going to be separated. There were was spirited bidding for the female, but no one wanted to bid for her and the two boys as a package. Clay had seen all he wanted and turned away appalled at the total lack of humanity that he had witnessed. He had no reason in his past to give much thought to the question of slavery, but as he left the auction and returned to his carriage, he held a firm conviction that the "peculiar institution" was indefensible.

When Clay returned to the hotel, there were no messages for him. It was apparent that the Secretary of War would not be summoning him and that was fine with him. He was in a mood to get on his return journey to the West, winter or no. Captain Richardson had been right when he advised him not to linger long in this city. He had just set about sorting his few possessions out and started packing when there was a knock on the door. A messenger awaited him as he opened the door.

"Message from Secretary Crawford, sir," the messenger announced as he handed him an official looking envelope.

The message, written in a flourishing scroll, requested that he call upon the Secretary a 9:00 A.M. the next morning. He arose early, breakfasted and took his leisure in reading the morning paper. The compelling news of the day was the anticipated debate between Clay, Webster and Calhoun over the issue of slavery and the admission of Missouri to the union as a slave state. The petitions of California, Oregon and Utah for statehood rode in the balance. The recent attempt to settle the slavery issue with the Wilmot Proviso, allowing each state to decide the issue of slavery within its borders had not passed the Senate, but had added fuel to the simmering controversy. Clay decided that if he was to remain in Washington for a few more days, he would take the time to attend the debate in the Senate chambers.

As he was leaving the hotel, the clerk called him over to the desk to ask if he would be staying on. "It appears that the town will be full of reporters and spectators for the coming debate. We are asking all of our guests to confirm their reservations and if possible to share their accommodations."

"I have a meeting with the Secretary of War this morning and will have a better idea regarding my stay by this afternoon and will advise you upon my return, but as for sharing my room, the answer is no."

The clerk took the news that he was meeting with Secretary Crawford with a look of surprise and interest. "You will find him to be a most artful inquisitor, I am advised," the clerk volunteered. "You may find that the gathering press will be on your door step if you have matters of importance to discuss with the Secretary."

The clerk had obviously meant his remark as an invitation for Clay to reveal the purpose of his meeting, but Clay did not take the bait, asked if there were any further messages and left for his meeting.

The government offices were but a half mile from his hotel and the weather being mild, he decided to walk. The city was coming to life and Pennsylvania Avenue was alive with carriages and drays. The clattering of iron wheels upon the cobblestones, the clomping of hundreds of shod feet gave a discordant rhythm that blended to the sound of the newsboys hocking their editions, the calling and whistling of the draymen and the murmur of the many voices of the gathering throng headed up the hill to the capital. About him were the people whose business it was to decide the great issues of the day and to guide a great nation toward its ultimate destiny.

Clay wondered as he gazed about at the important looking, scurrying multitude if any of them had any comprehension of the frontier beyond the Alleghanys, the mountain range that formed the limit to their known world. Yet it would be the officials and their lackeys in this remote and disconnected place who would decide the fate and fortunes of the thousands of people who now inhabited the distant lands beyond the Mississippi; lands more vast, diverse and bountiful than their limited imaginings could ever comprehend. The thought that he knew those lands, the emigrants and the natives that inhabited them gave him a feeling of relevance as he proceeded up the hill to his meeting with the Secretary.

As he climbed the many steps of the capital building and passed under the chandeliered portico into the massive entryway, Clay could not help but feel the omniscient presence that was the heritage and power of a great and thriving nation that was now extending itself to the shores of the world's two great oceans. The gilded frames of a dozen portraits adorned the walls depicted the images of those great men who had risen to prominence as the leaders of this great nation that was now demanding its place in the councils of the world. The future of that nation was inextricably entwined in its westward expansion and in the hearts and ambitions of the men who advanced the frontiers ever westward. Within the august halls of that nation's capital building Clay could feel the destiny of that nation as he could the pulse that drove life in his own body.

He enquired at the reception desk in the vestibule where he could find the office of Secretary of War Crawford. [15] The harried official behind the desk gave him a quick glance and checked a recording book on his desk.

---

[15] New Georgia Encyclopedia: George W. Crawford (1798-1872)tp:www.geogrgiaencyclopedia.com/nge/Article.jsp?id=h-3244

"May I assume you have an appointment? What is the name, please?"

Clay responded by handing the receptionist his engraved letter requesting his appearance.

"Yes, yes, I see your name is here. Head to the top of the stairs to your left. You will find a receptionist there who will advise the Secretary of your presence."

The receptionist pushed Clay's letter across the desk and was already engaged in addressing another petitioner as he did so. Clay took the letter from the desk and headed up another long stair case to the second floor where he was met with a line of people who were like him seeking a visitation with some government official. Clay was now in a large hall or lobby where there were dozens of other people milling about or standing in line before a number of receptionists. Clay found the receptionist who had a plaque in front of his desk identifying him as the receptionist for Secretary of War Crawford. About the desk mingled a number of men in the uniforms of the army and navy, some with gilded braid on their uniforms that evidenced the rank of generals, colonels, admirals, and captains. There were others of similar import in civilian dress each no doubt with some important matter to discuss with the Secretary. Clay assumed he would have to wait until each of these dignified looking solicitors would be attended to before he would see the Secretary.

As Clay waited in line, the large mahogany door behind the receptionist opened and a harried looking official hurried out and stepped behind the receptionist. He looked at the appointment sheet before the receptionist and looked about the room, "Is there a Clay Anderson present?" he enquired.

As Clay stepped forward from his place in the back of the line, the others who had been waiting in front of him gave him an appraising, inquiring look, aware that the Secretary's interest in this young man exceeded his interest in their concerns.

"Yes, the Secretary will see you now," Clay was advised as he moved to the head of the line. Before they passed through the doorway into the Secretary's office, the clerk who had asked Clay to step forward stopped and looked about the room: "There you are Captain Gunnison, the Secretary wishes to see you also, please come along."

Clay stepped aside while a uniformed officer of about Clay's height and build came forward and preceded Clay as they stepped into the reception area where several clerks were busily engaged in moving paper work about or drafting various documents. The Secretary's clerk opened another door and ushered both Clay and the Captain into the office of Secretary Crawford, who, as they entered stood at a large window overlooking the construction site of what would one day be the Washington Memorial. As he turned to greet his guests, he remarked: "A marvelous feat of engineering and a well deserved tribute to our greatest patriot. Now gentlemen please sit down, I have several things to discuss with you before this matter gets into the newspapers."

Clay was puzzled at the comment, having no idea of either the importance of or the public interest that might abide his report. The Secretary, unlike so many of his contemporaries, had a clean shaven face, thinning gray hair that fell in ringlets about his ears. He was dressed in what appeared to be the basic dress of Washington's officialdom, a black suit and trousers, a black vest and cravat and a high collared white shirt.

"This report you brought from Fort Boise," the Secretary said holding the report before him, "is most distressing. The report regarding the troubles in Oregon where your friends were murdered indicates that we have but another wild tribe to subdue. The situation you came across in Utah is another matter all altogether. You suggest that it may not have been Indians that fell upon this wagon train. From reading your report, I have a grave suspicion that you are correct. It doesn't sound like Indian doings what with the men all killed away from the women and children and there being no small children or infants left on the scene. I have had Captain Gunnison here look over this report, oh, by the way, have you gentlemen been introduced?"

Having taken care of the formalities, the Secretary proceeded: "The Captain spent a winter with the Mormons and in fact wrote a book about his experience. I wanted his opinion on the suggestion that Mormons could be involved in this business. Correct me if I am misstating you Captain, but it appears to be your belief that the Mormons, at least those you knew would not be involved in such a matter. However, you also suggest that based upon the report by Mr. Anderson here, you are inclined to accept the fact that this was not Indian business. Is that correct Captain?

Captain Gunnison studied Clay for a moment before he responded. "Based upon the facts as presented, I would have to believe these men were lured away from the wagons by white men and murdered in a manner that would not be likely if Indians had done the killing. I would not think that the men would separate themselves from the women and submit to type of depredation as evidenced in the report if they were dealing with Indians. The Indians about this territory, the Piute and Utes don't take captives and they don't do a clean job when they set about killing settlers."

"Well gentlemen, that leaves us with a problem. When this matter gets to the press, they may inflame the public against the Mormon and we will have more of the killings that drove them from Missouri. Even if they are convinced that it was Indians, these two massacres being reported at once what with what happened at the Sublette Cut Off last year will bring a cry of vengeance that will cause further troubles with the Indians that the army is not prepared to handle"

Clay studied the features of the Secretary with renewed interest. If the army was not to handle this affair, than who was? Clay was getting the impression that the Secretary didn't want to deal with more Indian troubles and was even more reluctant to have suspicions about a possible Mormon involvement enflame the public. It was becoming even more obvious that this meeting was not about interviewing Clay about the details of the dispatches, but was more about controlling the release of the information. His suspicious were confirmed with the Secretaries next question.

"Have you been approached by the press, or a Congressional delegation?"

"Sir," Clay responded, "I have discussed the details of the dispatches I delivered to you with no one since I arrived here and am not particularly inclined to be interviewed by the Press or anyone else. My employment was to deliver the dispatches and that I have done."

"Very good, very good," the Secretary remarked. "It is a messy business and can get out of hand quickly. I have to report this matter to the President and the Congress and the Press will soon be at your door. I would only caution you to be most discrete with them and don't let them stampede you into saying things that you are not certain of and be certain not to say any outrageous things that will end up in headlines."

Clay was at the point of irritation and was about to end the interview when Captain Gunnison intervened.

"Our press has no bounds for its appetite for stories coming from the West, particularly ones that will stir up their readership. You have seen a great deal that will interest them. Kit Carson was recently in town and the press and the public made his visit into a circus. He is quoted as having said the most outrageous things and accomplished impossible feats. The Secretary does well to caution you on these matters for I suspect you are a man of some principle and would not take kindly to being made to look the fool."

"If the Secretary will allow me the time, I am more interested in your travels. I gather you have seen a good deal of the territory along the frontier. I have been commissioned to do a survey of a possible transcontinental rail route and would be most interested in your sharing with me your observations."

Turning his attention to the Secretary, Captain Gunnison apologized for his intrusion, "I'm out of place to interject myself . . ."

"No, no," the Secretary interrupted. "You bring up the very point I was going to ask our friend about."

Turning then to Clay, Secretary Crawford continued. "The route you took from the Oregon Territory and indeed on to Washington from Fort Boise is along the very route that Congress has asked the Captain to survey. Any information you can give us regarding your travels will be most helpful. We have expanded this nation from sea to sea in less than a decade, now we must tie it together."

The meeting thereafter turned to matters of more interest of Clay and taking advantage of a large map on the Secretary's wall, he related where his travels had taken him. His description of the terrain along the route was noted by the Captain as he took notes and interjected a number of questions as did the Secretary.

"My inclination, the Secretary remarked is that the nation must be bound by a railroad running both to the Pacific Northwest and on into California. But these matters must await a further look. My many thanks for your efforts on behalf of the government, Mr. Anderson, but I must get on to other matters. I will be having a reception at my home tomorrow evening and I would hope you would have the time to attend. There are a few people you should meet. People who will be most interested in your observations. I will see that you receive a formal invitation."

At that the meeting was over Clay and the Captain departed together. When they reached the reception area, only six people remained of the many who had gathered earlier.

"What happened to all the people who were waiting when we went in?" Clay asked the Captain.

"Most of them come here every day hoping to see the Secretary and sell him on some scheme or invention they have come up with. No doubt they were told that the Secretary would not see them today and they left. Most of them will be here again tomorrow. It's the way things work in Washington. The hope of a government contract, especially for weapons would make most of these fellows rich. The generals and officers are here to urge the Secretary to add appropriation requests in the next budget for some project they favor."

"I would expect that some of them will be calling on you, knowing that you have gained the Secretary's favor."

When Clay returned to the hotel, the lobby was abuzz with a multitude of reporters from papers all over the East who had read the content of the dispatches Clay had brought from Fort Boise. Clay was not aware who they were or what their intention was, but as he entered the lobby, the clerk gave a nod to the assembled reporters and they fell on Clay like the wolves from the plains. He was asked a dozen questions at once and had no chance to answer one when another was pending.

"Who do you think killed the emigrants in Utah Territory?"

"Have you killed any Indians?"

"Is the Secretary of War going to send troops out to give them Mormons their due?"

"Were them emigrants scalped and mutilated?"

"What did you tell the Secretary?"

"How come you didn't get kilt with them other men in Oregon?"

In exasperation, Clay pushed his way through the crowd and ran for his room where he locked the door and would not answer any of the knocking that resounded through his room and his brain. This then is what he had been warned about. The incessant questioning could well lead one into a trap, for they gave you no time to think before they demanded answers to yet more provocative questions. After the reporters had exhausted their futile efforts for an interview and left Clay some solitude, another knock came at his door.

"Get the hell out of here," Clay shouted.

"It's a message from Secretary Crawford, Sir. I am his messenger."

Clay remembered then the invitation that he was to receive and opened the door and accepted the message that invited him to a formal reception at the home of Secretary Crawford the next evening. "Formal attire required," the invitation stated, a requirement that left Clay with a problem as he had no formal attire. Upon inquire at the front desk; Clay was advised that such attire could in fact be rented.

"Many of our guests have had to rent formal attire. Few pack such things when they travel," Clay was told.

Clay's experience with such functions was limited. The only time he had worn formal attire was at the funeral of his mother. He felt stiff and constrained in the high collared stiffly starched shirt, the tightly wound cummerbund and shoes that were half a size too small. Although he felt discomforted by the formal dress, Clay was anxious to attend a high society Washington function if for no other reason than to test the warning he had received from Captain Richardson at Fort Boise. Since arriving in Washington D.C. Clay had seen little of the fairer sex and spoken to none. His young blood and sexual interests were more of a driving force committing him to attend the function than was his interest in again meeting members of the Washington officialdom. His thoughts of sexual matters were much affected of late by the stripping of the female slave at the market place. He felt ashamed to have a prurient interest in the disgracing of the unfortunate, dishonored mother, but he could not erase from his mind the nubile delights that such a body could provide. His hope now was to find some more suitable subject upon whom he could direct his rising passions.

There was a long line of carriages waiting to deposit their passengers at the portico entrance of the pretentious, colonnaded Crawford mansion. Ladies in elaborate, colorful dresses and capes were escorted from the carriages and hurried into the warmth of the mansion, while the gentlemen mingled about greeting each other and taking their last draw from their aromatic cigars. Clay was one of the few guests who arrived singly and passed through the throng of lingering guest without notice.

An elaborately liveried servant met him at the entrance and inspected his invitation and then bowed at the waist with a gesture of his hand waived him inside. He was met by a milling crowd of mostly ladies, who were waiting to pass off their capes and coats to pertly dressed maids and then join their escorts as they were passed through the presentation line were Secretary Crawford and his wife would welcome them. Clay's acutely developed senses were immediately assaulted by a mired of scents radiating from the warming bodies of the ladies in the foyer. He though he must be near the rose garden, but realized it was not the season for such odors to be permeating the air.

How long, he wondered, had it been since he last smelled the scent of perfumes? How long had it been since he had seen the coiffured hair of a finely dressed woman. Was it that trip to St. Louis before they departed on their westward trek when he purchased the passions of a lady of the evening? Or was it the more subtle and innocent presence of his mother as she dressed for a night out with his father? He found the smell intoxicating and lingered for a moment in the foyer observing the disrobing of the ladies who when loosing the security of the coats and capes exposed an abundance of inviting white flesh about their neck and bodice. Most of the ladies were of a motherly, matronly configuration and not of interest to him, but there were there among the ladies the young and the vivacious whose presence radiated the sweet invitation of possible pleasures.

His observations were interrupted by someone grasping his elbow. He turned to see Captain Gunnison at his side resplendent in his dress blue uniform, sword and all.

"It is a sight to behold, is it not? Like a covey of swan gathering at some favorite nesting ground. I venture to say you will have many of them seeking your attention before this evening is over."

Clay looked at the Captain quizzically, "Why should they even notice my presence. Indeed none have noticed me yet," He responded with a rueful smile.

"I have been ignored thus far in spite of my goggling."

"Have you not read the evening papers? You now have a reputation that even the Lord himself would envy. The great Indian fighter, explorer, survivor of untold hardships, young, eligible and innocent are now your indelible legacy."

Clay was at a loss to respond. He had not read the papers, being engaged in preparation for his attendance at the Secretaries reception.

"Surely you jest," Clay responded, the horror of the revelation apparent on his troubled features.

"No, I fear I have not even done justice to the effusiveness that describes your exploits. I believe the Secretary suggested that you had best prepare yourself for these eulogies."

Clay was in a quandary now wondering what he had said when confronted by the reporters in the hotel lobby that might justify such unlikely reporting of what he considered his modest exploits and victimization by circumstance.

"I gave them no reason for such ridiculous speculations," Clay retorted. "There must be some error, sir in what you report."

The Captain smiled and suggested that they best proceed through the reception line as the crowed in the lobby was thinning. "I am sure as the evening progressed that you will have ample confirmation of my report."

The conformation came soon enough as they were introduced as they entered the hall and proceeded to the expected greeting from the host and hostess.

"Captain of the Army John Gunnison and Mr. Clay Anderson," the uniformed soldier announced as they entered the hall and handed to the soldier their invitation.

The murmuring in the room ceased and those in hearing of the announcement turned their attention to the reception line as Clay approached the Secretary. "Have I not been correct, my good friend," the Captain murmured at this side.

Clay's immediate thought was to turn and run out the door, but that option was closed as the Secretary firmly grasp his hand. "It appears Mr. Anderson, you have become the guest of honor which is all well and good as the president is indisposed and has sent his regrets."

"I have done nothing to deserve any attention, Mr. Secretary. I have not read the reports that have been published in tonight's paper, but Captain Gunnison has filled me in on some of the details, none of which appears to have any validity."

The Secretary gave him a knowing smile and placed a reaffirming hand on his shoulder.

"It matters little now what the truth may be. You are cast in a mold that most in this town would die to inhabit. Your fame, whether deserved or not, is now your currency. Spend it wisely."

At that the Secretary turned to his wife. "This is the young man who has risk life and limb to bring the dispatches that have been reported in tonight's papers."

"Oh, Mr. Anderson, I am delighted you have come. You must let be introduce you to my guests," she said effusively. "They will be delighted to meet you. Please permit me," she urged as he put her arm through his, left the reception line and moved him into the large foyer where she set about with dispatch and obvious pleasure to introduce him to her many guests.

Clay was rushed through the crowd of Senators, Congressmen, Ambassadors, government officials of all descriptions, newspapermen, businessmen and the many friends of the Crawford's. To Clay the entire process was not only the source of embarrassment, but added immensely to his desire to escape what he felt was a charade. He could find no appropriate words to respond to the effusive greetings and endless questions and reverted to muttering responses that seemed to make little difference to the guests. It appears they wanted most to say they had met with the "great warrior of the west" as one guest referred to him.

When the guests were finally called to dinner, Clay was ushered to a seat near the head of the table and seated beside his hostess on the left and to his right a young lady of considerable beauty dressed in a pink frilly gown with a bodice that caused Clay to blush as he was caught by his dining partner staring at her attributes. The young lady, rather than being offended, merely smiled at him,

"You have been out west for a long time haven't you?"

"Yes I have, I apologize for starring at you like that," Clay responded.

"You need not apologize for behavior that is a consequence to my provocations. What good is a dress if no one finds it's wearer of interest?"

Clay took a moment to gaze more completely at the lady to his right. She had flashing brown eyes, an engaging smile, features like those of his mother, with high aristocratic cheek bones and dark brown hair that was drawn like a bun atop her head with cascading ringlets that added an intriguing comment to a hair arrangement that no doubt took her all afternoon to perfect.

"My name is Jessie Fremont. My husband is an explorer like yourself."

Clay's embarrassment returned. "Please Mrs. Fremont; do not compare my modest exploits with those of your husband. I have done nothing to deserve the attention that I have received here tonight. I do hope you will introduce me to your husband before he leaves."

"My husband is in California at the present and in dire circumstances." As she said this, she gave a conspiratorial look at the hostess seated next to Clay. Her husband as Secretary of War would have some say in her husband's circumstance since Fremont had accepted a commission. "The Army wishes to discipline him for insubordination. It appears he has been too bold in his efforts to bring California into the union and has run afoul of General Kearny's ambitions."

"You are talking of matters that I have no knowledge of, Madam. I trust you husband will prevail," Clay replied hoping to steer the conversation onto subjects of more interest to him. He was disappointed that the lovely lady who was his companion was married and at that married to the famous explorer and surveyor of the west.

"I find it admirable that you so readily reject the adulations that have been cast upon you, but surely you do deserve some of the credits that have been attributed to your travels and adventures," Jessie Fremont offered realizing that the young man next to her was ill at ease in his present circumstance.

"Thank you for your kindness," Clay replied, but I have done nothing that deserves the attention I have been subjected too. I know dozens of men on the frontier who are more deserving than me of the gratitude of these people."

"My husband would be most please to meet you. He admires men of modesty and honesty. But there is yet another I would like to introduce you to before you depart. My father, as you may know, is Senator Tomas Hart Benton from Missouri. He has a great interest in the expansion of the frontier. His present interest is in a transcontinental railroad. He would be most interested in meeting you and getting your impression of the lands over which you have traveled. California must not only become a state, it must be tied to the union with more solid bonds."

The evening was not going well for Clay. He not only found himself in the ridiculous role of the hero of the frontier, he was now being hustled by a Senator's daughter to become involved in yet another situation that could lead him into more embarrassment.

"I'm sure the Senator has more to do with his time than to listen to stories of my misadventures," Clay replied dismissively.

"On the contrary, few have taken the trip from the center of the Oregon Territory eastward through the great basin. Besides, there is a great deal to be known here about the Indian tribes in the area. I insist that you meet him, now say that you will," Jessie implored placing her hand over his and looking him earnestly in the eyes.

Against his better judgment, Clay, succumbing to the pleas of the lovely guest whose intimate touch had the effect intended, consented to the meeting.

Further conversation was interrupted when the dinner was served. Clay was treated to a variety of dishes that were wholly unfamiliar to him, from the turtle soup that started the procession of lavish dishes, to the Cherries Jubilee that concluded the meal; Clay was bewildered by the variety and quantity of the courses that were served. The wine that was served with each course consisted of an interminable variety of flavors, few of which he found to his taste. When the meal finally ended and the gentlemen began to retire to the library for cordials, cigars and discourse, Jessie Fremont took Clay by the arm and escorted him to the far end of the table where several men lingered in serious discussion before retiring to the library

"Father, I would like you to meet Clay Anderson. He is recently from the Oregon Territory and the subject of all the articles in tonight's papers. I told him you would be interested in meeting him. Clay, please meet my father Senator Benton."

At the introduction, the Senator summarily dismissed the other guest he had been conferring with and grasped Clay's hand and gave him a firm grip and placed his other arm about his shoulder ushering him along to the library.

"My good man, I have much to discuss with you. Every since I heard you were in town I have been meaning to get in contact with you."

Senator Benton was a tall, heavy set man with a flowing main, a clean shaven face, and a prominent nose that was the one disfigurement his daughter inherited. He spoke with a loud authoritative voice as if he were speaking on the floor of the Senate. Clay was generally familiar with the career of Senator Benton who, though a slave owner, had recently split with his party's Sothern Democratic base over the spread of slavery into the new territories. His voice was raised in opposition to Henry Clay's advocacy for the expansion of slavery and his opposition to the National Bank and paper money had given him the nickname of "Old Bullion," a moniker that seemed to blend with his character.([16])

After they entered the library and were tendered sherry or brandy Clay found himself surrounded by a group of prominent appearing men as the Senator undertook what turned out to be an exhaustive, pertinent, and intense interview that drew the attention of most of those who were present. Surprisingly, the Senator seemed more interested in the Indian situation on the frontier than any other topic. The Senator, as Clay recalled, had been an advocate for the removal of the Indians from the land where white settlers would likely claim. He had been instrumental in devising the policy that drove the Seminoles and Cherokee from Florida and Georgia and resettled them in the parched regions of the Oklahoma territory.

"What tribe was responsible for the three slaughters you witnessed?" The Senator asked.

"How many members were in the hostile tribes?"

"What part of the territory did they claim as their tribal grounds?"

"Was the land that you crossed level enough for a railroad to pass over?"

To each answer, the Senator had some further question until Clay became fatigued and perplexed and finally asked the Senator a question that halted the interview and scattered the ranks of the assembled listeners.

"How is it that there exists in the nation's capital, a nation that extols the virtues of free men, a slave market where women, children and their men are sold like cattle at auction?"

To Clay's surprise, the Senator was not offended by the question, but responded with candor.

"That is a matter that troubles the President and is part of the debate now in Congress. It is unfitting to have such activities in the shadow

---

[16] Thomas Hart Benton (senator) hptt://en.wikipedia.org/wiki/Thomas_Hart_Benton_(senator)

of the Capital. I trust the matter shall be resolved in this session if the compromise Webster and Clay are working on come to pass."

"But then, that is another matter, son. I would like you to appear before the Indian Affairs Subcommittee. The report you have brought to Washington requires some further investigation and obviously some military response. Your appearance will assist the nation greatly in setting a more vigorous Indian policy."

"I am not certain I am the man you want to testify on that question. There must be dozens of other men who are more aware of the Indian difficulties in the West than I am. I have met a number of officers in the army who have had more contact with the Indians than I have. Surely you would do better to relying on career solders then people like me."

"Son, you have been witness to the bestiality of these red men on three different occasions. You have seen the mutilated bodies of innocent women and children. You have seen brave husband and fathers struck down by the savages as they stood to defend their innocent families. You better than anyone else can testify as to the atrocities that have been visited upon the unfortunate emigrants who have done no wrong except to seek land and a home for their families. You speak of the military and their interest in the matter. It has been my experience that their only interest is in protecting the savages from the invasion of their sacred hunting grounds. They blame not the insufferable savagery thrust upon the settlers and their children by the hostile tribes, rather they tend to blame the settlers for trespassing upon land the Indians have no real claim to; land that is there for the taking. No, I suspect the army is derelict in its duty to the citizens and does not want to be called into the fight."

Clay found it difficult to express himself against such a formidable advocate who had neither empathy nor concern for the welfare of the native Indians. In spite of the loss of so many innocent people many of whom he had called his friends, Clay felt little enmity for the Indians who lived by a simpler more basic nature, a nature that drove them to defend lands long held sacred by them from the intrusion of those whose claim would exclude them from trespass. The Indians of the west had no conception of deed claims upon lands that had since time immemorial been free land that no one could claim; land that only their Spirit Gods could possess and over which they had free passage.

"Congress is considering a Homestead Act," the Senator continued, "that will allow every emigrant who will improve land to settle it and claim it. The thousands who are trekking forth on their westward journey will lay claim to a great unsettled territory from which no foreign power could thence expel us. If we do not settle that land and hold it firmly to the bosom of the union, we may well lose it. You, Mr. Anderson, can add assistance to the great westward destiny that is the inevitable heritage of our great people. The natives that now possess the untilled soil of such abundance will one day be displaced from it either by citizens of this nation or of another. The meek may indeed inherit the earth; but we must first settle it."

Clay was certain that what he was being exposed to was a word picture of the future of the west. There was an inevitability inherent in the Senator's vision that Clay knew was inescapable. The multitudes that arrived each day in the ports of the east bolstered by the untold numbers of venturous Americans who traveled the Oregon Trail and Santa Fe Trail each year would inevitably change the character of the west forever. The talk of the railroad and the telegraph extending from ocean to ocean along with the settlers thronging westward, spelled the doom of the native culture that Senator Benton and his like neither respected nor cared to acknowledge.

Clay agreed to meet with the committee as requested by the Senator, but not for the purposes the Senator anticipated. When he heard that the meeting would not be for another week and that he would have to stay in town that much longer, Clay considered withdrawing his offer, but before he could do so, the doors of the library were thrown open and the men, along with their bilious clouds of cigar smoke, filtered out into the main room to join the ladies, to extend their thanks to the host and to retire from the evening's event.

That night, Clay gathered together as many newspapers as he could and retiring to his room and read with disgust the exaggerations and inventive reporting that detailed his adventures crossing the continent. He thought then of the words of Captain Richardson and the observations of the lawyer Lincoln. The press wanted a hero to write about and the truth would be no obstacle to their enterprise. He thought also of the words of advice from the Secretary given at the reception line. He could do little to change what had become his reputation; all that mattered now was how he would spend the coinage that was his legacy. As to that, Clay's mind was becoming firmly set against allowing himself to be treated as a passing novelty to be used as entertainment by Washington's elite.

As he stood by the hotel window the next morning viewing the scene, he could see the Capital building with the scaffolding enshrouding its top most portion like a spider's web. To the right of the capital building and but a short distance from it was the embryonic beginnings of the Washington Monument. It too was shrouded in scaffolding and was a beehive of activity. To many the building of an obelisk of such staggering height was an unimaginable feat. It would eventually rise to a height of 555 feet, but few could know that day that the events occurring on the floor of the Senate would soon cause a rift in the national populace that would prevent the completing of the monument for another forty years. ([17]) Clay's reading of the event surrounding the construction of the monument lead him to further inquire into the life of Major Pierre Charles L'Enfant, the man who first proposed a memorial to the first president. Why would a Frenchman, he wondered, be the proponent of a tribute to an American president?

Having little to do with his time as he awaited his appearance as requested by Senator Benton before the Senate Committee on Indian Affairs, Clay decided to wander over to the Smithsonian Institute and see what he could find out about Major L'Enfant. He discovered that the Major, at age twenty two became inspired by the vision of the struggle the American colonials were engaged in to divest themselves of the arbitrary rule of the King of England. Although an avid student of painting and sculpture his sensitive disposition was no impediment to him when he came to America with Lafayette and enrolled in the Continental Army as a Captain and served with distinction during the Revolutionary War. L'Enfant was gravely wounded in the battle for Savanna and upon his recovery he served on Washington's staff and was promoted to Manor. His experience during the war and his service on General Washington's staff led him to become a great admirer of General Washington.

At the end of hostilities, L'Enfant performed his greatest service for the fledgling nation he had adopted. Through the offices of then President

---

[17] Washington Monument http://www.cr.nps.gov/nr/travel/wash/dc72.htm

Washington, he was appointed the chief architect for the design and building of the nation's capital. It was a great novelty for a people to engage in a project that called for the creation of an entirely new city as its capital, a city that would uniquely claim the heritage of a new nation. The large malls, the broad boulevards, especially Pennsylvania Avenue were features he insisted upon. His design of the capital and its many buildings in the classical Roman columbular architecture gave the young nation a claim to the greatness and strength of another great Empire. ([18])

That evening when Clay had some moments to himself for reflection, he began, for the first time in his young life, to appreciate the nation to which he now claimed citizenship. Although it now had certain geographical boundaries that could define it as a nation, its people were not so easily defined. Many who now claimed American citizenship could not claim that right by birth. They had either just arrived from a foreign land that claimed their birthright, or their forbearers were so recently arrived that they had not completely shed the customs of another culture.

Clay recalled the members of the wagon train that his family had joined in their westward trek. The train was made up of Germans, Irish, Britons, French, Swedes, Norwegians, Italians and he knew not how many other nationalities. He grew up in Illinois amid people who spoke many languages. Here in Washington, the Capital of the nation, the melding of the many cultures of immigrants made the difference between the various nationalities less apparent. It was here and in the other great cities of the East that the nation and its character were being forged. Those who wandered across the vast expanses of the west may be the settlers that would lay claim to the vast continent, but they were but the flock and here in Washington and the centers of the east, were the leaders who would define their rights, their heritage and their nationhood. Yet, like the many columns that gave support to the structures that housed its government, many nationalities could claim a contribution to the structure of the nation here being forged.

The great challenge to that nation and its proclamations of freedom and equality were now being subjected to the severest, most challenging

---

[18] Pierre Charles L.'Enfant, Maor, United States Army http://www.arlingtoncemetery.net/l-enfant.htm

test. As one of its great leaders would one day declare, this great nation could not long survive half slave and half free. To Clay there was a further question that troubled him. Could a nation driven by the lust for the lands and the fortunes abounding in its western regions lay claim to its humanity if it drove from those lands and into extinction the peoples who had so long possessed it? Ironically, Clay discovered, Lawyer Lincoln whom he had met in his trip to the east when he served in the Congress, had raised that very issue when President Polk and the Texans drove from the southwest the Mexicans who had prior claim to those lands. The Native Americans had claims that preceded even those of the Spanish through whom the Mexican's rested their claim. Unlike the Mexican government, however, the Indian Nations had no unity and their migrant nature made it difficult to determine or even address their claims to any particular lands. Their disunity, Clay realized, would be their gravest misfortune.

To Clay's disappointment, he was notified the next day that the committee meeting that he was scheduled to attend had been postponed for two weeks because of the debate now raging over what was to become known as the Missouri Compromise that would allow slavery in part of Missouri, but extend it no further. Even though the compromise appeared to be favored as the best hope of saving the union, its ratification of the provisions of the fugitive slave law would make it impossible for the anti-slave northerner contingent to accept its provisions and to let rest the matter of slavery. The outlawing of slave markets in the nation's capital was a concession that to the anti-slave contingent meant little as a bargain, for the detestable nature of the conduct was enough alone to condemn it.

Clay was seriously considering departing on his way to the Oregon Territory, when he became deluged with invitations to all forms of parties and celebrations. It was as if the pending compromise had set free the pent up spirit of the Washington establishment and they were ready to turn to more pleasurable matters. Clay did not have unlimited funds and turned down a number of the invitations only to find a more insistent one at his door the next day. It was at a reception by the British Ambassador where Clay once again came across Captain Gunnison. He saw the Captain wave to him and beckon him across the room where he was in conversation with two other officers. As he was introduced, Clay was advised that they were all Army Engineers and had been discussing the expansion of the western rail road to the Pacific coast. Captain Gunnison, Clay was advised had just been given the assignment to survey a transcontinental route and would be leaving in the spring to commence that survey.

"Mr. Anderson, I am delighted to see you here tonight, it saves me the trouble of having to run you down. I am in need of several scouts to accompany my detachment and your name is on the top of my list. What do you have to say about that proposition?"

"It sounds interesting, Captain. Do you want my answer now or may I have the leisure of communicating my answer in a couple of days? It is rather sudden you know."

"Of course, of course," the Captain replied with a chuckle. "These matters do take some time; we will have to have a contract and all that. I just wanted to plant the idea in your mind and get you thinking about it."

"I am flattered that you would consider me Captain, your offer may be timely. I have used up all the vouchers I was given for this trip and am now living off of my own recourses which are not unlimited."

"Yes, that is a matter that we can take care of," the Captain assured him as he gave him a card with his address. "Please come by within the week and we can get this matter settled. I am counting on you."

Clay was turning to leave, when the Captain placed his hand on Clay's arm, "That reminds me Mr. Anderson, there is someone here who has asked me to introduce you to him. I think you will find him of some help with your current situation."

The Captain ushered Clay to the far side of the room where several gentlemen were lounging in overstuffed leather chairs having a cigar. One of the men, a tall handsome clean shaven man who when he stood, was a head taller than Clay, stepped forward as Clay and the Captain approached.

"Ah, Captain you remembered. I thank you. And this gentleman by your side is the man I have been wanting to meet every since I saw him get past that imbecile who guards Secretary Crawford's office door. My name is Oliver Winchester. I own, among several ventures, the Volcanic Repeating Arms Company. I doubt that you have heard of it, but that is a fact I intend to remedy. Come sit down and let's have a chat before that pesky hostess ushers us off to dinner."

"What kind of rifle do you own, young man?" Winchester asked.

"As a matter of fact," Clay responded, "I sold my Hawkins in Chicago. It seems there were no buffalo around there and packing that rifle around rather interfered with my opportunities for friendly discourse."

"Yes, yes, I imagine it would. We are attempting to become a civilized society, but I fear the discourse here in Washington would attest otherwise. But let me get to my business with you, young man. You have a reputation as a plainsman, and Indian fighter and a general all around hero."

As Clay started to protest the assertion, Mr. Winchester merely smiled, "I know there may be some exaggeration in the reports I have read, but that only makes you more important for my purposes. I want you to come out to my friend's country place and have a friendly little hunt with me and several of my associates. Without beating around the bush, I have a new rifle I would like you to try out. If you like it, I would hope to induce you to endorse it and say a few kindly words about it that I could use to impress some of these obstinate generals who are still equipping the army with muzzle loading rifles. Do you have any objection to a little time in the country and some hunting?" ([19])

Clay was delighted to accept the offer and get out of the city. "You name the time and place, and I will be there," He replied.

The next day Clay checked out of the Willard Hotel and at the appointed hour he found a carriage awaiting him and was soon on his way to meet Oliver Winchester. The carriage was closed and comfortable, with maroon velvet seats and was furnished with a matching wool lap robe. Clay could not help but notice the elegance of the carriage with its highly polished brass lanterns and trim. The matched Chestnut horses were no doubt Hamiltonian. They moved the carriage with a graceful, steady pace that soon had them outside the city and traveling over unpaved, rutted roads. Clay breathed deeply of the clean, crisp air that bore the scent of a recent rain. The pungent smell of wood and coal fires, animal waste and human garbage had made travel about the city an unpleasant experience for one like Clay who had been on the frontier.

A decanter of spirits had been provided for the trip and a humidor was stocked with cigars, both of which Clay declined but he did discover that

---

[19] Oliver Fisher Winchester-Wikipedia http://en.wikipedia.org/wiki/Oliver_Winchester

one of the decanters had a punch type drink that he found enjoyable. Clay had made some inquiries about Oliver Winchester and was surprised to discover that he was a man of considerable wealth, which he had suspected on their first meeting, but his wealth came from the textile mills he owned not from fire arms. Whatever the source of the man's wealth, Clay welcomed its embrace.

When the carriage turned off the main road and onto a long driveway lined with stately oak trees, Clay became aware that he was not visiting a hunting lodge as he had anticipated, but the grounds of a plantation. Clay had seen many towns in the west that were less populated then the sprawling plantation with its many barns, sheds and rows of slave cabins. The main house was a large two story white building with the familiar columned facade that graced so many of the Southern estates he had visited. Over the driveway at the gated entrance was a large wooden arch with the inscription "Welcome to Twin Oaks".

As soon that the carriage stopped under the portico, a servant appeared as if out of nowhere and opened the carriage door. Clay stepped out to be greeted by a liveried, silver haired Negro who spoke to him in a hearty, welcoming bass, "Mr. Anderson, welcome to Twin Oaks. The gentlemen await you in the study. Please follow me." As he turned to lead the way he instructed the other servant to, "Take Mr. Anderson's luggage to the blue suite."

Clay, realizing that his hunting clothes that he now wore, which were in fact his buckskins and moccasins from the frontier, were wholly unsuited for the occasion suggested to the elderly butler and that perhaps he should change before the meeting.

"I was instructed to bring you directly to the library, sir. Don't concern yourself about your dress. The gentlemen are in their hunting attire also."

Clay had but a moment to take in the magnificence of the entrance way that was dominated by a large ornate chandelier, a large Persian rug, and only a modicum of furniture, all of which gave emphasis to the large staircase that led to the upper story. A number of large carefully crafted doors lead off the entrance way one of which the butler swung open with a surprising ease for such a large entry and Clay was ushered inside. As the door closed silently behind him Clay felt diminutive and ill at ease as he surveyed a room where a huge fireplace radiated warmth and brightness in a room the size of most hotel lobbies. Cases of books lined one wall while the outer wall was graced by the mounted heads of game animals, most of which Clay had never seen before. Large overstuffed leather chairs were arranged in several conversation groups about the room. Further light was added to what would be an otherwise darkened room by the two chandeliers that seemed to match the one that impressed Clay as he had entered the mansion.

Two men who had been relaxing in front of the fire stood up as he entered and stepped forward to greet Clay. Clay recognized one of them as Oliver Winchester and was soon introduced to the other as Oliver's close friend Roger Mansfield. "Mr. Mansfield is the proprietor of this modest little estate that I mistakenly call the hunting lodge, for that is what always brings me here, a good hunt."

"I hope I have not misled you too greatly as I see you have come dressed for the hunt."

"I fear I was misled, I must apologize. I did, fortunately bring with me my entire wardrobe as I did not intend to return to Washington. If you will excuse me I will find my belongings and dress more appropriately." Clay responded.

Roger Mansfield who had stood beside his friend with an amused expression retorted. "You are a man of the frontier and I should not expect you to dress otherwise. You are perfectly welcome as you are. I suspect you would not be comfortable in city dress, so let's not worry the matter more. I have been most anxious to chat with you, please come by the fire and have a cordial and let's get acquainted. Oh, I must be the one to apologize now," he said as he turned to the far side of the room where Clay now noticed a third person was present.

"May I present my niece, Fay Mansfield. She will attend the hunt, it being her last respite before she leaves for New England to enter into matrimony with the scallywag who stole my princess from me."

As Miss Mansfield crossed the room, Clay's breath came up short. It was as if he were seeing Jenny again removed from the course frontier and cast into the womb of the abundance she deserved. Clay had flashbacks of that night when Jenny and his brother announced their engagement. He felt again the disappointment that came with the announcement. Jenny,

Clay felt, could never debase her effervescent spirit to fit the strictures his brother's wife would have to bear.

Fay wore what must have been the latest fashion in riding apparel; it was a tight split skirt, a white frilled blouse that accentuated an ample bust that was tightly embraced by a red felt vest. High leather boots graced what Clay imagined as firm rounded thighs. She removed a broad brimmed hat as she approached Clay and with a flick of her head sent a cascade of auburn hair whirling about her shoulders. She had dark brown, almost black eyes like an Indian's and a swarthy complexion. She moved like a gazelle, light and quick, and was before him in a moment. Clay was struggling for composure as she extended her hand. Clay didn't know whether he should kiss the hand or shake it. So he merely held it as he studied a face that was all too familiar to him.

"Forgive me if I stare," Clay finally remarked as the hand holding become embarrassingly long, "But it seems I have known you before. My brother's intended has a remarkable resemblance to you. I didn't think such beauty could be duplicated." He said as he released her hand and instantly felt he had overstepped the limits of proper manners by his last remark.

"You are a discerning gentleman indeed," Roger Mansfield offered. "Her coming marriage will break a thousand hearts."

Fay, who had stood observing Clay's reaction to her presence, had an enigmatic smile as she accepted Clay's admiration. "And I thought you men of the frontier only admired horses. I am flattered."

Sensing the mischiefness in her manner, Clay responded; "A good horse in a land of danger can save your life, a good woman in good society can give you a life."

"I know nothing of that land of danger you have visited, but rest assured you will need more than a fast horse when that good woman you speak of sets her cap for you."

"I have been about Washington society for several weeks now and have had no confrontations that put my virtue in danger," Clay replied.

"Don't assume too much. I have heard the ladies speak of you and you are in mortal danger of being drawn into the spider's web," Fay teased. "You had best carry your rifle at the ready," she said as she lowered her gaze to the rising mound in Clay's trousers.

"Well, well, enough of this." Roger interjected; you two are getting us nowhere. Let's have that cordial and get on with talk of the hunt and let Mr. Anderson tell us about that wild land he has recently visited."

"You men go ahead and smoke your smelly old cigars and have your chat. I must change out of this riding habit and dress for dinner," Fay remarked as she walked past Clay giving him a warm smile and a wink that left him wondering if there was more to her actions than he should hope for.

Clay was anxious to get to his room and to change into more appropriate attire for the diner hour, but was unable to find a point in the conversation where he could politely excuse himself. He was distressed to hear these men of means discuss westward expansion in terms of national necessity. Each of the older men looked upon westward expansion in different terms. Roger felt that it would eventually lead to a conflict between the northern Free states and the southern slave states. Roger was the owner of what Clay suspected to be several hundred slaves. To him, the right to move his slaves freely into the new territories was as he stated a property right granted in the Constitution.

"This land I own has been handed down through several generations, and the soil is worn out. I need new lands in those western territories to keep Twin Oaks viable. This Missouri Compromise that those politicians claim will save the Union will only exacerbate the final solution that must allow citizens to move about the nation unrestrained by these silly notions that the slaves ought to be free. Free, indeed! They couldn't survive without our protection."

"We've been over these matters before, Roger," Mr. Winchester responded. "We have many freed slaves up North and they get about just fine. Their real problem is that they are forever caught up in the wrangle between the Abolitionists and the Democrats. You say they couldn't survive without your assistance. If your assistance was more akin to exploiting their talents and minds rather than their labor, perhaps they could better prove their worth as citizens."

Clay was discomforted by the bluntness of the discourse and was reluctant to engage either in debate. As long as they limited their questions to him about the conditions of the western lands, he felt comfortable, but the question was finally put to him by Roger he could no longer remain neutral.

"What is your opinion in the matter Mr. Anderson: should the territories be open to all, or just those who want to farm the land with their own labor?

Clay had been giving this matter a good deal of thought over the past several weeks and his response came without consideration for the sensibilities of his host.

"The western lands are not suitable for the slave culture you people have enjoyed here in the South. There are no lawmen to enforce your laws regarding runaway slaves. There are harsh winters during which you would have to feed and house your slaves without productive labor to keep them duty bound. There are marauding tribes who would steal your slave and take them into Mexico beyond your reach. You reside here in a community where there is acceptance of your culture. There is no community system beyond the Mississippi that would protect you from revolt or unrest among your slaves."

Clay was warming to his subject now and ignored discretion. "As the soil that claims the labor of your slaves becomes depleted, the justification for their bondage must also die. It is convenient to your argument to refer the black man as less than human. If he be indeed mere "property" than he can claim no greater expectation than could a cow or a horse.

"I and many others do not accept that assumption. I have not spent a life time among them as have you, but those with whom I have associated are more like me than not and are no more dissimilar to me than any other stranger I could come upon,"

As Clay was about to add more to his assertions, he heard hand clapping from behind him. It was Fay. "Well said Mr. Anderson, I have been telling Uncle that he and the other plantation owners should manumit their slaves and be done with this rancor that will bring the North and the South into eventual conflict." Fay had slipped into the room to advise them that dinner would be ready soon.

To Clay's relief, Roger seemed to take no offence at his remarks or to those of his niece.

"You put your case well, young man and it will give me pause for thought. Now let's be on with dinner."

There were other guests for dinner. Clay didn't know if they arrived just for dinner or were guests who had been invited like him for the hunt. The conversation centered on matters of local concern such as the latest social event or the price of cotton. Clay found little interest in the conversation but did find some interest in the repeated glances that came his way as the other guests seemed distracted by the presence of a stranger visiting from regions remote to them. The questions he got were perfunctory until Fay turned the conversation to embrace him.

"Mr. Anderson here would disagree with you Mr. Clayton. He thinks we should not press the issue of extending slavery beyond its present limits. Isn't that correct Mr. Anderson?"

Clay hadn't been much interested in the conversation and had let his mind wonder. When the attention of the guests fell upon him, he was ill prepared to become the center of attention.

"I can't imagine my opinion on the matter is of much interest." He finally offered, realizing that he could not dodge the issue as the room became silent as the guests awaited his response. "I have no dog in this fight. My opinions are just that and being a stranger in this company, I would not wish to offend any of the guests whose views on the matter of slavery are based upon interests more vested than mine."

"I say," came the response of a young gentleman who Clay had been introduced to earlier, but whose name he had already forgotten, "We seem to have found the rare Yankee who knows his place."

The insolence of the remark brought a surge of anger to Clay and he started to respond when Fay interjected: "Well, Byron you certainly are one to know one's place, now aren't you."

Clay saw the immediate flash of anger on Byron's face as he turned to face Fay. His fist was clenched about his napkin, the veins in his neck and temple seemed to visibly pulse, yet he said nothing.

Clay realized that Fay had put Byron down brutally and that his response to the impertinence was unnecessary. Apparently no one else in the room except Fay and Byron were privy to the circumstances that created such a violent reaction to Fay's remark. All the guests were silent as they looked to first Fay and than to Byron wondering what currents were running between them. Clay realized that he had become the innocent trespasser in dangerous territory and that Byron would spill his hate and vengeance upon him for the embarrassment he had suffered this night.

The next morning a buffet breakfast was prepared as the guest assembled for the hunt. Clay, dressed in the only clothes he had brought for the hunt, clothes suitable for what he expected would be an experience similar to the hunting he had done on the plains. The rest of the guests were dressed as if they were going on an English Fox Hunt, with high polished boots, jodhpurs, brass buttoned coats and frilled shirts. While the other guests refrained from comment, Byron did not.

"What the devil kind of hunting kit is that?" He remarked as he entered the room where the rest of the guests were gathered. "Are you hunting boar or squirrel?"

Although Byron laughed at his suggestion, the rest of the guests turned away and busied them with the breakfast attempting to ignore the rudeness underlying the remark. Clay felt his face grow crimson and glanced briefly at Fay who was watching the two of them with an amused smile on her face as if she had been expecting the confrontation. After hesitating to gain composure, Clay responded:

"Well, I do apologize for my dress, but you see, I came prepared to kill a bear if I found one, not to mate with it."

Clay watched as Byron's right hand instinctively moved with a practiced reaction to this inside coat at the waist band. Clay knew in the circumstance Byron would not pull a weapon, but he had caused by his retort to make Byron give away the fact that he carried a pistol in his waist band and was inclined to use it.

The others found Clay's retort amusing and several of the guests tittered and guffawed.

"We shall see who will do the dancing," Byron responded as he turned and left the room.

Again Clay found himself perplexed at the confrontation, wondering why he had so quickly and irrefutably alienated Byron to the point where he was certain if the two of them had been alone, Byron would have drawn down on him.

He looked to Fay for some understanding and saw only an impish smile on her face. He was, he was now certain, part of a competition Fay and Byron were engaged in and he was determined not to be their pawn.

To his surprise, Clay was not part of the hunt that had been planned. Mr. Winchester had other plans for his presence at Twin Oaks. When the buffet was completed and the guest participating in the hunt had left the dining room, Oliver Winchester ushered him to the gun room that was located in the large stable behind the manor. Seated before a work bench, making adjustments to a gilded rifle set in a cradle before him was a man in brown tweed clothes, of a formal set. He didn't seem to notice the entrance of the two men who were beside him before he looked up.

"Oliver, glad you are here; I want to show you some adjustments I have made to the breach of our new rifle. I have strengthened the ejection spring to avoid the fouling we encountered when we last tried it. See here what you think, the man said as he handed the handsomely engraved rifle to Oliver Winchester. Oliver took the weapon and worked the lever action rapidly ejecting shells that rattled across the floor.

"Yes, yes, George, I do think you have solved our problem," Oliver observed as he turned and handed the rifle to Clay. "What do you think of our little baby?" He asked Clay.

Clay was fascinated by the rifle he held and inspected. He was familiar with the Hawkins, Spenser, Sharps and Henry rifles used by the mountain men and the many of the pioneers heading west, but they were nothing like the weapon he held in his hand which was much lighter, more balanced and had the feel of destructive assurance.

Clay picked up the cartridges that had been ejected onto the floor of the gun shop and examined them and then intuitively loaded them into the rifle and repeated the process of ejecting them.

"I presume these things you call cartridges will fire. If you can produce a gun like this I would think you could sell all you can make."

"Yes, well, that's the problem. The army is getting its budget cut each year now that that Mexican mess has been resolved. You can't get them interested in new weapons. That's where you come in to the picture and why I invited you to Twin Oaks. I need someone to prove this gun and make it popular in the West. The government seems a poor option at this time and perhaps the success of the rifle in the West will encourage Congress to vote funds to arm our soldiers with something better than those smooth bore saddle guns that are slow loading and inaccurate at any appreciable distance. What I'm suggesting is that you keep this rifle as your own and take it out West with you and introduce it to the frontier."

Clay extended the rifle at arm's length and inspected the craftsmanship that had molded this fine weapon. He could hardly believe that Oliver Winchester would gift him with this prize.

"I really don't know what to say. It is improbable that one man could go out west and introduce this weapon to the public. A man becomes lost in the immensity of the West and few would even notice him." Clay responded as he handed the rifle back to George.

"Don't worry about that young man. You will not be the only one who will be given one of these rifles. I intend to advertise it and use your name and the names of other well known men of the West as those who endorse my rifle. Now take that rifle and let's go out and do some shooting."

To Clay's surprise the rifle was extremely accurate and even when he fired it as rapidly as possible he could hit his target.

"I suspected you were an able man with a rifle," Oliver Winchester observed. "Now what say you about my proposition?"

Clay sat in his room at Twin Oaks admiring the hand crafted rifle. George had provided him with a wooden case with extra parts and tools to repair the rifle if necessary and assured him that he would provide him with ample cartridges which were being produced by the Spencer Arms Company. There was to be no hunt and for that he was relieved. He was anxious to get back to Washington and on his way back to the frontier. He had forgotten all about Byron, Fay and the intrigue in which he had become an unwilling participant.

The dinner that evening was again formal and was to Clay both distracting and boring. Fay was seated at the other end of the table and Byron sat next to her and that was fine with Clay as he wanted to avoid and further confrontations that might, if occurring without the presence of others, become nasty. Clay did not feel comfortable and would be glad to leave Twin Oaks and to leave Fay and Byron to their own devices.

Clay excused himself from the usual after dinner gathering in the library and went directly to his room. He noticed that something was amiss. The rifle he had placed with caution and the window table had been moved, as had been the wooden box with the parts and tools. At first he suspected the maid had been in to clean his room, but then he noticed his kit bag had also been inspected and his clothes had been rummaged through. What bothered him particularly was that he knew the maid had cleaned his room that morning and suspected she would not have the effrontery to rummage through his things. But why he asked himself, would anyone give a particular damn about his possessions? And why had they been so bold as to leave evidence of their intrusion?

Clay instinctively walked over and locked the large mahogany door. After inventorying his possessions once more to find that nothing was missing, he undressed, washed his body at the basin of water that had been provided and slipped into bed. The hour was late and he felt the need for rest and was soon deep in sleep. It was the instinct possessed by one who was accustomed to sleeping in semi awareness of danger that caused Clay to awake abruptly and reach for the knife on the stand beside his bed. He was certain he was no longer alone. The moon, covered with a cloud layer cast but a dim eerie light through the one window he had left open to allow in the chill, refreshing air. Still, he could not make out any form, but heard the slight rustle of garments as someone moved toward his bed. His muscles tensed as he prepared to confront the intruder. He heard the intruder climb onto his bed and knew that it was time to strike as he rose with his knife at the ready; he was interrupted by a husky female voice. It was Fay.

"Where are you big fella, are you hiding under the bed?"

"Shit!" he exclaimed, "What are you doing here; I came near to driving a knife into your belly."

"Is a knife all you have to drive into a girl? That seems so crude. Now climb back in bed like a good boy and we will see what else you have to offer."

Clay stood in silence for a long period trying to sort things out in his mind. Fay was soon to be married. She and Byron had drawn him into some kind of web of intrigue. Was this visitation to bring him pleasure or pain?

"You do like women, now don't you?" Fay asked, interrupting his introspection.

Clay could now make out the outline of her body as she rested on an elbow looking in his direction. He was certain she had cast off her nightdress and lay naked in his bed. He remembered her lithe, curvaceous body as exposed in her riding habit when he had first been introduced to her. He wanted that body then and he wanted to possess it now. Before he climbed back into bed, he listened intently for any other presence and was certain they were alone.

Clay's limited experience with women had been a chance encounter or two with Indian maidens he had slept with when he trapped alone around the Great Lakes and one dreadful encounter with a prostitute in St. Louis before the wagon train started westward. He was not prepared for the encounter with a woman of Fay's experience and passions. She drove him to desperation and then drained him of his substance again and again until he could no longer respond to her incessant desires.

"My God, woman," he muttered as he pushed her off his body onto the bed beside him. "You could drive a man to his death bed with your appetite. I need a rest. But most of all, I need to know what the devil is going on. How did you get into my room? Why is a beautiful woman like you who is about to get married jumping a total stranger?"

"My grandfather built this house and this was the bridal suit. He wanted his own access to the room and built a secret passage way between his room and this. That panel beside the fire place is the passageway between the rooms. I have the room that was my grandfather's. As to your other question, my coming marrage is one of convenience. I don't love the old fool who will be my husband, but I need the security of his fortune. My father was brother to your host. He died of consumption while we were living in France. He was the French counsel at the time. Needless to say, I grew up in France, a land where a young lady with a lust for life will gain a prospective for life and love that is a bit chancy here at home. Let's just say, I need my male companionship and you were the best prospect."

"What about this Byron fellow. You seem to know him and he no doubt has an eye for you. Why not him rather then me?"

Fay seemed amused by the question and grabbed Clay's penis as she answered. "God was not kind to Byron. His prick wouldn't satisfy a chicken which I am told some men fancy. I told him to quit bothering me and to find his relief down in the salve quarters. I need a timber like this one," she said as she stroked Clay's penis trying to bring it back to life.

"Now I understand why he felt chagrined at the dinner table the other night when you put him down. I can also understand now why he feels hostility to me if he thought you were taking my side in an argument. You have injured his pride in a way few men could forgive. I suspect that is why he has singled me out for his anger."

"You may be right there, but there is more to it than that," Fay responded.

I knew Byron when we were children. His family owned a large plantation on the tidewater and my grandfather knew his family well. Grandfather used to exchange visits. Byron and I often played little games in the hay loft. That's how I came to know of his limitations. His family lost the plantation when the soil gave out. Byron went away to Europe for a long spell and spent some time in Russia. He has an income from some source he will not disclose. Some suspect he may be in the pay of the Tsar. I find it all quite intriguing and am enjoying toying with him. That's some of the stuff I was involved with in France. Everything over there is mystery and intrigue and I enjoy playing with Byron knowing he's up to some devilment he won't or can't disclose."

Fay had, during their conversation stimulated Clay's member to a standing position and mounted him once more.

As Clay awoke the next morning, he was alone in his bed, Fay had returned to her room and left him drained and exhausted. He knew he had to make it to breakfast to avoid any speculation as to why he was absent. Clay, as he dressed thought over the events of the past evening. As Fay had suggested, there was more to Byron's attitude toward him then mere chagrin over the size of his privates. He suspected also that there was more to Fay's conduct than a desire to be bedded. Clay decided that he would extend his stay at Twin Oaks. There was something afoot and he wanted to see the end of it.

BOOK IV

JENNY

Jenny stood at the gate of Fort Boise and clutching the arm of William, watched with anguish as her brother and father rode off into a distant unknown land to claim their fortune in the gold fields of California. Since she had been betrothed to William, her father had treated her differently. It was as if she were no longer his concern. Every time she asked about matters affecting their journey or their future in Oregon, he had deferred and told her to take the matter up with William or Paul Anderson. She had never felt more alone. He brother who had been so much a part of her life was her last real connection to her family in light of her father's attitude and the loss of her mother. Yet, James too was riding of into a land unknown and may never be seen again.

The tears came in a rush. The efforts to hold them back only made the final spasm of despair worse and she drove herself into William's arms unaware that he was also struggling with his emotions knowing his brother was also among those whose fortunes would now be decided by circumstances beyond their knowledge or control. This was not to have been the culmination of their trek across the Great Plains. They had all planned a future together in Oregon. It would not be the same without Clay and James. They would have many moments of anguish as they speculated over the fate of those two young and spirited men.

Jenny's wagon had been brought forward and would now be a part of Paul Anderson's entourage. William would help with hitching up the wagon and see to her needs. Mrs. Whitman assigned herself the duty of seeing to Jenny's wellbeing and comfort. Since Jenny would be staying at the Whitman Mission until William became established in Oregon City and called for her, it seemed natural to accept her courtesies. She did not, however, favor the attentions of Reverend Whitman who began treating her as an acolyte and started giving her instructions in matters of religion that he felt essential for one who was about to become a teacher at his mission.

"These heathens need to be brought around to the only true religion. Their soles face damnation unless they accept the teachings of our Lord. It's our duty to lead them along the path of redemption. Their sins are outrageous and you will need the strength of His word to deal with them." The Reverend admonished her.

It was a relief to Jenny when the wagons had all been repaired and ready for their final push on to Oregon. It was but a few days travel to Immigrant Crossing on the Snake River where they would once more ford the Snake River, for some, the last time. Jenny was up early and prepared their breakfast. Having been able to get fresh provisions at the Fort, they had eggs, bacon and biscuits and for once the biscuits didn't have weevils in them. The Coffee was fresh and strong and the aroma brought the men from their beds rolls.

"Jenny," Paul Anderson remarked, "it's good to have a woman's cooking again. These boys of mine could find any number of ways to turn good grub into a bellyache."

Jenny was getting used to the frequent compliments of Paul Anderson. It was clear to Jenny that he was pleased that she was to become part of the family. Without her father to lean on, she found great comfort in Paul's attentions. Melody was Jenny's constant companion and together they would drive the Rawlins wagon on westward.

The grasslands and sage brush that spread endlessly beyond them had now turned amber as the relentless rays of the summer sun had drawn the moisture from the land. The flowers that were once so plentiful and pleasing were long gone; had cast their seeds upon the land and withered away. The air had the hint of the coming fall and the nights had grown colder. The heat of the sun that had been so tormenting during the long trip across the Great American Desert was now tolerable as the autumnal equinox drew the sun to the southern latitudes. To those who journeyed on, each was thankful for their good fortune in reaching the last leg of the journey well before the snows of winter were due. They knew some of the wagon trains would not be so fortunate. Wintering on the plains had brought disaster to a number of trains in previous migrations and the slackers of this year's migration would meet a similar fate.

The Snake River was a half mile wide at Immigrant's Crossing when the Anderson train lined up along its banks. They would camp that night on the eastern shore and cross over in the morning. Trees would be cut and the logs tied to the wagons to float them across the river. The river was too wide to use ropes from bank to bank to help the wagons across, so riders would tie onto the wagons and use their horses to guide the wagons across. It would take a full day to make the crossing. Camped on the other side of the river, the immigrants could make out an Indian encampment. The Reverend Whitman advised them they the Indians were Nez Perze and friendly.

Soon enough, canoes set out from the Indian camp no doubt intent on bartering with the settlers. When the Indians arrived and banked their canoes, Jenny noticed that these Indians were different from the Plains Indians they had encountered. They were tall, well built and some quite handsome. The leader among them spoke English and welcomed the strangers to his land. He then set about informing them that there was bad blood with the various Shoshone Indians to the south and they had best travel close to the river and not try to go south.

Jenny clasped her hands to her breast, her breath became labored. She felt a sudden faintness and fell into the arms of Paul Anderson.

"My God, My God, James and Father are headed that way. Can't we go stop them?"

Jenny realized then that Paul Anderson was also tense and alarmed by the news. His younger son Clay was also in danger. "They are too long gone now. If there is trouble to be had, I would dare not send more men to such an uncertain fate. There are plenty of them and they are well armed. That mountain man went to join them. I'm sure he will see them safely to California."

The news spread about the camp like a prairie fire and soon one could hear wailing about the camp as wives and mothers of those who had headed to the promised fortunes of California heard the news imparted by the Nez Perce Chief. That night the Reverend Whitman held a prayer session for those who now feared for the fate for loved ones now venturing ever further into a hostile land.

Once the crossing of the Snake River had been made, the train struggled over mountainous terrain and followed the path of rivers and streams as they approached the formidable Blue Mountains. The mighty Cascade Range lay beyond the Blue Mountains and then they would come to the alluvial plains of the Oregon coastal range. Paul and William Anderson would be making the entire trip. When they reached the confluence of the Snake and Columbia Rivers they would then decide whether they would raft down the Columbia to Oregon City or take the more arduous path over the mountains. Paul Anderson would first deliver Jenny to the Whitman Mission where she would await the summons of William once he had found a home and established himself.

"I do hate to leave you behind, my dearest," William had assured her. "But we don't know what Oregon City has to provide. The frontier towns are usually rather shabby places and I don't intend to have us living in some chicken coop. I am sure there is a need for lawyers and I should be able to get established quite soon. Once I have a decent home built I will come for you."

William's intentions were stated in a manner that left little room for debate, yet Jenny pleaded for him to take her along. She told him of her discomfort with the Reverend Whitman.

"I would gladly share that chicken coop with you William. I can't stand the thought of being away from you. You don't even know how long it will be. It may take months for you to get established. Please let me come along. Many other women have followed their men to the end of the trail. You know from our travels together that I can manage."

At her pleading, William drew her into his arms and held her tightly for a moment then held her apart as he kissed each of her eyes, her nose and then her mouth. Jenny melted into his arms and would have submitted to him then and there. She wanted to be a part of him, to be with him and to care for him.

"You are indeed a strong woman and a beautiful one and I want you always by my side. But I am certain I can get established much faster if I do not have to start making a home immediately upon my arrival. I want time to build you a fine house and to get established. I don't want my lady living in a hovel like a hermit. I have many more pleasant plans for you Jenny. Please accept my decision."

Jenny huddled in the warmth and security of William's strong arms could offer no further objection to William's proposal. And so it was that on their arrival at the junction of the two great rivers, Jenny followed the Whitmans to their Mission. William remained behind and the remainder of the train preceded westward to Oregon City its final destination.

Jenny was disappointed at what she saw of the Whitman Mission. The word Mission had impressed upon Jenny's mind a large fort like structure with exterior walls of adobe and a large ornate church within the protected confines of the walls. Instead she found a two story house that was the living quarters of Narcissa and Marcus Whitman. There was an adobe Mission building that served as the school and headquarters of the mission, several storage sheds a large garden and a windmill. There was a corral that contained several horses and three cows. Chickens and other creatures wandered about the place. The structures were unpainted and blended into the barren hill country about it. There was a small flower garden and some fruit trees.

The Mission was situated on a dusty plain overlooking the Snake River. A number of Indians wandered about the property, some of them apparently employed by the Mission, other itinerates wandering about. They were not of the handsome breed like the Nez Perce that she had recently encountered. They were smaller, dressed in loincloths and vests that added little to the concealment of bodies that were unclean. A number of children trusted to the care of the Whitmans lived at the Mission and there were a number of emigrants who had stopped to rest at the Mission or to seek medical help.

They had hardly set foot on the Mission property when Marcus Whitman was scurrying about chastising the natives for their lack of clothing and purpose.

"Marcus will never succeed in getting these natives to act like white men but he won't quit trying. I'm afraid he only makes them agitated." Narcissa remarked as she ushered Jenny and Melody into the main building.

There was much that Marcus found wanting as a result of his absence and he spent most of the day of their arrival scurrying about the mission issuing orders, admonishing the natives and inventorying the stores.

Narcissa led the girls through the house which contained a large kitchen area, a parlor and several bedrooms on the lower floor. Jenny and

Melody were given a small room to share on the upper floor of the house which had two small beds. a dresser, a chair and a bowl and pitcher for washing. There were several pegs on the wall to hang clothing, a picture of some wildflowers no doubt painted by a not yet accomplished artist. The picture did, however lend what little color there was to the austere room. The window was curtained by several flour sacks and the floor was rugless. The girls were left alone to unpack their few possessions and Narcissa soon returned with a picture of warm water, several towels and a wash cloths.

"We will have dinner at 6:00; the Reverend insists that we dress in our best for the table. I hope you have a nice dress. Do you?"

Jenny had one fine dress that her mother had given Jenny after her mother had became too thin to wear it without alterations. Jenny also had the dress her mother had bought for her at the Independence store before they started their journey westward. Her mother seemed to have anticipated that her daughter would soon be a bride and bought her a beautiful blue dress just for that occasion. Jenny had no intention of wearing that dress to please the Reverend Whitman. She placed it carefully in the bottom draw of her dresser still warped in the paper from the Independence store.

Melody left the room and went downstairs to afford Jenny and opportunity to bathe. As Jenny undressed to wash the trail dust from her body, she took the mirror she salvaged from her mother's possessions and took a good look at her nakedness for the first time since she had left home. She was pleased at what she saw. Firm full breasts crested with deep brown nipples, a firm belly and slim waist. Her modesty prevented her from viewing her lower regions. She was satisfied that she would make a suitable bride for William and that he would find in her all he wanted. She opened once again the gold locket William had given her and studied the expressive warm face of his mother. She held the locket tightly in her hand as it was all she had of William until his fortunes improved and he sent for her.

The dinner, though plain in its fare was plentiful. Before they ate, the Reverend subjected them to a long prayer, reciting his hopes for the Mission and the success of his efforts to civilize the savages. After dinner they retired to the parlor where he read to them from the bible and instructed them as to the meaning of the passages. Jenny and Melody felt compelled to listen and both feigned interest, while Narcissa busied herself with sewing, giving her husband an occasional nod or comment. Thereafter, Jenny also brought some sewing or needle work to the parlor after dinner and suffered the tedium of the recitation.

Jenny met Reverend Spalding as he passed by the Mission one day to greet the Whitmans on their return. She learned from their discussion that he and Marcus had come west together; had been sent to the Oregon Territory by the American Board of Commissioners for Foreign Missions to establish missions. Once they arrived in the West, they took independent courses. The Reverend Spalding started a mission among the Nez Perce at a place called Lapwai. Jenny would later learn that The Reverend Spalding had sought Narcissa' hand in marriage but had been rebuffed. As it was she could tell from their demeanor, that Reverend Spalding was quite solicitous toward Narcissa, but often curt when discussing Mission matters with Reverend Whitman. She found the Reverend Spalding to be even more austere and unpleasant than the Reverend Whitman and was glad to see him depart [20]

Having set matters at the Mission in order, Reverend Whitman set about the task of encouraging the native Cayuse Indians to bring their children to the Mission school. Jenny waited with great apprehension for his return. She had attended school back in Missouri, but had no idea how she should teach the natives who knew not her language. Narcissa had conducted the school and established the course and Jenny found Narcissa was reluctant to relinquish her position. Jenny wished Melody was beside her to help her during this difficult time, but Narcissa insisted Melody care for the number of infants about the Mission who were too young for school yet always underfoot.

Giving Jenny her instructions, Narcissa admonished her, "The Reverend insists that we convert them, so our teaching must lead them to the path of the Lord. I doubt you will ever teach many of them to read or write, but if we can teach them our language, we can save their soles."

Jenny lay awake that night in bed and considered the instructions she had received. She had not been prepared to become a missionary's instrument of revelation. She honestly thought she would be a teacher. She

---

[20] End of the Oregon Trail Interpretive Center, http://www.endoftheoregontrail.org/road2oregon/sa07whitman.html

had no aspirations toward soul saving and made up her mind to take an independent course. After all, what could the Reverend do about it? If he refused to let her teach the natives, that would be a blessing. Jenny, in but a few days was finding life at the Mission too constrained for her liking. Her independent nature would tolerate only so much of the Reverend's domination.

When the Reverend returned from his visitations among the natives, he was much distressed by their lack of enthusiasm for the opportunity he offered for the instruction of their children. He did receive assurances from the Chief that several students would be provided, but was in no hurry to comply with the Reverends demand. Jenny spent some time cleaning up the school house and making things ready for the students who were yet to arrive. She found that there was but a meager inventory of supplies but an abundance of hymnals. The students arrived two weeks after the Reverend's visits and consisted of eight young maidens three young males and two braves. A number of white children attended the school which included the half breed children of Joseph Meek and James Bridger and the seven Sager children the Whitmans adopted after their parents perished on the way west. ([21])

The first day's efforts consisted of attempts to learn the names of the students and get them to pronounce her name. Once that was done, Jenny tried to use their names and the meaning of their name to get them to understand the English meaning behind those names. After a full week's effort, and much unsolicited assistance from Narcissa, Jenny had accomplished little and the natives among her student body steadily diminished. To her surprise, when the subject was broached with the Reverend Whitman he was not upset.

"We can only try; they are a stubborn, ignorant lot and may never find the way to redemption. If you have too few students perhaps you can assist me in the infirmary. If they have no desire for knowledge, they certainly have an abundance of ailments."

And so it was that Jenny found her teaching limited to a few young girls and one young Indian brave who were eager to learn the ways of the white man. She spent more and more time in the infirmary and found

---

[21] End of the Oregon Trail Interpretive Center, supra.

that far more interesting than teaching. The Reverend had formal medical training and had a basic understanding of the diseases and ailments that affected the natives and was fairly successful in ministering to them. Jenny was a quick learner and found some solace in assisting in the infirmary. To her surprise, she was finding more pleasure in the company of Marcus than Narcissa, whose Eastern upbringing had made her a poor fit for life on the frontier. She was impatient with the natives who were employed by the Mission and was not averse to striking them to get their attention or obedience.

The weeks began to drag by and turn into months. The last wagon trains of the season would soon come and be gone and winter would be upon them. . The Reverend was often gone attending to the sick in the villages or visiting the Mission saw mill in the Blue Mountains. Jenny busied herself when not at the school, helping Narcissa in the kitchen, with the mending, and putting up preserves. She spent long hours gazing across the inhospitable terrain hoping to see a messenger coming to summon her to Oregon City and to her new home. Winter passed and spring came and no call came for her. Soon even summer was past, the last wagon trains were again wending their way to the new lands in Oregon, yet no call came for her. As the trains passed, the Mission supplied them with provisions to complete their journey. It became evident to Jenny that the Reverend was finding that converting the natives was hopeless and that his services could be better spent rendering to the immigrants, supplying them, affording safe passage and repairs and allowing them a point of rest before their last great struggled over the Cascade Range or rafting down the turbulent Columbia.

Jenny was nearing the point of desperation as the last trains of her second season at the Mission come and went. She contemplated riding along with one the trains to Oregon City. Surely, William had sent for her and the messenger had gone astray. Mail service was non-existent and depended upon giving a letter to the next man heading east. When Jenny reached the point of utter despair, Joseph Meek whose daughter was under the care of Narcissa visited the Mission and brought with him the long awaited letter from William.

My Dearest Jenny,

I am sorry it has taken so long to communicate with you. I have sent several letters, but none have reached you. The first messenger lost his life on the Columbia rapids. The second one returned without reaching your Mission. It has been most difficult finding a suitable building lot and the material to build a house as everything is in short supply. I have, however, succeeded in finding a beautiful lot overlooking the falls of the Willamette. It is a ways from town, but the town will soon be growing that way. Congress has made Oregon a Territory and we now have our own governor. The dispute between the United States and Great Briton over who owns the Northwest has been settled and America now extends up beyond the Puget Sound. I have been retained by the Provisional Government to draft the new codes and am most busy. Father's paper is prospering and will be a great asset to us if I decide to get into politics which is a matter I am considering. As my days are most busy, my nights are endless as I can do not but think of you by my side. Had I the choice again to make, I would have brought you with me. Now, however, we are but a few months apart. I shall call for you in the spring and we will have a wedding that will set the town on its ear. Be patient my dearest, we will have a life time together.

Your Loving William.

Jenny clutched the letter to her heart and tears of joy rolled without restraint down her cheeks. Life again had meaning and she took to her tasks with renewed intensity. Soon she would be leaving this Mission and this boredom and begin her life as the bride of what she was certain would be one of Oregon's most prominent citizens. She tried to picture the house she would share and how she would furnish it. Would there be places to buy furniture or would she have to have it made. What about draperies and rugs. Her mind was filled with hope and planning. Yet, high in the mountains where the Cayuse villages were preparing for winter, terrible events were occurring that would change forever the hopes and dreams that were budding in Jenny's young, innocent breast.

OREGON CITY

The trail beyond the Mission at Waiilatpu, where he left Jenny in the care of the Whitmans, was even more arduous than the Anderson's had anticipated. The decent from the Blue Mountains was the most hazardous and difficult of any passing they had made along the trail. Each wagon had to be roped down the last decent of over three thousand feet onto the plain below. By the time they reached the settlement at The Dalles, the Andersons and the rest of the train headed over the newly completed Barlow Toll Road. It was an awesome sight for the immigrants who had traversed the desolate plains of the Great American Desert to pass through the mighty stands of Douglas Fir, Hemlock, Ponderosa Pine, Fir and an endless variety of deciduous trees as they passed beneath the breathtaking spectacle of Mount Hood, with its gleaming mantel of white.

In reaching Oregon City, the wagon train came upon the first incorporated city west of the Rocky Mountains. Situated near the falls of the Willamette River, water power was available for the operation of the flour mill and a saw mill. The town boasted a population of over five hundred people and was the seat of government for the newly formed Territory of Oregon. Plated originally by Dr. John McLoughlin, the Hudson Bay factor, it had one main street appropriately named Main Street that constituted the business district. ([22]) As the Anderson train made its way down the street, crowds gathered to cheer their arrival and welcome them to the Oregon Territory and the end of their long, pilgrimage.

They camped outside of town and most were soon heading for the land office to process their claims for the 640 acres of free land that was being offered to the male head of the household. Others, not having seen a semblance of a city since leaving Independence set out to wander through

---

[22] End of the Oregon Trail, City of Oregon City http//www.ci.oregon-city.or.us/community-develop/planning/historical_context.htm

the town and its several shops. A few headed for the nearest saloon of which there were several along Main Street. Paul Anderson headed into town to see what his prospects might be for starting a newspaper. Upon inquiry, he was told to talk to a man named George Abernathy who knew all about the business prospects in Oregon City and the Territory. Abernathy as it turned out was interested in getting a newspaper established and offered to assist Paul in getting it off the ground.

When told that William was a lawyer and wanting to start a practice, Abernathy informed William that the town had a real need for a lawyer.

"There's all kinds of land squabbles and we are right in the middle of organizing a Provincial Government and we could sure use a good lawyer to help us through the hurdles."

Within a few weeks father and son were busily employed in establishing their respective businesses. Their big problem was finding suitable accommodations as there was a shortage of housing and building materials. The solution came when George Abernathy had a tenant move out of a store front to a new location. The building was a two story affair and Paul took the lower floor for his newspaper and William used the upper floor for his law office and living quarters. William was hoping to have sent for Jennie within a few months, but the lack of living space prevented him from doing so. Things were happening back in Washington D.C. that was putting Oregon on the fast track to statehood and the demands on Williams practice gave him little time to think or to do anything in regard to establishing a home for him and Jenny.

The gold boom in California was placing a big demand for lumber and the local mills were unable to produce more lumber to meet local demand. New mills were sprouting up but local interests were having difficulty bidding against the California purchasers, particularly so when a new shipping company that owned its own ships moved into the market. William had the unusual problem of representing the company on a local level while at the same time knowing that this very company was making it difficult for him to realize his own ambitions to build a home and a new office. His dealings were with a man name Captain Gray who represented a company named Little Flower Enterprises. His latest instructions from the Captain were to find lumber mills and timber land to purchase.

"I represent a young fella with more money than he knows what to do with and he plans on being a big player in settling the frontier."

"Well, you might tell me who he is, it seems rather important for a lawyer to know who he's dealing with."

"Ain't authorized to do that. He's formed this here corporation so's I and others can make his deals. He don't want people knowing about him. Has something to do with the source of his fortune. All I know about it is he made a big strike somewhere and he's been secretive about his affairs like most of them who find a bonanza is. I can sign any papers you need signing and put the money in your hands. That seems to be all that needed, ain't it?"

"Well, I'm not comfortable with the arrangement, but if he is dealing through a reputable bank, I guess that attests to his character." William admitted, knowing he would get no more information from the Captain.

"If you are that confident in him, you might drop by the Pioneer Bank, before you leave town and set up a five thousand dollar drawing account that I can use to make the deals we've discussed."

William thus became a participant in the business of his future brother in law without actually knowing who it was who was adding to his fortunes.

Paul Anderson was becoming ever more involved in the efforts to carve out of the vast Northwest a state and was eager to meet each new arriving vessel to get what news he could and to interview the leaders of each new emigrant train arriving in Oregon City. He was not surprised when the fortunes of far away Oregon became embroiled in the controversy over slavery in the South. The big debate in Congress was over the Missouri Territory. The Northern Congress men did not want to admit the state as a slave state, but wanted California into the Union to balance the scales in Congress between the slave and free states. Oregon was now bundled into the process and it appeared that both territories would be drawn into the Union without the normal process of first establishing themselves as a Territorial possession. Things were indeed moving fast and his efforts were taxed to the limit. Virtually ignored in the process of developing the Oregon Territory was the Indian land claims. The large tribes that had dominated the vast fertile plains of Oregon that were now being deeded to the white settlers had been decimated by the diseases the white man brought west.

Of the numerous tribes numbering into the many thousands of members that had inhabited Western Oregon when the fur trappers came west, now only a few hundred remained and than even those few were on the decline and would soon be extinct. Of those white men moving west, there was little concern for the plight of the red men. They were but a nuisance and the sooner gone the better. Many of those coming west carried the memory of depredations imposed upon them by the red men and had no sympathy for the natives. Whenever Paul's newspaper raised the issue of settlements with the natives, a matter for which he had some empathy, he was staunchly rebuked. "Let sleeping dogs lie." He was told. "Them Indians got no use for this land, they ain't done nothin' with it when they's been here for thousands of years," Others remarked. The other tribes that lived along the Columbia River, lived off of the plentiful foods supplied by the Columbia and had no particular claim to the lands beyond and no interest in the white man's possessive nature.

In the Eastern plains and mountains of Oregon, however, the Shoshone and Cayuse Indian tribes were smoldering with resentment over the invasion of their lands. Paul Anderson was too astute a newsman to not know that the rush to statehood would soon incubate a smoldering fire of resentment that would cost many on both sides to shed blood over the disputed lands in Eastern Oregon and the now forming Washington Territory. But few would listen to his words of caution. America's "Manifest Destiny" was the driving sprit of a nation that neither saw nor would tolerate any limitations to its dreams of Empire and fortune.

Paul looked to the Missionaries who where flooding west to establish their claims on the souls of the natives for support in his native Indian concerns. Although most had come west to establish missions among the natives, most found that endeavor unrewarding and soon either left missionary work to pursue their own fortunes or tied their fortunes to the emigrants who were becoming more and more of a factor in the territories of the west. The natives had few advocates and those who would plead their case were ignored.

CENTRAL OREGON

Father sun was slipping below the Spirit Mountains, casting its last glow across the undulating hills in the valley below. Running Deer had been watching the small train of wagons wending its way southward. From where he sat, erect and relaxed on his pony, he could see a great distance. At first the small train was but a cloud of dust. It came slowly into view, three wagons with twelve pale faces, twelve oxen three cows and four horses. It would be an easy matter to dispatch these intruders. The meat of the oxen and cattle would be a welcome addition to their winter stores. Perhaps they would have tobacco, sugar and coffee. He knew his braves would be anxious to get some of the white men's spirit water, but Running Deer saw no purpose to the silliness that the spirit water brought to his braves and hoped that none would be found. Much of what the white men brought into their land was welcome, the cooking pots, coffee, tobacco, sugar and salt. The guns and animals they could use, but he always feared contact with these people because he knew they carried diseases for which their medicine men had no cure. The spirits of the old ones had spoken to him. He must let none of these white men invade their lands. He had seen how it was with his brethren along the Great Sandy River. Once the white men entered upon the sacred lands, they settled on it in ever greater numbers and could not be driven away, for they came like the flood waters that drove all before it.

In the ravine behind him, forty warriors awaited his command. He turned to them and motioned them to follow him down into the valley below. The small train had crested a small hill and was now out of sight. The white eyes would be setting up their camp for the night, and judging from what he had observed, they would be ill prepared for what awaited them as the first light of the new day would blind them as Running Deer and his braves drove among them.

As he rode down into the valley, he had thoughts of the last ambush he had lead against a far more formidable group of invaders. He wondered if the one called Grizzly Rawlins whose life he spared had lived to tell other white men never to enter these lands. Unconsciously his hand moved to his thigh were the discomfort of the broken bone that had been set by the white man still gave him constant reminders of his debt to the young man who'd chanced upon him as he lay deserted and dying. He wondered why the young man had not killed him and taken his scalp. Would he have done different? He had felt conflicted by the event when he returned to his people and consulted with the shaman. Was the compassion of the young white man a sign that they should live in peace with these people?

"I have been to the land over the Spirit Mountains," the shaman had told him. "These white people have taken the land of our brothers. They have given them sicknesses that have made many die badly. They will do the same to your people. Let them not pass into our lands. You are our war chief and must protect your people."

Running Deer knew the shaman was right. He had paid his debt to the white man. His duty was now to his people. As they charged the camp the next morning, Running Deer was surprised that these white men did not fire their weapons. Many, seeing the charging Indians did not stand and fight, but knelt on their knees and pressed their hands to their chest. Others ran or hid. His braves, their blood burning with the lust for killing spared none of the invaders and quickly dispatched them saving their ammunition and bludgeoning most of them with the war clubs. As Running Deer rode among them, he noticed their strange dress. He recognized them as the ones called Missionaries. They were the first to come before the tide of white men came. They would tell the natives to live in peace while the other white men stole their lands, fornicated among their women, made mad men of the braves with their spirit water. It was good to be done with these people. Their deed, however, did not go unnoticed.

Running Deer had instructed his braves to throw all the dead into the wagons, pull the wagons together and set them afire. The smoke could be seen for miles and that is what attracted the attention of Sturgis Warren a down on his luck prospector who had left California and decided to prospect among the Blue Mountains. He had seen Indian sign and was proceeding cautiously. He knew nothing of the Indians in this territory, but had come across the signs of a massacre by a clump of Cotton Woods where he had sought cover the night before. The bones and assorted clothing and gear had been scattered about, but Sturgis guessed that there must have been more than a dozen men who met their fate at the Cotton Wood camp. Some of the sculls had been crushed with war clubs. Broken arrows lay about. He guessed that the bones had been laying here bleaching for a year or two. He searched about for any sign of who these people were. It was then he found the crude graves in a ravine. Scratched on the surface of a flat rock were the names, Wayne Rawlins, Franco and Parker.

Following the smoke sign, Sturgis came upon the murdered Missionaries. He could not tell how many people had been killed as the fire had done its work. The sweet, pungent smell of burnt flesh was in the air. Searching about the site, Sturgis found the Bibles and Hymnals that had been scattered about along with other sigh that indicated these people were Missionaries, although he could find no other identification as most of the Missionary's belongings not stolen were thrown into the fire. Sturgis had seen enough of this land inhabited as it was by hostile Indians. He knew he must not only get out of this country to save his skin, he must tell others of what he had seen. These Indians must be dealt with before they commit any more depredations.

Sturgis knew there were settlements over the mountains toward the Oregon Coast. He knew nothing of what lay ahead if he continued north, so he turned toward the mountains. Before he reached the mountains, he came upon a fast flowing river and decided to follow it northward. His travels were arduous and he proceeded with great awareness. Within a week, Sturgis came in sight of a mighty Columbia River and followed the Oregon Trail to the Mission at The Dalles. He was there advised to head on into Oregon City and impart his sad news to the Provisional Government that was being organized there.

"We don't have the means here to deal with those savages," Sturgis was advised. Sturgis arrived in Oregon City during a raging down pour. Not knowing where he would find the Provisional Government, Sturgis noticed the newspaper office and headed for it. When he entered, the newspaper office he noticed a flurry of activity in the back of the counter where Paul Anderson and his helper were busy setting type and running the shuttle on the press. A young man lounged in a chair reading one of the papers that had been pulled from the press. They all stopped to look at the drenched prospector who entered the office, dripping water on the floor and rubbing his face with a soiled looking bandana.

"What can we do for you, stranger? Paul asked as he wiped the ink from his hands onto an old towel. "Don't have much time to be visiting or taking ads, I got to get this newspaper out."

"Don't mean to be vexing you none," Sturgis replied. "My name's Sturgis Warren. I be need'n to find where the government office is so's I can report some bad doings over them mountains."

This comment stirred the newsman's interest and he stopped his typesetting and came to the counter. William, always interested as were most of the people in town, in any news from the outside, stood also and walked to the counter.

"My name is Paul Anderson, I own this newspaper, and this here is my son William. I can tell you rightly enough where the government office is, but I am a news man and if you have any news, I sure would appreciate it if you can tell me what it is that brings you here."

"Well," Sturgis replied, I guess it ain't confidential. Everybody's got to know about it in time anyways. I come up from California traveling up through the center of this Territory, having crossed over the Sierras. About six days or so from here I came across the signs of a massacre. Been some time ago, maybe a year or more. Don't know if anyone about knows them people or knows they ain't comin' home. Come another day's travel, I came upon a bunch of Missionaries that met the same fate, but that was just a day old then. The wagons were still smoking."

Paul turned to Davie, his helper and instructed him to stop printing tomorrow's newspaper. There was going to be a special edition.

Paul grabbed some newsprint and proceeded to take down Sturgis's accounts, preparing his article for what would be a special edition. This was the biggest story his young newspaper would handle. After asking all the usual questions he asked him:

Any idea who these people where at the first site? Any identification left about?"

"Yah they was," Sturgis replied and he fumbled inside his coat and pulled out a yellowed scrap of paper. They was a grave of a sort and someone scratched these manes on a rock besides it."

Sturgis strained his eyes to make out the charcoal scrawl he had made. "This here's faded some he remarked as he angled the paper this way and that. "Seems this here's a "W" something Rawlins, and this other is Franco or some such and a fella named Parker. Weren't no other markings."

Sturgis was startled as Paul let out a wail and fell into the chair behind the counter. William grabbed Sturgis's arm holding the note. "Let me see if I can read what you have there.

William's face drained of color as he read the markings on the note handed to him. "My God he muttered. How can this be? William remarked as he laid the paper on the counter and with his elbows resting on it held his hands over his face in obvious distress.

Sturgis was struck dumb. "What the hell is going on here?" he asked. "You know these people?"

William looked at him red eyed, "Sorry about the way were acting, but yes we did know these people. They came west with us on the same wagon train. One of them was my brother; another was my future brother in law. We knew them all." William said in a voice barely audible. "You are the bearer of truly bad news."

William instructed the young man at the press to show Sturgis where the Town Hall was, the building that served as the city and the Territorial headquarters. When you've done that, get word to George Abernathy about the news Mr. Warren has delivered."

After the two left the office, William walked over to where his father sat, tears welling in his eyes and his chest heaving. William knelt beside him and placed an arm over his shoulder and together they grieved for the loss of one's son and the other's brother. The newspaper shop stayed open late that night and when its publication was delivered the next morning it contained large, bold headlines: SAVAGES MURDER EMIGRANTS. There followed the details of the story as told by Sturgis and a list of the names of those who were among the victims. The list included Wayne Rawlins, James Rawlins, and Clay Anderson, Johnny Two Shoes Franco, Festus Parker, and the other members of the caravan that had left Fort Boise for California. It mentioned that the train involved in the second massacre was believed to have been a train of Missionaries looking for a suitable site to establish a Mission among the Indians.

As the news reached the streets, the reaction was instantaneous. Volunteers were coming in from all the nearby farms and from the city to form a regiment of militia to avenge the killings and halt any further violence. Within two days the volunteers were organized, armed, equipped and headed East over the Barlow trail to central Oregon. There were eighty men in all under the Captaincy of George Abernathy. William Anderson was among the volunteers. He had to argue at length with his father to persuade him to remain behind.

"The Territory will need a newspaper now more than ever. There will be dispatches to publish and you will have to hold the community together while most of its leaders are gone. Besides, Paw, your days in the saddle are over. It will be a long hard journey and the weather is not good. We have enough young men to do the job. You stay here where you can do the most for the people."

Paul Anderson reluctantly accepted his son's advice and not long after the militia left town he was writing an account of its membership and mission. He advocated that the Territory establish a permanent militia. "This will not be the last time we will have need for the services of a well armed and trained militia," he advised his readers.

Within seven days the militia reached the scene of the Missionary massacre and buried the charred remains of the slaughtered Missionaries. There was little evidence to identify the members of the small group so the common grave was identified only as the "Missionary's Rest." It took them several more days to find the place where the members of the Anderson Train met their end. Again, the bones were placed in a common grave. William found the place where Wayne, Parker and Franco were buried and wondered as he viewed it who had placed these remains here and made the markings on the stone. There must have been a survivor to have done this, but who would it have been and where was he now? He had looked over the collected ruminants of the slain and tried to see if there was any trace of his brother's belongings. He knew the Indians would have taken anything of value. He looked for signs of James Rawlins like the knife and necklace James always wore. He found nothing. Of the skulls and bones that lay about, none were identifiable. It was then he remembered that in his haste to help organize and equip the militia he had completely forgotten to notify Jenny of the loss of her brother. There was no way to remedy that now, he knew, but hoped his father would think to send her the sad news.

The militia had sent scouts out to try to find traces of the Indian Village that was responsible for the slaughter of so many of their kind. The scouts found no trace of an Indian encampment. To them any encampment would do, they were in a mood for killing. Their travels in the land of the Shoshone were not unobserved. Running Deer had been made aware of their presence and his scouts kept the militia under constant observation. He knew their purpose. He had no intention of meeting these well armed and vengeful men in combat. He knew he had to keep them away from his village and that left alone, they would soon find it. He decided to divide his braves into several bands and to make false trails that would lead them east and south and away from the Indian villages. Perhaps he could lead them about until their supplies were gone and he would have a chance to defeat them. Maybe they would split up and follow different trails and he could fall upon them individually. Soon the lands about would be in the grip of winter. If these men were not fools they would not be long in the land of the Shoshone. He must keep them busy until they leave.

After several days, Running Deer was satisfied that his plan was working. One band of braves had tied brush behind their ponies and drug them along making great dust clouds at a distance from the militia. The militia drove hard after what they thought was an Indian village moving away from them. After a day and a half of following the trail that vanished among a large outcropping of lava rock, the militia turned back only to sight another dust trail far to the north. When that trail finally ended in endless marsh lands about a large alkaline lake, George Abernathy had had enough. The men and animals were worn, their supplies were running low and the sky had the ominous presence of storm clouds.

"It's time to go home boys," He told them. "Whoever it is that we're pursuing ain't about to be caught before we be down to crawling after 'em. If we don't get out of this country before the snow flies we may end like the pile of bones we buried back at them Cottonwoods."

The lust for revenge had waned as the militia wandered aimlessly about the deserted lands of central Oregon. Each man knew he and his animals were at their limit as they turned north in defeat and headed home.

For William, the return trip had been agonizing. He had wanted to exact some revenge for the loss of his brother and others whom he had known. Every since the debacle with the Mapes Train, William had harbored a distrust and a growing hatred for the natives. To him they deserved the epitaph of savages. This land would never be safe for the white man until these people were driven out. They contributed nothing constructive; they stole, butchered and plundered not only among the settlers, but among their own people. He would do what he could once he returned to Oregon City to establish a permanent militia that could respond to the deprivations of the red man and drive them from the lands that would better be used by the continually arrive emigrants. The land was too bountiful to be left to the vicissitudes of the feckless people. Congress must be urged to send regulars soldiers into the west and protect the innocents from the mindless violence of the Indian tribes.

So it was with a new purpose that drove William once he had returned. He had much support among the settlers. The remnants of the Hudson's Bay settlers were opposed to his plans for vengeance and extermination of the red man, but their dominance of the affairs of the Northwest was a thing of the past. Dr. McLaughlin, the tall, silver haired ex Hudson Bay Factor, in particular pleaded for understanding and moderation. "It has been their land for centuries unrecorded. You cannot expect them to capitulate to the throngs of settlers that are settling on the hunting grounds. Have patience and negotiate. There must be an accommodation that will bring peace to all. I have dealt with them for years without rancor. They are like children and do not understand our ways. Give them time."

"He got along with the natives because he needed them in his fur trading business. That business has gone and the Indian is of no further use," William responded sarcastically to this plea.

The Territorial government responded to the demands made by William and those of a like mind who constituted a large majority of the community and thus was established a militia that regularly drilled, was well supplied and prepared to respond to the next outrage by the savages. William was made a Captain and was commissioned to venture to Washington D.C. that next spring and urge upon Congress the need for the establishment of a military presence in the territories. Already William was being looked upon as one of the leaders of the community and a man slated for greater things. Once William had set the course for the protection of the community, he set about the task of finding a home for himself and Jenny.

A new mill had opened up and he was quick to establish a commitment for timber and lumber for a home. The lot he found was one owned by

Dr. McLaughlin whose claim to the land in an about Oregon City was sometime ignored and at other times acknowledged. James chose to deal with the old factor knowing he was a man who still claimed some influence among the settlers. The good doctor had always been hospitable to the Americans and during the decline of the fur trade had been instrumental in aiding many of the settlers who had arrived in Oregon depleted of supplies and funds. Even the Reverend Doctor Whitman had used his hospitality when he first arrived in the Oregon Territory. Many of the missionaries had spent their first days at Fort Vancouver and had relied upon Doctor McLaughlin's experience in dealing with the Indians and establishing missions among them.

The lot he purchased had a view of the river and the Falls of the Willamette. He was sure Jenny would find it acceptable and sent her a letter advising her of the choice. His mind was unsettled over the question of advising her of the death of her brother and Clay. Someone, or maybe several of the caravan to California, he was certain, had survived. What else could explain the graves of those buried? The fact that the only marked graves were those of her father, Parker and Franco could well mean that those close to them may have survived. The most likely people to have honored the three whose graves were marked could have been either Clay or James. As to her father's death, he felt it best to be with her when she was given the news. That could be very soon now.

The last train to reach the Whitman Mission that year was delayed due to a severe outbreak of measles that had taken the lives of several of the children. Dr. Whitman took in a number of the still infected to his infirmary. Unfortunately, the members of the train had traded with and associated with the Cayuse and within a few days the fever raged through the villages of the Cayuse, decimating the tribe, especially the children. It was a grim meeting of the elders of the village when they met to discuss the virulence that had beset them. Their medicine men were helpless to respond to this strange malady.

"We have taken our people to the white man's Doctor and even there they die. The white children walk away while ours are buried," the once war chief relayed to them. His rheumy eyes wandered about the room to focus upon their chief.

"Word has now come that the white eyes have killed our brother Elijah Hedding the son of Peu-Peu-mox-mox the chief of the Walla Walla's. They have set out poison about the mission to kill our animals, the woman of the white doctor has taken a stick to our women when they do not respond; they insist we give up our ways and become farmers. Before we are all placed in our graves, we must have vengeance." Having said that the old chief pulled his soiled blanket about him and lapsed into silence.

The young war chief Tamahas, who had lost a daughter and brother to the white man's disease rose slowly to his feet to respond. His face was grave and the flickering light from the fire gave face his countenance a deathly look. ([23])

"You are right brother to speak thus of these people. They have been in our land several moons now and have given us nothing but disease and heart ache. They care not what is our heritage from our fathers and insist we live like them. Their school teaches our children to ignore our ways and become weak. Patua struck the hat from the white chief's head and he would not strike Patua for the insult. He is weak and is no good as a healer. He has let out children die and he must now die."

There were murmurs of assent about the lodge, but none would speak further. All that needed to be said had been said.

JAMES

James visited the home he had purchased one last time before heading back to the Little Flower Mine and its namesake. He was pleased to see that work was already in progress. The new contractor that Mr. Poindexter had hired was sitting in the middle of the large, cavernous living room behind a make shift desk studying an array of plans garnered from the original architect. As James' boots struck an echoing cadence as he strode into the room, the contractor look up in irritation, ready to demanded to know who he was and what the hell he was doing walking into his construction site.

---

[23] For the grievances of the Cayuse and the details of the Whitman Massacre. See End of the Oregon Trail Interpretive Center, supra; Dryden's History of Washington, Cecil Dryden, Binfords & Mort, (1968) p 98.

"Don't mean to interrupt the work I'll be paying for my good man, but I would like to know what it is my money is purchasing if you've the time," James retorted. The contractor seemed more distracted by James than interested in James' presence, but putting aside his spectacles, he recognized James and pushed aside the papers he was studying and rose to meet him.

"Yes, yes, I apologize for my brusqueness, but I got to get this place weather proofed before more weather damage occurs. It's bad enough as it is what with this place standing empty for so long. What can I do for you, young man?"

He then gave James an overview of the plans and his progress. As James had anticipated, the plans called for a Victorian design that was not to his liking.

"I don't want to live in a house designed for some French nobleman. I am a man of the west as is my wife and I intend to live in a home that has the taste of the America I know, not some foreign country I have no relationship with or interest in. I believe I let my preferences be know at out last meeting. You can burn these plans and hire a new architect and start this project all over even if it means tearing down this whole damn place. I hope that needn't be required, but let's not waste time trying to make a palace out of a pumpkin."

The contractor, Carl Jorgensen, rose slowly to his feet and studied the man standing before him. James was wearing what had become his standard apparel; a black frock cut away coat, black pants tucked into black polished riding boots, his bear claw necklace that stood in prominence on the back ground of a white, open collared shirt. His Bowie Knife was partially hidden by his coat, but its handle was jutting forward within ready grasp. The contractor, said nothing, but slowly rolled up the plans he had been laboring over and walked them over to the fireplace where a fire had been blazing away in an attempt to drive the dampness from the house. He threw the plans into the fire and then turned to James.

"Seeing you standing their in them duds of yours, it's obvious that the house I'd build by them plans wouldn't suit you at all. You seen any of them Mexican haciendas? I've an inclination that you'd be finding them more to your liking than this place," Jorgensen advised, assessing James with more interest. "I don't know how one of them places would fit in this here neighborhood, but you might give some thought to what you really want. I could show you a few of them places and we could start from there. I wasn't all that excited with them plans I was given. All them big shots that's gotten rich out here in the West seem to want to turn European once they's make their fortune."

Jorgensen and James rode out into the vineyards north of town and viewed some of the country homes build for the Mexican land owners. James was impressed. Jorgensen then made arrangements to have James meet with the man who had designed several of these estates.

The office of Jose' Hernandez, was located out near the Presidio that James had visited on a previous trip. As their carriage past the Presidio grounds, James noticed to his satisfaction, that there were signs that the complex was being rehabilitated. The movement of the Army into the west was a sign of stability and a confirmation of nationhood that the recently acquired territory much needed.

Hernandez, a native Mexican now living in an acquired territory of the United States, had clearly suffered from the loss of his clientele, many of whom had sold out and returned to Mexico. He welcomed James with a warmth and sincerity that won James' confidence. Hernandez had a portly stature that evidenced a hearty appetite and the grand life style that he had once enjoyed. He wore a mustache that dominated a face creased with wrinkles that marked the lines of his ready smile. He had a full head of gray streaked hair that he allowed to grow down to his shoulders. The space in his hacienda that was devoted to his business was littered with rolled up plans and had pinned to the walls replicas of villas he had designed or had proposed as designs. James answered the questions the designer usually asked to get a feel for his client's interest. James was impatient with the process, and having viewed one of the presentations on the wall, finally walked over to where it was pinned, and told the designer, he had in mind a design similar to the one shown.

Hernandez, recognizing that James had chosen the design of one of his dream homes he had never been able to sell, but had always wanted to see built was delighted with this strange Americano's selection and launched into a spirited explanation of the design and its possibilities. He made hurried sketches of the interior lay out and following James' approvals and disapprovals, soon garnered a feeling for James' preferences and was ready for some serious work.

James told him to do his best; he liked the way he was going. Giving the architect a card to call upon his banker for an advance, James completed his business, thanked Hernandez and was on his way after but a few hours.

Before he left, he assured Hernandez that he had confidence in his designs and abilities. "You are a good man. I am confident that between the two of you, you will build me a home that will suit me and my wife to be. By the way, I must inform you that she is a native, or as you people would refer to her, she is a squaw. But never doubt that she is a lady of good sense and I want you to keep in mind that what you build must be a tribute to her. I owe her my life and more. You might want to think of some features that would be attractive to her" I'm not talking about any basic design changes; I just want her to be comfortable."

As James left the home of the architect, he realized to his satisfaction, that he had not only made a critical decision on the design of his new home, he had announced to the architect a decision that had for many months troubled him, and that was about the future that he and Little Flower would share. He had one further major problem to confront, and that concerned the future operation of the Little Flower mine. His center of operation and interest was now gravitating toward California. He could not continually be traveling from one place to the other and living one life with Little Flower in a lodge on the frontier and another life as a businessman in San Francisco.

Above all, James wanted Little Flower to be a part of his entire existence, not just a companion during his occasional visitations to the mine. It would be a great imposition and transition for her to move to San Francisco, but her recent effort to please him with the dress she made from the pattern books he gave her was a promise of a changing disposition. Little Flower clearly wanted to please him and do the things that would bring her into his orbit. Yet, James knew, it would be a far different matter to live together at the mine than it would be when he and Little Flower set up housekeeping in the midst of a city struggling to gain respectability and status.

James was assured that his wealth insulated him from the recriminations that would arise from his marriage to a native. Little Flower would have a far more arduous task to gain an existence in a white dominated community that had an abhorrence toward intermarriages. James now realized that by naming the mine and shipping company after Little Flower, he was subliminally giving her a status that would help breach the gap between what was considered respectable society and her native origins. He now appreciated the efforts of Cactus Jack to teach her English and to help her to read the language. He must, as soon as they established their residence, hire her a tutor.

But then there was another matter to be resolved and to confront that situation, he took the steamer to Sacramento the next morning. When he reached the offices of Robert Peters, he found that the office had been closed for lunch from noon until two o'clock. He knew where he could find Peters and headed to the restaurant where he had been introduced to the acting Governor and explorer, John Freemont. His instinct was correct and he found Peters at a table at the rear of the restaurant in conversation with a well dressed, portly man who, as he spoke was leaning on a gold tipped cane. Peters recognized James as he entered and ushered him over to the table.

"I want you to meet Mr. Leland Stanford. He's trying to interest some of our citizens in the prospect of building a railroad from St Louis to San Francisco. I think he may want to talk to you; I sure don't have the means to invest in such a risky scheme" Although Peters left the impression that James had some wealth, he was still discreet enough not to reveal the source of that wealth which was a matter of confidence between them. Mr. Stanford gave James a studied look of a businessman appraising a prospect and then offered him a hand.

"Our statehood is assured, but we won't really be part of the Union until we are connected by more than horse trails. This is a great and prosperous state and we need to move products between the east and west more expeditiously than sail boating around the Horn. What may I ask young man is your interest in California?"

James now gave Mr. Stanford a studied look. He had heard of Mr. Stanford's various business interests that included banking, land development and politics. James realized that men like this would be the future of California and it would do him no harm to confide in him.

"Right now, I am invested in shipping, lumber and some mining interests. I have purchased property for a home on Beacon Hill, but it is in the building state at present. I believe it is not far from your home."

Mr. Stanford gave James a more appraising look. His gaze rested on the Bear Claw necklace. "I suppose there is some story behind that necklace of yours that might tell me something of the man wearing it," Stanford stated showing some interest in that story."

"Let me just say, but for this necklace, I would not be here today. It is a talisman I'm bonded to. It was given to me by a chief of the Shoshones. I claim not to have slain the animal whose claws I wear."

"You only make my curiosity more acute young man, but let us not dwell on that matter now." Stanford responded, turning now to face James and directed him to a chair opposite him. "Railroads are springing up all over the east and soon there will be a good connection between the eastern seaboard and St. Louis. It's only logical that some enterprising interests will want to move rail lines westward. I intend to be a part of that effort and when you have the time, I would like to show you the prospectus that we are making up. If you have an interest in the matter, I would like you to meet with my other investors. I don't wish to pressure you at this time, but do keep my offer in mind."

Mr. Stanford handed him his business card and then excused himself stating he had other business to attend to in Sacramento and than must catch the steamer back to San Francisco.

After Mr. Stanford's departure, James and Peters made small talk about the mining business.

"I stopped by your office and I see you are now able to take a little time off for lunch. I suppose that means the mine claims are down and your business is also," James suggested to get a reaction that might confirm his observation.

"Well, you are correct there, things are slowing down. Most of the miners are off looking for other employment and many of the once promising mines are now marginal at best. There's still plenty of gold out there, but its coming under the control of eastern businessmen and the old prospectors are cashing in their claims for a more settled life in the city."

This was the response that James wanted and he now broached the subject that brought him to Sacramento.

"I would suspect an enterprising man such as you would be getting a little restless, what with things slowing down," James suggested as he waived away the approaching waiter.

Peters leaned back in his chair and gave James and appraising look. "Now I don't suppose you rode that smoke stack of a ferry boat just to come up here and lament with me over the decline of the mining about here. What's on your mind?"

James admired a man who could get to the point of a matter and smiled at Peter's confirming that his purpose was more than a visitation.

"You are correct to suggest that I have more in mind than asking about your welfare. You have been discreet enough to keep my affairs confidential and I admire you for that. You have knowledge of mining and I suspect you are a good businessman. I haven't confided in you regarding my actual claim and where it is, but I think you are aware that it is a substantial find and will take several years to work. I have a partner who actually found the claim. He is a prospector and knows something about gold mining, but he isn't interested in running the type of operation needed to exploit the find. I made this trip to enquire as to your interest in taking over the supervision and the development of the claim. Would you be interested in such a proposal?"

Peters did not immediately respond to the inquiry, but sat for a moment studying the young man who had made him an offer he must seriously consider. He had known James for several years now but really didn't know him at all. He had been tight lipped about his activities and now wanted him to tie his fortunes to James' star. Would it be wise? He asked himself. Although business at his office had not been flourishing of late, it was still a good business and he was comfortable with his position. Yet, he knew he would never get rich unless he like so many others in the California Gold Rush took a gamble or two.

As James sat waiting for a response, Peters pulled the gold chain about his waist and withdrew from a vest pocket a gold watch which he flipped open and noted the time. When the watch opened, it played a waltz tune that was unfamiliar to James, but was a tune he found quite pleasing. He must get one of those watches for Little Flower.

"It's time I was getting back to the office. Why don't you come along with me and we will discuss this matter further. I can't give you an answer right away; I have the wife and my business to think about. I'll need to know a lot more about this mine of yours before I can give serious consideration to your offer."

After discussing the matter for several hours, it was decided that Peters would let his assistant run the office and he would ride back to the Little Flower Mine with James and make an appraisal of the property and its prospects.

"I have studied mining for a number of years and have a general idea of the machinery and equipment it would take to mine your property, but until I can inspect it I don't know if I can handle the job or for that matter whether I would want to," was Peters' last comment. That satisfied James and they settled on a date for departure earlier than James wanted, but a date that would allow Peters to return to Sacramento before winter closed the passes.

James had wanted to follow up on the invitation extended by Leland Stanford, but the accelerated departure date left him little time to buy the supplies, mules and other items he needed for the return trip to the mine. He made a hurried trip to see what progress Hernandez was making on the design of his new home. It was confirmed that Jorgensen would have to tear down the existing structure and start over. "You wouldn't have liked the results anyway if I had to salvage what's there," Jorgensen advised him.

Next James did some serious shopping for Little Flower. He bought her more material and sewing items, some store made dresses, shoes and under things that were recommended by the dry goods clerk, a fur coat, leather boots, a fur hat, gloves and finally a gold watch that played a waltz tune when opened. For Jack he bought tobacco, a knife, a new rifle, a coat and some boots. Remembering Jack's nearsightedness, he went to an eye doctor and with his advice selected several eye glasses of various strengths that might help Jack's nearsightedness. It took four pack mules to carry all the supplies he had gathered, but once gathered, he was on his way. As he arrived in Sacramento a heavy rain was falling. James was not displeased by the inclement weather. Few people would be about to notice his passing through town and that was to his liking. There was still the worry that some gold seeker would know who he was and would follow James to his claim. It would be difficult to hide their trail with so many animals. When Peters joined him he also had a pack mule and his horse to add to the train.

Fall had gathered in the hills as they traveled northward, the Oak trees, the Cotton Woods, the Larch and Maple trees were shedding their turning leaves covering the ground with a gold and red carpet. The Mulberry and Chokecherry bushes added their pageant of color on the ridges above. The rain that had brought gloom to their departure from Sacramento had moved off into the mountains to add a dusting of white that added a distinct contrast to the rolling hills through which the little train passed. Had it not been for the dire warning that the Modocs were ravaging the outlying settlements the passing of the small train would have been a passage through a veritable paradise. At Sutter's Fort, they joined an army troop under the command of General Canby that had been sent north to drive the Modocs back into the Klamath Lake area in Oregon Territory.

Unlike the civilian population that had no compassion for the natives, James found the General to be sympathetic to the struggle of the Modocs to keep the growing tide of settlers off of their traditional hunting grounds.

"It is my duty to defend the frontier against these attacks from the natives, but it is the settlers themselves who usually provoke them. When they find land they want, they take it and will defend it with their lives. The government gives them a title and ignores any claim by the natives. The army is committed to defend land claims that to my thinking ought not to be granted without some settlement with the natives. The use of force will not bring a satisfactory result I fear," the General confided to James as they moved northward.

James was impressed by the General, whose uniform was an amalgamation of civilian and military ware. His broad brimmed hat and his canvas coat were of his own choosing. His troops, however, seemed well disciplined and were all in standard military dress. The General was, James observed, a man of independence not customarily found in uniform. It was also obvious to James that the General would deal with understanding and sympathy with the natives. This generosity would one day cost the General his life and bring upon the Modocs the final and fateful vengeance of the white man's army. ([24])

The rampaging tribes moved northward ahead of the pursuing troopers and left the path clear for James and Peters to pass on into the lands that

---

[24] See: Lost River, Paxton Riddle, Berkley (1999)

would one day be the Nevada Territory where Little Flower and Cactus Jack awaited James' return. When they reached the place where James and Little Flower had first established their encampment, James was panic stricken to find the camp ground deserted. In fact he could find hardly a trace that they had ever been there. It was Jacks' jackass Daisy, who having heard their arrival came out of the woods to investigate. Soon after the donkey's arrival, James could hear Jack cussing Daisy and calling her back. As Jack came into the clearing and spotted their presence, James could see he was armed and being near sighted was approaching them slowly with his rifle at the ready.

"Put down that rusty old rifle of yours before it blows up in your face," James joyously shouted. "Where is Little Flower? What happened to the lodge we built?" James next demanded.

"Tarnation," Jack shouted back, "It's about time you got your sorry butt back here. We had to move the camp back up stream. There's been people snooping about the valley. I ain't got no sleep for months keeping watch about here. Little Flower's back up in the woods where she's been pining away for you."

When Jack noticed Peters standing by the creek looking about, he again raised his rifle and squinted in his direction. "Who's that snoopy fella down there nosing around?" Jack demanded, "He with you or should I blast him one?"

"As I told you, you best put that damn rifle away before you get yourself hurt. That there is Robert Peters. I told you about him. He's the Assayer from Sacramento. If all you say about this find of yours is true, we may hire him to manage the mine. We discussed the need to get someone to take over the operation. He's going to look things over and see if he'd be interested. Don't go shooting him."

"Now I'm going up ahead to find Little Flower while you and Mr. Peters get acquainted. You can trust him so don't be hiding anything from him you secretive old bastard. That bay mule with the white face has a few things I bought for you; you may want to check 'em out. You and Peters stick around here till I call you." With that admonition James took the lead rope of the other mules and headed up the creek to where Jack and moved the camp.

Jack had moved the camp abreast of the pond where James and Little Flower had loves first encounter. That thought pleased James and he left the mules and his horse at a distance and walked to the lodge. As he approached he heard the melodic humming of Little Flower as she hummed one of the many tunes Jack had taught her. As he got closer the humming stopped.

"Is that you Jack," Little Flower called from inside the lodge. There was cautiousness in her voice that caused James to wonder just how troubled the camp may have been in during his absence. James didn't answer Little Flower's call, but moved to the door of the lodge and having the gold watch in hand opened it and held it just inside the door while its tinkling merry waltz broke the frozen, cautious silence that had followed Little Flower's call.

To his surprise, Little Flower remained silent and there was no movement to be heard from inside the lodge. Inside the lodge, Little Flower had no conception of what that musical thing was that was playing the pleasant tune. She remembered, however, how the white men would dangle such things before the Indian maidens at the white men's Forts to induce them to submit to sex. She clung tightly to the large pistol that James had given her and now raised it toward the door and remained silent. When Jack did not respond to her call, she knew that a stranger was about the camp and she now feared for Jack's safety and her own. After a moment however, she noticed something familiar about the beaded glove that held that tinkling obstacle dangling inside the door.

"James, James! Can that be you?" she asked tentatively.

James then swept aside the lodge door and stepped inside. His eyes not having adjusted to the light he did not see the pistol in her hand until she uncocked it then threw it to the ground and sprang to embrace him. James was immediately aware that there was more to the tight eager embrace than a reward for his return. There was an element of desperation about the embrace that unsettled him.

After she had smothered him with a dozen warm, moist kisses, he was able to put her at arm's length where he could study her beautiful, but troubled face. Tears were running without restraint down her cheeks and she quickly moved back into his arms and squeezed him with an intensity that further alarmed him.

James moved her over to her bed robes and sat her down and knelt before her holding her tear covered face in his hands.

"You must tell me what has happened here, Little Flower, I could sense the fear in your voice when you called to me. Jack was running around down below ready to shoot me. Please stop crying and talk to me."

With great effort, Little Flower composed herself. "You must hold me and I will tell you," Little Flower responded as she moved within his sheltering arms.

"Several days ago," Little Flower said tentatively as if testing the correctness of the white man's numbering system Jack had taught her, "Two strange men came into our camp down below while Jack was up stream. They wanted to know why I was here and who was with me. I spoke to them in my language as I didn't want them to know anything. They looked in our lodge and threw things about and than looked about the camp. They demanded to know if there was gold in the creek. They seemed to know there was as Jack had set up a, what do you call it, a sluice box? Then they came at me and pushed me to the ground and one of them tried to hurt me. Daisy had run up the trail to where Jack was and warned him of the strangers. He came back and shot the man who was trying to hurt me. He hit him in the leg and they both threatened to come back and take our gold. They said they have friends and wouldn't be bothered by a little old man and a squaw."

"I was so afraid," Little Flower continued as she moved even more tightly into James' sheltering arms. Looking at him tentatively she said in a hesitant whisper, "I didn't want them to kill our baby, James."

James was stunned into silence. First, his entire being was seething in a rising anger toward those men who had invaded the camp and threatened Little Flower and Cactus Jack. He wanted to hunt them down, but then thought he knew nothing about where to look for them. But then they had threatened to return. James' mind was racing as he devised a suitable reception. But than what was it Little Flower said? He looked at Little Flower now with a keener interest. Now that she had stopped crying and whipped the tears from her face he could see that was a new radiance about her. Even though she now sat staring at her hands folded in her lap, distraught over James' silence, he could detect the difference between the young girl he had left behind and the woman now burdened with a thickening womb of motherhood.

James placed his hand under her chin raising her face to his. "Did I hear you right Little Flower? Are you really pregnant? Are you carrying our child?"

"Yes, James. I have your child within me."

James was speechless and conflicted. His anger at the attack on Little Flower dominated his thoughts, now there was the possibility that the intruder could have killed his child also.

Little Flower mistook his silence for disapproval of her pregnancy and tears again began to flow.

"You no want baby," she murmured as she pulled away from him. "I so sorry."

James, realizing that his reaction to Little Flower's announcement was being misread, pulled her back to him and kissed the cheeks down which tears were again freely flowing.

"Please, Little Flower give me a few minutes to control my emotions. First, you tell me that you have been attacked and that there will be a mission of retribution against us. If I'm to be a father I have a good deal more to fight for.

I really don't know how I feel about the baby right now. Give me some time to let this entire news settle in."

James then remembered that he had left Cactus Jack and Peters in the meadow below with instructions not to come into camp until he called for them. It was getting late and the air was turning chill. Standing and pulling Little Flower to her feet, he led her from the lodge. "I have brought someone with me you must meet. If he agrees with the offer I made him, we can leave this place and raise our son in a place where he won't be threatened."

"Maybe boy," Little Flower offered speculatively as she moved under James' proffered arm. "Maybe girl."

Before they reached the meadow, James stopped her and turned her once again to face him so he could look down into her now dry, dark and expressive eyes. "I've thought about it long enough. I like the thought of having a child with you Little Flower, but you know what that means don't you?"

Little Flower looked up at him quizzically, uncertain of what he was asking her. Her quizzical, uncertain look gave her face an expression that he found appealing. "You must become my wife. We will not bring up our son in the Indian way. He will have a father and mother and his father's name."

"Maybe girl," Little Flower repeated, moving again under his strong, sheltering arm. She felt the warmth of acceptance creep into the womb that sheltered their child.

When they reached the lower meadow, they found Jack and Peters in earnest discussion. Jack was as usual talking with his hands, his arms flailing about pointing to various objects along the steam bed where they stood. Jack stopped short when James and Little Flower approached.

"Thought you might have left us here all night," Jack said giving Little Flower a conspiratorial smirk in response to the serene expression that gave radiance to her face.

Peter's reaction to the appearance of Little Flower was observed closely by James. Most white men would have a noticeable reaction to the introduction of an Indian as a white man's intended spouse.

When the introductions were made, James noticed little if any change in Peter's expression.

"I can now understand," Peters responded to the introduction, "Why James named his mine after you. Such a name owned by such a lovely lady would surely bring good fortune."

Little Flower, responding as she had seen white men do when being introduced, extended her hand to Peter's, who to Little Flower's consternation, stoop to kiss it rather than shake it. She looked to Cactus Jack in confusion, and seeing his smile, took no offence to the intimacy.

Cactus Jack had built a lean-to that he now shared with Peters. As they sat about the fire partaking of Little Flower's perpetual stew, James quizzed Jack about the two men who had invaded their camp. Jack, after finishing his diner had been sitting by the fire examining the new Sharps rifle James had bought for him.

"Yeh, I aimed to shoot his balls off. Had I had this here rifle and these spectacles you brought me I'd neutered the bastard." Realizing his profane utterances was made in front of Little Flower; Jack flushed and apologized to her.

James ignored the profanity and enquired further as to whether he had wounded the assailant sufficiently to give him a noticeable wound.

"Oh, he'll be limping about for some time. I don't expect him back right soon." Jack responded, spitting on the ground beside him in a show of contempt.

James and Little Flower took comfort from each other that night, but as Little Flower in contentment succumbed to sleep, James stayed awake, his mind troubled by the threat that now hung over them. He knew it would be fatal to allow the strangers to pick the time and circumstances of the next confrontation. He had no intention of allowing anyone such an advantage. He resolved to take the offensive. He would go after them. Cactus Jack had surmised that the strangers had come up from a small settlement to the south along a river flowing from a great lake two days south. Jack speculated they would return there and collect the thugs that would form his band of claim jumpers. It would no doubt take several weeks if not months for the wound Jack administered to heal. It would be easy to identify a crippled man and he would go looking for him.

Little Flower was upset when she awoke the next morning to find that James had already left their lodge. She was even more distressed when she stepped outside and saw James saddling his horse. When he told her what his intentions were, Little Flower was distraught.

"There will be many of them. You can't fight all of them," she pleaded, "You must not go."

"I doubt they have had the time or the inclination to gather a group of renegades yet. I intend to get them before they have time to do so and before they are prepared to fight. You know that them kind will steal in here and try to ambush us. I don't intend to wait around and take a bullet in the back and have you and Jack killed in the process." James then took her back inside the lodge and sat her down. "You carry our child. I want you to have faith in me and not worry yourself while I am gone. Jack will be with you and Peters has promised to say until I return. He is a good man and good with a rifle. It is a good time for me to go."

James traveled south and was soon able to pick up the trail of the two men who had invaded their camp. He was pleased to find evidence that they had been riding slowly and had often stopped and dismounted. Jack's bullet had done its damage and one of them was having difficulty staying mounted. He found further signs of bleeding along with discarded wrappings from the wound they were treating. James had only a general idea as to where they might be, but he now had a blood trail to follow. One of the horses, he noted had thrown a shoe, the other was pidgin toed and had been recently shod.

It took James three days to reach the large lake Jack had described. He then followed the river flowing from its south shore hoping to find the small community Jack had described. Within a day's ride he came to the small collection of false fronted buildings and tented structures that made up the settlement. Camped about the river on the edge of town was a small wagon train that had no doubt stopped to rest before heading over the Sierra Nevada Mountain Range which loomed ominously to the west of town. As night was settling into the valley along the river, James rode through the town to find a suitable place to lodge, but although there were several saloons, an eatery, a store and several other business establishments, he found no rooming house and decided to head back to the wagon encampment and spend the night with the emigrants.

The emigrants were a sorry looking lot; they had been urged to take a new route south from Fort Bridger to California being assured that the route was across flat lands with plentiful grass and water. The trail they took led them instead over some of the most inhospitable land of the western high desert. Water and feed was scarce, the trail unmarked except for the tracks of a larger train they were supposed to join, but that train had not waited for them and had now passed on to California. Meeting the Captain of the Train, a man named Donner, James advised him that he was probably too late in the season to make it over the mountains and that he had best wait out the winter where he was. [25]

"Ain't got the supplies to rest here. The big snows ain't come yet and we aim to get over them mountains into California. We took a vote on it and were going to chance it tomorrow."

James looked at the tired animals, the poor condition of the wagons and the haggard expression that vested the face of each of the wagon members and again advised Donner against the venture.

---

[25] For a description of the Donner parties travels and disaster, see: Wagons West, p303-370, supra.

"It will take strong teams and stout hearts to pass over those mountains; I don't see that in this camp. You best heed my advice. I've been over those mountains several times now and wouldn't be trying the passage with a bunch of wagons this time of year."

"I thank you for your concern, stranger," Donner replied with a weary resignation, "But we got to chance it." Having communicated his resolution to disregard James' advice, James said no more about the matter.

The next morning James watched with a troubled heart as the Donner Party headed onward to what would be one of the West's greatest wagon train disasters.

As James walked his Appaloosa down what passed for the main street of the settlement, he found little activity and at the one eatery in town, he was the only patron. It was obvious that as the last wagon train headed onward, the town would be folding up for the season also. Eggs, a passable steak and biscuits were the only fare offered. The proprietor, a large overweight German wrapped in an apron that had no doubt served him since spring, wanted to know where James had come from and where he was going. "Don't get many lone strangers wondering through here," He remarked.

James had no desire to discuss his business with the fat German and ignored the question which seemed to arouse the suspicion of the proprietor even further. "I see that necklace of yours and that big knife. You a lawman or what? You don't look like the usual traveler we get comin' through here."

James finally turned to him and dismissively remarked that he was merely passing through. "You have a doctor in this town?" he asked.

"Not as such. The barber next door pulls teeth and sets limbs. He's the best we got. If he can't fix them he buries them. You hurt?"

"If he's good at barbering I will pay him a call," James responded, again ignoring the question.

The Barber, like his neighbor next door, had no customers and was sitting in the barber chair reading a well traveled newspaper. He sprang to his feet as James entered. "What can I do for you stranger?"

James stood for a moment and looked about. To the rear of the room, exposed by a drawn curtain, stood a metal bath tub. Tacked to the wall next to the tub was a fading sign advising that the price of a hot bath was

25 cents. Along the opposite wall from the barber chair was a long wooden table covered with a sheet upon which was displayed a number of what appeared to be doctor's tools. In back of the barber chair was a large mirror suffering from a peeling back side that left one's viewing problematical. The barber, a tall, thin stooped man with long disheveled hair which he now swept back with his hand, leaving his hair looking plastered down, waited in anticipation for James' answer.

Noticing James looking at the tub the barber offered: "Got hot water on the stove. Can have you a bath ready in a minute if that be your pleasure."

"I'll have that bath and then a shave," James answered removing his coat and exposing his Bowie Knife that drew the barber's attention. "Ain't seen one like that a'fore. You could knock down a bull with that thing. Ever kill a man with it?"

"Don't have to," James responded. "I just scare them to death with it."

The barber, not a man of great humor seemed to accept the jest as fact and hurried off to prepare the bath.

As James sat for his shave, the barber tried to make conversation talking about the coming winter, the passing wagon train that was headed for trouble and like the German next door tried to quiz James on his business in town if any.

Changing the subject, James asked him if he did much doctoring. "Don't do much. Set a limb or two, sew up some cuts and pull some teeth." The barber offered off-handedly. "Most folks about here doctor themselves."

"Would you have happened to doctor a fellow with a gunshot to his right leg recently?" James asked, trying to sound only slightly interested.

The barber gave him a furtive look and fell silent. "Cat get your tongue?" James finally asked.

"It ain't considered healthy about these parts to go asking about people who's been shot." The Barber stammered. "I don't go tellin' who I treat, ain't good for business, sides being bad for you health."

"Fella' who was shot was a friend of mine. I'm just interested in his good health." James offered as he pressed a twenty dollar gold piece into the barber's hand.

The barber looked at the coin and then at James; frustration written across his face. Beads of perspiration were gathering on his upper lip. James was certain from the reaction that the barber had treated the man, yet had reason to fear him. James waited while the barber struggled with his greed for the gold and the fear for his safety.

"He's a bad one, he and that side kick of his. Whoever shot him should have finished him. He's in a killing mood. His name's Bedford. He hangs out most of the time at Mary's Saloon down the street. Don't know what he and that pall of his named Barlow do for keep. Some suspect they rob travelers. I'd stay clear of them two was I you." Having said that the barber pocketed the coin and finished shaving James' weathered face. James gave the man a two dollar gold piece to cover the 25 cent bath and 50 cent shave and left.

Mary's was not open and would not open until noon, so James rode out of town to where he had camped along the river to await the nightly gathering at the saloon. His thoughts were with those who had left the encampment on their way to California. He saw to the west the gathering of clouds that would no doubt bring foul weather in the high Sierras. James changed from his tailored riding clothes that he had purchased in San Francisco into an old pair of trousers and a coat that he had borrowed from Jack, a coat that had seen service a few years beyond its intended use. He rumpled up his hat and rubbed it with the powdered dust that was left by the parting wagon train. Feeling he looked disheveled enough, he rode into town as darkness enveloped the campground.

As James entered the Mary's Saloon, there were only a few patrons leaning against the bar and several others playing poker at a table near the stairs that led up to the cribs where the services of the less then lovely ladies, now arrayed in remnants of once stylish dresses waited in another corner. James moved to the bar where the bar tender, who was dressed in black with a frayed gold vest, was busying himself cleaning glasses and arranging them in ready reach for the nightly trade. James laid a gold piece on the counter as the waiter stood before him and pushed it slowly toward him while watching his reaction. The bartender looked first at the coin then quizzically at James.

"What's your drink, stranger? You can buy most of what I got for that gold piece." The Bartender, who James was to later learn, was called "Pokey" by the trade, kept his eye on the coin as he spoke.

"I don't want your whiskey, but I do have a favor to ask. I want you to take one of those bottles and pour out the contents and fill it with tea, or coffee until it has the color of your whiskey. When I return and ask for a bottle of whiskey, you are to give me that bottle and glass and then you are to ignore what happens next. Do you understand me?"

Pokey, studied James for a moment, his smallish red rimmed eyes darting furtively about and then up the stairs where James assumed Mary, the proprietor might be watching. The bar tender moved his hand quickly and swept the sovereign into his vest pocket.

"Is that all you want for your money?" Pokey asked, again giving a quick glance at the stair well.

"Only one other small item. When I pay you for the bottle, I will give you a large coin. I want you to bring me as many coins as you can in change and just lay it on the table. I will leave you with a few coins when I leave for your efforts."

James had a hearty supper at the town eatery and returned to Mary's to find the hitching rail crowded with horses. Inspecting the lot, he found the pigeon toed animal and the one with a missing front shoe that he had followed from the mine. As he entered Mary's he made a point to stagger a bit and headed for a table near where a poker game was still in progress. There were six men at the table, one of them had a make shift crutch leaning on the table beside him. As James sat down he knocked over one of the chairs and plopped heavily into the other, muttering to himself as he reached beside him and set the other chair aright.

Pokey was soon at the table. "What will it be, Mister?"

"I'll have whiskey. Just bring me the bottle," he slurred as he slapped down a gold coin. He glanced at the table where the poker game was in progress and noticed to his satisfaction that the two men he trailed from the mine were watching him with interest. He gave them a belligerent look and turned away from them. When Pokey brought him the bottle, he managed to spill some of the liquid as he poured himself a shot glass full which he quickly downed and filled his glass again. Pokey had done his job and the liquid tasted like weak coffee.

When Pokey returned with the change for the two dollar bottle, he made sure to drop it on the table as instructed with a clatter. A side glance, told James that the two men he had followed were watching him with interest. James sat for an hour nursing from the bottle until he clumsily knocked it off the table allowing it to clatter on the floor beside him. James muttered to himself, grabbed a few of the coins, leaving two five dollar gold pieces for Pokey and then staggered out the door. As he left he noticed the two men stand and cash out of the card game. They would be following him out and that was what James was hoping for.

As Pokey came to the table to retrieve the promised coins, he found he was face to face with the man called Barlow, who swept the two coins from the table before Pokey could reach them and put them into his pocket.

"See here, Mister, them coins is mine," Pokey told Barlow. "What's left on the table belongs to me."

Barlow stepped toward Pokey and with his face within inches of Pokey's, replied with a gush of stale whiskey breath. "I believe that fella forgot these here coins. I'll just be takin' them to him." The menace in the Barlow's voice was clear to Pokey and when Barlow's partner limped up beside him and give him a sinister smile interjected: "Now you wasn't gonna' steal that man's money was you?" Pokey knew he had best back off. He returned to his station behind the bar and watched the two men leave. He had a suspicion that they would not be returning. He was certain he had not misread the stranger who gave him the gold coin. That man had a score to settle with the two men who followed him out and Pokey's hopes rode with the lone stranger.

James leaned against the far end of the hitching rail for a few moments until he was certain the two men were following him. The clump, clump of the wooden crutch approaching the door was evidence enough that he was being followed. He staggered slowly to the end of the board walk, and fell as he stepped off the planking into the muddy walkway leading beside Mary's Saloon. James got up cussing and staggered down the alleyway, steadying himself against the side of the building as he went. Half way down the alleyway an empty keg sat next to the door in back of the bar. James sat unsteadily upon it and made out as if he were getting sick. He could see from the light streaming through a small window in the door beside him, the two men, one on crutches, approach him. James was ready, his plan working to perfection.

The one called Barlow walked to the front of James chuckling to himself; he turned to his partner who approached more slowly, "This is too easy."

Barlow withdrew his pistol and holding it by the barrel end made ready to deliver a crushing blow to James' head, now bent between his legs.

Before he could deliver the blow, Barlow felt his breath gush from his lungs as a heavy blow was delivered to his midsection. He dropped his gun and staggered back against his partner looking down at the protruding handle of James' Bowie Knife that had been driven upward from his belly into his chest cavity. He died with the shock of recognition frozen on his face.

The man on crutches quickly pushed his dead partner away and James waited until he could reach for and draw his pistol. As that pistol came to bare, James' pistol spoke first and a bullet tore into the assailant's heart and threw him against the opposite wall. James was bending over Barlow retrieving his knife when the door behind him swung open and Pocky stood in the door way surveying the carnage.

Saying not a word, Pocky walked over to where Barlow lay and retrieved the two gold coins from the dead man's pocket. By then several other curious citizens had followed the sound of the shot to see what was amiss. All that looked upon the dead men agreed with the comment Pokey now made. "They had it coming. Now maybe all them robberies will be done with."

Seeing the barber who had served him the day before, James pressed a gold coin in his hand. "This should take care of the burying," James told him as he turned away, walked back up the alley, gathered his Appaloosa and rode out of town.

Upon returning to the mine, James was relieved to find that everything was in good order and that Peters had completed his examination of the property and was eager to make a deal and take over the mining operation.

"This area will produce a fortune, and it should take several years to retrieve all that ore. I have made out a list of the machinery and equipment I will need. I can go over it with you when you are ready."

By the time they had completed reviewing all the possibilities and necessaries, James was anxious to get the small party on its return journey.

"I don't intend to spend the winter here, not with Little Flower in her condition. Peters suggested and Jack and James agreed that it was too late to head over the mountains and that they should go south and come up through Southern California along the route Kit Carson and Kearny had mapped on their mission to claim California for America. They spent a day covering up any evidence of their occupation of the claim, and rode south as storm clouds gathered over the mountains to the west.

CLAY

Clay had another visitation from Fay the next night and after their love making he tried to discover more about this mysterious and beautiful lady who so willingly gave herself to him in spite of the fact that she was soon to be married.

"I thought I told you," she answered as she rolled over on her back exposing the perfect mounds of her inviting breast, "I'm not marrying for love. My intended is a bore, he's much older than I, but he is as rich as Midas. He has a villa in France, a country home in Surry, an apartment the size of the Acropolis in New York, a yacht that could be a Commodore's flag ship and he has agreed to set me up with a substantial account if I marry him."

Fay began stoking him again. She wanted more. "Now don't be silly and worry about my intended busting in and committing an act of jealous rage. We have our understanding. Do you want to go to Europe with me? You can be my gigolo," she said teasingly.

"You tempt me, but I doubt that you would be satisfied with me for very long, and it's a long swim back." She ignored his remark and mounted him again.

Clay slept late the next morning and when he came down for breakfast, he was informed that Fay and Byron had taken and early morning ride and would not be back for some time. Clay returned to his room which had been made up by the upstairs maid who Clay noticed had finished with Byron's room and headed down the hall. Clay went to Byron's room and found the door had been locked. Fortunately all the keys to the upstairs room used a common key and Clay let himself in. The room was neat; Byron was an orderly person putting everything in its proper place. As Clay went through the drawers looking for any information that could reveal Byron's identity, he left things in disorder. Whoever had gone through his room had shown no regard for his intrusion. Clay meant to return the favor. If it was not Byron who had searched his room, he would expect him to protest vehemently about the trespass. Clay found nothing of interest in the drawers, about the bed or anywhere else in the room.

On a stand next to the bed was a carpetbag that was emptied of its contents. Clay picked it up and thought it too heavy for an empty bag.

Searching it, he found that it had a false bottom which he pried open with his knife. In the compartment he found what he was looking for, there was a good many bank notes and correspondents between Byron and some Andri Ustinoff at the Russian Embassy in Washington D.C. It was obvious that Byron was a paid informer for the Russians, but what purpose he had for spying on him Clay could not imagine.

Clay had been allowed access to the Secretary of War's office, was known about Washington and had his recent connection with Winchester Fire Arms and its owner. None of these things, Clay thought should make him an object of scrutiny by a foreign government agent. Perhaps it was his employment by Gunnison and the survey of a rail route that was of interest, Clay conjectured. Russia had after all a lingering claim to northern California and lands to the north, including Alaska. That was the only meaningful connection Clay could come up with. From what he had learned in Washington, Clay was well aware that the Russians had a suspicious and intriguing nature.

Upon leaving the room, Clay made sure to leave the carpetbag in a different position on the stand wanting Bryon to know he had returned his favor.

Clay busied himself in the gun room after his search of Byron's room. Although Mr. Winchester had left, citing commitments, George had stayed on as a guest to repair and service the large collection of guns owned by Roger Mansfield. Clay found the many weapons from around the world fascinating and was eager to assist George. By the time they left the gun room, it was time for afternoon tea and cordials in the large study/trophy room. Clay and George entered the room after most of the other guests had been seated and were engaged in conversation. Byron and Fay had returned. Clay noted that they had changed out of their riding habits. Byron had returned to his room and had no doubt discovered that someone had visited him and discovered his clandestine involvement. Clay was aware that Byron was scrutinizing him as he entered the room and took his seat opposite the host. Clay ignored Byron until Byron addressed him.

"Have you had a busy morning," Byron asked him with obviously feigned interest.

"Why yes," Clay responded returning the insincere smile. "There are many matters of interest in an estate as large as this. I confess that I am given to snooping especially so when matters of foreign interest are concerned." Clay gave special emphasis to the word "foreign" and was rewarded by the confirming cold, hostile stare Byron gave him. This, Clay knew, would not be the end of the matter. Byron was clearly not a man who liked to be challenged. Clay was sipping a brandy when the gathering was interrupted as the butler entered and handed an envelope to Roger Mansfield. Roger reached in his breast pocket and retrieved a pair of spectacles and studied the envelope for but a moment and then turning to Clay remarked:"I believe this is for you, Mr. Anderson. Clarence can't read, you know, so he always delivers these messages to me."

When Clay noted that the envelope had come from the offices of Senator Benton, he excused himself and stepped to the fireplace to open and read the letter where there was both better light and with his back to the group, a little privacy. He gave a glance at Byron and noted he was watching him now with not hatred, but interest.

The note advised Clay that a Senate Committee had finally made time to look into the matter of the several massacres and the report that Clay had delivered to the Secretary of War. "You must return without delay," the note ended. Clay placed the letter into his vest pocket and asked Roger Mansfield if he could have a moment with him in the anterior room.

"I have been summoned to Washington and I must leave immediately." Clay advised his host. "I trust this matter will remain in confidence as I have reason to believe that my return was intended by the Senator Benson to be discrete."

"I understand," Roger assured him. "I will tell Clarence to have the carriage ready within half an hour. Leave by the kitchen entrance and your departure will be unnoticed."

Clay thanked his host for both his cooperation and for his hospitality then hurried upstairs to pack. It occurred to him as he exited the mansion by the rear entrance, that Roger must have had some suspicion or knowledge that the person who Clay was intending to deceive as to his departure was one of the guests. Had he also known that Byron was a foreign agent Clay mussed as the carriage made its way to Washington in the gathering darkness?

Clay had the driver drop him off at the Willard Hotel and was grateful to discover that rooms were available. The Willard was the living quarters of many of Washington's more prominent officials when Congress was in session. Senator Benson was at his residence and had asked in his note that Clay call upon him once he arrived in Washington. Clay left a note at the registration desk to be delivered to the Senator and retired to his room, expecting that the lateness of the hour would preclude any meeting until the next morning. To his surprise, he received a request to meet with the Senator immediately.

As he was ushered into Senator's study, the Senator was standing across the room conferring with a short, heavy set, officious looking man who with his eye glasses and mutton chop whiskers gave the appearance of a miniature reproduction of the Senator. When Clay was announced the Senator handed the shorter man the papers he had been glancing at as the two men were conversing, removed his reading glasses and dismissed the man whom Clay assumed to be one of the Senator's staff and ushered Clay to a nearby chair. The Senator dropped his heavy frame into the opposite chair, retrieved a gold platted container from the table beside him and removed a cigar, offering one to Clay who declined.

The Senator made an elaborate production of wetting; clipping and lighting the cigar, while at the same time studying Clay as if he were trying to read his thoughts. He next offered Clay a cordial, which Clay also declined. The hour was late and Clay was anxious to have this interview concluded and get to bed. It was obvious that the Senator had little regard for the lateness of the hour.

"I have read most carefully your report to the War Secretary. Since you have been absent from town, we have had the benefit of the official army investigation by a Lieutenant Abrams from Fort Boise. He like you has concluded that the slaughter of those unfortunate settlers was not the usual atrocity one expects from savages. The rumor is going about that these folks were murdered by Mormons no doubt the result of some incompatibility. What say you to that?"

The Senator blew a cloud of smoke into the air above him and then settled his stern gaze on Clay. Clay thought again of the warning given to him by the Captain at Fort Boise. "Don't get embroiled in the intrigues and politics of Washington. Those people can destroy an innocent fellow like you and care not about the consequences to you."

"I don't know anything about the matter other than what I reported to the Secretary," Clay replied wondering why he was being drawn into the matter and why the Senator was interviewing him at this odd hour of the night.

The Senator's set aside his cigar and placing a heavy firm hand on Clay's knee, leaned towards him and spoke in conspiratorial tones as if his words might be overheard by some hidden intruder. "I must know more about this matter. Some of my brethren on the hill are talking about a punitive expedition against the Mormon settlement at Salt Lake."

Clay stood up and moved away from the Senator. Standing in front of the large window overlooking the Capital building, its portico aglow with gas lamps revealing the coming and going of dozens of civil servants serving a government never at rest, Clay pondered the gravity of the situation that confronted him. When Clay walked back to face the Senator, Senator Benson had relit his cigar and sat relaxed in his chair giving the appearance of impartiality and at best mild interest.

"My report to the War Department is as complete as I could make it. I have nothing more to offer on the subject and see no purpose in my appearance before Congress. I have no desire to become involved in a matter of such serious consequences as a Mormon War if that is what is to come of the matter."

"You are reading much too much into my comment. No *war* as you call it is contemplated. Perhaps if such is intended, you could discourage it, if that is your inclination," the Senator responded, now watching Clay more intently. "The West is the future of our country and must be settled by men of peace and industry. This Mountain Meadows matter and these other massacres cannot go unchallenged. We must bring law and order to the territories and it appears that the Army is the only agency that can do the job. Those savages who killed your friends in Oregon will kill again. You cannot want that to happen. The Army as you may know is not particularly inclined to become the buffer between the natives and the settlers. Your testimony could be pivotal in this matter. You alone have seen the carnage and have suffered the loss of your friends. Your testimony could be most helpful."

"I have seen the carnage as you describe it and but for the grace of the Almighty, I would have been among them when the attack occurred. I was off hunting for game and returned to witness the awful vengeance that few could contemplate. The mutilation, the senseless desecration haunts me nightly. I do not know the men who do such a thing and would be glad to see them suffer for their cruel, unwarranted actions. But I have seen also the horrible death inflicted upon those savages as you call them; by the diseases we have brought among them. I have seen their women ravaged by drunken rouges; their once able warriors reduced to drunken dependence. The settlers that you talk about are indifferent to the needs of the Indians to hunt and roam the lands they claim. The Indians have reason to be hostile and if you send the soldiers among them there will be war. As to the Mormons, I have no knowledge of their complicity. I only know that the Mountain Meadows slaughter was not done alone by Indians, though there was evidence that they may have been involved. It may be that they were and should be brought to justice. You have your report from Fort Boise. You don't need my testimony."

The Senator now rose to his feet. He was obviously disappointed in the way the interview was going and wanted to impress upon Clay the importance of his participation in the upcoming Senate hearing. He was a man accustomed to having his way and could get petulant with those who opposed his views. Clay hoped he had not gone too far with his comments, but his mind was set and he wanted a way out. The Senator was now facing him; drawn to his full height he was impressive. He had held vast audience spell bound with his oratory and physical presence. In the halls of Congress he was the one solid, uncompromising voice that supported President Polk's dream of the American Empire. He represented the state of Missouri, gateway to the west. He had no affinity for the native population and like the Mexicans in the Southwest; they were an impediment to the expansion of America across the continent and must be either eliminated or restrained.

"You surprise me lad," the Senator responded with a warm and fatherly air. "I did read your report. You must admit it was somewhat brief. Secretary Crawford's testimony before the Committee was given yesterday. He seems to have been much impressed by your interview with him. I am certain you would be well received and could add a great deal to the proceedings. Come, now lad, let's have no misunderstanding. Your country needs your help."

Although the Senator's remarks were meant to persuade Clay to cooperate, they had the opposite affect; his remarks made it clear to Clay that his testimony was intended to buttress the demand for Army intervention and retaliation. Clay struggled to think of a way out of his dilemma. He wanted no more of politics and no more of Washington. He knew from the treatment the press had originally given him that he could as easily end up the goat and not the hero of the Senate proceeding, for there were those in Congress and the press who were as strong in their opposition to the intended policy as Senator Benson was in favor of it. The Press would not treat him kindly if he looked the fool in a business in which he was a novice.

Clay stepped away from the Senator and returned again to the window and viewed once more the Capital building still to gain the majesty of its intended skyward ascent. Carriages were lined up at the White House for another of the many state functions that dominated the social scene of Washington during the winter. Soon all of those finely dressed dignitaries and socialites would be retreating to New England or to their home states as the sweltering heat of the Washington summer and the diseases nurtured in the putrid swamplands about the capital would distress their comforts and to Clay, suspend their meaningless existence. Clay had never felt so alone and so desperate to return to the West. He was in the center of the power of ambitious men who were forging their dreams and careers and using people like him as the stepping stones to immortality.

The Senator had moved beside him and stood like him viewing the busy scene below. "You are looking lad, upon the pulse of a nation which has no limit upon it greatness. It must grow and expand and claim its place among the great societies of the world. Beyond our shores are the Old World powers whose quest for riches and might have laid claim to all we now posses and would control it still except for the stern resolution of men who wanted to be rid of their insufferable wars and interference. We have claimed a great land and now we must settle it and hold it. It will give us the riches and power to defy the tyranny of the Continental powers that would humiliate and dominate us if we vacillate. We need men of vision and strength. Young men like you must shoulder the burden of our great destiny and set the pathway to our glory. We ask little of you, yet you may help unleash the great forces that will make that Capital over there the center of the world."

Clay felt a shiver go down his spine from the sheer weight of the oratory that had been directed at him. The vision of America's greatness was a moving anthem that stirred the sole of all patriots and Clay considered himself among those elite. Yet, the tapestry that had been woven before his eyes, made Clay feel not inspired, but humbled. He felt far too insignificant in the events of this strange city to ride the horse presented. The Senator's ambition, Clay realized, would destroy lesser men who opposed him. Clay did not want to be that man.

Clay turned to the Senator now and addressed him in as sincere a manner as he could, hoping his sincerity would overcome the Senator's passion.

"I arrived in your city unknown, having accomplished little but having witnessed much. Your press made me out a hero and I am no hero, for I have never been tested except by circumstance. I have been invited to mingle with the rich and powerful who saw me not for who I am, but for what they wanted me to be. I have learned a good deal about these people and find few I admire among them. You paint a great vision for a nation that deserves its place among the world's great powers. That nation, however, will not be built by the fickle, self absorbed people who parade about in those fancy cloths and decorous carriages out there. I am certain your Congress will have a good deal to do with the matter of our nation's place in the world, but right now that Congress is more concerned with who controls it, the slave states or the free states than it is about that great destiny you foretell. I can do more for the future of this country by going back to the West than I can by an appearance before Congress. It is the West that will lead this country into the future, a future the bitterness and divisions over slavery in your Congress would deny us."

"You question my ambivalence concerning your attitude toward the Indians whom you deem a mere nuisance. Yet, your own daughter has confided in me that your son-in-law, Colonel Freemont, has found the natives less detestable than you have and has spoken out for them. Kit Carson and General Kearny who you have met have also cautioned against the cruelty that your policy might bring upon the natives. I shall head west in the morning Senator and wish you the best." Having spoken his final words Clay turned and left the room without looking back at what must have been a very agitated Congressman.

A fog had settled over the city as the warmth of the sun drove from the earth the long present frost. Clay was up early and drafted a letter to be delivered to Captain Gunnison informing him that he would meet the survey expedition upon its arrival in St Louis. He ended the letter with a description of his encounter with Senator Benson and expressed his hope that the encounter would not affect his employment with the survey. "If it should, please advise me by telegraph and I will not delay my departure for California."

Clay was not surprised to find that the rail lines he had traveled but a year before had been extended and that he was able to reach Chicago in less than three days. The accommodations, however, had not much improved and his ride in coach class was over crowded with emigrants, their children and their baggage and even a few of their domestic animals. The change of trains from one railroad to another was always eventful as families fought to stay together and move their many possessions from one terminal to another. Clay, having but one piece of luggage and his Winchester Rifle, was always able to find accommodations, but upon several occasions had to relinquish his seat to some aged parent or pregnant woman and find a place in the isle where the drafty railroad car kept him in constant discomfort. These people were mostly from Central and Southern Europe and their conversation was harsh and unnerving to Clay. Clay found it almost humorous to think that these people were the ones Senator Benton referred to when he talked of nation building. With the isolation on the Western lands, it would take decades for these people to assimilate into a nation the Senator envisioned.

It saddened Clay to think that these people had no conception of what lay ahead of them. They had invested all they possessed in a trip that would lead them into a hostile frontier without law and little authority. They would claim lands that others had possessed for centuries longer than their race existed. They would be faced with the harsh elements of weather and the interminable loneliness on the prairies that would drive many of them insane and would break the spirits of others. As he viewed the passengers in the car as they left Chicago, he tried to pick from among them those who would survive and those who would perish. In the end he gave up, for it was a saddening effort and would serve no good end. Providence alone would decide the issue. Clay had purchased enough food to last him to St Louis, but found as the trip progressed that the hunger filled eyes of several of the children made eating in front of them impossible. He distributed most of his food among them. How, he wondered, could these people survive the difficulties of the trail west if they could not buy food enough for their children on this short trip?

St. Louis had changed in the short interval when he had entered its portals and headed on his journey to Washington to deliver his dispatch to the Secretary of War. Many of the clapboard businesses that that had lined the main street had been replaced by solid brick structures giving a permanence to the town that it had lacked when he had seen it last. The snows of what must have been a severe winter were still in evidence along the streets that were bordered with the residue of the blizzards that had swept through the city. The gray residue of the winter fires of wood and coal that had warmed the inhabitants of the thousand houses that now formed the city had given the banks of snow an austere presence that blended with the clouds that held back the penetrating assault of the sun's soon encompassing warmth.

Clay was glad to leave the company of the emigrants whose companionship reminded him of the brutal and endless travails of the passage along the Oregon Trail that he had so recently experienced. The streets of the city at noon day were filled with the commerce of hopeful merchants who would soon be outfitting the hoard of emigrants who would soon be thronging through the city. The board walk along Main Street was crowded with ladies in hoop skirts and fur lined coats and their handsomely attired escorts who seemed impatient to be at their business. Mixed among them were plainsmen who had loitered through the winter and were, like Clay, itching to be on their way once again.

Clay found a suitable room at the newly completed Gateway Hotel, named no doubt for the promise of the city's dominance in the westward migration. Unlike the leisurely pace of Washington, and the organized pace of Chicago, St Louis was a frenzy of activity. Steam boats were in abundance at the wharfs along the Mississippi, disgorging their cargos of merchants, itinerants, emigrants and merchandise. The draymen who struggled for space along the crowded streets, the neighing and braying of hundreds of agitated animals, the shouts and curses of the teamsters gave promise of the tide of emigration that would soon overwhelm the city and enrich those who had the foresight to seize the opportunities that fortune presented.

From the farms and plantations across the plains and up and down the river, the inhabitants were crowding into the city to sell their produce and to purchase the supplies for the upcoming planting season. Their wagons and animals added to the confusion on the overcrowded streets. The calicos and ginghams in checks and prints of the country people added a luster to the otherwise conservative dress of the town's people as they passed along the street gawking in the widows where the wares of the day were displayed.

Senator Benson had labored long and hard to make St Louis the gateway to the west. His efforts would be rewarded if the rail lines heading westward would make the city the terminal point. The survey that Captain Gunnison was charged to undertake would be the fulfillment of the Senator's hopes.

Clay found that the Captain had responded to his letter and a cable was waiting for him at the Western Union office. It informed him that Congress was embroiled in another controversy over the entrance of California and Oregon and at present all thought of a punitive expedition against the Mormons was on hold. There were to be no repercussion from his encounter with the Senator and Clay was instructed to start gathering the supplies necessary for the survey. Clay's first trip was to Fort Leavenworth outside of the city where his horse had been left in the care of the army. There he made arrangements for the forty animals that would be needed for the survey party. He found that the other supplies that would be needed were in abundance and at good prices. That was a condition soon to changes as the wagon trains assembled.

Within a week Captain Gunnison arrived and took over the planning and outfitting, leaving Clay little else to do but to prepare the wagons and animals. Within another few days, the entire crew of twenty five had gathered and preparations were soon under way to depart St. Louis.

"I want to be ahead of the wagon trains, even if we have to face some foul weather," Captain Gunnison advised the crew. The Captain had done extensive survey work as a member of the Topographical Engineers and had even spent time surveying parts of the Utah Territory. The present survey would traverse territory known both to the Captain and to Clay. It was the intention of the Captain to reach the Salt Lake area and winter in that region. ([26]) Their work began in the town itself where a suitable terminal site was selected and a location best suited for a crossing of the Mississippi. Clay, unfamiliar with the work of a survey crew was fascinated with the process used to select routes, determine elevations, calculate the curve of the road bed, find suitable points to cross rivers or gorges, and of importance to locomotives needing fuel and water, to determine a route that would offer both in sufficient quantities. As the survey continued, the Captain even selected sites he thought suitable for towns.

"Railroads need people and commerce to support them," the Captain advised, "There's no point in looking only for the best or shortest route if you take the road to places no one wants to go."

It didn't take Clay long to understand the Captain's objective and he became more and more valuable to the Captain as he ranged far and wide picking probable routes that traversed lands that would one day produce the crops and attract the people who would make a transcontinental railroad profitable. The survey was, however, a good deal slower then Clay had anticipated. By late summer, they had not reached Utah, but their presence and purpose was being observed and reported to the Mormon settlements.

The Mormon's knew of Captain Gunnison who had spent a winter with them on a previous survey. The Captain's book, *The Mormons,* had been published several years before and had not been well received by the Mormons. They had fled from the persecution of the Missouri settlers and then had been forced from Illinois. They were not interested in having their present settlements publicized, nor were they anxious to see a railroad cross their state bringing untold numbers of unbelievers into their midst. Clay reported to the Captain that their progress was also being observed by the various Indian tribes along the route, some of whom Clay reported would probably turn hostile if they knew the purpose of the survey.

---

[26] See; Gunnison, John Denver & Rio Grande, http://gostdepot.com/rg/history/gunnision%20john.htm

The Captain seemed unconcerned with the probable danger. He had, he advised, fought the Seminoles and Cherokees in Florida and lived among the natives in previous expeditions out west. "We have our orders and must proceed. If we are threatened, we will fight. If we need assistance the army will provide it." Clay though the Captain's confidence was misplaced. Their party was too small to handle a serious attack and they were hundreds of miles from any army post. But as the Captain said, the survey must go on and Clay did his best to scout the trail ahead for any danger. A good deal of his time was spent hunting game to provide meat for the survey party and every time he fired his new rifle, he would wait in some concealed spot to see if his shot would attract the attention of some wandering band of Indians. On one such occasion a small band of hunters came upon the scene of a buffalo he had shot, and not seeing him, claimed the cow as their own. Clay rode on without contesting the kill. It was enough to know that Indians were in the area and that was a matter he should report to the Captain.

On occasion, the survey party's course would bring them within sight of or upon the Oregon Trail where they would meet with the emigrant trains heading west. These meetings were a welcome respite from the lonely work the men in the survey crew were engaged in. It was a chance to get what news could be had and to be among their own kind. The trains along the trail had increased in numbers and there seemed to be no end to them. As soon as one was past, another would appear on the horizon. But as summer waned and the days grew shorter and the nights colder, the wagon trains could no longer be seen snaking their way along the trail to Oregon. It was time, the Captain remarked one day, to think of finding a suitable place to winter.

"The snows will be coming early this year," he predicted as he gave Clay instructions to ride ahead and scout out a place to winter the survey crew. "I suspect we will have a month's work yet, before winter. Find a place with timber so we can build some shelter."

Clay left the next morning riding on within sight of a great mountain chain that was even now obscured by a thick cloud layer that would no doubt blanket the far peaks with their first of many snows. The terrain was rugged, with many deep ravines that had been carved by a thousand melting snows from the mountains to the north. Instinctively Clay turned southwestward, knowing he would find a river that would lead him to suitable ground for a winter encampment. The river he came upon was fast moving and teaming with spawning salmon whose instinct for spawning had taken them across half a continent. He followed the river for several days before he came upon suitable ground for a winter encampment. The river at this point ran slow and deep. A meadow that gave evidence of many wandering herds of elk, deer and buffalo descended gently to the river bank where across on the far bank a mountain stream purged its turbulent waters into the growing volume of what would be a mighty river driving relentlessly to the far ocean that Clay was yet to see. Clay spent several days at the meadow watching the comings and goings of the game that seemed indifferent to his presence.

When Clay rode back to the survey crew to advise the Captain of his selection, the Captain dispatched several of the crew to proceed with Clay and lay out a campsite. "You might smoke some of those fish you saw and start gathering meat for the winter," Captain Gunnison instructed. "If there are any Indian encampments about, you might trade for some furs and hides."

Although Clay had seen some sign of Indians, the sign was old and he assumed like the survey crew, that the Indians had headed for their winter encampments and would not be easily found. None-the-less, after he had settled the men into the meadow and selected the best site for a winter lodge, he left them to cut the timber and erect a log enclosure as he swam the river and headed into the mountains beyond in search of an Indian encampment. He was not pleased to find sign on the far side of the river. Their activity had been observed. The fact that the Indians had not tried to contact them and engage in trade was not a good sign. Clay knew little of the natives in the area and had no idea if they were friendly. When he lost their trail after several hours he grew even more worried. Whoever they were, they didn't want to be discovered. This also was not a good sign. Clay decided that it would not be wise to move further into the mountains where he assumed the Indians had headed. The survey crew was well armed and was composed of soldiers, many of whom had experience with the natives. He doubted that they would have any trouble with what few Indians might be in the vicinity.

After several weeks, Captain Gunnison and the rest of the crew arrived at the winter camp. The Captain took charge of the activities and left Clay and several of the other more talented hunters free to stock up the winter larder. Mr. Winchester's assistant had fashioned a scope to be mounted on the rifle furnished to Clay. It had taken some time to adjust the scope to the velocity and range of the Winchester. It not only provided better range, but gave Clay the advantage of searching beyond the range of the other hunters for available game.

It was while sitting in camp sighting his Winchester to the stream across the way that he was able to watch several Grizzly bears, over seven feet tall enter the stream and with their powerful arms sweep salmon onto the bank and then devour them. While searching the landscape about the stream for other Grizzlies, his scope came to rest on a small band of Indians astride mustangs almost fully hidden behind some bushes. The Indians were observing their camp. After studying the Indians for a few moments, Clay noticed that one of them stood out from the rest. Although dressed like a native, he was light skinned and had a disturbingly familiar look to him that bothered Clay, but he could not place the face. Clay gave the scope to the Captain, who identified them as Pahvant Indians who the Captain thought were friendly,

"They're curious no doubt. We would be too under the circumstances."

"Captain I know you have some experience with the Indians and have been out in this country before, but if you want my advice on the matter, I think we would be smart to build a stockade around our little settlement. There aren't that many of us and we have no idea of what those Indians might think of our presence about here."

"I'll give some thought to your concerns, Mr. Anderson, but for now let's just concentrate on getting our winter quarters in order. I hope you can find some more elk and buffalo. If we can't trade with the natives, we are going to need more hides to get through the winter."

When Clay asked the Captain if he had noticed the light skinned warrior, the Captain acknowledged that he had. "I've seen it before. The Indians have been raiding white settlements out here and down south for years. They have white children they have raised as their own. They are best left with the Indians. Most are more Indian the white."

Clay accepted the Captains explanation, but something about that face still disturbed him. The Captain, having thus dismissed his concerns, Clay took some comfort in the fact that his suggestion about a stockade had not been totally rejected and rode out with his two companions in search of more game.

On the other side of the river, Byron, unlike Clay, knew who he was observing. From his search of Clay's belongings during his stay at Oakmont, he knew of the survey expedition and its purpose. Russia's claim to California was tenuous, but they had no desire to see the presence of more Americans on the Pacific Coast. The building of a transcontinental railroad that was the purpose of the Gunnison survey was not in Russia's long range interest. Even though England had recently reached an accommodation with America over the Oregon Territory, Russia remained suspicious of America's westward expansion. The Russian Ambassador had instructed Byron to follow the progress of the survey crew and to report that progress and the proposed route of the railroad. Byron, however, had greater ambitions. That man in buckskins watching him from across the river was a man he wanted dead. He had laid his plans with care and within a few days, before the survey crew had a chance to construct a barricade, the survey would come to its end.

Byron could feel the pulse of excitement consume him as he anticipated the destruction of the encampment across the river and the death of Clay Anderson. Byron's jealousy toward Clay over his involvement with Fay Mansfield while staying at Oakmont had driven Byron to distraction. He had known Fay when they were both young and inquisitive. He had ignored her as young boys often did, when their families visited. But when Fay's awkwardness of a young girl who seemed to be all legs and flailing arms, turned almost overnight into the grace of blooming womanhood, Byron found her more appealing at each meeting. As young teenagers, Byron had tried to seduce her on several occasions, or to at least engage her in passionate embraces and exploration. She had resisted most of his efforts, but when he persuaded her on one visitation to follow him into the hay barn he thought his chance had arrived. He had observed Homer, the huge slave his father had bought in Cuba leading a young buxom half caste slave into the barn, he knew what was about to happen. He had snuck into the barn and hidden behind the sacks of grain and watched Homer perform his duty.

When he first watched with fascination his undressing of one of the slave girls and then mounting them, Byron had been unable to contain himself and drew down his pants and stroked his erected penis until he ejaculated just as the couple beyond him in the hay mound reached the frenzied heights of their passion. When he hinted at what had happened in the barn, suspecting that he would have the pleasure of seeing Homer put to the whip, his father surprised him by admonishing him not to interfere in Homer's business.

"I bought that big black nigger for a breeder. He'll produce offspring that will bring five thousand at auction. But don't go thinking you can be bedding them slaves. Homer's likely to take unkindly to your intrusions and I don't want no son of mine hanging around the slave quarters. If you need relief, and I suspect you are getting to that age, there are places in town where a gentleman can get entertained. In a few more years we'll see what can be done for your excitable condition. But for now, stay away from that barn."

As Byron led Fay into the barn he held her hand tightly and urged her to be silent. As they crawled into position behind the manger, he could feel her excitement mix with his anticipation. Although he had not told her what was about to happen, when she saw the tall black Negro fondling the young girl as he stood towering above her, he could feel the rush of excitement gather in Fay's body that was now pressed close to his as they drew together in their secret place. Homer soon had the girls dress pulled over her head and kissing her breast set to work removing her drawers. The young girl was panting almost like and animal and pressing her breast hard against his moist lips. Homer had her undressed and laid her gently upon the grain sacks that he had conveniently arranged. He then stood over her and dropped his pants, exposing a mighty erection that brought and audible gasp from Fay. Byron was at first afraid her gasp might have been heard, but Homer was too busy with his seduction to have heard Fay's gasp.

As Byron glanced at Fay to caution her against any further exited bursts, he noticed the intensity of her gaze as she watched with obvious fascination as he now kneeled over the slave girl. They were watching the scene from the back as Homer's muscular flanks hovered above the girl.

When the slave girl reached out to Homer and guided his huge penis into her, Byron could see from a side glance that Fay was now pressing her hands against her breasts and breathing heavily. She was on her knees, but her legs were spread apart and her hips were moving in rhythm with the couple before them. Byron could stand no more and pulled down his pants and pulling one of Fay's hands free, placed it on his engorged penis. Fay seemed not to notice, she was mesmerized by the rising passion of the couple before her. Her hand none-the-less grasped his penis and began stroking it. Byron put his hand to her breast and fumbled with her bodice to gain access to her flesh. Fay, to his surprise, helped him pull her breast free of its encumbering clothing and gasped as he placed his lips upon the exposed breast and suckled it.

Byron tried to get Fay to lie down, but she would not take her eyes from the scene before her. Byron was fumbling now to get his hand under her skirts, but before he could, his juices spurt forth in a mighty stream, covering the front of Fay's dress. It was as if Fay had been slapped in the face. She looked at Byron's instrument that had spurt forth its fluids with a shocked expression and then burst out laughing. Pushing him on his back she ran from the barn pulling her dress back over her shoulder as she ran. Byron looked once at Homer, who was now rising from above the slave girl with glowering anger over the interruption of his pleasure. Byron rose and fled after Fay frantically pulling up his pants as he stumbled from the barn.

He did not see Fay again for several months. His mind had been troubled every since their encounter in the barn. Why had Fay burst out in laughter? It seemed a strange reaction to the passions of the moment. When he maneuvered her into the privacy of the tack shed at this father's plantation where they had gone to select saddles for a promised ride, he tried again to renew the interrupted conquest. Fay pushed him away and with a humiliating laughter that still rang in his ears informed him that he was terribly ambitious to think he could pleasure a woman with his little spout.

"When you can show me an instrument like that Homer had, I might be interested," she admonished. "Until then pleasure yourself."

The burning insult registered like a violent tornado in his mind when Fay defended Clay at their first meeting and that anger increased to murderous intensity when he discovered that Fay had slept with Clay during his stay at Twin Oaks. Byron had taken care of Homer by falsely accusing him of spying on his sister when she bathed in a nearby pool where the coloreds were forbidden to trespass. He took satisfaction in fact that his father had immediately sold Homer to a plantation owner on the Louisiana Delta, an area known for its virulent diseases, particularly malaria. Now it was time for further vengeance.

Byron had trailed behind the survey crew, bored by its leisurely pace. He knew in time his opportunity would materialize and he would see the last of Clay Anderson. On a number of occasions he had Clay in the sights of his Henry rifle, but he did not kill him then because when the deed was done, he did not want the act to be traced back to him or to his Russian connection. His opportunity came unexpectedly when he observed a band of Pahvant Indians approach one of the wagon trains with what appeared to be a desire to trade. The Settlers panicked at the sight of the band of warriors, about twenty five in number and started shooting at them, dropping several of them from their ponies. Byron fallowed the warriors back to their camp and at some risk contacted them. Their chief could speak a smattering of English and Byron after camping with the tribe for several days gained the Chief's confidence. The Chief was being pressured by his braves to retaliate against the white people for their killing of the braves that had approached the wagon train.

Byron convinced the chief that the wagon train was too large for his people to attack. Besides, there were other trains along the trail that would send aid to any train they attacked. There was a smaller party of white men in the vicinity that they would outnumber. A party that was some distance from the wagon trail and would be more vulnerable. Besides, he advised them the party he had in mind was charting the course of a giant steel engine that would bring into their lands thousands of white people who would settle on their hunting grounds. It took a good deal of effort to get the Chief to envision a railroad and the trains that would use it. The Chief conferred with several members of his tribe some of who had actually seen such and engine. The prospect of such a machine coming across their lands bringing thousands of white settlers turned the Chief into his ally. These white men must be stopped. Killing them would also avenge the death of his comrades and satisfy the need for revenge among his other warriors. There would be dancing and celebrating that night. Tomorrow they would attack the camp across the river.

The game was moving. Whether it was the intrusion of the survey crew into their grazing lands or the normal movement in anticipation the coming winter, Clay was not certain. He had to wander further away from the winter camp searching for sign. It was not until the coming of darkness that they came upon a group of deer and antelope grazing in a large mountain meadow. They were able to kill four large does before the herd scattered. After dressing out their kill, they made camp for the night with the intention of returning to camp in the morning. They were within a mile from camp when they first heard the repot of fire arms. Clay knew immediately that his fears of Indian attack had been confirmed. The men turned loose their pack animals and drove hard for the encampment. By the time they arrived, the firing was desultory, but the screaming of the wounded and the war whoops of the Indians filled the air. Clay and his fellow hunters rode to a small ridge overlooking the camp and were soon firing down upon the warriors who were busy stripping the bodies of the killed and finishing off the survivors. Clay saw that Captain Gunnison was one of the last to fall and fired a volley at the warriors that surrounded him.

Clay wished he had time to remove the scope from his rifle as it was hindering him in finding quick targets. He wanted to find the Chief among the attackers as that might stall the attack. It was while moving the scope from group to group that he found that familiar face that he had noticed among the Indians watching the camp from across the river. The attempt at disguise had been abandoned during the melee. Clay saw the hate contorted face of Byron who seemed to be searching for someone among the dead. Clay did not hesitate to line up the sights and send a bullet directly into Byron's contorted face. He saw him crash backwards and writhe in agony and then lay silent in death. But now the focus of the attack turned upon them. Clay had a brief moment to reload his Winchester. The attacking Indians were bewildered by the rapidity of the fire that was directed at them as they attacked. Clay and his companions were hunters and did not waste their shots. But it was Clay's repeating rifle that finally drove them back. Several of the survivors in the meadow below were running to the sound of their guns and the hunters tried to protect them. Only one of them made it.

As the warriors assembled in the meadow below, it was obvious to the hunters and Clay that they would soon be out flanked and that their position against the fifty or more warriors was untenable. They fired a few well aimed shots into the group that brought down several warriors and then retreated back up to where they had tethered their animals and reluctantly left the warriors to savage the remains of their comrades. There was no pursuit; the Indians had had enough of their withering fire.

Fort Hall was the nearest military establishment. The small group of survivors headed north to deliver to the commandant the news that the Gunnison party had been slaughtered. Clay puzzled over Bryon's involvement in the events leading to the Indian attack. He knew Byron had some involvement with the Russians, but could not believe that the Russians would have any desire to get involved in this type of international confrontation with America. Could Byron's hatred toward him for the events occurring at Twin Oaks justify Byron's involvement in events at the winter camp? Clay did not want to think or even mention to the others that the murder of all their comrades was the result of circumstances that were personal between Clay and Byron. But what was Byron doing among the warriors that attacked the camp? Clay knew he would probably never have an answer to that question and when the events were reported to the Commandant at Fort Hall, he made no mention of the white man who had participated in the attack.

Clay wrote a long dispatch to be delivered to Oliver Winchester informing him of the success he had had with the repeating rifle and how he was able to hold back the Indian attack with the aid of the other hunters because of the fire they laid down. He knew it was the type of information that would help the Winchester Arms Company and the type of report that Mr. Winchester had hoped to gain when giving him the new rifle. When the news did reach Washington it had an entirely unanticipated result and had Clay known his refusal to mention the involvement of a possible Russian agent in the events would lead to unwarranted speculation, he would have most probably revealed Byron's participation in the attack. As it was reported, the press began speculating that the Mormons had precipitated the Indian attack as they had at the Mountain Meadows Massacre. It was retribution, they speculated, for Captain Gunnison's book about the Mormon's written after his first winter spent at the Mormon Salt Lake settlement.

When Clay's report of the affair was published, Clay once again became the subject of wild exaggerations and was once again made into a hero. Dime novels soon appeared extolling the imagined and invented feats of Clay Anderson, "Hero of the West." As for Clay, he faced the prospect of wintering at the Fort and to once again postpone his anticipated journey to California.

JENNY

Jenny did not know the cause of the interruption to her slumbers and lay in bed steeped in that early morning fog that bedevils one who has been deep in sleep and reluctant to shed the shroud of a pleasant interval and confront the cares of a coming day. Then she heard it again, it was Doctor Whitman in a heated discussion in the kitchen below. Who was he quarreling with she wondered? But then she heard the guttural, discordant sound of an Indian shouting in anger. She could not make out the words or the cause of the disagreement. Then she heard the screaming of a child, followed by the noise of a scuffle and then the sound of something falling on the floor. By now Jennie was out of bed scrambling to get dressed. Melody was sitting up in bed with a look of terror on her face.

Jenny was uncertain as to the cause of the commotion below, but Melody, who had lived through the terrible events at the Sublet Cut Off, knew instinctively what was amiss. Then there was the report of a rifle from the kitchen below. Jenny looked out of the window into the receding darkness of the coming morning and saw a number of Indians running about the compound several coming in and out of the mission buildings. One of them stopped and aimed his rifle at the house below where Jenny was now standing by the window. The shot was followed by screaming from the parlor below. Jennie heard one of the children below wailing in fear and shouting, "They killed Doctor Whitman, They killed Doctor Whitman."

"Mrs. Whitman has been shot," screamed another of the children. Jenny, who had been about to run down the stairs hesitated. What was happening in the rooms below struck fear in her heart. She looked back expecting Melody to be following behind her. Instead Melody was sitting in the middle of her bed sobbing hysterically. Jenny, remembering that Melody's misfortune at the Sublet Cut Off, realized Melody was losing control of her emotions. Jenny went back to comfort Melody, holding her tightly and trying to find words of comfort, words that did not come. The shouts and screams of the children from the rooms below drove from her mind any words of comfort. As she sat holding Melody, she heard the feet of the children as they scurried up the stairs. The children came bursting into her room; their faces streaked with tears and eyes wide in fear. "They are going to kill us!" shouted one of the Sager children. They threw themselves on the bed where Jenny sat trying to comfort Melody.

For the rest of the day and onto the night, the survivors remained in the upper rooms of the Mission house as the Indians wandered about the premise. Below, Doctor Whitman lay dying of his wounds and Narcissus lay on one of the upstairs beds slowly bleeding to death. Jenny found she could do little but comfort the children. Melody had slipped into a senseless trance. The Indians fearing that the upstairs survivors were armed were reluctant to come up the stairs and stayed below demanding that everybody come out. That next morning, the Indians said they were going to burn the house down unless everyone came down. Mrs. Whitman who had survived the night told them to obey the Indian demands as they had promised to treat them fairly.

"We have no choice," she told them. "We must save the children." Jenny and Mr. Kimball, one of the Mission helpers carried Mrs. Whitman down the stairs and placed her on a sofa. Mr. Kimball and Mr. Rogers proceeded to carry Mrs. Whitman from the house. One of the Indians called Frank, struck and killed Mr. Rogers who dropped his end of the sofa spilling Mrs. Whitman on the floor where she was set upon by several of the Indians and killed. Jenny tried to pull the Indian brave away from further mutilating the body of Mrs. Whitman, but was thrown to the side. She then thought of Melody and ran back up the stairs to bring her down. Melody was still on her bed babbling incoherently, spittle running down the side of her mouth. One of the Indians had entered the room, but would not approach Melody, but seeing Jenny enter the room, he grabbed her by the hair and forced her back down the stairs.

Jenny stood outside the house with the captives as the Indians proceeded to kill the remaining men and larger boys. She tried to comfort the terrified children, but the fear within her was so compelling that she could offer scant help. She could not believe what was happening to them. Many of the Indians were known to the Mission. It was difficult of Jenny to accept that they had turned into their assassins. Several of the women were pleading with the Indians to spare the men, but they were beaten for their effort. After the men were murdered, the Indians roped the women and children together and marched off toward their encampment in the Blue Mountains. ([27])

Jenny tried desperately to stay on her feet as the band of captives moved further and further into the vast wilderness of the Blue Mountains. One of the women was always falling or staggering out of line, pulling the rest of the bound hostages with them. The Indian braves, herding them like cattle beat the stragglers with their bows or war clubs. The terrain they traveled over was rock strewn and after traveling many arduous and torturous miles the shoes she wore were but tatters as was her dress which had come into contact with the many thorn bushes along the meager trail. Only once had they been allowed to stop and rest as the warriors drove them on as if expecting immediate pursuit. The children had been lashed onto the backs of the horses and mules that the Indians had stolen from the Mission and fared better, but were now crying for water and the comfort of those whom they feared had forsaken them.

Although the women had pleaded with their captives on behalf of the children, they had been ignored. As the heat of the sun bore upon them and their own thirst and hunger obsessed them, even the women grew silent and struggled to keep the pace and thus avoid the punishing blows that awaited the stragglers. As they proceeded higher into the mountains, the air had the bite of the coming winter, the vine maple, aspen and alder where in transition, their golden and yellow leaves giving the valleys the captives passed through the look of a splendor that gave a bitter irony to the struggling captives that passed in their view.

---

[27] The Whitman Mission, End of the Oregon Trail Interpretive Center, Supra; Dryden's History of Washington, supra (p 98)

As the descending darkness filled the valleys the temperature dropped quickly adding to the misfortune of the struggling captives. When the Indians stopped for the night, they gave little heed to their charges, but did allow them to drink from the clear mountain streams that cascaded down the valley. They were given scraps of food, but denied the warmth of the fire. Jenny and the other women drew the children close to their shivering bodies to give them what warmth they could. For three nights the captives were herded further and further into the remoteness of the Blue Mountains. The further they went the more desperate their plight became. Some had expected immediate pursuit and rescue. When they finally reached the Indian village on the far side of the Blues, their hopes of rescue fell away to solemn despair.

The village inhabitants surrounded the captives as they were herded into a circle in the middle of the camp. There followed a lengthy debate among the tribal members. Jenny and the other women attempted to interpret and translate the various arguments that were advanced. It appeared that some of the tribal members were totally opposed to the actions taken by what appeared to be a renegade band of the tribe. Others claimed their right to the prisoners and attempted to justify their actions by declaiming the Whitmans and the Mission. After several hours of argument, a number of the members of the tribe walked away to their lodges in a manner that seemed to display their rejection of the actions taken by the renegade braves. Jenny for a moment harbored the hope that the dispute among the tribe would lead to their release or at least to lenient treatment. She could have not been more mistaken.

The Indian women came first among them and selected various of the children and dragged them, most of them screaming and struggling to their lodges. The ten women that were remaining then became the subject of further argument as the braves stood about pointing to one or the other of them and laying their claims. Jenny felt all hope fade, replaced by a growing terror as one of the braves, a large and unfriendly looking brave with a face scared by signs of a long ago struggle with the white man's pox, kept pointing at her and arguing vehemently with the others. It appeared to Jenny that none wanted to confront his challenge. The brave, Jenny recognized as one who had brought his young son to the Mission school when she first arrived at the Mission, stepped forward, grabbed her arm and pulled her from the little cluster of horrified women. The other braves stepped forward and pulled from among the captives the one that they had claimed.

Jenny recalled that Dr. Whitman had referred to the brave that was now pulling her toward his lodge as one of the Cayuse chiefs the Hudson Bay men called Henry. She knew he could speak English and tried to plead with him to spare her from what she knew would be her disgrace. He paid her no heed, but upon reaching his lodge he threw her inside and entering the tent himself gave harsh instructions to the squaw that sat cross legged tending a fire in the center of the lodge. Henry then left the lodge leaving Jenny to confront the squaw that looked upon her not with kindness, but with contempt.

The squaw, a short, heavy set Indian with the lines of age creasing her harsh stern face, gave Jenny a strident command that Jenny could not understand as she sat cowering on a pile of robes. The Indian gave her another command and became irritated when Jenny looked at her uncomprehendingly which seemed to give the Indian further irritation. The Indian then picked up a stick and began beating Jenny cross the back driving Jenny away from her to cower on the far side of the lodge. In frustration, the Indian woman threw the stick aside and began tearing away the now tattered dress that Jenny clung to in desperation. The Indian woman succeeded in tearing the dress away and then threw at Jenny's feet a leather smock and shouted more instructions at Jenny. When Jenny again looked at her in confusion, the woman grabbed her stick again an approached her. Jenny realized, before she was struck again that she must shed the rest of her clothes and put on the smock, which she quickly did as the squaw looked at her nakedness with obvious derision.

Jenny reached for a robe to cover herself, the smock leaving most of her legs exposed and barely covering her breasts. The squaw pulled the robe away and motioned her to sit before her. To Jenny's surprise, the woman started picking the burrs from her hair that had become entangled there during the march to the village. When she was done, she combed her hair with a crude comb fashioned from some animal bone and then proceeded to braid it in Indian fashion. She then rubbed her cheeks with what Jenny assumed to be a berry juice or some mixture thereof. It then occurred to Jenny that she was being prepared for some sort of wedding or other ceremony where she was to be given as the prize to Chief Henry.

Although Jenny knew that no good end could come to her captivity, the ever nearing prospect of her disgrace was sending her heart racing. She looked about for a way to escape, but none presented itself as the Indian squaw was careful to keep her body between Jenny and the lodge opening. As she sat there being groomed for the Chief, tears began to stream down her cheeks the sight of which made the old woman smile and chuckle to herself. It was then the squaw noticed the necklace about Jenny's neck and she tore it from Jenny and held it in one hand admiring it while holding Jenny by the throat as Jenny struggled to retrieve her necklace. As Jenny gave up what she knew was a hopeless struggle, she felt more naked than ever. The taking of the necklace stripped Jenny of her last vestige of her past and her future.

Jenny tried to recall the dying words of her mother telling her that she was a very special person who would gift her intended with the prize of her youth and innocence. She thought of the last letter from William telling her of the house he was building for her and the grand life they would have when she reached Oregon City. What would become of all those dreams and hopes? Jenny knew how any white woman who had slept with an Indian was looked upon by the other whites as if they were lepers. How could God let this happen to her? How could Chief Henry and the other Braves who had been among the white people turn on them this way? When the old lady was done preparing Jenny, she moved over to the entryway of the lodge and busied herself working on some moccasins, leaving Jenny to her thoughts and forebodings.

WILLIAM

The weather had turned into the gloomy, rainy days of early winter as the clouds fought their way past Mt Hood on eastward and the sun was allowed a brief sojourn along the Columbia Gorge. William rose early as was his habit. It was to be a busy day. His name was being offered up as the Territory's representative to Congress and he had to meet with the prominent citizens of the area to assure his selection. The wagon trains from the east brought into the territory hundreds of new residents, many of whom were seeking his services to perfect their land claims, settle disputes and draft a number of legal documents as the emigrants were forming businesses, partnerships and new companies. Today was also the day when the contractor was to began the finishing work on the house he was building for Jenny. He would be sending for her soon as he did not intend to let her spend another winter at the Whitman Mission. He missed her greatly and wanted to get his life in order and Jenny's presence as his wife was part of his overall plan in his visions for the future. It was the balance he needed for a successful political career. William had lasting memories of his mother and how valuable her role had been in giving stability and warmth to the home his father had provided. He could not think of Jenny without his memory returning to that near reverent moment when he gave Jenny the ride back to camp; the feel of her warm yielding body pressed against his back as the rode to camp; the stirring it gave him in his loins; the need for a woman that it brought out in him, a need he had tried to ignore as he plotted his future. Jenny was the missing ingredient in the promising life he felt would be his.

As he labored at his desk putting the final touches on a legal document he was preparing for the new Governor, he gave little heed to the thundering approach of a horse up Main Street. It mildly annoyed him as he had drafted the ordinances that forbid racing horses up and down the main street of Oregon City.

Absorbed in his drafting, he was only subliminally aware that the horse had stopped outside of his office building. When he heard the clomp of heavy feet on the porch below and then the clumping of those feet as someone was racing up the stairs to his office, William laid down his pen and waited impatiently as the figure of Dr. McLaughlin's assistant Charboux crashed open his office door and stood breathlessly before him.

"You got to call out the Militia Captain; the Cayuse Indians have gone on the rampage. They attacked the Whitman Mission, killed most of the men and ran off with the women and children. Dr. Whitman and his wife have been murdered."

William sat in stunned silence trying to digest the news he had just received. It came slowly to his consciousness that his Jenny was now in the hands of a bunch of renegade Indians and would no doubt be subjected to brutal degradation by her captives. A wave of guilt came over him as he realized that Jenny stayed at the Mission at his insistence. When he met her again, if he ever did, she would no longer be the youthful, innocent bride who would be the center piece of his ambitions. Those and a dozen other thoughts of Jenny were now swirling though his mind.

Charboux stood before the silent unresponsive lawyer. He had expected the Captain to respond to the news by springing into immediate action. He repeated his message expecting to stir this comatose figure before him into action. William lifted his gaze from the desk before him and stared at Charboux trying to collect his senses. Trying to put reality to the news he had just received. Charboux became confused and uncomfortable under William's uncomprehending stare.

"Did you hear me Captain?" He asked. "Dr. McLaughlin is on his way upriver now and will try to bargain for the release of the prisoners. Are you going to call out the Militia?"

William stood slowly and spoke as if speaking to himself he muttered, "My God, I knew those people. Jenny, my intended wife was there. Have you heard anything about where they have been taken?"

Charboux reached up and pulled his stocking hat from his head, releasing a cascade of unruly hair damp with sweat from his furious ride. "I'm sorry Captain, I didn't know. I should have been more respectful."

"You couldn't have known, friend. I must think of the others now, not just my Jenny. Please go down to the church and have the rector ring the church bell. He knows what to do to gather the militia. I'll be down shortly. I must collect my wits. I fear I'm in a bit of shock."

After Charboux left his office, William walked over to the front window and stood gazing with a heavy heart at the almost completed house nestled on a small knoll overlooking the Willamette River; the home, but for a few weeks more, that would have been the safe haven where he and Jenny would have started their lives together. His mind was conjuring up images of the ugliness that must now be Jenny's fate. He closed his mind to the thought that there may now never be a Jenny in his life. She could be dead; she could be brutalized beyond redemption.

William walked over to his desk and took from the bottom drawer a bottle of whiskey and a glass and set them on his desk. He kept the liquor mainly for clients and seldom drank in the office, especially not before noon. But now he needed a drink. He was surprised to see his hand shaking. He had a hard time pouring into the glass and not splashing the liquor on his desk. Even as he brought the glass to his lips, his hand was unsteady and he dribbled liquor down his chin and wiped it away with the back of his hand. He poured another glass and walked back to the window and drank it more slowly looking once again at the now lonely looking house that would no longer be his harbor of joy.

As he sipped his whiskey, his hand steadied and his mood changed. Below him, militia members were now heading down the street to the church in response to the call to arms. William felt a seething rage build within him. He was focused now on the savages who had so dramatically altered his carefully laid plans and his future that seemed so assured but moments ago. He was reminded of the many Indians he had met along the trail west few of whom he found any use for. He was reminded of their indolence, their child like submission to the vices rampart about the various Forts and settlements he visited on the way west. He remembered the brutality visited upon the emigrants at the Sublette Cut Off. He quickly turned from the window, throwing his glass against the wall where it shattered into a thousand pieces as the remaining liquor ran in a growing stain down the wall. He was going down the stairs two steps at a time just as his father turned the corner to head up to his office.

"What is it William, what has happened? Why are they calling the Militia?"

William stopped abruptly as he came face to face with his father. He tried to come up with the right words to respond to the inquiry.

"Father, Jenny is in great danger. The Cayuse Indians have overrun the Whitman Mission. It appears that the Whitmans have been murdered and the women and children taken captive. I don't know how to put it any better. It is terrible news. I know how you loved Jenny. We must try to save her and the other captives. We will be leaving as soon as the men can return equipped and armed. I don't have the time now father to discuss this news with you. Please forgive me but I must meet with the men."

William clasped his father to him quickly and then hurried down the street where the men were gathering. When he got there, the news of the massacre was already being announced to the crowd and the men were growing more agitated as they responded to the report of the details. Few of them present had not at one time passed by the Mission; most knew many of the Mission people. It was then he noticed Joe Meek standing at the edge of the crowd with tears streaking down his face. Joe, like William had left loved ones in the care of the Whitmans. Joe Meek left his children. His girls were now captives of the Indians. If any man among them knew what fate awaited his children, it was Joe Meek. Jim Bridger whose daughter worked at the Mission would soon be among the mourners. William recalled the Sager children who had been left at the Mission when both of their parents died. There were many who would morn their losses this day.

William strode swiftly up the front stairs of the church and turned to address the crowd. As William turned to face the gathering, the men fell in to silence and moved closer to hear his command. William studied their stern resolute faces for a moment before he spoke.

"You all know the news by now and I don't want to take a lot of time discussing what happened. For now our only concern must be to get on our way to try to rescue the captives and punish the murders of those defenseless people at the Mission. I don't know how long we will be gone. Remember how we spent last fall just trying to find the Shoshones. I want to take twenty men and get started right away. We will take minimal supplies, but don't forget to bring all the ammunition you can carry. There will be some killing to be done."

Williams' reference to killing brought a cheer from the crowd. "We'll kill all them bastards," someone shouted. "There won't be any of them left to do any more mischief." That remark brought a further round of cheering.

William knew he should restrain these men and keep them in line, but he found he was pleased at the sentiments expressed.

"Let's get started then!" William shouted over the crowd that was steadily growing. He then named the men he wanted to return within the hour to start east. He gave instructions for the rest to come well armed and well supplied later and set up a rendezvous point.

When William returned within the hour with his best horse and arms; he was taken aback to see his father waiting with the men, well provisioned and intending to ride with him.

"Dad, you can't be riding off with us. You need to get the news published and keep things going here. Damn near every able bodied man will be heading east within a day. Someone has to keep the store."

Paul Anderson looked his son squarely in the eye. "I listened to your advice the last time you rode with the militia. You may order these other men about, son, but haven't seen the day yet when you can tell me where I'm to be. There ain't a pup here that I can't out ride or out shoot. Don't be wasting your time. I'm going!"

William knew he had been bested and merely smiled at the plucky old man and after inspecting the men and their mounts, saddled up and rode east.

They picked up the trail of the captives on the south of the Snake River and followed it into the mountains. The Indians had taken care to sweep their trail and on the second day, the Militia lost the trail and began wondering up one valley and then another finding nothing. Charboux, who had trapped in the Blue Mountains in the past suggested that they split up.

"I don't 'spect them Indians be lookin' for a fight. We could cover more area if we was to break up into small groups. There be a large valley where the Powder River runs into the Snake. I guess we'll be findin' them savages somewhere in that valley. Best we send some men up river and some down and a few to scout out the streams and valleys that feed into the Powder."

The plan was adopted and the search began in earnest. On the third day out, they ran into the first of a small band of Indians in winter camp nestled into one of valleys. These Indians claimed to have no knowledge of the affairs at the Mission. None-the- less the Militia men searched the camp for any sign that the captives had been there. They found only remnants of white man's clothing that were no doubt the product of trade and barter. One of the braves in the camp claimed to have seen a band of Cayuse heading up river from where they were. It was more than ten days now since the captives had been taken and the first powdering of snow was coming down as William lead his small band up river. No man needed to say it, but each of them was aware that the cold mountain air would compound the suffering of the women and children. They had to find them before the snows filled the valleys and made rescue impossible.

The horses were faltering under the pressure of the pursuit and they labored hard to maintain their footing over the boulders and rocks that were packed into the valleys and low lands they had to travel. As they labored, they emitted great puffs of vapor that hung in the frigid air.

William had sent runners back to bring up the rest of the militia and their much needed remounts and supplies. They had little choice but to halt and rest their horses and await the arrival of their comrades. It was a frustration to all of them to have to halt their search when they felt they were getting closer to their goal. It was again at Charboux's suggestion that they pick the strongest of the remaining horses and that five of the men scout ahead.

"If'n we can locate them Injins afore the rest gits here, we kin maybe palaver with them without gittin' into a big fight. If they's to see us comin' with a big force, they may do somethin' bad to them captives."

William and Charboux picked the best horses and three other men to ride with them. When they were ready to leave camp, Paul Anderson was by their side. William knew better then to oppose him. His father had not only taken a liking to his future daughter in law; he had taken her on as a special charge when he was entrusted to take her on to Oregon. Since the news of her father's death in Central Oregon had reached them at Oregon City, Paul's feelings for his intended daughter in law had become more and more paternal. William was not surprised to see that his father had indeed exhibited the strength and endurance that humbled some of the younger men in the militia. Paul had a mission, and William was not about to interfere.

They had a cold camp that night, nibbling on the last of their hard biscuits and jerky. When they awoke the next morning, the sky was threatening and a cold wind was pushing down the valley ripping from the deciduous trees along the creek the last of their withering, dying leaves. William rose slowly from his robes, finding that his muscles were unresponsive, that his joints ached from the cold night spent on the ground. The other men were stirring, and not to his surprise, his father was already up, tending to the horses, checking their hoofs, looking for saddle sores and other signs of injury. As he checked his rifle to be sure it was ready for use, he noticed that Charboux was not in camp. His bed roll was neatly rolled up across his saddle, but he was gone. He walked over to where is father was inspecting the animals.

"Have you seen Charboux?" he asked his father.

"He's gone up stream to scout. He said he'd be back within the hour."

As he was standing talking to his father, William looked up stream and saw Charboux leaping over boulders as he hurried back to camp. William realizing that the Hudson Bay man's haste meant trouble awoke the other men and told them to check their weapons.

When Charboux reached the camp he quickly reported that they had been under observation. "We'd best be gett'n after 'em, they knows we're comin'."

The trail up the canyon was hazardous. The early morning mist had been settling on the frozen ground encasing the rock outcroppings with a thin coat of ice. The sun struggled to penetrate the mist and as the militiamen rode up the trail, they could see only a short distance ahead and were fearful of an ambush. The smell of wood smoke was the first sign they had that they were nearing the Indian camp. William told the men to hold back and that he and Charboux would make contact with the Indians to determine if they were friendly. "You stay close on our tail and keep us covered. I don't want the lot of us exposed to their guns if they intend to fight. Besides, I don't want them to know how few of us there is."

"I fear they already know that much," Charboux volunteered. "I don't 'spect they want to fight or they wouldn't let us near their women."

But one hundred yards further they came upon the camp. As Charboux had predicted, the Indians were expecting them. In a small clearing there were about twelve lodges and no sign of activity about them except for a few camp dogs that were now challenging the advance of the two white men. Standing at the edge of the small village confronting the advance of William and Charboux were eight warriors, one decidedly taller than the others who stood before the rest of the warriors. The Indians were all dressed in buckskin clothing, several wrapped in firs, but none of them were armed.

"They aim to palaver," Charboux whispered to William. Best let the rest of the men come forward and back our play." William signaled the remainder of the party forward and had them stand back at the ready as Charboux and William approached the warriors, holding up their right hand with palm forward, the sign of peace. The taller Indian returned the sign and then spoke in his native tongue several words that William could not understand, so he turned to Charboux for an interpretation. As William studied the tall Indian he noticed the pock marked face that gave the man a menacing appearance. He was indeed menacing, he was broad shouldered and muscular. His hair was thick and hung about his shoulders in greasy strands. His mouth had what looked to be a perpetual and challenging sneer.

Charboux did not bother to translate the Indians words, instead he stepped forward and pocked the Indian in the belly with the muzzle of his rifle to which the Indian made no response. "I know who you is," Charboux addressed the Indian. "You be the one they calls Chief Henry. I's seen you about the settlements and I know you speak English so's you best be doin' it. These here men came to claim them hostages you made off with from the Mission. Now where are they?"

Chief Henry gave Charboux a stern look and with his hand pushed his rifle barrel away from his mid-section. "You talk in riddles Charboux. We have no captives. Search my camp. We have done nothing to the white men at the Mission."

William now stepped in front of the Indian. "We know how you lie to the white men. We will burn your village to the ground if you do not tell us where the captives are hidden. I have no patience." At that remark Chief Henry step aside and looked beyond William to the four men who were still mounted and held their rifles at the ready. "You speak big talk for one with so few."

The Chief looked about to his other braves and made a remark that brought laughter among them. William took the action of Henry as an insult which was no doubt intended. "You are a fool to think I come with so few men. There's many more coming behind me with many rifles. I came to negotiate. If I must kill every damn one of you to get the prisoners back, I will do so gladly. Now don't waste any more of my time. Where are the captives?"

The demeanor of Chief Henry changed and his tone was much more conciliatory when he responded. "I know the white man has invaded our lands with many guns and would gladly fire upon us. But we have no white people hidden among us. You must look further. We will help."

William was vexed by the answer and was considering the possibility that they had confronted an innocent band of Indians when from behind him a rifle shot rang out, so close that William thought that the shot was aimed at him, but from the side of vision he saw the head of Chief Henry disintegrate as a bullet entered his forehead and splattered his brain matter on the braves behind the Chief. He turned quickly to fend off the attack only to see that his father had ridden up close behind him. Paul's rifle was still held at the ready and the smoke of the recent discharge was rising from the end of the barrel.

Everyone stood for a moment in shocked silence and then there came a wailing from the women in the lodges. The other braves stepped back as if awaiting the cascade of bullets into their midst. No one was more shocked than William. His father had always been a man of restraint and understanding when it came to the Indians. His shooting of the Indian was the more shocking as it came from the gun of the man William would lest suspect of violence.

"What the hell have you done, father?"

Paul made no answer but slowly dismounted his horse and walked up to the body of the dead Indian. Bending over him he grabbed something about the Indians neck and jerked it loose. He then walked up to William and handed him, without comment, the locket that had been William's; his engagement gift to Jenny.

William held the locket in his hand. It was fortunate that the wearer of the necklace lay dead before him. He knew not what rage would have descended on the Indian had he noticed the locket before his father did. But one thing was certain. These Indians were not innocent of the atrocities occurring at the Mission. He turned to Charboux. "Tell these people that I want every one of them lined up here before us. I will start shooting them one by one until they come out with the truth. I want to know where the captives are being held."

Although William was unconcerned about how badly he was outnumbered and that it was unlikely he could carry out the threat, he could care less at the moment, his rifle was ready and he was burning to unleash its furry. The Indians, however, were more convinced, for as William stood before them in an obvious rage, the rest of the advance party was filing into the valley and lining up behind William with their rifles at the ready.

When the word spread about the camp of the intended action of the white chief, there was more wailing and crying from the women and the children, feeling the terror that swept the camp at the killing of their chief, the elders came forward. Before things got out of hand, another of the Indians stepped forward to speak for the tribe. "I am called Tamsuky by the white people. These people are not the ones you want. The captives are with another village further west. We were sent from the village to decoy the white soldiers so the others could get away. We will take you to them. Most of my people have rejected those who killed the Mission people and carried them away. We knew there would be soldiers coming after us."

It took most of the remainder of the day to question the villagers. William wanted all of those who had been involved at the Mission to be taken back for trial. After they had gathered three more of the braves and placed them under arrest, they left the village with Tamsuky to find the prisoners. Tamsuky, Charboux informed William, was one of those who had been at the Mission.

When the advanced party of the Militia came out of the valley where they had found the Indians, they came across the relief party carrying their supplies and remounts. To William's consternation, he was told that his chance for vengeance against the tribe that held the captives was an opportunity now lost. The agents of the Hudson's Bay Company had ransomed the captives and they would soon be heading back to the Walla Walla Mission. William's only recourse was to send out messengers to demand of the village that they surrender to them all of those who had been involved with the Mission incident. The Militia road back north. Few among them were relieved to hear that the intervention of the Hudson Bay officials had avoided the confrontation with the Indian tribes responsible for the massacre at the Mission. There was rather resentment against the company that still held a British presence and influence in the Territories. None among them wanted a peaceful resolution of the matter even though they were thankful that the women and children were now free. For William there was now a confrontation within his inner self. Word was filtering back as to the indignities inflicted upon the captives. Apparently all of the women had been beaten and repeatedly raped. Could he now accept such a woman as his partner for life? Had she been too damaged to be the companion he envisioned? Could she stand beside him in the halls of the influential and not be forever a symbol of the disgrace she had endured? Was he man enough to comfort her and to accept her for the different person she must now have become, a person who has lost her innocence and who has been violated by savages?

The Militia arrived at the Mission before the captives had returned and waited for their arrival. There was an odd assortment of people congregated at the Mission. A number of survivors who had escaped the attack were in attendance as were a number of settlers from around the area. Several members of the Hudson Bay Company were in attendance most notable among them was Dr. McLaughlin. All of the members of the Oregon Militia remained at the Mission as were a motley assortment of local Indians who had been hangers on at the Mission. The Reverend Spalding and his wife had left the Lapwaii Mission and were also in attendance. When at last the captives were seen approaching the crowd moved into the center of the Mission compound to greet them. A lane had opened up and the survivors walked slowly and despondently toward the Mission. Soon some of the children in the tattered clothes and tear stained cheeks were being embraced by relatives and friends and lead away to the comforting arms of those who had suffered the anguish of their captivity. The women, dressed in an odd assortment of native garments and the salvaged remnants of former dresses and coats found themselves in the discomforting gaze of those who felt compassion for their travails, but uncertainty as to how to approach them. That they had been severely treated was evident from their tattered clothes, bruises and scratches about their bodies and the vacant look in once bright and searching eyes. Most of them were listless and walked slowly forward as if in a funeral march, looking not ahead, but at the ground just ahead of their feet.

First one, than another member of the crowd stepped forward, wrapped their arms about a loved one or acquaintance and led the former captive away and into the crowd. Few of the captives had tears left to shed, but there was the sound of sobbing from the crowd of observers, most who could only imagine the shame and hurt that each captive must now somehow adjust to. In the back of the crowd, mounted on his horse where he could see over the heads of the assembled, William could not at first identify Jenny. When he finally did so, his heart rose in his throat and faintness blurred his vision. He knew the moment had come when he would either accept her or live with her disgrace, or he would move on and reorient his life in the realization that Jenny would no longer be a part of that life. Almost without conscious thought, he pulled the reigns of his horse to the left and his horse carried him away from the crowd and on to his return trip to Oregon City.

Paul Anderson had been seated on his horse beside his son, hung his head in sadness for he knew the import of his son's action. He did not turn to follow his son, however. Rather he spurred his horse forward toward the now lonely, desolate figure that looked so small, so fragile and so afraid.

PAUL

Before he reached Jenny, Paul dismounted his horse and pulled his saddle coat from the back of the saddle. He dropped the rains and as his horse had been trained to do it stopped and waited for its master's return. Paul draped the coat over the shivering body of Jenny who still stood looking disconsolately at the ground before her. His action caused Jenny to start and she looked at him for the first time and after a long moment seemed to recognize him. The look of a lost child that appeared to him made Paul hurt the more for the torment that he knew she had endured.

"You are safe now Jenny and among your friends". For the first time Jenny looked into the crowd that was now breaking up. Paul knew she was looking for the one friend whose compassion and acceptance would do the most to start the healing that she so desperately needed.

"He has gone Jenny, I am so sorry. They have prepared some warm food and hot coffee for you. They even have some decent clothing for you. We'd best get over to the infirmary before it's all gone."

Jenny allowed Paul to place his arms about her and lead her toward the infirmary where volunteers had made ready for their return. Jenny stopped as she passed the Mission house where she had last lived in a world now lost.

"I must see to Melody," she said in a mere whisper.

Paul then turned her to face him and with his hand gently raised her head so she would look him in the face. Paul struggled to come up with the right words and the most comforting words that must be said to bring Jenny back to the reality that she must now accept.

"Melody has gone. She suffered too much from the terror inflicted upon her and has not recovered. She has been taken to Fort Vancouver and will be sent by vessel back to the East. Hopefully, in time, her mind will mend."

Jenny returned her gaze to the ground before her and they walked together to the Infirmary. Paul had been on the scene when they brought Melody down from the upstairs room where she had remained in incoherent babbling and often violent thrashing as gentle hands tried to feed and administrate to her.

As with Jenny, Paul felt a responsibility toward the poor, now deranged girl who had last been placed in his charge as they proceeded on the last leg of their journey to Oregon. He remembered the beautiful but troubled girl who had suffered the loss of her family at the Sublette Cut Off and who tried so valiantly to bear her loss and suffering. Jenny had been the catalyst whose friendship had given Melody the strength to recover from her loss. To Paul who had lost his only daughter at the age of three to a case of strep throat that gradually choked her to death, had looked upon his two charges as family, the daughters he could have had.

He knew his son Clay, now also among the lost, killed by the senseless act of another Indian tribe, had been attracted to Melody and had he lived and Melody not suffered this last tragedy, they might well have found a life together. He might have enjoyed the bounty of their union. But there would be no intimate love for Melody now, no home filled with children, no warm hearth where she and her family could gather on those inhospitable winter evenings. She would now be confined to a convent or mental institution back east at some unknown location where she would waste away a precious life that once held so much promise.

As he thought of Melody and the loss of her, he felt the finger that had pulled the trigger blowing out the brains of Chief Henry, tighten as if having the chance once again to avenge the indignities that had so disrupted the fortunes of those he loved. Even now as he walked about the Mission grounds he felt an entrenched hostility toward the indolent river Indians who loitered about the premises. Once having looked upon them with compassion; the rightful possessors of the bountiful lands over which they passed, he now looked upon them as obstacles that belonged to the land as did the troublesome wolves, coyotes and other scavengers that fed off the bounty of others.

Paul took care not to push too hard on Jenny to form plans for her future. It was clear, however, that the Mission that could have provided a place for her was now to be abandoned. After but a few days the grounds once the location of productive activities, was fast losing its population. Everyone was leaving or would soon be heading on to other Missions or to their homes.

"Jenny," he finally approached her, "we must find a place for you. The Mission is to be closed. I want you to come back to Oregon City with me. I have room for you there. You can help me with the newspaper until you can start anew."

Jenny, who had spoken but a few words let out a long sigh. They were sitting at a bench before a crude table that held the tailings of a meal that Jenny merely moved about her plate, eating only small morsels with a lassitude that evidenced her disinterest not only in eating, but in living. After a moment, Jenny laid aside her fork, surrendering to her lack of appetite. Without looking at him, speaking more to her plate then to him she responded.

"It would not be right for me to go to Oregon City. William would find my presence disturbing. I could not bring him more pain by being where I would remind him of his rejection of me. I understand why he no longer wants me for his wife. I don't put the blame upon him for matters neither of us could have anticipated. If I am to have any future, it must be elsewhere, but I don't know where to go. I'm thinking I should go back east to my uncle who now works my father's old farm. I don't know if even he would want me, but I don't know what else to do."

That Jenny could now be so rational and so understanding of William drove a wedge of pain into Paul's heart. He loved his son. He loved this girl. He would never, however accept William's lack of compassion and understanding. Even if he could not any longer consider Jenny as his bride, he could surely have confronted her and been more of a man in the face of the misfortune that neither of them could have avoided.

"It is not a time to travel east. Winter is already upon us," Paul explained, "We must find some place where you can spend the winter and maybe even start a new life before you have to accept the prospect of heading back east. Let's have a talk with the Reverend Spaulding, or that group from the Mission at The Dalles. They may have a solution."

Paul found the Reverend Spaulding preparing to leave. He and his wife had the wagon loaded and were saying their farewells. The Reverend was amenable to delaying his trip and talking to Jenny. After several hours, he reported back to Paul that Jenny had agreed to go to the Lapwaii Mission with him. He had a place for her in the school they were building and was more than glad to have her assistance. Paul went immediately to consult with Jenny. He questioned whether she was really prepared to be among the Indians again. The Lapwaii Mission was far removed from the Oregon Trail and other white settlers.

"I don't fear them," Jenny responded to his questioning. "They can't do me any more harm. Mr. Spaulding tells me that the Nez Perce are a far friendlier tribe and have never taken up arms against us. He tells me they are more intelligent and eager to learn unlike the Indians about here. I don't see that I have any other options."

"Dr. McLaughlin could offer you shelter for the winter. You don't have to accept the Reverend's offer."

"I don't want to just idle about the fort. I must have something meaningful to do," Jenny responded.

"I would rather you come with me, Jenny, but you seem to have your mind made up. I must accept your decision, but please be careful. If you ever need me, I'll be there as soon as I can get there."

Jenny, to Paul's pleasure, finally turned to him and fell into his arms where he could finally hold her and feel the comfort of her needing him, at least, if not as her father, surely as a father figure. He held her tightly for a long moment and then kissed her cheek.

"You are still my Jenny," He whispered in her ear. Her tear touched his cheek and as her body convulsed in gathering sobs he knew that her healing had started.

Paul, mounted on his horse, watched the small wagon disappear over the rise of a small hill and then turned about and headed back towards Oregon City. Several members of the militia, who had remained behind, fell in beside him. Others of them remained behind to see to the burial of friends and relatives among them were Joe Meek and Jim Bridger. It was a solemn party that rode west. Each man was burdened with thoughts of the deeds that had brought them to the Mission, and each in his own way would not again trust the natives nor tolerate their misbehavior.

The Cayuse Indians who had attack the Mission had created a tide of resentment that would bode ill for their entire Indian Nation.

When Paul arrived in Oregon City, he was not surprised to find that his son William had already sold the house he had been constructing in Oregon City. William was in the process of arranging for the removal of his office to the new and rapidly growing town of Portland, just a few miles from Oregon City, but with the availability of sea commerce, was fast out pacing Oregon City as the center of commerce.

"I have nothing but bad memories here," he told his father. "I need to make a new start."

Paul accepted his son's assessment with silence. Jenny had now become an unapproachable and unmentioned barrier between father and son. As William set about moving his office and possessions to Portland, Paul busied himself with his newspaper. His assistant, Billy Morrison, had put the paper to press in a much abbreviated form. One of the projects he had in mind was to print a complete report of what had become called the Whitman Massacre in time to deliver it to a departing ship that was scheduled to leave in two days headed for Boston. The publication would be the first complete report to reach the east and would add prestige to his newspaper. When the publication was off the press, Paul took the first editions and rode to Portland to deliver it to the Captain of the *Atlantic Bell*. Paul found the ship completing its last preparations for sailing. Boarding the ship, Paul found the Captain busy in his cabin working on the manifest with the Purser. The Captain was glad to oblige Paul and promised to have the copies forwarded directly to Washington.

"I'll be heading there myself after arrival. Congress is talking about the problems with the crossing at Panama. Seems that Columbia is trying to impose a big transit tax. Them buggers is a bunch of bandits."

As Paul was saying his thanks and farewells, the Captain stopped him as he reached the rail to depart down the gangway.

"My Cabin Boy has cleaned out the passenger cabins and he has a bunch of newspapers and books the passengers left on board. Would you want to look them over? You might find a bit of news that would interest you."

Paul accepted the bundle of papers and books with alacrity. He had never thought of calling on the vessels as they arrived to get copies of the publications the passengers had brought with them. He had sent Billy Morrison to interview the passengers on occasion to get the latest news from the East, but he had never thought to ask for their discarded newspapers. Paul placed the bundle in the back of his trap and rode back to Oregon City with the intention of reading the publications that evening.

After eating his lonely dinner that he had usually shared with William, Paul was at loose ends when he remembered the bundle of books and papers he had left in the trap. After retrieving them he stoked up the fire, lit his pipe and settled back in his overstuffed leather chair. He had beside him a crystal decanter of Port and poured himself a liberal serving.

The first item he retrieved from the bundle was a copy of the Washington Express. He took a publishers appraisal of the printing style and print type before getting about reading the contents. He made some mental notes of the style that was used in presenting the news and saw some features he would copy for his coming editions. The large headline in bold print read "Gunnison Party Murdered by Savages." This item peaked Paul's immediate interest as he had just edited a similar report and read on avidly to compare his style of reporting with that used by the author of the article in the Washington Express in reporting on another Indian atrocity. Half way through the article, his let out a gasp and let his pipe fall from his mouth and clatter on the floor. He studied the line in the article in a trance like state, unsure of what he saw before him.

"The only survivors of the massacre were the members of a hunting party led by Clay Anderson, who had recently been the toast of Washington. Mr. Anderson, who was a scout for the survey crew, arrived on the scene of the attack in time to observe the action and with a newly developed repeating rifle managed to slay many of the attackers before he had to withdraw from the camp site when he and his outnumbered party was put in jeopardy."

Paul hurriedly rummaged through the remaining publications and though some contained nothing on the massacre of the Gunnison Party, those that did reported on the involvement of the party's scout Clay Anderson. In his haste rummaging through the newspapers, Paul did not notice that a novelette had fallen to the floor beside his chair. Paul now took a long draught from the glass of Port he had previously poured and ignored and quickly poured another. Was it possible, we wondered, if this Clay Anderson was indeed his son? How would he ever know?

It was when he reached over to pick up the assortment of newspapers to study them in more detail hoping to find some further mention of the Gunnison party that he noticed the novelette that had fallen away from the pile. Picking it up and turning to the front cover his gazed transfixed upon the illustration on the cover of the novel captioned: *"Clay Anderson: Hero of the West."* The illustration had a distinct resemblance to his son Clay. Paul thumbed through the novelette and found other illustrations of the "Hero of the West." In the other illustrations the resemblance to his son Clay was unmistakable. Paul quickly rose from his chair, retrieved the box of newspapers he had carried in and threw the newspapers and the novelette in the box and then shouted down the stairs to Billy Morrison to hitch up his trap. As soon as it was ready, Paul drove the trap at a break neck speed toward Portland.

When he reached the now deserted main street and pulled up in front of William's office, Paul was not surprised to see that there was still a light casting a shadowy glow in the interior. Paul found the door unlocked and burst in without knocking. William, who had been absorbed in the task of drafting a new Ordinance to implement the Land Claims Act recently passed by Congress for the purpose of legalizing the many land claims that had been made by the emigrants, looked up in irritation at the intrusion, expecting to see some drunken intruder who had just lost an altercation at some grog shop and would be wanting legal retribution.

"Dad, what brings you out this time of night?" as he asked the question, he could not but notice the agitation on his father's face and feared that he had hastened to Portland with news of another Indian deprivation.

Paul rushed forward and dropped the box of newspapers unceremoniously atop the documents that had just recently been the center of William's attention. "Look at this," Paul demanded as he pulled the top paper from the box and handed to William.

William immediately noticed the headline proclaiming another Indian massacre and assumed that this was the news that brought his father rushing to his office. He sat back down to give the paper a leisurely review. "No, No, not that. Look down to that third paragraph."

When William saw the name of his brother, he like his father felt his heart leap. He read the remainder of the article and then looked up to his father whose face was brimmed with expectation. "Could this really be Clay?" William asked uncertainly.

Paul put the novelette in his hand and waited to see if William came to the same conclusion he had. William's responds was to rush to the front of the desk and embraced his father and they did a little jig about the office whooping and shouting their joy.

William retrieved a bottle of whiskey from a cabinet and poured two generous portions and father and son toasted their good fortunes.

"If he is still alive, why do you suppose he hasn't written to let us know?" Paul asked his son.

"We don't know that he didn't. There just is no way to be sure that any letter would get through from where ever he is. From the article, it doesn't sound like he was in Washington when this report was made. If he was, a ship would be delivering any letter he might have sent. If he tried to send it from somewhere between here and St Louis, God only knows if it would ever reach us."

"Joe Meek headed back east to advise Washington of the Whitman Mission incident," Paul remembered. "If he passes through the Forts along the way which he most likely will, maybe he will bring us some word. Otherwise we'll have to wait until the wagons roll again and quiz the new arrivals. If he doesn't choose to contact us, I don't have any idea how we will every locate him. Meanwhile, I'll start meeting the ships that arrive. I never thought of getting my news from the discarded publications the passengers carry aboard."

WASHINGTON D.C.

It was ironic that "Old Rough and Ready" Zackary Taylor who had fought the Indian wars along the Northwest Territory and held off the entire Mexican army of twenty thousand with a force of a fourth that size; who always exposed himself to the guns of his enemy and survived a fusillade of bullets and shells, should die so suddenly and ignominiously of a fever after attending the dedication of the Washington Monument. Millard Fillmore, an unassuming and colorless Vice-President, took over the office of the President. His greatest claim to fame had been his efforts to gain approval of the Compromise of 1850 while a member of the Senate from Louisiana. He came into office with a conviction that the Taylor Administration had been the silent, dominant force in the attempt to defeat the compromise he fought so desperately to achieve, the compromise he was certain would prevent the Union from fracturing over the question of slavery and its expansion into the Western Territories. Because of his belief in the perfidy of the Taylor Cabinet, Fillmore sought and obtained the resignation of entire Cabinet that had been appointed by President Taylor.([28])

With his influence as the Chief Executive, Fillmore was successful in his efforts to enact into law the Compromise of 1850. To the anti-slave element of the population, the compromise was an act of perfidy. The most obnoxious provision of the Act was the mandate that the states above the Mason-Dixon Line would have to assist in the capture and return of the slaves who would flee to the north. Millard Fillmore was impervious to the lot of the slaves and placed the preservation of the Union as the prime objective of his administration.

Fillmore's house cleaning of the previous administration brought into the office of the War Department a southerner by the name of Charles Magill Conrad. He was a tall, austere man who, unlike the men of his time, was clean shaven except for a mustache that he kept neatly trimmed. He had clear blue penetrating eyes that gave evidence of an inner strength that had been honed in his rise from poverty to prominence in his home state of Louisiana. He was considered to be an excellent choice for his office, for there was during the formation of the Fillmore Cabinet, a desire to maintain a balance between the northern and southern influences in the national politic.

Since the War of 1812 with Great Briton, America had not been under the threat of the European powers. Andrew Jackson's defeat of the British at the Battle of New Orleans, had given to the nation a conviction that it had no formidable threats from abroad. The successful conclusion of the Mexican War had removed from the public's mind the necessity for a large military presence. Thus it was when Secretary Conrad took over the

---

[28] The American Presidents, supra. (p. 106)

office of Secretary of War; he found that he was presiding over an office of declining importance in the view of a Congress that was distracted by the question of slavery and the necessity of paying for the cost of the war with Mexico. ([29])

Secretary Conrad had a great capacity for work and was a man who delved in detail with the passion that often obscured his view of the larger issues facing the nation. But then the larger issue, that of slavery, was an issue that most politicians found excuses to avoid. The Compromise of 1850, which in effect over rode the Missouri Compromise, an earlier solution of the slavery question that had let Missouri into the Union as a slave state, but barred the extension of slavery into the other territories gained by the Louisiana Purchase, was a solution that gave political shelter. It was, however, but a bridge over a torrent that would soon take the lives of a half a million and more of the youngest and bravest of the Nation.

Unlike most bureaucrats holding position of prestige, Secretary Conrad did not distance himself from petitioners by placing between them a desk of great dimensions, ornately carved and laboriously inlaid with teak, mahogany, oak or cherry wood. The Secretary preferred a large table where he could place various separate piles of paperwork dealing with the competing interest that demanded his attentions. On one pile, setting at the end of orate table dominating his office was the current military budget that Congress was now considering. Another pile contained the reports from the various departments dealing with Indian affairs, another pile dealt with the personnel matters of the Army; who would be assigned where and who would be promoted or demoted, yet another pile held the files of the numerous petitioners who wanted patronage appointments or contracts. As demanded by the press of duty, the Secretary would move from one pile to the other unconcerned about clearing off his desk to make room for the next batch of paperwork as his attentions drifted from one matter to the other.

The Secretary was deeply involved with juggling the figures in the Army's annual budget in preparation for an appearance before the Appropriations Committee of the House. The Army, expanded to 40,000 men to deal with the Mexican invasion, was now being dismantled. A

---

[29] Charles Magill Conrad, http://www,army.mil/cmh-pg/books/sw-sa/Conrad.htm

Congress that had now turned its attentions to domestic concerns was unwilling to spend on a military that had no war to fight in deference to domestic matters where constituency could be built. Reducing the Army to its pre-war level of less than 10,000 men without fomenting dissent in the Army and damage to the Party's patronage was a monumental undertaking in itself. Every decision he made would be the wrong one for many. There was also a demand by a few radicals from the northern states that the present Army remain intact. The recent meeting of the coalition of southern states demanding separation from the Union over the slavery issue prompted these radicals under the banner of the Do Nothings, to demand a large army to intimidate the south and prepare for what was believed to be an impending insurrection. The Secretary, being a southerner himself, held little sympathy for their demands. The President, on the other hand would not support a large army, for he felt he had solved the problems presented by slavery in the south with the recent compromise.

A new pile of paper work had been placed at the far end of the table that could not be long ignored and was troubling the Secretary's mind, distracting him from the budget. The southern states, bordering the Caribbean had long been agitating over the question of Cuba. The presence of Spain in the Caribbean was a problem in itself, but the despotic rule that existed on the island, the prospect of its riches, drove many in the state of Louisiana, his home state, to demand that the United States invade the island and displace the Spaniards. This request had been ignored.

Unfortunately the hot heads in Louisiana, assured by Cuban dissidents that there was large popular support for an insurrection, organized their own invasion of Cuba. Their invasion was quickly suppressed, many of them were killed and over fifty were now held captive and had been taken to Spain for trial. Realizing that the Spanish question now resided in the office of the Secretary of State Daniel Webster, some of the captives were known to Secretary Conrad and he felt compelled to intervene on their behalf and was contemplating what military response might be appropriate when he was interrupted by the entrance into his office of his secretary. Knowing that his superior would object to his intrusion, the secretary approached uncertainly.

"There is a messenger from Oregon who insists upon seeing you. He says it is important. His name is Joe Meek. He is the Provisional Marshall of the Territory and he claims that the message is from George Abernathy the Provisional Governor."

Secretary Conrad set aside the papers he had been studying. His eyes were tired and he was getting nowhere trying to juggle the accounts to cover the needs of the shrinking Army. He put on his coat and walked over to the small side desk and seated himself before he instructed his secretary to show the messenger into his office. For once, he welcomed an interruption.

The Secretary was startled by the appearance of Joe Meek who entered his office still wearing the tattered and soiled buckskins that he wore on his trip of some three thousand miles. The man who stood before him now was clearly exhausted to the point of collapse. His red rimmed eyes, scraggly beard and hawkish nose gave him a frightening appearance.

"You had best sit down," the Secretary instructed him waiving him to the chair across from his desk. "You look like you could use a bit of rest."

Joe sat down as directed but after traveling so many difficult and dangerous miles to get to this point, he was suddenly too exhausted and disoriented to speak. At a young age Joe Meek had headed west and spent a decade wondering among the western lands as a trapper and fur trader. He had married several Indian wives and had several children by them, children he had left at the Whitman Mission to be educated and cared for. He had served the Provisional Government and had been appointed marshal for the Territory. He was a fabled story teller and his sudden inability to converse with the Secretary when he had such important news confused him. [30]

After a long silence, during which Joe Meek realized with embarrassment that he should have taken time to bathe, shave and change clothing before entering an official government office, sat looking at his surroundings trying to organize his scattered thoughts. The steely gaze of the Secretary gave him further discomfort, but he finally stammered out an apology for his appearance and suggested that maybe he should return later in a more presentable manner.

---

[30] Oregon Blue Gook; Notable Oregonians; Joseph Meek-Trapper, Lawman; http://bluegook.state.or.us/notaable/notmeek.htm

"Your appearance be damned, man. I was told you had some important news. Let's be out with it. I have other matters to attend to." The Secretary had not intended to be curt, but it was his manner when interrupted.

Joe sighed a mighty sigh and irritated by the Secretary's curtness gathered his thoughts. "I left Oregon on the First of December and rode here with hardly no rest and near kilt six horses on the way. I didn't want to wait around sprucin' up when I got things to be said." Joe began, "They's been an Indian raid on the Whitman Mission at Walliatpu. Them Cayuse Indians kilt the Reverend Whitman his wife and sixteen young boys and older men. They's taken all the women and children hostage. I fear they may have done them harm."

The Secretary pressed Joe for more details, making notes on the foolscap before him. When he had gleaned from Joe all the facts he though necessary, he called his assistant into the room and gave instructions to provide Joe with a voucher for the next several days and then he returned to the table where the Army budget was awaiting his attention. The Secretary well knew that the Congressmen who just two days ago were criticizing him for his plans to expand the Army of the West would now be demanding that action be taken to provide protection to the settlers. Now, however, it would be their idea for which they would expect due credit.

The news that two servants of the Lord had been brutally murdered by their intended beneficiaries, would drive the Legislative agenda as the press fed fire to the flames of indignation. The fact that a number of women had been taken hostage would only add to the public's passion. There would be a demand for immediate vengeance and the Army would be unable to respond. The country along the Oregon Trail had less than two equipped companies of ready soldiers and they were far removed from the site of the Whitman massacre. This was not a problem peculiar to the Oregon Territory. The Polk Administration had added to the Union the vast Territories of Texas, California, New Mexico and Utah and the reduction of the Army to 7,000 would leave this frontier undefended.

Perhaps, the Secretary mused, Congress would now be willing to consider his proposal to establish a trained and equipped volunteer Army Reserve that could be called out to defend the settlers and pacify the western tribes. Like other officials before and after him, the Secretary believed that the solution to the Indian problem was to teach them to be farmers and give up their wandering and warlike ways. At the present time, the entire west coast was under the command of Department of the Pacific headquartered out of the Presidio near San Francisco. The Secretary sketched out proposed military Districts for the west to present to Congress. The Oregon Territories would be commanded under a separate district to be located out of Vancouver. It would be up to the commander of the district to locate forts at appropriate places, but the Secretary noted that there should be a fort established at the area near where the Whitman Mission stood.

The Secretary searched over the military roster to determine who he would propose to command the new district. The war with Mexico had created in the Army a number of eligible officers who had distinguished themselves in that contest. Among the names he considered was that of Col. Robert E. Lee, Col. Thomas Jackson (later known as "Stonewall Jackson"), Col. George Pickett and Col. George Wright. He selected General John E. Wool in overall command and Col. Wright as second in command of the new northwest district. He recommended the appointment of Captains George Pickett, Philip Sheridan and Col. Edward Steptoe to serve on General Wool's staff. Having dealt with the immediate problem created by the Cayuse attack, he turned his attention to building and strengthening the military outpost along the remainder of the Oregon Trail. Joe Meek had given him disturbing reports regarding the rising hostility of the northwest tribes, including the Yakima, Spokane, Okanogan, Shoshone, and Snake tribes.

JAMES

During the trek south, James relied upon Cactus Jack to guide them as he claimed to have traveled through the southwest desert lands before during his days prospecting. It was Daisy, however, that had an uncanny sense of smell that led them from one water hole to another in a land that would be the death bed for many an emigrant who would follow the unmarked traces to California. They came upon a great depression where even during what was the middle of winter; the temperatures were extremely hot during the day and near freezing at night. As James looked to the north, he could see a mighty mountain, often shrouded in clouds that rose thousands of feet above the land they traversed. Cactus Jack and Robert Peters were fascinated with the rock outcroppings and were continually delaying their journey as they pounded on rocks with their pointed axes. Though nothing seemed to come of the effort, they would not relent.

Several of the rock cliffs they explored were pronounced to have "promising," samples, but the material was of metals that did not interest them. James, because of his concern for Little Flower's comfort, did not protest to the leisurely pace of their travels. As they rose above the valley floor and headed westward, they came upon the remnants of a wagon train that was no doubt running out of water or supplies as it headed into the mountains. Cactus Jack, after studying the sign pronounced that the train had recently passed, but he could not tell exactly how long ago because strong winds had obscured the trail. Possessions from the train were discarded along the trail as the travelers were trying to lighten their load.

The wagon tracks indicated that there were three wagons that were moving on. Whether the train had consisted of more wagons as it came out of the desert, they could not tell, as they had intersected the tracks that were heading northward as they were headed more to the south. James was not much interested in following the tracks because of his concern for Little Flower whose pregnancy was becoming more evident and her time was drawing near. They decided to wait under a prominent Palo Verde tree while James rode the wagon trail for a distance to determine if their help may be needed.

After riding the trail for several hours, James could see in the distance a gathering of vultures circling. He spurred his Appaloosa and proceeded at a steady ground covering trot to where he found a mule that had been cut from the traces of a wagon and left to die. Although the desert creatures had been at the carcass, James guessed that it had been dead for no more than a day or two. As he rode over the crest of another ridge, he found an abandoned wagon at what had been a camp site. He had left instructions with Cactus Jack and Peters to follow after him if he did not return by night fall. He stopped at the camp site by the wagon to await their arrival and ate a meager meal of biscuits and jerky as night fell. The next morning, while waiting for the others to catch up with him, James walked about the camp site to check for further signs. It was then he discovered a shallow grave covered with rocks and a crude marker with only the name Max McGreevy written in charcoal that was already fading. The grave had been hastily prepared as whoever survived, was in a hurry to move onward.

James was now anxious to be moving as whoever was ahead on the trail was clearly in need of help, yet all the supplies that he had that would be of assistance to any party in distress was on the pack mules being trailed along with Little Flower and the rest of his band. By noon they arrived and James had one of the mules loaded with only some extra food and water and again drove ahead to assist the travelers. For most of the day, he found only the remnants of the small train strewn about the trail. He found several more graves more dead mules and the last of their wagons abandoned. Dismounting at the last wagon, he suited the tracks. There were three adults and six children moving on foot beyond the last wagon. Within a mile, he found the body of a man, whose thin, emaciated frame was resting against a bolder where he no doubt had spent his last conscious hours watching the others move slowly out of the vision of his now sightless eyes. James did not stop to bury him as he knew Cactus Jack would do so when he came upon him. James drove his Appaloosa to a fast trot along the trail of that now seemed to be wandering aimlessly across the hot, dry high desert trace.

The second man, who appeared to be in his forties lay alongside the track where his strength and will deserted him. James tried to revive him when he found a fluttering pulse and a feeble but conscious effort to cling to life. As James tried to pour water past his blistered and parched lips, the man could not swallow it and it ran down his cheeks. Next James pressed a wet cloth against his lips and tried to squeeze droplets of water onto his swollen tongue, but still there was no response. The man's eyes flickered for a moment as if trying to recognize the stranger, who had stopped to give him aid, but then his eyes closed and James felt the death rattle consume his frail body and James held him tightly as he passed onto the his final reward. He was saddened to find near the man a small grave. He wondered if it was the graves of the now dead man's child.

James propped the body against the base of small outcropping where it would easily be seen by Jack as he followed along the trail. The trail of the last survivors commanded James' attention. He knew he was close behind them and was desperate to reach them while there was yet a chance to save them. The fact that there were tracks of many small footprints drove him to press his now tiring Appaloosa to even greater efforts. As James rode along the trail, he could see where the young ones were stumbling and falling and soon he was demanding even more from the Appaloosa.

James came upon them suddenly as he approached a large Ocotillo cactus that sent its spindly barren arms toward heaven as if in supplication for its need of water. They were huddled together in the meager shade provided by branches that were gray and lifeless. The woman sat Indian fashion, her legs crossed, and her back straight holding a small bundle against breasts that hung against her bony, meatless frame like empty pouches. She was trying to get the babe to suckle, but it had given up its feeble attempt to draw moisture from the body of a mother who was as withered as the cactus under which she sought shade. The five children who appeared to range from a young teen age daughter to a small toddler, sat listlessly about the mother staring quizzically and fearfully at James as he approached.

The mother, seeing James approach covered herself and tried to rise, but fell back spraddle legged and although she tried to speak, her voice was raspy and inaudible. James quickly dismounted. Taking a tin cup from his saddle bag, James went among the children and gave them each a half cup of water which was consumed in frantic gulps. Each begged for more, but James knew he must not allow them to drink their fill as they would just vomit it back up. He gave the mother a half cup. She ignored her need and tried to pour the water into her baby's open unresponsive mouth. The water ran down the babies dirt encrusted face. James took the baby from its mother's weakening grasp and holding it in his arms, wetted his kerchief and first cleaned the babies face and eyes and then put the wet end in the baby's mouth.

James was afraid at first that the baby was dead, for it did not respond and he could not detect any breathing. The mother watched him and when the baby did not respond began to moan and rock back and forth holding out her arms for the baby. James, ignoring the mother's plea kept wetting the kerchief and forcing droplets into the baby's mouth. After several long desperate moments, the baby started sucking at the cloth. James kept adding water to the kerchief and forcing it into the baby's mouth until its eyes fluttered and then opened. It was soon making the suckling sounds that brought a look of joy to the mother's sun baked and blistered face.

James gave the baby back to its mother and refilled the cup and demanded that the mother drink before she in her turn started squeezing droplets into her baby's now yielding, eager mouth. The other children were starting to stir and move about now, so James gave them each a small amount of water and a biscuit. He was amazed at how soon the bit of water and a little food rejuvenated the little travelers. Next James crumbled a biscuit into the cup and made a soft porridge and gave it to the mother who used her finger to place droplets of the food into the baby's mouth. James had been too involved with the task of reviving the baby and tending to the children to converse with them, but when the children had each eaten another biscuit and had more water, the oldest of them, a young girl with her hair in pigtails with large blue inquisitive eyes broke the silence and asked him: "Who are you, mister. How did you find us?"

"I picked up your tracks coming out of the desert and followed them here thinking you might be needing some help. Like you, I was headed for California. Now why don't you tell me who you people are and how it is that you ended up out here alone?"

"We was with another train," the girl responded, "They got the sickness and Papa and Mr. Henderson was going on ahead to get help. Papa lost the trail when that big wind came up and we just wander about hoping to find water and help. We ran out of water and the animals started dying and then Mr. Henderson and the three men he hired just died off. They was givin' all their water and food to the young ones. My Papa he's back there. Did you see him?"

James looked into the girls large enquiring eyes and didn't find within him the heart to tell her that all of those left behind were dead. Which one was her father he did not know, but he suspected it was the one who sat facing the trail, watching his family wander on as he lost his strength and will to lead them.

"July, you mustn't bother the man with those questions, "the mother intervened to James' relief. "See that the young ones gits cleaned up if the gentleman can afford to give us some more of that water."

"The young girl, who the mother called July, gave James an appraising look as if still expecting him to answer.

"I'll get you that water, July, but as to your Daddy, I would not know him and can't say if he's coming."

James hated to leave the girl with hope when he knew there was none, but it was her mother who must deal with this matter he told himself as he handed July a canteen. James then walked over to where the mother was feeding the baby and knelt down beside her.

"My name is James Rawlins, mam, what might your name be and where is it you were headed?"

The mother giving him only a furtive glance as she concentrated on the babe in her arms spoke softly in a voice that was weak and raspy. "We be the Martin family, my name is Emma. We were headed to a place called Los Angeles. Henry, he's my husband had a brother there who wanted his help in a freighting business he started up. I was hoping you might have come to Henry while he was still alive, but I gather you found him dead sittin' back there." She looked at him now for confirmation of her assumption.

"I came across two men back there who weren't buried. One died in my arms the other was dead when I got to him. I'm sorry mam, but there's no need in my being evasive, but I don't want to be the one to tell your babes what came of their father."

"That ain't no matter of yours, I'll tend to that. Now that you have found us, what is to become of us? You ain't got enough food or water there to get us out of this infernal desert." Emma had now turned to James and was studying his face with only that concern that a mother would display; a mother who had struggled so valiantly to save her children and feared that salvation might be an allusion. James could now see that beneath the weary countenance of a face too long exposed to the harsh desert heat and winds, there was a woman of great determination and strength. Her features gave evidence of a woman who once would have been attractive, with large steel gray eyes a straight thin nose over a mouth that was wide and expressive.

"You look young to have such a large brood," James remarked after studying her more closely.

"They ain't all mine, only the babe here and two of the young ones. The older ones be the Summers children. Mr. Summers was the last man you found along the trail. He gave me the last of his water, weren't but a cup full. I was sure we was to perish here where we sat. None of us had the strength to get on. Weren't no place to go anyways. Might as well sit here and die as anywhere."

"There are others following along behind me and we have enough food and water to get you through to California. Ain't no need to talk more of dying. I'll get some shade for the young ones with that tarp I got on the mule. We'll rest here and be ready to travel when the rest catch up with us. Can I get you more food, I 'spect you gave all of yours to the children? You'll be needin' your strength. You've got a passel of charges here and we still have a ways to travel."

James cut some of the legs off the Ocotillo cactus and set up a shelter and then tended to his Appaloosa that had expended its strength to reach the survivors. After watering the Appaloosa, James let him loose to scrabble about the desert to find what sustenance could be found. James needed only to whistle and the horse would return to him. As he turned to tend to the mule, he nearly fell over July who had been standing behind him unnoticed.

"Mrs. Martin said you came across paw and he won't be coming after us as he promised. Can I go see him? I don't want him lying out here for the buzzards to eat. I want to bury him. Can you take me to him?"

James knelt before July and grasped her by the arms, wanting to hug her and comfort her. Her request tore at his heart and he didn't know how to respond. The lump in his throat prevented him from speaking for a moment. She looked so much like an adult with the expression of concern on her face. Her heroic control of her emotions as James knew she was holding back a flood of tears, made it more difficult for James to tell her that they could not go back. They must now conserve all their water, food and strength to get out of the desert.

"There are people coming after me. They probably have already buried your father. We must think now of all the young ones. We have to go on to California. I don't want to worry the others, but I know I can trust you to hold a secret. I told Mrs. Martin that we have plenty of food and water because I want her to use what I have to get her and the children ready to travel. There's more food and water when the others get here, but I don't know how far we have to go and whether we have enough food and water to get there. You'll not tell the others, but I want you to be my helper and keep the children encouraged. I don't think Mrs. Martin has the strength to care for all these children. She gave too much of herself to get all of you here.

July stood before him, her dress tattered and torn by the brush and cactus of the desert, her shoes scraps tied together with rags, her freckled face, that had since been washed, bore a stern intense expression as she weighted the request James had presented. He could feel relaxation pass through her tense thin body as she accepted his challenge.

"I'll do it, mister. Papa told me to look after the little ones. We buried my momma back there. I wisht they was together. I don't know your name, what is it?" James stood now, relieved at the strength and hope that possessed that small frame now that she was given a duty and responsibility. To James' surprise, as he turned to walk back to where the others were, July took his hand and held it tightly as if to draw from that contact the strength she would need.

James was successful in shooting a large desert hare and the small group of survivors had rabbit stew and biscuits for dinner and then huddled together under the tarp to await the arrival of Little Flower, Cactus Jack and Robert Peters. James had given his saddle blanket and what covering he had to the smaller children for their protection against the cold. As he laid down with but his saddle for a pillow, he was not surprised when July snuggled close to his back so that they might share their warmth. James had remembrances of his long trip from Oregon when he and Little Flower were driven to embrace each other to survive the frigid winter nights. He had thoughts of those long ago winter nights when he and Jenny, then still young and pre-pubescent, shared their warmth against the cold of a night separated from them by only the cedar shingles that formed the roof over their head.

As the night falls swiftly in the desert like a curtain quickly drawn, so the morning comes with the golden rays of the sun bursting over the far horizon, turning night into day in what seems but a moment. The small encampment was slow to stir as the welcoming warmth of the sun drove the chill from the air and the bodies that had shivered through the desert night found comfort. As James felt the sun's warmth, he too was reluctant to rise, but when he finally stretched and started to rise, he realized that July was lying in the cradle of his arm, her curly tussled blond hair but inches from his cheek. James had ridden hard to find the survivors of the train and had fallen into a deep sleep undisturbed by the young body that curled about him. Having experienced the comfort and pleasures of a women's body, James was at first alarmed at the intimacy of the contact and quickly looked about to find Mrs. Martin awake and smiling at him.

"Don't take no mind to the girl. She was close to her papa and mamma and the family all slept in one bed coming over the tail. She needs some comfort. The little ones were wrapped around me all night. I didn't have no room for another."

"How old is the girl?" James asked.

"I believe she be fifteen. She's had to do a lot of growing up real swift like. I fear for her. Her little sister and brother ain't got the jist of their loss yet, but she's knows her loss and is taken it like a soldier. She may be taken hard to you, she needs a man about. She was real close to her father."

James was uncertain that he wanted to be adopted by the little girl lightly snoring at his side. He was about to become a father on his own and was hardly ten years senior to July, not an age to have the emotional attachment that July was seeking.

"I suggest you look upon her as your younger sister till we can get her among her folks," Emma suggested, sensing his discomfort. "I'd not want her to get hurt just now by you putin' her off."

James thought over this suggestion as July started to stir and with a sudden jerk raised her head and looked into James' face with obvious confusion. James, knowing the cause of her alarm, patted her shoulder. "It's alright July, you are safe. Shall we feed the babes now?" James gave no further thought to his assumption of the role of July's protector. The more he thought about it later, however, during the morning, the more comfortable he felt with the prospect. As he watched July scurry about taking care of her little brother and sister, the more admiration he had for her. She was indeed a little soldier. James studied her a little more closely as she moved about the camp, busily engaged in comforting the little ones. He could see the rising mounds of her gathering breasts, the shapeliness of the youthful body that gave substance to the loose colorless dress she wore. He could see that once her face had shed the abuse of her recent experience, she would be a presence that would, with but a few years maturing, be a welcome addition in the company of men.

By noon, James could see in the distance the approaching figures of Little Flower and her escorts. He yearned to have Little Flower back with him and would be glad to have Daisy back wandering about looking for water. The arrival of Little Flower and the two men, Daisy, the horses and pack mules, caused quite a stir among the children. As James stepped forward to assist Little Lower in dismounting and to welcome her back into is embrace, he did not notice the reaction of July and Mrs. Martin until he turned about to introduce them. Little Flower's protruding mid section left no doubt of her condition. The disapproval on Mrs. Martin's face was ill disguised. The look on July's face was a look of curiosity or confusion. Little Flower was dressed in a buckskin ridding shift that was liberally adorned with fringes and beads as were her calf high boots. Her dark flowing hair had been put up in two braids and she wore an eagle's feather in a beaded band about her head. Little Flower looked at the curious little faces lined up before her with apprehension. She felt immediately the disapproval growing ever more apparent on Mrs. Martin's face.

"This is Little Flower who will be my bride as soon as we can come across a preacher who will do us the honor," James offered in response to the curious glances. Mrs. Martin said nothing, but busily engaged herself in tending to her baby without further acknowledgment. July, on the other hand moved forward again taking James by the hand. "Is she with your baby?" July asked as she looked up to James.

James knelt in front of July again gripping her slender arms as he held her attention. "Yes, July, this is my wife and she is carrying my baby."

James waited, expecting July to turn away or to show her distaste in concert with Mrs. Martin. July looked beyond him then taking in Little Flower who was standing resignedly waiting for what she knew would be further rejection. As hard as Little Flower had tried to accept what she knew would be her discomfort among James' people, she felt that she had James' love and that was more then she could have expected. Why she should care what this little waif thought of her she didn't quite understand, but she did sense that there had developed some special relationship between James and the young girl and that the girl's acceptance was important to her.

"Will she be my friend like you?" July asked, lowering her eyes in supplication. James pulled her into his arms then and gave her the hug that he had wanted to give her the day before. "She will indeed be your friend as will I." At that assurance, July walked over to Little Flower and took her by the hand. "Please come meet my brother and sister." She pleaded as she motioned the siblings to come forward.

James looked to Little Flower and detected moisture in her eyes as she grasped July's hand and moved over to be introduced to July's siblings. While all this was going on, Cactus Jack retrieved from his pack some hard candy he was hording, candy he had purchased at the last outfitting, and passed it out among the children. James was disturbed by the reaction of Emma to the arrival of Little Flower. They had many more miles to travel together and he did not want the hassle of having to deal with dissention. When things had settled down and Cactus Jack had the children enthralled in his story telling, James took Emma aside and asked her directly the reason for her attitude.

Emma looked at him sternly before answering. "God did not intend that the white man should marry his lesser children or to beget mixed children who will find no place." Emma's stern disapproving look started a rising furry in James and he had to check himself before the responded. This, James knew would be a confrontation he would have to face many times as he and Little Flower raised their family amid a population that bore an intolerance toward people whose skin was of a different blend. Taking a deep breath, letting his temper cool, James responded:

"You mentioned your God. He sounds like a God who would treat differently among his created children. I do not believe in that God. The God I believe in is a merciful God who sent us on this course to find you. If Little Flower was not with child, we would not have made this journey and you and these children would have perished. Little Flower is a strong and loving person who has done you no harm. She doesn't deserve your scorn. You alone with these children have survived a terrible ordeal. You have been given a new life. I would hope you would live that life according to you Lord's teachings and not your own prejudices. It's a matter you must deal with and I will say no more about it. I will only say this: I will not tolerate any disrespect toward Little Flower from you or from anyone else."

James did not wait for her response, but walked away from Emma to tend to the animals and to get assurances that Cactus Jack and Peters had indeed buried the body of July's father. If they had not, James intended to back trail and make good on his promise to July.

Emma was a strong and domineering woman. Had she not been, she would not have survived this latest ordeal. She had lost only one battle of wills with a pliant husband who usually assented to her demands and that was his decision to leave their home in Kentucky and head west. She only relented when she took stock in what a decade of hard work had yielded them from the rock strewn patch of land that she and Ralph had struggled upon so long and hard to gain so little. It had been a long time since any man dared to talk to her as had this man James Rawlins.

As she thought about what he had said, she realized that perhaps it was the lack of resolution and submissiveness of her husband Ralph that had been the most distressing part of their relationship. Rather than resenting James' harsh words, she felt comforted by them and took his admonishment to heart. She realized she must start anew a life without possessions or funds. This Little Flower, with her strong loving young man was indeed to be envied and not disparaged. Yes, she thought, she must be quite a woman to command the respect of James Rawlins. She must depend on this man to carry her and her little ones out of this desert. His assertiveness and confidence was reassuring. She would gladly submit to his will.

The next morning, James distributed the children among the animals. Little Flower, knowing the difficulty Emma would have carrying her baby, had fashioned an Indian style carrying pack that held the baby securely to her back. The smaller children were carried in front the men and the younger ones rode on the back of their saddles, all except for July who rode astride Daisy.

"That animal be a bit testy, she's used to wandering about some, but don't you worry, she will follow along in time." Jack advised her.

And so it was that when they reached a ravine through which there was a dry stream bed, Daisy took off wandering up stream until she stopped and sniffed the ground and began pawing. July was puzzled by this action and being unable to get Daisy to return to the trail dismounted and stood aside watching her paw the ground, After a time, she could see moisture rising from the depression that Daisy had dug. July turned to call to the others about Daisy's find only to see the others had noticed her absence and followed her and Daisy up the ravine.

The trace of moisture had driven Daisy in to a greater effort until by the time the others arrived; there was a pool of muddy water clearly evident.

Cactus Jack talked Daisy away from the hole and in time the water cleared and they let the animals have their drink before refilling the canteens.

"That Critter is worth its weight in gold," Peters remarked to Jack's pleasure.

"She be that," Jack replied, "got more smarts than most people I knows. Only thing is she can get you water, but I ain't learned her yet to find me food."

For three more days the little band traveled westward until they came off the large desert plane and followed a tree lined fertile valley down into a large basin where they could see in the distance several rancheros, surrounded by orchards, vineyards and tall cottonwoods. James did not know how hospitable they would be received at one of the Spanish Land Grant rancheros. While in San Francisco during his last visit, it had become apparent that the gathering throngs of American settlers would pay little heed to the Spanish grants even though they gave title to lands now held for generations of Mexican citizens. Some of these grants held title to lands encompassing many thousands of acres of the most desirable lands in California. It would take days to travel the boundaries of some of the rancheros.

When at last they rode upon the central plateau and approached the first of the rancheros, a group of six vaqueros rode out to meet them. They were men whose large sombrero, colorful vests and breaches, gave them an appearance of the banditos who were known to habitat the Mexican provinces. James rode forward to greet them telling the rest of the band to remain at a distance until he could determine if they would be hostile to their intrusion. Each of the Vaqueros was well armed and several of them held their rifles across their saddles at the ready.

As the Vaqueros reached the spot where James awaited them and could see that the group he was leading consisted of mostly women and children they began pointing and gesturing toward them and talking among themselves in Spanish, a language James did not understand. It was evident, however, that they had decided he was no threat and those that had been carrying the rifles at the ready, sheathed them and rode forward. The Appaloosa that James was riding fascinated them. They were men who lived on horseback and knew fine horses as a well as any, yet they had never before seen an Appaloosa and rode in circles about James studying and discussing the features of the Appaloosa. James waived Parker forward, knowing he spoke Spanish, and soon he and the leader of the Vaqueros were engaged in discussion while James dismounted and held Caesar as the rest of the Vaqueros likewise dismounted and engaged in an extensive examination of this strangely marked horse.

When Parker finished his conversation with the head Vaquero, he reported to James that they were welcome to cross the lands of Victor Sanchez and they should stop at the Ranchero as the land owner would greet them warmly since they were not settlers seeking his land.

"It appears he has had some trouble since Freemont and that Navy Captain declared the territory free from Mexico. He doesn't want any trouble and wants to know all about your travels. He appears to be a talkative fellow."

By the time James turned to advise the rest of the party of the welcome, the Vaqueros had ridden back among the children and were urging the small group with gestures to follow them back to the Hacienda. The closer they got to the Hacienda the larger it appeared. When they came into the courtyard, they were greeted by the host who had been informed of their arrival and their ordeal by one of the Vaqueros who had ridden on ahead. Behind him stood six women who James guessed were household servants. They came forward when the children were lowered off the horses and escorted them through the vine covered entrance to the Hacienda and on into a large courtyard that was dominated by a large fountain which in turn was surrounded by the U shaped main structure of the Hacienda.

Victor Sanchez was not tall, but had a dominating appearance. He was dressed in a black coat with gold braid on the lapels, breaches with gold stripes down the sides and black boots that were shined to a luster. His hair that hung to his shoulders was wavy and in color was not gray, but silver. Beside him, clasping her hands in front of her was Victor's wife whose stout features made Victor's robust presence seem less dominating. Her expression was like her husband's warm and welcoming. She went immediately to Emma and spoke in halting English: "You must come with me. We will put fat back on those bones! I have mid-wife for baby, much milk."

James watched with amusement as Victor's wife overwhelmed Emma with her solicitous concern. During their trip, Emma had caused no problems and seemed to have accepted James' admonishment. James was satisfied that Emma had made a commitment to opening her views regarding those she had cordoned off from her acceptance as being unrespectable. She would, James mused, find a real challenge to her prejudices if she still harbored them within the embrace of this hospitable Mexican family. Little Flower had expressed her concern for the baby Emma was carrying. Little Thaddeus was continually fussing and crying.

"The baby is starving," Little Flower advised, "It needs its mother's milk and Emma has none."

James, Victor, Peters and Cactus Jack had taken the animals to the stable to be fed and watered. The next time James saw little Thaddeus, the baby had been wet nursed and was gurgling contentedly in the arms of Mary Sanchez whose ample frame made an embracing cradle for the now contented baby. Emma, sitting beside her on a long leather couch, held her two younger children, one on her lap and the other at her side. James noticed for the first time since he had rescued Emma and her band that she had taken time to comfort her other children. July had been the substitute mother, while Emma tried vainly to keep the baby alive. The look on Emma's face was no longer a mask of concern, but showed instead the look of relief and fatigue. When Mary Sanchez was satisfied that little Thaddeus was asleep, she handed him to the mid-wife and hustled Emma and the children off to the rear of the house.

"Now we must get you and the children bathed and out of those awful clothes. Then we will have a fiesta to welcome you the proper way." As she hurried off, Mary was talking excitedly in Spanish to the house servants giving them instructions for the promised fiesta. Little Flower followed after them, carrying one of the Martin children and Emma the other. July followed after them carrying her younger brother and leading Linda.

As James watched the women and children leave the room banded together, the ethnic mixture of the group, the diverse languages gave him a feeling of satisfaction that he could not quite identify. It was Victor who put words to his thoughts.

"What a rare and representative spectacle there is there," he said pointing to the group, "it is the future of this land. There is the native who preceded us all, the blood of the Spanish who came to this land a century and more before the white man. And then there are the white people who now come in droves with so many of their young. We Mexicans have held this land but have never populated it like the Americans will. That is our misfortune. We have divided the land into great estates and know not our neighbors. We live a great distance from each other and are more concerned with our own empires then that of the government that abides six thousand miles from us and worries little about our welfare. Those little ones will be the future of this land, for they will populate it as we have not. May we all live in peace. There now I have said a toast and have not passed out the wine. Your throats must be parched. Forgive me for my neglect. I have the finest wines in the land that is produced from my own vines. Let's get the dryness out of your mouth and when the ladies and children have done with the bath, you must follow them."

True to the information the Vaqueros had provided them, Victor Sanchez was a generous host and a man of considerable verbosity. As they sat waiting for the ladies and children to return, Victor held their interest in relating the history of his land grant that dated back to his great-grandfather who laid claim to the grant after serving the King of Spain as Ambassador to France. "He brought with him the vines that now grow on the estate; The Pruto Picudo vines from Zamora, The Pedro Xime'nez from Valencia and the Negro de Madrid from Toledo. He brought the Cabernets and Merlots from France. They thrive in this climate, but," he added with a chuckle. "We make more wine than we can consume. You must help me dispose of my stock."

"What else is it you do produce on your Estate?" James asked as he looked about at the richly furnished room.

"There is little to trade. Mostly hides and tallow. The beef we have so many of we cannot sell the meat. Some fruit and produce we sell, but it must travel too far to be good income. Most of what you see was built on the wealth of my family, not from the income the ranch produces."

"There is a great need for what you could produce up north where a stake can cost a man a day's diggings and eggs sell at a dollar apiece." Parker interjected.

"Yes, Yes, I know that, but how do we get it there. I cannot travel that far with what I have to sell. If they want my wine and beef up north, they should come and get it."

James began to understand why California had not prospered under Spanish and Mexican rule. These large land owners had contentment about their status and found no dignity in the give and take of commerce and little ambition for it. James realized that the words of Victor were prophetic. It was not in the American spirit to sit on such vast wealth and ignore its potential and to sit back and let the world come to them. This genteel society that Victor and his countrymen had enjoyed for a century would not last long under the challenging ambition of the thousands who were now traveling west and would soon flood this land.

After James and the reluctant Jack had their turn at the bath, and put on clean clothes, they returned to the Veranda for wine and cigars as the women prepared the meal and the children were either playing or napping. James' natural curiosity soon turned the conversation back to the potential commerce in the central basin of California. Victor told him about the availability of water to the south, the great salt sea, the palm trees and date palms that grew in abundance further south. "The soil about here will grow most anything. Right now it grows grass for the cattle is all," Victor remarked. "The more the work the more the worry."

Unlike James and Peters, Cactus Jack found little interest in the talk of farming. Once it became obvious that there was no gold or silver to be found in the central basin, Jack wandered off to find the children and to tend to Daisy. Unlike the others, Jack did not find the comfort to be afforded by the large estate to be to his liking.

"Once a man gets used to living under a roof," Jack had admonished James when he had first been ask to leave the mine, "the sooner is they'll be measuring him for his coffin."

After a day of rest, James was burning to move on to the coast where they could travel by boat to San Francisco. His mind had now turned to thoughts of his house now under construction, his shipping business and in developing the Little Flower Mine. His mind was further consumed by the possibilities that seemed to abound in the central valley. Remembering his conversations with Leland Stanford and the eagerness with which that man had promoted the idea of a transcontinental railroad, James could, after his discussions with Victor, understand the promise that transportation would hold for development of California. Unlike Leland Stanford, however, James was very familiar with the mountains and deserts that a transcontinental railroad must traverse. It was not the type of venture he wanted to risk his capital on. Yet, a railroad running north and south in California had great promise to this thinking. If there was ever a link up to be had with a transcontinental railroad, an existing north and south rail line would be worth a fortune. The more he thought of these prospects, the more anxious he was to be on his way.

When Mary heard him talking of leaving, she became very concerned. "But the baby is not well. It needs time to nurse and get fat. Emma is skin and bones; she must have time to get her strength."

To James' surprise, Emma was reluctant to leave. "You go on without me if you must. You have brought me and my babes out of the desert and have done enough. These good people have urged me to stay a little longer and I feel I must."

July was another matter. July, once their ordeal in the desert was over, seemed to lose her affinity towards Emma who had forced upon July the care of her two small children as she struggled to save the baby. Little Flower urged James to stay a few more days until all of the children were a little stronger. She suggested that they take July and her brother and sister with them.

"They have lost their parents. They have no one to go to. We should not leave them here. July says they have an aunt and uncle somewhere in the gold fields up north. Maybe we can find them."

James relented on the suggestion that they stay on a little longer because he wanted to take up Victor's invitation to visit the other rancheros in the valley. He was not prepared to commit to the suggestion of taking July and little George and Linda on as a responsibility. Jack and Peters, eager to provision the Little Flower Mine and get it into production, headed on to Los Angeles. By the time James returned from his tour of the valley rancheros, he was even more impressed with the potential that was the promise of the central valley. Little Flower had spent her time getting familiar with the Summers children and by the time James returned, she was more insistent than ever that they should take the children with them and find their missing relative.

"How do you know this relative will want anything to do with them? He may have a family of his own and no room for more."

"Then we must find a place for them. We cannot leave them here. Mary will be leaving for Mexico City to visit her relatives."

James knew there was little alternative except to take the children with them. No doubt in San Francisco, there would be facilities to care for orphaned children. Perhaps, he suggested if there were no orphanages or willing relatives in California, they could contact relatives of the children back east.

When July along with her siblings came into the living area upon hearing of James return, James was stunned at the change in her. The sack like dress she wore when he found her was replaced with a dress that had been altered to fit her. It had a low bodice, flounced sleeves, and a skirt that came to mid calf. The dress fit her tightly about the waste and the green and red trim on the otherwise white dress accented the now tanned skin that no longer bore the ravages of the desert march. Her hair was swept behind her head in braids accenting her high cheek bones. Color had been added to her lips and cheeks giving her a more mature appearance. James no longer saw a young girl, but the promise of an attractive woman. Like July, the little ones were outfitted in Mexican clothes that had been hand me downs from the smaller children on the estate. July stood expectantly before him and James sensed that she wanted his approval.

"You look very nice July. The rest and food has served you well." James wanted to say more, but before he could, July skipped across the room and threw herself at him wrapping her arms about his waist.

"Will you take us to San Francisco, now?" She pleaded. Her plea was not that of the woman he had observed but a moment ago, but that of a young girl adrift in a world that frightened her. It was also evident to James that her concern was also for her young brother and sister, who clung back from July's advance with apprehension shrouding their now clean and sparkling faces.

"You have been worried that I would leave you, is that what troubles you? I found you and I am going to keep you until we can find a good home for you," James assured her. "You will be going with us to San Francisco." The little ones George and Linda, reacting to the excitement in July's voice clapped their hands in delight, but rather than running forward to join their sisters embrace, they rushed into the arms of Little Flower who had been standing aside expectedly awaiting James' response to the children's pleas. July soon joined them as they started jabbering excitedly.

"You are a bunch of conspirators." James remarked good humouredly as he realized that the little drama he had just been the brunt of had been staged and that the delight of the children was in part the joy they felt for the success of their little plot.

Before they left the ranchero, Emma had requested of James that he look up her brother in law and advise him of the death of her husband and the plight she and her children now faced.

"I'll want him to know before I get there what happened to us. I'll need his help, but I don't want to just show up on his door step one day and say here I am."

James had every intention of calling on her brother-in-law. The fact that he was trying to establish a freighting business had been much on James' mind as he became more familiar with the potential of the inland valley and its lack of commerce. When it came time to leave, James talked to Victor about buying several horses as Peters and Jack had taken most of the mules and horses with them. Victor, however, no doubt with Mary's urging suggested instead they take his coach on to Los Angeles.

"Your woman should not ride a horse. It may bring the baby too soon. My coach is comfortable and the road ahead is not good. I have errands to attend to and will be going anyway."

When they were ready to leave, the Vaqueros brought to the front of the Hacienda a large coach that was all black except for the gold crest on the door, on the trim around the box and on the wheel spokes. The coach was pulled by a matched set of six gated palominos. The livery was all black and highly polished with a plums attached to the center of each horse collar. The vaqueros were now dressed in uniforms of thigh high black boots, white breaches, crested polished steel helmets and red coats. Each carried a lance with red and green streamers. When Victor came from the Hacienda he was dressed in a similar uniform to that of the vaqueros except for the helmet that had been replaced with a tricon. On each shoulder he had gold epaulets to signify rank.

James and Little Flower marveled at the display of elegance. Although their host had been gracious and unassuming while they were his guests, it was now quite evident, that Victor Sanchez was a nobleman. It was Victor's misfortune that he held his title by inheritance from a long declining empire that no longer had relevance in these far off lands that were now being drawn into an orbit of alien ideology that would have little respect for the pomp and ceremony now on display.

James, though impressed by the grandeur that was the tradition on the California rancheros, knew that this display of authority was in part to demonstrate to others the power and influence these noblemen had in conformation of their superior estate among the subjects of a sovereign. Their reliance upon blood lines, inheritance and tradition would ill suit them when confronted by the coming rush of men whose reliance was upon their wit and ambition; men who measured success not by blood lines, but by accumulated wealth and the accomplishments that created that wealth.

During their drive that took several days, Victor advised them of the need for his visit to Los Angeles. The fate of the land grants was much in doubt as the war with Mexico had not gone well and California was to be ceded to the United States. There was talk of a new government being seated. There was word that the United States had given recognition to the land grants which Victor and the other Spanish descendants relied upon. There was a Treaty of Guadalupe Hidalgo that brought an end to the war and Victor wanted to read for himself the words of that document. When arriving at Los Angeles, James was not impressed with the town. Unlike San Francisco that could boast of a fine harbor and forested hills, Los Angeles, except for the ocean front, looked like the desert lands from which James had recently departed. There seemed little excuse for the town site, except that the discovery of gold had boosted it to prominence as thousands of prospectors had flooded through its port and many had now settled there.

If the town had Spanish and Mexican origins, it had already lost much of that heritage as the streets were alive with men of all nationalities who had traveled from the far corners of the earth in the quest of gold. To James, the bustle of commerce and the urgency that seemed to infect the city was a welcome departure from the indolence of the past several weeks. He was quick to say his farewell and extend this gratitude to Victor, who himself was anxious to peruse his inquiry and hastened on. Peters and Cactus Jack were still in town and had fortunately arranged accommodations for James and his party as hotel space was limited. He found them in earnest and extensive discussions with a ship captain in a café next to the hotel. They had before them a large list of items they wanted the Captain to carry around the horn and were haggling over the price. James was introduced and sat down with the group, but did not interfere as he thought the negotiations were going well. After a while, he excused himself and upon inquiry was directed to the freight office where Emma's brother-in-law might be found.

Near the edge of town, James found the offices of El Central Freight Services. There was a large platform fronting the street loaded with an assortment of boxes and crates stacked in rows. At the back of the platform was a two story structure where James found the door marked "office" and entered. The office, like the dock area was strewn with boxes and crates which Jim assumed were awaiting pick-up by some local merchant. At the back of the room sat a man whose bald head, sat atop thick broad shoulders that were hunched over as the man was studying a pile of invoices. He had broad red suspenders over his gray homespun shirt. When he heard James footsteps he looked up hurriedly and waived him to a chair opposite his desk.

"Sit. I'll be but a moment." As James sat watching him, he could see the man was writing figures on the invoices, no doubt his freight charges. Now and than the man consulted a chart before entering a price. "Got to get this done before I can deliver this stuff," He muttered as he worked.

"Georgia," he shouted as another man entered the office. To his command a tall, large framed, plain looking woman, dressed in black with her hair done in a bun atop her head entered from the back room. "See that John here gets his shipment. It be the one in the corner there." He handed her an invoice which she took over to the corner and identifying the shipment, told the man called John that the charges would be five fifty. They chatted about the weather as she gave him his change and a receipt and she asked about his wife who apparently had been ailing. When the customer left she looked at James and enquired if she could assist him. Did he have a shipment to pick up?

"No," James answered, "I'm afraid I bare sad tidings. I have a message to deliver, not freight."

At that the man before him dropped his pen and demanded. "What is it then?"

"I have just traveled across the desert from the east. I came across a wagon train that ran into trouble. Most of the members had died of disease or starvation by the time I reached them." Although James was trying to think of an easy way to break the rest of his news, the man's brusque manner seemed to demand that he say what he came to say and be done with it.

"I am looking for the brother of Curtis Martin. I assume that you are that man." When the man before him nodded in assent, Paul continued. "Your brother did not make it. He died of starvation and thirst trying to save his wife and children."

James then remained silent for a moment to get the man's reaction before he went on. The man whose name was Chester looked at him blankly for a few moments then slowly rose from his chair to reveal his full burly frame.

"Are you sure it was him? He asked his voice unsteady and no longer assertive.

"I did not know your brother. But the wife survived and has made me her messenger. I carry her words." Behind him he now heard the sobs of Chester's wife. She covered her face and quickly fled the room through the door that she had entered.

"What of Emma and the kids," Chester asked his back now turned away from James. "They all survived. I was asked to tell you that she would be coming on in a week or so and that she had lost everything and will need your help."

"She'll have that stranger. Now if you will excuse me I must be alone. He followed James to the door and closed it behind him. James heard the lock fall into place as he walked off the landing.

James had made arrangements to sail on to San Francisco on one of the ships controlled by the Little Flower Line. It was loading at the harbor and would not sail for several days. Little Flower had made good use of the time and had bought new clothes for the Summers children and spent her time with the young ones who were still suffering from the trauma of their desert survival. Although little Linda would converse readily with Little Flower and July, she like young George would fall silent in the presence of James. When he tried to urge George into conversation, he would scurry away to the embrace of Little Flower or July.

"What bothers the child?" James asked Little Flower in exasperation when another effort at communication had failed.

"You scare him with that necklace and your big knife. You are all dressed in black. He thinks you are a demon."

"You must tell him that I must be strong so that I can protect him. Tell him that the bear claws and the knife will keep the evil away from him. Tell him that July does not fear me and that he will be safe as long as I am here to protect him."

"I will tell him these things you ask," Little Flower responded, "but I must warn you that if he comes to you he will trust you and you must never hurt him."

That night after they had fed the children and were putting them to bed, July came into the front room. "George wants you to come to him. Papa would always help him with his prayers before bedtime. He wants you to say his prays with him."

James looked at Little Flower who was busy brushing Linda's hair as Linda sat in Little Flower's receding lap imitating Little Flower's actions as she combed the hair on the doll that Little Flower had purchased for her that afternoon.

"I told him the things you said," Little Flower told him in answer to his inquiring look. "Georgie no longer fears you. He wants to be your friend."

When he entered the bedroom where July and her siblings shared a double bed, George was sitting on the edge of the bed, hands crossed in his lap, his gaze fixed on the floor before him. James sat on the bed beside him, but said nothing waiting for George to make the next move.

"I don't know what to pray for." George finally said. "I used to pray for mama and papa, but they have left me."

James put his forefinger under Georges chin and turned his small tear stained face to him. "Your mama and papa still need your prayers. They have taken a long journey to heaven and you prayers will help them on their way. You have other friends now and your sisters. You should give thanks that they are with you. There is much to be thankful for and you should be brave. Pray for strength and courage."

George seemed to think about what he had said for a long time and then looked up to James. "I don't know those prayers, will you help me?"

"I know all the right words," James replied, "now come kneel beside me and say the words as I do."

As they were finishing breakfast, James looked up to see the tall burly figure of Chester Martin enter the café glancing about among the patrons. When his eyes rested on James he hurried forward.

"I come to offer my apologies for being so abrupt with you the other day. I didn't even ask you your name or thank you for your efforts in saving Emma and her children or for that matter being good enough to bring me the news as sad as it was."

Little Flower, aware that the men were about to talk of matters she didn't want the children to hear, excused herself and hustled the children away. James assured Chester that he took no offense and could understand his distress at receiving the news so abruptly.

"My brother was not an ambitious man, but I did want him in the business. He was good at figures and such and could have run the office. The wife helps out, but she would rather be home tending to the orchards and running the house. I wouldn't need either of them in the business except for them damn gold strikes. Every time I train people, comes word of another strike and off they go. But, then that be no concern of yours, I just wanted to come by and thank you.

"How did you know where to find me," James asked.

"That part was easy. I just ask about for a man wearing a bear claw necklace and a big toad sticker of a knife. Ain't many that fits that description."

James invited him to sit, ordered more coffee and began questioning him about his business, making mental notes as the conversation went on.

"I mainly deliver the freight that goes to and from the docks. I deliver to the mines in the mountains and once in awhile take a load up north to San Francisco. Can't do much more as the cost of things is so high what with this rush for gold. Meant to be running up and down the coast by now. The sailing ships ain't much interested in that traffic. Treacherous sailing and not enough trade to fill their bellies. I need more wagons and teams. Been building the wagons myself in a shop out back of the place."

When James interest in his work became obvious, Chester, saying he had to get back to work invited James along to look over things if he cared to. By the time James looked over the wagons, the shop and smithy, the stock and the layout of the business he left Chester to tend to his affairs, asking as he left if he might return the next day.

"I like what you are doing here and see some opportunities I'd like to discuss with you after I give matters some further thought."

"You're welcome to come by any time," Chester assured him.

"The land in the inland valleys is very fertile." James began, "I cannot see the land going undeveloped what with all of the people flooding into California, especially when statehood is granted which appears likely and soon. These cities along the coast are going to grow and will be needing the products from the farms about. The ships will be arriving in even greater numbers bearing hulls full of goods that must be transshipped. There will be a great need for your wagons and it will not be just up and down the coast. The gold fields and settlers will need all kinds of material and few will have the time to haul it themselves. But for the long haul up and down the coast, your wagons will in time be too slow and limited. There is much talk of railroads and one day they will come and replace your wagons on the long halls."

Chester was listening intently and nodding his head in agreement as James talked. When James hesitated he interjected. "Seems like you have done a lot of thinking on the matter. You said you might have more to say about some proposal. What is it you have in mind?"

James smiled at Chester, "You are a man who likes to get to the point of things and I like that. Here is my proposal, I don't expect you to jump up and embrace it until you have had time to think it over."

James then laid out the plans for the incorporation of the freight company under the name of Little Flower Transportation and Railroad Company. They would be half owners. James would give him a draft for fifty thousand dollars to buy wagons and mules and to establish his freight routes.

"I know it sounds presumptuous to have the word railway company in the name, but I want to establish the thought and eventually the reality that we will own the rail line up and down the coast. People are already talking about a transcontinental railroad and making plans. When it comes, I want to have the railroad that connects with it and moves the freight up and down the coast. I would expect you as manager to know the routes that would be the likely route of the railroad. We will buy as much of the land as we can along the proposed right-of-away while the prices are cheap. That way when the time comes to build the road, we will have the cost advantage. If we pick the sites well and as towns spring up along your route, we can buy up the land others might need and we can use. I control much of the shipping up and down the coast and will use only your company for transshipments. We will divide the profits, but until I say likewise, all of my share of the profits will go back into investment. You will do as you like with yours, but you will have to agree never to compete against my interest. If you need more money, I will make it available. That will be my part. You will run the business."

Chester had asked for the two days to give more thought to the proposal and then came to James' hotel with his answer.

"You talk a mighty interesting game." Chester responded, "But I don't know you and don't want to get all exercised lest I know you can deliver. I don't have all that much in the company, but it's mine and I ain't a risky man. I ain't wantin' to sound ungrateful, but I need to know more about you."

"You don't hurt my feelings any," James responded. "I wouldn't expect any other response from a man I'd do business with. It just happens that my partner in the mining business has made a substantial deposit of gold in The Cattleman's Bank here in town. You can follow me down the street and we can make arrangements for the deposit I promised. By now he's had time to check with my bank in San Francisco and can tell you what I have up there to back my play."

After a visit to the bank, Chester was satisfied. "I guess we will be doing a little business. There's a lawyer here in town who can write this all up and get us a corporation going if that would suit you. I have only one other problem and that the name of the company. That Little Flower stuff don't sound right for a freight company. You got any objections to a different name?"

"That name must stick. I have personal reasons for wanting that name on the business. We can haggle over a lot of issues, but the name can't be changed."

When the little party finally boarded ship to sail north, the arrangements for the Little Flower Transportation and Railway Company were completed and Chester was busy hiring teamsters and buying every freight wagon he could find and was buying materials to make what he could not purchase. As they sailed north, James took Little Flower on deck and they stood watching the scurry of the deck hands as the sails were set and the schooner took to the wind.

"I promised you," James told Little Flower, "that as soon as we reached town, we would get married in the white man's church. I talked to a number of preachers, and none of them would marry us because you are an Indian. I wanted to tell it to you straight. We will have these difficulties. It doesn't change in any way my feelings toward you and my intentions, but before the baby comes, we must be married. I know it is not important by your customs, but we will be living in the world where it does matter."

Little Flower made no response, but looked ahead into the wind, her hair now loose and unbound tailed in the gathering wind. James, fearing she was upset over the betrayal of his promise placed his arm about her shoulders and pulled her close and she rested her head on his shoulder. He could not tell if she was disappointed or merely stoically considering the import of his words. As they turned to return to their cabin and take shelter from the cool coastal breeze, a thought struck James and he pulled her hurriedly to the Captain's cabin where he knocked hurriedly on the door and without waiting for an invitation, barged into the room to find the Captain fussing with some brass instruments. The Captain whose quarters were off limits to anyone first looked up in anger at the intrusion, but upon recognizing James gave deference to the man who owned his ship.

"What may I do for you, young man? You look to be troubled."

"I heard once that the Captain of a ship has the authority to marry passengers aboard his ship. Is that true?"

"Well, now," the Captain responded relieved that the visitation was for matters of personal concern and not business," I certainly have the authority, but I have never performed the service. Are you intending that I should marry you to this lovely child?"

"Will you do it?" was James response.

"You give me until tomorrow while I fuss through my papers and find the right words for the ceremony and get familiar with the paper work. It would be my honor to be the man who performs the ceremony. I will talk to the cook and see if he can get us a little something to add to the occasion."

The next afternoon, the captain had the crew luff the sails and let the ship rest in the wallows of the restless sea. The crew stood on deck in solemn rows as the Captain read the words of the ceremony from the paper he held in the same hand in which he held the Bible. His other hand rested on the hands of the bride and groom that were joined before him. The crew, like the Captain had never seen a marriage conducted at sea. Their curiosity was not as great, however, as was their expectation of a pint of rum at the conclusion of the ceremony. The cook had indeed worked his miracle and had a sugar frosted cake prepared. The ceremony was brief and attended by July who was the bridesmaid. James had George stand beside him as his best man. Little Linda stood between them looking up quizzically at the adults who were acting so strangely. Little Flower had put on her white calf skin dress and moccasins. To James, she had never looked lovelier. The budding of the baby within her womb, gave her a look of peace and contentment that had been hidden of late by the ordeal of the trek across the desert and with the burden of dealing with the needs of the children.

CLAY

As the winter snows receded from the plains and the coming of spring filled the air with the promise of warmth and the return of the growing season, Clay was preparing his kit for the trip on to California. His Winchester had been cleaned a dozen times, his hunting knife honed to a razor's edge. His clothes had been mended and his boots resoled. His horse was fat and ready for the trail. A few more days and he would be headed west again. He was not alarmed when the Sergeant approached his bunk and announced that the Major would like him to stop by his office at his convenience. Clay followed the Sergeant back to the officer's quarters and bid him good day as he entered the Major's office. The Major, as was his practice, was pacing back and forth from wall to wall obviously engaged with some troubling thought.

"Thank you for coming Mr. Anderson. Please be seated. I must have a word or two with you."

Clay took the seat offered and waited with unconcern for the Major to finish his thoughts and tell him why he had sent for him.

"I have received dispatches from Washington. I must commit a company of my men to General Kearny who is having troubles with the Pueblos, Comanches and Apaches in the Arizona and New Mexico Territories." The Captain then hesitated studying Clay's reaction to the news. Clay merely looked at him with an expression of a man mildly interested but curious as to why the Major was taking his time explaining Army matters to him.

The major then sat down at his desk and picked up the dispatch and held it before him. "I understand that you are preparing to move on to California or Oregon, where ever it is you intend to go, but it says in these dispatches that you are to be assigned as a scout to the Company I am sending south. Please explain to me why your name should appear in these orders."

Clay looked at him in amazement and a total loss for words. "Are you sure it's my name in those dispatches?" He finally stammered.

The Major handed him the dispatch and pointed out where his name appeared. "That is you isn't it?"

"Well, I was a scout for the Gunnison party, but that party was wiped out," Clay explained.

"Yes, yes I know that, but did you sign a contract?"

"Yes," Clay responded, but that was to scout for Captain Gunnison."

"Do you have a copy of that contract?"

"No, I don't. I lost it somewhere out in the wilderness when the wolves took down my pack horse."

"Let me guess," The Major speculated, "The contract you signed that you thought was with Captain Gunnison, was in fact with the U.S. Army. I am also speculating that it was for a three year term as is usual for those contracts. Does that refresh your memory?"

Since Clay made no answer, the Major continued. "Now I just suppose when they were putting together the force to assist General Kearny they were looking for scouts and come upon a contract with your name on it and with the term of the contract running for another two years. These here papers constitute my orders and unless you can convince me otherwise, I am to send you along with that force either willingly or under a condition of arrest. What have you to say to that?"

Clay had nothing to say. He sat before the Major, his mind racing over the events that had slipped from his concerns. Did the contract really commit him for three years? His mind clicked on his stay at Twin Oaks. The last he recalled, the contract was with his papers during his stay, but he had not seen it since. Had Bryon taken it? Why had they chosen his name for this assignment? Could this be retribution by Senator Benson for Clay's rejection of the Senator's request that he appear as his witness before Congress? He knew he would never have answers to these questions. He also knew that without proof of his duty term, he must accept the assertion of the Major. He was not about to go south in chains.

The Major had been standing behind his desk waiting for Clay's answer. Clay finally stood also and extended his hand to signify his commitment. "I'm your man Major. You don't have to wait about for me; I've been ready for a month now. When do we leave?"

The sun had not yet claimed the vast lands beyond the Mississippi River as the gates swung wide and the Calvary troop from Fort Laramie began to file out two abreast and start their long journey to Santa Fe. They were soon out on a prairie shrouded in the white mantle of a late winter frost and fog that drove the cold of the fading night deep within the shivering bodies of soldiers not long from their warm bunks. There was silence along the column of men wrapped in capes and coats and huddled close over their mounts. Their horse's steel shod hoofs made a crunching sound as they stepped upon the frozen ground; the cold unyielding leather of three dozen saddles creaked in protest to the movement of the animals beneath them. The jingle of metal from kits and bridles added to the discordant reassuring rhythm familiar to these men now on the move.

Their bent and huddled figures gave the troop an appearance more of a funeral procession then it did of a lethal military force on an urgent mission. Though yet in small numbers, this small force would be augmented as it drove southward until it reached the formidable numbers that would bring devastation upon a civilization of peoples who had lived for centuries in the heart of a forbidding land known to only a few. The Pueblo and Apache Indians had prospered beyond the records of history from the plunder of other weaker and more vulnerable tribes. When the Spanish came to the southwest with their horses, cattle, sheep and wealth, they only enhanced the prospects of plunder for the tribes. While the

Spanish maintained a military presence they did in some small way inhibit the raiding on the settlers. The Mexican government that succeeded the Spanish authority was weak and corrupt and constantly in rebellion. It afforded little protection to the farmers and settlers in what was referred to as the New Mexico, the lands north of the Rio Grande and Pecos Rivers.

When President Polk sent the American Army to claim the territory for the United States, the United States inherited the endemic problems of the raiding and plundering that was to the native population a way of life. Unlike the governments before it, however, the American government acceded to the pleas of the local population now being augmented by the growing addition of Americans. The order was clear to General Kearny, "clear the land of the native menace and make it safe for settlement." The Army of the West was fast being augmented in response to that order and Clay Anderson was the first of the army scouts that would lead the assembling Army of the West on to Santa Fe.

They followed the Platte River toward St Louis, retracing the route that Clay had followed westward with his father's wagon train. The trail was now a permanent scar on the plain as the wagon trains, hundreds of wagons strong along with thousands of their live stock had left a trace across the land that would be a permanent record of their passing. Their destination for the first leg of their journey would be Fort Leavenworth outside of St Louis. The Fort was first built to quell the rebellious tribes that the government had removed from the lands east of the Mississippi to facilitate the settlement of lands east of the Allegany Mountains.

Colonel Kearny had been assigned to Fort Leavenworth and was instrumental in bringing the tribes under the control of the army. When the Mexican war was declared, the fort became a major supply center for the advancing American soldiers. It also served as a major supply point for the western forts along the Oregon and Santa Fe Trails. When the small contingent from Fort Laramie reached the fort, it would be joined by other elements of the mounted infantry heading to Santa Fe. By the time they left the fort, they were four hundred strong, equipped with cannon and the supplies capable of waging relentless war.

The Santa Fe Trail traversed lands where wandering bands of Indians and renegades often fell upon unsuspecting and poorly armed wagon trains and supply trains. The passing column of soldiers came upon the signs of many burned out or scavenged wagon trains that had lost their battle with raiding parties; parties intent on either stopping the flow of emigrants or merely plundering the bounty they carried.

Clay and the other scouts leading the party south found abundant sign of these renegades, but there were none of them foolish enough to attack, or for that matter to be even sighted by the long line of soldiers moving slowly and purposefully through their domain. Bent's Fort, which had been the jump off point for Zachery Taylor's army when headed for Monterey, and a major trading post on the frontier, lay in wasted slumber when the troop arrived at its door. The rumor that the Fort had been abandoned because of a pestilence made the area a poor site for a bivouac, and the Troop moved past the Fort giving little note to what had been the first major presence of Americans in the Southwest.

Clay, unlike the soldiers in the Troop was not committed to the military line of march and wandered off to the old fort to vent his curiosity. When he passed by the crumbling walls that once stood as a formidable barrier to any raiding band, he noticed a lone horseman astride a large bay mare standing as a lone silent sentinel in the middle of what was once the central plaza where a broken flag pole served as a final reminder of the Fort's demise. Clay recognized the man as one of the scouts who had joined the column at Fort Leavenworth and rode over to where the man he knew only as Vasquez stood his lonely vigil.

"I hear this was once a bustling place," Clay spoke as he too looked about the burnt and broken timbers that once were the interior quarters of the Fort.

Without looking at him Vasquez answered in a reflective manner, "T'was that pilgrim, It was winter digs for all them mountain men that's all gone now. I was here in '34 and '36 when this here place was as busy as a bee hive, what with all them trappers sellin' their beaver and other hides. Them Bent boys got rich off them fella's. Gave them gold for their plunder and then took it back sellin' 'em whiskey and provisions. Married my first squaw here in '34. She died on the Yellowstone when them Flatheads raided our camp and took all our plunder. Left me and Bridger to walk out of there with but our rifle and shirt. [31]

---

[31] For a description of the Fort and the Bent brother's enterprise see: Bent's Fort Overview and History, http.//www.scsc.k12.ar.us/2003outwest/williamsA/default.thm

Clay looked the man over more closely. What he thought at first was a man his age; he could now see the weathered and whiskered face of a man much older. Once Clay induced the man to speak, there seemed to roll from his storied mind an endless series of events that were long pent up in the man and now found release.

"I know'd all them fella's. Old Beckworth, Bridger, Jedediah Smith, Kit Carson, Sublette; you name 'em, I know'd 'em. Hear tell, Kit's been made a Colonel in this man's army and is goin' to be leadin' this pack of rascals one'st we reaches Taos. Be good to set these tired old eyes on that old varmint again. Ain't seen him since he went wanderin' off with Freemont. Married him one of them Spanish ladies from Santa Fe and raised himself a passel of kids. Hear he was over in California shootin' up them Spaniards and takin' over the whole damn state. That man's wandered about like a coondog huntin' possum."

"I almost met him when I was back in Washington," Clay offered. "He made some impression. I found it hard to live up to what they expected of me after they had met Carson."

Vasquez now turned to study Clay for the first time. His old eyes still had the clear penetrating gaze of a man long in the wilderness and accustomed to reading terrain as well as a man's face for any sign of danger.

"You be that man was with Capt. Gunnison?" He asked after looking Clay over, studying his horse, rifle and clothes in that order.

When Clay answered that he had been with Gunnison at the ambush in Utah, Vasquez was soon off on another story of his wonderings.

"Capt. was a good man. Was with him in '49 when we went snoopin' around that Mormon territory for the Army. They's always wantin' maps and things. Them Mormons was a bit prickly about his snoopin'. They's been hassled some and don't take to strangers much."

Clay rode along with the old mountain man as they resumed the tail heading to Taos. As he rode along he, listening to Vasquez recount his many adventures when only a few of these brave independent men ventured beyond the Mississippi. Vasquez mentioned a name that brought a flood of emotion from the Clay's remembered affections.

"One'ct spent a winter trappin' with a fella named Franco, only name the man had far as I knowed. He could shoot a squirrel in the eye at a hundrert yards. Best damn shootin' I ever saw. Ain't no Indian got near us most times, what with them knowing he could smell them a mile away and bust them in the head with a ball afore they could get within range with them flintlocks them damn Hudson Bay people give 'em."

"I was with Franco and Parker in Oregon Territory when they were killed in a Shoshone raid," Clay volunteered.

Vasquez pulled his horse up short and turned to face Clay. "What's that you say, boy?"

Clay, having assumed that Vasquez would have heard of the massacre, told him the story of how he had returned from hunting to find all members of the California bound party slain and then carried the news back east. While he spoke, Vasquez remained silent and Clay thought he could detect gathering moisture in the old trapper's eyes.

"Them was good men. Knowed 'em well." Vasquez muttered, as they resumed ridding. He then related to Clay stories of his trapping days with the two mountain men.

As they rode on to Taos, Vasquez had purged himself of his remembrances of his days when he and his compatriots rode without fear into lands unknown in search of beaver and adventure. Vasquez rode the last miles in a brooding silence. Clay rode beside him in his own silent world thinking also of those whose lives had once been a part of his and whose lives were now committed to the memories of those few who loved them.[32]

Clay's thoughts turned to his brother and father, whom he was certain were now prospering in Oregon. Thinking of all of those who had been taken from him, his heart now ached for a nearness to his father and brother. He had tried to write to them on several occasions, but the letters remained unsent. Every time he tried to address the subject of William and his marriage to Jenny, the pen that swept so swiftly over the pages spilling forth word upon word, became deadened and his hand unable to respond because of the distractions of a mind obsessed by thoughts of the things that might have been.

How foolish he had been to carry his love for Jenny in his heart and to leave the many words he had rehearsed over and over again left unsaid.

---

[32] There was a mountain man named Vasquez and his exploits paralleled those of most of the mountain men. See: The Mountain Men, George Laycock, The Lyon Press (1988,1996) p. 98

William had always been bolder than he when it came to perusing those things he wanted. Little did Clay realize that one of the things William wanted was Jenny for his wife. By the time William had made his proposal, the game was over for Clay and he was conflicted over his loss of her and the good wishes he knew he owed to the two who meant the most to him. It would have been a natural course for him to head to Oregon to be with William and his father, but his feet would not turn westward and his course turned to California. So when the Colonel advised him that he was ordered to New Mexico, it really made little difference to him. Like many of the men that composed the troop of soldiers to which he was assigned, the thought of an Indian campaign meant the prospect of excitement and adventure that was the spirit of the frontier and the lust of the young.

As the Troop passed through the portals of Apache Canyon where the Mexicans, under command of the governor of Santa Fe, had made a last desperate attempt to fend off the invading American army under the command of Colonel Kearney, the Troop could see the remnants of wagons whose owners had suffered the depredations of the Apache tribes that still roamed unchecked in the New Mexico Territory. Clay and the other scouts had been sent ahead to make sure that canyon was clear of ambushers, as the high walls surrounding the trail's narrow course through the canyon could mean disaster for the Troop. The further they traveled into the New Mexico, the more discomforted Clay became. The land was unlike that along the trails he had followed across the Great Plains. The mountains, canyons, and rock formations that covered the land made it impossible to observe the dangers that could confront the Troop. A band of a thousand warriors could lay concealed in many places along the trial and not be detected.

The landscape itself varied from barren waste lands that harbored no vegetation to areas where Joshua trees would grow in abundance and than further on at a different elevation, the mighty Saguaro cactus spread their majestic arms in charactures that often had a human resemblance. The Ocotillo, their spiny arms growing in clusters that may be green during the rainy season then drop their mouse ear leaves and appear dead and gray in the dry seasons, grew where the Saguaro found sustenance. The dreaded Jumping Cholla cactus that sent is spinney branches out with clusters of thorns pods that seemed to jump at the animals or men whenever they foolishly ventured too close to their domain gave a hostile presence to the land they claimed. Prickly Pear and Beaver Tail cactus, with their long strong needles spread in great clusters and gave shelter to the critters of the desert from ever present coyotes and wolf packs. The green Creosote Bush gave much of the land the mistaken impression of lushness. At the higher elevations great stands of timber, the magnificent Ponderosa Pine, bull pine and valleys of aspen and laurel presented a beauty and verdance that gave promising relief from the desert about them. As Clay and the Troop rode through the land, Clay was conflicted over whether he was entering God's country or Hell itself.

The temperatures were the hottest he had ever experienced. At night, when relief was expected, the barren rock strewn land held the heat until the searing morning sun could reclaim the land and drive it again to oven like discomfort. Having seen some of the verdant lands on the trail to the Oregon Territory, Clay found himself questioning the wisdom of any government that would commit the lives of its soldiers to secure this mostly inhospitable land. If the Navajo, Comanche and Apache wanted to have this land to themselves, Clay thought it would be wise to let them have it. To him, it made more sense to drive the white man from the area and let the Indians have it.

As they entered Taos, the small community turned out to watch the Troop pass along their dusty main street to bivouac on the flat plane near town near the abandoned remains of Taos Pueblo where the bloody American siege ended the Taos Revolt and the last resistance to the American occupation. ([33]) Nearby was a bubbling brook that would allow the troops to wash the layers of dust from the depth of their pours. Their sweating bodies had held the trail dust against their skin until their skin had become irritated and chafed. The townspeople were largely of Mexican descent and stood in moody silence as the troop passed before them. The troop was but one more reminder to them of their subjugation and demotion in status.

The Mexican population had made their own accommodation with the natives and the Mexicans were usually as active as the natives in the plundering that had become a way of life in the Southwest. More than a few

---

[33] See: Blood and Thunder, Hampton Sides, p176, supra.

of them held captured natives as slaves and were not interested in American interference with their system of forced bondage. Their's was a system that had mutated over a century and a half before the first Americans ventured onto their lands. Those first Americans were the trappers that found in Taos and Santa Fe winter quarters and some a permanent residence. The most famous citizen was Kit Carson whose adobe home fronted the street along which the Troop passed. He and his Spanish bride stood with their small brood of children watching stoically as the dust laden troopers passed in an endless column before him. To Carson, the coming of the troops meant that once again he would be leaving the embrace of a family he was finding more and more to his comfort.

Kit Carson had wandered through the mountainous west with Freemont on hazardous adventures of discovery; he had lead Kearny's Army on to California and was with him as he fought the Mexican regiments to gain control of those far off lands. He had traveled to Washington and met with Presidents who sought his counsel. He felt no elation in being once again called from his home in the service of his country. He was a man, however, who knew these lands and the wandering tribes better than any man alive. The nation demanded his service and his duty was to respond and he accepted once more the call to arms.

The Scouts, who had ranged about the countryside to assure the troop's safe passage, were the last to pass through the town. Upon reaching the small assemblage on the front porch of the Carson house, several halted and dismounted to be greeted with the whoops and embrace of Kit Carson as he welcomed each into his home. Among them was Clay Anderson who followed the urgings of Vasquez to come and meet the Great Scout. Clay found Carson to be deceptively plain in appearance, his broad thin lipped face; wide set blue eyes and long hair would have made him inconspicuous in any gathering. He was not as tall and formidable looking as Clay had come to expect. He was short, but his stocky body evidenced a strength that had prevailed in many a skirmish. Clay found the contrast between this plain looking man and his strikingly beautiful wife interesting. She had a refinement that sharply contrasted to the humble surroundings of the roughly furnished home where her husband now entertained a trail worn and rowdy contingent of men who claimed an affinity with her husband that few could command; an affinity born in distant lands where mutual danger forged everlasting bonds.

By the time they left the Carson home, Clay had a clear impression of the man who was now a Colonel in the American Army, and the man who would command the troop he had been assigned to. Carson exuded a confidence of command that gave Clay a feeling of assurance about their mission. His impression now that he reached camp was lost in the fog of all the strong corn liquor that Carson had liberally provided. He and the other scouts fell from rather than dismounted from their horses.

"Drink your belly's full my lads, tomorrow I take command and you'll not have a drop until we finish with our business." Carson advised them.

Colonel Carson was true to his word. The troop was put through a rigorous drill and maneuver training to prepare them for their journey into the lands of the Navajo. They spent most of the summer in training and on patrols into the desert lands in pursuit of the allusive bands of Navajo, Apache and Cheyenne Indians who were relentless in their efforts to drive the white man form their territory. When they found the villages of the Indians, they would destroy their lodges and crops and drive them on into the high desert where sustenance was denied. By the time winter was approaching, General Charlton, who had taken over the Command of the Army in the New Mexico Territory, had devised his plan to bring the warring tribes to heel.

"You will find them Navajos to be an allusive bunch," Carson advised. "We will have to separate into company and squad units in order to cover the area and bring them to stand and fight. That Chief of theirs, Manuelito, is a crafty old fox and will lead you all over the place and ambush you when you are the most vulnerable. You scouts has got to keep an eye out and not be leading your troop into no traps. Once you make contact, it'll be up to you scouts to get the word out so we can close in on the devils while they are out in the open. Once they get into the hills and valleys, they disappear like the ghosts they claim lives in them mountains. I don't intend to let the Navajo off this time. We will find where they live, where their crops and animals are, and we will destroy everything we find. When them devils can't feed their women and young ones, they will come to terms. Out there somewhere, they have a large village where they winter up. We'll be finding it and drive them out onto the plains where we can deal with 'em."

Clay and the other scouts, like the troops about them sat in silence as Colonel Carson gave them their plan of battle, each now realizing the seriousness of the engagement they were to undertake. To Clay and many of the others, they had been preparing for a battle with the armed and trained warriors of the Indian nations. The prospect of waging war against the villages, the women and children, destroying homes and crops was a different matter, and some did not take kindly to the prospect. A number of the scouts had lived with the Indians and even married their women as had Colonel Carson before he married his present wife. These Trappers had little animosity toward the Indians and respected their customs and even understood their hostility toward the white men who invaded their territory.

"Wagh! That uniform old Kit put on done changed that child," Vasquez muttered. "Don't want no part in them doing's." Having said that Vasquez walked away from the assembled troops. Clay, intent on learning his assignment, paid no further attention to Vasquez assuming he would see him about camp latter on. Vasquez, however, had disappeared and when the troop moved on, he was not among them.

Santa Fe was the troop's last stop as they passed through the town to Fort Union to take on the last of their provisions before they headed westward. Clay had been assigned to a company under the command of Lt. Lewis, a lean clean shaven officer fresh from a military school in Virginia. He seemed to be one of the few who always had a clean uniform and was constantly on the lookout for slovenliness among the troops. Clay was glad he was a scout and not under the officer's direct command. Lt. Lewis' self assurance and disdain for the enlisted men under his command, in Clay's mind would not serve them well once they left the structure of the regiment and the Lieutenant could exercise his own initiative. After several days of travel, they broke down into smaller units as had been the plan. Lt. Lewis led a company of two dozen men that included Clay and took a center march, having the two other companies flanking at a two to five mile distance. The plan was that the company would converge if there was danger of a sighting of a large village and that the other companies further on would be notified to draw in toward any sighting.

As they had been advised, the Navajo were allusive and too experienced to be drawn into a pitched battle with the troops. Clay, riding in the lead found numerous sign of passing bands that to him meant that they knew the soldiers were coming and were evading them. For days they wandered through uncharted inhospitable lands where the vegetation consisted of cactus, mesquite, Palo Verdi, and creosote brush and dried out stream beds. It was now winter in the high plains and the temperatures were continually dropping, especially at night when the water in their canteens would freeze. Upon reaching a large cottonwood camp ground through which a clear cool mountain stream scrambled along over moss covered rocks and boulders, the squad under Lt. Lewis stopped to bivouac for the night.

Clay, being cautious, rode up the valley from which the stream flowed to determine if there was any danger. After riding for an hour up the rock strewn canyon where scrub oak trees grew in abundance, Clay stopped short as he came upon fresh sign made by an Indian pony. Clay took his rifle from its scabbard, dismounted to study the sign more closely. As he waded the creek from bank to bank, he could see where a large number of unshod horses were being ridden up the creek bed. He could not determine the number and leaving his horse behind followed the creek until he came upon a clearing about a large pool. A band of Navajo were camped just beyond that clearing, concealed by the woods and underbrush. Clay could not estimate the number and thought better of trying to move around them to get a better look. The rock laden terrain above the stream could not be easily traversed without dislodging rocks that would slide down hill and give away his presence.

Clay retraced his steps with caution and reached camp as darkness was gathering. A number of the soldiers were starting fires in order to prepare their evening meal. Clay ran quickly to the fires and began to kick dirt on them much to the agitation of the soldiers who jumped up to confront Clay and drive him away from their fire cursing him as they did. The Lieutenant, who had been close by writing his report called over to Clay: "What are you doing Anderson? Let them solders be. If you have a problem, you take it up with me!"

"Were not alone Lieutenant," Clay responded. "There's a war party of Navajo further up the canyon. The smoke from them fires will bring them down on us."

The Lieutenant and the rest of the squad gathered hastily about Clay to get his report. "I couldn't get a close look at them, Lieutenant, so I can't say how many there are. They are less than a mile upstream. They look to be making camp for the night."

"Is there any way out of the canyon?" The Lieutenant asked.

"I have no idea; I couldn't get around them to scout out the rest of the canyon. I would guess that there was. I can't imagine they would be headed up that way if there wasn't a trail out the other end."

"I suspect they have seen us and are running from us," the Lieutenant mused. "They can't be many of them if they turn and run from this small group."

"I can't confirm that Lieutenant. They could as well be expecting us to follow them into a trap."

"I doubt that Anderson. They've been running from us ever since we've been dogging them around this damnable country."

Clay offered that in any event they were probably outnumbered and he should be on his way to find the other troops and bring them in. If they could capture any members of this band or for that matter follow them, they might be able to find out where their main village was and the campaign could be brought to a conclusion. That was the objective Colonel Carson had laid out.

"That won't be necessary, Anderson. I will decide what is to be done. Right now, we don't want those savages wandering off or sneaking up on us. I want you to head back up that valley and make sure they stay put for the night. At first light you come back and let me know what you can of their strength and intentions."

"My directions were to ride out and inform the other troops when we made contact." Clay retorted, "You don't have enough men to be sittin' around here wondering what those braves are going to do."

The Lieutenant looked at Clay now, his steel blue eyes like flints. "Anderson, if you look upon my shoulders, you will see that I wear the rank of an officer in this army. I take orders from my superiors officers, not from civilians. I also interpret those orders. I will take care of dispatching any messages; you get your butt up that valley and do the scouting you are paid to do!" Saying that the Lieutenant turned and gave instructions to his men to bring their mounts in closer to camp and prepare a perimeter for the night.

Clay spent a fitful night. He had crawled as close as he dared to the Indian camp and curled in between two rocks where leaves of the cottonwood and willow trees made a soft bed. He dozed occasionally, startled awake now and then by the sound of an owl, the rustling of the leaves or the call of a coyote seeking its mate. Dawn came late in the canyon and Clay's anxiety rose as he could hear sounds about him, but could not see the source. When light made its way into the canyon, Clay could see movement in the direction of the Indian camp, but after watching for a while, he satisfied himself that they were not preparing to decamp. The fact that they remained mostly hidden bothered him. He could not determine their number and found their behavior unlike a war party that was unaware of the army's presence. There was no milling about and talking among them. They seemed to be waiting for someone, possibly the soldiers. It would be a good place for an ambush.

When Clay returned to report his observations to the Lieutenant, the men were preparing to move up the valley. The Lieutenant was dividing his force up, so that they could move up each side of the valley. He wanted to keep to the high ground, but when Clay told him that there were mostly cliffs lining the valley, the Lieutenant didn't listen.

"Lieutenant, I still don't know how many hostiles there are up there, they stay hidden like they was expecting an attack. I would advise you not to go up there until the rest of the troop arrives." As Clay suspected, the Lieutenant hadn't sent messengers out as he had been ordered to do before engaging the Navajo.

"Anderson, I thought I made myself clear. I am in command here. If you want to run around trying to find the support troop while these hostiles escape, you go ahead. I intend to engage them and drive them to their camp."

"You are making a mistake" Clay advised. "It's obvious that you haven't been on the frontier long and don't know the Tribes. They kill fools like you and they will have a butcher's holiday with these troops. I'm fairly certain they outnumber you."

The remark raised the Lieutenant's ire. He was not going to be called a fool by any man. "Anderson, you are being insubordinate. I can't shoot you, but I'll have you in chains if you don't get on that horse of yours and get the hell out of here. I'll see you at a court of Inquiry."

Clay mounted his horse and turned one last time to respond to the Lieutenant's remark. "And I'll see you in hell, Lieutenant."

Clay rode hard to the northeast as the snow began to embrace the landscape, turning the land into featureless whiteness. In hopes of finding a contingent of troops Clay rode to the northeast. It was not until noon when cresting a large rise that he made out the sign of a moving column. The column turned out to be the main force under command of Colonel Carson. When Clay came upon them and reported to the Colonel the predicament of Lieutenant Lewis, the Colonel immediately cut out a company of Calvary and leading them himself rode to the relief of the soldiers he, like Clay, believed to be in peril. When they reached the camp site, the horses that had been left tended by a single trooper as the other soldiers advanced up the valley on foot were gone. The mutilated remains of the private left behind to tend the horses was all that was left of the campsite save for the scattered ruminants of the soldiers kits. The Colonel was in no hurry to rush up the valley. He knew he was too late and he knew what he would find. Instead, he saw to the burial of the trooper and waited for the rest of the troop to arrive.

"I know this valley," Carson told his men. "There is a passage out the back end and I assume the Indians have taken it. Anderson, you take two troopers and scout up there until you find the missing men. If there are no more hostiles about send one man back with word of what you find. You and the other troop follow up the valley to make sure it's clear. About three forth of the way up you will find a trail cutting up over the side. I expect you'll find that the Navajo have taken that trail and are long gone. It shouldn't be hard to follow their tracks in this snow."

Clay walked among the mutilated bodies of the troopers now frozen and covered with a blanket of snow. He tried to identify the body of the Lieutenant. All of the bodies were stripped naked; most had been disemboweled, scalped and punctured with arrow and bullet wounds. The Lieutenants' body had been given special attention. Along with the other acts of mutilation, his ears were missing and his eyes had been poked out. Was he alive when these acts were committed? Clay wondered. The evidence about the scene indicated that the troopers had put up a good fight, but were hopelessly outnumbered. Clay felt again the nausea that gripped him before when he came upon the bodies of those who have fallen victim to the vengeance of the local tribes in Oregon. It was the belief of the more hostile native's tribes that mutilation of their victims would strike fear into the hearts of their enemies. They had no appreciation of the difference between their usual foes and the white armies they now confronted. The mutilation they left behind did not frighten the white soldiers, it only inflamed them to demand acts of equal retribution. It drove from their hearts what little compassion they had for their adversaries. When the troops were again on the move it was with a new determination to find and to destroy forever the vitality of the Navajo.

Colonel Carson had sent Clay and five troopers northward to follow the trail other scouts had reported.

"That probably is the bunch that butchered our soldiers," Carson observed. "After counting coup like they's done they'll be headed back to their village to brag and celebrate. That's what we've been waitin' for."

The terrain over which they were headed was high desert. Clay followed the trail of the retreating Navajo through canyons that had in millenniums past been carved by unimaginable forces of nature through the sandstone that dominated the landscape. The red rock canyons wandered through river beds that had not seen the flow of water for a century or more. The floor of the canyons was silt over which now gathered a frozen crust of snow. The horses labored to keep pace with the retreating Indians. Great pinnacles of sandstone rose as high as mountains and stood alone as silent sentinels of their ancient past. Clay was certain that their pursuit was being observed from these many promontories.

The Colonel had been purposeful in sending such a small body to trail the natives as they would no doubt feel unthreatened by such a small band and confident in their ability to deal with their pursuers if they felt threatened. That thought did not comfort Clay or the troopers whom he led. The Colonel had wisely brevetted Clay as a Second Lieutenant giving Clay the right to order the troopers into the heart of the Indian nation. Clay had little doubt but that the warriors they were persuing would turn upon them before the small troop could close in on their village.

On the third day of their pursuit, they came upon a steadily flowing stream that had its source in a large red rock canyon. The trail of the retreating natives followed the stream into the Canyon. Clay was certain that they had gone as far as the Navajo would let them go and if they followed that trail further, they would be ambushed in the canyon. Clay halted the troop and waited for the darkness of night to conceal their movements.

"I'm guessing that these tracks lead to the village we've been looking for and that if we follow the trail any further, we will not be coming back. I want you men to head back to the Colonel and advise him that we've located the winter camp. I intend to follow along the ridge of the canyon to make sure. By the time the Colonel gets here with the main body, I will know for sure if I'm right."

The troopers made haste in preparation for their departure, and none questioned the wisdom of Clay's decision to carry on the scout alone. Clay ordered them to keep a camp fire going until midnight and then slip away. "I want time to get up on that rim before they know I am not riding with you. I want you to take my horse so that they will think I have ridden with you. Where I am going, I will not need a mount, and if I am detected, a fast horse wouldn't do me much good anyway. Tell the Colonel I will see him coming and meet him at this site. If I am not here he can write me off the roster. You troopers ride fast. I won't be surprised if the Navajo pursue you when they find out you are not going to ride into their trap."

As Clay watched from the rim of the Canyon the next morning, he was confirmed in his suspicions when he saw a group of forty warriors ride out to inspect the deserted camp site where the troopers had camped. They rode off in pursuit. Clay could only hope the early start the troopers had would be enough to keep them ahead of the warriors who were now in desperate need to cut them off before they could deliver to Colonel Carson the location of their camp. Fortunately, the snow had not fallen on these high plains and the troopers would not leave a discernable trail. If the warriors overtook them, Clay would be left fending for himself hundreds of miles from help and with scant provisions in a frigid, desolate land. He had but three days of food and water and only a faint reckoning of his location and the route back to Santa Fe.

As Clay made his way from boulder to boulder and bush to bush along the rim of the canyon, he could see that he had indeed found the winter camp of the Navajo. The further he progressed along the ridge, the more he could see in the canyon below the villages, the orchards, gardens and granaries of the Navajo. What he saw was a veritable paradise where the Navajo had created their own conclave sheltered from their enemies. Their defense was the canyon itself that could be defended against any tribes that sought to enter their domain. ([34])

Near the end of the canyon, Clay could see a large promontory rock where, as a last defense, the Navajo could retreat. He had scouted the valley for several days and was now in haste to return to the mouth of the canyon where he could meet the troops who should be coming by now. He had traveled at night to make more speed. However, when the dawn came crawling over the far horizon, he could see no sign of the troops. Not until late in the afternoon did he observe the movement of a contingent of what he hoped were troopers coming toward the canyon. To his disappointment, the band was far too small to be the Army with its large contingent of troops, supply wagons and artillery caissons. As he watched the gathering formation, Clay realized it was the returning warriors who had taken off in pursuit of the troops he had dispatched to find Colonel Carson.

As The band of warriors passed below his vantage point, he could see that they were waving trophies on their spear points. He could not make out what all of the trophies were, but he could see that several of the warriors were clad in blue jackets, and some had on the blue hats worn by American soldiers. They were also leading horses upon which were draped the bodies of their dead. It was little satisfaction to Clay to note that the troopers had made the Navajo pay dearly for their small victory.

The sun took command of the sky, giving but slight warmth to the desert above the canyon. Clay sat viewing the vast desolate lands that surrounded him and tried to review his options. In the valley below was a verdant land that could provide water and abundant food. There were horses aplenty. He considered the prospect of stealing several horses and some food and then flee across the desert in hopes of finding the Army. Clay could see that the entrance of the canyon was under the continual observation of sentries. Patrols were occasionally set out, no doubt to observe the movement of the soldiers. It would be almost impossible,

---

[34] For a description of the Canyon de Chelly and Fortress Rock and the campaign to defeat the Navaho, see Blood and Thunder, supra.

Clay concluded to enter the valley and get away with what supplies and horses he would need to get back to the Army. He could follow on foot the river flowing from the canyon as far as it would take him. He had no idea whether that route would take him closer to or further away from the searching troops. If there were hostiles moving about, they would no doubt be following the river also. The last and least appealing alternative was to fill his water bottle from the river during the night and then take off on foot across the desert in hopes of finding some element of the searching troops. Upon consideration, he determined that the later alternative would be the most consistent with his mission.

Before the moon could bask the landscape in transparent daylight, Clay gathered up the saddle bag he had stashed and proceeded across country so he could approach the river through an arroyo that would provide cover from the now observant, wary Navajo sentries. He tried as best he could to conceal his foot prints as he crossed the sandy beach to the water's edge, but knew he could not completely hide those prints. He hoped that the fact that he wore moccasins would delude the Navajo into believing it was one of their tribal members who had left the prints. Heading up the arroyo, he tried to move from rock to rock and leave no print. He knew, however, that only an intervening dusting of snow would serve that purpose. He had one further consideration, and that was that he would have to travel only at night. The necessity of traveling unobserved militated against daytime travel. Clay surmised that the troop would have headed northward from the point he had left them at the Oak tree Canyon and headed in that direction. Unbeknownst to Clay, the troop had headed eastward by north to resupply and await word from him and other scouts before redeploying

Each night, as dawn approached, Clay was careful to select a hiding place on high ground so he could observe the trail behind for pursuers and the terrain ahead for any sign of the approaching troops. On the second day out he observed what he thought was a band of Navajo on his back trail. They appeared to be carefully searching along the route he had taken. They had discovered his presence and would soon over take him as they had the advantage of horses. As darkness fell, Clay had only one alternative. He needed to ignore his efforts to hide his trail and take off at a ground covering dog trot to try to outdistance his pursuers and to reach the troopers before he was captured.

Clay had heard the stories of mountain men like John Colter who had been able to run at full speed for most of a day to out distance his Indian pursuers. Colter, however, did not accomplish his feat in a desert where the land was soft and yielding and covered with cactus. Colter's pursuers were not mounted. Clay ate the rest of his food knowing he probably would not be needing more. He loaded what bullets he had into his belt pouch and discarded his saddle bag, keeping his water bottle and blanket. His Winchester was his only impediment to the sprint he knew he would have to win, yet the rifle was his only hope for survival if indeed he had any such hope.

The pursuing Navajo were still but a speck on the desert floor on his back trail when Clay took off at a determined sprint that he hoped he could maintain throughout the day. He was sure he had gone little more than five miles when his breath became labored and rasping, his mouth as dry as tinder and his lungs aflame. Each stride was becoming increasingly difficult and his calf and thigh muscles were cramping. The rough terrain, the cactus and resistant desert bush were cutting away his leggings, and turning his moccasins into shreds. His feet were now bleeding. He paused for a moment to regain his breath and looked behind. His pursuers were coming upon him fast now. They no longer needed to try to follow his tracks, he was now in sight and they were coming straight on. Clay saw another mile or so ahead a tall panicle with a rock strewn base where he might make a stand and started once more his labored sprint, hoping to make the high ground before the Navajo ran him down. The Navajo, realizing they now had their intended victim, slowed their pace to save their horses giving Clay the chance he needed to reach the high ground he chose as his last stand.

Clay scrambled up the rock strewn face and fell exhausted behind a large sandstone bolder. To his good fortune, the approaching braves were not making haste, but upon reaching the point where he had taken his stand dismounted their horses and stood discussing their plan of attack. Clay had chosen his spot well, for the braves could not charge up the face of the rise on horseback. Clay counted eight braves, several armed with old muzzle loaded rifles, the rest with bows, arrows and lances. Clay, by force of will steadied his hands and sighted on the warriors where they were, unknown to them, within his field of fire. He held that fire, a plan forming now in his clearing mind.

Clay suspected, as it turned out that the Navajo would assume he had a single shot rifle and that their advantage would be in approaching as close to him as they could, induce him to spend this rifle charge and then attack before he could reload. As the braves assembled below him Clay drew a bead on one of the braves that had an old flintlock and waited for him to come half way up the slope. They were moving from rock to rock, whooping and challenging him to shoot. When he was certain of his shot and the braves had come to within fifty feet of his position, he shot the one brave, sending him sprawling down the hill. He then stood up and fumbled with his rifle in the pretext that he was trying to reload.

The braves now stood and attacked. As they came ever nearer, Clay shot first the other rifle carrying brave and then proceeded to shoot the other braves as they came on. Once the braves realized that he was not stopping to reload, they hesitated in confusion giving Clay a clear shot. As the last Navajo came upon him and before Clay could aim his rifle at him, the brave wielding a tomahawk threw it with his full strength at Clay, just as Clay sent a bullet into his heart. The Tomahawk came at Clay as if in slow motion tumbling end over end. Clay had not the quickness remaining in his weakened condition to dodge the missal that now struck him with the terrific impact, throwing him backwards unto the rock strewn ground. It was Clay's intention to capture one of their horses and some of their water and food and proceed onward after he had time to rest. His hope was dashed when he struggled back to his knees and saw in the distance that the one brave who had stayed behind to tend the ponies, went riding off leading all of the horses. For all his effort, Clay had not advanced his prospects by but a day or more when he would parish either from the cold, further pursuit by the Navajo or from lack of food.

Clay lie back down and felt the shoulder what had received the impact of the tomahawk. The blade had driven deep into his flesh and had broken his collar bone. As he lay on his back gasping for breath, the pain of the wound grew and consumed what strength remained in his weakened body. After but a few moments he lost consciousness.

The sun was reaching its mid-afternoon zenith as Clay passed in and out of consciousness. His vision was playing tricks on him and he could not focus his eyes on the terrain below. He finally collapsed in the shelter of the large bolder he had used as his protection against the Navajo. He was soon in a fitful slumber, trying occasionally to revive himself; his strength was ever waning and he knew he was bleeding, but had not the strength left to tend to his wound. He finally fell into a deep sleep. The sun had moved westerly and was driving its meager warmth against his body, yet he did not respond. Something did however, disturb him and he tried to sit up and defend himself.

It was the sound of footsteps moving over the loose rocks of the slope, but Clay's senses could not identify the sound, he only knew there was danger close at hand. He struggled to sit up and raise his rifle, but the rifle was lead weight in his hands and it fell in a clatter by his side. A shadow now hovered over him, and whoever it was had his back to the sun and Clay could only see a silhouette, but couldn't make out any features. He awaited the blow that would surely come next, a blow he had not the strength to fend off.

"You're one sad looking Pilgrim. You plan on resting here much longer?"

The voice was familiar to Clay, but his mind was too muddled to even understand what was said. The figure was now kneeling beside him, holding a wet cloth against his face and wiping the grit from his eyes. Next he felt the trickle of water against his lips and as he tried to respond he chocked as the water passed down his throat. The gasping revived him and he grabbed the water bottle being pressed to his lips and began taking large droughts of the life giving liquid. The hands were now pulling away the source of water and Clay fought desperately to hold on.

"You best hold out a bit, young fella. I ain't got a whole lot of that stuff."

Clay lay back and looked without recognition at the figure beside him, trying to make his mind function. Then it came to him. It was the mountain man Vasquez who had found him.

"Where did you come from?" Clay asked in a croaking whisper.

"I was sent out looking for your carcass when we found you wasn't among them soldier's bodies we came cross back a-ways. Figured them heathen had taken you back to camp for a fry and it warn't much use looking. But old Kit insisted. Heard all that shootin' you was a-doin' and came to have a look. Sound carries here-a-bouts. Then I sees all them dead folks on this here promontory and came to have a look. You did them fellas some real hurt. That thar repeatin' rifle done saved your sorry hide, young 'un."

"But I thought you had taken off back at Santa Fe."

"Did, but old Kit ran me down and called me out. Seems he thinks I owed him one fer when he shot that old Grizz off my back upon on the Yellowstone. Now let's have a look at that shoulder of yours. Seems a bit of a mess."

Vasquez half carried Clay down the slope and set him against a bolder wrapping him in a blanket. "You best take a good pull and this, lad," Vasquez offered as he handed Clay a bottle of whiskey. "It's all the medicine I got. Take all you can as you'll be need'n' it when I fix that gash you got."

Vasquez started a fire using the greasewood bushes about the landscape.

"This will serve as a signal fire for them troops who's wondering about."

Clay passed out when Vasquez pulled his shoulder into position and strapped his arm to his body. Vasquez lined up the broken bone the best he could then sewed up the gashing wound with cat gut he carried for such purposes. Vasquez had seen the Missionaries tie wounds together and knowing the hazards of the wilderness, added the Missionary's tools to his kit. When he was done he poured some of the remaining whiskey over the wound and wrapped Clay back up and restocked the fire. It was dark when Clay next gained consciousness. He found himself lying on a wagon bed wrapped in blankets with a sputtering lantern hanging over his head. Colonel Carson was kneeling beside him talking to the Army surgeon.

"That scout did a smart job of setting the shoulder. I'd not done better myself. He should be alright, but won't be traveling for awhile," the doctor was saying.

Clay tried to sit up, but the sharp pain drove him back to the blankets.

"Don't try to move, Anderson. All I need to get when you are able is a report on what you found. Do you feel able now?"

The doctor raised him slightly and gave Clay another shot of whiskey tinted with laudanum. "Get what you can Colonel, he'll be asleep soon. That wound has got to be hurtin'," the doctor advised.

Clay gave the Colonel a report of his observations and the directions to the Indian encampment.

"By your description, that must be that Canyon de Chelly I've heard talked about. We clean that out and this campaign can come to an end and we can get out of this frozen wilderness. You've done well, Anderson, now get some rest and we'll be getting you out of here."

Clay was taken back to the warmth of the Army hospital at Santa Fe to heal from his wounds and exposure. He received in scattering details the progress of the Colonel Carson's campaign against the Navajo. The summer campaign that drove the Navajo from their villages and crops, sending them further and further into the desert, had proved successful. When the Colonel finally confronted the Navajo in their stronghold at the Canyon de Chilly, the tribes had been reduced to starvation and were suffering greatly from the weather. There was little fight left in them and they had agreed to come out of their ancestral lands and submit to assignment on a reservation where the government would care for them and teach them to farm and live in confinement. Clay well knew what fate now awaited the belligerent Apache, Comanche and Cheyenne. But Clay now had a way out of the Army. Being given a commission, he could now resign it and move on.

As Clay lay in bed recuperating from his ordeal, he was presented with a small wooden box that had arrived by freight wagon from St Louis. It was shipped to him by the Winchester Arms Company. Taking his skinning knife from is kit, Clay anxiously pried open the box, eager for any diversion from his confinement. Inside he found, neatly waxed and packed over five hundred rounds of the latest cartages for his rifle. Also enclosed were a number of newspaper clippings, exaggerated editorializing on his recent experiences on the high desert. He read the articles with amusement, wondering as he did how the report on his adventures came to be recorded and forwarded to Washington. Also included were several volumes of the "Adventures of Clay Anderson, Hero of the West." There was also enclosed a sealed letter written in the Hand of Oliver Winchester himself.

My Dear Mr. Anderson,

I forward to you the latest rim fire cartages that have been developed by my associate. You have done exceedingly well in promoting my repeating rifle and I sincerely appreciate your efforts, as hazardous as they may have turned out to be. I am enclosing herein a bank draft for $1500 dollars to back up my assurances that you would be rewarded for your promotion of my rifle.

Of passing interest to you, I have news of a friend of ours, Fay Mansfield to whom I believe you took some fancy while you visited at Twin Oaks. She did not marry her intended, but recently married the Grand Duke of Austria and is now touring New England. I mention this as she enquired regarding your wellbeing when I lunched with her last. She asked that I mention her if I should correspond with you. For reasons of state, considering her new nobility, she declined to address you directly although she asked that I pass on her best regards.

Your friend and confidant,

Oliver Winchester.

Clay lay back on his bed, holding the letter to his breast allowing pleasant memories of his nights with Fay to possess his thoughts. Soon, however, the woman in his reveries was no longer Fay, but Jenny. Allowing his flights of fancy to substitute Jenny for Fay in his moments of passion during his stay at Twin Oaks, he quickly shook off the reverie with a feeling of guilt. He was coveting his brother's wife. He then studied the bank draft enclosed with the letter. He had saved most of his army pay of thirty dollars a month, but knew that was a poor investment on his dreams of one day being a land owner and rancher. At last he had the means and purpose to pursue his travels to California where he thought he could find the fulfillment of his dream. Oregon was always on his mind, but he was not ready yet to face his now extended family. By now he imagined that Jenny would have given birth to a nephew of two cementing forever her distance from him. Word had reached him when he left Fort Laramie of the massacre at the Whitman Mission in Oregon Territory. That event meant no more to him then news of the other depredations occurring though out the West. He had no way of knowing that Jenny had been one of the victims of that event.

As the Spring warmth brought renewed energy and hope to the citizens of Santa Fe, they gave witness to the growing bands of Navajo who were, in compliance with the surrender declaration of General Charlton, moving south onto the designated reservation at Bosque Redondo, where many would perish and none would prosper. Clay made one last call at the home of Kit Carson, whom he found to be suffering from some malady that gave him remittent chest pains, pains he was finding difficult to ignore. The old plainsman gave him advice and directions concerning his travels to California and suggested to him that if he was looking for land, he should look near to the growing town of Los Angeles an area that had pleasant weather and healthy soil.

Clay joined a wagon train heading for California that had trekked from Independence, Missouri along the Santa Fe Trail, a train that would beyond Santa Fe, be passing through the lands of the Apache. The train members were eager to have a man of Clay's reputation join their ranks as the trail beyond Santa Fe was unprotected by the Army. The route of the Mormon Battalion that had passed through these lands was pursued by the wagon train. The train was composed of forty wagons most pulled by oxen. A herd of over fifteen hundred horses and cattle moved with the train as it headed west onto the desert lands Clay had so recently scouted in the cold of winter. The prospect of riding once more through Indian lands did not please Clay. He had had his fill of the suffering the settlers and the natives inflicted upon each other. But if it was on to California, he had to cross one more time the disputed lands of the desert tribes.

Carson's advice to follow the trail of the Mormon Battalion was based on the assurance that the more southerly direction would afford them the benefit of finding the Gila Indians who were generally hospitable and would resupply them from their abundant crops of fruits, melons, dates and vegetables. From there, Carson advised, they should follow the Gila River to the Colorado River and then cut directly west and avoid the mountains and the great desert that ran through the east of the great Sierra Range.

"The heat in them deserts, by the time you gets to 'em will boil your blood," Kit had advised.

As they proceeded west, they came across groups of Navajo moving on to their new reservation. Some under Army escort, most traveling alone. For the most part, the Navajo were in an impoverished state, suffering from lack of food and clothed in tatters. Their resistance to the white man had cost them dearly.

As they crossed from the lands of the Navajo, the oxen were already showing signs of trail fatigue. The soft sandy soil they encountered wore on their hoofs and made the burdens they pulled that much more difficult. When not on the soft ground, they would be moving across lava beds that cut at their tender hoofs. The horses and mules and tailing livestock suffered less, but many were favoring their sore hoofs when it was decided to rest the animals at a large mountain meadow where grass was abundant that the native pine and soft wood trees were abundant. They were entering the country where the hills were once again red sandstone. The valleys through which they would travel were circumscribed by the cliffs of the red rock. It was while waiting to refresh their animals, the scouts reported that a band of Apache were in the vicinity and were observing their camp.

Clay rode out to parley with the Apache with the wagon master, a man named Christianson who could speak in the universal sign language of the Plains Indians. They found the Indians to be belligerent. They demanded horses, guns, ammunition, sugar and whiskey if the wagons were to be allowed to pass. As Christianson did his bargaining, Clay did his best to size up the disposition and the size of the Indian encampment. He was not pleased to see that there were no women among them and that their ponies were painted and cropped; a sign that this was a war party. In the meadow near their camp was a large herd of horses. The horses were not the common Indian pony, but the more blooded lines found on the Mexican Ranches to the south. This was indeed a raiding party and they had no doubt taken scalps and would be eager to take a few more.

The Chief was about the ugliest Indian Clay had ever seen, with deep set snake like eyes, a large once broken nose that gave his weathered face an unbalanced appearance. The Chief had a large scar on his forehead where part of his scalp was missing. He was a large man with massive shoulders and arms. His gestures as he made sign were quick and indicated his impatience. The bargaining was not going well.

"That's one surly bastard that Indian is," Christianson remarked as they headed back to the wagon train. "When I told him there would be no guns or whiskey he said he might just take them if we didn't want to give them up." His sign wasn't that good, but the look on his face told me all I wanted to know. I think we're in for it."

"Best I can make out," Clay offered, "Is that they have some eighty to a hundred braves in their band. They are well mounted and have our men outnumbered."

"The chief said he would be along shortly to collect his bounty. We'll circle up and wait for him."

"Might I make a suggestion?" Clay proposed, "That group has been out raiding and are heading home. Their blood is up. No doubt they have swept through some small towns or farms and are high on their successes. I'd not want to invite them into a fight. I have a plan that may send them on their way without letting blood."

As the Apaches approached the laagered up wagon train, they stopped some hundred yards short of the camp and then lined up in a long line behind their chief. Their weapons were in evidence and they did not appear to be coming to parley or accept the ransom that had been offered. As they awaited the envoy from the wagon train to come out and parley with the Chief, some of the braves were shouting and taunting the members of the train. It was an ugly scene. To their bewilderment, however, the white men were not cowering. They watched as one of the wagons was pulled aside and there came from the protective circle a long file of armed riders who lined up in a long line in front of the wagons facing the Apache. The Apache could now see that there were one hundred and fifty armed and mounted men lined in front of them, more than their number.

When Clay and Christianson rode out with a pack horse loaded with the bounty Christianson had agreed to give him, the belligerence had gone from the Chief and he was sitting astride his pony in serious thought.

These white men were mounted and ready to fight and there were more of them then he had expected. When Christianson offered the bounty, the Chief motioned for his companion to take it and turned his horse and road away, the rest of his band following behind.

As they returned to the wagon train, the mounted defenders were waiving their hats and whooping and hollering at the success of their ruse. All of the women in the train had been dressed in men's clothing and were mounted and supplied with rifles, some with only broom sticks. None-the-less from a distance they appeared a formidable force ready for any encounter. The unanticipated problem caused by the rouse was that many of the women, once unencumbered with the heavy skirts, petticoats, and other unsuitable wear, refused to give up their pants and shirts and for the remainder of the journey would continue to dress in the pants and coats supplied them. Many of them would now ride astride the horses as did the men. A few of them even cut their hair short suggesting that it was cooler and more comfortable. Having used the women in the guise of men, the men were now helpless to demand that they give up the rouse the women now embraced. Clay found the turn of events he had precipitated mildly amusing, but several of the men were heard to mutter his name derisively about camp.

When out scouting, Clay came to a fast flowing river and followed it until, reaching the flat land he found what he had been told would be the Gila Indians. The party then followed the river southward toward the Gila settlement. They came upon wandering groups of Indians, but most were more curious then aggressive and were interested in trading not warring. When the train reached the Gila Indian settlements they found the Indians to be hospitable and thriving along a river that provided them with water for their varied agriculture. The train spent several days at the settlement repairing wagons, re-setting their wagon wheels and trading with the natives. History would not treat well with these friendly Gila Indians. Soon the white settlers would arrive and divert from their villages the vital water source that had sustained the Gila for centuries.

After a day's travel, they came to the Colorado River and followed it until it turned west. Finding a suitable ford, they crossed the river and headed northwest. After traveling for four days along a desolate, barren terrain that skirted a large salt lake, they came upon verdant lands with palm groves and artesian springs. Ahead of them loomed the San Bernardino Range that once passed would leave unencumbered their route to their destination of Los Angeles, where the wagon train would split, some going on north and others settling on the coastal plain around the small but thriving port city of Los Angeles.

Clay and a few others without family and wagons, headed on alone at this point saying goodbye to friends and comrades. When Clay road down into the coastal plateau he was immediately impressed by the groves of orchards and vineyards that surrounded the small community. Clay had no intention of becoming a farmer plowing the lands and planting yearly crops, but the thought of being an orchardist appealed to him and he resolved to look into the matter. The one thing that appealed to him the most was to settle down. He had finally, after thousands of miles of wondering throughout the west, reached the fabled shores of the Pacific Ocean. This was a suitable end to his wanderings.

Clay was not impressed with the city of Los Angeles, the population made up of itinerants of many nationalities, most who had abandoned the ships that brought them to the shores of California, were rowdy and shiftless and contributed little to the community. The largest portions of the population of 2,000 people were either Mexican or Gabrielino Indians. ([35]) Most of the houses were small adobe structures that were common along the coast were timber was not plentiful. Yet, after a few hours spent in the town, he could see the potential of this land blessed by God's nature. The coming wagon train and the others that would follow would bring the needed civilizing influence.

A large solon advertised rooms and meals and Clay enquired inside. When shown a room he would have to share with another tenant, he opted out and searched about town for some home owner who would rent him a room. It appeared that few people were offering rooms, leaving Clay to the bleak prospect of camping out along with a number of other itinerants. After a few days spent looking about, Clay was fast losing his attraction for the town, especially when, upon seeing the orchards and vineyards up close, orchards that had looked so promising from a distance were mostly

---

[35] The History of Los Angeles County California; http://www.laavenue.com/LAHistory.htm

Mission properties where irrigation works had been constructed. The rest of the land about the town was dominated by large ranch owners who held their claim from Mexico and Spain. Many of these owners did not even live upon their lands and resided in Mexico City. These rancheros were mostly engaged in raising cattle. Their largest market was the sale of hides and tallow.

After making a number of inquiries about purchasing land, he became even more discouraged. A William Workman, who claimed to own 50,000 acres of land and Henry Dalton who claimed to own three large rancheros, each advised him that they were not in the mood to sell land, but that their biggest concern was in protecting the titles they claimed from Mexico. ([36]) Each of them, along with a number of other land owners, purchased their property from departing Mexicans. The American takeover of California was a work in progress and the institutions necessary to carry out the provisions of the Mexican treaty of capitulation were unresponsive to their demands that the land titles of the Mexican and Spanish grants be protected. Their problems were exacerbated when the new emigrants squatted on their lands and the local authorities would do nothing to remove them, their sympathies being with the squatters.

The Mexican government, after its invasion by the American armies, was in chaos and could not lend support to the land claims of the land owners. Amidst this confusion, Clay decided not to purchase any property, but instead, following the advice of the land agent in charge of recording deeds, went south of town along the coast and laid claim to a 500 acre tract, by outlining the boarders of his claim and then filing his description of the claim at the land office. He felt confident that his claim would not be disputed as part of the land was polluted with a black oozing oily substance that made the land unsuitable for agriculture. Clay's interest in the claim was based not upon the land but upon a picturesque bay and a promising location for a future home.

Having completed his business, Clay went down to the water front and booked passage on the *Pilgrim*, a sailing ship that had recently arrived from Peru to trade for hides and tallow, offering to the residents such

---

[36] Inventory of the Henry Dalton Collection, 1819-1942, bulk 1840-1883; http://content.cdlib.org/view?docId=tf5d5nb00qt&doc.view=entire_text&brand=oac

goods as tea, shoes, shirts, Chocolate and candle molds in exchange. It was heading to San Francisco to complete its trading and then was off to China. Clay reluctantly sold his horse for $500 to the rancher Workman. He now had the nest egg he felt he would need to buy land or a business in San Francisco.

The ship he sailed on was one of the new Yankee Clipper ships that was setting sailing records on virtually every trade route and were giving the American shipping interest a decided advantage over the other commercial nations. The China trade was fast becoming the province of American shipping interests. Clay noted this fact and had a number of discussions with the ship's Captain as to the types of products that would be of interest to the China traders. Tallow and hides dominated their interest, but than that was all that had been available.

"Could sell some of the wines they produce around here, though," The Captain said. "Could sell that down in them South American countries where we trade. They have European tastes down that way. Some of them grain crops we're getting out of Oregon is doing good in the Orient. Furs and hides is still big in China. A fella could make some money if he brokered them products. Right now we have to go around scouting up our cargo. Cuts down on our sailing time."

When Clay arrived in San Francisco, he was immediately impressed with the busy harbor and the obviously burgeoning community situated on the hills above. At the harbor he was even able to hire a carriage to take him to the nearest hotel where he booked a room. After wandering about town and checking out the various business interests, he decided that he should bank what money he had and cash the bank note he held from the Winchester Arms Company. The bank nearest his hotel and the one that looked to be the most prosperous was the Ramsdale Bank.

JENNY

Jenny slowly recovered from her ordeal during captivity. The wounds she had suffered from beatings and sexual abuse healed, but her mind was burdened with periods of despair during the days and her nights were filled with nightmares that allowed her only fitful periods of sleep. The

Reverend Spalding assured her that prayer and time would do the healing, but Jenny found she could no longer pray to a God that had allowed her to be treated so poorly. After several months of listlessness during which she was allowed to indulge her grieving, she received from William Anderson a letter that left her even more desperate for some hope. He explained in cold lawyer like language that his law practice was prospering, but that he would be too engaged in the activities dealing with the Territorial government to pursue their intended nuptial vows and that she should feel free to accept other suitors. Jenny was not surprised by this revelation; she knew when William had ridden away on the day of her release that her hopes of marriage were over. She was not even sure she would have been able to face William if he had confronted her. She was seeped in bitter shame at having lost her virginity and having been used so brutally. What had she left to give a husband?

It was the second part of the letter that drove her into a deeper and more desperate despair.

I was awaiting a more appropriate time to inform you of the fate of the party that split off from the wagon train at Fort Boise.

Your brother and father along with my brother Clay were a part of that party. We received the sad news that the entire party had been set upon by hostile Indians and that they were all murdered. I rode with the militia to the site of the Indian attack. We were able to identify the body of your father as he had been placed in a marked grave, but were not able to find the remains of several of the members including that of your brother James. Of course when we reached the scene, it was not possible to make positive identifications. We have since received news that suggests that my brother Clay survived the event, but we have not heard from him. With all our prayers we hope that James also survived, but we have no way of confirming that fact. I dearly hope that this news does not add too gravely to your distress, but I find it to be even crueler to allow you to hope for some reassuring contact from your relatives when such hope may well be futile.

Jenny found that there was no depth to her despair. She stopped eating regularly and declined even to concern herself with her appearance and hygiene. She willed herself to die, but knew that somehow it was her fate to suffer and to live. After several more weeks, Eliza Spalding could stand no more. There was much work to be done about the Mission and she had intended that when she took on the task of helping Jenny recover, she would also gain a help mate about the Mission.

She found Jenny sitting on a bench in the church, looking at the crucified Christ whose picture hung over the rough hewn alter. Sitting beside her and taking Jenny's limp and unresponsive hand in hers, she squeezed it hard until Jenny turned to her and struggled to pull her hand away.

"So you do have some feeling. I began to have my doubts. Now just how long do you intend to waste away what life the Lord has allowed you."

"Your Lord has no concerns for me," Jenny answered, again turning her gaze to the image before her.

"You received a letter the other day. Was there news in that letter that has caused this new, deeper despair that seems to have possessed you?"

Jenny's response was to pull the letter from the side pocket of her dress and hand it to Mrs. Spalding without comment.

After Eliza read the letter she put and arm around Jenny's shoulder trying to give her comfort, but found no response.

"You mustn't blame the Lord for you sorrows, Jenny. He is your salvation."

At that remark, Jenny finally looked into Eliza's eyes and Eliza drew back when she saw within those eyes a troubling look of hatred."

"Your Lord may favor you, but he has deserted me and left me to suffer. Why would he commit me to this living Hell I have suffered if he was at all concerned?"

"The Lord does his work in ways we do not understand, but there is always a purpose we must try to understand. That is why I thought it best to have a talk with you, Jenny." Eliza took Jenny's hand again and waited until Jenny faced her once more.

"Jenny, are you with child?"

Jenny looked at her in stunned silence. "I….I…don't know." She replied bewilderedly. Jenny had been too obsessed in her grief and losses to have even considered the consequences of the abuse she had taken.

"When did you last have your flow?" Eliza asked.

"I….don't remember. I thought that the hurt I suffered was the reason it didn't come, but I didn't even consider that I would be pregnant."

"Let me see your breasts?' Eliza demanded.

Jenny was too startled by the request to respond. Her first sense of modesty returned as she held her hand to her chest as if to ward off and invasion.

"Jenny, don't be silly, I just want to see if your breasts are swelling. That is a sign of you possible pregnancy. Now let's have a look."

Jenny was now curious also and lowered her bodice looking with interest at whatever sign there might be."

"Just as I expected," Eliza pronounced. "Your nipples are enlarged and your breasts are full. Jenny you are with child."

Jenny suddenly grabbed the front of her dress pulling it as if she could somehow purge from her body this unwanted creature forming within her womb.

Eliza grabbed her wrist and restrained her. "Jenny, you must try to come to yourself. You have been wandering about in a fog of self pity. You have now been given the gift of a new life and you must be preparing yourself."

Jenny looked at Eliza in disbelief. How could this woman expect her to relish the thought of carrying within her a child conceived in an act of hate and violence? How could such a child grow up to be less than the monster that defiled her? Jenny's mind was now flooded with the events that shattered her once hopeful life. In her mind she saw the hate filled face of the Indian that took out on her frail young body all the vengeance that had filled his soul as one of the white man's outrages after the other had hardened his heart to steel. How could a child thus conceived be blessed?

"I know what is in your heart, Jenny. Few could face what you have faced, nor could they face what you must still endure. You must be brave. You must turn to God. He has a purpose to be served. This baby you carry must be very special."

Jenny turned away from Eliza and the tears of outrage spilled forth from the depth of her soul. She had shed no tears; not during the assaults upon her, not after her release, not upon reading of her father and her brother's murder, but now they burst forth in torrents that could not be restrained.

When at last the tears could flow no more and Jenny regain her composure she turned at last to Eliza, "These savages have stolen my honor, they have murdered my father and brother. How could I possibly give life to another of them?"

"I do not know what the Lords purpose is but . . . ." she could not finish her sentence. Jenny stood before her know shouting in anger. "Damn you and your Lord. I don't want to be part of his plan. I don't want this baby." Jenny then turned and stormed from the church.

Jenny, emotionally exhausted from her encounter with Eliza and the relief brought on by the release of her pent up anger and tears, fell into a deep slumber for the first time in months and awoke feeling strangely euphoric. The sun was sending dust motes whirling about the small, sparsely furnished room she had been assigned at the rear of the school house. When she came storming into the room and threw herself on the bed, she had neglected to pull the near threadbare curtain across the window and could now see on the hillock behind the Mission a solitary doe looking over the scene below, sniffing the air and then turning and vanishing in a few bounds up the hill and out of sight. Jenny felt a bonding with the deer in the sense that she too could be free now that she had found her release through tears and relinquished anger. Then darkness filled the room as if storm clouds had gathered to blot out the promise of the coming day. The baby! She now remembered the baby and she quickly rolled on her back and felt her stomach to confirm the horror that had driven her from her melancholy into a fit of panic just a few hours ago.

There was a small lump there in her abdomen. She reached up and put her hand down her bodice and felt her now growing, full breasts. It was true, she now knew, she was pregnant. The thought brought her upright on the bed and she began pounding her stomach with balled fists intending to drive the intruding growth from her. In this frenzy, she did not notice that the door had opened and someone now stood at the end of her bed observing her frantic efforts.

"You hurt baby, it die in you and you die too." Jenny looked now at the intruder. It was the Nez Perce Indian they called Molly. Like most of the Indians, they had no appreciation for the privacy concerns of the white man and entered their houses without knocking or introduction.

"What are you doing here?" Jenny demanded.

"I sent by Miz Eliza. She say you need me."

Jenny, in her confusion, stared in puzzlement at Molly. "Why would I need you? The last thing I want about me now is an Indian. Go away!"

Molly was indifferent to the command, and picked up the water bucket and poured water into the bowl on the stand beside the bed. "Need wash. Clothes torn. I fix."

Jenny demanded once more that Molly leave her room, and once again Molly ignored her and stood silently awaiting Jenny's response to her suggestion.

In frustration, Jenny rose from the bed and splashed water on her face, removed her dress and threw it on the floor. Molly retrieved the dress and left the room, slamming the door behind her.

After Molly left the room, Jenny latched the door, removed the rest of her clothing and for the first time in many days bathed herself with a wash cloth. It occurred to her that this Molly might know of some Indian concoction that would abort the fetus growing within her. That thought gave her some hope for the coming day. Jenny put on a clean dress and was busy combing the tangles from her matted hair when Molly again entered the room. She had with her a small, probably two year old boy with big brown eyes and the light completion of a breed who stood looking shyly from around his mother's skirt at Jenny.

"Bring food," Molly announced as she placed the plate of eggs, ham and toast in front of Jenny. Jenny's impulse was to hurl the plate and its contents at Molly and order her again from her room. The aroma of the food, however, overcame her anger and she proceeded to eat it with an eagerness that she had not felt for some time. Molly stood watching her until she had finished. Jenny then turned to her, "Now what is it you want?"

"You angry. I know feeling. I no want boy here. White men come to camp, kill men rape women. This boy seed of white man I no know. You have boy too. No one want you now. Must have son."

Jenny struggled with the meaning of Molly's words and starred at the young boy while the sense of what Molly had said sunk into her reluctant brain. The boy was beautiful. His shyness was appealing. Jenny realized that she had been hateful toward Molly and that it was unlike her. Her anger and frustration were dominating her actions. Molly, Jenny realized was trying to convey to her the sympathies only one who had shared a similar fate could appreciate. Some of what Liza had said also came to rest in her consciousness. Liza had said the words her own mother would have probably tried to convey to her were she alive.

She must decide whether she would live on with a meaningful life, or succumb to her despair. James and her father were now gone. She was the only Rawlins left and she was soon to have a child. That thought now rested heavily on her mind. She thought again of the last words of her mother. They were full of love and hope. Much had changed to blunt the promise contained in those last words. There would be no marriage and blessed giving of her woman hood to the man she loved. As Molly had just said, she was no longer a woman to be desired among her own people and would probably never marry. The life within her was her only future. These thoughts came upon her like a revelation and she wondered if indeed the Lord had somehow intervened to resurrect her from a life without purpose. Molly, standing patiently before her, now holding her son by the hand had uttered words that now had a profound meaning to her. Jenny looked again to the young boy.

"What is his name?" she asked.

"His name is Franklin. He need white man's name. The day of my people is over. He must grow up white. Must learn language. You teach?"

Jenny took another longer look at Molly now. There was a wisdom, purpose and determination in this woman that appealed to Jenny. She had been wrong to treat Molly as some bothersome squaw. Molly was upon appraisal not as tall as Jenny, but more firm of body. She had the oval face characteristic of her tribe with eyes that had an oriental cast and a mouth that was firm set giving Molly the general appearance of either sadness or inevitability, Jenny could not determine which. Jenny, who had lingering thoughts of the Indian squaw who had mistreated her during her captivity and who had prepared her for her captor's amusement, looked upon all Indian women with the same hatred she felt for the Indian that had assaulted her. She could not now see in Molly the image of the woman that had aided in her violation. These people were indeed not all the same. In time Jenny would even come to realize that the violence that was her lot while in captivity was in part a reaction to a history of abuses that transcended her person, but which made of her an object of retribution. She would never forgive those who had kidnapped her and who had killed

Dr. Whitman and his wife, but she would grow to understand the reason for their hatred of the white men who had invaded their lands and spread among them the white man's deadly diseases.

As Jenny undertook the task of teaching young Franklin the English language and to do his numbers, she soon had a small following of other students of the Nez Pearce tribe attending her classes. It was a needed diversion for Jenny and she found in her pupils the hope of a new understanding between the races. She became more and more acceptant of her condition. The growing size of her belly became a conversation between her and Molly.

"It grow big. It be boy." Molly assured her.

When the time came for delivery, it was Molly who assisted Eliza Spalding with the delivery. As predicted it was a boy who Jenny quickly named Wayne James Rawlins in memory of her lost father and brother. The baby, with its dark brown eyes, black hair, had a fair complexion much like that of young Franklin. He had Jenny's distinct features, angular face, smallish nose, expressive lips and round eyes. There was no doubt however, that Wayne James was a half breed. Jenny now had the same worries that had plagued Molly. Would her child be accepted in the white community where his only future might lie? As the boy grew he took on the stature of his grandfather, broad shoulders and a lanky body. He remembered how fragile James had been as a boy and was glad to see that Wayne James had not inherited from her mother's side as had her brother James. But things were not going well at the Mission. The Spaldings were dissatisfied with their progress at civilizing the Nez Pearce and the Mission funds were drying up as the Eastern Church found more productive uses for its funds.

When Wayne James had reached the tender age of three, Henry Spalding came to Jenny's room to advise her that the Mission would be closing and that she should find a husband to take care of her and the little one.

"You can't be serious," Jenny remarked. "Who would have me but one of those ill tempered sots that wants a house slave. Who would take me and Wayne and treat us as they would a new bride. I could not take Wayne into such a relationship. You know I am right, now please don't set about finding me a husband. I will have to find another position for myself at another Mission."

"I believe there is a Mission being planned among the Spokanes," Spalding offered. "I will see if I can help you there. I fear, however, that there may be trouble with the tribes. The new Territorial governor in Olympia, Governor Stevens, is going among the tribes demanding that they give up their lands and accept reservation life. That is one of the reasons this Mission is closing."

The gold rush to California had brought prospectors from all corners of the earth in search of gold. Silver deposits were being found through the west and the rush was on for the riches hidden in the folds of the earth. The Army had been successful among several of the tribes to confine them to their traditional hunting grounds on the assurance that the Army would protect them from the incursions of the white settlers. The Army of the West, however, was limited in men and recourses and scattered too thinly across the vast frontier to be effective in controlling the migrating hordes of emigrants and the thousands of prospectors none of whom respected the limitations agreed upon between the Army and the tribes. In what was now the Washington Territory, the allure of precious metals in the lands of the Okanagan, Spokane, Yakima and Coeur d' Alene tribes had brought on a host of miners determined to find their fortunes. The intervention of the Army was resented by those who looked upon the lands of the West as theirs to claim and plunder.

When the Indians retaliated against the intruders, it was the Indians who were most often arrested and often hung. The resentment among the tribes had driven them into confederations and stimulated Washington to increase its efforts to confine the tribes. In the process, the sympathies were more often in favor of the settlers and miners, driving the Indians ever back into lands that could not sustain them. The Nez Perce had received the emissaries froom the Yakima and Okanogan and Spokane tribes to join their federation and drive the white men out of their territory. Once banded together, the tribes greatly outnumbered the Army in the region and the settlers now resident in Oregon and Washington. It was a time to act and the blood of the tribes was stirring. The Nez Perce Chieftains were not prepared to engage the white man and declined to join the confederations. Up in the Okanogan country, gold had been found and the miners moved into the territory reserved for the Okanogan tribes.

Several of them were killed and the Army was called out to arrest the Indians responsible.

The Army of the West had spread its forts across the frontier and one of its locations was at Walla Walla near where the Whitman Mission once afforded its relief to the wagon trains from the east. It was from this Fort that a detachment was ordered to move into the Okanogan and protect the white miners from the hostility that was running high among the Okanogan, Palouse, Coeur d' Alene, Yakima, Colville and Spokane tribes. Several miners had been recently killed by the Palouse Indians, miners who were trespassing on what were designated Indian lands. At the time, the Army did not consider the Indian's reactions to be unreasonable and the sympathies of the Army were with the Indians. But the tide of history turns often on trivial events that are but the catalyst of a ground swell long rising.

JAMES

Upon his arrival back in San Francisco, James was relieved to find that the construction of his new home was nearly completed. Jose' Hernandez had successfully incorporated the features that they had discussed before his departure to the Little Flower Mine. There was but one problem. The home was unfurnished and James was at a loss when it came to furnishing a house. To his relief, John Pondexter, hearing of his arrival made an early call, and finding James and his small brood without furnishings to settle into their house, advised them that the matter could be handled quite expedisously should they hire the services of what James later found to be John's mistress, a woman who held out her services as an interior decorator. It was a new profession, John assured James, but quite common in the eastern cities. Angeline, to James' amusement, was an over energized, diminutive spirit who had been born and raised in New Orleans and having inherited a sizable fortune from a husband who died in a duel, came to California to start a new life.

She had a swarthy complexion that James suspected might indicate some mixed blood. Her hair was dark and full, cascading in ringlets about her strikingly beautiful face. Although just over five feet tall and trim of figure, she had a presence and assurance that dominated in any group she fell in with. Within but an hour or two, she had decided what furnishing would be required, had beds and bedding delivered and had hired for James a Mexican cook and a house maid. Before the next day was out, furnishings began arriving to compliment the Mexican flavor of the house. She asked James few questions about his desires taking the authority upon herself to tell him what it was he needed.

When it came to Little Flower, however, Angeline's personality did a metamorphosis. She treated Little Flower as if she were a princess, making certain that the home she was furnishing was to Little Flower's approval. Little Flower, in her turn was concerned that the children had suitable accommodations. James had come to San Francisco with the intention of finding a home for the Summers children, but without any special thought given to the matter, the children were soon incorporated into the Rawlins household and discussions of their future were lost in the bustle of settling in the new home and arranging schooling for the children. Little George was now a constant companion to James and whenever the opportunity allowed, George would accompany James on his errands and was ever curious about James' activities.

July proved to be a devoted companion to Little Flower and as Little Flower's term was near, July's assistance in performing the many errands and that were now becoming a burden to Little Flower made her position in the order of things ever more welcome. When James was able to get away from the confusion of organizing his home and venture into town to tend to business matters, he was not surprised to find that his plans for Little Flower's integration into the white community was having the intended results. Little Flower Shipping and Navigation Company was a prominent tenant on the water front and many of the businesses and residents of San Francisco had used its shipping services. Peters and Cactus Jack had caused a sensation when they reached San Francisco ahead of James and began placing more orders for mining equipment and advertising for miners. The news of the Little Flower Mine was now causing a wave of new speculation and another gold rush into the Nevada Territory. .Advertisements were daily appearing in the papers soliciting freight for the newly formed Little Flower Freight Company offering freight services between San Francisco and Los Angeles. James now understood why Angeline was giving such deference to Little Flower and was treating him so indifferently. This realization brought a smile across James' face as he walked into the Ramsdale Bank.

"You are a welcome sight, Mr. Rawlins," was James' greeting from the head clerk as we enquired after Mr. Ramsdale. "We were hoping you would be back soon. The Bank has had to hire two new clerks just to handle all of the business that is coming our way from your enterprises. I will introduce you to them. Mr. Ramsdale is out to lunch and will be back soon. He will be most delighted to see you in town again."

As James waited for the return of the Banker, he was introduced to the new clerks and began his inspection of the accounts. He was deep in this process when Mr. Ramsdale returned and greeted him effusively. James spent the remainder of the afternoon conversing with the banker and completing his review of the accounts. The Little Flower enterprises had accumulated a good fortune in his absence and had spent a good deal of it purchasing new ships, buying several saw mills in Oregon and 150,000 acres of timberland in the Oregon and Washington territories. The land holdings of the various enterprises encompassed six blocks along the water front which holdings included the Cactus Jack Mission. James had brought six more pouches of gold dust and turned that over to the banker as he concluded his visit.

"You must come to dinner," the Banker offered. I have a number of people I would like you to meet. You are one of our leading citizens, yet very few have even seen you than alone met you."

"I will take you up on that offer, but right now my wife is with child and I would not like to attend any functions until she is delivered and recovered."

Banker Ramsdale was taken aback by this revelation. "You married. When did this take place? There are a number of documents we must prepare. I will need her name and the particulars of the marriage."

The Banker had moved to his desk after having risen to walk to the door and bid him James goodbye.

James looked at the banker for a long moment, realizing that even after all the dealings they had together; his banker hadn't the slightest idea who Little Flower was. To him, Little Flower was only a business. Mr. Ramsdale was a discreet banker and asked no more questions than were necessary and did not pry into his client's affairs.

"Sit down," James suggested to the banker, "You have some catching up to do."

James then told the banker the story of his escape from Oregon, how he ended up with the mine and what his relationship was with the Indian woman who saved him and had been his companion these past several years. "You mention that there are papers she should sign. She is a Native, a Cree Indian from someplace in Canada. Unless I am mistaken, she is not entitled by law to own land in this state and is virtually a non-citizen so I don't think there are any papers that need to be prepared. I would ask you to investigate these matters and if she can hold land and own a business, I would like her name added to that of mine. I don't think that is possible according to the lawyer you sent me to unless things have changed since the new government has been organized."

James noted the confusion cross the banker's face, and the redness engorging his face. James tried to read whether it as embarrassment for his lack of awareness, or embarrassment at finding he had a client with an Indian wife. Was the banker offended by the fact that James had been cohabitating with an Indian and conceived a child out of wedlock? It crossed James' mind that the Banker was now trying to find a diplomatic way out of his recent dinner invitation.

"You caught me completely unprepared for that revelation" Banker Ramsdale responded. "To be truthful with you, James, I had been preparing a business plan for you that would have written the name Little Flower out of your corporate dealings. It seemed an unsuitable name for an enterprise. I am embarrassed that I should have assumed that you had no good purpose behind the use of the name. Please forgive me my presumptions."

"Mrs. Ramsdale will insist that I make certain that your new bride be introduced to San Francisco society at one of her social occasions. Do promise me that, or I shall be ostracized in my own home. I hope I do not offend you by suggestion that Little Flower will now be as famous as Pocahontas and Sacajawea and will be the toast of the town."

"I must also make my confession," James responded. "It was my intention in using her name to create just the situation you now describe. I am pleased at my success. I hope I have not created a great hoax when everybody realizes that she is but a name and can own nothing."

"Then let us hope, James, that some of these knot heads in Sacramento will realize the foolishness of declaring the first Americans unsuitable to be owners of lands we have claimed from them."

As James left the Banker's office, he was euphoric over the success of his scheme to give Little Flower an identity that would supersede the prejudices against her race. Walking swiftly through the lobby, he did not notice the young man in a buckskin jacket sitting in the foyer awaiting an audience with the Bank's president. He at first heard a muttered exclamation from the man that was hardly audible and he did not slacken his stride, "My God, is that you James?"

As he reached the door the stranger rose to his feet and shouted his name so loudly that it echoed throughout the bank, stopping all activity as the customers and clerks looked with alarm at the man now rushing toward the gentleman who had just reached the bank's entrance. James' hand dropped instinctively to the hilt of his bowie knife as he tuned to confront the man rushing toward him. The man had him in his grasp and was dancing him about the foyer of the bank before it penetrated James' mind that he was in the grasp of his lost companion Clay Anderson. Their whoops and hollering drew Banker Ramsdale from his office to view the strange encounter. Realizing that he was witnessing a rare reunion, banker Ramsdale ushered the two men into his office and left them there to enjoy their occasion in privacy.

One customer of the bank, however, was not distracted by the scene in the bank, but being a reporter for the local paper thought there might be a story in this encounter. As the confusion reigned, she slipped behind the reception desk where she could read the entry on the guest register. Her suspicions were confirmed. The man who created the scene was the famous frontiersman, Clay Anderson, who had been dubbed by the Eastern press as "The Hero of the West".

After Clay and James had spent several hours relating their respective experiences after they last shared a camp in Oregon, they left the office of banker Ramsdale to confront a throng of curiosity seekers among them members of the local press the latter of whom were pressing forward asking questions faster than they could be answered. To their relief, Banker Ramsdale had ordered a coach and once they were ushered through the throng in the bank lobby, the coach rushed them away from the even larger crowd that was quickly gathering in the street in front of the bank.

Clay, completely bewildered by the reception he was receiving found it difficult to explain the paradox to James. "I ain't done nothin' to deserve all this attention."

James had other concerns for his friend. "They will hound you to death. Where are you staying?"

When Clay identified the hotel he was staying at, James insisted that he come to his home and stay with him until all the excitement subsided. "We'll send the coachman down town to get your things. You won't be given a moments peace if you stay where you're registered."

Clay and Little Flower were delighted to meet once again. Their common bond with her late husband Parker gave them each a comfort in the company of the other. There was a long period of excitement in the home that night and the children were drawn up in the furor. July, who was experiencing the coming of her woman hood, found in this new stranger a center for her youthful admiration. George and little Linda were wide eyed as the stories of past encounters were related and once again relished by the teller and the hearer.

Late in the evening after little George and Linda had fallen into slumber and had been carried off to bed, Little Flower excused herself and she and July retired leaving the men alone to reminisce. The discussion had turned to family. Jenny had been on both of their minds. James announced that after Little Flower gave birth and was able to travel, he intended to go visit his sister whom he assumed was settled in Oregon City, raising a brood of young Andersons. Clay admitted that he had been negligent in his duties to family and would like to accompany James on his trip to Oregon and visit with his father and brother. When it came to Jenny, however, he could not bring her name to his lips.

It was not a surprise to either James or Clay when the newspapers hit the street the next day with all kinds of exaggerated stories about Clay and his heroic past and his meeting with the now famous businessman James Rawlins. Both James and Clay stayed out of sight for the next week hoping that the furor would subside. Little Flower could not, however, wait out her pregnancy and gave birth to a Wayne Parker Rawlins on the third night of Clay's visit.

When Clay mentioned to James that he was intending to investigate the possibilities of becoming a freight broker, James enthusiastically encouraged his interests. He arranged a meeting with Captain Gray who had just purchased two of the new fast Yankee Clipper ships and was intending to expand Little Flower Navigation Company's reach to the Orient. James arranged for warehouse space to be made available for Clay's business and gave him his recommendation to Banker Ramsdale who was more than pleased to be part of the new venture by extending the bank's credit. Soon Clay was swept up into the excitement of his new enterprise. He was buying large lots of hides, tallow, wine, furs and through the offices of Captain Gray, had contacted a factor in Hong Cong as his agent to sell his products and in turn buy and ship back to the states tea, porcelain, furniture, rice, silk, and spices. Up and down the coast he found ready markets for his products and was soon chartering the entire cargo space on the Yankee Clippers flying under the Little Flower flag.

While Clay was busily engaged in getting his business off the ground, James turned his attention to the matter of getting Little Flower introduced to the community she was now a part of. Here again, he found the assistance of Angeline most valuable as she gave Little Flower instructions in etiquette and tried to familiarize her with the more influential members of the community whom she would meeting. A wardrobe was also in order, but Angeline insisted that Little Flower not give up her identity and try to imitate the matrons of the city. "You have a beautiful body and you shouldn't try to hide it behind all that flounce and foolery that is the fashion in the city."

With the help of a seamstress, Angeline and Little Flower designed a wardrobe that accented her ancestry and with the judicious use of materials and design were both interesting and provocative. The dresses were not dissimilar to the one Little Flower had designed for herself from the materials James gifted her with at the mine. Accenting her outfit for her début, James had a jeweler design from her normal headband one that was studded with diamonds and rubies. It was too Little Flower her most cherished possession.

"You are a Princess;" Angeline assured Little Flower, "Don't worry about what others do. You must be yourself. You must create interest and talk. That's what society in this town is all about; talk, talk, talk."

Little Flowers appearance at Banker Ramsdale's home created a social sensation. No one present seemed at all concerned about her linage, but all were interested in her struggles to survive as she nursed James back to health and struggled south through the winter snows to where the Little Flower Mine was found. In their mind, Little Flower's identity with the newest gold bonanza was all the credentials she needed to be the honored quest at the Ramsdale function and others that would follow. James could not have been more pleased and he often faded into the background and let Little Flower glow in her own charming light. James noticed a radiance about her that he attributed to her new motherhood and the assurance she now gained as a social icon.

Very little had been discussed between Little Flower and James as to the welfare of the children. The children were accepted as a part of their family without much thought given to the matter until one Monday morning a stranger came calling at the Rawlins residence.

"I'm the Uncle of that brood of children you brought out of the wilderness and I came to claim them," the stranger announced after he was ushered into James' study where James had been reviewing the latest output reports from the Little Flower Mine. James looked at the man for a long moment. His clothes, though clean were threadbare. He was tall, thin and gangly in appearance. He had thick black eyebrows, a long thin nose that that lost itself in an unkempt mustache. His skin had a grayish pallor to it like one who had spent his life in a coal mine. Little George, who had been playing with his toy soldiers across room, ran out into the hallway upon hearing the demands of the stranger and was heard calling to his sister July.

James, knowing the effectiveness of Indian stoicism when confronted by the demands of a stranger, did not respond, but merely stared the man down until the stranger cast his eyes downward toward his feet and began to crumple and uncrumple his felt hat which he had removed upon entering the study.

"I do recall the children had mentioned having an uncle. I made inquires as to their kin and have found none that they admitted to. Just who the hell are you and what interest do you have in these children."

"I'm their uncle through marriage. I married Cora Appleton who be the sister of this broods mother. Cora, bless her soul, has passed on. She got the cholera coming west. I figure it be my Christian duty to see to the upbringing of her kin and not leave them be in the hands of a stranger."

James, although he could have invited this stranger to sit, felt it best to leave him standing. James suspected that this man was up to no good.

Taking a sheet of paper, James asked the man what his full name was, where he lived and what he did for a living. When he asked him if he had enough money to take care of the children, the stranger, who now identified himself as Albert Knutson told James that that matter was none of his business. James was still trying to read in the face of the man any signs of real compassion or concern for the welfare for the children and could detect none. When James asked him how he knew that the children were even in his care, Knutson admitted that he had read of the matter in the local papers. James' rescue of the children and Emma Martin and her children had been written up with the series of articles that related the stories of his reunion with Clay.

James was trying to make up his mind if Knutson was not a mere impostor seeking some payment for a claim or whether he was an actual relative whose demand would be respected in a court of law. Either way, James was beginning to suspect that the man's interest was more in a money settlement than for the welfare of the children. It was while these thoughts were swirling about his brain, that July entered the room and slipped up beside him, placing her arm about his shoulders. James could feel the tension in July's body as she leaned over and whispered in is ear.

"I don't like him. Don't send us away with him, please, Oh Please!"

"Do you know this man?" James asked her.

"He's our uncle." Saying that July, demanded of the stranger, "Where is Aunt Cora?"

"Why your dear Aunt done passed on coming over the Oregon Trail. There's just me and you children left now and I come to claim you."

James could feel July quiver at that last comment by Knutson.

"We are happy here," July responded. "Go away!"

By now Little George and Linda had come into the study. Linda crawled onto James lap and peered apprehensively at the stranger. George stood beside his sister July and gave the man a defiant, angry stare.

James, knowing that Knutson had a relationship to the children, and that he had no filial claim, decided that the best course was to stall for time and get his lawyer involved. He had no intention of turning the children over to this man, especially when he noticed the lascivious look on his face as Knutson ran his eyes up and down July's slim body now ripening into womanhood.

"It doesn't appear that the children share your enthusiasm for a family reunion," James remarked, "but let us not get over wrought about this. You come into my home and start making demands I am not prepared to meet. Come back in a few days and I will have an answer for you."

"You'll do no such thing," Knutson responded, his eyes narrowing and face contorting. "Them is my kin and I will be taking them now." At that Knutson pulled from his pocket a paper and threw it on James' desk. The paper was an order signed by the Justice of the Peace ordering James Rawlins to surrender unto Albert Knutson the custody of the named children.

"You git smart with me and I'll have the sheriff on you. That there is an official order and you best obey it."

Little Flower had now entered the room and stood at the doorway, a terrified look upon her face, her hands held tightly to her chest.

James, affronted by the belligerency of Knutson, knowing he would never give up custody of the children to this man, gave Linda over to Little Flower and walked over to the coat rack where his bowie knife now hung and strapped it about his waist, put on his hat, picked up the order from his desk and turned to Little Flower, "Would you be so kind as to have the carriage brought about. Mr. Knutson and I are going to see this Justice of the Peace."

Little Flower bade the children to follow her and headed down the hallway to order the carriage.

"I ain't goin' nowheres with you. I'll be taking my kin and leaving by myself!"

James now turned to confront Knutson, his hand on the hilt of his bowie knife. "You are standing in my house. You will make no demands of me. You will come with me peacefully, or I will carve up your sorry ass and take you in pieces."

Clay, who was still residing in the house, now entered the room. He had overheard the shouting and came to see what the problem was. Clay crossed the room to where the two men confronted each other, James about to spring on Knutson, and Knutson now backing away. As Knutson turned to rush out the door, he ran into Clay who grabbed him by the scruff of his neck, half lifting him off his feet.

"The man says we are going to see the Justice of the Peace. You best be coming along, I know this man when he pulls that knife. It ain't too pretty."

Things had gone all wrong for Albert Knutson. When he read the article in the paper and discovered that the children were residing in the home of a multi millionaire, he devised a scheme to extort money from James believing James would not be willing to turn the children over to him. He was a frequent visitor to the Gold Dust Tavern where a fellow patron was a Justice of the Peace with a weakness for good whiskey. Over a period of a few weeks, he had met and become a confident of the Justice and it was the Justice who, upon hearing of his intentions had issued the order in question, assuming that his friend Albert would be successful and have ample funds so they could indulge together in their habit. The Justice did not have a clear head when he signed the order, for a justice of the Peace had no authority to enter such and order. This was the flaw in Knutson's scheme that James, knowing a little about the law from all his business dealings, suspected.

James and Clay set Knutson on the seat opposite them as the carriage proceeded toward the business district. Noticing that Knutson was getting fidgety and looking toward the door of the carriage as if he might bolt through the door, James and then Clay set their leg to rest in the seat opposite them, blocking the door. Knutson, even though the weather was moderate was sweating profusely as the carriage stopped in front of the Law offices where James dismounted and soon returned with lawyer Madison in tow. The carriage then proceeded to the office of the Justice of the Peace where the four of them entered the Justice's court where he was listening to arguments from two litigants, one of which had supposedly killed the other's pig that was trespassing on his garden plot. As the four of them sat on the bench awaiting the completion of the trial, the Justice was scrutinizing them and became distracted from the proceedings before him. James carefully watched the expression on Knutson's face to see if he would attempt to warn the Justice of the reason for their presence. The lawyer presenting the case for the pig owner, noting the Justices distraction and the affect it was having on his presentation asked for a recess which was quickly granted.

James' lawyer was quick to his feet and before the Justice could retire to his chambers, laid before him the Order of Restitution and demanded if the Justice had indeed signed it.

"That's my order, now what is this all about?" The Justice demanded.

"By what authority did you enter it? Do you usually enter orders without notice to the other affected party?" The attorney asked.

The Justice looked the order over and then looked at Clay, James and Knutson still sitting in the front row bench. "If these are the people involved, then let's have our hearing," the Justice responded, trying to gain command of the situation.

"Let's not be in such a hurry, your honor," the attorney responded. "I believe the civil code requires that the children in question be present and represented and that the court has the duty to interview the children to determine what is best for their welfare. But than I wouldn't expect your honor to be knowledgeable of these things since his court has no jurisdiction in the matter. My suggestion, your honor, is that you revoke this illegal order and bring an end to this charade.

The justice was red faced by now and knew he was in trouble. His position was by appointment, and the lawyer standing before him and his prominent client could make real trouble for him. As for Knutson, the Justice felt no obligation.

"Do you have such an order ready?"

"My clerk will have it here shortly."

Knutson was ready to bolt for the door and be done with the affair, knowing he had been bested, but a firm grip on his arm held him vice like to his spot.

"We are not done with this thing yet. I am advised by my lawyer that what you have tried to do is a fraud and I can have you put in jail. I am a reasonable man, however," James advised Knutson. "Let's have an end to this matter once and for all. My lawyer is preparing papers stating that you relinquish all claims as kin to the Summers children. If you sign those papers, there will be a stipend awaiting you. Not what you expected, but enough to get you well out of town. Do you understand me?" James was now face to face with Knutson, the menace written clearly on his face.

"Don't like this damn town much anyway," Knutson responded as he now shuffled his way out of the court under the watchful eyes of Clay and James. The papers were signed that afternoon, but before James left his lawyers office he instructed the lawyer to start the necessary proceedings for his and Little Flower's adoption of the Summers children.

James had one other visitation that summer, this one not so contentious. Cactus Jack called at the Rawlins residence one afternoon with a long face under the pretense that he wanted to see the children. July and Little Flower had been spending some time with Jack at Jack's Mission and James assumed the visitation had something to do with the Mission. Cactus Jack hung around for the afternoon had lunch with the family but remained silent most of the time. After the lunch, James herded Jack to his study.

"You been walking about with that hang dog look long enough, Jack, now what is it that bothers you?"

Jack looked at him, letting out a long, deliberate sigh. "My Daisy died last night". He tried to say more, but his throat was constricted and the tears started flowing. James stepped to the decanter on the side board and poured a strong shot of Cognac and handed it to Jack.

"I am so sorry, Jack. I know how much she meant to you. She was more than a friend could have been."

When Jack took a few swallows of the Cognac and regained his composure, he continued. "She was a sweet thing. She saved my sorry ass more than once. I don't know how old she was; found her wandering about in the desert. She came to me wanting water and has been with me some twenty years now."

James was not surprised when Cactus Jack informed him that he was done with his travels and wanted no more to do with the Little Flower Mine.

"I got enough to do at the Mission. The Banker's wife has been a big help, but says we need to do something about the orphans that's gathering about. I got me a plate full. If you can keep puttin' money in my account from the mine diggings, I will find a way to spend it. I'll be settlin' down now and you've got to handle matters from now on without me."

James assured him that the Mission would be adequately funded. "You are still part owner whether you work the mine or not. I will see that you get progress reports to see how things are going."

"Don't be botherin' me with all that stuff. I knows you will do right by me. I trust you like you was my son, which you most are."

James gave the old man a hug and walked him to the door with his arm about his shoulders. "Everything I've got, Jack came to me when you wondered into my camp and found the gold that was right under my nose. I'll do right by you Jack, you're not to worry."

James sat for a long time in his study lost in his memories of Cactus Jack and their time spent together at the mine. Little Flower wandered in and interrupted his reveries.

"Where is Jack? Has he gone?"

James told her of Jack's real reason for his visit. Little Flower responded, "he's been more than a friend. The time I spent at the mine with him while you were gone, he treated me as his daughter and made me feel good. I will go see him tomorrow. He will hurt a long time over his loss of Daisy. I love that old man like a father. He needs our company. I will ask him to come stay with us. The children will love it and he could use their company."

James, sitting now in his overstuffed chair with Little Flower on his lap, kissed her neck. "You are right, he shouldn't be alone now. We have enough room in this house to run it as a hotel. It would be good to have him about."

His encounter with Cactus Jack and the confrontation over the children brought to James a yearning to see his sister. He had planned to see her last year, but his business and the business that was keeping Clay engaged kept the two friends from setting a date for the visitation. Now Clay was somewhere in the Orient making business arrangements and would not be back for several months. James now resolved that upon Clay's return, they would book passage to Oregon.

WILLIAM

The seasons in the Willamette Valley came and went presenting to the newly arrived settlers a land of plenty and a perfusion of dramatically pleasing vistas. They had abandoned homes in lands of privation and continual conflicts, sailed the violent seas on barely commodious vessels, traversed a continent in a foreign land and joined with fellow travelers who had traveled not so far, but had shared in the desperate days along the Oregon Trail, where each day brought grueling confrontations with a hostile nature and occasional brushes with hostile Indians. Now settling upon claims honored by their government and challenged by the natives, they turned with a vengeance against those natives who respected not their claims nor understood nor accepted the laws upon which they were based.

The native Indians, often driven by hunger as the game once abundant vanished under the relentless hunting and land clearing of the settlers, often fell upon the wandering livestock of the settlers in need of food. Often, the natives would attack and kill the settlers in their homes in hopes of driving them from the land once theirs; land that belonged to no one but the great spirits the natives revered. The natives watched with disdain and incomprehension as the white man with their instruments and chains measured off sections of their heritage and claimed the lands within their markings as theirs alone. They watched these white men mark trails that the great emergent trains would follow as the white men swarmed into their lands. They witnessed the coming of the prospectors who wandered among them digging about the land in search of metals the Gods had planted. They had no comprehension of the system of wealth that drove these miners ever deeper and in ever increasing numbers onto their hunting grounds.

For every deprivation the Indians visited upon the white settlers, the retaliation was relentless, violent and clearly out of proportion to the wrong done. When the Indian killed a white man he was hanged. When a white man killed an Indian, he was honored. The Natives were insulted by the injustice of the settlers and their conception of justice. Of the Cayuse Indians who had attacked the Whitman Mission, many who were innocent and who had not participated in the event were taken to Oregon City and subjected to the white man's conception of justice and were hung without honor in a way that insulted the custom of the Natives. The "Great White Father" whom they were told would protect them if they surrendered their lands, was far away and not available to their petitioning. The agent of the "Great White Father" named Stevens came onto their lands and demanded they sign papers giving them their richest lands in exchange for promises of protection from the white man and on the assurance that the "Great White Father" would provide for their needs. This man Stevens did not understand that in the Indian Nation no chief could command the submission or loyalty of all the tribes nor could any tribe make treaties that bound others. For his own convenience this man Stevens appointed chiefs among the tribes and negotiated with them for the removal of the tribes to the reservations he selected. Yet the wise men of the Indian Nation counseled submission to these unequal demands. There would be no peace and the killing would go on until the last red man was killed if some accommodation could not be reached.

It was not just the white man's militias that raided their villages that drove the elders to submission; it was also the arrival of more and more of the white man's regiments of organized soldiers that convinced the elders to submit. They knew that in time the white man's soldiers would overwhelm them and their chance of settlement would be diminished. Yet the braves, who were born to war, would not listen nor would they respect the words of the white man who were usually the first to ignore the promises of the "Great White Father" and trespass indiscriminately upon their lands. The time for words had passed and the flame of hatred spread across the lands of the Northwest William had been sent from Salem as a representative of the Oregon Governor to petition the Army to send a punitive force into southern Oregon to drive the Rogue River Indians back onto the reservations and punish those who had been raiding the settlers in central and southern Oregon. As a former Captain of the State Militia, William, who was also one of the state's best known lawyers, was considered the most promising representative to persuade the man that the Oregon Governor knew to be a reluctant warrior. General John E. Wool looked at the young lawyer sitting before him with disdain. The General, now in his seventies, had a long and lustrous career in the service of his nation. He distinguished himself along with Chief of the Army Winfield Scott in the War of 1812. He was able to mount the first organized resistance to confront the British as they marched upon Washington D.C. He served with Zachary Taylor with distinction in the Battle of Buena Vista in the Mexican war and had there been honored for his bravery and initiative. He had been a reluctant participant in the tragic removal of the Cherokee nation from Georgia and Tennessee to the desolate lands west of the Mississippi. He was now the Commander of the Department of the

Pacific presiding over a territory well beyond the means of his underfunded and under armed peace time army. ([37])

He had witnessed with contempt the efforts of Governor Stevens to settle the Northwest Indians onto reservations with treaties he knew to be unequal and mostly unacceptable to the majority of the tribal members. The General was under the impression that the Army was best suited to deal with the Indian question and that the civil authority was driven by greed and hatred. "The only good Indian was a dead Indian" was a slogan much in vogue among the settlers. The General felt that the Army's best purpose was to prevent the settlers from encroaching on the Indian lands and that in most of the confrontations, the Indians were more often justified in their retaliations.

Keeping the white man away from the Indian lands was the Army's policy under his command and Governor Stevens was a major interloper in that effort. The General had before him as he sat facing the young lawyer the most recent report from Captain Smith at Fort Lane. The Captain reported that when attempting to remove 400 Indians to a reservation in western Oregon from Eastern Oregon, the citizens of the territory had threatened to kill all of the Indians. One had been murdered when in the protection of the soldiers. He had the recent report also on his desk of the treatment of the friendly Yakima Chief Peu-peu-mox-mox, who had come under a flag of truce to meet with a volunteer militia troop only to be murdered and mutilated.

The General had recently declared all of Washington east of the Cascade to be off limits to white settlement, an edict that had infuriated Governor Stevens and had been generally ignored by the emigrants. The General was certain that the main cause of the hostilities in Oregon were the result of the public demands by many of the citizens and several newspapers for the extermination of the Indians. Twenty –five friendly Indians had recently been killed in southern Oregon as they were headed for a reservation under orders of the Army. The militias that were running rampart in Oregon were killing innocent Indians, women and children included. The General had warned Governor Stevens that his conduct must be stopped, the militias disbanded and the Army would take charge

---

[37] John E. Wool-Wikipedia, http://en.wikipedia.org/wiki/hohn_E._Wool

of all further activity regarding the Indians. This, and the edict regarding Eastern Washington, would soon terminate the General's command as Washington would side with Governor Stevens.

When history records an accumulation of grievances, one risks presumption to declare that any one wrong was the catalyst that drove distrustful men to impose upon others the brutalities of war. The conditions that underlie the start of hostilities were numerous. To the red men it was the festering indignation over the unequal retribution for the wrongs committed by but a few of their number. The insistence of the white men to indiscriminately and indignantly hang Indians perceived to be involved in depredations was a continuing irritant. The flood of prospectors and settlers onto the lands Governor Stevens and the Army said would be theirs, justified in the minds of the Natives, their retaliation against these trespassers. To be punished for defending what was said to be theirs was a wrong they could not accept.

To the white man, it was their intolerance for the customs and conduct of a race they chose to disdain. They were driven to self righteousness by the concept of "manifest destiny" a concept that justified their possession of "uninhabited" lands and to claim those lands for America. It was the same obsession that justified the European nations, under the euphemism of "the white man's burden" to subjugate the black and brown races of Africa and the Far East. One could not ignore the singular greed and opportunism of the individual that clothed himself in the flags of nations.

The flames in the northwest were finally ignited when an emissary of Governor Stevens was brutally murdered while attempting to reach the Governor who was than in Eastern Washington Territory. There was also the recent murder of the friendly Yakima Chief Peu peu mox mox, referred to in the report to General Wool, who had approached a militia group under a flag of truce. His body was dismembered to provide souvenirs for the militia members. Militias in both Oregon and the Washington Territory were organized and, along with regular army troops went into the field to fight a number of skirmishes, some successful, others disastrous.

In Oregon, William was once again called to duty and headed a troop of volunteers sent to quell the rebellious Rouge River Indians. His efforts to persuade General Wool to send troops into southern Oregon had not succeeded, for the General did not want his troops serving with what he considered to be a rouge militia. William had a troop of forty men who were well armed and experienced. Many had ridden with him into Central Oregon in search of the Indians who had attacked and killed his brother's party. William felt good to once again take command of the troops. He, along with many of the members of his troop had festering resentment against the Indians and wanted them destroyed as a menace and this was the time for doing. The Rouge River country was unlike any the volunteers had fought in before. The rugged hills and narrow valleys were heavily forested and thick with vine maple, scrub oak, and a variety of other bushes that made travel difficult. Along the valleys were scattered the remnants of the wagon trains and the graves of many that had followed the Applegate trail into Oregon.

As they proceeded into the southern plane along the Umpqua River, they found to their distress the burned out lodging of a number of homesteaders who had claimed their lands in the fertile valleys along the river. What settlers remained had built block houses and were prepared to defend themselves until relieved by the Army that had come and gone to no benefit. Other volunteers were added to their ranks as they headed into the Rouge River Valley where the volunteers were certain they would finally confront the hostile tribes.

Their first contact was but distillatory firing from the thickets, meant to harass the troops. William, finding the trails too narrow and the terrain too difficult, finally ordered his men to dismount and proceed on foot.

"You make easy targets sitting on top of your horses. Get down where the brush will give you protection. We'll have to root these savages out and force the fight."

For an entire day they struggled through the rugged hills along the passes heading south and east, but could not engage the Indians who were determined not to become engaged in close contact with the better armed volunteers. As night began to fall, the men of the volunteers were exhausted. Many were suffering from sprains and bruises as they struggled through the rocky canyons and over ridges. When William called a halt and assembled the men to turn them back, they came under heavy fire from the Indians who surrounded them. William, ordered his men to charge up the valley. Taking his pistol and slinging his rifle over his shoulder, he charged ahead to lead his men into the battle they had been waiting for. William had taken but a few lunging steps forward when a well aimed bullet entered his forehead and brought him down. William never saw the Indian who had fired the shot, nor would that have mattered. He died instantly, his revolver still clutched in his hand, his mouth still uttering the call to arms.

The loss of the popular Captain William Anderson and the defeat of the volunteers on the Rouge River was a hard blow for the settlers of Oregon to accept. Soon they had organized a retaliatory raid, knowing that the defeat of the volunteers would encourage the Indians to even more and more brutal raids. Soon a contingent of 400 volunteers and soldiers were headed into southern Oregon with orders to find and destroy the Indian villages and drive the hostiles onto their reservations. How many they killed was a matter not discussed, but killing Indians was their obsession that festered in the minds of all.

STEPTOE

The rising hostility among the Native tribes against the white settlers necessitated the presence of the army in the Walla Walla area where the Cayuse, Spokane, Palouse, Coeur d'Alene and Yakima tribes were confederating. This hostility resulted in the construction of Fort Walla Walla near the site of the abandoned Whitman Mission. Command of the fort was given to Colonel Edward Steptoe, a veteran of the Indian wars in Florida and along the old Northwest frontier. He gained his military credentials, like his contemporaries in Mexico during the Mexican War where he earned distinction at Cerro Gordo and in the Battle of Chapultepec. His years of service had not come without sacrifice. At the time of his assignment to Fort Walla Walla, he was suffering from ill-health and a possible heart ailment. When word reached Colonel Clark, the successor in command to General Wool, that the Eastern Washington tribes were raiding and that prospectors in the Colville vicinity had been killed, Colonel Clark ordered Colonel Steptoe to lead an expedition into the area and settle the tribes and reassure the settlers. ([38])

---

[38] History Link Essay: Yakima, Palouse, Spokane, and Coeur d' Alene warriors rout U.S. Ar… Http://www.hitorylink.org/essays/output.cfn?fiel_id=5162

Colonel Steptoe sat in silence contemplating the orders he held in his hands. He had read them several times and finally set them aside and moved across the clapboard floors of his sparsely furnished office and stared out at the parade ground where a desultory effort was been made to bring discipline to troops that had minimal motivation. The Colonel regretted the necessity that underscored the orders. Colonel Steptoe had been sent into the field against the Cherokee in Florida and was a reluctant participant in their removal from Florida to the lands west of the Mississippi. He had fought the Seminoles and helped subdue that tribe. Since being stationed in the Northwest, he had fought in several encounters one along the Columbia River at the small settlement at Cascade. He had fought in the defense of Fort Dalles and also Fort Walla Walla where he was now in command. His sympathies were with the natives who he felt were merely reacting to the continued encroachment on their lands. He knew General Wool had held the same sympathies. The Army officials in the West reluctantly responded to their orders to quell the tribes, knowing they were usually striking against the innocent rather than the instigator.

The natives were no match for the Army of the West as they had no understanding of tactic and fought more as individuals and tribal units than a unified force. Time was running against the natives and he must now go into the field one more time to restrain them before they crossed the boundary where their hostilities would demand that the Army become once again the unwilling instrument of their subjugation.

Looking again at the parade, his thoughts returned to the slack performance of the troops. Perhaps this new assignment would serve to motivate the troops and provide an opportunity for training. Most of the troops had never been on a serious patrol let alone faced hostiles. The Colonel had been successful in pacifying the Cayuse tribes and had good relations with the Nez Perce and Walla Walla tribes and had little reason to believe that he would not be able to deal with the restless tribes to the north. The Spokane, Coeur d'Alene, Yakima and Colville tribes had given Governor Stevens cause for concern, but the Army had generally sided with the tribes. Yes, this would be a good exercise for the troops he concluded as he called for Lieutenant Gaston, his Executive officer.

"We'll be taking a little trip up to Fort Colville and settle down the tribes. Those prospectors have been stirring them up. We'll take three companies of Dragoons and a Company of the 9th Infantry mounted. See to the details."

Steptoe returned to his desk and sat down as a slight dizzy spell overcame him. He loosened the color of his tunic and took some deep breaths as he felt that familiar fluttering in his chest. "The damn heat," he muttered. He considered consulting the medical officer to see if there were not some potion he might prepare to alleviate the symptoms he had been experiencing, but decided against it. He had sought medical advice before and was advised that his heart was not strong. The medicines they gave him did little good and usually made him feel worse.

On May 15, the Colonel stood before the assembled troops and as the sun cast its first rays across the parade, he moved among them to inspect their gear. He was not comforted by what he saw. These troops were mostly raw recruits and unlike the troops he commanded at Vera Cruz and Cerro Gordo, they appeared ill suited for the task that lay before them. But then, the Colonel mused, what soldier is ever ready for his first confrontation on the field of battle. It was comforting to the Colonel that a battle was unlikely. Their mission was to show the flag.

The troop had moved but a short distance from the Fort to the ferry operated by the Nez Perce at Red Wolf's crossing of the Snake River when it became obvious that the wagons were to heavily loaded for the terrain. The Colonel ordered the troop to return to the Fort where much of the supplies and ammunition was unloaded. The column of 158 men then proceeded with its mission armed with two howitzers.

The troops proceeded in a long column following the established trail that meandered through the gentle rolling hills of the Palouse. About noon one of the scouts came galloping up to the Colonel and reported: "There's hostiles gathered ahead of us. Mostly they's keepin' to the ridges and ain't doin' nothin' but watching."

'Keep an eye on them Sergeant and don't let them come among us. I doubt they mean any harm."

As the troop moved on in a long file the mood of the Indians began to change and they started taunting the troops waving their rifles, bows and spears and at times made feigned charges at the troops. The Colonel noted that most of the Indians were dressed in their war bonnets, were painted and rode ponies that were also decorated with the war signs of the tribes.

Steptoe for the first time began to assess his situation. His scouts had reported that there were somewhere between 800 to 1200 hostiles on the hills above the column. His force which seemed so formidable when it started its march north now seemed inadequate. "What tribes are up there?" Steptoe asked his Executive Officer.

"I make it to be a confederation of the Spokane, Palouse, Coeur d'Alene, and Yakimas. I'm told that Chief Kamiakin may be leading some of them," Lieutenant Gaston reported."I suggest, sir, we try to parlay with them. Things could get out of hand if one of them fires into the Troop."

Colonel Steptoe was not pleased to hear that the Yakima Chief Kamiakin was with his tribe on the ridges above. Kamiakin had led his braves against a punitive expedition lead by Major Haller and drove Haller from the field at a battle along the Yakima River a few years before. He had since attacked the small settlement at Cascade Falls on the Columbia River and had been hunted by the Army every since.

Near evening the troop approached a small lake and halted. Steptoe was soon visited by several Spokane Chiefs who wanted to parley. When Steptoe advised them that his mission was not hostile to their interest the Chiefs expressed their doubts.

"You bring big guns and travel onto our lands far from the trail to Fort Colville," one of the chiefs responded. "My people do not want you on our land."

"We have no quarrel with your people. We have come this way because your tribe has always ferried our soldiers across the Spokane River," the Colonel retorted.

"No use ferry, most go back," was the Chief's adamant response. Hearing this news, the Colonel knew he would have to abort his mission and bivouacked for the night.

The troop spent a restless night as the Indians, camped about them kept up a constant drumming. The troops got little sleep as they were treated to the constant war whoops and war chants of the Indians as they prepared for the coming confrontation. The Colonel knew he was in a desperate situation and that his troops were badly outnumbered. More braves would probably be joining the hostiles by morning. His intelligence was not good but he knew he was outnumbered at least seven to one. He now had cause to regret his decision to unload the wagons at the Fort. As a precaution, the Colonel dispatched one of his scouts Wie-cat back to the Fort with a request for reinforcements. Wie-cat, believing the situation of the soldiers was hopeless, rode instead to the camp of the Walla Walla Indians and urged them to attack the now lightly defended Fort. The next morning when the troop mounted up and headed back toward the Fort, the Indians became more emboldened believing that the troop was in retreat and intimidated by their presence. Their actions became ever more provocative.

At mid morning one of the Palouse braves fired into the troops. The Infantry Company was ordered to return fire to drive the braves back. Their first volley dropped several of the Coeur d' Alene chiefs who were riding in front of their warriors. This action enraged the Indians and the battle was on. From atop the ridges the Indians began firing into the ranks. Their trade rifles, though not the best rifles available, were far superior to the weapons provided the troopers. The Jaeger rifles furnished to the Infantry, could not be reloaded while the soldiers were mounted, the muskatoons carried by the Dragoons were short-ranged and inaccurate.

The Indians were yelling taunts as they fired from the ridges and the Colonel knew they could not withstand the constant assault. He ordered Lieutenants Taylor and Gaston to clear the ridges. He watched in horror as both of his able young officers were felled as they drove up the ridges to dislodge the Indians. The effort to dislodge the Indians was, however, successful and the troop in a long file fought their way back toward Fort Walla Walla. When the Indians attacked the center of his column and drove off his pack animals, the Colonel ordered his troops toward a high promontory and formed a defensive perimeter. The soldiers fought desperately the remainder of the day as the Indians mounted attack after attack. As night fell and the natives returned to camp the Colonel called his remaining officers together to inform them that they would stand and fight to the last man.

"We're not with you on that one Colonel," one of his officers responded. "We're down to but a few rounds of ammunition per man. We ain't got our sabers, they was left at the Fort. We will be overrun by noon. We best run for it."

The Colonel had been in enough battles to know that once his troops were in the open they would be scattered and killed indiscriminately. He did not want his men to die so ignobly. It would be a slaughter. Five of his men including two of his best officers lay dead already and fifteen troopers were wounded.

Before the Colonel could issue his command to dig in, one of is Nez Perce scouts was seen approaching with Sergeant Beeker. "What is it Sergeant?" Steptoe demanded.

"The scout says they ain't gaurdin' the trail east of here and he can lead us out of this mess."

The Colonel was quick to act upon hearing the scout's report. To his assembled officers he ordered: "Every man is to discard all but absolutely essential gear, cut up the blankets and muffle the horses hoofs, see that every piece of equipment that can rattle or make noise is muffled, disassemble and bury the howitzers, leave three men behind as a rear guard to keep the fires going so the hostiles will think we're still here. Tell the surgeon to get rid of all the alcohol he's got and make sure no spirits are left about to rile up the savages any more than they be.

Within an hour the troop was on the move. The Colonel stood beside the trail and watched each man as he rode past; issuing instructions to any trooper who had not complied with his orders. As the troopers headed off the mountain and turned south, the Colonel waited for the first report of a fire arm, as he was certain their luck could not hold. After they had gone but a mile the Colonel ordered the pace quickened and as the dawn approached he received reports that they were not being followed and they had indeed escaped. The Colonel did not doubt that they would soon be pursued and pressed his troops even harder. They reached the Snake River crossing exhausted, hungry and thirsty to be greeted by Chief Lawyer of the Nez Perce with a large contingent of braves. To the Colonel's relief, the Chief was riding under the banner of an American flag and was on a mission to rescue the troopers. Chief Lawyer provided cover for the troops as they fell exhausted from their saddles and rested. But unlike the troops, exhausted from several days of battle, the Colonel could not rest.

As he stood by the banks of the Snake River, looking across to the Fort he commanded, he well knew that when he crossed that river, his ordeal would be over. It was a comfort to him to know that his troop was now safe and that he had lead them out of harm's way. To his regret he also knew that as this chapter closed, so would his Army career. He had fought for his nation in the Seminole War, had fought for his country to the gates of Mexico City and fulfilled so many of those dreams had had obsessed his days as a Cadet when he attended that Citadel on the Hudson. He proudly wore the emblem of a field officer, a rank not earned by many. He had earned that distinction for valor and for the victories that attended his efforts. What was ending this day would earn him no distinction. He had failed in his duty and he knew the consequences. The pain in his chest had increased during the night. He needed rest and was anxious to get across the river to the Fort.

As he stood ruminating over his fate, he had not noticed that Chief Lawyer was now standing by his side.

"Tomorrow we take you across river to Fort. There you be safe," the Chief remarked, interrupting the Colonel's thoughts.

The Colonel now turned to the tall, stern countenance beside him. The Chief was wrapped in a trade blanket and like the Colonel was staring across the river.

"I thank you greatly for your loyalty to the Army and certainly for your assistance today," the Colonel responded. "But I fear this is not the end of the matter. Across that river, there will soon be arriving another thousand and more wagons bringing the settlers and adventurers that have a hunger for your lands and the land of those tribes that attacked us at To-Hoto-Min-Me. Those tribes have brought shame upon the Army that has been their friend and protected them and their land from settlement. Now the Army must save face and it will march against them in far greater numbers than I command. The braves who fought against us showed great courage. They know not, however, what they have brought onto themselves by what they have now done."

"Our soldiers have been trained in the art of war. Our lessons go back to the days of the Romans in Centuries long past. We have learned the art of war in a thousand battles in lands far away and those braves who drove my troops from the field will soon face a vengeance that will destroy them. They will lose their lands, the settlers will take them and their way of life will end. Your people, the Nez Perce, have been our good friends; let us hope your good deeds will be remembered." Having said that the Colonel turned and walked away into the darkness.

At Fort Vancouver, Colonel George Wright solemnly read the report received from Colonel Steptoe. The loss of two promising young Lieutenants and the embarrassment of the army at the battle of To-Hoto-Min-Me (later referred to as the Battle of Steptoe Butte) in Eastern Washington Territory was now a festering issue between the civil government and the Army. The Army was being accused of precipitating the now raging frontier war because of its misplaced sympathy for the Indians. Colonel Clark, now promoted to General ordered Colonel Wright into the field to quell the rising rebellion. Colonel Wright felt sadness for his old friend and fellow soldier, Colonel Steptoe whose foolish mustering of an ill-equipped expedition had given the Indians the opportunity to drive the Army from the field. The days of leniency were now past. The burdened now fell upon his shoulders to redeem the Army's prestige. He had treated in the past with the tribes and knew well who the ringleaders were. They must now be brought to justice, disarmed and driven onto the reservations Governor Stevens had designated. Eastern Washington must now be open for settlement. The Native Tribes had played their last hand. Colonel Wright would now assure that it was the loser's hand.

Colonel Wright assumed the Command at Fort Walla Walla and bid his old friend Colonel Steptoe farewell as the Colonel headed east into eventual retirement and an early death. Colonel Wright would not make the same mistake as did Colonel Steptoe. He trained his troops well and rearmed them with new long range Springfield breach loading rifles. When his contingent of over five hundred soldiers headed north, it was a formidable presence, but that did not discourage the tribes from trying to repeat their performance against Colonel Steptoe but a few months before. As the Indians rode the ridges and started firing down on the troops they discovered that the soldiers now had superior weapons and were picking them off at a greater distance than their own bullets would carry. Colonel Wright was able to drive the tribes from the ridges and confront them on the prairie in an area known as Four Lakes where their superior tactics and organization drove the tribes from the field. When the Indians retreated into the woods where they thought they could better confront the cavalry that drove into them in waves, the Colonel did not peruse them, but instead brought up the cannon and drove them from the woods and again into the open where the cavalry cut swaths through their ranks driving them into disorganized retreat. The army severely battered the Indian tribes and the tribes retreated toward the Spokane Falls, where Colonel Wright pursued them and set up camp along the river.

The next day, the Colonel was informed that the Indians were moving their horses north and preparing to renew hostilities. The Colonel reacted quickly, rounded up over five hundred of their horses and shot the lot of them in one bloody, terrible slaughter. The Indians knew they were now at the army's mercy and asked for terms which were summarily rejected. Colonel Wright demanded their complete surrender. As the tribes gathered to capitulate, Colonel Wright arrested those among them he suspected of instigating hostilities or of killing any of the settlers. The suspected offenders were summarily hung at a tributary of the Spokane River, later known as Hangman's Creek. The Northwest Indian war was over. ([39])

JENNY

Jenny stood on the steps of the small mission school as the Spaldings rode away, leaving behind them the bitter sweet memory of their labors which held such promise in the beginning but became a promise lost in the frustrating endeavor to reform an Indian nation that had no understanding of the white man's religion and would not convert to the worship of the white man's spirits. Chief Joseph of the Nez Perce had urged Jenny to stay on and continue to operate the school which was having some limited success in teaching if not converting the young pupils who were attending her school at the insistence of the Chief. Jenny found little satisfaction in the work she had undertaken. Her students were steeped in the traditions of a proud race and gave scant attention to Jenny's lessons. Their great Chief could send them to the school, but he could not make them learn, nor could Jenny.

Franklin Washington, Molly's son was the exception. He learned to read within a few months and was becoming affluent in the white man's language. His penmanship lessons were troublesome to him, but his efforts

---

[39] History Link Essay: U.S. Army Colnel George Wright hangs Yakima and Palouse prison…; http://www.historylink.org/essays/output.cfm?fiele_id=5141; See also Dryden's History of Washington, supra. P 136-140

at making letters and signs held his fascination and he would not give Jenny any rest until his lessons were mastered. James Wayne was another matter. He found no interest in the schooling his mother provided, but wandered about the Nez Perce lodges seeking friends and playing with the Indian children until he was indistinguishable from his half kin. He insisted on wearing the clothing worn by the Indian children and went with them when they were instructed in the use of the bow and arrow, the war lance and the war club. He played their games with an intensity that won the admiration of the elders. When word spread throughout the Nez Perce nation that the white soldiers were at war with the Palouse and Cayuse tribes, young James Wayne found company in the band of young braves who wanted to join the fight and drive the white soldiers from the hunting grounds that had been the sole province of the Natives since time began.

James Wayne was only four years old, but was old in the ways of the natives with whom he found companionship. Jenny did her best to dissuade him from his pursuing a course she knew would bring him disappointment. The white soldiers had driven the Indians onto their reservations and their day of glory was past. They were a declining race and Jenny did not want her son to share their disappointments. The advice given to her again and again by the Reverend Spalding to marry a white settler and raise her son as a white man, weighted heavily upon Jenny's mind almost daily. Living among the Nez Perce gave her few opportunities to meet white men. Her greatest impediment however was that she was not inclined to be bedded by any man. She had limited experiences with the passions that motivated the relationships between men and women. She had only her memory of her period in captivity. That memory made her mind and body revolt at the thought of male contact and the brutality and invasion that was part of their passions.

Yet, her mind became conflicted when her thoughts returned to the companionship of her brother and her brief relationship with William Anderson. These men had treated her respectfully and she could not believe they would be capable of the brutality she had experienced. When she received word from Paul Anderson that William had been killed fighting Indians her thoughts became even more ambivalent. She believed that her captivity and treatment had some part in William's obsession to punish the Indians who rose in rebellion. She sorely missed the promise she once had in the dreams of a life spent in the comfort and security of William's world. She wanted to have hope for a future and the prospect of having a home, but her mind became blank and dark when she tried to envision that future.

Also troubling Jenny was her relationship with the Nez Perce Chief Joseph. Her ability to speak the Chinook language and understand and speak the language of the Nez Perce had placed her in the position where the Chief would call upon her to sit with him in councils with the white representatives who had now turned their attention to placing the Nez Perce within the confines of a reservation. The Chief was adamant in asserting his belief that he and his people had been promised lands that included the Blue Mountains and the Grande Ronde Valley of Oregon which were considered the tribe's historic hunting grounds. The government representatives were equally adamant that the Indians were to have a far smaller parcel, none of which included the Blue Mountains or the Grande Ronde Valley.

Jenny well knew the history of the Nez Perce. This tribe had a long friendship with the white settlers. They had given aid to the Lewis and Clark Expedition when it arrived in their valley weak and starving. They had aided many a distressed wagon train that had used up its provisions or became lost on the trail west. The tribe had provided scouts and soldiers for the army. Their Chief felt justified in his demands and certain of the promises that had been made to the Nez Perce. A great sadness griped Jenny's heart when she saw the tide of events now turn against the friendly and loyal Nez Perce Indians. It was a welcome relief when one of the missionaries called upon her seeking her help in establishing a school among the Spokane Indians who were now settled on their reservation. Jenny did not want to be present when the rising difficulties between the government and the Nez Perce erupted into conflict.

JAMES AND CLAY

James and Clay boarded the *Grizzly Rawlins* on a bright spring morning to start their long delayed voyage to Oregon and to reunion. Captain Gray no longer had the time to Captain the vessel that had been the flag ship of the expanding Little Flower fleet. He nonetheless saw them off, handing over to James a number of portfolios outlining the extent of James' interest in the Northwest.

"I'm interested in gettin' one of them paddle wheelers operatin' between that new Portland city and The Dalles. Now that Oregon has become a state and the Eastern Washington Territory has been opened up for settlement, there's likely to be good business up that river. You might want to have a look at them prospects. There be a lot of them emigrants still headed down that river."

To James, the prospect of a new venture added excitement to the trip north. He was also interested in following up on several suggestions that his mine superintendent Peters had presented concerning mining prospects in the Okanogan and Couer d'Alene regions. To Clay, there was also another purpose then to visit his family. He had enjoyed the rapid and successful expansion of his brokerage business, but at the height of its success, he had come to realize that his heart was not in it. His thoughts always returned to ranching. Now that the territories of Eastern Washington had been opened for settlement, he wanted to study the possibilities of ranching and settlement in those opening territories. Before he left San Francisco, he had sold his business and had a sizable cash balance available to now pursue his dreams. But first there was the matter of a reunion with William, Jenny and his father; a prospect that rested uneasily upon his emotions.

As Captain Gray had warned them, the passage up the Coast to Oregon was a treacherous passage; the winds seemed to be forever driving the ship toward the jutting rocks that abounded along the coast line. The swelling waves gave James and Clay no rest from the continual rolling and pitching of the schooner. Little Flower and the children were mostly confined to their cabin, either from sea sickness or from the danger of the angry sea. The passing over the bar at the Columbia River was another confrontation with the furry of nature that made all aboard apprehensive. When the boat finally settled into its birth on the Oregon side of the river, both James and Clay found that their land legs were unsteady and their walk uncertain. Little Flower and the children were badly in need of rest and James took rooms at a nearby hotel. Clay swore it would be his last venture on the seas.

"I've been twice to China and back, but never have I feared so much for my sorry ass."

Clay had no idea where to find his family. When he asked about his father at the local newspaper, he was informed that his father was still publishing a newspaper from Oregon City. When he asked about William, the newspaper publisher looked at him sternly, studying Clay's innocent expression.

"You best ask your paw about Captain Anderson," the publisher responded. "I ain't got any news of him."

Both James and Clay were puzzled by the publisher's response to the question regarding William, but rather than linger any longer in Portland, they hired a carriage and headed for Oregon City. Once they reached Oregon City, it was not difficult to find the newspaper published by Paul Anderson. On the main street the large plate glass window in the two story frame building had an inscription that read: *The Oregon Independent, Paul Anderson Publisher.*

Paul Anderson had been spending more and more time at the newspaper office. The loss of William had been a difficult blow and he felt the need to absorb himself in his publishing business. When he went home, which was upstairs, he found himself too troubled to rest and too ready to resort to his liquor cabinet. Thus it was, when there came a rapping on the door, he was too consumed in typesetting to notice the disturbance. Clay tried the door when there was no response to his rapping and finding the door unlocked, entered the office. Clay recognized his father at a table in the press area behind the counter, bent over the type plate. There had been an aging in his father that was immediately evident to Clay. His hair was now completely gray and thinning, his body, once broad and strong looked shrunken and stooped. He wore spectacles that hung on the end of his nose and a mustache that was white as snow emphasized the wrinkling of his features.

When James and Clay stepped up to the counter and clapped the bell that had been placed there, Paul finally looked up, and impatiently waived them off: "Put your ad in the box there and I will get to it tomorrow."

"I ain't got no ad Paw. It's you I came to see."

Paul froze over the type plate letting the words uttered in a once familiar voice settle in his mind. He now looked up, removing his spectacles and studied the strangers demanding his attention.

"That can't be you, can it Clay? These old eyes ain't so good now days. Is that you Clay?" The voice of his father was shallow and raspy and Clay was gripped with emotion.

Throwing aside the gate, Clay moved quickly to his father grasping him by the shoulders. "Can you see me now Paw?" Clay felt the frail body of his father now grasp him as Paul tried to steady himself.

"Where have you been boy?" Tears were now forming in Paul's eyes and his body began to tremble as he held tightly to Clay. "I've needed you boy. There is much to tell you."

Clay led his father over to a chair and sat him down and knelt before him. "I'm sorry Paw. I've not been a good son. Maybe someday I will be able to explain to you why I couldn't write."

Paul now noticed the other stranger standing aside as the father and son had their moment. A new sorrow possessed him as he recognized James and knew of the hurt he must bring upon these two young men. "Let's close this place up and go upstairs. We have much to tell each other and I am in need of some brandy before we get to the telling."

Paul poured them each a full glass of brandy and sat down in his favorite chair. "I know you will be wanting to know about William, he began," but without saying more, he pointed to a full page article framed and hanging on the wall. "You best read that and save me from the pain of telling."

James and Clay went to the wall and together read the article that was William's obituary. It was now Clay who found his eyes flooding with tears. When they both had finished the reading they turned to Paul with the same question on their lips: "But what of Jenny? There is no mention of his wife in this article."

Paul rose slowly and walked to his desk where he retrieved another article. He handed it to James. "Please forgive me, James, but I find it difficult to talk of these matters. You can read what happened to your sister in this article."

The newspaper he was handed was yellowed and aged. James felt tightness in his chest grip him as he thought he had been handed another obituary. Distressed as he was, when he finished the article and handed it to Clay, he was relieved to know that his sister was still alive. She had suffered, but she was still alive!

"They never married," Paul now informed James. "She did have a child as a result of the incident with the Cayuse. She was with the Nez Perce for some time, but is now somewhere near Spokane Falls. I hear from her now and then. She has had a hard life. You must go to her."

Clay noticed that even though his drink was still hardly touched, that his father had drained his glass and was pouring himself another drink. Clay swiftly finished his and joined his father. They had much to discuss and he needed to relax and let the words flow more freely. James was quick to join him and refilled his glass.

Oregon City was fading into the annals of Oregon history. The Capital had been moved to Salem and Portland, because of its access to the navigable Columbia River was becoming the center of commerce. When James and Clay returned the next morning and Paul heard that James had brought his family which to his surprise consisted of three young children a new baby and his wife, he suggested that they rent a house and settle them in before they headed on to find Jenny.

"William built a nice home in Portland. It's been empty for a while. I couldn't bring myself to sell it. You could put up your family there until you return. Most of the Indian troubles are over. The Army has put the tribes on reservations, but there are still a few bands of renegades who might find a family traveling alone a tempting target. There are no decent roads and nary a lodging place to be had. You best bring Jenny back here. Maybe she will listen to you. It seems she fears rejection because of her captivity and what with having a mixed breed child."

The reference to a mixed breed child brought a smile across James' face. "I'm sure we can make her comfortable with that circumstance. You must come and meet my family. I will accept your offer of the house if it will not create a problem. I do believe my family is a little weary of traveling after that voyage up the coast and will not be anxious to undertake a coach ride that could well take several weeks."

Paul gave James the direction to William's house and taking Clay with him hurried off to open it for its new residents. Clay walked up the steps from the carriage way, through the large mahogany doors into the entrance way of William's home desperately saddened by the thought of things that should have been. This fine home was where he had expected to find his brother and Jenny. Now, walking through the large well furnished empty rooms, rooms that now smelled of the stale air of disuse, Clay tried to envision his brother's presence in each room and was confronted with the realization that he missed his brother terribly. When he entered the upstairs bedroom, he noticed, hanging on the mirror of the dressing table, the locket William had given Jenny; the locket that had been given to him by their mother.

Clay grasped the locket and held it tightly in his hand. His thoughts were of the two women against whose breast the locket had rested. He was trying to conjure visions of each, but the visions would not come.

"It's yours now," he heard his father say as his father entered the room. Clay dropped the locket into his pocket and together Clay and his father went about the house opening windows and doors in hopes of driving from the house the staleness that held captive the essence of a life now forever gone.

Clay had gone downstairs to check out the outbuildings while Paul went into his son's library to see if there were any knick knacks or mementoes that should be placed beyond the reach of children. Several documents lay on William's desk. Paul noted that they were drafts of land sales documents involving timberlands in the Cascade Range. The pen last used in its drafting was still in the inkwell that was now without the ink that had long since evaporated. William had left in haste when the summons came to him to call out the militia. Paul sat down in this son's chair and the memories of his lost son cascaded though his mind. He held close to his chest the last documents upon which William had spent his energies. Tears were welling in his eyes and this throat was constricting when his reveries were shattered by the sound of children's scampering feet and their shrill voices in the hallway below. James had arrived with his family.

Paul put the papers in a side drawer and sat for a moment listening to the commotion below. A smile came to his face. It was fitting that this big house should be filled with the delightful squeal of children, Paul thought. His thoughts had often dwelt upon the promise that he would one day have little grandchildren playing at his feet. Jenny and William would have made him a most happy grandfather, but alas he told himself he must forget those dreams and accept what promise the future might now bring.

Clay was back and James and Jenny who were like his own family may soon be together under this roof.

With a brisk stride, with his shoulders thrown back, Paul left the library and headed down the stairs and into the parlor where the voices of the children and admonishing adults could be heard. He stopped abruptly in the door way when he saw standing in the center of the room and Indian princess more beautiful than any he had ever seen. She was holding in her arms a small dark haired, tanned skinned, dark eyed baby that was pulling at his mother's blouse. James, who was standing by the window, looking down on the river below, held the hand of a small boy with curly blond hair that hung long over the color of a sailor suit the boy wore. A young woman sat in a chair across the room with a small blond haired girl in her lap holding before the child a picture book that held the young girl's attention.

James now turned from the window: "Oh, there you are Paul; I would like to introduce my wife and children to you. I believe you have seen Little Flower before probably at Fort Boise when she passed through with Parker, looking to join up with Franco and our group. Young George here and Little Linda are the ones I found in the desert along with their sister July. Little Flower and I have adopted them and they are now our family along with our son Wayne whom I fear is a little testy and hungry right now."

Paul could find no words to express his surprise at the appearance of Little Flower. He had indeed met her at Fort Boise and remembered seeing her at Fort Laramie. He remembered her as shy and reticent. Her dress on the frontier hid from others the voluptuousness of the youthful body now displayed before him. The clothes she now wore were not the conventional dress of the women of Portland; her dress was shorter, tight fitting and had features of her Indian heritage offset with a beaded belt that was wrapped about her waist. She wore a head band that sparkled with inset diamonds and rubies that gave the impression of the richness that accented the attention paid by her dressmaker to show off the perfection of her stature.

James mistook the confusion on Paul's face for shock at the presence of Little Flower in the home that had been built by his son, now dead at the hands of the Indians. James wondered if he had been wrong to bring Little Flower into his home and feared that matters would now become unpleasant and he be asked to leave.

"I thought you knew about Little Flower," James said in apology. "I should have been more thoughtful."

Paul looked at James now, his composure restored. "Of course I knew about your wife. Clay told me all about how you two survived together in the desert. I am stunned by the transformation she has gone through. I do remember her from Fort Boise. When she and Parker came through looking for Franco, I tried to hire him to guide our train on to Oregon. But that's not what made me look so foolish. It's the name Little Flower. William did not know either her or Parker. He had mentioned he was doing some work for a Little Flower company out of San Francisco on a number of occasions, but I never connected the name with this young lady. I was just looking over some of his papers upstairs and it involved the Little Flower Logging Company. Is this just coincidence or is this young lady the Little Flower referred to in those documents?"

Paul now went to Little Flower and extended his hand and held it warmly when offered. "You are welcome here Princess. Now what can we do to calm that little babe of yours? There is no food in the house. We might persuade Clay to handle that situation. Come and I will show you the rest of the house."

As Paul moved over and extended his hand to little George, George puffed up at the recognition of his manhood that this gesture indicated. "Are you my Grandfather?" He precociously demanded.

"Well now," Paul responded. "Your papa has lost his father, and I have lost a son. I just might be interested in the job if it's being offered."

James and Clay headed East up the Columbia River to find Jenny, leaving Little Flower and the young ones in the care of Paul Anderson who found the role of surrogate Grandfather to his liking. Little George was fascinated by the printing press and the creation of the images that it produced and became a regular companion to Paul and insisted on accompanying him when Paul went to the newspaper office. Little Flower, once her arrival in Oregon had been announced in Paul's paper and the story of her social status and her adventures became known, was now in demand in the celebrity starved functions about Portland and Salem.

July, who now accompanied Little Flower, was herself creating a mild sensation. She was now of marriageable age and was finding the attentions she was receiving at times amusing and at other times annoying. With the assistance of Angeline and the approval of Little Flower, July had designed a wardrobe much like that of Little Flower's. Her skirts were worn tight to her body, revealing her youthful figure and her blouses had the provocative low cut bodice that was fashionable in Paris. The skirts revealed her trim ankles and her shoes were low cut, resembling moccasins. July enjoyed reading the social portions of the local papers that usually contained the shocked critique of her attire by the prudish editors. Little Flower's untoward dress was acceptable, because she was a native. But for a young, unattached girl of marriageable age, such dress was considered shocking.

July's unreciprocated adoration of Clay presented her with a standard that she found no suitors could meet. July viewed most of the young men in Oregon to be course and aggressive and unschooled in the art of courtship. July had no intention of submitting to the courtship of anyone who would impose upon her the condition of living in Oregon and never returning to San Francisco. Her familial relationship with George and Linda, their dependence upon her, also prevented July from considering seriously any attempts at courtship. Yet, the more stand offish she became, the more passionate was the response to her rejection. A sensation was caused when two of her would be suitors set off one morning to engage in a duel; each believing the other had been the cause of July's rejection. Fortunately, to the relief of July, Marshal Meek was informed of the event and cooled the passions of the adversaries by advising them that neither would be acceptable suitors if they engaged in an illegal duel and one ended up dead and the other in the territorial prison.

James was relieved to let all these family and social matters rest in Little Flower's hands as he headed up the Columbia River to investigate the possibilities of starting a scheduled paddle boat operation up and down the river and to then proceed to Fort Walla Walla where he was certain he could receive news of Jenny's whereabouts. Although James had seen the Mississippi River and the Missouri Rivers at their spring turbulence, he found the Columbia River a far different experience. The river was in most places fast flowing; it had treacherous rapids, eddies and whirlpools. Along the way he viewed the progress of raft and flat boats that carried down steam the emigrant families completing the last leg of their journey to the land of promise. It was indeed a hazardous venture and many would lose their lives or their possessions or both on the hazardous trip downstream.

James and Clay hired the local Chinook and Umatilla Indians to carry them and their few possessions upstream in their dugouts. They discovered that these Indians, who lived off the abundance of the great Columbia, were generally lazy and prone to thievery. They had to constantly watch their possessions and sleep with one eye open. Finally James, who had discontinued wearing his bear claw necklace and bowie knife, put them both on one morning and found, as he hoped that the Indians now feared him and curtailed their thievery. James became convinced on his journey that there was indeed a need for larger boats on the river.

When they finally arrived at The Dalles, they were glad to leave the river and head on to Fort Walla Walla on horseback. When they arrived at the Fort, Colonel Wright was still in command and was engaged in the process of settling the tribes of Eastern Oregon and the Washington Territory onto their reservations. A number of the Chiefs and Elders, along with a number of braves were being held in confinement awaiting trial and punishment for various transgressions, most of which involved leading war parties and murdering white settlers. A gallows had been constructed in the center of the parade ground the use of which now awaited the determinations of Colonel Wright as to which of the Natives would be released and which would be hung. There was no hope of a prison sentence; the verdict would be either freedom or death by hanging and the judgment would be summary.

The officer of the day greeted James and Clay and offered them accommodations in the barracks reserved for single officers which was located in a row of buildings that made up the Fort. Fort Walla Walla had no walls or palisades as did the other forts along the frontier. Across from their quarters, the army had built a temporary corral like enclosure with several lean-tos where the captive Indians were being held awaiting trial and sentence. As James stood observing the captives from across the parade ground, the door to Colonel Wright's office swung open and two soldiers proceeded to escort one of the Indians back to the holding area. The Indian, although wrapped in a blanket over his buckskins and was without head gear, walked with an airy dignity which lead James to believe he was probably one of the Chiefs. As he watched the small procession cross the compound, he noticed that the Chief had a slight limp. The longer he watched the more disturbed he became. There was a familiarity about the Indian that started James mind into motion.

He was interrupted in his thoughts when the Colonel's orderly informed James and Clay that the Colonel sent his compliments and asked them to join him. Colonel Wright stood to greet them as they entered his office and walked forward to clasp their hands.

"I have heard of you," he remarked to Clay. "You scouted for Captain Gunnison and Colonel Carson as I recall. I could have used your services had you come a few months earlier. Colonel Steptoe remarked about your services with Gunnison. He was commissioned to investigate the possible Mormon involvement in that mess and to punish the Indians involved. He left for assignment back east a few months ago. You and he would have had a good deal to talk about."

The Colonel, who had just recently been brevetted a General in recognition for this quelling of the uprising, was tall and clean shaven unlike most of the officers Clay had met who generally were adorned with facial hair. His eyes betrayed the fatigue of his recent ordeals in the field and in increasing demands for retribution against the tribes that were flowing by currier into the Fort.

James asked him about the Indians who were being held captive and what their fate would be. "Most will be hung. It's an unpleasant business, but this fighting and killing must be ended," the Colonel responded.

"I have a folder on my desk of a massacre down in central Oregon. If I'm not mistaken young man, your name is in that file. Are you the same James Rawlins that was listed as missing in that affair?"

James and Clay related to the Colonel their memories of the event and went over the Colonel's list of the victims. "You will be glad to know gentlemen that the War Chief who instigated that raid is now in my custody. He has had his trial and will be hung tomorrow."

"Would that Chief's name be Running Dear?" James enquired.

"That's the one. I interviewed him before I sent for you. He admitted to the whole business. His band also slaughtered a group of Missionaries not long after they wiped out your party."

James could not share the Colonels enthusiasm for bringing an end to the life of Running Dear. He remembered how he had first met Running Dear when he was dying of his wounds back in Nebraska Territory and how they had formed a brotherhood when James nursed him back to life. Although he remembered little of the massacre at the Cottonwoods, having been knocked unconscious early in the fighting, he was informed by Little Flower of how the Chief had spared his life and spared that of Little Flower so she could nurse him back to health.

"I would like to meet with Running Dear if that would be possible." James advised the Colonel. "He killed my father and my friends, but he spared my life."

Colonel Wright gave instructions to his orderly to take James to the prisoner. " He has been taken to the brig where we hold those prisoners who are to be hung. They get testy when they know they are going to hang."

James found the Chief sitting on a wood framed bunk in an otherwise unfurnished room. A trade blanket was wrapped about his shoulders. His hair hung in greasy strands about his shoulders. The dignity that dominated the Chief's appearance that James remembered was evidenced only in his solemn facial features that were now turned to the lone source of light from a small barred window. James could see that the Chief's lips were moving and as he approached the cell where the Chief was confined, James could hear the Chief sing his death song.

As James was let into the cell and given a chair the Chief did not at first acknowledge his presence and continued his chant.

"I have come to say farewell my brother."

The Chief fell silent and now looked at James. The light was not good and the Chief did not recognize him.

"If you are the white man's prayer maker, I do not want your prayers. I do not want to go to your heaven. I will go to the hunting grounds where my father and his father await me. You may go now."

"I have no prayers to give for you my brother, I have come to say farewell."

The Chief studied James more closely now. "I remember you. You have changed much. I am glad that you have lived. I did not know if you would. How is it that you are here?"

James told the Chief that his presence was mere happenstance. He also told the Chief how he had survived and was now traveling to find his sister. "I did not know that you had been captured or that you were sentenced to hang for what happened so long ago. I did not travel this long distance to talk against you before the General's Court nor am I here to watch the soldiers take the life I once saved."

"It has been a long battle, the Chief responded, "We fought the white man until all our villages were destroyed, our children hungry and crying, our women grieving for their dead. We once owned these lands and hunted from where the sun comes up in the morning sky to where it leaves at days end. The game was in great numbers, our children cried not from hunger, but from the great joy of living. Our braves were feared far beyond our lands and their grandfathers' rested in peace. The white man came and gave use his sickness, stole our lands, killed the game that fed us and then demanded we give them more. Would not any man rise to fight these people? Why is it I must die while the Blue Coats and white men who have raided our villages and killed our women and children live?

James thought for a long time before he could answer. "There is no good answer to that question. Our ways are very different. As your braves wandered far from your villages to bring war to your brethren when there was a time for peace, so it is with my people, they want ever more land and will wage war to take it. Peace is the result of victory when your enemy can fight no more. Our cause may not have been just, but it is the stronger. I can shed no tears for your losses. Among those that died when you raided our camp were my father and my dear friends. We did not come to fight or settle upon your lands, yet you killed all without question. These lands have been stained with the blood of many innocent people and many who took to the lance and sword. The blood will flow until one or the other can fight no more. The killing must end before your people are no more. If it is your life that must bring this end, then it is as it should be."

There was a long silence in the room. The Chief turned again to the window. "I once saved your life and in turn you saved mine. You gave me another great gift. The woman you spared so she could care for me is now my wife. She has given me a son. I will tell him of you and he will be proud of his blood for you have been a brave Chief and fought well for your people."

"Yes I did fight. I fought until I could fight no more. I fought until the arms of my braves could rise no more. The Blue Coats who came upon our lands grew large in numbers with each battle. They brought with them their big guns. Their rifles were many and ours were few. They brought their war to our villages and left us weak with hunger. There is no more war within us. It is good that you have a child of my blood. Together we may now live in the bosom of our women. Our blood will be one. Goodbye my brother."

The Chief turned again to the window and resumed his death song.

James and Clay made a point of leaving the Fort before sun rose. Neither wanted to bear witness to the hanging of Chief Running Dear. Their trail north followed that of Colonel Steptoe whose defeat had given rise to the acts of vengeance that they sought to avoid by their early departure. The rolling plains and hills that but a short time before were teaming with warriors were now barren and transitioning from the green of spring to the yellow of a sun baked summer. The flowers that had grown in profusion were now shedding their seeds that would be sheltered by the dry earth to await the coming of a new spring. Soon the plow would turn these lands into abundant fields and witness not again the passing of the red men whose presence left the land unburdened by their trace. Both James and Clay, whose lives had been so intimately affected by their travels through the wilderness that had been the west, felt the pangs of nostalgia as they traveled through a land they knew would soon be invaded by the throngs of emigrants whose wagons were now coming by the thousands across the trail to Oregon. The red men had lived with this land for times unknown and left it unchanged. Within but a few years it would be changed forever. A great nation was forming and the tide of its rising would submerge in its passing the week and irresolute.

As they came upon the great butte where Steptoe took his stand, they witnessed a detachment of soldiers removing the bodies of their dead comrades from the temporary graves where they have been interned during the Colonel's retreat. The great butte that dominated the land could have been, but for the vacillation and lack of military skills of the Natives, the burial ground for Steptoe's entire detachment. It now stood as a reminder of the red man's desperate struggle against the inevitability of the driving vision of the white man's manifest destiny.

JENNY

Jenny stood sweeping the porch of the small reservation school where she held regular classes for reluctant students whose attendance varied with the weather which was now optimum thus leaving her classroom empty. James Wayne was off fishing with the boys who declined her educational efforts. A movement in the distance attracted her attention. On the road leading to the mission compound she could just make out two horsemen approaching. The persistent summer had turned the land tinder dry and she could see the dust trail made by horses hanging in the lifeless air. It would no doubt be some traveling officials, she presumed. The Reservation was constantly being visited by government agents whose attentions generated many reports, but little in the way of measurable results.

Jenny, having finished sweeping the accumulated dust from the porch sat down on the lone chair and glanced again at the strangers riding toward the Mission. They were still far off and Jenny could only make out that they were well mounted and rode their mounts with the authority of men accustomed to the saddle. There was little to attract her interest, the days accumulated one upon the other without distinction. Just to view a movement on the road became an event of interest, so she sat watching the riders move toward the Mission speculating whether they were actually government officials or just some of the many speculators who had been passing through of late looking for opportunities.

There came a nuzzling at her elbow that distracted her. She reached down to stroke the offered head of Champion, James Wayne's adopted mongrel that had been off chasing rabbits when his master joined the other boys the test the waters of the Spokane River. Champion was not content to be stroked and pushed at her until she gave him her attention. Jenny then realized that he was thirsty and that his water bowl was empty.

"You should have let those rabbits alone and you would be down by the river by now and had all the water you needed," she admonished Champion as she walked over and retrieved his empty water bowl and walked over to the well and filled it.

She became distracted by the wilting rose bush she had brought with her from Lapwai and had planted near the well. She drew more water and poured it at the base of the rose bush watching the dry soil absorb the moisture as fast as she supplied it. She had forgotten about the strangers who were now within hailing distance of the mission. Champion drew her attention back to the strangers when he started barking and ran from the yard toward the road. Her attention was directed toward Champion. She did not want him scaring the horses and drawing the anger of the strangers. Her calls went unheeded and she turned to pick up a stick or anything that would draw the dog's attention. She grabbed the broom she had left on the porch and went down the steps and after Champion, who seeing her wielding the broom, now left the strangers and sought his shelter under the porch. The strangers were but a few yards away when she turned to them to apologize for the dog's behavior. Her words stuck in her throat; she dropped the broom and ran into the waiting arms of the now dismounted James.

Clay remained saddled as he watched the gleeful reunion of brother and sister. He had spent many nights lying awake trying to remember Jenny's face, her physical presence, the sound of her voice and even her touch. Now he was finally close enough to touch her and he felt the timidness that had once prevented him from approaching her return. He had watched her closely as the rode into her yard. As she was concentrating her efforts on the barking dog, he could see that the only change he could detect in her was her loss of the vibrancy of her youth. Her face was thinner and evidenced the ordeals she had been through. But now as she embraced her brother, smoothing him with kisses, he could see the transition in her face back to the more youthful girl he remembered.

"Well, Clay Anderson. Are you going to get off that horse and let me hug you?"

"I was afraid you might put that dog on me again or whap me with the broom," he remarked as he dismounted to find Jenny within his grasp. He felt her firm warm body pressed against his. She pulled his head down and gave him a warm kiss. He instinctively pulled her closer and held her kiss longer than she had intended. She pulled back and gave him an inquisitive look. He felt the redness rising in his face. Had he gone too far?"

"Now Clay," Jenny remarked pulling back, "You are no longer the bashful boy I remember." She grabbed his hand and that of James and led them to the school house. "I have some water tinted with wild berry cooling in the well. I want to hear everything you two have been up to. I didn't think I would ever be seeing you two again. I have so much to tell you, but that's not all pleasant. Let's hear about your absence and what kept you away. I have missed you both so very, very much."

James Wayne stopped up short when he entered the school house and heard the animated conversation coming from the small room behind the school that served as his and his mother's living quarters. He had come home excited and wanting to show his mother his catch. He had caught three fine rainbow trout and knew his mother would be pleased with his efforts. He moved slowly through the school room and peered cautiously past the doorway that had been left open to allow the heated air to circulate through the cramped quarters. He saw James first and stood fascinated by the man dressed in black with the prominent bear claw necklace. He knew it to be an Indian trophy and signified bravery. He saw then the large knife with a sheath decorated with Indian beads and designs. He then noticed the other man dressed in buckskins and moccasins. These were not the same white men that he was familiar with, the ones who looked upon his tanned skin and black hair with disdain whenever he was introduced as Jenny's son.

James was first to notice him. "And this must be my name sake and nephew standing there in the doorway. Come in young man that big catch you got there must be getting weighty."

Jenny rushed to her son's side and took him by the hand. "Come and meet your uncle, my brother James. I've told you about him. And this is Mr. Anderson. I've told you about him also. He's the man you read about in that book Paul Anderson sent to us." Turning to Clay she said teasingly; "He's the "Hero of the West." James felt his cheeks flush at the reference to a heroism that he knew to be more invention then fact.

"He is a fine looking young man," Clay responded. "You must be proud of him."

James Wayne was unfamiliar with compliments and looked at the man sternly, waiting to see disapproval cross his handsome, tanned face. Instead he saw only a warm, sincere, inviting smile. "Where did you catch those trout? I bet you learned your fishing skills from one of these friends of yours. I don't see any fishing pole. You must show me how you caught those fine fish."

At that remark, Jenny relieved James Wayne of his and catch. "This will make a fine dinner. I will get them cleaned and ready. You stay here and entertain your uncle and Clay."

James Wayne stood awkwardly in the middle of the room, not knowing what was expected of him. "I have a young son who looks a lot like you," James offered in way of conversation. "He is your cousin." Noticing the doubting look on James Wayne's face," James continued. "Oh yes, young man he is half Indian and half white just like you."

This revelation puzzled James Wayne. His treatment among the white population left him with the certainty that he was different and not acceptable. This man seemed proud to have a half breed son.

"You two have some socializing to take care of," Clay interjected. "I'll excuse myself and go help Jenny with that cleaning job she's got herself into."

Clay found Jenny at a side table attached to an outbuilding that served as a kitchen and storage area. She was looking down at the three large trout with a look of disdain. As Clay approached Jenny admitted to him that she hated to clean these smelly creatures, but that she did enjoy eating them.

"I'm an old hand at this job, just stand aside and we'll have these trout in the frying pan in a minute. Do you have a fire going in that stove?"

Jenny went to the stove and shook the grate and added some kindling and had a fire going in a few minutes. Clay brought the fish in and took over the job of flouring them, and putting them in a large skillet amply supplied with bacon grease. Jenny stood aside, grateful to have someone else preparing the meal. How long had it been she tried to remember since she had someone else do the cooking while she had the leisure of just watching. They fell into an easy conversation and as the cooling of the night brought relief to the land they finished their preparations and called James and James Wayne to join them. When James Wayne appeared, Jenny noticed immediately that he was wearing the bear claw necklace James had placed around his neck. When Jenny asked whether her son had wrestled it away from James, James Wayne responded proudly, "Uncle James said it was mine."

Jenny looked at James in surprise. She knew the history of the necklace and how attached James was to it. "It's his," James offered. "I've found it a bit troublesome to be wearing it now days. It seems to draw too much attention. You best adjust it a bit, but it now belongs to my nephew." As he made his announcement, James Wayne smiled and took his seat beside his uncle at the table. Jenny could not help notice the sudden change in her son. He was open and cheerful, asking questions and listening carefully to the answers, answers that stimulated more questions. He had his uncle's complete attention and was blossoming in his presence. The advice of Reverend Spalding came again to her mind. Her son needed a man about.

For several days, James and Clay rode about the land east of the reservation, traveling to Spokane Falls, the Coeur d'Alene area and up as far as Fort Colville. They spent the last few days just visiting and talking about the country they had inspected. James noticed with amusement that Clay found every opportunity he could conjure up to be with Jenny. It was Clay who had insisted that James Wayne be given a horse and accompanied them on several of their trips. But then it was time to leave. James had many business matters that would by now need his attention. He missed Little Flower and his new family. It was time to approach Jenny about leaving this mission and returning to Oregon with them.

James found Jenny unreceptive to his urging. He knew there was a problem in Jenny's mind regarding her son and how he could manage in the world of the white man. "He needs to choose who he is. I'm sure he'll find it much easier to adjust once he is with my family. Little Flower is a great influence."

"It is your family James. I must make my own way."

"Nonsense Jenny, it's your family too. You and James Wayne need family. You have been through a lot. It's time to heal and to get on with your life."

Jenny would not relent. James crawled into his bed roll that night unsettled about the prospect of riding off the next morning and leaving Jenny behind in this land so far removed from those who loved her. He took no notice that the bed roll beside him was unoccupied that night. When he awoke he hurriedly saddled his horse and packed his bed roll. He was upset that Clay was not about and preparing to leave. He walked into the school room and found Clay and Jenny seated side by side on a bench. James Wayne was stretched out asleep on the bench, his head resting in his mother's lap. It came to James that Jenny and Clay had been up all night.

"Are you going to saddle up, or am I going to have to do it for you?" He asked Clay. He then noticed that Clay was holding Jenny's free hand. Around Jenny's neck hanging in prominence was the locket that had once before been her token of betrothal.

"I'm afraid you are going to have to ride on alone, James, unless of course you want to stay around for the wedding. Jenny and I will be staying here. We are where we want to be."

EPILOGUE

Clay and Jenny settled on land once the summer home of the Yakima Indian tribe in a fertile valley where the grass grew in abundance and their herds multiplied. Often at night as the sun receded beyond the majestic crest of the Cascade Range, Jenny would sit in contentment on the veranda of her new home and watch the valley below where Clay and her son Wayne move the cattle about from pasture to pasture as they settled them for the night. She often had visions of the hundreds of Indian ponies she had once observed in this valley and she often thought of the people that had once lived in freedom in this valley, a people now confined to reservations and limited by laws the white man imposed. As they came in ever increasing numbers onto their land, the tribes rose against the gathering tide of emigrants, but they had not the strength to resist those who would possess that land and spread the power of America from sea to sea. The settlers and adventurers who had driven the red men from the land were now its possessors and they thought not of the wound they had left on that land. Others would one day rise in indignation at the injustices done, but for now the West was won and the land was at peace.

On the far away frozen plains of Montana on a day yet to come, the last act of the Northwestern Indian resistance would ebb away as Colonel Miles confronted the desperate Nez Perce Indians who sought to escape their reservation and flee to Canada and freedom. Chief Joseph had fought a long and brilliant campaign to bring his tribe to but a few miles from freedom only to be confronted by the American soldiers who bared their way. Chief Joseph's people were freezing and starving and could fight no more. His words of contrition would be the epitaph of the western tribes. As Chief Joseph handed over his rifle in surrender he pointed to the west and the setting sun and told his captor; "From where the sun now stands, I will fight no more forever." ([40])

---

[40] War Chief Joseph, Helen Addison, Howard and Dan L. McGrath, Caxton Printers, Ltd. (1941) p. 282

www.ingramcontent.com/pod-product-compliance
Lightning Source LLC
Chambersburg PA
CBHW030105100526
44591CB00009B/283

TABLE OF CONTENTS

Chapter 1. A Good Time to Pray 1

Poetry which are prayers, about prayer, or are an encouragement to pray written by Poet: Bob E. McGlothlin

Chapter 2. Acronym Mania 47

A two-part series of acronyms

Part One: Acro"NAME"ia 47

Acronyms from people's first names by Poet: Bob E. McGlothlin

Part Two: Acronymia 153

Acronyms from words by Poet: Bob E. McGlothlin

Chapter 3. God Bless You 191

Poetry written with the intent to bless by Poet: Bob E. McGlothlin

Chapter 4. Inspirational Thoughts 249

16 short poems by Poet: Bob E. McGlothlin

Chapter 5. Let This Light So Shine 267

A collection of 25 of the best poetry by Poet: Bob E. McGlothlin

Chapter 6. Some Angels 309

Angel poetry written by Poet: Bob E. McGlothlin

Acknowledgements 323

Poet Bio 325

My Testimony 327

Now a little more about me 329

My Family Background 335

FROM THE POET'S PEN

Dear Reader:

It is my sincere desire that God will use these words of prose to inspire and encourage you to view life from a completely different perspective than what you are used to. You see, many of us go through life experiencing difficulties, trials, tests, temptations, and troubles of all kinds; and, many times, we only focus on the negative aspects of each situation. When we do this, it makes it very hard to see God's wisdom and purpose in allowing us to go through each situation; unless, of course, we can learn to change our focus. So, I hope that God will use these words to encourage someone to look beyond the way things appear; and try to view life's situations as God sees them. As you prayerfully read the following pages may you receive an impartation of God's grace and power to overcome during the troubles of your life.

Now, although each poem carries a unique message of its own; I believe, if you approach this book as a total complete message in its combined form, it will greatly enhance your life.

Bob E. McGlothlin

Chapter 1

A GOOD TIME TO PRAY

A Good Time To Pray

When you're living your life
Behind closed doors,
And you're hungry for light,
And ready for war;
When you want to revolt
Against your own ways;
This is a good time
To kneel down and pray.

When your life is a mess,
And all out of sorts;
And you're getting real tired
Of the enemy's darts;
And you're not real sure
To him what to say;
This is a good time
To kneel down and pray.

When you're looking for answers,
And are finding none;
And your life has ceased
To be any fun;
To find peace of mind,
You can't find the way;
This is a good time
To kneel down and pray.

When all is in order,
And nothing's amiss;
Everything's going right,
Your life is in bliss,
And blessings just cross
Your path day to day;
This is a good time
To kneel down and pray;

For we never know what
The future may hold;
Or what's coming up
Just down the road.
Around the next curve
Something might say,
"You'd better take time
To kneel down and pray."

Elevate Me, Oh Lord

Elevate my thoughts, oh Lord,
That I may catch a glimpse of yours.
Elevate my ways, oh Lord,
That I may walk on Heavenly shores.
Elevate my love
That I may love the unlovable.
Elevate my sensitivity
That I may touch the untouchable.
Elevate my knowledge
That I may,
Above all,
Know You.
Elevate my vision, oh Lord,
That I may see the invisible.
Elevate my faith
That I may taste
The ultimate victory.
Elevate my wisdom
That I may be wise enough
To obey Thee.

Dear God

I know I don't deserve
The kindness you have shown
All these years.
Oh, my, haven't they flown?
Please forgive me for
All the wasted time,
When I should have focused
Upon what was Thine.
Help me now to see
How to be so wise
As to redeem the time.
Oh, please, open my eyes
To see the quickest way
To win souls to thee;
For Lord, I'm looking
For more than two or three.
Jesus, I'm asking this very moment
For you to use my life
To help many people
Find eternal life.
Direct my steps, oh Lord,
As I walk each day.
Help me to be more sensitive
Is what I really pray.
I ask this all above
In Jesus precious name.
Lord, it is Your will
That I want to claim.

Drive And Pray

When the storm is raging,
And its pouring all around;
And you don't want to chance
Getting on the road to town;
But you need something desperately,
And have to anyway;
You get out in the weather,
And just drive and pray.
When you hit a patch of water
Which makes you hydroplane,
You then begin to panic
For steering is insane;
You call on the name of Jesus
And control is then restored,
It makes you very thankful
You've come to know the Lord.

God Bless You

May the Grace of God be with you
In all you try to do.
May God's Spirit be ever present
And may your heart be ever true.
May His blessings over take you
In an awesome way.
May you always remember
To seek the Lord and pray.
May you never think too highly,
Taking pride within yourself;
So, you may always then exalt Him;
And find spiritual wealth.
May the Love of God find a place
Deep within your heart;
And fill you with compassion;
While meet other's needs you start.
May you live in great expectancy
Of the things that God will do.
May your faith be ever growing,
And God's presence ever new.

Four Cedar Walls

Four cedar walls,
In this attic so high,
Oh, so alone,
So alone am I;
Locked up in this closet
So that maybe I
Can pray past my fears.
At least I can try.

Four cedar walls,
If they could testify;
They'd tell you of how
Very hard I did try.
They'd tell of all
The tears I did cry;
Locked up in this attic,
In this attic, so high.

Four cedar walls,
One window, one door;
Day after day,
I'd seek Him some more;
So, afraid of what
I was seeking for;
Yet earnestly seeking
Locked behind this great door.

One week went by;
Then went by two.
If I do not find Him;
Oh, what should I do?
Stay locked up behind
All fearful and blue
These four cedar walls;
Just what should I do?

Four cedar walls,
I can't stay right here;
Locked up behind
These four walls of fear.
I've got to step out;
Step out now by faith;
If I'm ever going to find
Some more of God's grace.

Though I'm not real sure
Which way I should go;
If I stay right here,
I know I won't grow.
So, I'm stepping out.
I'm telling fear, "No;
You can't hold me here;
I'm going to go."

So, by facing those fears;
I now have gained faith;
And found that my God
Has given more grace;
And all that I've needed
To run this great race.
Now, I'm determined
To just keep in pace.

I Go To Jesus

Where do I go
When bitterness knocks
Continually upon
My heart's lock
Trying to gain
An entrance here
To fill my life
With pain and fear?

I go to Jesus
In times of prayer,
And ask Him to answer
My times of despair
Through forgiveness, peace,
Joy, and hope.
Through these He'll give me
The means to cope.

What do I say
When anger beckons
For me to seek
Revenge to reckon
To someone for
The hurt they've caused?
Through their selfish intent
My life they've paused.

*I go to Jesus
In times of prayer,
And ask Him to answer
My times of despair
Through forgiveness, peace,
Joy, and hope.
Through these He'll give me
The means to cope.*

*Where do I go
To flee from pain
Caused by life's
Uncertain rain
That daily pours
Upon my soul
In its attempt
To take control?*

*I go to Jesus
In times of prayer,
And ask Him to answer
My times of despair
Through forgiveness, peace,
Joy, and hope.
Through these He'll give me
The means to cope.*

God, I'm Sorry

God, I'm sorry
For letting things in my life
Get so out of hand;
How my life just spins around
As if there is no plan.
I just cannot control
The daily shifts
That life sends my way.
Just help me, Lord,
To just hang on
To Your hand, oh this I pray.

Forgive me, Lord,
If I let any of my desires
Take precedence
Over Your Divine purpose
That you've directed
For my life to stand.
Teach me, Lord,
To take dominion
Over these carnal desires;
Then fill me with Your Holy Love
And consume me with Your fire
While directing me by Your hand.

Revive my heart,
Dear Precious Lord,
Through a Baptism
Of convicting grace
That'll draw my soul
Into Your presence
With a desire
To seek Your face
In a brokenness of spirit
With a contrite heart;
So, You won't find me despicable;
And turn Your eyes
From my part.

Consume me with
A burning zeal
To accomplish Your Divine plan
That my life,
Oh, Precious Lord,
Can serve Your awesome command
With all my heart,
My soul, mind, and strength;
For with Your grace and anointing, Lord,
I will go the length.

I Asked; He Said

I asked God for Holy Fire.
He said to bring a sacrifice.
I asked God for friends unending.
He said to lay down my life.

I asked God for His Holy love.
He said to keep His commands.
I asked for wisdom and knowledge.
He said to take a firm stand.

I asked God for living water.
He said to bring Him praise.
I asked for bread from Heaven.
He said to walk in His ways.

I asked for His loving kindness.
He said to be kind to man.
I asked God for His salvation.
He said to obey His plan.

I Need To Be Wanted, Lord

Whether, or not I succeed
Or fail, live or die,
Whether, or not I go to Heaven
Or in Hell I fry.
Lord, I need to be wanted
And needed by someone
That longs to be with me
To live and have fun.
I need some help and incentive
To work my way free
From this snare that I'm caught in;
Yes, from this sin disease.
Please forgive, oh Lord,
And help me please to find
My way back to You,
Your presence and peace of mind.

Forgiveness, Peace, Joy, and Hope

Forgiveness answers
The bitter demands
Of anger's lack
To understand.
Peace can only come
Through simple trust
In the one that knows
Much more than us.
Joy is the fruit
Of the faithful stand
For truth and mercy,
And God's plan.
Hope, my friend,
Anchors the soul
In the presence of Him
That makes us whole.

I'm Sorry, God

I'm sorry, God,
For this mess I'm in.
It's really all because
I have committed sin
In allowing another master
To lead my soul astray.
I find now that I'm adrift
So very far from the way.
I am very sorry, God.
I do so want to find
My way back to You
Who is so loving and so kind.
To think that you've waited,
Longing for this very day
That I'd turn again to You
And with humble heart pray.
I'm really very sorry, God.
Will You please forgive
And lead me back again
To the way so that I can live,
For as yet I'm still drowning
In so much debt and despair
That I'm even wondering
If anyone even cares.

Just An Acquaintance

Just an acquaintance,
That's all He tiz.
I met Him while
About my biz.
He called me with
A voice so strong
That I talked with Him
All night long;
And when He left
My company,
Somehow I felt
That I was free.

As I lived
My life awhile,
I noticed Him watching
Me with a smile.
Not a word
Did He speak to me.
Just a longing
In His eyes, I'd see.
Although He made
His presence known,
I waited just
A bit too long.
When finally, I thought
I'd look His way,
I noticed that
He did not stay.

Just an acquaintance,
That's all He tiz;
So, I went on
About my biz.

A day or two
Went by so fast.
I turned and looked;
And there He passed.
I quickly tried
To catch up to Him.
Again, too late;
He's getting dim.

Just an acquaintance,
That's all He tiz;
So, I went on
About my biz.

A month or two
Went by so fast.
I heard him calling
As I passed;
But too busy
Was I right then.
When I turned, and looked;
He was gone again.

Just an acquaintance,
That's all He tiz;
So, I went on
About my biz.

*A year or two
Went by so fast.
I heard Him crying
As I passed;
"Come unto Me
All ye that labor.
I'll help you through.
I'll be your Savior."*

*Just an acquaintance,
That's all He tiz;
So, I went on
About my biz.
A decade or two
Went by so fast
I heard Him weeping
As I passed.
This time I stopped
To take a look;
And caught a glimpse
Of the cross, He took.
I saw Him suffering*

There for me;
So that I
Might be set free;
And when I
Identified
With His pain,
I had to cry.

Then again,
We talked awhile;
And once more
I saw Him smile.

No more, said I,
Will this Man be
Only an
Acquaintance to me.
I'll seek Him out
Each, and every day.
I'll look to Him;
And I'll pray.

Look To Jesus

When what to do
Is not real clear;
And your nerves
Are knotting up with fear;
And it's all you can do
To hold back the tear;
Look to Jesus.
He will help you find the way.

When the answers are just
Too hard for you to find;
And you have just got
Too much on your mind;
And if only you could
Just relax and unwind;
Look to Jesus.
He will help you find the way.

When you are lonely,
And feeling blue;
Others have just
Been untrue to you;
And there is so much left
For you to do;
Look to Jesus.
He will help you find the way.

When life has dealt
To you a bad hand;
And there are some things
You just don't understand;
And you feel you are standing
In a strange land;
Look to Jesus.
He will help you find the way.

When you are sick,
Longing to get well;
The last time you felt good
Is hard for you to tell;
And you just feel like
Giving out a loud yell;
Look to Jesus.
He will help you find the way.

Lord, Be My Umbrella

Lord, I know
That this rain
That's falling all around
Is so necessary to life;
So, I'm not asking
For this rain to stop;
Just help me with the strife.
Now Lord, I may be tired,
And do not really
Care to be drenched;
But I do so desire
That through this rain
This long drought be quenched.
So, I'm not asking
For this rain to quit;
Just be my umbrella, oh Lord,
And keep me from getting wet.
Lord, let this rain continue to pour;
Cause all that are around here
Really do need it more.
Just let your grace spread out its wings;
And cover my life during this storm.
"Be my umbrella," is what I sing;
While this my strength is worn.

Lord, Bless This Mess

Lord, bless this mess
That I must eat;
And make it taste
So, good and sweet;
And bless the hands
That made this mess;
And let them know
That they are blessed.

Lord, How Much Do I Love You?

Lord, how much do I love You?
Let me count the ways.
I love You so very much,
That I'll give You all the praise.
And as I live this life,
I'll do my very best to
Live it in such a way
That it will be pleasing to you.

Lord, Why?

Lord,
Why is it so hard
To climb over this wall
That I have allowed to grow
Oh, so very tall?

Am I so afraid
That I might just slip,
Lose my hold, and fall;
Or is it because I lack the faith,
And don't believe in myself at all?

Lord,
You know that I
Desire not to dwell alone.
Oh, if I could just have
A friend to talk to
On the phone.

I'm trying to live
In such a way that
Would be pleasing to You;
And by Your grace
I have kept myself
Morally clean and pure.

Haven't I yet proved
To be faithful enough
For You to bless me with a wife;
Or is it really
Your perfect will for me
To remain single
The rest of my natural life?

Well Lord,
I'm not real mad
Or angry at You at all.
I just wish
That Your will
Was much easier to find,
That's all.

Lord, Cleanse Me

Lord, cleanse my mind
With Your Word.
Help me heed
To what I've heard.
Lord, cleanse my soul
Of what it's wrought,
And help me live
By what You've taught.
Lord, cleanse my mind
With Your Blood.
Wash my soul
'Neath the crimson flood.
Lord, here's my heart.
Cleanse every part,
And Lord please,
Give to me
A brand-new start.

Making Peace

Stormy days
And stormy nights
Can fill our hearts
So full of fright,
If we have not
Made our peace with God.
Troubles that come
Into our life
Can fill our hearts
So, full of strife,
If we have not
Made our peace with God.
When we face
Anxiety,
We'll wonder how
We could get free,
If we have not
Made our peace with God.
When we live
Unto our self,
We'll never find
Eternal wealth,
Until we have
Made our peace with God.

Oh God, I Seek

Oh God, I seek forgiveness for
All the things that I've done
That grieve your heart and make you want
To from my life depart.

Oh God, I seek direction in
This my desolate life
How that I may please You again
And receive Your help with strife.

Oh God, I seek Your face that I
May know just how You feel
About those things You love the most
So I can serve You with zeal.

Oh God, I seek to know the path
That You will choose for me
For I'm convinced within my heart
Your path will set me free.

Oh God, I seek an open door
Through which I can now walk
And find Your power and the strength
To my old ways then depart.

Oh God, I seek to love Your more
So, I can continue to serve you
From a heart that's filled with love.
I'm not trying to please a man
Unless it takes it to please You;
For Your favor is what I long for.
Help me keep a heart that's true.

Open Up Your Heart

Open up your heart,
And let Jesus in;
And your life will never
Be the same again.
Listen to His voice,
Harken to His call;
For Jesus will be
Your all in all.

Quicken Me

Quicken my eyes to see
What you would have me to.
Quicken my ears to hear
Your Word which is so true.
Quicken my mouth to say
What you would have me to say.
Quicken my heart, oh Lord,
In every way.

Quicken my feet to walk,
Oh Lord, in your steps.
Quicken my faith so that,
Oh Lord, it is felt.
Quicken my mind to think
All the right thoughts.
Quicken my heart to know,
Oh Lord, that it's bought.

Show Me, Lord

I wish that I
Could pin point
Just what You're
Trying to say.
I know You're trying
To speak to me;
And so, I'll just
Watch and pray.
I feel Your presence lingering near,
And knocking on my heart's door.
So, here I am, oh Lord.
Come and sup with me some more.
Help me to hear and understand
With an open heart;
And respond to Your presence
Right from the very start.
What must I do, oh Lord,
To stay within Your Grace;
To stay within Your favor
Traveling at Your pace?
I want only to move forward;
Not to stop, or fall back.
I want my life to please You;
So, help me stay on track.
Speak to me, dear Jesus.
Give me wisdom from above;
Fill my life completely
With Your compassionate love;
So that I might act more wisely
Than I ever have before
And once I do I'll even seek
To love You all the more.

What Do You Want From Me, Lord?

What do you want from me, Lord?
Do you want most of my time;
Or maybe, you want the knowledge
That you planted in my mind?
Is it possible you want my dreams;
Or perhaps, my life long plans?
Could it be you want my feet;
So, you can help me make a stand?
Should I give to you my hands;
So, you can work my messy life out;
Or maybe, you want my faith;
So, you can chase from my life doubt?
Are you asking for my eyes;
So, you can show to me the way;
Or should I give to you my knees;
So, you can teach me how to pray?
Though Lord somehow, I know
That you really want all these;
I kind-a-think my heart
Would make you the most pleased.

The Hour Of Prayer

Twas the hour of prayer,
And no one was there,
And all because
They did not care.
What a horrible shame;
Because Jesus came,
And found the place empty
Again, and again.
In His Word, you know,
He said He would show
Where in His name
We would gather;
To forsake us
He said, "No."
His promise is there
For us to claim in prayer;
So, my friend,
Why weren't you there?

The Time To Pray

*Struggling hard
To find his way,
He would not take
The time to pray.
Stumbling here,
And stumbling there,
Loaded down
With so much care;
Though it was now
Late in the day,
He would not take
The time to pray.
Continuing down
This lonesome path;
Sometimes feeling
Satan's wrath;
Still burdened down
As he walked in the way,
He still would not take
The time to pray.*

*So,
Please take time to Pray.*

Two Prayers

The prayer of the heart
Is faintly heard,
Until expressed
With the word.
The prayer of the soul
Is crying out,
And will be heard
Without a doubt.
When will God answer?
What will God say?
Yes!
Amen!
Believe!
Today!

What Your Presence Means To Me

What does Your Presence,
Oh Lord,
Mean to me?
It means life,
And liberty.
It means hope,
And to be free.
It means love,
Joy, and peace.
It means there shall be
Many new releases.
It means righteousness,
And law.
It means that my life
Will be worth living
After All.
It means provision,
And satisfaction.
It means that my life
Won't just be a reaction.
It means purpose,
And fulfillment.
It means my life will have
A Divine in filling.
It means power,
And authority
Over things or spirits
That desire to have control of me.
It means that my eternal destination
Will be to spend Eternity with
The Lord of all creation.

Upper Room, If You Can

Upper room,
If you can speak,
Then tell us of
Those that weep
For loved one's lost
And dying souls,
And their desire
To make them whole.

Upper room,
If you can sing,
Then sing the songs
That warriors sing
When waging war
In heavenly realms
For new souls to win
And join in hyms.

Upper room,
If you can cry,
Cry out for those
That will soon die
Without the Lord
Making residence in-
Side their hearts,
New life to win.

*Upper room,
If you can love,
Then love all who
Seek God above,
Whether for themselves
Or another's woes.
Just love all who
To you come and go.*

*Upper room,
Oh, you can speak,
And sing, and cry,
And love the weak;
For you can speak
Through prayers prayed,
And sing through songs
By broken hearts made.*

*You can cry through those
That weep in prayer
For lost loved ones
And for others they care.
You can love through those
That love so much
Because they spent time
Seeking God to touch.*

So, upper room,
Do speak, and sing, and cry aloud,
So that all who visit you
Can love the crowd,
The masses of people
That still do not know
The impact of love
By those that to you come and go.

You Are My Reason

Lord, You are my reason for living.
Yes, You are my reason to be.
Oh, You are my hope of salvation;
For through You I have been set free.

Chapter 2

ACRONYM MANIA

PART ONE:
ACRO"NAME"IA

Amanda

Amazed by her beauty,
Mystified by her presence,
Alarmed by her receptiveness,
Nurtured with her essence,
Disarmed by her style,
Attracted by her smile;
And I would sure like,
*With A*MANDA*,*
To spend a little while.

Amber

*"A" is for A*MIABLE*;*
For she listens to instruction.
*"M" is for M*ERCIFUL*;*
For others, she feels compassion.
*"B" is for B*EAUTIFUL*;*
For she is a great attraction.
*"E" is for E*ACH TIME
She brings me satisfaction.
*"R" is for R*ESPONSIBLE*;*
For indeed she takes action.
*And her name is A*MBER*,*
Who knows how to get attention.

Andrew

"A" is for A<small>UTHENTIC</small>;
For he is one of a kind.
"N" is for N<small>EIGHBORLY</small>;
For friends is what he'll find.
"D" is for D<small>ELIGHTFUL</small>;
For he is fun to be around.
"R" is for R<small>ESERVED</small>;
For he is easy to astound.
"E" is for E<small>MOTIONAL</small>;
For he Feels your very need.
"W" is for W<small>ELL-BRED</small>;
For he came from special seed.

Anthony

The "A" is for he's A<small>DVENTUROUS</small>;
For he always out exploring.
The "N" is for he's N<small>OBLE</small>;
For his character is just adoring.
The "T" is for he's T<small>RUSTWORTHY</small>;
For you can count on him.
The "H" is for he's H<small>ELPFUL</small>;
For he's there when you need a hand.
The "O" is for he's O<small>BSERVANT</small>;
For he notices when things change.
The "N" is for he's N<small>EIGHBORLY</small>,
And meets no one he finds strange.
The "Y" is for his Y<small>EARNING</small>
To be all that he can be;
And there's no one quite like him,
For his name is A<small>NTHONY</small>.

Ashley (1)

"A" is for how ANXIOUS
That I am to actually meet you.
"S" is for how SWEET
That you seem to be.
"H" is for how HAPPY
I'd be just to get to see you.
"L" is for this LOVE INSIDE
That you can set free.
"E" is for EACH TIME
I find myself thinking of you.
"Y" is for this YEARNING
That's growing within me
To have my arms
All wrapped around you
Holding you, oh, so tight
You'll have to experience just to believe.

Ashley (2)

*"A" is for her A*ttitude
That is as sweet as a gentle rain.
*"S" is for her S*mile
That helps to ease life's pain.
*"H" is for her H*ugs
That welcomes you as a friend.
*"L" is for the L*ove *you feel*
As she welcomes you in.
*"E" is for her E*ntertaining way
he makes you feel at home.
*"Y" is for her Y*outhful glare
Even though she's grown.

Betty

"B" is for her B<small>ENEVOLENCE</small>;
For she is kind to those in need.
"E" is for her E<small>LEGANCE</small>;
For she's a woman of taste indeed.
"T" is for T<small>HANKFULNESS</small>;
For she is grateful for all that life brings.
"T" is for her T<small>HOUGHTFULNESS</small>;
For she's considerate of little things.
"Y" is for Y<small>IELDING</small>;
For she is submissive to her man;
And her name is B<small>ETTY</small>,
Who's always got a plan.

Brandi

Brilliant is her countenance.
Radiant is her smile.
Awesome is her presence.
Niceties are her style.
Dynamic is her essence.
Intriguing is her demeanor;
And just a little plain.
She is so rich in beauty;
And Brandi is her name.

Brittany

"B" is for how BRIGHT
That she seems to be.
"R" is for her RADIANCE
That shines so brilliantly.
"I" is for her INTUITION
That helps her see the need.
"T" is for she's TRUSTWORTHY.
You can count on her indeed.
"T" is for her TIMELINESS;
For she's Johnny on the spot.
"A" is for her ATTENTIVENESS
To every tittle and jot.
"N" is for that NEVER
Can anything get by her.
"Y" is for this YOUNGSTER
Can cause here quite a stir.

Burnell

"B" is for he's B<small>RIGHT</small>
And has a brilliant mind.
"U" is for his U<small>NDERSTANDING</small>
Of life's reasons and its rhymes.
"R" is for how R<small>ESPONSIBLE</small>
He really tries to be.
"N" is for that N<small>O ONE</small>
Will be like him, you see.
"E" is for E<small>VERY TIME</small>
He offers you his place.
"L" is for his L<small>ANGUAGE</small>
That's always so full of grace.
"L" is for his L<small>EADERSHIP</small>
That leads you to the next step.
And his name is B<small>URNELL</small>;
Who's so full of energy and of pep.

Cailynn

"C" is for the Care
That you have shown.
"A" is for her Attitude
That is as sweet as a gentle rain.
"I" is for she's Impulsive;
And spontaneously on the go.
"L" is for the Love
That she has to show.
"Y" is for her Yearning
To make a difference in life.
"N" is for that Never will she give in
To the pressures of daily life.
"N" is for that No one
Can anything get by her.

Carl

"C" is for his C<small>ONFIDENCE</small>
Which brings such comfort to me.
"A" is for his A<small>FFECTIONATE WAY</small>
He always sets my love free.
"R" is for his R<small>ESILIENCE</small>
To all of life's ups and downs.
"L" is for his L<small>IVELY WAY</small>
He brings my love around.

(Written for a wife to give to her husband or for a woman to give to her boyfriend or fiancé)

Cathrine

"C" is for the CARE
That you have shown to me.
"A" is for how ATTRACTIVE
That I find you to be.
"T" is for the TIMES
I'd like to spend with you.
"H" is for how HAPPY
I am when I'm with you.
"R" is for the RESPECT
I have for your opinion.
"I" is for how INVOLVED
I'd like you to be in my mission.
"N" is for how NICE
That I think you are.
"E" is for EACH TIME I see you;
You're the star.

Cathy

"C" is for the CARE
That you've shown to me.
"A" is for how ATTRACTIVE
That I find you to be.
"T" is for the TIMES
I'd like to spend with you.
"H" is for how HAPPY
I am when I'm with you.
"Y" is for how YIELDING
You are to God above.
And I wrote this poem for you;
With thoughts of purest love.

Charles

"C" is for the CARE
That he continually shows.
"H" is for the HAPPINESS
That he wants in us to grow.
"A" is for the APPRECIATION
He expresses to be alive.
"R" is for his REALISM;
For he considers what is true.
"L" is for the LOVE
He shows to me and you.
"E" is for his ENDURANCE;
For he's endured so many misdeeds.
"S" is for he SENSES
So many of our needs.

Christian

The "C" is for C<small>OURTEOUS</small>;
For he's polite indeed.
The "H" is for my H<small>OPE</small>
That he's of better seed.
The "R" is for R<small>ESPONSIVE</small>;
For he's quick to return your call.
The "I" is for I<small>NTUITIVE</small>;
For he's sensitive all in all.
The "S" is for S<small>KILLFUL</small>;
For how he handles today.
The "T" is for his T<small>HANKFULNESS</small>;
For he's grateful for each day.
The "I" is for his I<small>NITIATIVE</small>;
For prompting he doesn't need.
The "A" is for he's A<small>STUTE</small>
And sharp as a tack indeed.
The "N" is for that N<small>O ONE</small>
Is quite like this man of faith;
And his name is C<small>HRISTIAN</small>,
A man that tries to stay in shape.

Crystal (1)

"C" is for the CARE
That you continually show to men.
"R" is for the RESPECT
We have for your opinion.
"Y" is for your YIELDING;
For you yield to one and all.
"S" is for your SERVILE WAY
You help us heed the call.
"T" is for you're TRUSTING
With an open heart to give.
"A" is for your ATTENTIVENESS
To every moment live.
"L" is for you're a LEADER
Of those that you befriend.
And this all spells Crystal;
Whom we'll love through thick and thin.

Crystal (2)

"C" is for the C<small>ARE</small>
That Mom and Dad have for you.
"R" is for the R<small>ESPECT</small>
We have for your opinion that's true.
"Y" is for your Y<small>EARNING</small>;
To express yourself to one and all.
"S" is for through your S<small>ENSITIVITY</small>
You help us heed the call.
"T" is for you're T<small>RUTHFUL</small>
With an honest heart to give.
"A" is for your A<small>TTENTIVENESS</small>
To every moment live.
"L" is for you're a L<small>EADER</small>
Of those that you befriend.
And this all spells Crystal;
Whom we'll love through thick and thin.

Curtis

"C" is for the C<small>ONFIDENCE</small> he expresses
Which brings such comfort to me.
"U" is for the U<small>NDERSTANDING</small> he possesses
of life's seasons, you see.
"R" is for the R<small>ESILIENCE</small> he has
To all of life's ups and downs.
"T" is for he has a T<small>RUSTING</small> N<small>ATURE</small>
Which is one thing about him I have found.
"I" is for he is I<small>NTELLECTUAL</small>,
And just one of a kind.
"S" is for he is S<small>ENTIMENTAL</small>,
And lets his feelings just shine.

Damone

*"D" is for she's D*ARLING*;*
For she is sweet as she can be.
*"A" is for she's A*NGELIC*;*
For she's an angel, you see.
*"M" is for her M*YSTERIOUS LOOK
That's always in her eyes.
*"O" is for she's O*LD-FASHIONED*;*
And her traditions are no surprise.
*"N" is for she's N*EIGHBORLY*;*
For a stranger, she doesn't know.
*"E" is for how E*LOQUENT
Her speech is although.
*And her name is D*AMONE*,*
A woman who's mind
Is all her own,
A true one of a kind.

Danielle

*"D" is for D*ARLING*;*
For she is sweet as she can be.
*"A" is for A*NGELIC*;*
For she's my angel, you see.
*"N" is for N*EIGHBORLY*;*
For a stranger, she doesn't know.
*"I" is for I*MPULSIVE*;*
For she's spontaneously on the go.
*"E" is for E*LOQUENT*;*
For she skillful with her speech.
*"L" is for L*OVING*;*
For she cares enough to reach.
*"L" is for she's a L*EADER
Of those that she befriends.
*"E" is for E*ACH TIME
A gift that she will send.

David

"D" is for his D<small>YNAMIC</small> personality.
"A" is for his A<small>NALYTICAL</small> mind.
"V" is for that he's V<small>ERY</small> extraordinary.
"I" is for that he's the I<small>NTELLECTUAL</small> kind.
"D" is for his D<small>RAMATIC</small> expression
That we are seeing most all of the time.
And all of this spells "D<small>AVID</small>"
Who really is one of a kind.

De'mone

*"D" is for her D*YNAMIC *personality*
That is quite a sight.
*"E" is for she's E*FFICIENT;
And competently gets things right.
*"M" is for she's M*ERCIFUL;
For her compassion brings us through.
*"O" is for she's O*RDERLY
For she'll even organize you .
"N" is for that there's No one
That's quite like her.
*"E" is for she's E*LOQUENT
Which makes her look so fare.

Deena

The "D" is for how DARLING
That I think you are.
The "E" for EVERY DAY
I think you are a star.
The next "E" is for EACH TIME
You smile at me is bright.
The "N" is how NICE
You are within my sight.
The "A" is for this ATTRACTION
That I have for you.
And your name is DEENA,
A woman whose heart is true.

Devin

The "D" is for he's D<small>ELIBERATE</small>;
For he does what he plans out.
The "E" is for he's E<small>FFICIENT</small>
On each task that's he's about.
The "V" is for how V<small>IBRANT</small>
That he seems to be.
The "I" is for his I<small>MAGINATION</small>,
And how he wants to set it free.
The "N" is for that N<small>O ONE</small>
Will ever be quite like him;
And his name is D<small>EVIN</small>,
Who tries to be everybody's friend.

Dorothy

"D" is for her D<small>YNAMIC</small>
Personality.
"O" is for she's O<small>BSERVANT</small>
For everything she seems to see.
"R" is for her R<small>EALISM</small>;
For she considers what is true.
"O" is for she's O<small>RDERLY</small>
For she'll even organize you.
"T" is for she's T<small>RUSTING</small>
With an open heart to give.
"H" is for the H<small>APPINESS</small>
That she wants all of us to live.
"Y" is for her Y<small>EARNING</small>
To live a fruitful life;
And her name is Dorothy,
One whose patient in times of strife.

Dwayne

"D" is for how D<small>ARING</small>
That he seems to be.
"W" is for how W<small>ARMHEARTED</small>
That he is, you see.
"A" is for how A<small>CTIVE</small>
That he tries to stay.
"Y" is for his Y<small>EARNING</small>
To get me to with him play.
"N" is for there's N<small>O ONE</small>
That is quite like him.
"E" is for I'm E<small>NCHANTED</small>
That he wants to be my friend.

Dylan

"D" is for his DYNAMIC Personality.
"Y" is for his YEARNING
To be all he can be;
"L" is for his LEADERSHIP
That will lead us all the way.
"A" is for his ASPIRATION
To be someone someday.
"N" is for that there's NO ONE
That's quite like him;
And his name is Dylan;
Someone that is everybody's friend.

Elizabeth

"E" is for E<small>ARNEST</small>;
For she is serious about life.
"L" is for L<small>ABORIOUS</small>;
For that's how she handles daily strife.
"I" is for I<small>NQUISITIVE</small>;
For she's naturally curious.
"Z" is for Z<small>ESTFUL</small>;
For living life she is quite zealous.
"A" is for A<small>PPRECIATIVE</small>;
For she's thankful to be alive.
"B" is for B<small>RIGHT</small>;
For to learn she'll always strive.
"E" is for E<small>FFICIENT</small>;
For she competently gets things done.
"T" is for T<small>RUTHFUL</small>;
For she is the honest one.
"H" is for her H<small>UMOR</small>;
For she's quite unique at this;
And her name is E<small>LIZABETH</small>,
Who tells it like it is.

Ellen

This "E" represents her E<small>LEGANCE</small>;
For she is that to my eyes.
The first "L" represents her L<small>OVING WAY</small>
That she lifts my spirit so high.
The second "L" represents how L<small>IVELY</small>
And active she seems to be.
This "E" represents the E<small>NCOURAGEMENT</small>
Her spirit is to me.
The "N" represents the fact that N<small>O ONE</small>
Can be quite like her;
And her name is E<small>LLEN</small>
Who's given my heart quite a stir.

Eryka

"E" is for her ENTHUSIASM;
For she really gets into what she does.
"R" is for REALISM;
For she considers all of us.
"Y" is for her YOUTHFULNESS;
For she is so full of zeal.
"K" is for her KINDNESS;
From her this is what you feel .
"A" is for her AFFECTION;
For all of whom she cares;
And her name is ERYKA,
Who's ready to go anywhere.

Francis

The "F" is for her F<small>AITH</small>
That she expresses from day to day.
The "R" is for her R<small>ESPONSE</small>
To the Almighty when she prays.
The "A" is for the A<small>NGELS</small>
That attend when she's in prayer.
The "N" is for that N<small>EVER</small>
Will she loose for she will remain there.
The "C" is for the C<small>ARE</small>
She expresses to those in need.
The "I" is for the I<small>NCREDIBLE POWER</small>
She finds as God's Word she heeds.
The "S" is for her S<small>ACRIFICE</small>
That she renders unto the Lord.
And her name is F<small>RANCIS</small>,
Whom God will bless with a tremendous reward.

Gabariral

"G" is for the Grace
By which she carries herself.
"A" is for her Acceptance,
For as you are she accepts.
"B" is for her Benevolence;
For she is kind to those in need.
"A" is for her Attentiveness
To every little deed.
"R" is for her Realism;
For she considers what is true.
"I" is for the Illustrious way
That she speaks to you.
"R" is for she's Responsive
With real care for you and me.
"A" is for the Animate way
That she gets you to her way see.
"L" is for she's a Leader
Of many that she befriends.
And her name is Gabariral,
A friend that will be there
Until the very end.

Gwendolyn

"G" is for how G<small>IVING</small> that she must really be
To have raised such a great company.
"W" is for how W<small>ILLING</small> her sacrifice really is
To spend her life involved in another's biz.
"E" is for E<small>ACH ONE OF HER CHILDREN</small> call her blessed;
For they understand that she can stand the test.
"N" is for that N<small>O ONE</small> can comprehend her zeal;
Unless they understand that what's inside her is so real.
"D" is for her D<small>YNAMIC PERSONALITY</small> that's shining through
To bless all those around her, even me and you.
"O" is for how O<small>BSERVANT</small> that she really is
To watch all of her children, and understand their Biz.
"L" is for how L<small>OVING AND KIND THAT SHE AIMS TO BE</small>
So that all those around will by her be blessed, you see.
"Y" is for her Y<small>EARNING TO MAKE A DIFFERENCE IN LIFE</small>
By enduring every hardship and daily strife.
"N" is for that N<small>EVER WILL THIS WOMAN GIVE IN</small>
To the pressures of daily living that try to draw her into sin.

Harriet

"H" is for the HAPPINESS
That she brings into my life.
"A" is for the ACCEPTANCE I FEEL
When I come to her with daily strife.
"R" is for the REINFORCEMENT SHE GIVES
To character qualities that are true.
"R" is for the RESPECT
That for this woman from me is due.
"I" is for how INCREDIBLE
Life has been just knowing her.
"E" is for EACH DAY IS A GIFT
That I get to spend it with her.
"T" is for the TIMES WE'VE HAD
That I remember, oh so well;
For she is my Mom,
Who's been such a blessing I cannot tell.

(Written for someone to give to their mother)

Heather

"H" is for how HAPPY I AM
Whenever I'm with her.
"E" is for her ELEGANCE
That makes others seem like a blur.
"A" is for how AMAZING IT IS
That she's interested in me.
"T" is for this TERRIFIC FEELING I GET
Whenever it's her I see.
"H" is for this HEART-FELT LONGING I have
To spend some quality time with her.
"E" is for EVERY TIME we talk
My heart is completed stirred.
"R" is for how REAL
These feelings for her have become.
And her name is HEATHER
Who I believe could just be the one.

Jacqualine

"J" is for being
Just like Mom is.
"A" is for how Anxious I am
To tend to that grown up biz.
"C" is for how Careful I am
When I grab a broom and sweep.
"Q" is for how Quite I am
When it's time to go to sleep.
"U" is for that I Understand
That I'm just a child.
"A" is for how attentive I am,
Trying not to just go wild.
"L" is for Lively,
For that describes just what I am.
"I" is for my Imagination,
For I imagine as much as I can.
"N" is for that No one
Can ever keep right up with me.
"E" is for Each time
A grown up I want to be.

Jacqueline

"J" is for being
Just like Mom is.
"A" is for how Anxious I am
To tend to that grown up biz.
"C" is for how Careful I am
When I grab a broom and sweep.
"Q" is for how Quite I am
When it's time to go to sleep.
"U" is for that I Understand
That I'm just a child.
"E" is for how Every time
I try to keep from going wild.
"L" is for Lively,
For that describes just what I am.
"I" is for my Imagination,
For I imagine as much as I can.
"N" is for that No one
Can ever keep right up with me.
"E" is for Each time
A grown up I want to be.

Jacquelyn

"J" is for being
J̲u̲s̲t̲ like Mom is.
"A" is for how A̲n̲x̲i̲o̲u̲s̲ I am
To tend to that grown up biz.
"C" is for how C̲a̲r̲e̲f̲u̲l̲ I am
When I grab a broom and sweep.
"Q" is for how Q̲u̲i̲t̲e̲ I am
When it's time to go to sleep.
"U" is for that I U̲n̲d̲e̲r̲s̲t̲a̲n̲d̲
That I'm just a child.
"E" is for how E̲v̲e̲r̲y̲ t̲i̲m̲e̲
I try to keep from going wild.
"L" is for L̲i̲v̲e̲l̲y̲,
For that describes just what I am.
"Y" is for my Y̲o̲u̲t̲h̲,
For I'm much younger than I proclaim.
"N" is for that N̲o̲ o̲n̲e̲
Can ever keep right up with me.
All this spells J̲a̲c̲q̲u̲e̲l̲y̲n̲,
Who acts like she's twenty-three.

James

*"J" is for he's J*UDICIOUS*;*
For he is sensible in his ways.
*"A" is for his A*PPRECIATION
Of the blessings sent his way.
*"M" is for he's M*ERCIFUL*;*
For others, he feels compassion.
*"E" is for he's so E*FFICIENT
On each task, you'll be amazed.
*"S" is for his S*ENSITIVITY*,*
How he senses so many needs;
And his name is James
Whose words we should often heed.

Ja'vone

"J" is for he's Judicious;
For he is sensible in his ways.
"A" is for his Aspiration
To be someone someday.
"V" is for his vivacious ways
That inspires us one and all.
"O" is for he's Observant
For he seems to see it all.
"N" is for that there's No one else
That can make life seem so free.
"E" is for his Enthusiasm;
For he has a lot to see.

Jeff

"J" is for J<small>ESUS</small>,
The center of his life.
"E" is for E<small>TERNITY</small>,
The goal he keeps in sight.
"F" is for his F<small>AITHFULNESS</small>
To a holy God above.
"F" is for the F<small>REEDOM HE FOUND</small>
While receiving God's Holy Love.

Jenny

"J" is for JUDICIOUS;
For she is sensible in her ways.
"E" is for ELEGANT;
For she has cultured tastes.
"N" is for NOTEWORTHY;
For she is quite remarkable.
"N" is for NURTURING;
For she holds her children as treasurable.
"Y" is for her YEARNING
To be all that she can be;
And her name is JENNY,
Who is one terrific lady.

Jessica

*"J" is for her J*USTNESS*;*
For she cares for those
Who has wrong to them done.
*"E" is for her E*QUITY*;*
For she tries to be fair
To everyone.
*"S" is for her S*ACRIFICE
To do what she believes is right.
*"S" is for S*UFFERING
When people try to this fight.
*"I" is for her I*NSISTENCE
That the good prevail.
*"C" is for her C*ARING ENOUGH
That her opinion she must share.
*"A" is for the A*NSWERS
To all the questions
She must find.
*And her name is J*ESSICA*,*
Who for the underdog
Will always shine.

"For people that try to win this fight."

Jesus

"J" is for He's J<small>UST</small>
And righteous altogether.
"E" is for He's E<small>TERNAL</small>;
For He will reign forever.
"S" is for He's our S<small>ACRIFICE</small>
To redeem our souls from sin.
"U" is for that He U<small>NDERSTANDS</small>
What it takes for us to win.
"S" is for He's our S<small>ECURITY</small>;
Fir in Him we are secure.
And all this spells J<small>ESUS</small>,
The name of Christ our Saviour.

Karli

*"K" is because she K*INDLES
A flame inside your heart.
*"A" is for she's A*FFECTIONATE
And loving from the start.
*"R" is for her R*ESPONSIVE
Attitude of real care.
*"L" is for the L*OVE
That she has to share.
*"I" is for the I*NCREDIBLE WAY
She gets you to hear her;
*And her name is K*ARLI,
Who can really cause a stir.

Katherine (1)

"K" is for her KINDNESS
That she shows to everyone.
"A" is for her APPRECIATION
For all that her way has come.
"T" is for she's TRUSTING
With an open heart to give.
"H" is for the HAPPINESS
That she wants us all to live.
"E" is for she's so EFFICIENT
On each task, you'll be amazed.
"R" is for the RESPECT
She has for your ways.
"I" is for the ILLUSTRIOUS WAY
That she speaks her jive.
"N" is for that there's NO ONE ELSE
That can make life seem so alive.
"E" is for EACH TIME
She's met me at the door;
And her name is KATHERINE;
My great and wonderful Mother.

(Written for someone to give to their mother)

Katherine (2)

"K" is for how K<small>EEN</small>
Her sense of perception is.
"A" is for how A<small>CCOMMODATING</small>
To someone else's biz.
"T" is for the T<small>IMES</small>
She sacrificially goes along.
"H" is for H<small>OW OFTEN</small>
She loves to sing her song.
"E" is for her E<small>LOQUENT WAY</small>
Of showing you that she cares.
"R" is for she's R<small>ELIABLE</small>;
For when you need her she is there.
"I" is for her I<small>NTUITION</small>;
For she always senses your need.
"N" is for that N<small>O ONE</small>
Is quite like her indeed.
"E" is for her E<small>AGERNESS</small>
To always be your friend;
And her name is K<small>ATHERINE</small>,
Who's there through thick and thin.

Katya

"K" is for her kindness
That she has shown to me.
"A" is for how Attractive
That I find her to be.
"T" is for her Trusting heart
That causes me to care.
"Y" is for this Yearning I feel
Just to have her near.
"A" is for her Attitude
That's positively a plus.
And all these spells, "Katya",
Who wants her and I to be us.

Kay (1)

"K" is for K<small>INDNESS</small>;
For she's always been sweet to me.
"A" is for A<small>TTRACTIVE</small>;
For she's beautiful to see.
"Y" is for Y<small>IELDING</small>;
For she's submissive to those who care;
And her name is "K<small>AY</small>",
With whom I'd like some time to share.

Kay (2)

Kind at heart,
She makes her mark
By making you feel right at home.
Attentive indeed
To hospitable needs,
And will be 'til you're gone.
Youthful lady
That does not say maybe
When it comes to getting things done.
She's a marvelous lady
That is real pretty,
And K<small>AY</small> is her name.

Kayanna

"K" is for her K<small>INDNESS</small>;
For she's so kind to all.
"A" is for her A<small>CCEPTANCE</small>;
For she's quick to heed your call.
"Y" is for Y<small>IELDING</small>;
For she submits to those in command.
"A" is for A<small>CCOUNTABLE</small>;
For she'll tell you where she's been.
"N" is for that N<small>EVER</small>
Can you question her honesty.
"N" is for that N<small>O ONE</small>
Is quite like her, you see.
"A" is for her A<small>PPRECIATION</small>
For everything you've done;
And her name is K<small>AYANNA</small>,
Who likes life when its fun.

Kelsey

"K" is for Kindness,
For she's been so sweet to me.
"E" is for Each time
She lets her temper flare.
"L" is for her Lovely
And energetic life she leads.
"S" is for Sassy,
For she lets her opinions glare.
"E" is for Enthusiasm;
For she has a lot to see.
"Y" is for her Youthful glow
Which tempts you to even stare.
And her name is Kelsey,
To miss her life,
You wouldn't want to this one be.

Kendra

Kind,
Eager,
Nice,
Devoted,
Radiant,
Attractive

Ketura

"K" is for the Kindness
That you have shown to me.
"E" is for Enchanting,
For that's what I find you to be.
"T" is for the Time
I'd like to spend with you.
"U" is for this Undeniable feeling
That I have when I'm around you.
"R" is for the Reasons
I give myself to look your way.
"A" is for this Attraction
I feel toward you today.
And your name is Ketura,
Quite a lady indeed,
One that has my attention,
That I'm glad to have come to meet.

Kristy

*"K" is for her K*INDLY*
And warm-hearted smile.
"R" is for the R*EFRESHING*
Of her spirit with no guile.
"I" is for the I*MPRESSIONABLE*
Way that she greets you.
"S" is for her S*ERVILE WAY*
She helps you make it through.
"T" is for her T*RUSTING*
And open heart to give.
"Y" is for her Y*EARNING*
For a fruitful life to live.*

Kyla

*"K" is for her K*NACK*
For getting your attention.
"Y" is for her Y*IELDING*
To her Mom's contention.
"L" is for her L*IVELY*
And energetic ways.
"A" is for the A*NIMATE WAY*
She gets you to for her pray.*

Kyle

*"K" is for his K*NOWLEDGE
Of autos and of bikes.
*"Y" is for his Y*EARNING
To build that motorcyc'.
*"L" is for his L*OVE
For mechanics and the grease.
*"E" is for E*ACH TIME
He wants to be released
To work on an auto,
Or maybe on a bike.
*And his name is K*YLE,
My son who loves to bike.

(Written for a parent about their Son)

Laicy

"L" is for how lovely
I find this one to be.
"A" is for this Attraction
That longs to be set free.
"I" is for how Involved
I'd like to be in her life.
"C" is for this Closeness I feel
When I look into her eyes.
"Y" is for this Yearning
To spend more time with her;
And her name is Laicy,
This woman that has caused
Quite a stir.

Lakeiya

"L" is for she's a Leader
Of those that she befriends.
"A" is for Angelic,
For she's an angel to the end.
"K" is for her kindly
And warm hearted smile.
"E" is for Each time
She satisfies me all the while.
"I" is for Impulsive,
For she lives so spontaneously.
"Y" is for her Yearning
To be all that she can be.
"A" is for Authentic,
For she is one of a kind.
And there's no one quite like Lakeiya,
Whose life like the Sun does shine.

Laquanda

"L" is for her LOVING WAY
Of making you feel right at home.
"A" is for her ATTRACTIVENESS;
From her, your eyes long not to roam.
"Q" is for she's QUAINT
And petite in her build.
"U" is for she's UNIQUE
In how she aims to yield.
"A" is for ACKNOWLEDGMENT
Of all those that are near.
"N" is for that NO ONE
Will call her anything but dear.
"D" is for the DARLING
That she has become.
"A" is for the APPROVAL
She receives from everyone.

Lenora

"L" is for she's a Leader
Of many that she befriends.
"E" is for her Enthusiasm;
For she's exciting to the end.
"N" is for that there's No one
That's quite like her.
"O" is for she's Orderly
For she's an organizing girl.
"R" is for her Realism;
For she considers what is true.
"A" is for her Attentive way
That she keeps her eyes on you.
She has everything on the go,
Staying busy all the while;
And her name is Lenora,
A lady of class and style.

Lori

"L" is for her Loving approach.
"O" is for her Observant ways.
"R" is for her Radiant countenance.
"I" is for her intuitive gaze;
Her name is Lori;
And she's a real sight.
Just watching her
Makes me wish things were right
For me to pursue
A relationship with this
Beautiful woman
With a kiss.

Lynsey

"L" is for the Love
That I feel for you.
"Y" is for this Yearning
I feel to be near you.
"N" is for that No one
Makes me feel this way.
"S" is for the how Sweet
You are today.
"E" is for Each time
I get to be with you.
And "Y" is for Your beauty
That sparks these feelings so true.

Marentha (1)

"M" is for MIRACULOUS;
For God gave to her me.
"A" is for ANGELIC;
For she's my angel, you see.
"R" is for REMEMBER;
For I'll always remember her.
"E" is for EACH DAY is a gift
I get to spend with her.
"N" is for No one
Loves her like I do.
"T" is for the TIMES
That together we've gone through.
"H" is for the HAPPINESS
I have because she's mine.
"A" is for that ALWAYS
My love for her will shine.
And I get to be her DAUGHTER;
And Nikki is my name.
I am so very proud of her.
Of her I'm not ashamed.

(Written for a daughter about her mother)

Marentha (2)

"M" is for M<small>IRACULOUS</small>;
For God gave her to me.
"A" is for A<small>NGELIC</small>;
For she's my guardian angel, you see.
"R" is for R<small>EMEMBER</small>;
For I'll always remember her.
"E" is for E<small>ACH DAY</small>
I get to spend with her.
"N" is for No one
Loves her like I do.
"T" is for the T<small>IMES</small>
That together we go through.
"H" is for the H<small>APPINESS</small>
I have because she's mine.
"A" is for that A<small>LWAYS</small>
My love for her will shine.
And I get to be her D<small>AUGHTER</small>;
And Nikki is my name.
I am so very proud of her.
Of her I'm not ashamed.

(Written for a mother about her daughter)

Marie

"M" is for the MEMORIES
Of our growing up together.
"A" is for the ABUNDANCE
Of them that we treasure.
"R" is for the REMEMBRANCE
Of the good times that we share.
"I" is for the IMPORTANCE
Of showing that we care.
"E" is for EACH DAY
I often think of you;
For you are my SISTER,
And oh, how I do love you.

(Written for sisters)

Maureen

"M" is for how M<small>IGHTY</small>
She becomes in prayer.
"A'" is for the A<small>UTHORITY</small>
She has when she is there.
"U" is for the U<small>NDERSTANDING</small>
Nature of her ways.
"R" is for how R<small>ESPONSIVE</small>
That she is when she prays.
"E" is for the E<small>TERNAL VALUES</small>
That she holds.
"E" is for E<small>ACH BURDEN</small>
She takes to God so bold.
"N" is for the N<small>EW LIFE</small>
That she has found in prayer.
And her name is S<small>ISTER</small> M<small>AUREEN</small>
Whose heart is filled with care.

Melshika

*"M" is for the M*ysterious look*
That's always in her eyes.
*"E" is for the E*loquence*
Of her daily disguise.
*"L" is for the L*ogical way*
She plans her daily events.
*"S" is for S*cholarly way*
That her plans she presents.
*"H" is for the H*eadstrong way*
Way that she seeks to shine.
*"I" is for I*llustrious way*
That she speaks her mind.
*"K" is for her K*inetic personality*
That provokes you to act.
*"A" is for her A*ttitude*
That helps keep her on track.

Michael (1)

"M" is for how MEANINGFUL
Our relationship has become.
"I" is for how INCREDIBLE IT IS
That you and I are one.
"C" is for the CARE
That you've shown for me.
"H" is for HOW MUCH
My emotions have been set free.
"A" is for ALL THE TIMES
We've spent together.
"E" is for EACH TIME
Was special, no matter the weather.
"L" is for the LOVE
That I have for you;
For you are "MY MAN",
The love that's been so true.

(Written for a Wife or girlfriend about her man)

Michael (2)

"M" is for the MAN
You'll someday become.
"I" is for how INCREDIBLE IT IS
That you are my grandson.
"C" is for the CARE
That you've shown to me.
"H" is for HOW MUCH
That in you I believe.
"A" is for ALL THE TIMES
We have spent together.
"E" is for EACH TIME was special
No matter the weather.
"L" is for that in your LIFE
God has plans for you;
And you are "MICHAEL",
The grandson I love so true.

(Written for a Grandfather about his grandson)

Minnie (1)

"M" is for MAJESTIC;
For her presence demands respect.
"I" is for INCREDIBLE;
For she's better than the best.
"N" is for she's NOBLE;
For she's quite dignified.
"N" is for she's NOTABLE;
For she's the exceptional kind.
"I" is for IMPRESSIONABLE;
For she's made her mark on me.
"E" is for ELOQUENT;
For she articulates so beautifully.

Minnie (2)

"M" is for she's MOTHERLY;
For she has been that to me.
"I" is for she's INCREDIBLE;
For her love has set me free.
"N" is for that NO ONE
Will ever be quite like her.
"N" is for that NEVER
Will she be forgotten ever.
"I" is for the IMMEASURABLE
Mark she's made upon my life.
"E" is for the ELOQUENT WAY
She's helped me through my strife.

(Written for someone about an adoptive
motherly figure, legally or not)

Misty

"M" is for how M<small>ETICULOUS</small> <small>SHE IS</small>.
"I" is for she's I<small>NCREDIBLE TO KNOW</small>.
"S" is for her S<small>ENTIMENTAL WAYS</small>.
"T" is for she's a T<small>RUSTING SOUL</small>.
"Y" is for her Y<small>EARNING TO LIVE</small>;
   And her name is M<small>ISTY</small>,
   Who has a heart to give.

Mitzy

"M" is for how MILITANT
She is in prayer.
"I" is for how INVOLVED
She is in care.
"T" is for the TRUTH
She loves to proclaim.
"Z" is for her ZEAL
For Jesus name.
"Y" is for her YEARNING
By God to be used.
All of this spells "MITZY"
Who has higher things in view.

Monique

"M" is for MOTHERLY;
For she always looking out for you.
"O" is for OBSERVANT;
For she notices what you do.
"N" is for that NO ONE
Will treat you like she does.
"I" is for that she's INVOLVED
In blessing all of us.
"Q" is for her QUIET
Humble and meek spirit.
"U" is for she UNDERSTANDS
When you're going through it.
"E" is for EACH TIME
You meet her she's a blessing;
For she is MONIQUE;
Quite unique with her addressing.

(Written for someone about an adoptive motherly figure, whether or not legally)

Natasha

"N" is for she's Naive
And simple in her ways.
"A" is for she's Admirable
And worthy of some praise.
"T" is for she's Trusting
And believes without restraint.
"A" is for she's Affirming
To the antiquated and quaint.
"S" is for she's Sentimental
And romantic in her disguise.
"H" is for she's Honest
And fair in other's eyes.
"A" is for she's Affectionate
Towards he who is her man;
For she is Natasha,
Who loves to be romanced.

Nikki

"N" is for that Never
Have I seen her without a smile.
"I" is for Incredible;
For I'm amazed by her style.
"K" is for that Kindness
Is how she leaves her mark.
"K" is for Kinetic;
For her energy creates a spark.
"I" is for Intuitive;
For she's Johnny on the spot;
And her name is "Nikki",
A friend I like a lot.

Nuwanda

The "N" is for her NONCHALANT WAY
Of getting you to be involved.
The "U" is for her UNDENIABLE WAY
Of getting things resolved.
The "W" is for her WONDERING
What's in this life for her.
The "A" is for her ARTISTRY;
For she has an artful stir.
The "N" is for her NATURAL
Obsession with daily events.
The "D" is for her DEFIANCE
To allow anything to life circumvent.
The "A" is for her ATTEMPTS
To get so much more out of life;
And her name is NUWANDA,
Who faces head on her daily strife.

Ola

"O" is for she's O<small>BSERVANT</small>;
For that's what mothers are.
"L" is for the L<small>OVING WAY</small>
She treats her children as a star.
"A" is for her A<small>BILITY</small>
To know when things are wrong;
And her name is Ola,
The queen of her own home.

Orlando

"O" is for O<small>BSERVANT</small>;
For he notices most everything.
"R" is for R<small>EPUTABLE</small>;
For his reputation is on the wing.
"L" is for his L<small>AUGHTER</small>;
For he finds humor in each day.
"A" is for his A<small>SPIRATION</small>
To be someone someday.
"N" is for N<small>EIGHBORLY</small>;
For he's friendly to all who'll receive.
"D" is for D<small>ARING</small>;
For he'll try anything he can believe.
"O" is for O<small>PEN-MINDED</small>;
For he'll discuss most any topic;
And his name is O<small>RLANDO</small>;
If you tell a story,
He'll try to top it.

Pam (1)

Pretty
Awesome
Mamma

Pam (2)

"P" is for you're PRECIOUS;
For to us you're such a sweetheart.
"A" is for your APPRECIATIVE;
For you've been thankful from the start.
"M" is for the MYSTERIOUS LOOK
That's always in your glare.
And you are Pam;
Who we love through heartfelt care.

Pamela

"P" is for you're PRECIOUS;
For to us you're such a sweetheart.
"A" is for your APPRECIATION;
For you've been thankful from the start.
"M" is for the MYSTERIOUS LOOK
That's always in your glare.
"E" is for your ELOQUENCE
Which makes you look so fare.
"L" is for your LOVING WAY
You make everyone feel alright.
"A" is for your ATTENTIVE WAY
That keeps us in your sight.
And you are PAMELA;
Who we love through heartfelt care;
And when you need us, daughter,
We will certainly be there.

(Written for a parent about their daughter)

Perishes

"P" is for P̲r̲e̲c̲i̲o̲u̲s̲;
For she is so very sweet.
"E" is for E̲a̲c̲h̲ t̲i̲m̲e̲
She does some little thing so neat.
"R" is for R̲a̲d̲i̲a̲n̲t̲;
For she beams with care for all.
"I" is for I̲m̲p̲e̲t̲u̲o̲u̲s̲;
For she is impulsive, though she is so small.
"S" is for S̲p̲e̲l̲l̲b̲i̲n̲d̲i̲n̲g̲;
For your attention will not roam.
"H" is for H̲o̲s̲p̲i̲t̲a̲b̲l̲e̲;
For she makes you feel at home.
"E" is for E̲m̲p̲a̲t̲h̲e̲t̲i̲c̲;
For she feels your very need.
"S" is for S̲y̲m̲p̲a̲t̲h̲e̲t̲i̲c̲;
For she involves herself with sympathy.

Queen

*"Q" is for she's Q*UAINT*;*
And petite in her frame.
*"U" is for U*NIQUE*;*
For there's no one quite the same.
*"E" is for E*NTHUSIASTIC*;*
For she gets into what she's doing.
*"E" is for E*ACH DAY
She's really into off showing.
*"N" is for that N*O ONE
Can resist her charm;
*For her name is Q*UEEN*;*
Who is royally not the norm.

Robbie

Radiant,
Observant,
Bright,
Beautiful,
Intelligent,
Encouraging.

Rodney

"R" is for he's RELIABLE;
For I can certainly count on him.
"O" is for he's an ORGANIZER;
For he's coordinating everything.
"D" is for his DYNAMIC PERSONALITY;
For he draws people into his act.
"N" is for that NATURALLY
He leads people to the right track.
"E" is for his EFFORT
To keep everything going smooth.
"Y" is for his YEARNING
To always be on the move.

Romona

"R" is for RESERVED;
For she's careful
Who she lets close to her.
"O" is for OLD-FASHIONED;
For she holds to
The traditions of her mother.
"M" is for MANNERLY;
For she always uses
"Thank you" and "please".
"O" is for OBSERVANT;
For she notices
Whatever she sees.
"N" is for NEIGHBORLY;
For she takes time
To be a friend.
"A" is for ACCOMMODATING;
For she is gracious
And willingly helpful to the end.

Sharon

"S" is for she's Sassy
With attitude in her ways.
"H" is for how Happy
I get whenever I see her play.
"A" is for how Appreciative
She is just to be alive.
"R" is for her Realism;
For she's concerned with relational ties.
"O" is for she's Observant,
For everything she seems to see.
"N" is for that there's No one else
That can make life seem so free.

Shawn

"S" is for how Special
That you are to me.
"H" is for how Happy I am
When it's you I see.
"A" is for this Attraction
That I cannot deny.
"W" is for the Way
You capture me with your eyes.
"N" is for that Never
Will there be anyone quite like you.
The one that I love,
Miss. Shawn,
Yes, I really love you.

Shermichael

The "S" is for he's S<small>ENTIMENTAL</small>;
For he dwells on the good of the past.
The "H" is for he's H<small>ANDY</small>;
For he likes for things to last.
The "E" is for his E<small>XERCISE</small>;
For he's into working out.
The "R" is for he's R<small>ECEPTIVE</small>
To new ideas without a doubt.
The "M" is for he's M<small>ELANCHOLY</small>;
For he likes things organized.
The "I" is for he's I<small>NVENTIVE</small>,
A character to be prized.
The "C" is for he's C<small>ARING</small>
For his family and his friends.
The "H" is for he H<small>USTLES</small>
When working for their end.
The "A" is for his A<small>MBITION</small>
To be all that he can be.
The "E" is for he's E<small>NERGETIC</small>;
For he's got lots of energy.
The "L" is for his L<small>ABORIOUS WAY</small>
Through which he gets things done.
And his name is S<small>HERMICHAEL</small>,
A man that's continually on the run.

Sherriah

"S" is for S<small>ASSY</small>;
For she's so very opinionated.
"H" is for H<small>OTHEADED</small>;
For when her temper is abated.
"E" is for E<small>ACH TIME</small>
She lets her temper flare.
"R" is or her R<small>ESPONSE TO HER CHILD</small>
As she looks on with a proud glare.
"R" is for the R<small>EMARKABLE WAY</small>
She faces daily events.
"I" is for her I<small>MAGINATION</small>
Helps her work out her intents.
"A" is for her A<small>TTITUDE TOWARDS LIFE</small>
That will help her fight.
"H" is for her H<small>ONESTY</small>
That keeps her in the right.

Stacy

*"S" is for she's S*ASSY*;*
Somewhat adamant about life.
*"T" is for she's T*RUSTING*;*
And accepting her daily strife.
*"A" is for she's A*DVENTUROUS*;*
For she'll try most anything.
*"C" is for she's C*ARING
For all that life will bring.
*"Y" is for her Y*EARNING
To be all that she can be;
For her name is Stacy,
Who's wants to be set free.

Suzanne

"S" is for how SWEET
That she seems to be.
"U" is for UNDERSTANDING;
For she considers you and me.
"Z" is for her ZEAL
To make her mark upon your life.
"A" is for that with ATTITUDE
She attacks her daily strife.
"N" is for that NEVER
Will you see her sitting by.
"N" is for that NO ONE
Is like her in your eye.
"E" is for ENTHUSIASM;
For she has a lot of this;
And her name is SUZANNE;
Whose life you don't want to miss.

Tamiko

"T" is for she's T<small>RUSTWORTHY</small>;
And to trust her you can start.
"A" is for she's A<small>PPRECIATIVE</small>;
For she is thankful from the heart.
"M" is for the M<small>YSTERIOUS LOOK</small>
That's always in her eyes.
"I" is for the Illustrious way
That she speaks her jive.
"K" is for her K<small>INDLY</small>
And warm-hearted smile.
"O" is for she's O<small>RDERLY</small>
For she organizes with style.

Tommy

"T" is for the T<small>RUST</small>
That I've placed in him.
"O" is for he's O<small>BVIOUSLY</small>
Become my closest friend.
"M" is for the M<small>IRACLE</small>
That we found each other.
"M" is for how M<small>EANINGFUL</small>
Our feelings have become for one another.
"Y" is for this Y<small>EARNING</small>
For us to be as one.
And T<small>OMMY</small>, I'm so glad
That to me you've come.

Tonya

The "T" is for her Tempting eyes
With which she draws you in.
The "O" is for she's Observant
Of ways to please her men.
The "N" is for that Never
Will time with her be ever dull.
The "Y" is for her Yearning
To live life to the full.
The "A" is for her Attitude;
About her so much it does tell;
And her name is Tonya,
A woman that likes to excel.

Victor

"V" is for his VITALITY;
For he's vigorous
And full of life.
"I" is for his INFLUENCE;
For his sway will
Overcome much strife.
"C" is for he's CONSISTENT
In his daily affairs.
"T" is for he's TRUSTWORTHY;
You can be sure he'll be there.
"O" is for he's ORDERLY
And organized in his eyes.
"R" is for he's RATIONAL;
For he's intelligent and wise.

Willie (1)

"W" is for she's Willing
To always carry a smile.
"I" is for she's Incredible;
For I'm amazed by her style.
"L" is for the Loving way
That she lifts my spirit so high.
"L" is for how Lively
And actively she seems to fly.
"I" is for she's Intuitive;
For she's Johnny on the spot
"E" is for she's Efficient;
And competently gets things right.

Willie (2)

"W" is for he is so Willing
To always carry a smile.
"I" is for he is just Incredible;
For I'm amazed by his style.
"L" is for the Loving way
That he lifts my spirit so high.
"L" is for how Lively
And actively he seems to fly.
"I" is for he is Intuitive;
For he is Johnny on the spot
"E" is for he is very Efficient;
And competently gets things right.

Xavier

"X" is for his eXtra efforts
To become just what he desires.
"A" is for he's Admirable
For his spunk and his inner fire.
"V" is for he's Valiant
And bold to make a stand.
"I" is for he's Intelligent
And clever with his hand.
"E" is for he's Eager
To make his mark on life.
"R" is for his Resolve
To overcome daily strife.

Xena

*"X" is for her e**X**tra-ordinary way*
She can capture your attention.
*"E" is for **E**ach time*
She comprehends your intention.
*"N" is for that **N**o one*
Is quite like her.
*"A" is for that **A**lways*
She's causing quite a stir.

PART TWO:
ACRONYMIA

Angels

"A" is for the AWESOME
Presence that you feel.
"N" is for that NO ONE
Really comprehends their zeal.
"G" is for the GOD
Whom they serve both day and night.
"E" is for the ETERNAL REALM
In which they always fight.
"L" is for the LOVE OF GOD
Which motivates their work.
"S" is for the SALVATION OF MAN
For which they stay alert.
The BIBLE calls them ministers;
A flaming fire of God
Sent to help the heirs
Of the salvation of God;
We refer to them as ANGELS;
And often fail to see
That they are working day and night
To help and set us free.

Bible

"B" is for the Brightness
Of its light through all of time.
"I" is for its Instruction
To help us to tow the line.
"B" is for its Boldness
To tell it like it is.
"L" is for the Love
And grace to live like this.
E" is for the Enlightenment
We find within its text.
And its words are sent
To help us
To face what's coming next.

Birthday

"B" is for the BRIGHTNESS
Of the Sun that shines your way.
"I" is for how INCREDIBLE
I hope will be your special day.
"R" is for the RADIANCE
Of your smile as you are Blessed.
"T" is for the THINGS
You may receive from all the rest.
"H" is for the HAPPINESS
I hope this day brings to you.
"D" is for the DRAMATICS
Of many friends that are so true.
"A" is for how AWESOME
That I really think you are.
"Y" is for this next YEAR
In which I know you'll be a star.

Calvary

"C" is for the C<small>HRIST</small>
That died upon this hill.
"A" is for the A<small>WESOME</small>
Power of His will.
"L" is for the L<small>OVE</small>
He displayed in going there.
"V" is for the V<small>ICTORY</small>
He won for us to share.
"A" is for the A<small>NSWERS</small>
We can now have through His name.
"R" is for the R<small>EDEMPTION</small>
That His spilt blood became.
"Y" is for His Y<small>EARNING</small>
For us to come to Him.
And all of this spells C<small>ALVARY</small>
The altar for all sin.

Christian

The "C" is for Courteous;
For he's polite indeed.
The "H" is for my Hope
That he's of better seed.
The "R" is for Responsive;
For he's quick to return your call.
The "I" is for Intuitive;
For he's sensitive all in all.
The "S" is for Skillful;
For how he handles today.
The "T" is for his Thankfulness;
For he's grateful for each day.
The "I" is for his Initiative;
For prompting he doesn't need.
The "A" is for he's Astute
And sharp as a tack indeed.
The "N" is for that No one
Is quite like this man of fate;
And his name is Christian,
A man that tries to stay in shape.

Christmas

"C" is for the CHRIST CHILD
That was born upon this day.
"H" is for the HOLINESS
Of God upon display.
"R" is for the RIGHTEOUSNESS
That was shining all around.
"I" is for the INCREDIBLE THING
That happened in this town.
"S" is for the SUFFERING
That He had to go through.
"T" is for the TRUTH He brought
To deliver me and you.
"M" is for the MIRACULOUS
Way that Jesus came.
"A" is for the ANGELS
Who revealed to us His name.
"S" is for the SALVATION
We now have through faith in Him.
And all of this spells CHRISTMAS,
The day it all began.

Covenant

"C" is for the COMMITMENT
That true COVENANT requires.
"O" is for the OBEDIENCE
That true COVENANT inspires.
"V" is for the VICTORY
That total commitment can bring.
"E" is for the ENCOURAGEMENT of having
Someone to which you can cling.
"N" is for the NEARNESS you feel
Whenever you do commit.
"A" is for the ASSURANCE of
The vows with which you are knit.
"N" is for NEVER forgetting
These vows that you have made.
"T" is for being always TRUE;
Never giving anything in trade.

Customer

"C" is for the C<small>ARE</small>
We should express to you.
"U" is for our U<small>NDERSTANDING</small>
That will help us to serve you.
"S" is for our S<small>ERVICE</small>
That you should find second to none.
"T" is for our T<small>IMING</small>
To help keep you on the run.
"O" is for our O<small>BSERVANCE</small>
Of your daily need.
"M" is for our M<small>ERCY</small>
To reach out to you indeed.
"E" is for E<small>ACH TIME</small>
You return right through our doors.
"R" is for you're the R<small>EASON</small>
That we open up this our store.

Drugs

"D" is for the D<small>ANGER</small>
They present to your life.
"R" is for the R<small>EALITY</small>
They distort in your sight.
"U" is for how U<small>GLY</small>
That you eventually feel.
"G" is for how G<small>RADUAL</small>
Your sanity they steal.
"S" is for the S<small>UFFERING</small>
People go through because of them.
And if you abuse D<small>RUGS</small>
You can be nobody's friend.

Easter

"E" is for EVERYONE
That's the reason that HE came.
"A" is for the AUTHORITY HE GIVES
Over sin and shame.
"S" is for the SALVATION we have
Through faith in HIS NAME.
"T" is for the TRUTH that sets us free
Again, and again.
"E" is for the ENCOURAGEMENT we get
From spending time alone with HIM.
"R" is for the REST HE GIVES
As we learn to trust in HIS NAME.
His EXAMPLE
Showed us HOW TO COPE.
His ASSURANCE
Gave our hearts NEW HOPE.
His SURRENDER
Brought us VICTORY.
His TOUCH
Gave us LIBERTY.
His EVERLASTING ARMS
Gave us real SUPPORT.
His REDEEMING BLOOD
Gave us A BRAND-NEW START.

Fasting

*"F" is for the F*LESH
That you are trying to overcome.
*"A" is for the A*NSWERS,
For you hope to get some.
*"S" is for this S*ACRIFICE
That you've chosen to give.
*"T" is for the T*RUTH
That you have chosen to live.
*"I" is for the I*NSTRUCTION
You desire to get through prayer.
*"N" is for the "N*O'S"
You tell yourself when you're there.
*"G" is for the G*RACE
Of God that waits for you.
*And F*ASTING *is one thing*
That will help you make it through.

Fellowship

"F" is for the F<small>EELING</small>
Of acceptance
That you feel.
"E" is for the E<small>NLIGHTENMENT</small>
That sharing His word
Can reveal.
"L" is for the L<small>IVES</small>
Of those who really care.
"L" is for the L<small>OVE</small>
That we so often share.
"O" is for the O<small>NENESS</small>
We feel with everyone.
"W" is for the W<small>ILLINGNESS</small>
Of all those that have come.
"S" is for how S<small>PECIAL</small>
Everyone is to you.
"H" is for the H<small>APPINESS</small>
That this can bring to you.
"I" is for your I<small>NVOLVEMENT</small>
In everybody's lives.
"P" is for the P<small>URPOSE OF</small> G<small>OD</small>;
For together we will survive.

Focus

"F" is for your F<small>AITHFULNESS</small>
That keeps you standing strong.
"O" is for your O<small>BEDIENCE</small>
That keeps you out of the wrong.
"C" is for your C<small>ONCENTRATION</small>
That helps you zero in.
"U" is for your U<small>NDERSTANDING</small>
That will help you win.
"S" is for your S<small>TEWARDSHIP</small>
That makes you worthy of trust.
And all of these will help you F<small>OCUS</small>
On the things that you must.

Frustrating

Frequently
Ridiculously
Underestimating
Simple
Temporarily
Agitating
Times
Involving
No
Gain

Now, that's Frustrating!

Heaven

"H" is because this is a HOLY PLACE;
For anywhere God dwells is Holy.
"E" is because this place is ETERNAL;
For it is not confined to the realm of time.
"A" is because of the ANGELS
That minister there to His Majesty.
"V" is because of the VICTORIOUS CELEBRATION there
Through Christ will be yours and mine.
"E" is because that ENTHRONED there
Will be the Jesus, Lord of all Eternity.
"N" is because that NO ONE goes there
Who did not let his light so shine.

Holy Ghost

"H" is for that H<small>ALLOWED</small>
Be His Holy name.
"O" is for His O<small>NENESS</small>;
For He's always the same.
"L" is for His L<small>OVE</small>
He manifested through the Son.
"Y" is for His Y<small>EARNING</small>
For us to Him come.

"G" is for the G<small>IFT</small>
That His Spirit really is.
"H" is for His H<small>ELP</small>;
So we can live like this.
"O" is for His O<small>MNIPOTENCE</small>
That created this whole wide world.
"S" is for His S<small>ALVATION</small>
That His great love unfurled.
"T" is for His T<small>RUTH</small>
That continually sets us free.

Honest

The H̲u̲m̲b̲l̲e̲ M̲a̲n̲ can learn
Wisdom from above.
The O̲b̲e̲d̲i̲e̲n̲t̲ M̲a̲n̲ can learn
How to truly love.
The N̲e̲w̲ M̲a̲n̲ can learn
New ways to know the Lord.
The E̲n̲d̲u̲r̲i̲n̲g̲ M̲a̲n̲ can learn
The rivers he can forge.
The S̲u̲r̲e̲ M̲a̲n̲ can learn
Just how much he can stand.
The T̲r̲u̲e̲ M̲a̲n̲ can learn
What it means to be a man.

Humble

The HONEST MAN can be
Safe from reprimand.
The UNDERSTANDING MAN can be
A safe and secure friend.
The MATURE MAN can be
A shelter from the storm.
The BRILLIANT MAN can be
A light shining in the mourn.
The LOVING MAN can be
A comfort to those in pain.
The ENCOURAGING Man can be
One to lift them up again.

Hunger

"H" is for How this
Makes you want to eat.
"U" is for this Unopened jar of pickles
You believe would be a real treat.
"N" is for your Need of more leverage
Just to open this jar.
"G" is for the Grunting you do
To try to win this war.
"E" is for Each time you try
A little harder to get this treat.
"R" is for the Relief you feel
When you finally get to eat.

Kindness

"K" is for it's the K<small>EY</small>
To being well thought of.
"I" is for it's the I<small>DEAL BEHAVIOR</small>
Towards the ones you love.
"N" is for that N<small>EVER</small>
Should you let this attitude slip from you.
"D" is for D<small>IFFERENCE</small>
You'll experience should you ever do.
"N" is for how N<small>ICE</small>
You feel when people to you are kind.
"E" is for the E<small>NCOURAGEMENT</small> you feel
When you keep them in mind.
"S" is for how S<small>ACRED</small>
Your memories of their kindness are.
"S" is for your S<small>ACRIFICE OF KINDNESS</small>
Can help you win your internal war.

Kiss

The "K" is for K<small>INETIC</small>
For the transfer of emotion.
The "I" is for I<small>NCREDIBLE</small>;
For it causes such commotion.
The first "S" is for S<small>ENSUAL</small>;
For it activates the senses.
The second "S" is for S<small>PIRITUAL</small>
For the moods that it enhances;
And if a K<small>ISS</small> is to be blessed
And fruitful in its essence,
It must be voluntary.

Lonely

*"L" is for the L*ONGING
For the fellowship of a friend.
*"O" is for this O*BVIOUS
Void that is within.
*"N" is for the N*EED *that*
You feel within your soul.
*"E" is for this E*XAMINATION
Of why you cannot feel whole.
*"L" is for these L*ESSONS *that you*
Learn through having this feeling.
*"Y" is for the Y*EARNING
To be with friends congealing.

Love

*"L" is for the L*ONGING*
Of the One True God
For someone with which to walk
And with Him through eternity trod.
"O" is for His O*MNIPOTENCE*
By which He created this world
When He spoke it all into existence
Causing His Word to be unfurled.
"V" is for the V*IBRANCY*
Of His Awesome Holy Presence
As He first walked with Adam
In the garden of His essence.
"E" is for E*TERNITY*
Which is what He wants to share
With those that choose to live for Him
With a life that's filled with care.*

Messiah

"M" is for the M<small>AJESTY</small>
Of the King of kings.
"E" is for the E<small>TERNAL</small> R<small>EALM</small>
From which He reigns.
"S" is for His S<small>UFFERING</small>
Through which He paid the price.
"S" is for the S<small>ALVATION</small>
Which I enjoy tonight.
"I" is for the I<small>NCREDIBLE</small> <small>POWER</small>
Of Jesus blood and name.
"A" is for the A<small>UTHORITY</small> He gives
Over both sin and shame.
"H" is for His H<small>OLINESS</small>
That His life displayed;
For He was M<small>ESSIAH</small>
Who gave His life
For ours in trade.

Mother

"M" is for MERCIFUL;
That's what she's been to me.
"O" is for OBSERVANT;
For there is nothing she doesn't seem to see.
"T" is for TRUSTWORTHY;
For there's nothing she can't be told.
"H" is for her HELPFULNESS;
That is more precious than gold.
"E" is for her ENERGETIC CALL;
That her children will always hear.
"R" is for her REVERENCE FOR GOD;
That motivates her children to fear.

New Year

"N" is for the NEWNESS
That a new year brings.
"E" is for the ENDINGS
That the old year sings.
"W" is for the WISHING
For that brand-new start.
"Y" is for the YEARNING
Of the anxious heart.
"E" is for the ENDURANCE
Of the by-gone-days.
"A" is for the ASSURANCE
That new hope is on its way.
"R" is for the RENEWING
Of commitments made;

Repentance

*"R" is for the R*ESISTANCE
That you feel within your soul.
*"E" is for that in E*TERNITY
You'll want to be fully whole.
*"P" is for your P*RIDE
That you must put to death.
*"E" is for the E*NCOURAGEMENT
Of God's Spirit to pass this test.
*"N" is for the N*EW LIFE
That this prepares you for.
*"T" is for when you T*RUST GOD
You'll begin to win this war.
*"A" is for the A*UTHORITY
In Christ, you will receive.
*"N" is for that you'd N*EVER
Thought you could believe.
*"C" is for the C*OMMITMENT
To Christ that you must make.
*"E" is for that E*ACH TIME *this happens to you*
You're that much less a fake.

SCAGG

Sincere
Confident
Appreciative
Go-Getter

Spiritual Warfare

"S" is for your "SACRIFICE"
Through which you enter this fight.
"P" is for the "POWER OF GOD"
That becomes your might.
"I" is for the "INSPIRATION"
Received through the Word and prayer.
"R" is for the "REALITY"
Of this Spiritual Warfare.
"I" is for the "INCREDIBLE POWER"
Of God's Holy Living Word.
"T" is for the "TRUTH"
That becomes your mighty sword.
"U" is for His "UNDENIABLE"
Presence that you feel.
"A" is for the "AUTHORITY OF GOD",
Your rightful place with zeal.
"L" is for the "LOVE" of God
That motivates your fight.

"W" is for the "WINNING"
That you expect to do tonight.
"A" is for your "ABIDING IN HIM";
For this will make you whole.
"R" is for the "RESISTANCE"
Of the enemies of your soul.
"F" is for the "FAITH"
That will give you strength tonight.
"A" is for how "ACCEPTABLE"
Is your good and faithful fight.
"R" is for your "RIGHTEOUS DUTY"
Which it is to answer God's Call.
"E" is for "ETERNITY"
The reason for it all.

Stress

Simply
Too many
Random
Enormously
Strenuous
Situations at once.

Thanksgiving

"T" is for the TIMES
That God has seen us through.
"H" is for HOW OFTEN
He has strengthened me and you.
"A" is for the ANGELS that
Are watching our every step.
"N" is for that NO ONE
Can do without His help.
"K" is for His KINDNESS
He displays daily toward us.
"S" is for the SUFFERING
Of the savior Christ Jesus.
"G" is for the GIFT
Of that precious Holy Ghost.
"I" is for the INCREDIBLE WAY
That He provides for this great earthly host.
"V" is for the VICTORY
That He bought for us to share.
"I" is for the INSPIRATION
Of His Word which shows us He cares.
"N" is for that NEVER
Will He leave us alone.
"G" is for that I'm GRATEFUL
For all that God has done.

Toothache

"T" is for the TIMES
That you cry out in pain.
"O" is for the word OUCH,
That becomes your refrain.
"O" is for the OVERALL
Suffering you go through.
"T" is for the TRUTH that
The only one to blame is you.
"H" is for the HYGIENE
You let slide from year to year.
"A" is for this AWESOME PAIN
That takes away your cheer.
"C" is for the COMFORT
You now receive from pain pills.
"H" is for the HEALING of this infection
That would cure so many ills.
"E" is for EACH TIME you thought
"If I'd only known."
I could have avoided this TOOTHACHE
That is now become full-blown.

Valentine (1)

The "V" is for the Voice
Of this one I love.
The "A" is for my Attraction
To this one, my special dove.
The "L" is for this Love
That I feel for her.
The "E" is for Each time
We get to spend together for sure.
The "N" is for that No one else
Makes me feel like this.
The "T" is for the Temptation
To give this one a kiss.
The "I" is for how Incredible
Are the times I spend with her.
The "N" is for that Never
Can I this feeling be anything but pure.
The "E" is for the Embrace
That will help me to show
How much that I care
To her get to know.

(Written for a Man to give to his
Girlfriend/fiancé/wife)

Valentine (2)

The "V" is for the VOICE
Of this one I love.
The "A" is for my ATTRACTION
To this one, my special dove.
The "L" is for this LOVE
That I feel for him.
The "E" is for EACH TIME
We get to spend together again.
The "N" is for that NO ONE ELSE
Makes me feel like this.
The "T" is for the TEMPTATION
To give this one a kiss.
The "I" is for how INCREDIBLE
Are the times I spend with him.
The "N" is for that NEVER
Will there be a closer friend .
The "E" is for the EMBRACE
That will help me to show
How much that I care
To him get to know.

(Written for a Woman to give to her
boyfriend/fiancé/husband)

Zeal

"Z" is for Z<small>EALOUSNESS</small>
For the worthy cause of Christ.
"E" is for E<small>TERNITY</small>,
A good reason to live just and right.
"A" is for the A<small>UTHORITY</small>
Of the Holy God of Heaven.
"L" is for the L<small>OVE OF</small> G<small>OD</small>
That will drive out all the leaven.

Chapter 3

GOD BLESS YOU

Accepted

To never be invited
As a guest to dinner,
Always the last one chosen
For a sporting team,
To be the object of
Every bully's scorn,
To be included is
Just a dream.

Isolated from my
Scholastic peers,
Not accepted by
The status-quo,
To just be asked
To tag along,
To soothe some pain
Or end some woe;

Living this life
So, all alone,
Without one close
Confiding friend,
Can be a painful
Road to trod
If left alone
'Till the end.

*But though man
May me
Not include,
And always leave me
'Till the last;
There is one thing
That I'm assured,
In God's Kingdom
The last is first,
And the first is last.*

*And though rejected
By peers quite oft,
And my opinion not
In this world respected,
There is one thing
Helps me endure;
In the beloved
I am accepted.*

Adversity

Adversity, adversity;
So, you find yourself in adversity.
Perhaps if you knew
What's just beyond you,
It might help you through
This adversity;
For lessons are learned through adversity;
And honor is earned through adversity.
Sins are shunned through adversity;
And battles are won through adversity.
Plans are set through adversity;
And needs are met through adversity.
Visions are caught through adversity;
And lessons are taught through adversity.
Warnings we heed through adversity;
And successful men proceed through adversity.
Spirits are worn through adversity;
But nations were born through adversity.
So, what is adversity;
But a blessing in disguise;
Sent to make you strong;
Intended to make you wise.

An Oasis In The Desert Of Life

All churches should become an oasis in the desert of life; for the Church of the Living God is supposed to be where the springs of living water come together to flow out. So, as you offer yourself up to the Living God in worshipful adoration and praise, open your heart and allow the fountain of living water to erupt within you to cause the Spirit of God to flow through you into the Sanctuary. This is how the Spirit of God can effectively move upon a sinner's heart, through the spontaneous eruption of praise and worship that invokes the outpouring of Holy Ghost conviction to draw that sinner's soul unto Him, the fountain of living water. In Jesus Christ's own words, "He that believeth on me as the Scripture hath said, out of his belly shall flow rivers of living water." What is it that causes these rivers to flow? It is a belief that erupts into thanksgiving which will lead into heart-felt praises that in turn transforms spontaneously into worship. For once you really believe in Jesus Christ "as the Scripture hath said," then you cannot help but to become thankful for the hope of eternal life in Him. A truly thankful heart can't help but praise the God of all the ages. And since "God inhabits the praises of His people," true heart-felt praise can only draw the soul into worshipful adoration of the Almighty God. Lost men should be able to taste of the living water as soon as they are in the presence of the Body of Christ, whether it is the local church or just one or two members of the Body. The springs of living water should be flowing through you continually, as you go through your day. Sinners that you come into your presence should have their appetite for the things of God provoked to hunger. They should feel the life-giver flowing from you, wooing them into longing for what you have. If those springs are not flowing from you, you should desire to find out why. You should seek to find out what it is that is clogging up the well-spring of life within you. Commit yourself to a season of fasting and prayer to unclog the well-spring of your soul so that those springs can flow once again. The lost members of your families cannot "taste and see that the Lord is good" if your well is clogged. The people you work with cannot "taste and see that the Lord is good" unless your well is flowing, unless the Spirit is really moving within your soul. Is the living water of the Spirit flowing through you? If not, then "it is time to seek the Lord, until He comes and rains righteousness upon you," until you have unclogged the well-spring of life within you, until you become a vital part of this oasis in the desert of life.

Ariel

Ariel is so sweet,
Yes, Ariel is so nice.
It seems like she's made
Of sugar and spice.
Although she is small,
An infant yet in size,
She is going to be
Quite a unique surprise;
For once she is grown,
It won't be too very long
Before she'll make
A decision so great
That'll affect so many lives
Of a generational size.
The impact of her life
Will be as a shining light
That'll shine upon men's path
Leading them away from Divine wrath
And into the loving embrace
Of a savior's amazing grace.

Bible

"B" is for the Brightness
Of its light through all of time.

"I" is for its Instruction
To help us to tow the line.

"B" is for its Boldness
To tell it like it is.

"L" is for the Love
And grace to live like this.

"E" is for the Enlightenment
We find within its text.

And its words are sent
To help us
To face what's coming next.

Definition Of A Bad Day

How do I define
A bad day?
Well, it's one where I
Forgot to pray;
Forgot to take
A solemn look
For instruction from
God's Holy book;
Forgot to listen
For His voice;
Forgot to make
That better choice;
Forgot to ask
For answers needed;
Forgot to let
My cause be pleaded;
Forgot to seek
His presence out;
Forgot to close
The door on doubt;
Forgot to knock
On Heaven's door;
Forgot to ask
My God for more.
Oh, how do I define
A bad day?
Well, my friend,

It's one where I
Forgot to pray.

God Bless You

*May the Grace of God be with you
In all you try to do.
May God's Spirit be ever present
And may your heart be ever true.
May His blessings over take you
In an awesome way.
May you always remember
To seek the Lord and pray.
May you never think too highly,
Taking pride within yourself;
So you may always then exalt Him;
And find spiritual wealth.
May the Love of God find a place
Deep within your heart;
And fill you with compassion;
While meet other's needs you start.
May you live in great expectancy
Of the things that God will do.
May your faith be ever growing,
And God's presence ever new.*

He Is Truly The Light

The hustle and bustle
Of this special season
Is all due to
One special reason.
It all goes back
To one Holy night
When Mary gave birth
To the One who is Light.
As she was in labor
Laying in the hay,
Some shepherds saw angels
And fearfully prayed.
The angels did charge them
That they should fear not,
But to look for Messiah;
This message they got,
"In the city of David,
Bethlehem, by name,
The Christ child is born
In a stable," though strange.
"You'll find Him therein
Wrapped in swaddling clothes
Lying in an old manger;
So, get up and go!"
They traveled a bit,
Until they did find
What the angels had told them
About in the night.
Some two thousand years
Has past since that time;
And this child has proven
That He is truly the Light.

The hustle and bustle
Of this special season
Is all due to
One special reason.
It all goes back
To one Holy night
When Mary gave birth
To the One who is Light.
After this birth
From a journey so long
Came wise men from the east
To honor His throne.
They stopped at Herod's Palace
Thinking their journey was through;
But discovered there was more
That they had to do.
Once back on the road
The Holy star did appear
To show them to Bethlehem
Where the Christ they'd revere.
Some two thousand years has past
Since that Holy night;
And this child has proven
That He is truly the Light.

Holiness

*You're not necessarily Holy
Whenever you dress the part;
For Holiness can only be obtained
Through surrender from the heart.
It's only through submission
To God's unfolding plan
Can one obtain a Holiness
That transcends the flesh of man.
It's when your flesh does not distract
From the Christ that lives in you,
Is when your Holy relationship
With Christ can then shine through.*

*Holiness is not about standards;
But standards are about Holiness.
Holiness is not about dress codes;
But dress codes are about Holiness.
Holiness is not about chaste conversation;
But chaste conversation is about Holiness.
Holiness is not about the company you keep;
But the company you keep is about Holiness.
Holiness is not about stewardship;
But stewardship is about Holiness.
Holiness is not about hair length;
But hair length is about Holiness.
Holiness is not about maintaining
The distinction between male and female;
But maintaining the distinction between male and female
Is about Holiness.*

I Asked; He Said

I asked God for Holy Fire.
He said to bring a sacrifice.
I asked God for friends unending.
He said to lay down my life.
I asked God for His Holy love.
He said to keep His commands.
I asked for wisdom and knowledge.
He said to take a firm stand.
I asked God for living water.
He said to bring Him praise.
I asked for bread from Heaven.
He said to walk in His ways.
I asked for His loving kindness.
He said to be kind to man.
I asked God for His salvation.
He said to obey His plan.

I Came Across

I came across
A stumbling block,
Stumped my toe
Upon a rock.
When I cried out
Cause of the pain,
Jesus cleansed me
Of the stain.
I came across
A path so wide;
And started down it
With great pride.
But when I found
Myself a ditch in,
Jesus helped me
To start again.
I came across
A falling star;
Began to follow
From afar.
But when I found out
Which way he led,
"Follow Me"
Jesus said.
I came across
A broken man;
And did not really
Understand;
And did not want
To get involved;
But Jesus said to
His problem, solve.

If His Hands

If His hands touch my hands,
Then our hands can play a melody.
If His mind becomes my mind,
Then our mind becomes Infinity.
If His word becomes my word,
Then our word becomes Authority.
If His life becomes my life,
Then our life becomes Eternity.
If His will becomes my will,
Then our will becomes Heavenly.
If His faith becomes my faith,
Then our faith becomes Victory.
If His love becomes my love,
Then our love can reach the lonely.
If His ways become my ways,
Then our ways become Holy.
If His thoughts become my thoughts,
Then our thoughts become Lovely.

In His Hands

In His hands
Are the oceans.
In His hands
Is the breeze.
In His hands
Are the mountains.
In His hands
Are the trees;
And whether or not
We know what
His word has revealed,
In His hands
His future plans
Here-to-fore
Have been concealed.

In His hands
Are the rivers.
In his hands
Are the streams.
In His hands
Are the storms.
In His hands
Are our dreams;
And whether or not
We have come
This to understand,
In His hands,
His future plans
By him

Can be revealed.
In His hands
Are our wants.
In His hands
Are our needs.
In His hands
Are our prayers.
In His hands
Are our pleas;
And whether or not
We know when
He has answered our prayers,
In His hands,
His future plans,
We know that
He is there.

In His hands
Are our losses.
In His hands
Are our gains.
In His hands
Are our chances
That we can
Begin again;
For whether or not
We know what
For us the future holds,
In His hands,
His future plans,
Can then
To us be told.

Inward Struggle

There's a battle going on;
And it's raging now within.
It's the flesh against the spirit;
And they both desire to win.
Before I became aware
Of this inward fight,
I continually made decisions
That proved not to be right.
Now as long as I'm aware
That this battle is a-raging,
I can control the outcome
By the choices that I'm making.
If I sit back and relax,
And take this fight for granted,
I'll find myself doing wrong
By this world enchanted.

Just An Acquaintance

Just an acquaintance,
That's all He tiz.
I met Him while
About my biz.
He called me with
A voice so strong
That I talked with Him
All night long;
And when He left
My company,
Somehow, I felt
That I was free.

As I lived
My life awhile,
I noticed Him watching
Me with a smile.
Not a word
Did He speak to me.
Just a longing
In His eyes, I'd see.
Although He made
His presence known,
I waited just
A bit too long.
When finally, I thought
I'd look His way,
I noticed that
He did not stay.

Just an acquaintance,
That's all He tiz;
So, I went on
About my biz.

A day or two
Went by so fast.
I turned and looked;
And there He passed.
I quickly tried
To catch up to Him.
Again, too late;
He's getting dim.

Just an acquaintance,
That's all He tiz;
So, I went on
About my biz.

A month or two
Went by so fast.
I heard him calling
As I passed;
But too busy
Was I right then.
When I turned, and looked;
He was gone again.

Just an acquaintance,
That's all He tiz;
So, I went on
About my biz.

A year or two
Went by so fast.
I heard Him crying
As I passed;
"Come unto Me
All ye that labor.
I'll help you through.
I'll be your Savior."

Just an acquaintance,
That's all He tiz;
So, I went on
About my biz.

A decade or two
Went by so fast
I heard Him weeping
As I passed.
This time I stopped
To take a look;
And caught a glimpse
Of the cross, He took.
I saw Him suffering
There for me;
So, that I
Might be set free;
And when I
Identified
With His pain,
I had to cry.
Then again,

We talked awhile;
And once more
I saw Him smile.

No more, said I,
Will this Man be
Only an
Acquaintance to me.
I'll seek Him out
Each and every day.
I'll look to Him;
And I'll pray.

Memorials

*When I remember
The by-gone-days,
Battles fought,
Victories won;
I often find
Myself amazed;
For many times
In days gone by,
I thought the end
Was just in sight;
Only to find God intervened;
And made a way I had not seen.
On these times
I dare not dwell
Too very long,
Lest I fail
To see the way
I need to go
To continue on
This Heavenward road;
But just from them
Glean some faith
To help me
Run in this race.*

My Guardian Angel

No one knows me
Like my Guardian Angel;
And, oh, how he must
Know me!
Oh, the things I put him through;
And all the misery!
Oh, how I take
So many chances;
And yet he's still out there;
Standing patient;
Taking glances;
It's how he shows he cares.
Yet one day
When I leave this world,
I think his job will be o'er;
But still I know
My Guardian Angel
Will stand by me some more.
So, here's to you,
My Angel;
For all the things, you've done;
And please be patient
As you keep me from danger;
Remember, I'm just a little one.

Options

You and me,
We have some options,
A choice of mere three,
When it comes to our friends and Hell,
And its certainty.

We can warn them before
With great hope, they'll prepare;
So that our friends will surely know
How to avoid going there.

We can arrive on the scene
When that death angel is them nigh;
And hopefully pull them out
Before any of them die.

Or, we can just remain indifferent,
Impervious to this hope;
And forget that God has placed
Into our hands
A rope.

Prisoners Of Time

While encapsulated in a capsule of responsibilities that dictate the responses that can be made; will you go in or out, up or down, right or wrong? There is no in-between. Each decision has eternal ramifications. Each decision affects the lives of countless thousands that follow through this capsule called time. Time is a ruthless warden that holds us prisoner within his defining walls. He stops for no man. His only governor is God's eternal truth. He challenges every man, and yet is challenged by no man. Man, outside of God's Divinely ordained plan, is no match for time. Time holds us captive until the day of our eternal release by the judge of the quick and dead, the Lord Jesus Christ. At that point, we will pass through the great barrier into eternity; and only then will we know how many we have hurt and how many we have helped while traveling through this capsule called time. Right now I am, you are, we all are prisoners of time. Time is continually escaping us; but we will only escape time by our Divine appointment with eternity. The appointed time of our departure is set. And only the governor of time can change that date. What shall we do with time? Or even yet, What will time do with us? Will it age us, starve us, weaken us, or strengthen us? Will it love us, hate us, mold us or shape us? Will it help us, hurt us, strip us, or skirt us? Just what will it do with us while we are still prisoners of time?

Revival Fires

Revival fires,
Start with me.
Help me burn out
All the chaff
As God's Spirit
Begins to expose
All sorts of carnal
Riff-raff.

As I seek
To kill my flesh;
By sacrificing
What it wants;
Revival fires
Burn through me;
Leave nothing left
To haunt.

Revival fires,
Help me find
God's anointing
And His Power
That will change
My life completely
Starting this very hour.

Revival fires,
Where's the spark
That will ignite inside of me
A Holy, Godly fire so bright;
That it will draw
All those around
To come and watch me
Burn tonight.
Revival fires,
Start with me;
For as I give
All of me
Willing to burn with
Eternal flame;
I invite the Lord of Host
To send His Holy Rain;
Not to put out
This Holy Ghost Fire;
But to feed this hunger
And enhance this desire
To seek after God
With all that's within
To secure a relationship
With my Eternal Friend.

Seeds of Eternity

Once you have visited the Realm of The Eternal, the realm of time seems to lose its appeal. Once you have realized the value of just the concept of Eternal Life, material things begin to lose their ability to entice you. But unless you cultivate these Seeds of Eternity, it is not long before you begin to reevaluate them according to the analytical philosophies of the human existence. The only thing you can never deny is the fulfillment that you felt standing in the Realm of The Eternal Spirit of God, that feeling that you never wanted to leave His Holy Presence, that desire to do whatever it takes to secure an everlasting relationship with Jesus Christ that would catapult you into Eternity with Him. Just how much is it worth to you to spend forever with the Creator of All Things, the Eternal One that is the very basis of all that True Love is? What scales do you use to measure an Everlasting Relationship with An All Powerful, All Knowing, Ever Existing God? How can it even be compared to this temporary limited existence we all know in this material world? Just the authority alone that believers obtain is invaluable; that ability to speak to situations and see them reversed right before your eyes; that ability to see beyond the appearance of things and understand the underlying motives of the hearts of people involved in specific circumstances. How can a price tag be too large to pay for such a gift? When you lay time right next to Eternity, just how do they compare? Is not time just a tiny spec and Eternity a continuous straight line with no beginning or end? Is not life without Jesus Christ the essence of all loneliness as well as the epidemy of chaos and confusion? God is a God of Order and Dominion; and contained within His Domain is real peace, and within His Order is true safety. Submission to His Plan brings real contentment and cleansing. So why stay outside? Come on in. Yes, come on into the Presence of The Eternal One where the light of His Existence will begin exposing the hidden attitudes of your heart to allow His Blood to cleanse your soul. Allow Him to walk the corridors of your heart, knocking on all the closed doors. And when He does knock, open them up unto Him so He can sup with you in Holy Communion. A Communion that is more than just a piece of bread and a cup of juice or wine; but This Communion is really your participation in a relationship with an Eternal God. The eating of the bread and the drinking of the cup merely signifies that relationship and reaffirms our covenant vows. The reality of that Communion is found in the Spirit, That Realm of The Eternal, that place of actual At/one/ment where our spirit becomes one with His Spirit, where our mind becomes one with His Mind, where our emotions mingle with His Emotions, where our will joins forces with His Will, and where our bodies become animated by the sheer joy of being completely engrossed in His Majesty. Once we find this type of Communion we will never want to let go of it; but, to the contrary, we will want to cultivate it often, pulling out all the weeds and grasses that would hinder the growth of such a relationship. Don't you want this type of relationship with the Lover of Your Soul? He desires that with you. That's why He invites you right now to come on into His Holy Presence and experience what True Communion really is.

Strongholds

There are many strongholds,
Of which some do stand out;
Like the addiction to smoking,
The drink, or to being all drugged out.
But there are some strongholds
That are not quite as plain;
Like that of prejudice,
Pride, guilt, or shame.
The stronghold of a grudge
Due to offenses, unforgiven
Opens the door for hatred
Of whom that one's resenting.
Strongholds are merely doorways
That allow manipulation
By demonic forces'
Attempts at intervention.
So, if one allows a stronghold
To exist within his life,
He should not be at all surprised
When he endures consistent strife.

That Dusty Old Book

*No one really knows the wealth
That's in that dusty old book on the shelf.*

*Men search for riches,
And then for fame;
And go through so
Very much pain;
Not really knowing
Of the great wealth
That's in that dusty old book on the shelf.*

*Men hunt for treasures
The whole world o'er,
Traveling from this,
And to that shore;
Not really knowing
Of the great wealth
That's in that dusty old book on the shelf.*

*No one really knows the wealth
That's in that dusty old book on the shelf.*

The End Of Time

We really need to think about the end,
Yes, the end of time;
Or at least the end of life,
The end of our chance to shine.
We need to consider how short the days,
The few we have yet left,
To redeem each, and every moment
Before they're victimized by theft.
Oh, the enemy of our souls
So, deceives us to distract
And keep us from the will of God,
God's plan for us to enact.
We must each find the righteous path
That God would have us to take;
So, by the rapture of the church
Each one of us could then escape
The perilous times coming on this world
That all who's left will see;
And before it's over
Only few will recover
To escape and then find peace.
So, let us all consider and think over
How to live our lives to shine
To lead many souls to a better place
W<small>HICH CAN BE FOUND AT THE END OF TIME.</small>

The Last Day Of Time

'Twas the Last day of time before eternity began,
And all around the world, life was still the same.
No one was repenting or living for Him;
Everyone was selfish and continuing to sin.
When all of the sudden came a giant blast,
The sound of a trumpet, Jesus coming at last.
He was riding a white horse and leading the way,
The Saints coming with Him all in bright array.
The armies were gathered and ready to fight;
But no match for the Master, who was shining the Light.
The mountain was split, that great Olivet,
When His feet came to rest, the battle was set.
He fought with The Sword that came from His mouth,
That brought judgment to all, East, West, North, and South.
As the battle continued over hill, valley, and plain;
The blood of men ran to the horses' mane.
Then spake the Lord Jesus, at the end of it all,

"It is finished,
The End of The Law."

The Letter

I know you would like to know Me, for the longing I see in your eyes reveals the hunger that is in your soul. But the busyness of your lifestyle is preventing you from seeking after Me the way that you would like to. You think that you are trapped in this lifestyle you are living in; but you just don't see that it is all in a choice. A simple decision on your part could turn your whole life around. And what appears to be major hindrances in your life would just vanish as if they never existed if you would only make up your mind to turn and seek after Me; for I am the Lover Of Your Soul, the All Existent One, the Almighty. And when you seek Me with your whole heart you will find Me; for every step you take towards Me, I will take ten towards you. For every word of praise, you render unto Me will hasten My advances toward you; for I long to caress you with My Spirit. I long to hear your heartfelt calling of My name; for you are the apple of My eye. I'm always pondering ways to get your attention. I search for ways to answer your prayers in hopes that you will notice. I stand at the gates of Heaven with My ear inclined towards you in the mere hope that your very next word could be your call; and I stand ready to answer you. So, come unto Me with your weariness and find rest. Come unto Me with your brokenness and find joy. Come unto Me with your pain and find healing. Come unto Me with your emptiness and let Me fill it to the full with My Love. If you will turn and walk towards Me, I will run towards you; for I love you. I am your Creator, your Friend, your Counselor, your God.

All My Love, Jesus Christ

The Lonely Side Of Christmas

Some people have never seen
The lonely side of Christmas;
That place that sorrow is in;
And the tears just won't pass.
As much happiness that
This holiday has brought;
Some have seen the lonely side
And the broken heart;
And all because a loved one passed;
Or maybe just forgotten,
To send a card, a gift which has
Some love inside begotten.
The lonely side of Christmas;
No one really wants to see it;
Until they find that it's them
That they're seeing in it.
So, when you're sitting home;
With family and with friends;
Enjoying opening presents;
And the fruit that giving brings;
Remember someone's hurting;
And in their hour of despair;
And at that very moment needs
FOR SOMEONE JUST TO CARE.

The Reflection

When people dress so Holy,
As I see you do,
They manifest the purity
Of a heart that's true.
Their dress is then a light
That is both seen and heard;
For it is reflecting the voice
That's hidden behind the word;
And when the heart is pure,
And the ways are clean,
The walk of man is faithful,
Then the light is seen.
Heaven's glory is then revealed
To mere earthly men;
The God of Heaven glorified
In the very end.

The Road To Bitterness

The road to bitterness
Is paved with stones
That harden the heart
Through many wrongs.

One of these stones
That is so there
Is that of apathy
That just does not care
How anyone feels
About what they've done
For they're just glad
That they've won.

The road to bitterness
Is paved with stones
That harden the heart
Through many wrongs.

Another stone,
Wouldn't you guess,
Is that old stone
Of unforgiveness
That holds the grudge
And won't forget
"Till all is paid,
The price of regret.

The road to bitterness
Is paved with stones
That harden the heart
Through many wrongs.

A third stone
That's cemented in
Is that angry stone
That just won't give in
Until avenged
Is their right
To get even
Through a fight.

The road to bitterness
Is paved with stones
That harden the heart
Through many wrongs.
Those that walk
Upon these stones
Become a prisoner
Of each, and every wrong,
For the pain
That each inflicts
Dictates to them
What kind of tricks
That they should do
So, to protect
Their selfish right
To their regret.

There's No One Quite Like Mom

She used to have such patience,
Much greater than that of Job.
She used to express a wisdom
That kept me on the go.
She seemed to understand
The greatest trials of life.
She also made for my Dad
Such a perfect wife.
When I look back
Over the years,
Now that I am grown,
I can't even remember
One little thing
That she ever did wrong.
I guess it's cause
When I look at Mom
And all the things she's done,
I see her through eyes
Of the purest love,
And remember only
The care and fun.
I guess if there's a reason why I've never settled down,
I've yet to find another woman T*HAT CAN WEAR HER CROWN.*

To My Beloved

You say all the right things. You never curse or swear. You don't go to bars, movie houses, or anywhere that would compromise your faith. When you go out from your home, you make sure you're modest in your apparel so you won't attract the attention of any unwanted suitors; but, yet there is something missing. You don't ever miss a church service. You're there every time the doors are open. You wouldn't even think of missing Sunday School. You even bring a visitor now and then. But, yet there is still something missing. You abide by all the standards of the local church. You even go beyond what is laid down by your Pastor. You keep your hair just right, your sleeves just right, everything in place. But, yet still something is missing. Your standards are supposed to reflect your inward character and the convictions that are produced by having a relationship with me; but you have turned them into walls and barricades to keep me out. They've become a place for you to hide. If you look right, talk right, and stay out of the wrong places you feel secure. You trust more in your standards than you do in your God. Your standards are given to you to protect our relationship, not to keep us apart. Why have you used them to lock me out? You use them as a defense against my wooing. You use them to cover your ears when I'm calling. You say, "I'm alright; I do all those things I'm supposed to." But I say, you're not alright. I miss those times when you'd spend hours with me in prayer. I miss those times when you'd spend time searching my Word for something I'd show you. You used to be so awed when I'd reveal my truth to you. But now the busy-ness of your life has you caught up in its care as if it has become your lover. You caress your busy-ness without even giving me one thought. What happened to my Word that said, "Acknowledge God in all thy ways; and He will direct thy path." I want to direct your path and show you how to handle those busy days. I would walk with you through them, and direct each step; but you won't even inquire of me. I'm sending you this warning. You're about to miss the mark of my high calling; and when you realize you missed it; then you will cry out to me. But you can come to me now. I'm waiting and will guide you through. I'm waiting and will deliver you; and we can have those times together, caressing each other in prayer again. All my love; JESUS CHRIST.

Trust The Nails

To open the doors
Never opened;
To try to find
New ways to soar
Above the average
And the mundane
To new heights
Of joy and pain;
For the higher you soar
Above all the rest
Can make the fall
An awesome test.
To climb the mountain
And cross the abyss;
To live in victory
With nothing amiss;
To believe for mercy
In the face of law;
To pass the test
Instead of fall.
The trials and tests
Of life will come.
You can count on this,
And believe this one;
But whether you pass,
Or whether you fail
Depends upon whether
You trust the nails.

Two Buds

Enclosed in a bubble
Of fear and rejection,
This bud would not open,
Not even one section;
For life had not dealt
The hand that he wanted.
In his mind he was tormented,
By rejection was haunted.
Withholding from the world
All his pomp and his splendor,
He kept to himself,
Not one service did he render.
What was the end
Of this bud that never flowered?
He was cut off and burned up
At the midnight hour.

Another bud on that
Same branch of the tree
Faced the same fears
And rejections as he;
Risked opening one section
At a time, just to see;
Found the light of the sunshine,
Bright warmth and victory.
The more he opened up,
The more that he found
How beautiful life was
Once he was not bound.

As a flower looking back
To when he was budding,
Wondered why he had feared
To let one blade, start to jutting.

Though fears and rejections
Of the past cloud your mind,
Open up to God
And His Church and you'll find
What you thought would just
Push you back in your shell
Are really the things He's sent
To help you get well;
For when you face fears
And rejection in life,
You gain faith and acceptance
In the sunlight.
So, open up to God
And His Church this very hour;
And you'll find the beauty
OF BEING A FLOWER.

Two Fires

Being a man
Of like passions,
I understand
Your desires;
How that you desire
Companionship sometimes
'Till it feels like a fire
Is burning on
The inside of you
Trying to take control;
But if you let it burn,
And then burn within your soul,
It just may consume you
From the inside out,
Until you're just out of control,
And losing this bout;
But you don't have to
Lose control of this desire;
But instead you can give
Yourself to another kind of fire,
Which is born out of seeking
After the most-High God;
And will help you take control
WHILE IN THIS WORLD YOU TROD.

Watching Jesus

Watching Jesus life
As I turn each page;
Changing life after life;
Calming storms which rage.
"What kind of man is this?"
Is what Saint Peter said;
"Why He just spoke to the storm;
And now the storm is dead."
Never had any man
Expressed such powerful words;
That even the common elements
Obey when they are heard.
Is it any wonder
That this man became
The central focus of history
With just the mention of His name.
Why, we even count our days
In reference to His time;
Yet His ways to men
Seem to be so hard to find.
Watching Jesus death
On the Cross of Calvary;
Watching such surrender;
Which is what really set us free;
Led as a sheep to slaughter;
Opening not His mouth;
Laying down His life for all;
East, West, North, and South;
At the end of life;

Forgiving all mankind;
Then giving up the Ghost;
So that we can find
A brand-new start forever
Outside the bounds of time;
Across the Heavenly Jordan;
Eternal life to find.

Watching the resurrection;
Such power never known;
Just as if the husbandman
A corn of wheat had sown;
Pushing death aside;
As if it were a stone;
Coming forth
Up from the grave
So, we won't fight alone.

What Do You Want From Me, Lord?

What do you want from me, Lord?
Do you want most of my time;
Or maybe, you want the knowledge
That you planted in my mind?
Is it possible you want my dreams;
Or perhaps, my life long plans?
Could it be you want my feet;
So, you can help me make a stand?
Should I give to you my hands;
So, you can work my messy life out;
Or maybe, you want my faith;
So, you can chase from my life doubt?
Are you asking for my eyes;
So, you can show to me the way;
Or should I give to you my knees;
So, you can teach me how to pray?
Though Lord somehow, I know
That you really want all these;
I kind-a-think my heart
Would make you the most pleased.

What We Should Desire

To be used
By Almighty God
To save this world
From the chastening rod;
This is what we should desire;
To be set aflame
With Heavenly fire;
To burn as a candle
In the dark of night;
Sharing with others
This Heavenly light;
To walk in paths
That are narrow and straight
That will lead us right to
Those Pearly Gates.

When Weakness Becomes Strength

There was a common man
That was plagued with sin
That could not in his own strength
Fight the battle to win.
When he would give it his all
It never seemed quite enough.
To overcome this wall
To him was much too tough;
Until he met the Savior,
Jesus the Nazarene,
The one who went to Calvary,
And died for you and me.
Once this meeting was over
He found such strength through Him,
His life was changed completely
Including his struggle with sin.
As he learned to pray in the Spirit,
And read God's precious Word,
He did increase in wisdom,
And learned to wield the Sword,
That Word of Truth that's mighty
To the discerning of spirit and soul.
It really wasn't very long
'Till he was completely whole.

Wisdom Is Available

*Wisdom is available
Unto the prudent man
That diligently seeks for
Understanding in everything.
But wisdom fleets away
From the slothful soul,
That just waits around
Never attempting any goal.
Whenever a man is diligent
In seeking after knowledge;
He digs deep to find it,
Then applies it like a wedge.
The slothful man is not interested
In ever coming to know
Anything that might mean
That he would have to grow.
For growth in the knowledge
And wisdom of life
Would place demands upon him
To stretch and to strive.
But there is one thing that this
Slothful man won't find;
Is that diligence would insure
A fruitful and productive life.*

Wondering

When I sit
All perfectly still,
Wondering if
I'm in God's will,
I think about all the times
When His will I did not find.
Then I think of all the ways
That my failures can be praised;
And before too long,
In despair,
I find myself
Wholly there.

But when I'm busy;
And a'doing
All the things
That I'm knowing,
His light's a'shining,
His Word's a'showing
The very way
I should be going.

Words

Words can be so right.
Words can be so wrong.
Words can be so weak.
Words can be so strong.
Words can be so false.
Words can be so true.
Words can make things old.
Words can make things new.
What is it that determines
How our words will be?
But how that they are used
By you and by me.

Words can be so blunt.
Words can be so kind.
Words can make you see.
Words can make you blind.
Words can be deceptive.
Words can be straight too.
Words can be real helpful.
Words can hinder you.
What is it that determines
How our words will be?
But how that they are used
By you and by me.

Words can be real smart.
Words can be real dumb.
Words can be real serious.
Words can be real fun.
Words can be real nice.
Words can be real mean.
Words can be real dirty.
Words can be real clean.
What is it that determines
How our words will be?
But how that they are used
By you and by me.
Words can be caring.
Words can also hurt.
Words can be sharing.
Words also can be curt.
Words can be real dull.
Words can be real sharp.
But one thing is for certain,
Words come from our heart.
What is it the determines
How our words will be?
But how that they are used
By you and by me.

Chapter 4

INSPIRATIONAL THOUGHTS

One

One
Is what we ought to be;
For God is one
Not two or three.
And when we come together in Christ;
We should be united
Through His life.
When division comes,
It's not the Lord;
But another who
Is tainting the word;
But when revealed,
We can only see
The power of Christian
Unity.

Everyday's an Opportunity

Everyday's an opportunity
For me to be
A friend to a brother
Or a sister in need.
Everyday's an opportunity
For me to see
How to be a blessing to Thee.

Lord, I want to be
A blessing to Thee,
A blessing to Thee,
A blessing to Thee,
Lord, I want to be
A blessing to Thee;
So, show me how to use
My opportunity.

What is Truth?

"What is truth?"
Someone asked.
"is it the pulling
Off of a mask?"
"Truth," I said, "is not a what.
Truth, my friend is a who.
For Truth is the one that
Created me and you.
And Truth is not an it,
As some would describe;
For Truth is Jesus Christ
Who's still looking for His bride."

Open Up Your Heart

Open up your heart,
And let Jesus in,
And your life will never
Be the same again.
Listen to His voice.

Harken to His call;
For Jesus wants to be
Your all in all.

Two Prayers

The prayer of the heart
Is faintly heard
Until expressed
With the word.
The prayer of the soul
Is crying out,
And will be heard
without a doubt.
When will God answer?
What will God say?
Yes!
Amen!
Believe!
Today.

The Reflection

When people dress so Holy,
As I see you do,
They manifest a purity
Of a heart that's true.
Their dress is then a light
That is both seen and heard;
For it is reflecting
The voice that's hidden behind the word;
For when the heart is pure
And the ways are clean,
The walk of man is faithful,
And the light is seen.
Heaven's glory is then revealed
To mere earthly men.
The God of Heaven is glorified
In the very end.

Playing Games?

If games with God
You must then play,
You must play well
Prepared to say
The reasons for
The games you play
Else you'll be found
In a bit dismay.

That Dusty Old Book

No one really knows the wealth
That's in that dusty old book on the shelf.

Men search for riches,
And then for fame,
And go through so
Very much pain,
Not really knowing
Of the great wealth
That's in that dusty old book on the shelf.

Men hunt for treasures
The whole world o're,
Traveling from this,
And to that shore,
Not really knowing
Of the great wealth
That's in that dusty old book on the shelf.

No one really knows the wealth
That's in that dusty old book on the shelf.

A Delicate Matter

Behold how delicate a matter
When hope grows on an elusive platter.
To destroy the illusion
Would throw the soul into much confusion.
To save the soul
From hopeless despair,
One needs to scrape the platter
With tender loving care.
Then when hope is fully resting
On a solid plane,
The illusion can be broken
With just a little pain.
Then when the pain subsides,
And peace returns again,
Hope can still grow
On solid ground within.

What We Should Desire

To be used
By Almighty God
To save this world
From the chastening rod,
This is what we should desire,
To be set aflame
With Heavenly fire,
To burn as a candle
In the dark of night,
Sharing with others
This Heavenly light,
To walk a path
That is narrow and straight,
That will lead us to
Those Pearly Gates

Counted Worthy

Feeling o unworthy
Of the blessings that God sends,
Makes it so very hard
Unto His will to bend;
For when the blessings come
We quickly watch them go
When we really should have invested
Then to watch them grow.

When we think of life,
And how we all have sinned,
Not one of us are worthy,
Not one of us should win;
But because of Jesus Christ
And the work of Calvary,
We can be counted worthy
And set completely free.

Wondering

When I sit all perfectly still,
Wondering if I'm in God's will,
I think of all the times
When His will I did not find.
Then I think of all the ways
That my failures can be praised,
And before too long, in despair,
I find myself, wholly there.

But when I'm busy, and a doing
All the things that I'm knowing,
His light's a'shining, His words a'showing
The very way I should be going.

Fight For The Right

I was looking for the light
When I entered a fight
Where everyone seemed in the right;
But only one was.

Although it was dark
I caught a glimpse of a spark
With the victorious remark,
"In the name of Jesus."

By the end of the fight
The room was filled with the light
Of the One who was true and right,
The Lord Jesus.

Looking For Love

Carefully,
Looking for love.
Wondering who
Might care enough
To risk
Exposing themselves,
Their inner self.
To love
Is to risk
Being hurt.
It actually hurts
To love.
But love also
Brings happiness.
In fact,
The hurts of love
And it's happiness
Are always extreme.
The question is,
Is the happiness of love
Worth the risk
Of the hurts of love?
God Thought so.

Hate

Hate, my friend,
Is a big mistake.
It'll turn you into a real fake.
Your dignity from you it will take.
Anything you do will be second rate.
It alone will determine your fate.
Change your mind before it's too late.
You'll find, my friend, a lot is at stake.
And another choice you can make.
Do it now, for Heaven's sake.
Don't delay, please don't wait.
You see, my friend, we all have a date.
If you want to see that Pearly Gate,
And absolutely avoid that fiery lake;
The wrath of God you can escape.
Oh, my friend, please Don't hate.

The Hour Of Prayer

T'was the hour of prayer,
And no one was there,
And all because
They did not care.
What a horrible shame,
Because Jesus came,
And found the place empty
Again, and again.
In His Word, you know,
He said He would show
Where in His name we would gather;
To forsake us He said, "No."
His promise is there
For us to claim in prayer;
So, my friend,
Why weren't you there?

Chapter 5

LET THIS LIGHT SO SHINE

Wisdom

Unlike some would believe,
Through academic study alone
Wisdom is not received.
If you would desire to be wise;
Just look to Jesus Christ;
See life through His eyes.
Look at the suffering and the pain
That He had to endure;
Then look at the Holy Ghost rain,
And the joy set before.
Understand, He did not have to
Give His life for us;
But He really wanted to;
For He really loved us.
Wisdom counts the cost
Before making the decision;
Then knowing what is lost
Is only and incision;
Understanding the reward
Is much greater that the cost;
And the joy set before
Is much greater that what is lost.

The Temptation

Trying so hard to resist
What this my heart desires;
For this attractive young woman
Had really sparked a fire.
Oh, the pain I feel inside
As this my desire burns.
Can I yet resist it
As my heart just yearns?
Oh, so afraid am I
That I might just sin
Against my Lord and Savior;
Yet I have hope He'll win,
And keep this my soul
Rightfully in his place;
So, I might yet win
In this life course race.
What then If I should stumble;
Yes, then if I should fall;
I know I have an advocate
Upon whose name, I'd call.
I would cry out for His mercy.
I would plead for the Blood;
And call on the name of Jesus,
Asking for the crimson flood.
Oh, the Blood of Jesus
That can cleanse each stain,
And lift this fallen soul
To restore it once again.
And I know without a doubt,
He will answer my call;
For He loves the repentant heart;
And He loves the sinners call.

To Overcome

To overcome;
What does it mean?
Is it getting high enough
For you to be seen?
Or it just beginning to dream?
Are there steps
To overcoming;
Or is that just
The way it seems?

To overcome means
To come over obstacles;
Small or large
Or even unseen;
Things like
Doubt or fear,
Depression or rejection;
Things like
Anxiety or confusion,
Unbelief or deception.

To overcome means
To have victory,
Not defeat;
Faith, not unbelief;
Truth, not deception;
And acceptance, not rejection.

The Power That Lies in Reach

To stand between
A man and death;
To take command
And conquer it;
To command the Angel
In Jesus name;
To fight the invisible;
And conquer pain:

Oh, the power
That lies in reach
When we heed God's Word
As we hear one preach.

To speak the truth
That frees from sin;
To fight the battle
Till the war you win;
To come to grips
With conviction's word;
Till the heart is clean;
Till His voice is heard:

Oh, the power
That lies in reach
When we heed God's Word
As we hear one preach.

To command in faith;
And see it done;
To walk so straight
The victory's won;
To see God's power
Right before your eyes;
To watch demons flee
To your surprise:

Oh, the power
That lies in reach
When we heed God's Word
As we hear one preach

To watch the Savior
Do His great work;
To save a soul
Through the new birth;
To wash away
The stain of sin;
To watch that soul
A new life, begin:

Oh, the power
That lies in reach
When we heed God's Word
As we hear one preach

True Understanding

The Bible says many things;
And most of them are clear;
But there are some things
That aren't so plain
Unless the Spirit's near.
True Understanding
Does not come
From reason or from rhyme;
But only comes
Through relationship
With the Lord through time;
For to view things
Through the flesh
Will just merely deceive;
But to view things
Through the Spirit
Will help you, to believe.

Fifth Sunday Dinner on The Ground

Chopped beef steak,
All nice and juicy;
Mashed potatoes and gravy,
Made by aunt Lucy;
Buttered corn and bread,
Piping hot to the touch;
And chocolate cream pie;
Just a little too much;
All this and much more
Is what could be found
At the first Pentecostal Church
Fifth Sunday Dinner on The Ground.

Fried Chicken in baskets,
A whole table full;
Catsup and fried taters;
Corn on the cob in the hull;
Black-eyed peas, butter beans;
And more of that such;
Fresh baked strawberry pie;
Now, ain't that too much?
All this and much more
Is what could be found
At the first Pentecostal Church
Fifth Sunday Dinner on The Ground.

Pastors and their wives,
Youth groups and choirs;
Evangelists would drive
For all sorts of hours;
Singing groups would come
With their bands, all in stride;
Just to come and sing;
And share their talents with pride;
All this and much more
Is what could be found
At the first Pentecostal Church
Fifth Sunday Dinner on The Ground.

Elders and Deacons;
Laymen of all sorts;
Board members and trustees,
All playing their parts;
Missionaries on furlough
Raising money for trips;
Politicians with their aids;
And so many more V.I.P.'s;
All this and much more
Is what could be found
At the first Pentecostal Church
Fifth Sunday Dinner on The Ground.

Shut Up Flesh

*Sometimes it's hard
To shut the mouth of the flesh,
That cries day and night
For you to satisfy its wish.
But when you are determined
To put the flesh to death,
And wrestle it down,
You will find peace and rest.
For with fasting and with prayer
You fight the flesh to win.
After this kind of struggle
The victory you will win.
But fasting alone
Cannot conquer this foe.
It takes the prayer of faith
To deliver blow after blow;
Till quiet and submissive
The flesh will follow behind
The leading of God's Spirit
And the Christian mind.*

Humble

*The Honest Man can be
Safe from reprimand.*

*The Understanding Man can be
A safe and secure friend.*

*The Mature Man can be
A shelter from the storm.*

*The Brilliant Man can be
A light shining in the morn.*

*The Loving Man can be
A comfort to those in pain.*

*The Encouraging Man can be
One to lift them up again.*

Hungry Believers

Hungry believers,
All across this land;
Trapped in their confusion;
Needing a hand;
They're crying out to Jesus,
Who is the Great "I Am",
And God has heard their cry;
So, don't you understand,
(That they're)

Hungry believers,
All across this land;
Hungry for the fellowship
Of the saints.
Hungry believers,
Crying out to Him,
Wanting for someone
Just to feed them.

Nothing Like Jesus

*There is nothing
In this world
That's like Jesus.
There is nothing
In this world
That's like Him,
Nothing that can save,
Or give you peace within.
No, there's nothing,
No nothing,
Nothing like Him.*

Honest

The Humble Man can learn
Wisdom from above.

The Obedient Man can learn
How to truly love.

The New Man can learn
New ways to know the Lord.

The Enduring Man can learn
The rivers he can forge.

The Sure Man can learn
Just how much he can stand.

The True Man can learn
What it means to be a man.

The Dark Corner

There is one sin,
And then yet another,
So, many times, repented of,
And yet not fully covered;
For there is yet inside
This calloused heart of mine
An old dark and dreary corner
Where no light has shined.
One day I know is coming
A revelation of His love,
That'll flood this old dark corner,
And envelop it like a glove;
Till revealed is the source
Of the snare of sin.
On that day I'll rejoice;
For that's when love will win.
Until then, I'll repent,
And then repent again;
Till the day love will conquer,
Till the day love will win.

Four Cedar Walls

Four cedar walls,
In this attic so height;
Oh, so alone,
So alone am I;
Locked up in this closet
So that maybe I
Can pray past my fears.
At least I can try.

Four cedar walls,
If they could testify;
They'd tell you of how
Very hard I did try.
They'd tell you of all
The tears I did cry;
Locked up in this attic,
In this attic, so high.

Four cedar walls,
One window, one door;
Day after day,
I'd seek Him some more.
So afraid of just what
I was seeking for;
Yet earnestly seeking
Locked behind this great door.

One week went by;
Then went by two.
If I do not find Him;
Oh, what should I do?
Stay locked up behind
All fearful and blue,
These four cedar walls;
Just what should I do?

Four cedar walls,
I can't stay right here;
Locked up behind
These four walls of fear.
I've got to step out,
Step out now by faith;
If I'm ever going to find
Some more of God's grace.

Though I'm not real sure
Which way I should go,
If I stay right here,
I know I won't grow.
So, I'm stepping out.
I'm telling fear, "No,
You can't hold me here.
I'm going to go."

So by facing those fears,
I now have gained faith;
And found that my God
Has given more grace,
And all that I've needed
To run this great race.
Now, I'm determined
To just keep in pace.

Making Peace

Stormy days and stormy nights
Can fill our hearts
So, full of fright,
If we have not
Made our peace with God.
Troubles that come into our life
Can fill our hearts
So, full of strife,
If we have not
Made our peace with God.
When we face anxiety,
We'll wonder how
We could get free,
If we have not
Made our peace with God.
When we live unto our self,
We'll never find
Eternal wealth,
Until we have
Made our peace with God.

The Finish Line

This man, though crippled
By arthritis pain,
Knew that he
Had much to gain;
So, with all his might
He did strain
To reach this Finish Line.

Though pain shot through
His joints so tight,
He still struggled
With all his might,
Knowing he'd lose
If he did not fight
To reach this Finish Line.

With stiffened up joints,
And determination of mind,
Careful consideration,
The next step to find,
With grace of a very
Different kind,
So, to reach this Finish Line.

*Though no one else
Was in this race,
He still struggled
To Keep In pace,
Hoping to find
A little more grace
To reach this Finish Line.*

*And when he made
His final step,
Tears did flow
As this man wept;
For thanksgiving of heart
Is what he felt
When he reached this Finish Line;*

*For because this man
He did obey
What Christ the Lord
To him did say,
In answer to
What he did pray,
His healing he did find.*

*Though you may suffer
When you choose to do
What Christ the Lord
Has told you to,
A special grace
Waits for you,
As you reach your Finish Line.*

Let This Light So Shine

How can I just sit
And watch a world go astray?
How can I stand by
While millions are held at bay?
How can I just not do
What God has called me to?
How can I love God
If I can't prayerfully love you?

No, I cannot sit
Idly by
While this world spins
Its way to Hell.
I cannot let
Myself stand still
While millions
Just scream and yell.
I can't continue
To hesitate
To heed this Gospel call;
But I must prove
My love for God
By loving one and all.
I must stand in the gap
And form a bridge
With my fervent prayer,
Showing everyone I meet
How much my God cares.
I must now step out by faith,

And do those things
That I'm afraid to do,
If I'm ever going to prove
That my love for God is true.
I must walk in the light,
And let God reveal
Those things that hinder me,
So that my worship
Of my Lord
Can be set completely free.

No, I cannot sit
Idly by
While this world spins
Its way to Hell.
I cannot let
Myself stand still
While millions
Just scream and yell.
I can't continue
To hesitate
To heed this Gospel call;
For I must prove
My love for God
By loving one and all.

This world must see
A man of God
Completely given to Him;
Not held back
From God's will

By some earthly whim.
They must see
A shining light
In answer to God's call;
One that will direct
The steps of many,
And lift up the souls that fall.
They must see
A man that's empty
Of his own selfish desires,
That's been set aflame
With the love of God,
And with Holy Ghost fire.

It's not enough
To just stand by,
And watch from the side line;
For I must plunge
Into the fight,
And let this light so shine.

No, I cannot sit
Idly by
While this world spins
Its way to Hell.
I cannot let
Myself stand still
While millions
Just scream and yell.
I can't continue
To hesitate

To heed this Gospel call;
For I must prove
My love for God
By loving one and all.

No, it's not enough
To just stand by,
And watch from the side line;
But I must plunge
Into the fight,
And let this light so shine.

An Artist Dilemma

An artist pondering,
"Just what should I draw;
Mountains, valleys,
Hills, or falls,
Trees, flowers,
Rivers, or streams,
People that are kind,
Or angry and mean,
Clouds, rainbows,
Fog that is thick,
A holiday scene
With good ole' Saint Nick?
Oh, how can I express
What I'm feeling today;
Draw an empty street,
Or maybe a parade?"

While pondering there,
A thought crossed his mind.
Then in just a moment,
He fell asleep for a time.
Then began he to dream
Of a time and a place
That no one had seen
Or been in that case.
He dreamed of a room
All colorful and bright.
He then saw himself standing
In a bright and shining light.

*Then as he looked closer
At himself standing there,
He saw several spots
That seemed covered with hair.
As curiously he looked,
And pondered some more,
He then saw a man
In the shape of a door.
"Just what are these spots
That I'm covered with?"
Asking the door,
He said, "What is this?"*

*"These spots are your sins
The light has revealed.
While you were in darkness,
They were merely concealed."*

*"What should I do
To be rid of these spots?
Should I see a surgeon,
And have him cut me a lot?"*

*"That's not the answer,"
The door said to him.
"You must first be sorry
For all of these sins.
Then walk on closer,
And step right through me,
And you'll find yourself
All clean and spot free."*

Then with a cry,
He showed his remorse;
And then to the door
He established his course.
Then as he looked down
To grab hold of the knob,
He saw just a name,
And started to sob.

"How do I open
This door to get in?
Please tell me so I
Can be rid of my sin."

"Just call out that name,
And step right on through;
For that name is what will
Open the door for you."

So, then he cried "Jesus",
And stepped right on in,
And found himself clean,
Set free from his sin.
Then he awoke,
And found he did know
About what to draw,
And which way he should go.

To the Bishop Family

To my niece,
Miss Emily,
Who is so bright,
And full of glee:
God has been good,
So good to you.
You must stay with God,
To him be true;
For the day will come,
And soon it will;
Temptation will come
For you to rebel;
But you must submit
To Papa's hand;
For in due time
You'll understand.

To Erica,
My sister's first:
Your dreams just might
Like bubbles burst;
Unless you learn
Your life to plan,
Find God's will,
Not some man's.
Aim at the mark
Of God's high call.
Aim with your heart
Then give your all;
For God has got
Great plans for you.
He's got a task
For you to do.

To my Sis,
With faith of gold:
Pray for your girls
To be firm and bold;
For in times ahead,
They'll face a lot.
They'll need your prayers
Against Satan's plot.
Teach them well
To live the Word,
And one day
They will be heard.

Now to the Priest
Of Sister's home:
Keep on walking,
In faith be strong;
For God's light
Will shine on you;
If you'll just
To Him be true.
Beware of pride.
It will deceive,
And lead you to
Untruth believe;
So, humble yourself
Before God now,
So, you'll be ready
When He shows you how
To walk completely
In holy light,
And to overcome
The Devil's fight.

Optical Illusions

Optical illusions present to us pictures that just aren't so. So, when we see an optical illusion, we find that reality is not as it appears to be. What appears to be real is not; and what appears not to be real is. Sometimes people are as optical illusions. On the surface, they appear to be genuine, but once you dig deep into the heart, they just aren't as they appear to be. Sometimes they appear to be phony on the outside, but, come to find out, they are genuine as pure gold. For this very reason, Jesus looks upon the heart. He doesn't judge by outward appearance. Though a man may appear to be a beggar outwardly, he could very well be a king on the inside. Another man may appear to be rich by outward standards, yet poor when you measure him up to Godly standards. A man may appear to be sick unto death by earthly standards, but getting ready to be made whole and complete by heavenly standards. For when you peer through these old earthly eyes, you can only view things according to earthly standards, but when you peer through heavenly eyes, you have an opportunity to view things by heavenly standards. You might say, "How can I view through heavenly eyes?" Well you pray for the God of Heaven to open your eyes to the heavenly. Then open your heart to receive what God will show you. You will find that God is more willing to reveal the Truth to us than we are to see it. For truth will cut away the spiritual cancers. Truth is the pin that pops our illusive balloons. Truth is the light that illuminates our darkness. Optical illusions can only be revealed by the introduction of truth. When truth is received, deception fleets away. When truth is loved, deception cannot find its way back into the heart, though it may seek diligently. A deep abiding love for the truth seals off all the inroads that deception once had into our hearts. This love of the truth will protect us from the optical illusions of spiritual darkness in our day. The Scripture teaches us if a man receives not this love for truth that God Himself shall send a strong delusion that that man should believe a lie and be lost. This is proclaimed in the Kings of the Old Testament, where Macaiah the prophet was sent to King Ahab to tell him that God was sending a lying spirit into the mouths of all the false prophets. Then Ahab followed the council of these false prophets and died in battle. Had Ahab received a love for truth in his heart, though God Himself sent a strong delusion, this love for truth would have protected his heart from believing the lie. But because he did not love the truth, the deception came and swept him away. You see truth is that two-edged sword of the Spirit that divides and makes the distinction between soul and spirit, good and evil, right and wrong. And our love for truth is our grip on that sword. You can hold truth with a fish grip or a death grip. And how you love truth will determine how you hold truth, whether, or not truth can be wrestled from you. If your love for truth is a fish grip, then you might drop it or it just may be taken from you with little or no effort by the enemy. But if you have a death grip on truth, then nothing will be able to take it from you. Consider that King David fought against the Philistines with such a grip on his sword that men had to pry it out of his hands after the battle. And if we hold (love) truth in this way, then we will not fall for the spiritual optical illusions of our day.

A God of Detail

God is not only so big that he created a galaxy, but he is also a God of great detail throughout all His creation. He paid enough attention to each intricate part of creation to give it specific design and detail. For example, the leaf structure of every kind of tree is different from every other kind of tree; and though each individual leaf of a specific tree is similar enough to identify it as a leaf of that kind of tree, it has enough individuality that it can stand alone. No other leaf is exactly like it. That speaks of a God of detail. Family members favor one another, but each person is an individual in character, personality, and looks. Just consider the awesomeness of universe after universe, all of which is help together by unseen gravitational forces; then consider the tiny ant colony and the order in which they conduct themselves. Consider humanity that wouldn't be able to survive the depths of the sea, and scientists tell us that they've discovered some varieties of fish that live there that would explode if they were brought closer to the surface. Now that speaks of a God of detail. Oh, how awesome is our God who is not only big enough to have created galaxy after galaxy, but is also concerned enough to pay attention to the details of life on any particular level.

Some Folks

Some folks walk
To the left'
While others walk
To the right.

Some folks walk
In the dark,
While others walk
In the light.

Some folks carry
Their burdens,
While others give
Theirs away,

By taking them to
The foot of the Cross
Each time they kneel
Down to pray.

Some folks hold
Everything in,
While others let
Everything out.

Some folks live
By faith,
While others live
By doubt.

Some folks believe
In God's mercy,
While others
In Justice Divine,

And live out their lives
In the constant fear
They'll never connect
Up to the vine.

Some folks hold
Grudges forever,
While others
Forgive right away.

Some folks never
Release love,
While others share
Theirs day by day.

The Revolution

Some revolt against system;
Some against regime;
Some against order;
Some against the mean;
But there is a revolution that is going on;
That for the most part, goes on unseen;
For it is a battle that is beyond this life.
It is fought in the heavens, not with gun or knife.
This war that's going on
Is almost not even heard;
For it is being fought
Through the Spirit, with the Word.
It's in man's imagination,
And it's in his heart
That this battle's fought,
Lost, or won in part.
Although the battle may go on
In an unseen realm,
The victory is seen
Just as clear as on film.
And when defeat is felt
Just as real as rain,
It is then revealed
Through one's pain.
Though victory is the lot
Of the determined man,
Defeat is the end
Of the double minded stand.
This revolution
Goes on and on through life
In the unseen realm
Of mental and emotional strife.

How Many

How many paths
Must I travel o're
Before I can find
Eternity's shore?

And how many places
Must I now see
Before there is found
A place for me?

And how many years
Must I now live
Before I have finally
Past love's test?

And how much knowledge
Must I now gain
Before God's wisdom
On my soul rains?

A Hand

If you've lost
Someone you love,
Just look to God
Who is above;
For he's bending down
With outstretched hand
Reaching for
The broken man.
A hand to heal
He does possess,
So why don't you put
Him to the test?
If you've lost
Your way down here,
Just look to God
Who's always near
To shine His light
Upon your path
And steer you round
Ole Satan's wrath.
A hand to guide
He does possess,
So why don't you put
Him to the test?
If you've lost
Your peace of mind,
Just look to God,
For He'll help you find
The way to peace

Through His powerful Cross,
And help you recover
Just what you've lost.
A hand to restore
He does possess,
So why don't you put
Him to the test?
If you've lost
A heart to live,
Just look to God;
For new life He gives.
He'll help you mend
That broken heart,
And show you a new
Place you can start.
A hand to renew
He does possess,
So why don't you put
Him to the test?

The Time to Pray

Struggling hard
To find his way,
He would not take
The time to pray.
Stumbling here,
And stumbling there,
And loaded down
With so much care,
Though it was now
Late in the day,
He would not take
The time to pray.
Continuing down
This lonesome path,
Sometimes feeling
Satan's wrath,
Still burdened down
As he walked in the way,
He still would not take
The time to pray.

Please take the time to pray!

Chapter 6
SOME ANGELS

Angel Business

Angels coming.
Angels going.
All along to us unknowing.
Here to guide.
Here to direct,
And reveal to us
The Christian sect;
Showing us
The path to take
So that we
Then can escape
The coming trials
And coming tests
That will fall
Upon the rest.

Angels standing.
Angels fighting.
All the while,
We are guided
By the movement
Of these spirits,
Even though
We fail to hear it.
Angels bowing.
Angels flying.
In great reverence
They are crying
Holy, holy,

Holy is He
That has come
With great victory.
When angels come,
When angels go,
Whether, or not
We ever know,
They are about
The Father's will,
And for us
They won't be still;
But they will stand,
And they will fight
For our salvation
Both day and night.

Angels

*"A" is for the A*WESOME
Presence that you feel.

*"N" is for that N*O ONE
Really comprehends their zeal.

*"G" is for the G*OD
Whom they serve both day and night.

*"E" is for the E*TERNAL REALM
In which they always fight.

*"L" is for the L*OVE OF GOD
Which motivates their work.

*"S" is for the S*ALVATION OF MAN
For which they stay alert.

*The B*IBLE *calls them ministers;*
A flaming fire of God
Sent to help the heirs
Of the salvation of God;
*We refer to them as A*NGELS;
And often fail to see
That they are working day and night
To help and set us free.

I Charge Angels

I charge angels
To go before me
And prepare the way
For the Word of God.
I charge angels
To clear a path
For this messenger
To safely trod.
I charge angels
To soften hearts
Of many a lost soul,
Them to prepare
To receive
A Living Word
That'll spare them from
The flames of eternal Hell.
I charge angels
To keep the way
Safe from the snares
Of the fowler's hand,
So, this messenger
Can yield to God
By reaching for
The lost man.
If the enemy
Tries to block
The path of this
Messenger,
I charge angels
To use faith to win
In this spiritual war.

*Angelic hosts
Look down on us
From Heaven's Holy place
To work for us
On our behalf
Because of Divine grace,
That favor of God
We don't deserve,
But receive unmerited,
Allows these angels
Of the Most High
To fight through Christ's blood
To bring our souls
Back into
Divine grace and favor with Him
So that we
Can know our God
And spend eternity with Him.
Oh, what love
Shown toward us
By Christ upon the Cross,
For through His surrender
Unto obedience in death
He did not suffer loss;
But gained a Church
That spanned two centuries
And still it marches on;
But soon the trumpet
Will blow from Heaven
And this Church will then be gone;
So, don't be left behind
When this Church flies away;
But make your peace with Almighty God;
And do it, yes, today.*

In This Ole Life's Game

When you entertain a stranger;
And he helps you to see
How to climb out of trouble;
And you work your way free;
Could this be an angel
That you have entertained;
Or just another player
In this ole life's game?

When your vehicle is broken down
On the side of life's highway;
And you look up to God
Cry out and pray.
Then someone comes along
Just in the nick of time;
And before too very long
You are doing just fine.
Could this be an angel
That you have entertained;
Or just another player
In this ole life's game?

When you're down sick,
And discouraged too;
Wondering if you'll get better,
Or what else you can do;
And someone comes to see you
That you just don't know;
And lifts you up in spirit,
Leaving you all aglow.
Could this be an angel
That you have entertained;
Or just another player
In this ole life's game?

You see,
The Word tells us be careful
Just who we entertain;
It just could be an angel
In this ole life's game.

My Guardian Angel

No one knows me
Like my Guardian Angel;
And, oh, how HE must
Know me!
Oh, the things
I put HIM through;
And all the misery!
Oh, how I take
So many chances;
And yet HE's still out there;
Standing patient;
Taking glances;
It's how HE shows HE cares.
Yet one day
When I leave this world,
I think HIS job will be o'er;
But still I know
MY GUARDIAN ANGEL
Will stand by me some more.
So, here's to YOU,
MY ANGEL;
For all the things, YOU'VE done;
And please be patient
As YOU keep me from danger;
Remember,
I'M JUST A LITTLE ONE.

Some Angels

Some angels have fallen;
Others stand their post,
Carefully attending
To the Holy Ghost.
Some angels are for battle;
Some are there to aid,
Whenever we are helpless,
And cannot make the grade.
Some angels are for good times;
Some are for the bad;
Some for when we're happy;
Some for when we're sad.
Some angels are there to nurse us
From sickness, back to health.
Some are there to help us
From poverty, back to wealth.
Some are there to hold us,
And keep us in the way.
Some are there to mold us
As we seek the Lord and pray.
Some are there to lead us,
And gently take our hand,
Taking us step by step
Out of a foreign land.
But all in all God's angels
Are there for me and you
To help us along the way
To walk a path that's true.

Warring Angels

*Warring Angels standing ready
To do battle on our behalf.
They are awaiting one simple thing
Before they step into our fight.
They're listening for the desperate cry
Of hungry hearts and thirsty souls
Crying out for Jesus Christ
To be made completely whole.
They're watching for decisive steps
Toward the good and righteous path
Before they move into position
To express a Godly wrath
Upon the enemies of the souls waiting
Prepared and dressed for that day
That her bridegroom will come and get her,
Take her away though come what may.
He'll move the heavens, need it be,
To make this day view bright;
For He's coming soon in glory
Showing the way for He is light."
Warring angels standing ready,
And ready now to fight
For the hungry and the desperate
To find their way into the light.
Of the many righteous saints
Expressing God's Holy Word
Authoritative to acquaint
Demonic forces with the power
Of the Holy One on high.*

So, beware, Demonic forces,
The Kingdom of God is very nigh!
Angelic forces standing ready,
Swords all drawn, shields raised high;
Standing on the edge of battle
Listening for the battle cry.
Demonic kingdom, be thou warned,
And tell your leader, "It won't be long.
Jesus Christ so soon is coming,
His banner waving, and waving strong.
He's coming for a bride that's
Prepared and dressed for that day
That her bridegroom will come and get her,
Take her away though come what may.
He'll move the heavens, need it be,
To make this day view bright;
For He's coming soon in glory
Showing the way for He is light."
Warring angels standing ready,
And ready now to fight
For the hungry and the desperate
To find their way into the light.

ACKNOWLEDGEMENTS

Firstly, I must give glory and honor to Jesus Christ, without which this book would not have been written. You see, He is my primary focus and inspiration. Secondly, I want to say thank you to some special friends, whose words of encouragement were not only timely but necessary for me bringing this project to completion. Special thanks to: Helen White, Barbara Nichols, Colleen Walthers, Marshal & Vani, Brother Welch, and many others. Also, a special note of thanks to Sister Vesta Mangun and all my friends at the Pentecostals of Alexandria for helping me to realize the value of my gift from God.

Poet Bio

MY TESTIMONY

All through school I sought one thing, to be accepted by the status-quo; but did not find that blessed thing; but tried real hard although. I got into fights, not once or twice, but nearly every day. Twas no fun, almost never won. As for them, it was just play. Whenever we'd move, it would repeat just as it was before. It got to where, when I'd come home, I didn't want to go back there anymore. No one knows the pain I'd feel day out and day in. Just the longing that I would have for just one Life-long friend.

Then one day when I was ten I met this neighbor girl. All summer long our friendship grew 'til her parents' plan unfurled. She moved away. I painfully stayed wondering why this had to be. Until I got down in my backyard, down on my bended knee. When I asked God to fix it all, this thing He did for me. He took the pain out of my heart; from it set me free. Before this time, I had not known If there really was a God. But since that day unto this one, in pursuit of Him have I trod. Although when I was only ten, I did not know His name; I asked my parents where I should start; "We're Baptist," they proclaimed. I don't remember but just once that we'd ever been to church. But I decided I had to know; so, I began my search. Then at eleven is when we moved to the country out on a farm, just walking distance from a Baptist Church; to go would do no harm. For the next six years, went faithfully, Wednesday, Sunday morning and night. Learned a lot of God's Word, to which I had no light.

At seventeen, when I saw a deacon curse and swear; got caught up in judging him, and fell prey to Satan's snare. The next four years, I started running around with the wrong crowd. Drinking, carousing, and doing things of which I'm not too proud. During

This time, just like ole Jonah, I ran off to another land. Only to find that God was there reaching for me with His hand. Again, I prayed on a hillside not ready to give in; but God was patient and so kind; and faithful to the end. Back in the States He came again; and called me by my name. Could not resist His audible voice so, I turned to Him once again. This time I knew beyond a doubt His presence is so real; and His hand was on my life; for His Spirit, I could sure feel. Again, I went to a Baptist Church; for this was all I knew; but soon God brought some witnesses to show me what was true. First a man from the Church of Christ showed me Acts 2:38; and said I must be baptized right if I want to see those pearly gates; but when I asked of the other part, about this Holy Ghost, he said it was not for today; then I felt, this must be a hoax. Two weeks past; and I met a man from the Assembly of God; who told me I needed the Holy Ghost to help me through life trod. But when I asked him about baptism, He said all ways are the same, so I decided to wait until More revelation came. One year went by; then almost two; and I had returned back home. Saw God do things in my life that could only have come from His throne. So, again I looked at the book of Acts, chapter two, verse thirty-eight. Again, asked God to reveal the truth. This time it really came. This time as I researched His Word, I met people both left and right that had obeyed this awesome truth; and now stood there as a light. So, I obeyed this Word of truth found in Acts two, verse thirty-eight. And found a friend that would stand by me all the way to those pearly gates.

NOW A LITTLE MORE ABOUT ME

At 15, I had very few friends. So, I began to spend much time with my Dad's animals and in deep thought about life. I began to express my thoughts on paper in the form of Poetry and much of my time I spent taking care of my Dad's animals I spent singing to them, making up songs then writing them down later. Although none of the music had the privilege of being written down, I hung on to the words. Many of my poems started out as unwritten songs. In 1994, as an accomplished poet I had an idea. Probably not a new idea, but it was new to me. There was one of my poems that I knew had some depth to it and I knew it was as good as "Foot Prints in The Sand." What sparked this idea was when I walked through a new store, on their walls, they displayed some decorative paper. I envisioned my poem printed upon some of that paper. So, I typed it up and then had it transferred on to one of those decorative prints. Next, I walked out on the street just a few feet away from the shop and ask a man if he would like to read my poem. He said, "Sure." I handed him a copy. He read it. Then I said, "You can have that copy for $1.00." He just reached into his pocket and pulled out a $1.00, and gave it to me. I started that afternoon with 5 copies on decorative paper. 2½ months later I had grossed $1,000.00 in just the sale of that one poem. And that was just one-on-one direct sales. I knew that I had something. I got busy working with other poems I had written as well. In about two years, not only had I saturated my local market, but my efforts sparked other poets in my area to do the same. So, my local market played out, so to speak. I knew that if I could somehow enlarge my market, I could do well just publishing and selling my writing. Another poet from Natchitoches, Louisiana heard about my business of selling my poetic works and sent me

A LETTER INQUIRING OF ME AS TO HOW I DO IT. SHE ALSO ASKED ME IF I COULD HANDLE HERS. BELOW IS A COPY OF THE TEXT OF THE LETTER I SENT HER IN RETURN IN SEPTEMBER OF 1997.

FIRST OF ALL, BOB'S POETRY SHOP IS, AT PRESENT, MERELY A BUSINESS NAME IN WHICH I CONDUCT BUSINESS USING MY POETRY AS THE BASIS OF A PRODUCT LINE. I'VE CREATED MOST OF MY PRODUCT LINE THROUGH USING THE EQUIPMENT AND THE MATERIALS HOUSED AT LOCAL SELF-SERVE PRINTING SERVICE; AND UTILIZE THE SERVICES OF THE SAME. FOR LARGE ORDERS, I UTILIZE THE SERVICES OF A LOCAL PRINT SHOP.

IT ALL STARTED WITH ONE POEM ENTITLED, "TWO BUDS," WHICH I DEVELOPED INTO A DECORATIVE FRAME-ABLE PRINT. THEN I WENT DOOR-TO-DOOR COMMERCIALLY SELLING COPIES OF JUST THIS ONE PRINT. AFTER 2½ MONTHS, I HAD SOLD OVER 1,000 PRINTS OF THAT POEM, ONE PRINT AT A TIME. THAT MARKET TEST WAS A HUGE SUCCESS; SO, I STARTED DEVELOPING MORE OF MY POEMS INTO THE SAME TYPE OF PRODUCT, AND FOUND THAT THEY ALSO BEGAN TO SELL. THEN I FOUND I COULD SELL LAMINATED PRINTS OF THE SAME. NOW, I'VE PUBLISHED A BOOK, AND MY NEWEST PRODUCT LINE IS CALENDARS AND BOOKMARKS.

RIGHT NOW, I'VE BEEN OPERATING A LICENSED BUSINESS WITH VIRTUALLY NO OVERHEAD (NO BUILDING, NO MACHINE MAINTENANCE, NO ELECTRIC BILL, ETC...) FOR THE LAST YEAR. I'VE SOLD THIS PRODUCT LINE FOR MORE THAN FOUR YEARS NOW. DON'T GET ME WRONG. I DO HAVE PLANS TO BUILD A SHOP THAT WOULD HOUSE TWO COMPUTERS, A LAMINATOR, A BINDER, AND SUFFICIENT STORAGE SPACE TO OPERATE A PUBLICATION AND DISTRIBUTION BUSINESS. AT PRESENT THOUGH, THE PHYSICAL SHOP IS MERELY A DREAM, A GOAL THAT I'M REACHING FOR. RIGHT NOW, IT IS JUST A PART TIME BUSINESS; BECAUSE I ALSO WORK A FULL-TIME JOB AT KFC HERE IN ALEXANDRIA.

So far, my most profitable method of distribution has been direct sales; although I do have some books in stores such as Books-A-Million, White Steeple Books and Music, King's Emporium, and the Baptist Book Store. I am also planning on using the Internet as well. I've tried distributing the poetry of two other writers in the past; but I've found that the biggest problem I have right now is tracking. I am currently not set up to tract sales sufficiently to produce or sell another author's work. As soon as I am set up, I plan to do just that.

About 50% to 75% of my writing is inspirational or Bible-based material. With this letter, I will enclose a couple of my most noted pieces. I have written tongue-twisters, romantic prose, nursery rhymes, Sunday School songs, and just for fun poems. I've been writing poetry for 27 years; and have probably lost literally thousands of pieces over the years; because I really didn't understand the gift that I had. Now that I have seen my work touch people's lives, I'm dedicated to the cause of publishing my work, hence the creation of Bob's Poetry Shop.

I want to thank you for your interest in Bob's Poetry Shop, and I'm open to further communication with you, even meeting you, should you so desire. Perhaps as fellow poets we can share some interesting inspirational moments. I will look forward to hearing from you again soon. If you have access to email, my email address is bps80 at hotmail dot com (no longer active).

Since this letter, I've changed the name to Bob's Poetic Ministries, and the new email address is apoetbob@gmail.com . And the book referred to in the letter is a poetry book entitled, "Let This Light So Shine".

In the meantime, I've written another book entitled "The Focused Fast," and I placed it first of all at a few local bookstores, then finally made it available online at www.bobspoeticministries.yolasite.com While the book was in the local artist section of Books-A-Million in my area, it achieved best-seller status among the local authors. But then Books-A-Million decided to change their purchasing policy and began requiring all local authors to have an ISBN and a bar code. In the short time that it was there I sold out of my first print of this new book. Then I decided to reformat the book and try to sell it as a correspondence course. I sold about 50 more, not through mail order, but as whole binders of the complete course. So, next I reformatted again, and sold it as a half size book (5½ X 8½). So, far I've probably sold about 250 copies, including the newest CD version. Being that it is now online, I just assumed it would fly. But I now know, without the proper knowledge of how to promote the book, it won't sell there either. This book is too important (not just for me, but for the masses that could be changed by its message) to just quit and give up. I've got to find a way to get the word out to people that will not only buy the book but also read it and absorb its message. Once in a while, a book comes along that has the power to change lives. And, believe me, this is one of those books. I've seen it work in people's lives already. One of the ladies that I ask to proof read the book told me that each paragraph she read sent her to her knees weeping. She had to pray through each paragraph. Now, I know that it won't affect everyone like that; but I'm sure there are others that will be affected that way.

Finally, I uploaded several books online that are presently for sale at the following sites: www.bobspoeticministries.yolasite.com; www.poetbob.com; www.poetbob.ws; www.poetbob.info; including a four volume set of my Inspirational poetry entitled "Becoming".

If you would like to be encouraged, strengthened, uplifted, or edified in anyway, take some time and visit my bookstores and review my books.

More Recently, I moved to the Paris, Tennessee area where I have spent much more time on the publishing end of my writing. And now, I have published 3 newer books, "Rivers of Inspiration", a best of collection of my inspirational poetry, "Becoming a Life Time of Prose", an attempt at an unabridged version of my inspirational poetry, and a new version of "The Focused Fast Training Course", a spiritual warfare training course.

My newest books being released this year are "Spiritual Warfare Basic Training", and "An Expose' of Prose". Not to mention, a new version of "Becoming a Life time of Prose".

MY FAMILY BACKGROUND

Born December 19th, 1954, the 5th of seven children of Elmo & Emma McGlothlin, I grew up in the Central Louisiana area. I attended Carter C. Raymond Elementary for about 6 months at the age of 5, then the family moved to Alexandria where I attended Cherokee Elementary for 6 months. Then they started me over in the 1st grade again at Horseshoe Elementary for 5 years. After which, we moved out to the Latania Community, just outside of Lecompte, Louisiana where I attended Poland High School (at that time, a 1 - 12 school) for the remainder of my basic education. After Graduating High School, I went 1 semester to LSU at Alexandria, LA, followed by 3 years and 2 months in the USAF. When I got out of the military, I took 1 semester at Louisiana College in Pineville. But due to a radical change in my life, I dropped out of college altogether to pursue a brave new goal in life, the Will of God. That radical change was an experience most call "the born-again experience". Just before I moved to Tennessee in June of 2006, my parents needed some help, so I took off 5 years to be there caretaker. In the middle of that 5 years is when the family moved my parents and myself up here to Tennessee. After their passing, I got work in a factory up here in Southern Kentucky.

www.ingramcontent.com/pod-product-compliance
Lightning Source LLC
Chambersburg PA
CBHW030106100526
44591CB00009B/300